Righteous by Faith Alone

Herman Hoeksema (1886-1965)

Righteous by Faith Alone

A Devotional Commentary on Romans

Herman Hoeksema

Edited by David J. Engelsma

Reformed Free Publishing Association
Grandville, Michigan

© 2002 Reformed Free Publishing Association
All rights reserved
Printed in the United States of America

No part of this book may be used or reprinted in any form without written permission from the publisher, except in the case of brief quotations used in a critical article or review

Bible quotations are taken from the Authorized (King James) Version

Book design by Jeff Steenholdt

For a catalog of books in the Reformed Calvinistic tradition, contact:
Reformed Free Publishing Association
4949 Ivanrest Ave SW
Grandville MI 49418-9709 USA
Phone: 616-224-1518
Fax: 616-224-1517
Website: www.rfpa.org
E-mail: mail@rfpa.org

ISBN 0-916206-71-8
LC Control Number 2001126951

Contents

Editor's Introduction		xv
A Word about Martin Swart, the Transcriber		xxi

Romans 1

Verses 1–4	Chapter 1	
	Separated unto the Gospel	1
Verses 16, 17	Chapter 2	
	The Gospel a Power of God	9
Verse 18	Chapter 3	
	The Revelation of God's Wrath	16
Verses 19–23	Chapter 4	
	Inexcusable Madness	24
Verses 24, 25	Chapter 5	
	Delivered to Corruption	32
Verse 28	Chapter 6	
	Given Over to a Reprobate Mind	39
Verse 32	Chapter 7	
	The Mutual Delight of Sinners	46

Romans 2

Verse 1	Chapter 8	
	The Inexcusable Judge	53
Verses 4, 5	Chapter 9	
	Despising God's Goodness	60
Verses 6–8	Chapter 10	
	The Revelation of the Righteous Judgment of God	68
Verses 14, 15	Chapter 11	
	The Gentiles a Law unto Themselves	76
Verses 17–21a	Chapter 12	
	The Vain Boast of Self-righteousness	83
Verses 28, 29	Chapter 13	
	The Impossibility of Religious Work-righteousness	90

Contents

Romans 3

Verses 3, 4a	Chapter 14	
	The Faith of God	97
Verses 7, 8	Chapter 15	
	A Damnable Inference	104
Verses 9–18	Chapter 16	
	All under Sin	111
Verses 21, 22	Chapter 17	
	The Righteousness of God Manifested	119
Verses 25, 26	Chapter 18	
	Christ the Demonstration of God's Righteousness	126
Verse 27	Chapter 19	
	Boasting Excluded	133

Romans 4

Verses 3–5	Chapter 20	
	Faith Reckoned for Righteousness	141
Verses 6–8	Chapter 21	
	The Blessedness of the Justified	148
Verse 11	Chapter 22	
	The Sign of Circumcision	154
Verse 17b	Chapter 23	
	Believing the Living God	161
Verses 23, 24	Chapter 24	
	Imputed to All	168
Verse 25	Chapter 25	
	Jesus Raised for Our Justification	175

Romans 5

Verse 1	Chapter 26	
	The Believer's Peace with God	182
Verse 2	Chapter 27	
	Standing in Grace	189
Verses 3, 4	Chapter 28	
	Glorying in Tribulations	195

Romans 5 (cont.)

Verses 6–8	*Chapter 29*	
	The Proof of a Marvelous Love	202
Verse 10	*Chapter 30*	
	Saved by His Life	209
Verses 12–14	*Chapter 31*	
	All Have Sinned	217
Verse 15	*Chapter 32*	
	The Abounding Gift	224
Verse 18	*Chapter 33*	
	Our Justification of Life	230
Verse 21	*Chapter 34*	
	The Reign of Grace	237

Romans 6

Verses 1, 2	*Chapter 35*	
	The Christian and the Sin-life	243
Verse 4	*Chapter 36*	
	Buried with Christ	250
Verse 11	*Chapter 37*	
	The Christian's Self-esteem	257
Verse 14	*Chapter 38*	
	The Justified Christian Liberated from the Dominion of Sin	263
Verse 23	*Chapter 39*	
	The Grace-gift of God	269

Romans 7

Verse 4	*Chapter 40*	
	Our Marriage to the Risen Lord	276
Verses 5, 6	*Chapter 41*	
	Serving in Newness of Spirit	283
Verses 15–17	*Chapter 42*	
	The State of Imperfect Perfection of the Christian	289
Verses 24, 25a	*Chapter 43*	
	The Wretched Christian	296

Contents

Romans 8

Verse 1	**Chapter 44** The Blessedness of Freedom from Condemnation	302
Verse 2	**Chapter 45** Spiritual Liberation	309
Verse 11	**Chapter 46** The Certainty of the Resurrection of the Saints	315
Verse 14	**Chapter 47** Sons of God Led by the Spirit	322
Verses 15, 16	**Chapter 48** Assurance of Our Sonship	329
Verses 17b, 18	**Chapter 49** The Suffering of This Present Time	335
Verses 19–22	**Chapter 50** The Waiting Creature	342
Verses 26, 27	**Chapter 51** The Groanings of the Spirit	349
Verse 28	**Chapter 52** The Assurance That All Things Work for Good	354
Verses 31, 32	**Chapter 53** God for Us	361
Verse 34	**Chapter 54** No One to Condemn Us	367
Verses 35–39	**Chapter 55** Separation Impossible	374

Romans 9

Verses 6–8	**Chapter 56** The True Children of Abraham	382
Verses 10–13	**Chapter 57** Jacob's Election	390

Contents

Romans 9 (cont.)

Verses 14–16	*Chapter 58*	
	The Righteousness of God's Sovereign Mercy	398
Verses 17, 18	*Chapter 59*	
	God's Raising Up of Pharaoh	406
Verses 19–21	*Chapter 60*	
	God's Absolute Sovereignty	414
Verses 22, 23	*Chapter 61*	
	God's Sovereign Dealings	422
Verses 24–29	*Chapter 62*	
	The Calling of the Vessels of Mercy	430
Verses 30–33	*Chapter 63*	
	The Realization of God's Sovereign Purpose	437

Romans 10

Verse 4	*Chapter 64*	
	Christ the End of the Law	445
Verses 5–8	*Chapter 65*	
	The Confession of the Righteousness by Faith	452
Verse 9	*Chapter 66*	
	The Certain Salvation of the Confessing Believer	459
Verses 11–13	*Chapter 67*	
	The Universality of Salvation	466
Verses 14, 15	*Chapter 68*	
	The Mission of the Preacher	474
Verses 16–18	*Chapter 69*	
	The Hearing of the Preaching	482
Verses 20, 21	*Chapter 70*	
	God Found by a Strange People	496

Contents

Romans 11

Verses 1–5	Chapter 71 The Ever Abiding Remnant	503
Verse 6	Chapter 72 By Pure Grace	510
Verses 7–10	Chapter 73 Obtained by the Election Only	517
Verse 11	Chapter 74 The Divine Purpose of Israel's Stumbling	524
Verse 15	Chapter 75 The Greater Glory of Israel's Reception	532
Verses 16–21	Chapter 76 Humility toward the Old Branches	539
Verses 22–24	Chapter 77 The Goodness and Severity of God	546
Verses 25, 26a	Chapter 78 The Mystery of the Salvation of All Israel	554
Verses 28–31	Chapter 79 Hated yet Beloved	561
Verses 33–36	Chapter 80 The Only Adorable God	569

Romans 12

Verse 2	Chapter 81 Transformation from Within	576
Verses 3–8	Chapter 82 Sober-mindedness with a View to the Gifts of Grace	583
Verse 9	Chapter 83 Love without Hypocrisy	591
Verse 12	Chapter 84 Patient in Tribulation	598
Verse 16	Chapter 85 An Exhortation to Be of One Mind	605
Verse 19	Chapter 86 Leaving Vengeance to the Lord	612

Contents

Romans 13

Verses 1–5	Chapter 87	
	Subject to the Higher Powers	619
Verse 8	Chapter 88	
	The Ever Abiding Debt	626
Verses 11, 12	Chapter 89	
	The Calling of the Dawn	633

Romans 14

Verses 1–3	Chapter 90	
	Receiving the Weaker Brother	640
Verses 4–8	Chapter 91	
	Always the Lord's	646
Verse 23b	Chapter 92	
	Always Living by Faith	652

Romans 15

Verse 4	Chapter 93	
	Instruction unto the Hope	659
Verses 5–9	Chapter 94	
	The High Calling to Glorify God	666
Verse 14	Chapter 95	
	The Church Filled with All Goodness	673

Romans 16

Verses 3–16	Chapter 96	
	Christian Greetings	680
Verses 25–27	Chapter 97	
	The Glory of the Only Wise God	687

Books in English by Herman Hoeksema   695

Index to Scripture References   697

Editor's Introduction

In the late 1930s, Herman Hoeksema preached a series of ninety-seven sermons on the epistle to the Romans. He preached the series to the First Protestant Reformed Church of Grand Rapids, Michigan, at that time a congregation of some five hundred families. These sermons are the content of the exposition of Romans in this book.

Hoeksema was in his early fifties at the time when he preached the series on Romans. He was then at the height of his powers as an interpreter of the Word of God. This renowned Reformed theologian was singularly qualified to explain the book of Romans. In addition to abundant natural gifts, wide reading, and disciplined theological study over many years as both a pastor and a seminary professor, Hoeksema shared the zeal of the apostle Paul for the glory of the triune God in His sovereignty. This enabled Hoeksema to explain Paul rightly in those areas, particularly predestination, where so many commentators faint and fail.

With the exception of the sermons on Romans 9–11, this exposition of Romans has never before been published.

The story of the existence of Hoeksema's Romans series is fascinating. The sermons were not recorded on tape when preached. Evidently Hoeksema's own outlines of the sermons on Romans have perished. But Hoeksema had a scribe. A member of the congregation, Martin Swart, took down ninety-six of the ninety-seven sermons as they were preached, using his own system of shorthand. Many members of the congregation, as well as Hoeksema himself, noticed Swart writing industriously while Hoeksema was preaching. Immediately upon arriving home, Swart wrote the sermon out in full, using a pencil. Later he transcribed the sermon into a spiral notebook, writing the final copy with a pen. Each of the transcriptions has a heading consisting of the sermon theme, the text, and the name of the preacher. Swart preserved the notebooks containing his copies of Hoeksema's sermons for his own use. The series on Romans, with many other sermons by Hoeksema, survives in these notebooks in the lovely, neat, and almost perfectly legible hand of Martin Swart. A facsimile of part of the first page of the first sermon of the Romans series in one of Swart's notebooks is shown facing the first page of chapter 1.

Before his death, Swart gave his precious notebooks to one of his sons. From this son, the Reformed Free Publishing Association borrowed the notebooks containing the Romans sermons and was given permission to publish the sermons. The RFPA expresses its indebtedness to Martin Swart for the existence of the sermons and its thanks to Jim Swart for access to them.

In 1940 the Doorn Printing Company of Grand Rapids, Michigan, printed the sermons on Romans 9–11 under the title *God's Eternal Good Pleasure*. The book was reprinted by the RFPA in 1979, but that edition is now out of print. The existence of this publication was of great importance to the editor of the present volume. It allowed him to compare a number of sermons as taken down by Swart with the same sermons as written out by Hoeksema himself for publication in *God's Eternal Good Pleasure*. The comparison established the accuracy of the Swart transcription. The accuracy extends not only to the explanation and doctrines generally, but also to the expressions and words. Swart took down what Hoeksema said—as he said it.

At the same time, there are significant differences between the sermons as Swart transcribed them and the sermons as Hoeksema prepared them for publication in *God's Eternal Good Pleasure*. The latter are much longer, more polemical, deeper, and more difficult to understand than the same sermons in Swart's notebooks. As Swart took them down, the sermons—even in Romans 9–11—are lucid, lively, and practical.

A striking example of the difference as regards practical application is the sermon on Romans 9:14–16. In Swart's version, much of the second part of the exposition applies the passage to the grievous reality of the perishing of a child of believing parents according to "the righteousness of God's sovereign mercy." Almost nothing of this appears in the version published in *God's Eternal Good Pleasure*.

There can be no doubt that Swart's transcriptions give us the sermons as Hoeksema actually preached them. When Hoeksema edited his sermons for publication as a book, he changed them significantly, though not substantially. He was writing for an audience different from the one to whom he had preached the sermons. That new audience included his theological adversaries.

It is conceivable that the comparative brevity of the sermons as taken down by Swart might be due to Swart's inability to take down everything that Hoeksema said. However, Hoeksema was quite deliberate in his style of preaching, so that it would not have been impossible for a determined scribe to take down nearly every word. If parts are omitted, the sermons themselves make plain that these could not have been main thoughts in the exposition.

In a couple of instances, Hoeksema changed the titles of the sermons when he published them in *God's Eternal Good Pleasure*. An example is the sermon on Romans 11:16–21. The original title was "Humility toward the Old Branches." In *God's Eternal Good Pleasure* Hoeksema gave it the title "Holy Branches." We have retained the original titles.

Some will welcome the publication of Hoeksema's sermons on Romans for the additional light that the sermons shed on the thinking of this notable Reformed theologian. Interpreting the epistle to the Romans required Hoeksema to explain virtually every cardinal doctrine of the gospel. On the foreground in the epistle, as the sixteenth century Reformation emphasized, are the fundamental truths of the gospel of salvation by sovereign grace. Foremost among them is the truth of the sovereign God Himself. Hoeksema sets forth God's sovereignty as few expositors of Romans have ever done.

One aspect of Hoeksema's own theology that is clarified in

Editor's Introduction

this exposition is his well-known contention that the attributes of God characterize God's own being apart from their manifestation in His dealings with His people. Some have severely criticized Hoeksema for this teaching. The Romans sermons make plain that Hoeksema understood this doctrine in a trinitarian manner. The sermons on Romans 5:15 and 11:6, for example, teach that God is gracious in Himself in that the Father sees and delights in His own beauty in the Son.

Another benefit of the publication of the sermons will be that it permits seminarians and ministers to learn from the homiletics of a gifted preacher. Even though the ostensibly sermonic has been edited out in the interests of producing a commentary, it is obvious that *Righteous by Faith Alone* was originally sermons. These sermons are models of homiletics. They are exegetically based and therefore strictly an exposition of the Word of God. Their themes are unerringly the one, main Word of God in the text. The divisions serve to develop the theme as well as covering all the material in the text. There are homely, effective illustrations.

The book should remind Reformed ministers of the great benefit to the congregation (as to themselves) of their preaching extended series of sermons on various books of the Bible.

The sermons are also exemplary in that they urgently apply the Word to the experience and life of the people of God. A deep concern of Hoeksema that runs throughout the exposition from beginning to end is that his audience might have the assurance of their salvation by believing the message of the book of Romans. Under such teaching, the Holy Ghost would not leave large numbers of the congregation "believing" with their heads, but forever doubtful of their own salvation.

Valuable as the present volume may be in these respects, its main worth is its commentary on Romans. Romans stands out in sacred Scripture as a full, clear, systematic statement of the gospel, as the Reformation had observed. Luther called the epistle "the masterpiece of the New Testament, the purest Gospel of all." Calvin declared that "this epistle, besides many other and singular graces found in it, has one [grace] proper and peculiar to it, which can never be sufficiently prized and esteemed; this is that anyone who has achieved a true understanding of it has as it were an open door through which to enter into the most secret treasures of Scripture." Hoeksema agreed. At the very end of his exposition of the epistle, he referred to Romans as "one of the richest and most beautiful parts of the Word of God."

The present work is a rather complete commentary. Even though it does not explain every verse, much less every word, it does explain all of the main sections. It was Hoeksema's practice in preaching a series to select the verse or verses that are central to the passage. In the course of explaining the verse or verses at the heart of a passage, he would also comment on the related verses. Often this was his introduction to the sermon. The exposition includes word study of the main words in the book of Romans. There is also analysis of difficult points of grammar and even discussion of different readings of the Greek text.

Nevertheless, consisting as it does of sermons preached to a congregation, the commentary is a *devotional* commentary. It functions as the epistle to the Romans itself is intended by the Holy Spirit to function, as instruction and edification of the beloved saints (Rom. 1:7).

The title of the commentary is really Hoeksema's own. Again and again he asserted that the main theme of Romans is justification by faith alone.

In the nature of the case, it took extensive editorial work to transform handwritten copies of sermons into a published commentary. In addition to the expected matters of grammar, the editor changed the more pronounced indications that the exposition was originally sermons; corrected scribal mistakes of words and ideas; added connections which, although implied, were missing; and occasionally rearranged material within the body of the explanation of a certain passage. In a few instances, the editor changed or omitted what were undoubtedly Hoeksema's own expressions to reflect the development of Hoeksema's own thought on the subject. One example is Hoeksema's statement, "We are co-workers with God" in the exposition of Romans 8:14. In accordance with Hoeksema's later repudiation of the notion that ministers and other saints are co-workers *with* God, this statement was omitted.

All footnotes are the editor's. In the body of the book the editor has supplied all the Scriptural references that appear in brackets. Hoeksema would often quote or paraphrase a text without indicating the source.

A challenging editorial task concerned the one sermon that was included in *God's Eternal Good Pleasure*, but omitted from the Swart transcriptions. This is the sermon on Romans 10:16–18, "The Hearing of the Preaching." We certainly did not want to omit the sermon from the present volume, but neither could we simply lift it from *God's Eternal Good Pleasure* and include it in that form in *Righteous by Faith Alone*. The differences between the revised sermons in *God's Eternal Good Pleasure* and the sermons as taken down by Martin Swart would have made this sermon incongruous. The solution was that the editor of *Righteous by Faith Alone,* with a bravery bordering on foolhardiness, severely shortened and simplified the sermon to bring it into conformity with the other ninety-six sermons in the book.

In such a round-about, arduous, and totally unplanned and unforeseen way does Herman Hoeksema's explanation of the epistle to the Romans finally reach the public, after more than sixty years. Mysterious, and fascinating, is the providence of God. In this, too, He is sovereign.

DAVID J. ENGELSMA, Editor
Professor of Dogmatics and Old Testament
Protestant Reformed Seminary

A Word about Martin Swart, the Transcriber

The man to whom we are indebted for the preservation of Herman Hoeksema's sermons on Romans, and therefore this commentary, is Martin Swart. Mr. Swart was a member of First Protestant Reformed Church, Grand Rapids, Michigan, from its origin as a Protestant Reformed congregation in 1924/1926 until his death in 1977.

Swart was a prominent member of the congregation. He was often elder. He was active in the English Men's Society, serving for many years as its president. As a lively member of the society, Swart wrote a number of learned essays on theological subjects for the benefit of the members. Some of these essays survive. They are remarkable doctrinal and church political studies for a layman who had only an eighth-grade education. Swart was one of many members of First Church during the ministry of Herman Hoeksema who became mighty in the Scriptures and learned in the Reformed faith under Hoeksema's expository, doctrinal preaching.

Martin Swart was a devoted disciple of Herman Hoeksema for the truth's sake. This motivated him to take down Hoeksema's sermons and then transcribe them by a laborious process into notebooks, which were carefully preserved, as described in the Editor's Introduction. Swart used these expositions of the Bible for his own study and edification. He intended that his children benefit from them as well. Swart's

Martin Swart (1891-1977)

xxiii

devotion to the truth of the Word of God as taught by Hoeksema also guaranteed that he would be meticulously accurate in recording and copying the sermons.

Born in 1891 in Friesland, the Netherlands, Martin Swart immigrated to the United States with his family in 1900 at the age of nine. The family settled in Grand Rapids, Michigan. He married Mary Smit in 1917 and worked as a woodcutter in furniture factories in Grand Rapids. Martin and Mary had six children, four of whom are still living. A son was killed on the battlefield in Italy in World War II. Swart's four surviving children and many grandchildren and great grandchildren are members of various Protestant Reformed churches. At the age of eighty-five, Martin Swart died in 1977.

DAVID J. ENGELSMA

the basis on which to be saved. It is impossible by our own effort, by our own attempt, to reach the word of life. And in that emptiness the word of the resurrection came and we say: I am saved by the righteousness of God which is in Christ Jesus.

  Text: Romans 1:1-4

  Rev. H. Hoeksema

  It is not known what is the beginning, and what is the origin of the Church at Rome. Certain it is that the Romish tradition, that Peter is the founder, and that he was the first bishop, cannot stand the test of scripture. We may believe, that if the Apostle Peter had been instrumental in establishing the Church at Rome, that at the time when Paul writes this Epistle, the Apostle Peter must still have been there, and that he must still have been, according to the Catholic claim overseer of the Church. And that is impossible. For Paul would never interfere in an other man's work. And he

Above is an excerpt from the first page of Martin Swart's transcription of the Romans sermons.

Chapter One

Separated unto the Gospel

Romans 1:1-4
Paul, a servant of Jesus Christ, called to be an apostle, separated unto the gospel of God,
(Which he had promised afore by his prophets in the holy scriptures,)
Concerning his Son Jesus Christ our Lord, which was made of the seed of David according to the flesh;
And declared to be the Son of God with power, according to the spirit of holiness, by the resurrection from the dead.

It is not known what is the beginning and what is the origin of the church at Rome. Certain it is that the Romish tradition that Peter is the founder and that he was the first bishop cannot stand the test of Scripture. We may believe, if the apostle Peter had been instrumental in establishing the church at Rome, that at the time when Paul writes this epistle, the apostle Peter must still have been there, and he must still have been, according to the Roman Catholic claim, overseer of the church. But this is impossible, for Paul would never interfere in another man's work. He would not have written this epistle.

Besides, in the long list of names mentioned at the end of the epistle, Peter is not even mentioned.

As to the origin of the church, there must have been a good deal of connection and traveling between Jerusalem and Rome. There were connections of business and the like. In addition, the large congregation at Jerusalem soon was scattered, due to persecutions. Undoubtedly many went to Rome. Perhaps the congregation at Rome was finally established by one of the helpers of the apostles, although it is not certain.

According to the evidence of the epistle, the congregation consisted of converts out of the Jews and Gentiles.

As to its contents, the theme of the epistle is clear. There was no particular reason in the congregation that caused the apostle to write this letter. There were no heresies and no particular sins against which the apostle is called to warn the congregation. He simply states that he longed to see them, but was prevented hitherto. And so he felt the need of writing them. What we have, therefore, in this epistle to the Romans is a quiet development of one theme. This theme is that a man is justified not by the works of the law, but by faith in Christ.

We find that there is a threefold division of the book. The first is that it is impossible for man to become righteous before God on the basis of works. The second is the expounding of the positive doctrine of justification by faith. And the third is the application of that doctrine of justification by faith to them who are so justified. Inasmuch as this is the main theme, and inasmuch as the faith by which man is justified cannot possibly rest on the word of man, the apostle introduces himself to the Roman church in the text as one *separated unto the gospel*. This is the theme of this part of the epistle.

A Significant Gospel

Notice that the apostle is speaking of the gospel of God. The *gospel*, as to the meaning of the word, is good news. It is a good message, a tiding of joy. As to the scriptural meaning, the gospel is, in the first place, a message from God. This is an essential element of the gospel.

In the second place, it is a message from God to His people as they are in this world. It is a message from God in this world of darkness, of sin, and of death. It is a message from God in the world in which His people are by nature children of wrath. It is a message from God in the world in which His children are loaded with sin and in which everything about them testifies of sin and of death. In this darkness comes a message. It is a message that comes from heaven, a divinely authoritative message, a message that is glad news.

The glad news consists in this: those who are in darkness see a great light, those who are in sin receive righteousness, and those who are in death receive life. This is the gospel.

The apostle tells us concerning the gospel that it is the gospel of the Son of God, Jesus Christ our Lord. He is the object of the gospel. It is concerning Him that glad news comes from heaven. It is the gospel concerning His Son, who as we know Him, as He stands with His face toward us, is the Lord Jesus Christ; and who as He stands with His face to the Father, as we do not see Him and know Him, is the eternal Son. As He stands with His face toward us, as we see and know Him, He is Jesus of Nazareth, who became like unto us and walked among us for thirty-three years. He is the object of the glad news.

If you ask, what does God declare concerning His Son, what is the contents of that glad news, the apostle mentions two facts. The first is His incarnation. The second is His resurrection.

"Concerning his Son Jesus Christ our Lord, which was made of the seed of David according to the flesh; And declared to be the Son of God with power, according to the spirit of holiness, by the resurrection from the dead"—this God declared concerning His Son.

According to the flesh, Jesus was made of the seed of David. *Flesh* in the text does not mean sinful flesh, but His human nature. It means His human body and soul. Jesus, according to His body and His soul, was made. He was made of the seed of David. That is, He assumed, He took upon Himself, that flesh, that body and soul. He took that flesh from the heart of the covenant line that was in David. According to prophecy, the heart of the covenant line runs through David's house. The covenant line is like a pyramid that has for its base the seed of the woman. For its apex it has the house of David. The last that we have in Scripture concerning the coming of the Son of God in the flesh is that He will take on the flesh and blood not merely of man, but of David. Jesus could not be a Roman; He could not be a Greek. But He took on the flesh from the heart of the covenant line. He was made of the seed of David.

This God declared. This is the gospel. This is the one fact of the gospel.

The other fact is the resurrection. God said concerning His Son that He was powerfully declared to be the Son of God, so that we also know Him as the Son of God by the resurrection from the dead. "Declared to be the Son of God with power, according to the spirit of holiness, by the resurrection from the dead," the apostle says. *According to the spirit of holiness* stands over against the flesh here. The spirit of holiness is not the Third Person in the Trinity. It is not the Spirit of sanctification, as the Dutch translation has it *(De Geest des heiligmaking)*. But the spirit of holiness refers to the divine nature of Jesus. God is a spirit. His nature is spiritual. The chief characteristic of God as a spirit is that He is holy. When the apostle says that He was "declared to be the Son of God with power, according to the spirit of holiness," the meaning is that Jesus according to His human nature is of the seed of David, but that according to His divine nature He is the Son of God. This is the gospel.

The powerful demonstration of Jesus as the Son of God is the resurrection. When He lies as a babe in Bethlehem, this does not become manifest. As far as we can see, He is just like any other babe. But when He rises from the dead, we have a powerful demonstration that He is the Son of God.

The gospel is glad news coming from heaven concerning the Son of God, whom as we see Him is Jesus Christ our Lord. What God declares concerning His Son is that according to the flesh He is of the seed of David, but according to His divine nature He is declared to be the Son of God by the resurrection from the dead.

Why does the apostle select these two truths? It is evident that these two truths mark the beginning and the end of His being with us. That period was *the* period. In that period the gospel is realized, the gospel concerning His Son. It is in that period that God comes from heaven in His Son, is with us for thirty-three years, and then returns. All that lies between that beginning and that end constitutes the gospel of our salvation. That is the only historical basis for all we believe. That is really the gospel.

What happened?

In the year A.D. 1, God came into our darkness. He came through His Son. Here there was nothing but darkness, sin, and death. The Son of God came into our darkness and death. If He were not the Son of God, there is no gospel. Then there is no hope. If theological modernism is correct, there is no gospel. On the incarnation of the Son of God hangs all the righteousness that is by faith. He entered into our life. He became like us in everything, sin excepted. He became a man among men, weak and suffering. Not only that, but He died. He died as all men die. But if this is all that can be said about Him, there is no gospel, for viewing Him as the Son of God entering into our night, we are watching and wondering whether He will come out of that night. No man ever did. No man ever entered into our night and came out of it. When the Son of God comes into our night, the question is, what will become of Him? In breathless expectation the church stands and asks the question "What will become of Him?"

He was raised! The Son of God came, He walked among us, He bore our sins, and with our sins He sank into death. But He was declared to be the Son of God in the resurrection. Upon the incarnation as the beginning, and the resurrection as the end, depends the gospel, the gospel of our justification. If that child of Bethlehem is not God, He did not bear our sin. And if He is not raised, He failed to atone. But in the resurrection He was powerfully declared to be the Son of God. This is the gospel.

Divinely Declared

This gospel God declares. We read in verse 1 that it is the gospel of God: "Paul, a servant of Jesus Christ, called to be an apostle, separated unto the gospel of God." It is the gospel of God. That is, God is the author of the gospel. God made the gospel. He conceived of the glad news concerning His Son to His people. God is the author of the gospel because He realized it in the fulness of time. In the fulness of time God rent the heavens and sent His Son into our darkness. He loaded upon Him our sin. He gave Him over to the death of the cross. He poured the vials of His wrath over Him. And He raised Him, He glorified Him, He set Him at His right hand in the highest heavens, He gave Him the Spirit without measure.

But the gospel is also the gospel of God in the sense that He declares it. He is the only one who is able to declare it. In the first place, this is because man is not able to understand and interpret that gospel concerning the Son of God. Suppose that it were left up to man to interpret the facts. He would never come to this gospel. All the philosophy of man cannot interpret that babe in Bethlehem. All modern theology, in interpreting that babe, sets aside God's interpretation of that babe, and then you have nothing left but that an ideal man is born. Modern theology is the setting aside of God's interpretation. After setting aside God's interpretation, it interprets that babe itself. Then you have nothing left, for there is nothing to see. From the human side, that babe is just like all others. This is modern theology also as concerns the cross. Set aside the declaration of God concerning the cross, and you have nothing left but the pitiful spectacle that a man is cruelly put to death, whether that man be guilty or innocent.

In the second place, the gospel must be declared by God because it is only on the basis of God's declaration that we can believe impossible things. I believe in such impossible things as the forgiveness of sins. That the God who is unchangeably righteous forgives sin is impossible. Yet on the basis of God's declaration, I believe that the impossible is possible. All such things that are contradicted by all that is around me, I believe. I live in the valley of death. I die and I am gone. In the midst of this, I believe that I have eternal life. All about me contradicts it. But I believe. Why do I believe? Did Moses say so? Then my faith is vain. Did Isaiah say so? Did Paul? Faith cannot rest on the word of man. If I am to be confident of righteousness and life in the midst of death, there is only one who can tell me. If there is ever to be glad news for me, it must be God who brings it to me.

This is what the apostle says. This is why he says, "the gospel of God, (Which he had promised afore by his prophets in the holy scriptures)," that is, in the old dispensation. He declared it through His prophets. He declared it as a promise. In the old dispensation God said, "My Son will come." His people suffered, but they clung to that Word of God. They died in that faith, not having received the promise. God finally declared it through His Son when He sent Him into the world. Through Him God spoke directly to His people. He said, "I am the way, the truth, and the life" [John 14:6]; "I am the resurrection, and the life" [John 11:25].

A Necessary Separation unto This Gospel

In the new dispensation, the apostle says, God still declares the same gospel. Paul means, "Don't take it as my word. If you ask me, 'How did you get it, Paul? Did you go to school to learn it? Did you prepare for it? Did you receive it by coming into contact with philosophers? What then?' the answer is, 'Paul, a servant of Jesus Christ, that is, His slave, who is to speak what He tells me to.'"

Called to be an apostle! It was far from the mind of Paul to become an apostle. So far was it from his mind that he persecuted the church and raved against the gospel. But Christ called him. He separated him unto the gospel. He so separated him that Paul became the instrument of the Spirit to receive the gospel and to declare it so that we have the gospel in the holy Scriptures. The Scriptures are God's testimony concerning His Son to His people.

The practical application is that upon the basis of God's declaration, as soon as the gospel speaks to our heart, we believe the impossible possibility that our sins are forgiven and that we have eternal life. The Son of God was made flesh from the seed of David.

Do you believe it?

The Son of God was raised from the dead.

Do you believe it?

Do you say of the Son of God, "Our Lord Jesus Christ, to whom I belong"? Then this gospel is yours, and you can rejoice and say, "I, then, having been justified by faith, have peace with God."

Chapter Two

The Gospel a Power of God

Romans 1:16, 17

For I am not ashamed of the gospel of Christ: for it is the power of God unto salvation to every one that believeth; to the Jew first, and also to the Greek.

For therein is the righteousness of God revealed from faith to faith: as it is written, The just shall live by faith.

The words of the text give a reason for something that the apostle had spoken of in the immediate context. There the apostle had said that all that is within him is ready to preach the gospel to them who are at Rome also. As the reason for that statement, or for something that lies at the basis of that statement, the apostle says that he is not ashamed to preach the gospel of Christ at Rome.

He was not ashamed to preach to them at Rome, as perhaps it had been slanderously said of him. To the contrary, he had long had the desire to visit them. This desire was perhaps born from the fact that the Roman church was well spoken of. Their faith was spoken of throughout the whole world. The reason was, perhaps, that they had suffered persecution and had endured. However that may be, the apostle writes that he always remembered them in his prayers. When he prays for the saints in Rome, he also makes request that the Lord may open the way for him to come to Rome. This is his desire.

He explains this desire as having a twofold reason. In the first place, he wants to impart some spiritual gift unto them, or as he explains it, "that I may be comforted together with you by the mutual faith both of you and me" [v. 12].

In the second place, he would like to preach in Rome so that he might have some fruit among them, even as elsewhere. But he had been prevented, hitherto, from coming unto them. The Lord had closed the way for him. But he longed to come, for he is not ashamed to preach the gospel in Rome.

He explains why he is not ashamed. The gospel is a power. It is not a word of man. It is not a philosophy. It is not an offer. But it is a power. If it were a philosophy or an offer, one might be ashamed of it. But the gospel is a power of God unto salvation. It is sure to have effect. That the gospel of Christ is a power unto salvation has its reason in this, that "therein is the righteousness of God revealed from faith to faith."

A Power, What?

The apostle says that the gospel of Christ is a power unto salvation. We must, therefore, ask three questions. First, what is a power? The answer is, the gospel of Christ. Second, unto what is the gospel of Christ a power? The answer is, unto salvation. Third, why is the gospel such a power? The answer is, because it is the gospel of God.

The gospel is glad tidings, a joyful message. This is the meaning of the word. It is a joyful message from God. This is essential to the gospel. It is a glad message from God concerning God's Son. The gospel is always this. It is a joyful message from God concerning God's Son that chiefly contains two elements. The first element is that the Son of God is, according to the flesh, of the seed of David. The second element is that He is powerfully declared to be the Son of God in the resurrection. These two elements must always be in the gospel. It is a message from God to His people as they are in the darkness of this world. This is the gospel.

In harmony with this, the apostle calls the gospel *the gospel of Christ*. Christ is the center of the gospel. The gospel has

Christ for its contents. It is the gospel of the whole Christ. It is the gospel of Christ as He was foreshadowed in the old dispensation. It is the gospel of Christ as he walked among us on earth for thirty-three years. It is the gospel of Christ as He interpreted Himself through the apostles. This is the gospel. It is the gospel of Christ because in the gospel Christ tells all about Himself—His incarnation, His walk here on earth, His suffering and death, His resurrection, His ascension. Having told all about Himself, He interprets Himself through the apostles. This is the gospel.

This gospel, the apostle says, this message from God concerning Christ, is a power. A power is, in general, virtue to accomplish something. Electricity is a power. Why? It accomplishes something. Wind is a power. Steam is a power. A power accomplishes something; it has an effect. That anything is a power must be seen by its effect.

The question is, therefore, what does the gospel effect? The text says that the gospel effects salvation. It has the sure effect of salvation. The gospel of Christ is a power. It is a power unto salvation.

Salvation from what? In general, it is salvation from this world and all that this world stands for. The gospel of Christ is a power to save from this world with its sin, with its corruption, with its misery, with its death. It is a power to save from the world in which we live, in which we are born, in which we suffer, in which we die. It is a power to save from the guilt of sin in which we are born, from the corruption of sin from which we cannot deliver ourselves, from the power of death by which we are held.

Salvation unto what? It is a salvation unto righteousness, both in the legal and in the spiritual sense. Therefore, when the apostle says that the gospel is a power of God unto salvation, the meaning is that the gospel of Christ has the inherent virtue of rolling away your sin, driving out your darkness, cutting the shackles of death, and translating you into a state of righteousness, of holiness, and of life. This transformation, which Scripture calls salvation, is the effect of the gospel of Christ.

Not, it *may* be.

Not, perhaps it *will* be, if you meet it halfway, if you accept it.

No, it *is*. The gospel *is* this power. It surely transforms. The gospel is a living, transforming power that, if it touch your inmost heart so that you are connected with it, drives away your sin, your darkness, your death. The gospel does that.

How is this possible? How can it be maintained that the gospel is such a power?

You understand, this can never be said about any word of man. The Bible as such, which is the infallible revelation of the gospel, never transforms you. If I should preach until midnight, my word would never transform you. You might judge it, you might agree with it or disagree with it, but my word would never transform you. If I should get down on my knees and beg you, my word would never transform you. My word has no power beyond the power of persuasion. Persuasion will never change anyone from a state of unrighteousness to a state of righteousness, from a state of corruption to a state of holiness, from a state of death to a state of life.

For this reason the gospel can never be an offer. An offer is powerless. I offer you something, but you shut your hand and refuse to receive what I offer. The power is gone. An offer has no power.

But the apostle says that he is not ashamed of the gospel of Christ, because it is not a human word, but the power of God. This is why he is not ashamed to preach the gospel, even in Rome. Rome may be powerful, but it has never seen anything as powerful as this. The gospel is a power. Why? Because it is the gospel of God.

What does this mean? First, it is the gospel of God because He is the author of it. Second, it is the gospel of God because He realized it. Third, it is the gospel of God in the sense that He declared it. He declared it throughout the history of the world.

But when now the apostle says that the gospel is a power of God, the meaning is that God also delivers this message into your soul. Only when, through the Word, the gospel is carried by God into the heart as a power that God uses, does it become a power unto salvation. When God carries the gospel into my heart, the effect is that I say, "I am a child of God, my sin is rolled away, I am delivered from the power of death." Though my conscience testifies against me, I know that I am righteous before God.

A Power, Why?

Why is the gospel a power unto salvation? The apostle says, "Therein is the righteousness of God revealed from faith to faith." This is not the reason why the gospel is a power, but why it is a power unto salvation. We can understand this in light of the following realities. In the first place, God is righteous, unchangeably righteous. The righteousness of God means that He always acts and thinks and wills in accordance with His holy being. God's righteousness is an attribute. God is righteous.

In the second place, this unchangeable righteousness of God as an attribute of God means that He can only love the righteous. He cannot love the unrighteous, for He is righteous. God is angry with the unrighteous. He is angry with the wicked every day. God cannot love the unrighteous. I do not say that He cannot transform them. This is just what we are talking about. But He cannot love the unrighteous. He hates all who are not in harmony with His being. He makes them the object of His wrath. Being the object of His wrath, they must perish.

In the third place, righteousness—that is, the state in which we are in harmony with Him and with His will according to His own judgment over us—is an indispensable requirement of salvation. Only the righteous can live.

But we are unrighteous. We are unrighteous in the sense that we have sinned. We are behind in our obligation. Our obligation is to love God with all that we are and have, and at all times. Not only are we behind in our obligation, but we fall behind more and more. For we are corrupt. Therefore, our state is such that we can never become righteous. Everything around us, even our daily newspapers, points its finger at us and tells us that we are damned. Everything within us and without us testifies that we are unrighteous, corrupt, damned. In every sense of the word, salvation is impossible because righteousness is unattainable.

In the fourth place, the text says that in the gospel of God, a righteousness of God is revealed. This does not refer to the righteousness of God as an attribute, but it refers to a righteousness that God has prepared and will give to you. The text does not mean that God is righteous, but it speaks of a righteousness that God has prepared and that He gives to His people.

It is the righteousness of God because God conceived of it in His eternal counsel. It is the righteousness of God because in time He realized it by blotting out the sin of His people. He realized it in Christ, on the cross. This righteousness of God, which He conceived of in His counsel and realizes in time in Christ, is declared in the gospel, in which the righteousness of God is set forth.

If this gospel is delivered into your heart, what do you do? You take hold of it. You believe. I do not say you *must* believe. I do not *persuade* you to believe. When the almighty power of the gospel comes into contact with your soul, what do you do? You believe. You surely believe. You absolutely believe. You cannot help but believe. God works this faith in your soul through the gospel.

A Power, unto Whom?

This is why the gospel of Christ is a power to everyone who believes. Whatever the phrase *from faith to faith* may mean (for this is not so easy to explain; in the original, Romans 1:17

reads, "out of faith and into faith"), it surely means that the gospel is a power out of faith and unto faith. For faith is essentially the tie that unites with Christ. This faith God gives through the gospel. Because faith is the spiritual connecting power with Christ, it is faith in the gospel. Because the gospel reveals Christ, faith is a certain knowledge of the gospel. Because faith is a certain knowledge of the gospel of Christ, he who believes says, "I am righteous before God." For this reason faith is a sure confidence, so that he who believes relies on that gospel. For the same reason he lives from that gospel.

The last clause of the text might be read, according to the original, "the just by faith shall live." That is, he who is righteous by faith shall live. But it can also be read, "the righteous, by faith shall live." It is my conviction that the apostle means both. The minute we look away from Christ, it looks hopeless. Therefore, let us clearly see the gospel of Christ. We must write death upon all our own works. When I have thrown away all my own works, then my eye, by the faith of the gospel, is fixed only upon the righteousness of Christ.

The apostle also means that the righteous out of faith shall live. Here there is so much that condemns us as unrighteous. But the time will come when God will cause us to become manifest, by a final justification, as perfectly righteous. The righteous by faith shall live.

Chapter Three

The Revelation of God's Wrath

Romans 1:18
For the wrath of God is revealed from heaven against all ungodliness and unrighteousness of men, who hold the truth in unrighteousness.

The text is an added reason for the statement of the apostle in verse 16. There the apostle says, "I am not ashamed of the gospel of Christ. I am not ashamed to preach it, to represent it, wherever the Lord sends me, even in Rome."

The first reason for this statement the apostle gives in verses 16 and 17: "for it is the power of God unto salvation to every one that believeth; . . . For therein is the righteousness of God revealed." Therefore, he is not ashamed of it. No one needs to be ashamed of a power that accomplishes such an effect. The gospel is no philosophy. It is not a human word. But it is a power.

The other reason why the apostle is not ashamed to preach the gospel is expressed in the text. It might be that although the gospel is such a power, men have no need of it. It might be that, although the gospel is the revelation of the righteousness of God that is by faith, men are not in need of this righteousness. But the apostle in the text tells us the opposite. Men need this righteousness, for the wrath of God is revealed from heaven against all ungodliness and unrighteousness of men who hold the truth in unrighteousness, that is, who hold *down* the truth in unrighteousness.

In order not to be ashamed of a thing that we represent, three things are necessary. First, the thing must do what it is supposed to do: it must do what we claim it will do. Second, the thing that we represent must actually be needed. Third, the particular thing that we represent must not only be needed but must also be unexcelled, so that nothing can take its place. *This* the apostle means in the context: "I am not ashamed of the gospel of Christ, for it serves its purpose; it is an efficacious power. I am not ashamed of the gospel, for it is needed, the world being full of unrighteousness. I am not ashamed of the gospel, for it is unexcelled. No human wisdom has ever effected what the gospel effects."

The wrath of God is still revealed from heaven.

In this light we must look at the text. The text in itself is negative. The purpose of the text lies not in itself, but in the gospel. The purpose of the text is to show that our need lies in the gospel and to create the feeling that we need the righteousness of that gospel.

The Wrath That Is Revealed

The wrath of God is emphatically the wrath of *God*. This wrath of God is *revealed,* the apostle says. God's wrath is the constant reaction of His holiness against all who refuse to seek and acknowledge Him as the highest good. It becomes active in the will and the power to curse. This is God's wrath.

God is holy. God's holiness is probably His most distinct divine attribute. When Scripture says that God is holy, it sometimes means almost the same thing as that God is God. God's holiness not only means that He is separated from all sin and corruption and unrighteousness, but it also means that He is separated from all creatures. God's holiness is that virtue in God by which He is entirely *other* from any creature. The distinctive virtue of God by which He is entirely *other* from the creature is this, that God is always motivated by the will to seek Himself because He is the highest good. Because God is the highest good, He must seek Himself. What is sin in us, namely, to seek ourselves, is virtue in God. God has His purpose in Himself in all that He wills and does. This is God's active holiness.

Because of this, God's holiness reveals itself in a twofold way as it comes into contact with different objects. God's holiness is mercy when it comes into contact with them who seek Him. This is the action of holiness. This same holiness becomes wrath, that is, divine displeasure, the will to curse, unto those who refuse to seek and acknowledge Him. This is the meaning of the apostle when he says that the wrath of God is revealed. The divine anger, the divine displeasure, the will to curse, is revealed.

When we speak of the wrath of God, we must be careful, first, that we have in mind the actual wrath of God. The wrath of God is not like the wrath of man. The wrath of God is not a sudden passing passion. God does not flare up in anger. God's wrath is constant. It never changes. It does not increase or decrease. God's wrath is not a sudden passion that soon passes and for which He is then sorry. No, God's wrath is constant. It is as constant as His holiness.

Second, this wrath of God has all the attributes of the divine being. As the wrath of God, it is omnipresent. It is everywhere. God is everywhere. God touches you, He besets you, He pursues you, He surrounds you. God is omnipresent. So also is God's wrath.

Third, the wrath of God is absolutely efficacious. That is, it cannot be resisted. It does what it wills. And it wills to curse. Therefore, if we would understand the reality of the text, we must understand that the apostle teaches that there is in this world, in this night of darkness in which we live, an operation of the wrath of God in everything. There is an operation of the wrath of God around you and within you. There is in this world a divine *No* to the sin of man. God says *No* always, constantly, eternally, in the world, everywhere. God says *No* to the sin of man. That God says *No* does not mean that He forbids it. When God speaks, there is power in that *No*. There is power in that *No* to curse. That *No* does curse, and from it there is no escape.

The Provocation of This Wrath

This *No* is constantly provoked by what men do in the world. The apostle speaks reality. He is speaking of the world. He is speaking of the world as it really is. He is speaking of the cultured, the civilized, world. He is not speaking of men in the wilds of Africa. He is speaking of Rome. He is speaking of men who stood at the pinnacle of culture. He is not ashamed to preach the gospel at Rome, for there the wrath of God is revealed.

This wrath is revealed today, as it was then. Men also hold this truth down in unrighteousness, but the apostle says that there is an actual operation of wrath in the world because the world provokes it. By what? The apostle says, by ungodliness, unrighteousness, and the wicked attempt to hold down the truth in unrighteousness. The apostle does not mean that this wrath is revealed wherever there is unrighteousness and ungodliness and wherever the truth is held down in unrighteousness. Rather, the apostle means that *all* men hold the truth down in unrighteousness. Men of learning, philosophers, men of culture, men for whom you take off your hat—all men in every station of life hold down the truth in unrighteousness. This is the reality of the world that provokes from heaven God's *No*.

What is this provocation? Ungodliness, the apostle says. Ungodliness is the opposite of the fear of God. The fear of God, springing from the love of God, is godliness. Godliness arises from the love of the true God—not *a* god, not a god who is nice and loving, not a god for whom you can do something, for whom you can work, to whom you can give a dollar in the collection plate. This god is just as much an idol as the heathen gods of wood and stone in Paul's day. This is not God. No, but

God! If you know who God is—the wholly *other* whom you must always fear, whom you must always love, whom you must always obey, whose will you must always do, whose honor you must always seek—and if, then, you love Him in reverent fear, there is godliness in the heart.

Ungodliness is just the opposite. Ungodliness is that you do not love Him, do not fear Him, do not care about Him, never reckon with Him, and act as if He is never there. Ungodliness does not mean that you curse and swear. This is hardly decent. But ungodliness is that God is not in all your thoughts. Ungodliness is that you breathe His air, eat His bread, drink His water, partake of His bounties, and never say, "Thank you." This is ungodliness. Ungodliness also characterizes modern philosophy (I mean philosophy that throws God away for the pleasure of saying that it cannot find Him). Philosophy is ungodliness.

The apostle says it is also unrighteousness that provokes God's wrath. Unrighteousness follows from ungodliness. To be unrighteous in the heart and in the walk is to be contrary to the will of God. Not to will what God wills: this is unrighteousness. The apostle charges that the whole world is characterized by this ungodliness and unrighteousness. No matter how cultured, how refined, how civilized, the world may be, the natural man is ungodly and unrighteous. This is exactly what you and I are by nature. And over against this ungodliness and unrighteousness is God's terrible *No*. It pursues you, it curses you, it drags you down, and you cannot escape it.

Why do men do this?

Why do men provoke the wrath of God so that it pursues them and curses them at every step?

Do they not know?

Yes, the apostle says, in the third description he gives of the world; they hold down the truth in unrighteousness. This is an ethical principle. This is the dominating principle in the life of natural man: he holds down the truth in unrighteousness.

Not *a* truth. Men seek after truth, as, for example, the truth that two times two is four. But *the* truth they hold down in unrighteousness.

What is the truth? The truth is God. The revelation of God—God as He is, God in His righteousness, in His holiness, in all His divine perfections—this truth, the apostle says, men *know*. This is what he says in the following verses. Men know this truth. This is why they say there is no God. This is why we have atheists. Atheism is not ignorance. We must not be deceived by what people call a difference of opinion or an honest error when it comes to *the* truth. When it comes to the truth of God, men hold this truth down; they suppress it in unrighteousness.

What does this mean? It means that men want to live in unrighteousness. They love unrighteousness and hate righteousness. Now comes the truth. As the apostle explains in the following verses, "That which may be known of God is manifest in them; for God hath shewed it unto them." They know God. When this truth comes to men, whether they be white or black or yellow or brown, whether this truth comes to them from creation or from Scripture, or when it comes to them in the very body of His Son, they say, "There is no God." Why? Because they hold down the truth in unrighteousness. And if the truth persists, as it persisted in Christ, they crucify Him. This is the world. This is you and I.

One must not try to evade the apostle's judgment by saying, "Yes, but there is common grace." There is no common grace. Do not try to light an oil lamp in our night. Our night is just as dark as the night in which Paul preached. Do not try to fix it up. Do not say, "I don't agree with you." This is not the question. It is the Word of God. The Word of God tells us that "the wrath of God is revealed from heaven against all ungodliness and unrighteousness of men, who hold down the truth in unrighteousness." There is no way of escape for man. You cannot change it.

The Revelation of This Wrath

In this night, the wrath of God is revealed. The apostle says that the wrath of God is revealed from heaven. We cannot see Him. If we could see God as the text pictures Him, the world would not have the peace that it seemingly has. God is in heaven. We cannot see Him. But He frowns from heaven. That is, His face is in heaven. But the apostle declares that in the world this wrath of God, this *No* of God, this will to curse, is revealed. This does not mean that God tells the world about it. But it means that this wrath is operating. It is plainly visible. We can plainly see God's anger. We can see it in its operation. It is plainly evident that God curses. It is revealed everywhere that God curses. Curses what? Sin? No, *men*—men who hold down the truth in unrighteousness.

This is evident in many things. The apostle in the verses following merely points to the general line in which this wrath is revealed. The apostle draws this line. The wrath of God takes hold of man and forces him, giving him over, from corruption to corruption. We can easily see what is the end of this pursuing wrath of God. The end is nothing less than hell. The wrath of God takes hold of the human race. It takes hold of you and me as soon as we become a part of that human race. And it brings the human race from corruption to corruption until the end comes, and the end is hell.

The wrath of God destroys individual life, family life, and the life of society. This is evident in our American family. The wrath of God is sweeping it on and bringing it from corruption to corruption. It is evident today in our economy how the wrath of God is bringing it from corruption to corruption so that today the whole world is crying for an economic savior.[1] The general line of the development of men who hold down the truth in unrighteousness is the way of destruction. There

---

1. Hoeksema preached this sermon in the late 1930s when the United States and other nations were suffering from severe economic depression.

is no way out. We must go on. There is no escape from this wrath of God. It pursues us every step of the way.

Is there no way out at all? Yes. In this night God declared the gospel concerning His Son, who became flesh. He took upon Himself our sin. He said, "It is my delight to do thy will, O God." And God raised Him from the dead.

What does this mean? It means that God said, "I stop saying *No* right here. There is no more wrath. I poured it out upon the head of my Son, and my wrath has been burned out in Him. He that believeth in me shall no more see the wrath of God." Therefore, he who says, "There is no hope for me," and says, "Be merciful to me a sinner," and seeks his righteousness in the risen Lord, will no more taste the wrath of God.

Having been justified by faith, we have peace with God.

Chapter Four

Inexcusable Madness

Romans 1:19–23
Because that which may be known of God is manifest in them; for God hath shewed it unto them.

For the invisible things of him from the creation of the world are clearly seen, being understood by the things that are made, even his eternal power and Godhead; so that they are without excuse:

Because that, when they knew God, they glorified him not as God, neither were thankful; but became vain in their imaginations, and their foolish heart was darkened.

Professing themselves to be wise, they became fools,

And changed the glory of the uncorruptible God into an image made like to corruptible man, and to birds, and fourfooted beasts, and creeping things.

The passage speaks of what may be characterized as inexcusable madness—the inexcusable madness of unrighteousness.

Let me illustrate. Imagine that in a dark night a car is approaching a railroad crossing while a fast train is coming down the tracks, rapidly nearing the road upon which the car is traveling. Some five hundred feet from the crossing a large sign tells the driver that the railroad crossing is near. The driver sees that sign. A little farther, the driver reads another sign: "Stop, Look, and Listen." He reads that sign. The signal lights are flashing, and the bells are ringing. The driver sees and hears it. He hears the shrill whistle of the train. But he drives on with the inevitable result that the car is smashed and its occupants are destroyed. What is this? It is madness. Yes, but it is madness for which there is no excuse.

Or imagine that in the city there is a third rail, highly charged with electricity. A large sign warns of the presence of that rail. It is properly fenced off to keep anyone from stepping upon that rail. Yet someone, in spite of the warning and in spite of the fence, climbs over that fence and steps upon that rail and is killed. What is this? Madness, you say. But it is inexcusable.

This illustrates what man does with the living God. That train is the almighty God, who holds His course, who does not change His way, who never stops. That living rail is God, who is a consuming fire for all who set themselves against Him. The mad driver is the sinner. The signs and signals are the things that are seen of God. These things are clearly seen. Yet natural man goes on, clashes with God, and is destroyed. This is inexcusable madness.

The text calls our attention to this inexcusable madness from a threefold point of view. It tells us, in the first place, what this madness is, namely, that "when they knew God, they glorified him not as God, neither were thankful." In the second place, it tells us that this madness is inexcusable when it says, "That which may be known of God is manifest in them; for God hath shewed it unto them." In the third place, the text tells us of the first result of the madness. It does not tell us the complete result, but it tells us that the first result is that men "became vain in their imaginations, and their foolish heart was darkened."

The Madness

The madness is that man knew God and glorified Him not as God. The apostle is speaking of man, that is, of the world as it lies in darkness, of the world as it lies apart from the gospel, as it does not have the light of the gospel. He is speaking of the world in which he is called to preach. We may say that he is speaking of the heathen world. Of this heathen world the apostle says that they knew God. Their foolishness and idolatry are not to be ascribed to natural darkness. It is often presented as if the heathen stand with outstretched hands waiting for the gospel. This is not the heathen world according to Romans. The apostle is speaking of the world apart from the gospel. Of this world he says that it *knew* God.

When the apostle says that the heathen world knows God, he means that they know God is, and they know God is of everlasting power. The apostle says this in verse 20: "For the invisible things of him from the creation of the world are clearly seen, being understood by the things that are made, even his eternal power and Godhead." By the eternal power of God, the apostle simply means the power by which He is able to do things. They know it. They know that God is and that He is of eternal power. Of course, the apostle means, too, that they know the stick they put in the ground is *not* God. They know this.

But they know more. They also know the divinity of God. God's divinity is what distinguishes Him from all creatures. God's divinity is what distinguishes Him from all that we see. As divine, He is not of this world. As divine, He is distinct from everything. As divine, He is wholly *other* from all that is called creature. The heathen know this. Man knows this. Man knows God's divinity. God's divinity is what is called His "holiness" in Scripture. God's holiness is that virtue in Him by which He demands that He must always be served, worshipped, glorified, praised, and thanked. Men know this.

Men know that God is not off somewhere in heaven. They know that there is power that surrounds them, a spiritual, living power that surrounds them and that demands of them that they glorify Him. This is the train of my illustration. Men know this. Yet they do not glorify God and thank Him.

To glorify God as God is to acknowledge that God is God, that He is good, and that He must be praised and worshipped. To give thanks means practically the same thing, only with the acknowledgment that from this God we receive all things. The food we eat, the water we drink, the air we breathe: all things we receive from Him. The heathen know this. They are conscious of the everlasting power and divinity of God.

Sin is not ignorance. Sin is corruption by which man refuses to acknowledge God because he loves unrighteousness. If a man loves unrighteousness, he cannot, will not, and cannot will to glorify God. He will not give thanks because, as the apostle tells us in verse 18, he holds the truth under in unrighteousness. Therefore, he refuses to go along with this power. He goes his own way.

This is madness. It is madness because, no more than that train, will God stop. The truth does not change because we do not want it. God goes on—everlasting power, everlasting divinity. The sinner crosses this everlasting power and divinity. It is madness because the sinner knows that coming against this power and divinity, he must be crushed.

The Inexcusable Nature

But perhaps there was an excuse. The apostle shows, in verse 20, that no man has an excuse to run against the living God and be crushed. An excuse is something that weakens or even removes the blame for a fault. If a man does not reach a certain place in time, although the sin of being late is there, yet it may be excused. The man may not have known; he may have been misinformed; he may have been detained so that he could not come on time. Therefore, he is excused.

So perhaps this man who runs against God has an excuse. After all, God is invisible. The apostle says so in verse 20. Philosophers say that God cannot be seen, is invisible, and therefore cannot be known. The atheist says, "Because we do not see God, there is no God."

But the apostle takes this excuse away. He shows that man is inexcusable. God has done something that makes him inexcusable. What is it? Why is man without excuse? The apostle explains that the invisible things of God from the creation of the world are clearly seen, being understood by the things that are made. Verse 20 is an explanation of what the apostle mentions in verse 19, where he has said, "That which may be known of God is manifest in them; for God hath shewed it unto them." That which may be known of God, or as the original has it, that which *is* known of God, means that what is known of God is manifest in them. Notice that the apostle does not say that it is revealed unto them. It is *manifest* in them. It is manifest in their heart and mind. The apostle does not mean that they have a revelation of God in nature, as it is frequently explained. It is manifest in them. God made it known to them. There is not a man who does not know that God is. God makes known unto man His eternal power and divinity.

The apostle explains this. "For," he says, "the invisible things of him from the creation of the world are clearly seen, being understood by the things that are made." By the invisible things of God, the apostle means all the virtues of the divine being. You cannot see God. God is hid. He is hid behind the veil of the material things. The essence of God is not seen. But the invisible things of God are seen, the apostle says.

This seems to be a paradox. The invisible things of God are seen. How? By the things that are made. The things that are made are the veil behind which God is hid, but the fact that God is behind the veil is *seen*. The reason is that all these things are words. They are words of God. When God made these words, what did He speak about? There wasn't anything to speak about except Himself. But the apostle says that the invisible things of God are seen. They are not merely declared. The apostle says that man sees them. The apostle does not mean that man *may* know God if he only takes notice of these things and that he may also *not* know God by *not* taking notice of them. No, the apostle means that man *must* know God. How does he know God? God brings these things into his heart and mind.

Creation is not a dead book. It is a living testimony. Through it God brings the invisible things of God into man's heart. Just as He brings the living testimony of the gospel into the hearts of His people, so He brings the living testimony of creation into the heart of man.

For this reason the invisible things of God are clearly seen. That is why it is a good remedy, even for the Christian, to escape from this sophisticated world for a time (for we live in a *very* sophisticated world) and go to the woods, lie on one's back, and say nothing. Don't say anything; don't spoil it by talking. Just look up at the sky, listen to the birds, and look at the trees, the flowers, and the grass. This will be the testimony: "God is! God is eternal in power and eternal in Godhead! God must be praised!"

They know God. They know His eternal power and Godhead. They know that He must be glorified and praised.

The Result

We would say that if man knows God in His power and divinity and knows that He must be glorified and praised, the expected result would be that man would glorify and praise Him, just as when the driver of that car sees the signs and signals and hears the train, the expected result would be that he would step on the brake and stop the car. But the apostle says that the expected fails. Man knows God and that God must be praised and thanked, but man does not give thanks.

Why not?

In principle, the apostle gives the answer in verse 18: they hold the truth under in unrighteousness. Men want unrighteousness. What do they do? They begin to talk. The apostle says that they became vain in their imaginations. Or, according to the original, they became vain in their own reasoning. Men began to philosophize about God. They set aside God's testimony concerning Himself because they wanted a god after their own heart. They did not want to let God tell them who He is. Then they began to philosophize. They said, "We will develop our own system of wisdom." This is philosophy.

Philosophy says, "We will determine our own god." This is also the philosophy for which we take off our cap. All philosophy is foolish, because it does not want God.

What is the result? The apostle says that man became vain. He became vain, empty, void of the knowledge of God. Man may reason the knowledge of God away—not in his deepest heart, for there he must know God. But man may reason so long that he reasons the knowledge of God away. Especially over generations this happens. He becomes vain. This is what the apostle means: knowing God, he did not glorify and thank Him, and he became vain. He became vain with respect to the knowledge of God. He became vain—empty—with respect to the knowledge of God.

What was the result? The result was that as soon as they so reasoned with regard to God, they clashed with the wrath of God. That wrath of God struck them. Their foolish heart was darkened. God showed them that their wisdom is foolishness. Professing themselves to be wise, they became fools.

You understand, God showed them the foolishness of their wisdom when He cast them down before the image of corruptible man and birds and beasts and creeping things. God said, "If you will not serve me, then I will make you fools." How does this become evident? By their idolatry. God made man foolish, and man made a picture of a corruptible man and of an ox and of creeping things. He said to that image, "Thou art my god. From thee do I expect help and deliverance and salvation." They changed, in their mind and heart, the glory of the uncorruptible God into an image made like to corruptible man and birds and four-footed beasts and creeping things.

I am not ashamed of the gospel of Christ, the apostle says, in the light of this explanation of man. I would be ashamed of it if the gospel had nothing to say to this man who so holds the truth under in unrighteousness. I would be ashamed of the gospel if it did not have a remedy. But it has, for in it is revealed the righteousness of God that is by faith in Christ Jesus.

I would be ashamed of this gospel if I had to come to this

world and offer the world this righteousness, for then it would be hopeless. Man does not want righteousness; he loves unrighteousness. All history shows that man does not want righteousness. God's invisible things are clearly seen. Although this is not the gospel, it testifies of this one thing: man does not want righteousness. In nature He holds the righteousness of God under in unrighteousness. If I *offer* this man the righteousness of Christ, he will also hold this truth under in unrighteousness. If he holds the righteousness of God revealed in nature under in unrighteousness, he will hold the righteousness of God revealed in the gospel under in unrighteousness.

But the gospel is not an offer. It is the power of God unto salvation. Just as God takes the testimony of nature and carries it into the heart of man, so He takes the testimony of the gospel concerning His Son and carries it into the heart of His elect.

I am not ashamed of the gospel of Christ, for it is a power. It is the power that the sinner needs to be saved from the death in which he holds the truth under in unrighteousness.

Chapter Five

Delivered to Corruption

Romans 1:24, 25
Wherefore God also gave them up to uncleanness through the lusts of their own hearts, to dishonour their own bodies between themselves:
Who changed the truth of God into a lie, and worshipped and served the creature more than the Creator, who is blessed for ever. Amen.

The main thought of this passage, in its context, can best be expressed by saying that sin is very successful and prospers in all that it wills, even unto the end. The reason for this prospering of sin is the wrath of God. The wrath of God prospers sin so that it reaches its purpose. From a spiritual point of view, the sinner does what he pleases. However, sin prospers more than the sinner originally planned. He cannot stop.

Let me use a figure. Suppose there is a steep, icy road that ends in a precipice. A man sets his feet on that steep, icy road. What will happen? He will go on. He will be prosperous in his slide down that road. Can he stop? No, he must go on. Why? You say, "Because of the law of gravitation." Perhaps this is correct. But what is the law of gravitation? It is the unchangeable operation of God in things. God pulls that man down. Will God stop because a man puts his feet on that slippery road? No. God does not change. What must happen if that man is to stop halfway, or rather, if he is to go up that steep road instead of down? You say, "It would take a miracle." This is a fitting illustration of the passage, in its connection.

The slippery road is the process of sin. The man who puts his feet on that road is the sinner, indeed the whole world. On this slippery road the whole world moves by nature. The power that pulls the world down is the unchangeable operation of the wrath of God. The wrath of God pulls man down from sin to sin until he reaches the precipice. The only power that not only will cause man to stop, but that will also cause him to go up, is the gospel. This is why the gospel is the power unto salvation. This is why the apostle is not ashamed of this gospel.

The wrath of God is revealed, the apostle has said. When the apostle says that the wrath of God is revealed from heaven, he does not mean that God in heaven is angry, but he means that there is an effectual operation of wrath in the world. This wrath is present. It is around us. It besets us on every side. It works. In the face of the operation of this wrath, men hold the truth under in unrighteousness. The truth is that God is God, that He is glorious, and that He must be praised and thanked. Men hold this truth under in unrighteousness. They want to be unrighteousness. Therefore, they hold the truth under in unrighteousness. As soon as they do, wrath is revealed.

How? God's wrath was revealed in that their hearts were darkened, so that they became religiously foolish. This is the punishment of their wanting to perform unrighteousness. Men held the truth under in unrighteousness, and God made them so foolish that they made themselves gods that were like corruptible man and birds and four-footed beasts and creeping things. Having made these images, they went on; and their hearts became more darkened, until finally they believed that these images they made actually were God.

This is always the case. Some people, for example, will find all kinds of excuses for not sending their children to the Christian school. They know better. They know that they should send them to the Christian school, but they seek all kinds of excuses. Once having started on this road, they must go on until they finally believe their own excuses.

So it is here. Man said, "I do not want to serve and glorify

God." He held the truth under in unrighteousness. God said, "Go ahead." Then man made images. He knew these images were not God. But God darkened his heart. Man was carried on until finally he believed that these sticks and stones actually were God. This is the course of sin. The next step is moral corruption. This is the inevitable result. A man is like his god. If he makes himself a god, he becomes like the god he makes. The reason is that wrath pulls him down. God brings His people into heaven. He also brings the wicked into hell.

This is the teaching of the text: "Wherefore God also gave them up to uncleanness through the lusts of their own hearts, to dishonour their own bodies between themselves: Who changed the truth of God into a lie, and worshipped and served the creature more than the Creator, who is blessed for ever."

This is the development of sin. Only one power can save man from continuing on this road of sin until he falls into destruction.

The Meaning

The text says that God gave them up to *uncleanness*. All sin is uncleanness. But if we read the rest of this chapter, we will see that the apostle means something specific. What the apostle means with *uncleanness* is that moral state of heart and mind in which man corrupts himself sexually. Moral filth is what the apostle has in mind. By this uncleanness the apostle means that God gave them over to such a condition of the heart, will, mind, and desires that they delight in sexual filth. The effect is that they dishonor their own bodies between themselves.

What the apostle means by this he explains when he says that this moral corruption is such that men lusted after men, and women after women. It began with corruption in the spirit; it ends with corruption in the body. This is heathendom. This is civilized Greece and Rome. This is reality. This is still the case.

The text is an explanation of many things we see around us. It is striking that the world that departs from God gives rise to all manner of uncleanness. Many of our movies would be out of business if it were not for the sexual filth shown in them. What is the reason for the sexually explicit pictures everywhere? Why must even ordinary ads contain unchastity? Unclean minds make unclean things. But remember, the text explains it as a manifestation of the wrath of God. The wrath of God brings men to hell. The wrath of God brings the world to destruction.

Mark well, the text says that God *gave them over.* People have tried to explain away the force of this word. They have even found in this chapter a classic proof for common grace. They say that God's giving man over to uncleanness does not mean that God pushes man into sin. This, they say, would be contrary to God's holiness. They say, rather, that it means God simply abandoned them. He simply let them go. He let them go as I let go my handkerchief so that it falls. God first held man back on the road of sin. This is called the restraint of sin. Then God let man go. He stepped out of man's way so that He did not hold him back anymore. Man then slipped down on the road of sin.

This is not so. Did you ever see the law of gravity stop anyone from going down? Romans 1 teaches that the wrath of God pulls man down. The word used in the original does not mean "to let go." It rather means "to push down, to deliver up." It is the same word that is used for delivering a prisoner into prison. You do not deliver a prisoner into prison by letting him go and letting him walk into prison of his own accord. The same word is used for the deliverance of Christ into the hands of wicked men.

In this same way God delivers men unto sin. He does so in His wrath. The wrath of God is revealed; it operates in the world. The effect is that men become religiously foolish and morally corrupt.

The passage teaches, therefore, that God punishes sin with more sin. The road of the world is sin, wrath, more sin, and more wrath.

35

The Manner

How does God do this? How does He do this without becoming the author of sin? How is it possible? How must it be explained that the wrath of God, which is the reaction of His holiness, brings the sinner deeper into sin. The text says that God does it through the lust of men's hearts. God gave them up to uncleanness through the lusts of their own hearts, to dishonor their own bodies between themselves.

The heart is the center of man's life from a spiritual point of view. Out of the heart are the issues of life. All our thinking, our willing, and our desiring issue forth from the heart. As the heart is, so is the man, spiritually, morally, ethically.

There is nothing wrong in the fact that the heart desires. The heart is made to desire. This is the purpose of the heart. But the normal desire of the heart, apart from sin, is that it desires after God. It desires to be pleasing to Him, to serve Him, to glorify Him. This is the normal desire of the heart. But these desires become lusts as soon as this heart turns away from God. Then the heart fastens itself on other objects, apart from God. It says, "I will no more serve God."

Upon what does the desire of the heart fasten itself if not on God? It fastens itself upon the creature instead of upon the Creator. It seeks things, and it seeks to press these things into the service of unrighteousness. This is lust. There are many lusts in the world: lust of money, lust of honor, lust of position, lust of the flesh, lust of the eyes, the pride of life. The lust of money is that we press it into the service of unrighteousness. This is why we have a depression.[1]

What does God do? He works upon these lusts by His anger. He does not let them go. He works in them. He works in everything. The purpose of God working in these lusts is to bring man as low as possible. Man says to a cow, "Thou art my god."

---

1. The reference, again, is to the economic depression being experienced in Hoeksema's day.

God says, "I will see to it that you fall as far below that god you made, as a worshipper ought to be below his god." Thus man comes to fall below the beast. He does things a beast would never do."[2]

God does it! God says two things to the sinful world. He says, "I will take your heart and guide you in the direction that will bring you lower than the beast you serve." He says also, "I will lead you to destruction."

The Motive

Why? The final reason for God's delivering sinners to destruction is expressed in the words *who is blessed for ever. Amen.* The meaning is that God is the only good. Being the only good, He is the only Blessed One. He is the only Blessed One as the triune God. As the infinite good, He wills to become manifest as the only Blessed One. He wills to become manifest as the one apart from whom there is no blessedness. There may never be anything in which God does not become manifest as the Blessed One.

There are two ways in which God becomes manifest as the only Blessed One. He becomes manifest as such by blessing those who fear Him. But with this same unchangeable will to become manifest as the Blessed One, God assumes an attitude over against the wicked. The result is that God manifests His wrath by making the wicked unspeakably wretched. Antithetically, it becomes manifest that God is blessed forever. Joy and glory are a testimony that God is blessed forever. Wretchedness and misery testify, antithetically, that God is blessed forever. There are but two powers operating in history, blessing and wrath.

The wrath of God is revealed when men serve the creature more than the Creator. This does not mean that they serve the

---

2. Hoeksema is describing the gross sin of homosexuality referred to in the passage.

Creator, too, and that they serve the creature more. No, the meaning is that they serve the creature *instead of* the Creator. They change the truth of God into a lie. And God pushes man down until it becomes manifest that sin is sin.

I am not ashamed of the gospel. This is the positive thought. I am not ashamed of the gospel. It is the power of God unto salvation. It is a power on the slippery road on which wrath pushes man down and on which all find themselves.

How can man be saved? By means of instruction? This is impossible. Salvation is not a matter of education. Man wants unrighteousness. What will stop him? Shall we give him an example? There is no example. The whole world is on that path. No, there must be a power that can change that wrath into uplifting love. This power we have in the gospel. The gospel is a power. It is a power to lift man up.

I am not ashamed of the gospel, for it is a power of God unto salvation. The righteous shall live by faith. He that believeth in Him shall not perish, but have everlasting life.

Chapter Six

Given Over to a Reprobate Mind

Romans 1:28
And even as they did not like to retain God in their knowledge, God gave them over to a reprobate mind, to do those things which are not convenient.

In my explanation of verses 24 and 25, I compared the way and development of sin to a smooth and slippery road upon which the sinner slides down to destruction. He is forced down by a power that the apostle described as the revelation of the wrath of God.

God is the doom of the sinner.

We may compare the development of sin as described in these last verses of Romans 1 to an organic growth. Sin can never stop. It must continue to work until it has corrupted every relation of life. This is not due only to an inherent power of sin, but it is also due to the fact that God *works* in sin. God is not the power of corruption. But God is the power that is able to cause the sinner to corrupt himself unto the very end. God works in sin, causing the sinner to go down from corruption to corruption and to destroy himself.

The beginning was that man did not want to glorify and thank God. By that beginning man stands opposed to the ever present and ever living God. In His wrath, the ever present and ever living God stands over against that sinner who will not glorify and thank Him. This wrath pushes the sinner down.

The apostle mentions three stages in this awful process. In

the first stage, the sinner becomes a religious fool, so that he bows down before an image made like corruptible man and birds and beasts and creeping things. When man refuses to glorify and thank God, the first downward step is always that man bows down before an image. It makes no difference whether he carves this image in wood or stone, as the heathen did, or whether he carves it in his mind, as do the modernists of today.

The second stage the apostle pictures in verses 24–27. God gave them over, the apostle says, to the stage that makes them lower than the beast. If a man wants to worship the beast, why should he not become lower than the beast he worships? But wrath does not stop with this one sin. God goes on. Sin does not stop. It goes on until it bears fruit in every relation of life; hence, the third stage is that God gave them over to a reprobate mind, to do those things that are not *convenient*.

What this means is described in the following verses. When God gives the sinner over to a reprobate mind, three things happen. In the first place, this sinner becomes filled with all manner of unrighteousness, such as fornication, wickedness, covetousness, and maliciousness. Being so filled with unrighteousness, he next becomes filled with all vices, such as envy, murder, deceit, and malignity. The final result is that he begins to act. When God gives men over to a reprobate mind, they become whisperers, backbiters, haters of God, despiteful, proud, and the like.

Is there any hope? What shall we do in such a world? Shall we build up institutions of education? With these institutions of education the world goes to hell.

Shall we reform this world? With this reformation the world goes to hell.

Shall we have federations? Men who slide down, when they federate, slide down together.

No. We shall say, "I am not ashamed of the gospel of Christ, for it is the power of God unto salvation."

The Meaning

The mind is man's moral judgment. It is that faculty of man by which he is able to distinguish between good and evil. It is that faculty of man by which he can distinguish between the truth and the lie, between righteousness and unrighteousness. Not only does the mind distinguish, but it is also the faculty that counsels the will. We might say that the mind is our moral attorney. It tells us what we should do and what we should not do. This is the function of the mind.

The text speaks of a reprobate mind. The original uses a word meaning a mind "not approved." It refers to a mind that has been put to the test and has failed. It is a mind that has been condemned and rejected. It is a mind that does not function properly. The proper function of the mind would be to distinguish between what is good and what is evil. Having so distinguished, it is the function of the mind to persuade the will to determine what is good. The function of the mind is not only to distinguish between good and evil, but also to persuade the will to determine what is in accord with the will of God.

A reprobate mind functions perversely. Suppose that one must give testimony in a certain case. A reprobate mind distinguishes between what is the truth and what is the lie concerning this case; however, at the same time this mind compiles all kinds of lies and persuades the will to tell the lie. This is a reprobate mind, one that distinguishes between good and evil but persuades one to choose that which is evil. Of this mind the apostle is speaking.

To this reprobate mind, God gave man over. This *giving over* is not meant in a passive sense. The word does not mean "to let go." God cannot let things go. A God who lets things go, we do not fear. The word means that God takes the sinner and delivers him up to corruption or, to change the figure, pushes him down from corruption to corruption.

God is the doom of the sinner.

When the text says that God gave man over to a reprobate mind, that is, when God gave him over to such moral judgment, the meaning is not that God makes man's judgment corrupt. His judgment is already corrupt. The mind is already corrupt when man refuses to glorify and thank God. It is already the judgment of a reprobate mind that changed the glory of the incorruptible God into an image of corruptible man and of beasts. God had already given him over when he fell into all kinds of bestiality.

Rather, the text means that God gave man over to bear the fruit of sin to its fullest extent in every relation of life. There is a working of God in man's soul, in his mind, in his will, in his desires. This working is a working of wrath. God works in this mind in wrath. In what way? He causes this mind to bear all the possible fruits of sin.

What are the possible fruits of sin? The next verse tells us. The result of God giving man over to a reprobate mind is that he begins to bear every possible fruit of corruption, so that he becomes filled with every possible unrighteousness. He does not become totally corrupt. He already was totally corrupt. But he bears every possible fruit of unrighteousness.

When God influences the thistle, it bears fruit. When God influences the good tree, it brings forth good fruit. When He influences the corrupt tree, it brings forth corrupt fruit. When God influences the sinner, he becomes filled with every form of unrighteousness.

What is this? The description in verse 29 lists fornication, wickedness, covetousness (greed of every kind), and maliciousness (the desire to do someone wrong).

When he has borne this fruit in its general motives, he bears still more fruit. He becomes "full of envy, murder, debate, deceit, malignity." Under the influence of God's wrath, the reprobate mind bears fruit.

So it was with the world of Rome. So it is with the world of today. If we scratch off a little of the varnish, what do we find?

We find these things. These things are boiling at the fountain heads of the world.

The Result

What is the result? This is expressed in verse 28. Man does things that are unseemly. The inner motives bear fruit in action. The man who is full of envy, et cetera, begins to act. What does He do? He does things that are unseemly. Notice that the text says that this is the intended result: "God gave them over to a reprobate mind, to do those things which are not convenient." This is God's purpose. This is the purpose of His anger. The purpose of God is not to hold the sinner back. The purpose is that the sinner become manifest in all his folly and corruption. If this is to become manifest, the sinner must *act*. God will not let the sinner rest until he does things in order that he may become ripe for judgment and that it may become manifest that God alone is good.

They do things that are not *convenient,* that is, things that are not fitting or proper. The emphasis of the text is that these things do not fit with the way God rules things. If I put my hand in the fire, God keeps right on working in that fire. The result is that I burn my hand. So God causes man to do things that do not fit with the way He rules.

What these things are the apostle indicates in verse 29 and following: whisperers (people who secretly talk about you), backbiters (wagging of the tongue when you are not present), haters of God (literally, in the original, *hated of God*), despiteful, proud, boasters, inventors of evil things (inventors of things with which to do evil), disobedient to parents (setting aside all authority), without understanding, covenant breakers (unfaithful in any relation of life), and without natural affection, so that the woman can give up the child of her bosom.[1]

---

1. In the 1930s this meant giving the child away; in our day it also means "murder the child of her womb."

This is the result. This was the case in the Roman world. These sins came forth out of that one sin of not wanting to glorify and thank God. These sins lie at the bottom of the woe of the world of today. It is these sins that destroy the home, that destroy society, that destroy the world.

What shall we do?

I will go a step further. These sins are in your heart and in my heart. I do not mean that every one of these sins is in the heart of every individual, but all these sins are in the hearts of men in general, so that the one manifests this sin and the other another sin. These sins are in your heart and in mine.

This is the doom of the sinful world.

God forces it down from corruption to corruption and into destruction, into hell.

The Reason

Why does God do this? The text explains it. The apostle says, *"Even as* is the sin, so is the punishment."

"Even as."

Even as what?

What was the sin?

The sin was that they did not like to retain God in their knowledge. That is, they did not want to keep the true knowledge of God in their mind. They knew God, but they did not want to keep this knowledge of God in their mind. The original uses a strong expression. The original means they did not think God worthy to keep in mind. They knew God. They considered whether they would keep God in mind. They came to the conclusion that God was not fit to keep in mind.

Why?

Didn't they know any better? Was it an error on their part? No. They wanted to live in unrighteousness. It was not an intellectual error. It was a moral question. They did not want to keep God in mind.

Even as they did not see fit to keep God in mind, so God

gave them over to an unfit mind, to do things that are unfit. Why? Because it must become manifest that he who does not think God fit to keep in mind must run to destruction.

What shall we do? Nothing—not if our intention is merely to reform the world by all kinds of human acts.

What shall we do? We shall conclude that it is hopeless. It is the wrath of God that is at the bottom of it all. It is the wrath of God that is at the bottom even of war, of the present confusion of the world, and of the depression.

What shall we do? Shall we call a Prayer Day? This is folly. Away with all that is of man! From the point of view of man, it is hopeless. Why? Because it is the wrath of God that takes hold of man and pulls him down into hell. Let us confess that it is really hopeless.

What shall we do? We shall say, "I am not ashamed of the gospel of Christ, for it is the power of God unto salvation." For what do we need? We need righteousness. We need holiness. We need a power to snatch us away from the wrath of God. The gospel is a revelation of the righteousness of God, which is by faith in Christ Jesus.

This gospel is a power. It is not an offer, but it is a power taking man out of the power of sin and lifting him up into the glory of everlasting life.

Hopeless—from the point of view of man, and of the world!

Full of hope—in the cross of Calvary!

The righteous shall live by faith.

Chapter Seven

The Mutual Delight of Sinners

Romans 1:32
Who knowing the judgment of God, that they which commit such things are worthy of death, not only do the same, but have pleasure in them that do them.

According to the general impression and opinion, the fire of the hotel in Lansing a few days ago was an awful tragedy.[1] Undoubtedly it was. We can only imagine a little of the horror of men and women trapped in a fiery furnace to be burned alive, or to find death in the icy waters of the Grand River. We cannot imagine the horror of it. We can also perhaps understand that the horror changed to righteous indignation when it was told us the next day that the fire was probably caused by the rowdiness of a drunken party.

Let us try to carry that awful picture just a little further. Suppose that fire was actually due to the rowdiness of drunken men. Suppose that the majority of these drunken men had escaped the fire. Suppose that some days later these same men, now sober, now at another party, are still reliving that night. They talk about the party they had, laugh about the things that took place at that party, and still rejoice in the drunken revelry, even though it was the cause of the awful death of many.

---

1. Preaching this sermon in the late 1930s, Hoeksema refers to a fire in Lansing, Michigan, that captured the attention of the public. It is worthy of note that Hoeksema would press such an event into the service of the Word.

You say, "That would be the depth of degradation!" Yet this is the picture the text gives of natural man. It is exactly this that characterizes him.

From this point of view, verse 32 is the climax of Romans 1. Paul does not hesitate to describe men who have been given over by the wrath of God to a reprobate mind as rejoicing to see men on their way to hell. This is the text. They know, the text says, that they who do such things are worthy of death. They know that this is the righteous judgment of God. They know, therefore, that they who do such things are on their way to hell. Although they know that they who do such things are on their way to hell, they not only do these things, but they also delight in them who do them. The text, therefore, pictures to us the mutual delight of sinners.

A Wicked Delight

This mutual delight of sinners is, first of all, a wicked delight. The apostle expresses this especially in the last part of the text. You understand that when the apostle says they not only do the things enumerated in the preceding verses, but that they also have a pleasure in them who do them, he characterizes their wickedness as being the depth of degradation.

That the passage is very real we can know from everyday life. The sinner seeks the sinner. Sinners delight in one another's corruption. This is evident not only from the text and in Paul's day; it is equally true in our modern world. All along the line you will find the reality of the text. You can start in the underworld. They not only have their robberies, their holdups, and their killings, but they also have their parties at which they tell about their robberies and the crimes they have committed, laugh about them, and rejoice in their wicked deeds. Anyone who does not rejoice with them has no place among them. Men come to the shop on Monday morning and tell all about how they spent the Sunday. They tell how they spent the pay they had received on Saturday in drunken revelry and filth, and they laugh about the things they have committed. They delight in each other's filth.

It is evident in the business world. Businessmen come together and tell about how they cheated and about the crooked deals they pulled off, and they rejoice in it.

We find these two things: men do such things, and they have pleasure in them who do them. When they come together, they agree together and laugh about each other's corruption.

Why is the delight that men have in each other's sin a worse sign of corruption than the deed itself?

The answer is evident. Sin may be committed because one looks for the fruit of that sin. Sin looks good to him, not because of the sin itself, but because of what it brings him. A man may tell a lie because it seems to him that in telling that lie he will be benefited. A man may be a drunkard, not because of that sin as such, but because he enjoys himself in the carnal lust of drunkenness.

But the apostle says that this is not all. Even if they do not do these things themselves, they have a delight in them who do them. Even if there is no personal gain in it, they have a delight in these things. They delight in such corruption. They will even try to make you commit these things. The drunkard likes to see you drunk. He will try to make you drunk. Men delight in one another's corruption and sin.

What does this mean? It means, in the first place, that the sinner loves sin for sin's sake. He has pleasure in corruption. He has pleasure in sin even if there is no personal gain in it. It is only in this light that we can understand the rest of the text. The sinner loves sin; he has pleasure in corruption. This is a very wicked delight.

In the second place, it means that the sinner who commits sin wants the darkness to prevail in general. If you ask, "Why does the sinner delight in them who commit sin?" the answer is that the sinner's great desire is that sin abound everywhere and in everyone.

Let us ask the opposite question: "Why does the sinner hate

the righteous?" Sinners hated and finally killed Jesus. The sinner hates the righteous, and he will in principle kill him every time. Why does the sinner hate the righteous? Because the righteous man, in his testimony and work, is a manifestation of the truth. That manifestation of the truth, as it is in the righteous, condemns that sinner. He hates that righteous man because the sinner wants to hold the truth under in unrighteousness in order to sin peacefully. The sinner wants to have company. He tries to kill the testimony of the righteous. This is natural man. They have pleasure in one another's sin although they know that they who do such things are worthy of death.

Let me use an illustration. Again, there is a steep, slippery road that ends in a precipice. Men are sliding down that slippery road. The text means that although they know they are sliding down it, they want to enjoy their slide. Although they know that at the end is the precipice, they want others to enjoy that slide with them, and they take them along.

A Cruel Delight

This is why the text calls our attention to a cruel delight. We must notice that this is an everyday delight. The wicked take each other along to hell. This is true of the father with regard to his son, whom he does not want to walk in the way of righteousness. This is true of the mother with regard to her daughter. This is true of the whole world. Knowing the judgment of God, that they which commit such things are worthy of death, they not only do the same, but also have pleasure in them who do them.

Notice that the apostle says that they know this way of sin ends in death. The question has been asked, "What death does the apostle mean? Does he mean physical death?" Then the apostle would mean they know that those who commit this corruption will die the physical death. This would not make sense. Besides, when Scripture speaks of death without further designation, it always means the final state of death; it means

49

eternal desolation. Death is hell; therefore, we may say that men who are on that sliding road know that the end is hell.

How do they know this? In the first place, they know it because God has revealed it from the beginning. The fact that death is the wages of sin, God has revealed from paradise. This revelation was not entirely lost so that men outside the church do not know that the wages of sin is death. This revelation was preserved. It has been declared throughout history that the wages of sin is death. Men hold this truth under in unrighteousness, but in their deepest hearts they know that the wages of sin is death.

In the second place, this is the clear testimony of general revelation. The apostle shows in this chapter how, by the power of the wrath of God, man is drawn to everlasting desolation. This is simply the direction of sin. Everybody can see that the direction of natural debauchery is physical death. When a man lives a life of spiritual debauchery, the result is more spiritual debauchery, and this is death.

Finally, there is the testimony of the Spirit of God in the heart, establishing this connection. The testimony of the Spirit in the heart of the wicked establishes this testimony: the end of sin is death. Knowing that they who do such things are worthy of death, they not only do them but have a delight in them who do them. The tender mercies of the wicked are cruel. They not only like to slide down themselves, but they want to take others along. They rejoice when others go along with them to hell. This is awful. This is the movement of sin in the heart of all of us. This is why sin is so terrible. We may try to cover up that sin as soon as it touches us personally. But we are by nature so corrupt that we not only commit these sins; we also delight in them who do them.

An Inexcusable Delight

This is inexcusable. The apostle does not say merely that they do these things and know the end is death. No, the apostle says two things. They know that it is the judgment of God. They know that they are worthy of it. They know that the judgment is righteous. Knowing the judgment of God, that they who commit such things are worthy of death, they are without excuse. They cannot say, and they do not say, "This is our lot; we can't help it." No. What they say in their own consciousness is this: "God judges me to be worthy of hell, and this judgment is correct."

How does man know it? How does man know the righteous judgment of God? God has revealed it. They know it because they know that God is. All men know this. Atheism is a philosophy. All men know that God is. All know that God is eternal in power and Godhead. All men know that this God must be glorified and thanked. This is the inevitable "Thou shalt" written in the heart of man. Knowing this truth of God, not wanting this God, and refusing to glorify and to thank Him, man knows that he runs into eternal destruction.

What shall we do? What shall we do if this is the condition of the sinner? What shall we do if man would rather go to hell than abandon sin? What shall we do? Shall we scare him into abandoning his way? Shall we preach hell and damnation to him? That will not help; they try that in the world. When corruption gets a little too bad, they say we must tell men what will be the consequence of certain sins. But the text says that men have a delight in the sins of others. These measures are doomed to fail.

Sometimes they say it in the church. They say, let us preach hell and damnation. It is all right to tell men about it, but if the purpose is to turn man from the way of sin, it is at the outset doomed to fail. Knowing that they who commit sin are worthy of death, they not only do the same, but have a delight in them that do them.

What shall we do? There is only one answer. The apostle gives that in verses 16 and 17: "I am not ashamed of the gospel of Christ." This gospel preaches the righteousness of God that is by faith in Christ Jesus. This gospel is the vehicle of the righteousness that descends from heaven. This righteousness can be had in the only possible way in which righteousness can be had, namely, by faith.

Therefore, the apostle calls this gospel *the power of God.*

The end of it is, "The righteous shall live by faith." He puts away all his own righteousness, all that is of self. He puts all his trust in the righteousness of God, which is by faith in Christ Jesus.

Chapter Eight

The Inexcusable Judge

Romans 2:1
Therefore thou art inexcusable, O man, whosoever thou art that judgest: for wherein thou judgest another, thou condemnest thyself; for thou that judgest doest the same things.

The apostle introduces this second chapter of Romans by combining it with the first when he says, "Therefore thou art inexcusable, O man, whosoever thou art that judgest."
Therefore.
The question is, "How? How is this particular man, whom the apostle addresses, inexcusable?"
It is evident that the apostle is introducing a new phase of the main theme of this part of his epistle. This main theme has been that the apostle develops a reason why he is not ashamed of the gospel of Jesus Christ. He is not ashamed of the gospel because, positively, it proclaims a righteousness that is free, that is by faith, that is without works. Negatively, he is not ashamed of the gospel, because the world is in need of just such a righteousness. It is impossible for man to attain righteousness. He is unrighteous, drawn down by the wrath of God, which is revealed from heaven. This the apostle developed in the first chapter.
It is not only possible, but it is also characteristic of sinful man, to look for an excuse. If what the apostle has written concerning the sinner is to take hold of the consciousness of man,

it is necessary that the sinner does not excuse himself anymore. As long as the sinner can find one excuse, he will not be receptive to the gospel. It is also one of the chief characteristics of the sinner that he will try to exclude himself from the company who are under the wrath of God. According to this tendency of the sinful heart, the sinner might say, "It is all true what the apostle has written concerning the world, but I am not part of that rebellious, vile, damnable world." He lifts himself above the world that the apostle has described and, instead of being a defendant, he makes himself a judge.

This tendency the apostle takes away. He says, "Therefore thou art inexcusable, O man, whosoever thou art that judgest: for wherein thou judgest another, thou condemnest thyself; for thou that judgest doest the same things." Then this *Therefore* becomes plain. For also in the last verse of the preceding chapter the apostle had said, "Who knowing the judgment of God, that they which commit such things are worthy of death, not only do the same, but have pleasure in them that do them." Therefore, you belong in this class, for you do the same things.

In the verse, the apostle places the individual in the class of those who are under the wrath of God.

The Judge

The apostle addresses a man. It is important that we see this. The apostle addresses a man who judges others. He addresses a man who does the same things while he accuses others. Notice that the apostle addresses this man directly. He points the finger at him and says, "Thou art the man."

The question has been asked, "What man does the apostle have in mind?" There have been many answers. The most common answer is that the apostle here addresses the Jews. They say that in chapter 1 the apostle addresses the heathen, and in chapter 2 he addresses the Jews. The reason for this interpretation is, first, that it is evident that the apostle begins a new phase of his main theme in chapter 2. Second, the apostle literally addresses the Jews in verse 17, where he says, "Behold, thou art called a Jew, and restest in the law, and makest thy boast of God." Third, the argument is that the apostle is speaking of one who judges another. It is characteristic of the Jews, they say, to judge others and to place themselves above those whom they judge. Therefore, they say, the apostle addresses the Jews.

I do not agree with this interpretation, even though it is the most general one. My reasons are, first, that the apostle says, "O man." He might have said, "O Jew," but he doesn't. He says, "O man." You can never interpret this to mean "O Jew." Second, the apostle adds, "whosoever thou art." This cannot mean the Jews only. Third, it is not true that the characteristic the apostle mentions is peculiarly Jewish. It is not characteristically Jewish. It is characteristic of every sinful heart. "Thou art inexcusable, O man, for thou that judgest another doest the same thing." This is not only characteristic of the Jew, but also of every sinful man.

Therefore, the explanation is this. In the preceding chapter the apostle had spoken of the heathen. Here he is speaking of man, including the Jew but not excluding the heathen. You may notice also that the apostle is using the singular. He does not speak of *men*. He specifically addresses *man*. It is important that we see this. The apostle means to point his finger at the individual man. Finally, notice this feature of the text, that instead of talking *about* man, the apostle is now speaking *to* him.

There is this difference between the viewpoints of chapters 1 and 2. In the first chapter, the apostle speaks of the heathen. In the second chapter, he speaks of man, including the Jews but not excluding the heathen, although he has in mind to apply it specifically to the Jews later on. In the first chapter the apostle speaks in general, but in the second chapter he uses the singular and points at the particular individual.

The question now is, how do you react when what the apostle says here is laid at your door? The apostle means, "Did you understand what I have developed here? Well, this applies to you." The text must be understood in this light. We must not say, "This is sound doctrine." The question is, when the word of God comes to us and says, "Thou art that man," what do we say?

The text says, "thou that judgest." The apostle says that man is a judge. Every man is a judge. He must judge. He must judge in a moral sense. This implies several things. It implies that we are able to evaluate a moral act. It implies that we are able to estimate the moral value of an act. It implies that we know the righteous judgment of God over the deeds of men. It implies, with a view to verse 1, that this man's judgment is not applied to himself but to others. This is his mistake. The word implies that this man condemns those whom he judges. Finally, the word implies that he expresses this judgment; he openly condemns them before others.

Let us understand that this man who judges does the same things he condemns in others. Notice that the apostle does not say, "You also sin." This is not the point. The point is that he who judges does the *same* sins. He condemns another who lies, and he lies himself. He condemns another who steals, and he steals himself. He condemns another who commits adultery, and he commits adultery himself. The same moral deeds that he condemns in others, he commits himself.

Let us see how characteristic this is of sinful man. There is nothing Jewish about it. We find it in our own hearts. How characteristic of the world that the world condemns the world in the things that the world does. You find it in your daily newspapers. A man condemns the thief and the bank robber. At the same time, this judge who condemns the thief, himself steals right and left. The banker cries bloody murder when one steals from him, but he does not care that after he has piled up the money of the poor, he closes his bank.[1] How characteristic of

---

1. Hoeksema comments on the social conditions during the years of the "great depression" in the 1930s, specifically the closing of the banks, which was when this sermon was preached.

one generation to condemn the sins of a former generation. How easily we can see, through the beam in our own eye, the mote in the other's eye. Have you ever noticed, while sitting in company and talking about another and what a slanderer he is, that all the while you are doing the same thing? In other words, it is possible for us to backbite in talking about the backbiting of others. In a word, it is characteristic of the heart of man that he judges another while he himself does the same things.

His Imagination

Why should man do this? The implication is that the man who so judges another while he himself does the same things tries to persuade himself that he is judge rather than defendant. Thus, he imagines that he can persuade God and others that he is with excuse. He lifts himself above all. He takes part with the Judge. He tells the Judge that he agrees with him. He tells the Judge that all those men before him are worthy of death. He makes himself a companion of the Judge in the courtroom. This man does it. Each man does it.

What a situation! Everybody is accusing everybody but himself. This is the implication of the text. This is terrible. Just imagine! In a courtroom there are one hundred men, and every one of them demands the sentence of the other ninety-nine. This is the world. The world is a courtroom. The judgment is not *coming;* the judgment is *every day.* It is true that there is a final judgment coming, but the world is a courtroom already. God judges every man, but in this courtroom every man stands before the face of God and says, "Yes, condemn them." Therefore, the apostle says, "Thou who judgest another condemnest thyself, for thou doest the same things."

The purpose of the sinful heart that so judges is to declare himself to be outside this judgment. Why does the sinner condemn the other sinner? What is the underlying idea? What is there in the sinful heart that makes a man do this? It is this: he means, "I am better than all the others."

You all know the story of David and Nathan. As long as Nathan is speaking of the other man, it is easy for David to condemn that other man. He condemns the other man in the thing that he was doing himself. When David says, "That man shall surely be put to death," he means by implication, "I would never do that."

Did you ever notice that if a man really comes to repentance, he talks about himself alone? He says, "Be merciful to me, a sinner." But as long as he talks about others, he means, "I am better."

Before himself, this means deceit. He deceives himself. Before others, it is conceit. Before God, it is self-righteousness. And this man who so judges will never be receptive to the gospel.

His Inexcusability

Therefore, the apostle says, "Thou art inexcusable, O man." Literally, the meaning of *inexcusable* is "to be without defense." When does a man have an excuse? In certain instances, he is excusable: when the charge brought against him is not true, when he is not under obligation, when he is morally not responsible, and when what is demanded of him is physically impossible.

But the apostle says that in God's courtroom man is *inexcusable*. In the day of judgment he will be *without defense*. In the day of judgment God will judge according to truth. The apostle really implies that God asks every man, "Have you anything to say? Have you anything to say for yourself?" And man will keep still. God will say to the others, "Have you anything to say for the defense of this man?" The world will say, "No, we have always condemned him."

He is inexcusable.

Why should he be inexcusable? The apostle says, "The things wherein thou judgest another, thou doest thyself." When a man judges others, he shows that he is not irresponsible. He shows that he can evaluate a moral deed. While he does so, he actually includes himself among them whom he condemns, for he does the same things.

What shall we say then? We shall say this. We will come down from the bench of our imaginary judgeship. We will take our place among the accused. We will stop judging the other; we will bring ourselves under the righteous judgment of God; and we will hear the word of the text: "Thou art that man."

However, we will never do this! We will never do it unless God takes this Word and inscribes it in our hearts so that we hear it as the Word of God: "Thou art that man." Then we will say, "Be merciful to me, a sinner."

This is the admonition of the text: "Come down from the bench. Come down to the floor of the courtroom." On the floor of the courtroom is a Lawyer. Man has no excuse. But for him who places himself on the floor of the courtroom, among the condemned, there is the righteousness of God. Jesus Christ is His eternal defense and apology. And we will say, "We, then, being justified by faith, have peace with God through our Lord Jesus Christ."

Chapter Nine

Despising God's Goodness

Romans 2:4, 5
Or despisest thou the riches of his goodness and forbearance and longsuffering; not knowing that the goodness of God leadeth thee to repentance?
But after thy hardness and impenitent heart treasurest up unto thyself wrath against the day of wrath and revelation of the righteous judgment of God.

The heart of Romans 2:4, 5 is undoubtedly expressed in the words *the goodness of God leadeth thee to repentance.* This is the undeniable truth around which the entire text in all its details is really grouped. It is the one certainty that can always be applied and always stands, to which there is never an exception: *the goodness of God leadeth to repentance.*

For this reason we must not change this statement to fit our notion of what the goodness of God ought to be. Poison kills, fire burns, and bread nourishes; so the goodness of God leads to repentance. We must not say, or think, or attempt to change the meaning of this statement into something like this: "The goodness of God *likes* to lead you to repentance." This is not true. Or, "The goodness of God *tries* to lead you to repentance." This is not true, either. Nor is it the meaning of the text. We must leave this word exactly as it is and say—just as we say poison kills, fire burns, and bread nourishes—the goodness of God leads to repentance.

It does this always. We may know it or not; it makes no difference—the goodness of God leads to repentance. You may take poison or you may not; it makes no difference—poison kills. You may put your hand in the fire or you may not; it makes no difference—fire burns. You may feel the power of the goodness of God or you may not; it makes no difference—the goodness of God leads to repentance.

But there are those who despise that goodness of God. Despising the goodness of God, they treasure up unto themselves wrath. It is to those that the apostle calls our attention in the text.

The Meaning

The apostle is still addressing the man of verse 1. He is not addressing any particular class. He is not addressing the Jew, nor is the Jew excluded. The apostle has in mind to apply what he has said to the Jews in a special sense, but here he is addressing man. He is speaking in the singular. This man, the apostle has pictured in a very peculiar and realistic light. In other words, he has pictured him just as he is. He has pictured this man as judging and condemning others while doing the same things himself. He condemns the liar, and he lies himself. He condemns the thief, and he steals himself. When he condemns the backbiter, he becomes a backbiter himself. This is characteristic of sinful man. God lets him do it in order to make him say that he knows the righteous judgment of God, so that he will be without excuse in the day of judgment.

The apostle asks this man (and this is the connection with verse 1), "How do you explain your attitude? How do you come to assume the attitude in which you condemn in others what you do yourself?"

How must this be explained? The apostle knows of but two possibilities. The first possibility is expressed in that first question in verse 3: "Thinkest thou this, O man, that judgest them which do such things, and doest the same, that thou shalt escape the judgment of God?" Is this the explanation? If this is the case, his attitude is explained.

Or—and this is the other possibility—is this attitude rooted in the sinful contempt in which you say, "I know that I shall be in the judgment, but I don't care"? As verse 4 puts it, "Or despisest thou the riches of his goodness . . . not knowing that the goodness of God leadeth thee to repentance?"

In the original, four words are used, where in our English translation of verse 4, there are but three. The text, therefore, should be read this way: "Or despisest thou the loving-kindness, forbearance, long-suffering, and goodness of God?" As to the meaning of these various terms, they are so related that goodness includes all the other virtues. God's loving-kindness is His goodness manifest. God's forbearance is His goodness manifest. God's long-suffering is His goodness manifest.

What is God's *goodness?* In the first place, God's goodness is that virtue of God by which He is in Himself infinite perfection. This is the background of all other goodnesses. God's goodness does not mean that He is our benefactor, that He bestows good upon us. God's goodness means that He is good in the sense of perfection. Because God is good in Himself, He also does good. God does good to all creatures. There is no exception. He does good to all creatures, organically considered and individually considered. God always does good. He does good to the wicked and to the righteous. When God blesses the righteous, He does good. When God curses the wicked, He does good. God would not do good if He blessed the wicked. God is in Himself good and the overflowing fountain of all goodnesses.

For this reason there is in the text mention of a threefold manifestation of God's goodness. These three are also related. God's *loving-kindness* is the first manifestation of His goodness. God's loving-kindness is His inmost desire to bless the righteous. The goodness of God so works and reveals itself that there is in God the eternal desire to bless the righteous. You can never say that of God's attitude toward the wicked. Then He would not be good. There is in God never a will, a desire, to make the wicked happy. We must understand this. The central thought of the text is to emphasize that it is impossible for God to bless anyone unless he comes to repentance. As long as he does not come to repentance, and despises and does not know the goodness of God, he cannot taste the blessing of God. We must understand, therefore, that the loving-kindness of God is that manifestation of God's goodness according to which it is His eternal desire to bless the righteous. This is why the natural man despises that loving-kindness of God. Man will never despise a general grace, but he despises the fact that God blesses the righteous.

The other two terms, God's long-suffering and forbearance, are again manifestations of the goodness of God as revealed in time. God's *long-suffering* is His desire to deliver His suffering people, but His waiting until all things are ripe. If I have my child on the operating table and that child begs me to stop, but I keep right on cutting into the live flesh until the operation is completed, I am long-suffering over that child. So God's long-suffering is His purpose finally to bring His people to glory while permitting them to suffer until the time is ripe.

God's *forbearance* is the antithesis of long-suffering. It is His will to destroy the wicked in the day of judgment while allowing them to prosper until that day. God's forbearance is this: I have a man in my home who eats my bread, drinks my water, wears my clothes, and sleeps in my bed. That man ignores me and abuses my children. I forbear from putting him out of my house until the time is ripe. This is God's forbearance. The forbearance and long-suffering of God are manifest.

The apostle asks the sinner, "Despisest thou the loving-kindness and forbearance and long-suffering of God; not knowing that the goodness of God leadeth thee to repentance?" To despise a thing presupposes that we come into contact with it to the extent that we know what we despise. The apostle means, therefore, that in some way, to some extent, man always comes into contact with this threefold manifestation of God, the heart of which is that the Lord blesses the righteous.

Despisest thou this?

It is emphatically in the church, where the goodness of God is bestowed, that the goodness of God is despised.

To despise a thing is to think nothing of it. To despise a thing is to judge it worthless, not to want it. Therefore, when the testimony is, "The Lord blesses the righteous," we simply ignore it and continue to walk in sin. Do you not see that the sinner, going on in his own way, despises the goodness of God?

Its Cause

How is this possible? The apostle says that the deepest cause is in the sinner's impenitent heart. "But after thy hardness and impenitent heart," the text says. The heart is the center of a man's life from a spiritual point of view. From the heart is the life of man as to its spiritual direction. An impenitent heart is a heart that *cannot repent*. It is not a heart that does not repent; neither is it a heart that cannot be brought to repentance. It is a heart that *cannot repent of itself*.

To repent is to change so that our judgment of our own sin is as God's judgment of our sin. An impenitent heart is the very opposite. It is a heart that loves sin, that seeks sin, that walks in sin.

That impenitent heart, the apostle says, is *hard*. It is not hardened. It is hard. "After thy hardness," says the apostle. Hardness is the characteristic of the impenitent heart. That heart is hard, so that it is not receptive for repentance. When that impenitent heart sits under the influence of the Word of God, even before that Word comes, it makes up its mind not to repent. An impenitent heart is always hard. It is not that the impenitent heart is first soft and that gradually that heart hardens. That heart is hard from the beginning. Every impenitent heart is hard.

It is true that there is a hardening of the heart in a natural way, but not in the spiritual sense. Even a hard, impenitent heart can become hardened in a natural way. When first that hard, impenitent heart comes under the influence of the Word of God, there are the pangs of conscience, a certain fear, a trembling before that Word. But under the influence of the goodness of God, that impenitent heart becomes hardened. We can see, often to our deepest sorrow, how the impenitent heart becomes hardened. With an impenitent heart, one does not know that the goodness of God leads to repentance. This is the immediate result.

The Arminian distortion is that God is good in the sense of being gracious to all. He is good in the sense that He likes to save all. Because He likes to save all, He tries to lead all to repentance. When He does so, there are some who resist that goodness of God. This is the Arminian distortion of the text.

But this is not the teaching of the text. The text does not say the goodness of God tries to lead you to repentance. The text makes a statement of fact. The text says that the goodness of God leads you to repentance. It is impossible, if you leave the text in its context, to elicit from it a general grace. Instead, it is a general statement of fact: the goodness of God leads to repentance.

This becomes manifest in those who come into contact with this fact. It is as though I would say, "Don't you know that fire burns you?"—meaning, of course, as soon as you come into contact with it. Or, "Don't you know that poison kills you?"—meaning, of course, when you come into contact with it. So the apostle says, "Don't you know that the goodness of God leads you to repentance?"—meaning, as soon as you come into contact with it.

The natural man does not know that the goodness of God leads to repentance. Does he not know the *fact?* He does. This is not the meaning. But he does not know it in the sense that he does not experience and taste that the goodness of God leads to repentance, and in the sense that he despises it. He despises the goodness of God as it becomes manifest in His loving-kindness, forbearance, and long-suffering, not knowing, in the sense of not experiencing, that the goodness of God leads to repentance.

Its Result

Is this the case? If it is, there is but one result: the man who so despises the goodness of God treasures up wrath against the day of wrath and judgment.

There comes a day of the revelation of the judgment of God. The passage warns, "After thy hardness and impenitent heart treasurest up unto thyself wrath against the day of wrath and revelation of the righteous judgment of God." We must not say that there comes a day of the judgment of God. This judgment is always present. But there comes a day when this judgment shall be *revealed*.

This judgment is now frequently covered up. It is so covered up that frequently we would say that God's judgment is not righteous. The wicked seem to prosper, and the righteous are in trouble. This judgment is so covered up that men have come to the conclusion that there is a general grace. God's judgment is now covered up, but there comes a day when that cover will be taken off. That is the day of the revelation of the judgment of God.

That day will be a day of wrath. For whom? For that man. It will be a day of wrath; that is, it will be a day of nothing but wrath. And that man treasures up wrath. He lays up wrath as one lays up a sum of money in a bank. He piles up wrath. He lays up wrath in the bank of God's judgment. He does that in all his life. He is always increasing his capital of wrath. He treasures up wrath against the day of wrath. You may call that "grace" if you please, but the apostle knows nothing of that.

What shall we say then?

I will conclude with the same words with which I started: "The goodness of God leadeth thee to repentance." If you have not come to repentance, you have never known the goodness of God. If in the midst of those men who despise the goodness of God you become a penitent sinner, what then? Is there any hope? I am not ashamed of the gospel of Jesus Christ: this the apostle still has in mind. I am not ashamed of the gospel of Jesus Christ, for in it is revealed the righteousness of God that is by faith in Christ Jesus. The righteous shall live by faith. Living by faith, they say this: "Being justified by faith, we have peace with God" [Rom. 5:1].

Chapter Ten

The Revelation of the Righteous Judgment of God

Romans 2:6-8
Who will render to every man according to his deeds:
To them who by patient continuance in well-doing seek for glory and honour and immortality, eternal life:
But unto them that are contentious, and do not obey the truth, but obey unrighteousness, indignation and wrath.

The apostle is still addressing the man to whom he had spoken in verse 1 of Romans 2. No longer is he addressing the Gentiles, nor is he exclusively addressing the Jews. But he is addressing man—any man, man in general and yet every man individually; not all men but each man, the apostle is addressing, both in the text and in its context.

This man is addressed as a sinner, such as he is in the sphere of this present world. The apostle had told him that while he exalted himself as judge over the deeds of others, he himself was doing the same things. Therefore, he was his own judge while he pretended to be a judge of others. This is characteristic of the sinner.

The apostle has asked this man two questions in order to obtain an explanation from him. The first question was, "Thinkest thou this, O man, that thou shalt escape the judgment of

God because thou judgest others in the things thou doest thyself?" Is this the explanation? Is this the reason why you assume that attitude in which you judge others in the things you do yourself? In other words, "Thinkest thou that by making thyself judge, thou shalt not be among the condemned?" This was one possibility.

Or this was the second possibility: "Despisest thou the goodness of God that becomes manifest in loving-kindness, forbearance, and long-suffering; the goodness of God that becomes manifest when God loves the righteous and hates the wicked; the goodness of God that leads to repentance? Despisest thou that goodness of God, not knowing it?" Was this the explanation?

But the apostle meant this: "Whatever may be the explanation, thou who judgest others and doest the same things art continually busy in heaping up wrath against the day of wrath and revelation of the righteous judgment of God." This is true. Therefore, the apostle has spoken of the righteous judgment of God.

What is this righteous judgment of God? What will be its procedure? How is it possible? In what possible state can a man stand in that righteous judgment of God? What must be the possible verdict? What must be the verdict of Him who will reward every man according to his deeds?

The apostle knows of but two possibilities. On the one hand [v. 7] are they "who by patient continuance in well-doing seek for glory and honour and immortality, eternal life." On the other hand [v. 8], it is possible that a man has been contentious and therefore did not obey the truth; he shall be judged worthy of indignation and wrath. These are the only two possibilities. There is no other, because God is the only standard. God is the Judge, but He is also the only standard according to which that judgment shall be.

We have in the text, therefore, the truth of the righteous judgment of God in its revelation. It is not the judgment of God of which the text speaks. The judgment of God takes place always. God always judges the deeds of men. But the text speaks of the revelation of this judgment of God.

A Revelation of All the Evidences

The evidences brought into this court, the passage says, are the works and the deeds of men. These deeds are not the objects to be judged. They are the evidences. The one to be judged is man. What must be made plain concerning every man is what he is worth; or rather, it must be made plain that every man is worth what God judges him to be worth.

God has no need of a day of judgment. He does not even have need of our works as evidence. God knows our works from eternity, and in this sense He has no need of a day of judgment. He knows who is worthy of eternal life and who is worthy of indignation and wrath. The purpose of the day of judgment is that everyone may justify God when He judges. God knows what every man's spiritual, ethical value is. But if God is to be justified, that is, if in the consciousness of every moral creature God is to appear as just when He judges, so that every man may be exposed as a liar and God become manifest as true, then the day of judgment must come. If this day is to be a revelation of the righteous judgment of God, God must produce His evidences. This He will do. He will produce His evidences, not to Himself, but to us, to every moral creature, to men and angels.

This evidence will be the works of man. The works of man will be the evidence by which his worth will be shown. God will render to every man according to his works. These works of man are all his activities between the hour of his birth and the moment of his death. They are all his activities in connection with his position, his occupation, and his relations.

These works are not limited to what is seen by men. They are not only the outward works that we see. No, they are all that man does between the hour of his birth and the hour of his death in the sense of speaking, seeing, hearing, thinking, willing, and desiring. They include the works that man never knew, or which he conveniently forgot. We do a certain evil, and then we conveniently forget about it. We like to remember our good deeds and talk about them, but our evil deeds we like to forget. Did you ever notice that when you commit a sin, you let a day go by before confessing that sin before the Lord? It does not seem so raw then. We forget about these evil things, yet all these sins God will produce.

He will produce them to your consciousness. He will convince you that they are yours. You will never say in that day, "I never did that." There will be no denial in the day of judgment. They will be brought to us as *our* works. God has a way of doing this.

He will bring these works as evidences before our consciousness and before the consciousness of all moral creatures, angels, and men. The Lord says that what has been done in secret will be preached from the housetops. That is, your works will be made perfectly plain to me and to all the world. He will expose your and my works to the world. Exposing them, He will cast the light of His own judgment upon them in order that the answer to the question as to the purpose, the motive—why did you do it?—may be plain.

A Revelation of Every Man Who Is to Be Judged

The apostle says that God will judge every man according to his works. Notice, not the deeds are to be judged. But *man* will be judged. Every man will be judged according to his deeds; that is, the real value of every man will be exposed as God sees his worth by the evidence of his works.

How is this possible? Why are a man's works evidence of his worth? The answer is that they are in relation to man as fruit is to the tree. By their fruit ye shall know them. As you know a tree by its fruit, so you can know man by his works. These works are his fruit. Accordingly, God will use all these works to show what you and I really are, and what we are worth. This must be revealed.

This day must come. It is coming. If this is the case, how shall we appear? In this revelation of God's righteous judgment, there will be only two potential outcomes with regard to those who are to be judged. The reason is that God is Judge, and He is the only standard by which man shall be judged. The only two outcomes are that we stand before Him as righteous or unrighteous.

Who are the righteous? Notice how the apostle describes the righteous. He describes them as those who seek for glory and honor and immortality—this, first of all. Second, they are those who seek for these things in the way of patient continuance in well-doing. The man who from the moment of his birth to the hour of his death has sought for glory and honor and immortality in the way of patient continuance in well-doing: this man shall be righteous.

When the apostle says that they seek for glory, honor, and immortality, he does not mean that this man seeks for *any* glory, honor, and immortality. In a way, all men seek this. But the apostle means real glory, real honor, and real immortality. If we seek this, we shall surely find it.

Real glory is essentially the glory of God. This is the only glory there is. If we seek this glory, glory being the radiation of good, then we seek God and His glory as our own. We may say, therefore, that if we seek glory, we seek God.

Honor is not any kind of praise, but honor belongs to God. If we seek the honor of God, we seek that honor of God by which He approves of us.

Immortality is a weak translation. The original means "incorruptibleness." If we seek incorruptibleness, we seek God and that blessing by which we may be incorruptible before Him. This is why the text says that we can seek this only in the way of patient continuance in well-doing. Well-doing is that which is in harmony with the will of God. If we do the will of

God, we seek Him. Continuance in well-doing means continuous, uninterrupted seeking of immortality. Patience means that we walk in that way no matter how much we suffer.

If we meet the day of the righteous judgment of God in this way, it will be all right. If from the moment of our birth to the moment of our death we have never sought anything but glory and honor and immortality, if we have never sought anything but God's face and fellowship, we will be righteous. Then, when we face Him in the judgment day, it will be all right. This is one possible outcome.

The other outcome is expressed in verse 8. Indignation and wrath will be for them that are contentious, and do not obey the truth, but obey unrighteousness. They are the unrighteous.

The word *contentious* in our Bibles rests on a mistaken translation. The original word really means "partisanship." What is a *partisan?* Let me illustrate. Take, for example, in the evil sense, a politician who uses the position in which he is supposed to serve the community not because he wants to serve the community, but to advance himself. This is a partisan. This is awful, but it is quite common in our day. Such a man uses his job for himself.

God has given man a position. His position is that he is king. God has appointed man to be king in creation. Why is man appointed king? In order that he should seek the glory of God. But he is a *partisan*. He uses his position in creation not to the glory of God, but to oppose Him and to seek self. This is the principle from which he lives. In this principle, of course, he disobeys the truth.

This is the other possible outcome. A third there is not. We shall appear in that judgment according to that one class, or the other.

Which will it be?

When God exhibits your and my works, and when you see those works and you say of them, "Yes, they are mine," what do you think it will be? Will it be one long way of seeking for glory and honor and immortality? Or will our works reveal the alternative: we have been partisans? Will they reveal that we have sought the world not for God, but for ourselves?

Which will it be?

A Revelation of the Final Verdict

The apostle does not answer, but he says that God will reward every man according to those works. To them who have been unrighteous, have been contentious, and have disobeyed the truth—to them God will give the reward of indignation and wrath.

When God gives His wrath to anyone, it means that He gives him the complete operation of His wrath and indignation. It means that He pours out the intense heat of His wrath upon all who have been contentious and have disobeyed the truth. All will admit that this judgment of God is just.

We can see this now. God is God. As God He says, "Love Me." This is good; all else is evil. God says, "Love Me." The sinner says, "I will not." He turns his back upon God until he stands before the face of God, and God shows to him that he is worthy of indignation and wrath, that he is worthy of hell. The sinner will say, "This is right; this is all I am worthy of." All who deny this here make God a liar, but there it will be different. No denial will be found there. All will admit that God is just. All the world will say that His verdict is right.

On the other hand, they who by patient continuance in well-doing seek for glory and honor and immortality will receive eternal life. Eternal life means the life that Scripture always pictures not only as everlasting, but also as the highest life. It is perfect fellowship with God.

You say, "How is this possible?" My answer is that it is impossible. If you ask, "How can anyone come to eternal life?" the answer is that it is impossible. It is impossible to come to eternal life if one from the moment of his birth to the moment of his death must, in the way of patient continuance in well-doing, seek glory and honor and immortality. The apostle means that this is truly impossible.

Because it is impossible, the apostle is still thinking of the main subject of the context: I am not ashamed of the gospel of Jesus Christ. There was only one among mankind who sought, in the way of patient continuance in well-doing, glory and honor and immortality. That was not a mere man. That was Immanuel, God in our human nature.

God did it!

Jesus Christ, from the moment of His birth until the moment of His death, sought glory and honor and immortality in the way of patient continuance in well-doing. Finally He said, "It is finished." He did so as the revelation of God's righteousness for His people.

Therefore, when we have seen that the case of man is hopeless, God comes to us with the gospel. He proclaims a righteousness that is His and that He has realized in Christ.

I am not ashamed of the gospel of Jesus Christ, the heart of which is this: the righteous shall live by faith.

Chapter Eleven

The Gentiles a Law unto Themselves

Romans 2:14, 15
For when the Gentiles, which have not the law, do by nature the things contained in the law, these, having not the law, are a law unto themselves:
Which shew the work of the law written in their hearts, their conscience also bearing witness, and their thoughts the mean while accusing or else excusing one another.

The thought in the immediate context of this passage is that God shall judge every man according to his works. The revelation of the righteous judgment of God in the day of Christ: this is the theme of the immediate context. This judgment shall be conducted according to our works. That is, our works shall be the evidence in this judgment. According to our works, our moral, ethical value will be shown. Our value will be shown not to God, but to us. It will be shown in order that He may be justified when He judges and that we may be found to be liars.

The apostle explains that the verdict will be such that they who sought for glory and honor and immortality in the way of patient continuance in well-doing will be rewarded with eternal life. Contrariwise, he who lived from the principle of partisanship, that is, he who used his position, place, and relation to God for himself, for his own advancement, and therefore disobeyed the truth, will receive indignation and wrath. In the following verses the apostle elaborates upon this verdict of

God. Tribulations and anguish will be upon every soul of man who does evil. But glory, honor, and peace will be to every man who worketh good. This is the revelation of the righteous judgment of God.

The apostle is addressing man. It is plain that he does not exclude the Gentiles. He is speaking to man in general, yet to the individual as well. He is speaking to man, not excluding the Jew, and having in mind to apply it presently to the Jew in particular. For this reason the apostle emphasizes that the Jew shall be first in that judgment. The Jew shall be first, as always. But also the Gentile shall be in that judgment—the Jew first, but also the Gentile—for there is no acceptance of persons with God. There is only one thing to be judged. This is whether man is ethically worthy of eternal life.

But now a question that some might ask arises in the mind of the apostle. They might say, "But we have the law." So the Jew reasoned. "God gave me the law, and the fact that God gave me the law is proof that I am righteous." The apostle takes this excuse away and says, "Not the hearers of the law are just before God, but the doers of the law shall be justified"[v. 13].

But the question arises, "How is it with respect to the Gentiles? They have no law. How can they know what is right or wrong? By the law is the knowledge of sin, but if the Gentiles have no law, how can they know?" The apostle has already said that as many as sin without law shall also perish without law, and as many as sin in the law shall be judged by the law. In other words, it is possible to sin without law, for, and this is the connection, the Gentiles who have not the law have the work of the law written in their hearts.

The apostle explains this, first, by saying that the Gentiles do the things of the law. They do not do *the things contained in the law,* as our English translation has it. This is not a translation but a commentary. The Gentiles do not do *the things contained in the law,* but they do *the things of the law.*

Second, because they do the things of the law, they are a law unto themselves.

Third, the truth that they are a law unto themselves is evident from two facts: even in the Gentile world the conscience witnesses; and public opinion sets its seal upon the truth that they are a law unto themselves.

What This Means

The Gentiles are a law unto themselves, the apostle says. The question has been asked, "What law does the apostle have in mind?" The question has been asked whether the apostle has in mind merely the moral law, the law of the ten commandments, or whether he has in mind the entire law of the Jews, the moral, ceremonial, and civil laws.

This question is entirely out of place and should not be asked. The apostle does not have in mind any specific law. What the apostle says is that the life of the Gentiles, in the external sense, is characterized by this: they have no law. This is the difference between the Jews and the Gentiles.

By *law* here is meant the external code, the written law, not the spiritual essence of the law. The apostle does not mean that the Gentiles are not under the law of God; this is just what he emphasizes. He means that the Gentiles have no *written* law, no *external* code of precepts telling them what is the will of God. There is no such revelation to the Gentiles as there was to the Jews. God spoke to the Jews in decalogue, in the law of the ten commandments. These ten commandments were real; they were written in stone. In that code God came from without to the Jews and said, "Thou shalt," and "Thou shalt not." The entire way, step-by-step, was externally mapped out for the Jew. He could walk that way blindfolded. Israel was bound, all along the way, by the external law. This the Gentiles did not have. The Gentiles are without law, in this sense.

These Gentiles are a law unto themselves. They are their own law, in a certain sense. That the Gentiles are their own law does not mean that they have the authority to declare what is right and wrong. This is not the meaning. Rather, there is in them a principle, a light by which, to a certain extent, they are able to declare unto themselves what is right and what is wrong. When they declare what is the will of God concerning right and wrong, they show that they have sufficient light to know the law that they do not possess.

If you ask how that is, the apostle explains that they have the work of the law written in their hearts. Do not mistake this phrase. That the Gentiles have *the work of the law* written in their hearts is by no means the same as having *the law itself* written in the heart. Scripture speaks of having the law written in the heart [Jer. 31:33; Heb. 8:10]. Scripture emphasizes that God's people have the spiritual principle of the law of God, which is love, written in the heart so that they have no more need of an external code. The heart is the center of man's life from a spiritual point of view. If God implants the spiritual essence of the law in the heart, the heart does what the law requires. But this is not the meaning here.

The work of the law does not mean the work that the law requires. Many interpret it this way. Some say that although the Gentiles have not the law, they are in a position to do what the law requires and be saved. Others say that there is a general grace by which God has written the work of the law upon the hearts of the Gentiles so that they do the things contained in the law. But this is not the meaning.

I call your attention to the fact that the text is an answer to the question, "Can the Gentiles be marked as sinners and perish?" Therefore, the apostle means that the work which the law does for the Jew—this work the Gentiles have written in their hearts.

What is the work of the law? It is, first, to express what is the will of God and to distinguish between good and evil. Second, the work of the law is to promise life to them who keep it. Third, it is to curse them who do not abide in all that is written in it. This is the work of the law. This is written in the hearts of the Gentiles.

They did not need the law to distinguish between good and

evil. Why? They had the work of the law written in their hearts; therefore, they had no need of an external law. Thus, the threefold work of the law is written in the heart of every man.

The Effect in the Gentile World

You might ask, "How is the work of the law written in the hearts of the Gentiles?" The answer is, by God Himself. God has written it in their hearts, externally by His revelation in nature and internally by the testimony of His Spirit in their hearts. This testimony of the law was not only in the hearts of the Gentiles, but also in the hearts of the Jews. This was not the distinction between the Jews and the Gentiles. The distinction was that the Jews had the written law *besides* having the work of the law in their hearts, while the Gentiles had *only* the work of the law written in their hearts.

What is the result? The result is that the Gentiles do by nature the things of the law. They do not do *the things contained in the law,* as our English version would lead us to believe. As we have pointed out before, this comments on, rather than translates, the original. The things contained in the law are to love God, above all, and the neighbor as ourselves. The things contained in the law are not to have any other gods, not to have any graven images, not to use the name of God in vain, to keep the sabbath, to honor your father and mother, not to kill, not to commit adultery, not to steal, not to bear false witness, and not to covet. If the apostle had said that the Gentiles do the things contained in the law, he would have said that the Gentiles keep all of the ten commandments. But in the context the apostle says that the Gentiles perish without the law. Therefore, we must understand that *the things* of the law are *the things* that the law did for Israel.

What did the law do for Israel? It divided all of life into several departments. It gave Israel precepts and clearly marked out what Israel had to do: "Thou shalt have no other gods; thou shalt keep the sabbath; thou shalt not kill; thou shalt not covet." All the time, the law drew lines before the consciousness of the people of Israel. This the Gentiles did for themselves; otherwise, they could not have made laws.

The Manifestation in the Life of the Gentiles

How did they do it? They had the law not to kill, not to steal. How did they have it? They had the work of the law in their hearts. That this is true is plain from the conscience, the apostle says.

What is the *conscience?* The word is a translation from the Greek. The first part, *con-*, means "with." The second part, *-science*, means "knowledge." Therefore, the word *conscience* is derived from a word that means "to know with." It means "to know something with another."

Let me illustrate. Someone commits a crime. Another is witness to that crime. He who commits the crime has knowledge of it. The witness also has conscience of it. That is, he has knowledge of it along with the one who committed the crime.

The word *conscience* also means "to have knowledge with ourselves." It means that we have knowledge with ourselves of the thing we have done, after we have done it.

Let me illustrate once more. A man does something wrong. Before he does it, he knows that it is wrong. And after he has done it, his own judgment condemns what he has done. This is *conscience*.

It is sometimes said that we must not do anything against the conscience, but strictly speaking, we cannot do anything against the conscience because the conscience speaks *after* the thing is done. For this reason the conscience is sometimes called "the voice of God." It condemns the wrong and approves of the good that is done.

It is true that the conscience can become very sinful. Sometimes man succeeds, to a certain extent, in silencing the conscience. A man can tell the conscience to keep still. If he says it often enough, he will put the conscience to silence. But the conscience never stops speaking. In the judgment day the conscience will bear witness with the law. This is what the Gentile does. His conscience bears witness. Because his conscience bears witness, it is a plain manifestation that there is the work of the law written in his heart.

The work of the law also becomes manifest in public opinion. There is a public opinion. You find it in your daily papers. What you find there is not a mere recitation. What you find is the judgment of men concerning the things that are done. How do men judge one another? They find lines between what is good and evil. Thus, there was a public opinion among the Gentiles. There was a public opinion by which they accused or else excused one another.

This does not mean that the Gentiles have grace. The fact that man can distinguish between good and evil, that he condemns the murderer and the thief, does not mean that he does not steal. But it shows that no man is excusable.

This is the theme of the apostle in chapter 2: "Therefore thou art inexcusable, O man, whosoever thou art that judgest" [v. 1]. Law or no law, man is inexcusable. You say that you have the law? It makes no difference; you shall be judged according to your works. You say that you have no law? It makes no difference; you have the work of the law in your heart. God judges man according to his works. Every soul that is not righteous will receive indignation and wrath.

What then? Is there no hope? There is no hope in religion, in going to church, in being baptized, in partaking of the Lord's Supper. There is but one hope. This is the righteousness of God in Christ Jesus that comes to them who have sought glory, honor, and immortality in the way of patient continuance in well-doing. The righteous shall live by faith. Therefore, as far as we are concerned in the matter, we must learn to write hell and damnation upon all that is of us. Having come naked before the Judge, we must learn to look at Him who is our righteousness and our redemption.

Chapter Twelve

The Vain Boast of Self-righteousness

Romans 2:17-21a
Behold, thou art called a Jew, and restest in the law, and makest thy boast of God,
And knowest his will, and approvest the things that are more excellent, being instructed out of the law;
And art confident that thou thyself art a guide of the blind, a light of them which are in darkness,
An instructor of the foolish, a teacher of babes, which hast the form of knowledge and of the truth in the law.
Thou therefore which teachest another, teachest thou not thyself?

In the words of this text, the apostle takes away a religion. He takes away a religion as the basis of our righteousness before God. It is his purpose in the first part of his epistle to the Romans to take away all that we have from the point of view of the question "How can one be righteous before God in the day when God shall judge the secrets of men?" From this point of view the apostle removes everything from us—even our piety, our religion, our Christianity. This is the essential meaning of the passage.

In the preceding verses the apostle had laid down the general basis for the address with which he now approaches the Jew. He had addressed man and had laid down a general principle, which he now applies to the Jews. This general principle, which lies at the basis of all other principles, is that God will judge every man according to his works. From this follows that not the hearers of the law are just before God, but the doers of the law shall be justified. Doing the law means nothing less than by patient continuance in well-doing, we seek for glory, honor, and immortality every moment of our life. There is no respect of persons with God. Jew and Gentile shall both be judged according to their works.

This general rule the apostle had applied to the Gentiles when he said that the Gentiles who have not the law do by nature the things of the law. Therefore, they are a law unto themselves, having the work of the law written in their hearts. For this reason we can say of the Gentiles that they who sin without the law shall also perish without the law.

Now the apostle applies this same principle to the Jews. He takes away their religion as a basis of righteousness before God. He also takes away all their privileges. Then he takes hold of their conscience and says, "Thou that teachest another, teachest thou not thyself?"

When we read these words, we must beware, lest we become filled with indignation at the self-righteous Jew. If we do, we are more self-righteous than the Jew. For this self-righteous Jew is a picture of what we are by nature. You and I are just what the apostle says here of the Jew. I am the worst Jew; next, the elders; then, the deacons; then, the teachers and leaders; then, the common members. But I am the worst Jew. I am not joking; I mean it. It is the mystery of the ministry of the Word that God chooses such a Jew as I am, who preaches but does not do as he preaches.

Don't you see that we can read the text this way? "Behold, thou art called a Christian, and restest in Reformed doctrine, and makest thy boast of God, and knowest His will, and approvest the things that are more excellent, being instructed in Reformed doctrine. Thou trustest that thou hast the purest form of the truth and that thou art an instructor of the foolish, a teacher of babes, a guide of the blind, and a light of them who are in darkness. Thou hast not only the form of the truth, but thou hast the truth itself. Thou, therefore, who teachest another, teachest thou not thyself? Thou who teachest that we must glorify God above all, glorifiest thou not God thyself? Thou who teachest that we must not seek the things below but the things above, seekest thou the things below?"

Our religion, our piety, our baptism, our doctrine, our Reformed convictions; still more, our repentance, our faith, and our hope are taken away as a basis of our righteousness in the day when God shall judge the secrets of men.

A Rich Heritage

A rich heritage the Jews had. They had the law. They had the form of knowledge and of the truth, as taught in the law. The law here is not the decalogue, but the Old Testament law in its entirety. The entire form of Old Testament doctrine is meant here. It is the Old Testament form of the truth, as given to the people by Moses. It includes the entire revelation of God concerning the Old Testament form of righteousness, not only the way in which the people must walk, but also all the shadows and types of Christ.

The apostle says, "Behold, thou art called a Jew." *Jew* means "glorifier of God." "Behold, thou art called a glorifier of God. Thou hast the law. Because of this law, thou hast a form of the truth and of knowledge."

The apostle does not say that the Jews had the truth and knowledge, but that they had a *form* of the truth and knowledge. This does not mean that the Jews merely had an appearance of truth and knowledge. The apostle has in mind the old dispensation. *Truth* must be understood in the sense of the apostle John when he says, "For the law was given by Moses, but grace and truth came by Jesus Christ" (John 1:17). What the Jews had was the form of the river through which the water of salvation was presently to flow. They had the form, the mold, the pattern of the truth. The form was waiting for the truth. They had the form of the truth and knowledge of God in the law.

We have more. Truth and grace have been revealed. We have the reality. We can, therefore, apply this word far more emphatically to ourselves. We can read it this way: "Thou hast the truth and knowledge." We have a system of that truth. We have a system of the truth in our doctrine and confessions. We have the reality of the truth in such a form that it is ready-made.

The apostle does not mean that we should despise these things, but he means that the Jews had a rich heritage in these things. So have we. The apostle brings out the riches of this heritage when he says, "Thou knowest the will of God." The Jew knew the will of God as manifested in the law. We know the will of God as manifested in Christ. That is, *theoretically* we know the will of God.

A Great Zeal

Knowing the will of God, the Jews (and we) are pictured as being full of zeal. This zeal becomes manifest in that the Jews approve the things that are more excellent. The meaning is this. The Jews knew the law. They systematized the truth of that law. With that system of doctrine they compared all other forms of philosophy.

We do the same. We know the truth in distinction from all false doctrine. Not only do we make this distinction, but as a result we approve of the truth. When an Arminian comes along, we condemn that Arminian and approve of the Reformed doctrine; that is, as the apostle means it, *theoretically* we do this.

The apostle adds, "approving of the things that are more excellent, they are confident that they are a guide of the blind." The Jews had a right to be thus confident. They had the form of truth and knowledge. They were a light to them who were in darkness and an instructor of the foolish. That is, they were a light to them who were outside the light of the truth, as revealed in the law. Because they had the form of knowledge and of truth, they were teachers of babes. The Jews were the only ones to instruct their children.

The same is true of us. Anyone who stands outside the church does not instruct his children, but we instruct our children. We need not be ashamed of it. We say that we have the truth and that we are a guide of the blind and a light to them who are in darkness. We also instruct our children. With right, we claim that we are the only ones who do this. The apostle approves of these things. They are a blessing. They are a tremendous heritage.

But from the point of view of the question "How can I be righteous before God?" all these things are worthless, and for more than one reason. These things cannot possibly be the righteousness with which, in the day when God shall judge the secrets of men, you and I can appear before God and be justified.

When that day comes, and we shall be judged by our works, we cannot say, "I have been a Christian," for then the Lord will say, "That was a privilege, but it is not a work."

In that day you cannot say, "I went to church and was a member." The Lord will say, "That was a privilege, but it is not a work that can be the basis of your righteousness before Me."

You cannot say, "I was Reformed and knew the truth." The Lord will say, "That was a privilege, but it cannot be the basis of your righteousness."

You cannot say, "I have rejected every heresy repugnant to the truth, and I have fought Arminianism and Pelagianism and all false teaching." The Lord will say, "That was all right, but it cannot be the basis of your righteousness."

You cannot even say this: "I have repented; I have repented of my sin; and because I have repented of my sin, I expect to be justified." Then the Lord will say, "Did you? Did you always repent? Patient continuance in well-doing: did you always do this? All your life?" Then you will have to say, "No, I repented once in a while." And our *impenitence* will be so great that we will be worthy to go to hell with all our repentance.

You cannot say, "I have sought the kingdom of God," for the

Lord will say, "Did you?" And the times when we sought not the kingdom of God, when we sought the world and ourselves, will be so great that we will be worthy of condemnation.

In the day when God shall judge the secrets of men, everything will be taken away from us.

A False Reliance

The apostle does this to us here. "Thou restest in the law," the apostle says. That was a false reliance. "Thou restest in the law." What does this mean? It does not mean that the Jews did not care about the law but would merely hear it. No, they rested in the law. They looked upon the keeping of the law as the basis of their righteousness before God. All the sacrifices told them differently, but they looked upon the law as the way to righteousness. Looking upon the law as the basis of righteousness, they kept it painstakingly.

The Jew did not have to be cut off from the church because he neglected his religious duties. Rather, keeping the law as a basis of righteousness, he rested in that. He said, "On the basis of keeping the law, I am righteous before God."

Do we not do the same thing? We do. If you will but candidly examine your heart and mind, you will find there that self-righteousness by which you rest in your religion. I do not mean merely that you rest in your churchgoing and other external acts. Rather, you and I say, "I am pious. I believe in Christ, and on the basis of this I will be justified." This the apostle takes away. This was the Jews' false reliance.

A Vain Boast

It became their vain boast. The apostle takes it all away. Remember, the apostle is preparing the way for the gospel. If the way is to be prepared for the gospel, all must be taken away that is of us.

Why?

"Thou boastest in God," the apostle says. "Thou restest in

the law and makest thy boast of God." In other words, the Jew boasted that God was his God. The apostle goes on to say, "Thou dishonorest God. Thou that preachest a man should not steal, dost thou steal? Thou that sayest a man should not commit adultery, dost thou commit adultery? Thou that abhorrest idols, robbest thou temples?" [vv. 21–23].

The Jews would say, "No, I don't. I don't steal; I don't commit adultery; I don't rob temples. I keep the law."

Putting the question to us, the apostle says, "Thou that teachest that a man should repent, repentest thou not thyself? Thou that sayest that a man should seek the things above and not the things below, seekest thou the things below?"

We say, "No, we are Reformed." We say, "I do repent; I do seek the things above; I do seek first the kingdom of God."

But the Word of God does not let us go so easily. The question is not, what do we do now? The question is, what will we say in the day of the righteous judgment of God? God will say, "Didst thou steal?" We will have to say, "Yes, in my heart I did." "Did you commit adultery?" You will have to say, "Yes, I did in my heart." "Did you really always repent? Were you never impenitent?"

The more we shall be questioned, the more we will say, where is my religion? If I come before God with my religion as the basis of my righteousness, I will be condemned. Therefore, away with all my religion as a basis of righteousness. Then there is nothing left but a poor, miserable sinner before God.

If this is understood and acknowledged, and we see and believe as a matter of living faith, then we have room for the gospel. In the day when God shall judge the secrets of men, we will say, "I plead not on my own righteousness, but on Thy righteousness in Christ." This is a righteousness that is perfect because God has prepared it. He has prepared it in Christ. He has revealed it in the gospel.

I am not ashamed of the gospel, for there is no other righteousness than the righteousness of God, which is by faith in Christ Jesus.

Chapter Thirteen

The Impossibility of Religious Work-righteousness

Romans 2:28, 29
For he is not a Jew, which is one outwardly; neither is that circumcision, which is outward in the flesh:
But he is a Jew, which is one inwardly; and circumcision is that of the heart, in the spirit, and not in the letter; whose praise is not of men, but of God.

The question that the apostle is answering in the context is whether a man can be righteous before God because of his religion. He is talking no more to man in general, as in the beginning of the chapter, but he is addressing religious people. He is addressing the religious man. He is addressing the church member, even though it is the church member of the Old Testament, the Jew. He is taking away his religion, his piety, and his religious good works as the basis of righteousness before God. This is the general thought of the context.

It was plain that man cannot be righteous by works and that the heathen cannot be righteous by works. But now, if a man is religious, cannot *this* be the basis of his righteousness before God?

Remember, the apostle is addressing not only the Jew, but he is also addressing the religious people of that day. Therefore, he is addressing you and me. He is answering the question whether church membership and all that stands connected with it cannot be the basis of our righteousness before God.

The apostle answers that if our religion is to be the basis of our righteousness, it must be one hundred percent perfect. If circumcision, which was the heart of the Old Testament religion, considered as a work, is to be the basis of my righteousness before God; if baptism, considered as a work, is to be the basis of our righteousness, then it is necessary to keep the law perfectly. For, the apostle writes in verse 25, "Circumcision verily profiteth, if thou keep the law: but if thou be a breaker of the law, thy circumcision is made uncircumcision." This is so emphatically true that if a Gentile who is not circumcised in the flesh keeps the righteousness of the law, his uncircumcision shall be counted for circumcision, and he shall judge the Jew, who by the letter and circumcision transgresses the law.

The reason for what he has said in the context, the apostle gives in the text. Your religion, your baptism, your church membership, your piety, your religious activities cannot serve as your righteousness before God. "For he is not a Jew, which is one outwardly; neither is that circumcision, which is outward in the flesh: But he is a Jew, which is one inwardly; and circumcision is that of the heart, in the spirit, and not in the letter; whose praise is not of men, but of God."

According to the context, the text emphasizes that if your religious righteousness is to be perfect before God *as a work,* you must be able to circumcise your own heart, and you must be perfect in your inward heart. Hence, the apostle shows us here the impossibility of religious work-righteousness.

Such a Righteousness Must Have Praise of God

The apostle says, "He is a Jew . . . whose praise is not of men, but of God." We would say, "He is a Christian whose praise is not of men, but of God." This means three things. In the first place, objectively it means that God praises us. To praise is to judge, to approve, and then to tell the one so judged and approved of that approval. God judges perfectly. He also judges thoroughly.

The apostle says that the man who would be righteous by his religion must not have his praise of men. Man cannot praise. When man praises anyone, it does not signify that the man so praised is righteous. Man praises according to the standard of man. His praise is sinful with regard to the motive. Mere sinful man praises from various motives. Not only is the praise of man sinful, but it is also external. Man can only praise what is external; he can only praise what he can see. Man cannot judge, and therefore he cannot praise motives. For these reasons, man's praise is meaningless as a criterion of righteousness.

Even a certificate of the church does not mean anything with respect to your righteousness before God. When the consistory gives you a certificate of membership and writes on it that you are sound in doctrine and in walk, you do not receive a passport into heaven. The consistory also praises what it sees.

Your praise must be according to God. But God judges perfectly. God approves only what is one hundred percent perfect. He does not approve anything that is not one hundred percent perfect. As God judges perfectly, so He judges thoroughly. That is, He judges according to the inmost root of the heart. What must our service be in order to be one hundred percent perfect so that it can be acceptable to God? It must be one hundred percent according to the will of God, and it must be one hundred percent from the heart.

In the second place, the phrase *He is a Christian whose praise is not of men, but of God* means that you do not seek anything *but* the praise of God. It means that in all your religious activity your only motive is to obtain the praise of God. Your motive must not be to have the praise of men. It is your one hundred percent desire that *God* praise you. From this, all our religious activity must spring if we are to be praised by God.

In the third place, that one's praise must be of God means that God judges because of what a man is and does. Therefore, one whose praise is of God, and who is righteous because of his religious activity, is one who has the Word and the testimony of God that he is righteous before God. You must have the testimony of God, through the Spirit, that you are righteous because of your religious activities. But this is impossible.

We would read verse 28 this way: "He is not a Christian who is one outwardly; neither is baptism that which is outward in the flesh. But he is a Christian whose praise is of God." If this is the case, we can have no moment's peace. There is no righteousness in being baptized, in going to church, in being a Christian, or in being pious. If our work must have the praise of God, and if whatever is not one hundred percent perfect before God cannot enter into the judgment, then I am lost.

Such a Righteousness Must Proceed from a Perfect, Circumcised Heart

For what is the case? If I am to be righteous, I must have a circumcised heart. If circumcision is to be the basis of my righteousness before God, I must have a circumcised heart, and I must circumcise it. Circumcision is not that which one performs in the flesh. If that were the case, if circumcision merely meant the cutting of the flesh, the Jew could say, "Yes, I am circumcised." The Jew could say, "I circumcise all my children, and I did it. If this could be the basis of righteousness, the Jew could become righteous. The apostle says, however, that this is not what circumcision is.

This is also true of baptism. If baptism was merely that we bring our babies to church and sprinkle a little water on them, we could say, "I baptize and am righteous."

When we read in the text that circumcision is not in the letter, the meaning is that it is not by the law. The letter is the law. The law had power to circumcise all children. The law was obeyed. The apostle is not speaking to those who were indifferent. He is speaking to the faithful Jew; he is addressing the religious Jew, who kept the law. All were circumcised by the letter of the law. But the apostle says that this is not what circumcision is. In like manner there is a baptism by the letter. There is an ordinance of baptism that is kept by the church. If this could be our righteousness before God, all would be righteous. But the apostle says that this is not true.

Circumcision is of the heart, in the spirit, and not in the letter. Circumcision was a sign. The negative testimony of circumcision was that a man could not bring forth children of God. The negative testimony of circumcision was that if God did not perform an operation upon the generations of Abraham, Abraham could not bring forth God's children.

Positively, circumcision was a sign by which God testified, and Abraham accepted, that God by a wonder of His grace would make of Abraham's children, children of God. Circumcision was a picture of the cutting away of sin.

The apostle speaks of circumcision of the heart. The heart is the center of our existence from a spiritual point of view. Our willing, our thinking, and our desiring is from the heart. As the heart is, so we are. If our heart is corrupt, our thinking is corrupt, our willing is corrupt, our desiring is corrupt. If the heart is good, if the heart is circumcised, the man has been circumcised and sanctified.

This is baptism also. Baptism is a sign. It is a sign of the same thing. There is no essential difference between circumcision and baptism. The only difference is that circumcision looked forward to Christ, while baptism looks at Christ as He has come into the world and made atonement. The Old Testament people of God must be circumcised to bring forth the Christ. But as soon as the Seed has been brought forth, it stands to reason that the sign is changed. When Christ has come and atonement has been made, there can be no more circumcision, but baptism.

If circumcision and baptism must be the basis of our righteousness *as a work*, all we do is perform the outward rite. We can never circumcise the heart. We can never baptize into Christ. If it is true that circumcision is a circumcision of the heart, and if baptism is a baptism of the heart, and if it is not our work but the work of God, we can never bring circumcision or baptism before God as work-righteousness. The apostle means, "It is impossible for any one to say, 'I am a Jew; I am circumcised,' or, 'I am a Christian; I am baptized; I observe all that stands connected with the church; and therefore I am righteous.'" Paul means, "Your religion must go!"

Certainly the circumcised Jew was justified, but not as long as he looked upon his circumcision as a work. For his circumcision testified of the righteousness that is by faith in Christ Jesus. As long as we look upon baptism as a work, it can never justify us, for we are not righteous. As it is with circumcision and baptism, so it is with all our works. Our religion can never be the basis of our righteousness before God.

Such a Righteousness Must Be Characterized by a Perfect Walk

What does the apostle say? "He is not a Jew, which is one outwardly." All who look upon the Jews as really being the Jews are condemned here. The Jews are not all Jews. What is an outward Jew, that is, a Jew in appearance? An outward Jew is one who was born of Abraham, who looked like a Jew, who was circumcised on the eighth day, who was brought up in the knowledge of the law, and who observed all the religious rites.

So it is with a Christian in appearance. A Christian in appearance is one who is born of believing parents, is baptized, is instructed in the Word, and is faithful in all his religious obligations. He is not one whom the consistory must run after to come to catechism. That is not even a Christian in appearance.

The apostle says, "He is not a Jew, he is not a Christian, which is one outwardly." Do not turn that around. The apostle does not say, "He is a Jew who is *not* circumcised." He does not say, "He is a Christian who is *not* baptized." A Christian will do these things. He will go to church and to catechism; he will observe his religious obligations. He wants to go to church. He likes to go there. He will sing praise to God and listen to His Word.

Rather, the apostle means that all you see of a Jew and of a Christian does not constitute a Jew or a Christian. The reason is that all these outward things can be accomplished by the outward flesh.

He is a Jew and he is a Christian who is one inwardly. He is a Jew and he is a Christian who is one in the hidden things of his heart. This hidden life of his heart will then become manifest in all his life as the spiritual background. Therefore, if you want to make your religion the basis of your righteousness before God, you must be able to say that in whatever you do, you are motivated one hundred percent by the love of God.

What is the conclusion? What is *your* conclusion? What is *my* conclusion? What is *our* conclusion if we review our religion? This: away with our religion as the basis of righteousness! Away with our piety! There is not one who on that basis would dare to stand before God and say, "Lord, I have been religious; on the basis of my work, make me righteous." Hence, there is nothing left; there is no righteousness with us. This is the conclusion.

Then the way opens for what the apostle means to teach. Only as we cast away all our own works is there room for the preaching of the apostle. The heart of this preaching is this: the righteous shall live by faith. When we stand in judgment (and we do—we stand in judgment now; this judgment will be revealed, but we stand in judgment now) and confess that all our righteousness is but filthy rags, God will speak to us and say that our sins are forgiven. The impossible possibility has happened: the unrighteous has become righteous.

I am not ashamed of the gospel of Christ.

Chapter Fourteen

The Faith of God

Romans 3:3, 4a
For what if some did not believe? shall their unbelief make the faith of God without effect?
God forbid: yea, let God be true, but every man a liar.

"For what if some did not believe?" This is a very real and extremely practical question. What if some do not believe? Then what will you say? Then what will your answer be?

Of course, you do not feel how cutting and practical this question is as long as you stay strictly with the text and ask, "What if some of the *Jews* did not believe?" But what if some of *us* do not believe? Putting the question in this form, it becomes more real to you and me. What if some of the children of the covenant do not believe? What if some of the children of our own church do not believe? Or if you want to feel it more intensely, what if some of them be your own flesh and blood? What if it be some of your babes, whom you brought up, whom you instructed in the fear and admonition of the Lord, and for whom you prayed, pleading, "Lord save them"—what if some of *them* do not believe? What will you say then?

This is precisely the question that the apostle asks in the text. True, he is speaking of the Jew. In the first part of the chapter, he has asked the question, "What advantage then hath the Jew? or what profit is there of circumcision?" This question arises in his mind because he realizes that the Jews will ask this question of him on account of what he had said. The Jew would say, "If it is true what you have written; if all are to be judged according to their works, the Jew first and also the Greek; if circumcision profiteth nothing; if the Jew has no advantage; if there be no difference between Jew and Gentile; if there is no respect of persons with God; what advantage, then, hath the Jew?" If it makes no difference whether you belong to the church or to the world, what advantage, then, is it to belong to the church?

The apostle answers, "Much every way." But the advantage of the Jew and the profit of circumcision must not be sought in anything that he is or does, but in the gift of God. The advantage of the Jew is not in his religion, is not in his being a Jew, is not in circumcision. Rather, the advantage of the Jew is this, chiefly: he has the oracles of God; he has God's Word.

But this raises another question. "If the Jew has the Word of God, what if some do not believe?" What is your answer? Do you turn Arminian? Do you say that through his unbelief man makes the faith of God of no effect? Do you then make God a liar?

The apostle answers, "God forbid: yea, let God be true, but every man a liar." This is the reason why some do not believe.

Revealed

The apostle speaks of the *faith of God:* "Shall their unbelief make the faith of God of no effect?" *Faith* in this connection does not mean "to believe." It does not mean faith in the sense of believing, as the word is used with respect to us. But *faith* in the verse has the significance of faithfulness. The apostle is asking, "Does the unbelief of them who do not believe make the faithfulness of God of no effect?" Faith in this sense is constancy. It is really unchangeableness. Faith in this sense is that in a certain relation one remains unchangeable. When anyone in a certain relation always reveals himself as he is expected to reveal himself in that relation, the particular party in this particular relation is *faithful*. In the same way, God is faithful.

Reverently speaking, God could not be anything but faithful. The root of God's faithfulness is His unchangeableness. He is, in the first place, faithful in Himself. As the triune God, He is the faithful covenant God. In the covenant relation of Father, Son, and Holy Ghost, every one of the three persons does that which is in harmony with that relation.

In the second place, the faithfulness of God means that He is constant, that He is unchangeable in His relation to His people. In respect to His people, He always stands in a relation of covenant friendship. He gives them life, forgiveness of sins, righteousness, and eternal glory.

It is especially to this latter faith of God that the text calls attention. Verse 3, therefore, may be paraphrased and expanded thus: "Does the unbelief of some who do not believe cause God to break His covenant relation with His people so that He does not save them, does not forgive their sins, does not deliver them from the power of death, and does not give them eternal life and glorify them?"

"Does the faith of God depend upon the faith of man?" This is the question.

The faith of God has been revealed, according to the context. The apostle says that the Jews had the oracles of God. The oracles of God are the Word of God. They are the Old Testament Scriptures. They are really the one Word of God. That the apostle uses the plural—oracles—is due to the fact that he refers to the different times in which that one Word was given. God gave His Word to Adam, to Enoch, to Noah, to Abraham, to Israel. This one Word of God became oracles. Those words, the apostle says, were committed to the Jews, or as the Dutch has it, they were *entrusted* to the Jews.

To have the Word of God is a trust. To have the Word of God is a terrible thing for sinful man. It is not just given to him, but it is entrusted to him. The apostle says that the Jews were entrusted with the Word of God, just as God has entrusted that Word to us. The chief content of that Word is the promise.

What is the advantage of the Jew? Or what profit is there in circumcision? Translating into New Testament language, we would say, "What is the advantage of the church, or what is the profit of baptism?"

Chiefly this: to the church the oracles of God have been entrusted. The advantage of having the Word of God is that the content of these oracles is the promise "I will establish My covenant with you." This is the content of that one Word of God. This is the content of the gospel. God says, "I will establish My covenant with you, I will redeem you from sin, I will deliver you from corruption, I will lift you up into glory." This is the advantage.

Questioned

What if some do not believe, some who had those oracles, some who were entrusted with that Word of God's promise? What if some of them do not believe? How do you explain this?

You understand that the apostle is speaking of an awful fact. The apostle asks, "What if some did not believe?" The apostle has been criticized because he says *some*. Because there were so many who did not believe, the apostle has been criticized for saying *some*. But he says *some* not because he did not know that there would be many who did not believe, but to compare this with the glory that is to be revealed unto them who are to be saved. Still it is an awful fact.

Oh, there is a world of trouble and sorrow in this question of the apostle—"What if some do not believe?"—for the apostle is not thinking of a few in his own day. Instead, he is thinking of all those who did not believe throughout the history of the Old Testament people of God. Ever since God spoke through Moses, there had been this *some*. They did not believe. Thus, they made God a liar. It made no difference how that Word came to them; they did not believe. When the oracles of God came to them, they said to the bearers of these oracles, "Get out of the way!" So they did in the desert; so they did with the prophets; so they did with Christ. The essence of this attitude with respect to the Word of God is that they called God a liar. As it was in the old dispensation, so it is in the new. When God commits His oracles to His people, this *some* is always there.

This is so awful a thing that those who brought these oracles to the people of God in the Old Testament, and those who bring them in the new dispensation, sometimes say, "Blot me out of the book of life. Rather than that my brethren perish, blot *me* out of Thy book." This was the testimony of Moses when he saw that some did not believe. The apostle Paul said, "I could wish that myself were accursed from Christ for my brethren, my kinsmen according to the flesh" [Rom. 9:3].

Is it not a grief when you have, say, a half dozen children who all receive these same oracles of God, and when they come to years of discretion, you see some of them go astray? Is it not a grief that no matter how you plead with them, there are a number of them who say to these oracles of God, "God is a liar"? Is it not a grief if in the congregation, after having labored with all your might, you see the same effect? Some do not believe, and the consistory goes after them, but they do not believe. And they say, "God is a liar." This is such a grief that it is killing.

What if some do not believe? What will you say then? This is the question. Shall we say that the faith of God is made of no effect? Shall we question the faith of God? This is possible in two ways. The first is this: God brings His Word to man. He brings this Word to the Jews, to the church, promiscuously. When He does, He says to everyone, "I promise to give you eternal life. I promise to forgive your sins, to deliver you from corruption, to glorify you." This is the faith of God. When some do not believe, their unbelief makes the faith of God impossible. Is this the explanation? Is there a general offer that is brought to everyone, head for head, and if one does not believe, he makes the faith of God of no effect? God forbid! Then the unbelief of man would make it impossible for God to save anyone.

Or the question of the apostle may mean that the faithfulness of God is not true. Perhaps it means that God is not faithful. Let no one say that he never alleges this. When we parents appear before the throne of grace and say, "Please save my child because we have the covenant promise," but the child does not believe, what then? What if God does not hear our petition? (Sometimes He does not.) What is your response then? Oh, we do not put it this way, but we experience this rebellion, this unbelief in our hearts, that says that God is not faithful. If faith is a gift of God and is included in the promise, and if some do not believe, does not their unbelief prove that God is unfaithful to His promise? God forbid! God forbid that our unbelief should make the faith of God impossible. God forbid that our unbelief should prove that God is not faithful to His Word.

Maintained

What does the apostle answer? He does not explain, but he throws this accusation far from him with "God forbid!" The explanation and purpose why some do not believe is that every man be a liar and that God be true. In other words, the purpose why some do not believe is that it may become ever increasingly evident that man is a liar and that it may become ever increasingly evident that God is true.

Man is a liar. We always lie about God, by nature. This is so strong that if we examine our heart, we will find that we are always lying about God because we do not want Him. This is so strong that if we examine our hearts as Christians and then read this Word, we find in our heart this testimony: we don't want it. Still stronger, this is so true that when our sinful heart overwhelms the principle of new life and we read this Word, we say, "I do not want it." This becomes evident. It becomes clearly evident. This becomes evident in the heathen world, but it becomes far more evident if the oracles of God come. This Word from which there is no hiding, this Word that speaks to you and to me directly, this Word says to us, "Listen to me. Listen to the Word that can bring you near to God." But unless God changes our lying heart, we will say, "I do not want it." This is why they killed the prophets. This becomes evident. That some who do not believe must have the oracles of God is in order that it may become evident that sinful man is a liar who always lies about God. This must become evident in the judgment.

It must also become evident that God is true. That is, although some do not believe, God fulfills His promise to everyone to whom He has promised it. The perfected church shall be an everlasting testimony that God is true, just as the outer darkness shall be a testimony that man is a liar. If we really take this answer, we have peace, for God does all things well.

What shall we say then? Shall their unbelief make the faith of God of no effect? No. But we shall say this: let God ever increasingly become true, and let man ever increasingly become a liar.

Chapter Fifteen

A Damnable Inference

Romans 3:7, 8
For if the truth of God hath more abounded through my lie unto his glory; why yet am I also judged as a sinner?
And not rather, (as we be slanderously reported, and as some affirm that we say,) Let us do evil, that good may come? whose damnation is just.

In the immediate context, the apostle removes from the sinner a last possibility of excuse. This is the purpose of the preceding four or five verses. The apostle presently intends to elaborate upon the positive message of the gospel. This message is that man is justified by faith through the righteousness that is of God and that He realized in Christ. If the sinner is to receive the positive message of the gospel, he must have nothing left that is of himself. There must be no possibility left for him to be justified by works.

Not only those works we might call the works of the law, but also our religion, our piety, our Christianity, must be taken away. They are no good as a basis of righteousness. Also every excuse of the sinner—that he shall not appear in the judgment, that God has no right to execute judgment upon him—must be taken out of the hand of the sinner, who always lies about God. He must stop lying about God.

In the context the apostle answers a possible objector who lies about God to excuse himself.

Let me use an illustration. A judge passes sentence upon his own son. That son has committed murder. He is tried in his father's own court. That judge expresses the verdict of the death sentence upon that son. By the verdict of that judge, the sentence becomes the occasion of commending the righteousness and integrity of the judge. The son, hearing that the judge is praised for his righteousness and integrity, turns around and says, "Because my sin commends your righteousness, you cannot condemn me to death." But the judge answers, "How shall I judge then?"

What is the flaw in the reasoning of that son? That although his sin becomes the means of the sentence, and thus of commending the righteousness and integrity of the judge, that sin does not become meritorious. That sin remains sin. Therefore, it is to be condemned.

So the apostle reasons in the context and in the text. The apostle had said that the faith of God is not affected by the unbelief of the sinner. He had said, what if some do not believe? Shall their unbelief make the faith of God without effect? God forbid! Yet their unbelief must show that all men are liars and that God is true.

The unbelief of them who have the oracles of God shows that although man may have the Word of God, he is still a liar. When they have the Word of God, this Word serves to bring out, even more, that all men are liars. But God gives faith to them who are heirs of the promise.

Now the objector states, "If this is true, if my unfaithfulness commends the faithfulness of God, then God is unrighteous if He brings wrath upon me." Or, as in the text, "If my lie must serve to bring out His truth, I cannot be judged as a sinner." In this case, the safest rule is this: "Let us do evil, that good may come out of it." This, says the apostle, is a damnable inference.

The Inference

The objector draws a conclusion. He draws a conclusion from Paul's doctrine. This is often done. How often do you not hear this conclusion if you insist upon preaching the sovereignty of God, if you insist that even sin and the devil are there by the will of God: "You make God the author of sin!" This is not the conclusion of those who hold to the sovereignty of God. This is the conclusion of the enemy. This same faulty reasoning we have in the text. From the doctrine of the apostle, the objector draws this conclusion: "Let us do evil, that good may come."

The question is, from what doctrine of Paul does the objector draw this conclusion? The answer is, from the teaching of Paul that even sin, evil, and all the powers of darkness exist, operate, and must redound to God's glory. The objector draws this conclusion from the teaching that all the lies of men must bring out the truth of God. This was the answer of Paul to the objector who had said, "What if some do not believe?" The apostle said that God must become ever increasingly true and man must become ever increasingly a liar. This must be the outcome. This will be the outcome. The apostle had stated that this was the purpose of God when He did not give faith to all. This was the issue. Faith is included in the promise. Why, then, did not God give this faith to all? The apostle answers that God did not give faith to all in order that it might become evident that God is true and that every man is a liar. This is the particular teaching of Paul from which the objector draws the conclusion "Let us do evil, that good may come."

There is a general principle at stake here. Sin has no purpose, no end of its own. The only purpose, the only end that sin can reach, is the glory of God. That is, God's purpose with sin is that it may become evident that He is God, that He is God alone, and that He is the only good. The powers of darkness must serve this purpose, and they must serve this purpose alone.

This is an important principle. To deny this truth is to deny the antithesis. This denial leads to dualism. You do not believe the antithesis if you do not explain sin and the devil out of God. Not to explain sin and the devil out of God leads to heathen dualism. This the apostle does not teach. The apostle says that sin is there to glorify God. The unrighteousness of man must bring out the righteousness of God. The lie of man must bring out the truth of God. This is God's purpose. This truth we must never surrender. This is the truth of truths. It is the truth that God is God.

What is the inference? The apostle says, "I speak as a man." It is the inference of a man. What is the inference of man? It is not the inference of an apostle. It is not the inference of a Christian, but "I speak as a man, as a *sinful* man."

What does sinful man say? He says this: "If what you have been teaching, Paul, is true, this is also true: my lie bears good fruit, it serves a good purpose, and it serves to bring out the truth of God. Therefore, my lie is really a necessary element in the glorification of God. If I do not lie, God will not be glorified. My unrighteousness commends, by way of comparison, the righteousness of God. All can see that I am unrighteous and that God is righteous. But my unrighteousness serves to bring out the righteousness of God. Hence, this is also true: God cannot judge me as a sinner. Why, then, am I still judged as a sinner? If the truth of God abounds more through my lie unto His glory, God cannot judge me as a sinner. Don't you see, Paul, that I am excused? Even though I am a liar and unrighteous, I cannot be judged, because my lie must redound to the glory of God."

There is one more step. From the doctrine that God is sovereign, this conclusion of the enemies also follows: "Let us do evil, that good may come." The apostle says these objectors alleged that this is what he taught; ". . . as we be slanderously reported, and as some affirm that we say," reports the apostle. This is an old method of opposing the truth. There were some who actually said about the apostle's doctrine that the apostle taught, "Let us do evil, that good may come." The apostle did not teach this. This was merely a conclusion of the enemy. The apostle calls it a damnable inference.

Its Absurdity

What is the error? What is wrong with this conclusion? They who draw this inference do not present the matter quite correctly. They say, "Our unrighteousness commends the righteousness of God." This is not quite correct. They make just a little mistake, but this little mistake is a serious error. Their statement is not quite true. The objectors state, "God's glory must abound through our lie." But this is not exactly the case. It should be put in a slightly different form in order to be true; otherwise, it is a devilish error. The lie of man does not commend the truth, but *opposes* it. The unrighteousness of man does not commend the righteousness of God, but opposes it. In other words, man does not glorify God when he lies. He does not glorify God when he commits unrighteousness. Man does not intend to glorify God when he lies or commits unrighteousness. His lie is not a work that can be put to his credit, for it was not his purpose to glorify God. A lie is always a lie.

Therefore, the truth must be put this way. God glorifies Himself through my unrighteousness. God glorifies His truth through my lie. My lie does not glorify God. God glorifies Himself. God always glorifies Himself. He glorifies Himself in the elect. We are not the meritorious glorifiers of God. God glorifies *Himself*. Even as He glorifies Himself in the elect, so He glorifies Himself in the reprobate. God does it. God uses man's lie and unrighteousness to His own glory.

The inference of the objector is absurd. God's glorification is a self-glorification. It is a glorifying of Himself in spite of sin and the devil. How, then, can the sinner ask, "Why am I judged as a sinner?" His lie does not glorify God.

If a man throws a child into the water and that child becomes the occasion for another man to show his bravery; and if he who had thrown the child into the water should want the credit, would he not be deemed mad? Or if the Jews who crucified Christ should say to God, "We are the cause that the blood of atonement was shed, and we want the credit," would that not be deemed insane? This is the absurdity of the objection of all the wicked. In the day of judgment, the wicked shall see and acknowledge that they have served nothing but the glory of God. But then they will not say, "This was our work." Rather, they will say, "We were the most absurd fools that ever were." The sinner is absurd. The devil is absurd. He is foolish. The absurdity of the fool will be acknowledged by the fool himself when it shall appear that God is true and that every man is a liar.

Its Damnable Character

This inference of the sinner is also *damnable*. Oh, we hear these things doctrinally. We hear people say, "You teach that God willed sin." This is true. But they add, "If this is true, then it is also true that God is the author of sin." When they say that, we must not withdraw our teaching, but we must say, "Your damnation is just."

When the apostle says that their damnation is just, he does not merely mean to express a general truth, but he means that of those who say these things about our doctrine, it is already evident that their damnation is *certain*. It is clear that they are hopelessly in sin. When the gospel is preached to them, and when it is preached to them that they can do nothing with a view to their salvation, it is evident that their damnation is just, because they turn this Word into a word of the devil. When men hear the gospel and subvert this gospel into the damnable doctrine, "Let us do evil, that good may come," then their damnation is obvious.

In addition, the apostle means that the damnation of those who thus slander the gospel and us is *just*. Why should they spread this slander? Was it a mistake? Was it a matter of intellect? Not at all. Their deepest purpose was that they wanted to lie about the living God. When they heard the truth, they wanted to show that it could be led to an absurdity. Their purpose was to lead people away from the truth.

People do the same today. When we teach that God is sovereign, also with respect to sin and the powers of darkness, people say that we make God the author of sin. Is this a mistake? No, their purpose is to oppose the truth. Their damnation is just.

Every excuse is gone. God glorifies Himself. He does so whether one believes or not. Evil is not to be put to our credit. There is no excuse left. There is not one who can appear before God.

Our salvation is that God brought light out of darkness, not we; that God brought righteousness out of unrighteousness, not we; that God brought life out of death, not we.

God is true. He is true as He became manifest in Christ. Him, God sent into death. Him, He raised from the dead. In Him, He revealed a righteousness with which we can appear before God, a righteousness that is of God through faith in Christ Jesus.

Believe in Christ. Believe in Him. That is, throw away all that is of self, something that we must do every day. It is not so easy to believe in Christ. Every day we must throw away all that is of self. When everything that is of self has been cast away, we will cast ourselves on Christ. Casting ourselves on Christ, we will be clothed with His righteousness, and we will say, "We then, being justified by faith, have peace with God through our Lord Jesus Christ."

Chapter Sixteen

All under Sin

Romans 3:9-18

What then? are we better than they? No, in no wise: for we have before proved both Jews and Gentiles, that they are all under sin;

As it is written, There is none righteous, no, not one:

There is none that understandeth, there is none that seeketh after God.

They are all gone out of the way, they are together become unprofitable; there is none that doeth good, no, not one.

Their throat is an open sepulchre; with their tongues they have used deceit; the poison of asps is under their lips:

Whose mouth is full of cursing and bitterness:

Their feet are swift to shed blood:

Destruction and misery are in their ways:

And the way of peace have they not known:

There is no fear of God before their eyes.

Romans 3:9–18 constitutes a perfect unity. We cannot, therefore, divide it very well without marring the whole. This passage is introduced by a question "What then?" that causes us to surmise we have a conclusion of what the apostle has said in the preceding verses. What then? How does the case stand? What is the case of a man? Of any man? What is the case of any man when God judges him? What can we say of any man as he is by nature, when he stands before God in judgment?

There is another question asked here: "Are we better than they?" This question really means, "Do we have an excuse? Can we bring something before God in defense of ourselves?" The answer is, "Not at all."

There might be several excuses. The apostle has treated them in the preceding verses. We might say, "We are Jews, we have the law, we boast in the law, and we are zealous in keeping it." Or to put it in New Testament terms, we might say, "We are Reformed, and we stand for Reformed doctrine." Shall we bring this before God in our defense? The apostle has said that these things are all very well, but they cannot serve as our defense before God, for God will judge every man, whether Jew or Gentile, according to his works. We cannot, therefore, bring our religion before God as a matter of defense.

We might bring for defense that we have many advantages. So did the Jews. We might bring as a matter of defense that we have the Word of God. So did the Jews. But you cannot bring this for your defense. Although you have these advantages, if you have been disobedient, God will wreak vengeance upon you, for He judges you according to your works. In this case, your unrighteousness will serve to bring out the righteousness of God.

But then a third excuse might be brought. If my sin serves to bring out the righteousness of God, my sin is meritorious. It serves to glorify God. But remember, *you* did not cause your sin to serve God's glory, but *God* causes your sin to serve His glory.

What, then, is the case of the sinner standing in judgment before God? It is hopeless. The sinner has no excuse. If he were only righteous, he would need no excuse, but the apostle says, "We have before proved both Jews and Gentiles, that they are all under sin" [Rom. 3:9].

The Meaning in General

We must understand that if this Word of God is to reach its purpose with us as we hear it, the issue is not so much whether we understand what the apostle here declares to be the state of the natural man. The apostle uses plain language. Neither is it so much the issue whether we assent to it as the truth. It is the truth, but this is not the issue.

The real issue is this: when we hear this word, what is the reaction to it in our own heart and mind? What the apostle says here is not pleasant to the natural man. It is small wonder that the natural man will not listen to it. If we put it bluntly, the apostle says just this: the natural man is an ungodly, unrighteous, lying good-for-nothing.

But this is not the worst. The worst we have in the first verse of the text. If the apostle had simply written that all are sinful, it would not be so repugnant to the natural man. If the apostle had just written what he did in verse 10 and had not written what he did in verse 9, the natural man would not object so much. If he had just written that all are sinful, man would have no objection. You can even emphasize the awful nature of natural man and paint him as dark as the apostle does here, and yet if you do not go a step further, the world will even like to hear it. The natural man likes to hear you undress man, providing you leave man just one thing, that is, that you leave him his freedom.

Just listen carefully when you hear one who is busy undressing the natural man. Then ask that person the question how he would picture that sinner over against his own unrighteousness. As long as you leave him the power to dress himself, as long as you leave him his freedom, it is not so bad. But say this to him—"You are under sin, you are a slave to it, sin is your master, and sin holds you in its power"—and natural man will cast this testimony far from him.

This is what the apostle does. He does not say all are sinful. No, he says all are under sin. This is a different matter. If you leave man under the impression that he can serve sin as long as he wants to, and that he has the power to break with sin whenever he wants to, then he is not offended. But this the apostle does not preach. Rather, the apostle says all are *under* sin. This means that sin has man in its power.

Sin is a power. It is a spiritual, moral, ethical power. The characteristic of this power is that it causes man to miss the mark. Sin is that power over him that causes him to miss the mark. Implied in this dominion of sin is, first, that the sinner does not *will* and cannot *will* the good, but that he can only *will* the evil because sin has dominion over his will. Second, it means that he cannot *do* good, and can only *do* that which is evil, because sin has dominion over him. Third, combining the other two, it means that the natural man cannot do what is good. He cannot reach the mark, which is God, and he cannot will anything but evil.

I will go a step further. The natural man, who is under sin, *may* not and has no *right* to do the good, for it is a privilege, a blessing to do good. Man under sin may not and has no right to do the good. He has but one right, and that is to be under the dominion of sin. This is the meaning of that one phrase *They are all under sin.*

You say that then the natural man is an object of pity. This is true. A natural sinner is an object of pity. There is no joy in sin, and the wages of sin are death. Is not the sinner, then, an object of pity? He is.

However, if you mean by this that the sinner is an object of pity rather than an object of condemnation, you are mistaken. You will soon detect his real nature if you approach him this way and tell him that he is an object of pity. He will tell you to mind your own business. Why? Because the sinner is bound from within, not from without. It is a bondage of the will; it is a bondage of the heart. It is a bondage that has its root in the fact that the heart, mind, and will are corrupt. Therefore, although the natural man is an object of pity, before God he is an object of condemnation. He is an object of condemnation because he loves sin. This is the meaning of being *under sin*.

The Specific Implications

As a result the apostle describes the specific nature of this man. He tells us what the sinner, who is under sin, looks like, and he describes what the sinner does, from a negative and from a positive point of view.

We ask, to begin with, what a man who is under sin looks like, no matter who he is, whether he be Jew or Gentile, whether civilized or heathen. He looks like this: "There is none righteous." Notice that the apostle quotes the Old Testament.[1] Notice also that he quotes Scripture with universal application. He says that it describes all men. "We have before proved," the apostle says, "both Jews and Gentiles, that they are all under sin . . . ; There is none righteous."

Righteousness is harmony with a certain standard. The standard is God. The standard is God's judgment. Man is righteous when his nature compares with the standard of God's judgment. The apostle says, "There is none righteous." Lest you think that there might be some mistake, the apostle adds, "no, not one." There never was one. There is no one righteous anywhere, in any country, civilized or heathen. God looked down from heaven upon the children of men, and when He did, there was not one righteous. There was not one in harmony with the standard of God's will. This is the general character of the natural man. If man stands naked before God, the sentence of God is, "You are not righteous." This is the same as saying you are unrighteous.

From this it follows, as the apostle continues, that there is not one that *understandeth*. This is one aspect of the unrighteous nature. This does not mean that no man has any sense. It does not mean that no man has any understanding of natural things. This is evident. Man has a keen understanding of natural things. This is not the issue.

Nor does it mean that no one has natural understanding of spiritual things. Every man does. He has natural understanding of such things as sin, God, grace, righteousness. He knows that God is. He knows that God must be glorified and thanked. He even expresses it. He expresses in the laws he makes that he knows righteousness. Man has natural understanding of

---
[1]. Psalm 14:1–3.

spiritual things, but he has no spiritual understanding of spiritual things. He does not acknowledge, and bring into practice, that God is the highest good. He does not understand spiritually.

The other aspect is that no one *seeketh* after God. This is the other characteristic of the unrighteous nature. Mark you, there is none: you can never find one man who seeks after God. It is sometimes presented differently. It is sometimes said that the heathen go about seeking after God. Don't you believe it! None seeketh after God. No man, whether civilized or heathen, seeketh after God. This seeking after God is not, of course, seeking where He is, how He is, and that He is. Rather, no one seeks to have fellowship with Him, to be near Him.

The Actual Manifestation

Being under sin will show itself in the actual manifestation of life. "They are all gone out of the way," the apostle says. The way is God's way. This is man's way to walk, but all are out of that way. They walk in their own way. They walk in their own desires, in their own lusts, in their own pleasures.

Because of this fact, the apostle says, they are all *unprofitable*. To put it very bluntly, the apostle means that all are good-for-nothings. This means that the natural man never does anything that benefits anyone. He is no good to God or man. There is profit in righteousness. There is no profit in unrighteousness. No matter what man strives for, there is no profit in him as long as he is unrighteous. This is terrible, but this is Scripture. The apostle draws a line through all our good works. He smashes all the images that we may set up of great men. You are no good, I am no good, to God or man unless something fundamentally changes in our nature.

It is still worse. "There is none that doeth good." *Good* has the sense of useful. What does the sinner do then? If he cannot do good, what does he do? Nothing? His condition is far worse. Listen: "Their throat is an open sepulchre; with their tongues they have used deceit; the poison of asps is under their lips: Whose mouth is full of cursing and bitterness." All these sins are sins of the lips, of the mouth, of speech, of books, of literature. Still worse! The apostle not only speaks of sins of the mouth. He says, "Their feet are swift to shed blood." They have the finger on the trigger all the time. They are at all times ready to shoot. One wrong word, one wrong act, and they are ready to kill.

What is the result? "Destruction and misery are in their ways." All that man touches, he destroys. He leaves destruction behind him all the way from paradise to the day of judgment. All his way is one way of destruction. All that he leaves behind is destruction and misery, "and the way of peace have they not known." All do this, not all in the same way, but all leave destruction behind them. There is no hope.

The apostle generalizes it when he says, "There is no fear of God before their eyes." The *fear of God* is loving reverence for Him inwardly. Outwardly it is reverence for God's precepts. The sinner does not fear God's precepts, because he has no fear of God inwardly.

What then? How does his case stand? His case is hopeless. What is your reaction? Do you say, "I know an old man, an old lady"? Do you say, "The case is not so bad with me"? What is your reaction? Do you say, "Man is not so bad as all that"? This is what they said in 1924.[2] They said that you must read this word of the apostle with a grain of salt. In the face of this plain language of the apostle, they said that man can still do good.

What is your reaction? Do you say, "I am glad that I am Reformed"? Do you say, "I believe it all"? This is all wrong. Put it away.

---

2. Hoeksema refers to the decision of the Christian Reformed Church in North America adopting the doctrine of common grace, which teaches that God restrains sin in the unregenerated so that they are not totally depraved, but merely partially depraved. Thus, supposedly, they are able to do much good.

But is your reaction this: the Word brings you to your knees? This should be the reaction to this Word. The case of man is hopeless, but there is a righteousness of God in Christ, sovereignly granted by faith in Him. Clothed with this righteousness, I need no righteousness of my own, for this righteousness is perfect. Then we say, "Yes, Lord, this is I, full of unrighteousness. But the righteousness of the gospel, which is by faith in Christ Jesus, is mine. I am righteous by faith in Christ Jesus our Lord."

Chapter Seventeen

The Righteousness of God Manifested

Romans 3:21, 22
But now the righteousness of God without the law is manifested, being witnessed by the law and the prophets;
Even the righteousness of God which is by faith of Jesus Christ unto all and upon all them that believe: for there is no difference.

It is plain that in the text the apostle introduces a new section of his epistle. This section forms a direct contrast with the idea that the apostle had been developing in the preceding chapters. This is evident from the first two words of the text, *But now*. What a contrast is introduced by these two words! It is the contrast between light and darkness, between the bondage of sin and the liberty in Christ, between life and death.

But now!

The apostle has summarized what he had taught in the preceding part of the epistle by saying, "By the deeds of the law there shall no flesh be justified" [3:20]. This is not because the law cannot justify, but the law cannot justify *flesh*. Flesh cannot be justified, because it cannot fulfill the law so as to be justified by the law. "*Therefore* by the works of the law shall no flesh be justified." This means that a man may exert himself ever so much to be in conformity to the law, and if then he places himself before the face of God, and God judges him, he will still be damned. There is no hope. It is all darkness. It is all damnation. There is no way out.

119

But now!

The apostle means, "I am going to present the other side of the case." *But now* we have a contrast between the works of the law and the righteousness without the law, a contrast between the hopelessness of the attempt to obtain righteousness by works and the certainty of the gift of righteousness by faith in Christ Jesus. "But now the righteousness of God without the law is manifested, being witnessed by the law and the prophets."

What Is Manifested

The apostle tells us that the righteousness of God is manifested. What does this mean? What is the righteousness of God? What is righteousness? What in general is the righteousness of God? What is righteousness by faith? What is the righteousness of God in the text? Some of these questions must be answered. The thought of the text is a fundamental element in our faith. It is of fundamental importance that we clearly understand that we are righteous by faith, that we are righteous by the righteousness of God and not by works. We have heard these things so often. Sometimes the things we hear the most often are understood the least. Therefore, let us consider this righteousness of God that is without works.

Righteousness presupposes that one is in harmony with a certain standard according to which he is judged. Righteousness is the state that is required of a moral, rational being. Righteous is what a spiritual, moral, rational being must exhibit according to a certain standard. Just as when you put up a wall, that wall must be in harmony with the plumb line that you drop alongside it, so righteousness is a spiritual, moral, ethical state consisting of harmony with a certain standard. The harmony between us and that standard is to be judged by a competent Judge. According to this Judge, the rational, moral being in his thinking, his willing, his desiring, his walking, his talking, and his acting—indeed in everything—is in harmony with the required standard.

If we bear this in mind, the question arises, what is the righteousness of God? What is this righteousness as a virtue, as an attribute, of God? How can God be said to be righteous? There is no standard by which God can be judged. God is absolute. God is wholly *other,* also in this respect: God is above all law. There is no law for God, for there is for Him no lawgiver and no judge. How, then, can Scripture say that God is always as He ought to be? There can be but one answer: God is His own standard and judge. He eternally passes judgment upon Himself and pronounces Himself righteous. Therefore, God's righteousness is, first, that God is spotlessly good in His being. Second, this spotlessly good being of God is the standard for all God's life. Third, God judges all His thinking, willing, and working to be in harmony with His being. This is the righteousness of God as a virtue, as an attribute.

But this is not *the righteousness of God* in the text. The text does not mean that righteousness is one of the virtues of God. It certainly does not intend to imply that the righteousness of God, as a virtue in God, was not manifest. This is plain from the context. The apostle has emphasized in the three preceding chapters that it was manifest. The question in the preceding chapters was, "How must we be righteous?" How can this relation be brought about so that when God judges between us and His perfect will, He pronounces that there is harmony? If this relation cannot be brought about, there is no life for us. Outside of this relation there is no blessing. What the world calls a blessing and what the theory of common grace calls a blessing is no blessing. It is merely success. And success is but an advance on the way to hell. A man may be successful, but if back of that success is not the verdict of God that the man is righteous, success is a curse. You must understand, therefore, that it is indispensable that God pass this sentence on us and say, "My verdict is that I find you righteous."

The apostle speaks of a righteousness *without the law* as well as a righteousness that is through faith in Christ. Obviously the reference is not to the righteousness of God as a virtue. But now is manifested that which we cannot bring about, namely, the relation in which we are in harmony with the standard of the perfect will of God. This is a righteousness of God in the sense that He is the author of it. What the flesh could not do by the law, God does. It is a righteousness of God in the sense that God conceived of it; God thought it out. It is a righteousness of God also in the sense that God realized this righteousness, not we. Our works had nothing to do with it. It is a righteousness that stands outside our works. This righteousness God gives to us. It is the righteousness of God for us. It is a righteousness of God that we receive of free grace.

The righteousness of God, in this sense, is *manifested*. Do not overlook this word. That righteousness is *manifested* means, in the first place, that this righteousness always was. By *always* I mean that it is eternal. Where? In God's mind, that is to say, in God's counsel. This righteousness was eternally in God's mind. It is essential that we maintain this. There is no change in God. It is not so, that in God, in God's heart, in God's mind, His people appear as sinners, so that God hates them and damns them, and then that God changes His attitude toward them and justifies them. This is impossible. In God's mind, in His counsel, God's people are righteous from everlasting to everlasting.

In the second place, that this righteousness of God is *manifested* implies that it was hid for a time. It was there, but it was hid. It was not hid in the sense that it was not declared, namely, in the Old Testament, for it was declared. The text tells us that this righteousness had the testimony of the law and the prophets. *The law and the prophets* is a standing expression for the Old Testament. That this righteousness had the testimony of the law and the prophets means, in a certain sense, that it was declared. Yet it was not manifested; that is, it had not yet come. This righteousness was in God's mind. His people knew that it was in God's mind. It was in God's mind to justify His people, but it was not yet accomplished. When the text says that the righteousness of God is manifested, it refers to the fact that the eternal idea in God's mind came out of God's mind. It was in God's mind, and God's people knew it. We may think of a monument that has not been uncovered. Everyone knows that the monument is there. Perhaps some also know something of what that monument looks like. But that monument is not manifested until it is uncovered.

Similarly, the righteousness of God is manifested when Jesus comes. This righteousness had been hid. It was hid in God. But God's people knew that it was in God. Now Christ comes. Christ suffers, dies, and is resurrected. The cross comes, and the resurrection. Bearing our sins on the cross, He brought about a relation of righteousness. In the resurrection God gave the verdict that His people are righteous. In the cross and the resurrection of Christ, the righteousness of God is manifested. The righteousness of God *to us* is manifested.

How It Is Manifested

This manifestation of the righteousness of God to us, we would never have understood if it had not been for the gospel. Suppose that God had not explained one word about His work, but had, nevertheless, sent Christ. The result would have been that historically He would have manifested His righteousness to us, but we would not know it. However, God explains. Accordingly, the apostle tells us that the righteousness of God had the testimony of the law and the prophets, that is, of the Old Testament. The entire Old Testament testified of the righteousness manifested in the fulness of time, the righteousness without the law. If God had not declared that He had in mind the justification of His people, they would not have known. But God told His people, through sacrifices, altar, priest, and prophet, that He had in mind to justify His people.

Therefore, the saints of the Old Testament were righteous in hope. Their sins had not really been blotted out. Their sins had not historically been blotted out. When Abraham sinned, no ransom was brought for his sin. How then could these people be saved? Because they had the testimony of the law and the prophets that God had it in mind to justify His people. They were righteous in hope, just as we are glorified in hope.

In the gospel God declares, "I justify you." This takes place through faith. More particularly, it takes place through faith of Jesus Christ. This is faith of which Christ is the object. Faith *of* Christ is the same as faith *in* Christ. In general, it is that adhesive power by which the heart, mind, and soul cleave to Christ. Faith is a spiritual adhesive power. It is a spiritual drawing power. This faith the natural man has not. It is a gift that God gives to the soul.

By faith the soul knows itself to be absorbed in Jesus. So absorbed is the believing soul in Jesus that if God drops the plumb line of His justice along one, He must drop it along Jesus. I, the believer, am so *one* with Jesus that I feel sure God cannot judge me without judging Jesus. I am so *one* with Jesus that God cannot say anything about me without saying it about Jesus. If He calls me a sinner, He must call Jesus a sinner. This is faith.

The text says that it is *the righteousness of God which is by faith of Jesus Christ*. It is the righteousness that God prepares for us and that He bestows on us through the instrumentality of the faith of Jesus. But even then it is His righteousness. He causes the soul to cleave to Jesus.

For Whom It Is Manifested

For this very reason the apostle says that it is a righteousness unto them and upon all them that believe. It is *unto* them because God eternally destined them to believe. It is a righteousness *upon* them because they are under the verdict of God's sentence. This is not because faith is a work. It is not because faith is righteousness. Nor is it because faith is the meritorious ground. But the explanation is that faith is the means by which the believer is incorporated into Christ, even as he has been incorporated into Him from eternity. There is an eternal corporation of which Christ is the head. Throughout history, believers are incorporated into Christ by faith.

There is no hope in your work and mine. Let your own work become void. Let it become void in your mind. It can be no basis for righteousness. It stands between you and your justification. Away with it! *But now* the righteous shall live by faith in Christ Jesus. The gospel always emphasizes this.

Believe!

Believers, believe! Believing, live and be saved, justified by faith in Christ Jesus our Lord.

Chapter Eighteen

Christ the Demonstration of God's Righteousness

Romans 3:25, 26
Whom God hath set forth to be a propitiation through faith in his blood, to declare his righteousness for the remission of sins that are past, through the forbearance of God;

To declare, I say, at this time his righteousness: that he might be just, and the justifier of him which believeth in Jesus.

There is no difference among men in this respect: all have sinned. There is no difference between Jew and Gentile. There is no difference between men of different stations of life. There is no difference between men of apparently different manifestation. All have sinned. All miss the mark. So the apostle has written in the context: "All have sinned and come short of the glory of God" [3:23]. The meaning is not that they fall just a little short of reaching the glory of God, that they attain in a measure to the glory of God but that they fall somewhat short. Rather, the meaning is that the glory of God is the only object for the rational creature to make his aim, or his mark, and all have missed that mark. It makes no difference what other aim, what other purpose, man may have, whether it be self, or society, or humanity—all have sinned, for all miss the mark. All fall short of the glory of God.

There is no difference also in this respect: there is only one way for all men to be justified. There is only one way of justification for all, namely, by a free gift of God. The motive of this justification is grace. The means is "the redemption that is in Christ Jesus" [v. 24]. This, too, is the context.

In the text the apostle says that God has set forth Jesus Christ as a propitiation, through faith in His blood, in order that He might prove His righteousness, that He might openly demonstrate that He is just when He justifies the ungodly. He set forth Christ that He might demonstrate that He was just when He passed by the sins of the old dispensation and that He is just with respect to the general truth that God justifies the ungodly.

The Content of This Demonstration

Let us clearly see the specific point of the passage. The point is not that Jesus is a propitiation for our sins. This is not the chief idea. The main idea is expressed in the *setting forth*. This must have the emphasis. To make the point plain, we must ask a few questions. First, is it not possible for God to excuse the sinner? Can not God excuse the sinner as, for example, a criminal is pardoned? No. This is impossible. God cannot excuse the sinner, or sin, because God is righteous. If God is to pardon sin, there must be a basis upon which that pardon can rest. Not only is this impossible on the part of God, but this is also impossible on the part of the sinner who is pardoned. The sinner could not enjoy this pardon and have peace with it. The pardoned criminal cannot be happy. He carries in his heart the testimony of his conscience that he ought to be in prison. He carries the testimony in his heart that the governor who so pardoned him is unrighteous, that he violated justice. Also, he has the testimony of those around him that he ought to be in prison. Therefore, if God would pardon the sinner, the sinner could not be happy. Bluntly speaking, he would have lost his respect for God. He would have lost his God. The pardoned sinner would have the testimony of his conscience that he ought to be punished. He would have the testimony in his heart that God is unrighteous, that He is not just. And he would have the testimony of others that he ought to be punished. Excusing or pardoning sin in this sense is impossible on the part of God. It is also an impossible way to happiness and peace on the part of the sinner. It is established, then, that God cannot excuse sin.

We can ask a second question. With this we come to the point in the text. Would it not be possible for God to establish a basis of justification for His people? Suppose that God had provided a basis of justification that satisfied His own conscience, but that he had not published it. Then sin would have been propitiated, and the basis for righteousness would have been established, but we would not know anything about it. Would it not have been possible for God to provide a basis for righteousness and not say anything about it? In this case, we would enter into glory as a sort of a surprise, not knowing why. In other words, would it not have been possible for Christ to have been crucified in some far off, forgotten place of the world and not have said anything about it?

The text says that this also is impossible. The reason is that God must not only be righteous before His own conscience, but also before the conscience of all rational creatures. When finally He shall take His people into glory, He may challenge all the world and ask whether He is not righteous in doing this. All the world must say that God is righteous. This is why Christ is set forth, is publicly shown, as a propitiation for sin in the cross. Christ is not crucified in some forgotten part of the world, but in the center of the world. He was made a public spectacle. In the resurrection God publicly set forth Christ as a propitiation for sin. Christ is *set forth*. This is the point of the text.

Propitiation is that which appeases. Propitiation is not the same as reconciliation. Reconciliation is the effect. Propitiation is the cause of reconciliation. Propitiation presupposes sin and that God is wrathful because of that sin. There is something that appeases this wrath of God. Because His wrath is appeased, there is grace on the part of God. God's wrath is not some passing passion. God's wrath is the constant expression of His holy and righteous will with respect to the sinner. Therefore, God's wrath cannot be appeased except by the bearing of that wrath. God's wrath must be poured out. God cannot deny Himself. His wrath is as constant as God is. It must be poured out. A propitiatory sacrifice is a sacrifice in which one is intentionally, from the principle of love, set forth to receive the wrath of God. If one loves God, loves God's wrath, loves to have God pour out that wrath upon him, and is able to bear that wrath to the full, this is propitiation.

This the sinner cannot perform. It is impossible for the sinner to bring propitiation. It is impossible for the sinner to bear that wrath of God to the end. There is no end. The sinner can bring nothing to God as the sacrifice of love. The position of the sinner is such that he daily increases his sins.

But the text says that God set forth *Christ* to be a propitiation. This indicates, for one thing, that God propitiates *Himself*. We don't. We don't appease God. We don't change God's sentiment with relation to His people. God provides for Himself a sacrifice, which is a sacrifice for the sins of His people.

Since the expression *set forth* means "to demonstrate publicly," it also implies that propitiation did not have its origin in time. It did not have its beginning in the cross. The cross is the setting forth of that propitiation. Propitiation was with God eternally. God's sentiment with relation to His people never changed. Propitiation was eternally with God. This is why we read of the Lamb that was slain before the foundation of the world [Rev. 13:8]. But this propitiation God has publicly shown. God revealed that which caused His wrath to be swallowed up. He sent Christ out of His counsel. He sent Him to the cross. In the cross God demonstrated that there was propitiation eternally with God. God completed that public demonstration when He raised Jesus from the dead, for in the resurrection we have God's answer: the cross is the propitiation for the sins of His people.

This demonstration, this setting forth of that propitiation, is the setting forth of a propitiation that is through faith in His blood. Such is the meaning of the text: "Whom God hath set forth to be a propitiation through faith in his blood." It is a propitiation through faith; otherwise, it does not work. God cannot be known to be propitiated except through faith. There must be faith as the adhesive power that unites us with Christ in order to know that God is propitiated. God sets forth Christ as a propitiation objectively, in the cross. Subjectively, God brings it to the heart and mind of His people through faith. This is also of God.

The Reason for It

Why did God so have to demonstrate His propitiation publicly? Because it seemed that otherwise there would be reason to accuse God of unrighteousness and injustice. Suppose God had kept it to Himself. Then it would have seemed that God was not righteous. Why? Because He justifies the ungodly. He does this. God justifies the ungodly. To justify the ungodly without propitiation is unrighteous. To justify the ungodly without a public demonstration of propitiation would leave the impression that God is unrighteous.

The reason, therefore, for this public demonstration lies in the fact that it pleased God to love a people. Loving them, it pleased God to bring them to glory in the highest sense. It pleased God to bring them into His tabernacle, there to taste that God is good. In order to lead them to that highest glory, it pleased God to lead them through the way of sin and grace.

Historically this people come into the world as ungodly. And God justifies them. The apostle emphasizes in the text that God did so in the Old Testament. The passage says, "to declare his righteousness for the remission of sins that are past, through the forbearance of God." It is too bad that our English translation uses the word *remission*. This is not the original Greek. The original means "to pass by." We must read the text this way: "to declare his righteousness for the passing by of the sins that are past, through the forbearance of God." That is why we have the word *forbearance* here. Forbearance means that God does not pour out His wrath now, but waits until the final day. The meaning is that in the Old Testament God passed by the sins of His elect. No propitiation had been brought yet. The saints of the Old Testament had sinned. Nevertheless, they went to heaven. Some even went to heaven publicly. Not only did they go to heaven, but also God gave them testimony that they were righteous. God justified them by giving them eternal life. He passed by their sins. The devil accused the brethren. All through the old dispensation the devil appeared as the accuser of the brethren. He claimed that they had no right to eternal glory, since "all have sinned and come short of the glory of God." In the Old Testament, God passed by the sins of His people. On account of that passing by of the sins in the Old Testament, and on account of the general truth that God justifies the ungodly, God sets forth in the cross that He has a right to justify the ungodly. The text is rich: "Whom God hath set forth on His own behalf as a propitiation, through faith in His blood, to declare His righteousness with regard to His passing by of the sins of the past; to shut the mouth of the devil and of the world; and to demonstrate publicly that He is justified in justifying the ungodly."

The Arminian conception of the text is this. God might righteously have condemned all, but He would not. Therefore, He set forth the cross. If one says, "Yes, God might righteously have condemned all," then God will receive him in mercy. But this is not atonement. This is not a demonstration of righteousness, but of unrighteousness.

This is not the text. The text is that Christ is the propitiation for sin. He is indeed the head of His people. He bears indeed the sins of His people. Because Christ is indeed a propitiation, the cross is the demonstration of the righteousness of God as He justifies the ungodly.

The Purpose of It

The purpose is that God must become righteous. This righteousness of God must become manifest before all, especially when He justifies the ungodly. He must become manifest before the devil as righteous. The devil knew that the cross was a demonstration of the righteousness of God. He no longer accuses you before the face of God as you believe in Christ. God has publicly shown His righteousness in justifying the ungodly. He must publicly demonstrate before all the world that He is propitiated. This is one more reason why the gospel must be preached to all.

It must be brought to the heart and mind of His people by faith. Do you know that if you believe in Jesus, you do not feel like a criminal? This is why we can look God in the face, thanks to His grace. When you believe in Jesus, you can look God in the eye. You have the testimony of being righteous heirs through Him who loved us unto death. This is the blessedness of God's people. That righteousness and mercy kissed each other: this is the blessedness of God's people.

When the final day shall come and God shall judge all according to their works, and when He shall judge them who believe in Jesus, He will pass this verdict upon them: "You are righteous." All shall declare that God is righteous when He judges the ungodly. And we shall see Him face-to-face.

Chapter Nineteen

Boasting Excluded

Romans 3:27
Where is boasting then? It is excluded. By what law? of works? Nay: but by the law of faith.

"Where is boasting then?" the apostle asks. That is, if the matter of a man's righteousness before God is such as I have set forth in the preceding verses, where remains any room for the boasting of men? The apostle had emphasized the truth that the sinner, that man, must be just by faith only through the righteousness that is freely given him of God. The apostle had said that there is no difference between Jew and Gentile as far as one's righteousness before God is concerned. From the point of view of his justification, there is no difference between man and man. All stand on the same level as far as their justification is concerned. One does not stand higher than the other. The level upon which all stand is that all have sinned. Since sin is the missing of the mark, all come short of the glory of God. In this respect all are alike.

Because of this, there is but one way in which man can become righteous before God: the way of justification. Man must be justified. There is no way of justification through the works of man. When we shall stand in the hour of judgment as sinners, there is nothing that can be said in our favor. Instead, God manifested His own righteousness. This is the righteousness He gives, He manifests, He realizes, and of which He is the Author. This righteousness He manifested in Christ Jesus and bestows upon His elect by faith. In order that it might become manifest that He is just when He justifies the ungodly, God not only gave Christ, but He also set Him forth, making Him a public show.

If this is the case, if a man must be justified by faith through the redemption that is in Christ Jesus, where, then, is boasting? It is excluded. According to the law of faith, there is absolutely no room for boasting. The law of faith excludes all boasting.

Therefore, two conclusions are true. If a man has ceased from boasting, you have in this a sign of his having been justified by faith. But if in his life you still find boasting, in the measure that you find it, you do not find the righteousness that is by faith. You can boast of your works, of your religion, of your piety, of your faith. You can boast of virtually everything, but as long as there is any boasting, there is not the true receptivity for the righteousness that is by faith, for the law of faith absolutely excludes all boasting.

This implies that if we would fully taste the blessedness of being justified by faith, we must fight, we must strive, to exclude all boasting. The truth is that we do boast. We boast of everything. We can even boast of not boasting. But if we would taste the blessedness of being justified by faith, all boasting must be excluded.

Excluded Because, according to the Law of Faith, Man *Has* Nothing

To boast is to attribute something to ourselves on the basis of which we may claim honor. Often in the world this boasting takes place over against others. We attribute something to ourselves, distinguishing ourselves from others in this matter, and thus boast against them.

Here boasting comes up in the matter of our justification. The question is this: when we are justified, when we stand righteous before God, is there in this hour of our justification anything for us to boast of? Is there in this justification anything to which we can point and say, "This is mine"?

The apostle says, "Boasting is excluded." *Excluded* is a strong word. To use a figure, we may think of a city. In this city righteousness dwells. This city is walled. Its gates are shut, so that there is no possible opportunity for anyone to enter this city. That is, neither boasting nor the boaster can enter this city. There are righteousness, peace, and joy in this city, but not boasting. Boasting is excluded.

Boasting, under this figure, might enter through three possible gates. Man might boast of what he has. Or he might boast of what he does; that is, he might claim entrance on the basis of his own acts. Or he might boast of what he is. It is of these three things that man can boast: what he has, what he does, and what he is.

The apostle says that all these three gates are shut. Where is boasting? It is excluded. In this city men do not boast of what they have, they do not boast of what they do, they do not boast of what they are; they boast only in the Lord. "Let him that glories, glory in the Lord" [I Cor. 1:31].

We can apply the exclusion of boasting to the system of truth. The apostle has been developing the truth of righteousness by faith. Now the question is asked, "In this system of truth, where is there room for boasting?" The answer is that it is excluded.

We can look at the exclusion of boasting once more in the subjective sense, for the apostle says that boasting is excluded by the law of faith. *Law* is not to be taken here in the usual sense. *Law* here has the sense of a rule according to which a thing works. It is the rule according to which faith works. According to this law of faith, boasting is excluded. We can, therefore, apply the apostle's teaching in the subjective sense. Suppose you have a man who is conscious that he is justified by faith. Where, then, in the heart of this man is there room for boasting? It is excluded. It is excluded according to the law of faith.

Notice that boasting is excluded because the law of faith leaves man nothing to start with. It leaves man nothing on which he can boast as a basis of righteousness.

The law of works, on the other hand, does leave man with reasons for boasting. The law of works is, "Do this and live." If a man is justified according to this law, he has plenty of which to boast. For the law of works is, "You shall love the Lord thy God with all your heart, and with all your soul, and with all your strength." To become righteous according to the law of works, man must have something to begin with. This something he must have is legal righteousness. If I am to become righteous before God according to the law of works, there must not be one single sin. I must be perfectly, legally righteous. I must be able to boast that I have no sin.

But there is more. I must not only be able to boast that I have no sin now, but I must also be able to boast of a certain inherent goodness. This is just what we see in the man who boasts in his own works. The man who boasts in his own works lives in the consciousness that he has a certain inherent goodness by which he can become righteous before God.

This is the law of works. We may be deceived by this law of works, even as Christians. Some people have had certain religious experiences, and they boast of it. Boasting of anything at all is an attempt to be saved by the law of works. The law of faith is this: God justifies the ungodly. You can emphasize every word of this statement. You can say, "*God* justifies the ungodly." Or you can say, "God *justifies* the ungodly." Or you can say, "God justifies the *ungodly*." This is the law of faith. The law of faith tells us that we are ungodly and that we must write condemnation on every one of our own righteousnesses. We have nothing to say but this: "I am ungodly." But this is nothing about which to boast. This is the law of faith.

Do not add anything to this. Often when speaking with people about their spiritual condition, we find that they are wavering on this point. When it comes to the question, "How must I be justified before God?" it is difficult spiritually to realize that all we must say is, "I am ungodly." We must say nothing else. We must put the period right there. We must let God say the rest. In order to be justified, we must say nothing more than just this: "I am ungodly." This is no boasting. This is the confession of the publican. This means humiliation.

Now watch out! Do not make this humiliation your boasting! Do not say, "God must justify me, but I must humble myself." You must not say anything but this: "I am ungodly." This is the law of faith. Do not say, "I must go to church"; "I must repent"; "I must pray." Do not say anything but just this: "I am ungodly." Where, then, is boasting? It is excluded. By what law? By the law of faith.

Excluded Because, according to the Law of Faith, Man *Does* Nothing

The danger is that man supposes, after making this confession, he must begin to do something. It would seem that if we confess that we are ungodly, it is time that we begin to change this. It would seem that we must do something. According to the law of works, we must. This is the first impulse in the sinful heart. This heart is so pharisaic. The law of pharisaism is rooted so deeply in our hearts that we say, "What must I do? I must do something." Let us say, "I am ungodly, but I must repent." No, you must not. Remember, I am speaking about the question "How must a man become righteous before God?" Must he do anything? No, that is the law of works.

The law of faith is this. God prepared your righteousness for you. It is all ready. You cannot add anything to this righteousness. You cannot add anything to it by your righteous works, by your piety, by your repentance, by your prayers. Objectively, this is the law of faith: God justifies the ungodly. Then do not try to become less ungodly. That does not help. You will remain just as ungodly as far as your justification is concerned. You must do nothing. Justification is finished. It pleased God eternally to justify the ungodly. As it eternally pleased Him, so He has done in Christ Jesus, now nineteen hundred years ago. The righteousness that we must have is finished. It was finished when God sent His Son into the world. It was finished when He sent Him to the cross. It was finished when He raised Him from the dead. To this work of God in Christ whereby He finished the righteousness that you need, you can add nothing by all your doing.

"Yes," you say, "but I must believe." Well, let us see. Perhaps there is still an element of boasting. You say, "There is a righteousness that God has prepared, but if I am to have this righteousness, I must believe." Well, then, let us persuade men to believe. Let us tell them that they are justified because they believe. This is the way it is generally put: "Because you believe in Christ, you shall become righteous before God." But this is not true. Your faith does not add to your righteousness. You do not become righteous on account of your faith.

Shall we put it this way then? "Faith is the principle from which we live. Because of this, we become religious, we become pious, we repent, we pray, and we do good works. Because of these works of faith, we become righteous before God." Not so! Works of faith do not make us righteous before God.

Shall we put it this way then? "Righteousness is ready, and faith is the hand that takes it." Then there is still something to boast of. Then righteousness is all ready, but it must be accepted by the hand of faith. This is not faith. Faith is not an act of ours. Faith is that power whereby we receive (do not change this into "accept"!) the righteousness of God in Christ. By faith we do not "accept." By faith we receive. But it is nothing to boast of that we receive something.

When you said, "I am ungodly," then God began to work. Do not say, "I then started to pray." This is not true. When you said, "I am ungodly," God began to work. I will go a step further. This is only true as far as your consciousness is concerned. God is even back of your confession that you are ungodly. But as far as your consciousness is concerned, you said, "I am ungodly," and you left it there. And faith is the power by which you receive the righteousness of God in Christ Jesus.

Where, then, is boasting? It is excluded. It is absolutely excluded.

Excluded Because, according to the Law of Faith, Man *Is* Nothing

But we are not at the end of the line yet. The law of works may still creep in. After all, the sinner may say, "I know where boasting comes in. It is true that faith is received; it is a gift of God. But to have the righteousness of God in me, I must be someone. That is, I must be a believer. And I must be a believer in distinction from others who are lost. I must be someone in order to have the righteousness of God in me. What I must be is a believer."

But I am *not* a believer. The last word is *ungodly*. We are not believers. We do not want righteousness. We are corrupt. We are enemies of God and of His Christ.

Where, then, is boasting? Faith is the gift of God. If God gives me faith, if my last word is that I am ungodly, if God lays in my heart the faculty of faith and brings to that heart the gospel, and if then that heart receives righteousness, where is boasting? It is excluded.

Are we there now? No, not quite. There is still a loophole. For the question comes, "How must it be explained that some believe and others do not?" The answer will most likely be that God gives this faith to His elect. There is no Christian who speaks any other language. Even the Arminian will say this. All Christians will say that God gives faith to His elect. But we must ask one more question. We must ask, "Who are the elect?" Then the Arminian will start his boasting. He will say, "The elect are those of whom God foresaw that they would be willing to receive this faith." The Arminian will say that the elect are those of whom God knew that they would be willing to receive this grace. This is a very fine point, but it includes the whole law of boasting. For if it is so, that God saw some distinction in man; if He saw that some would be willing to receive faith and others not, and He chose those whom He saw would be willing to receive faith, then their willingness is the point upon which they boast. I am willing to receive faith, and this is why God gave it to me. This is not the law of faith; this is the law of works.

The law of faith is this: God is merciful to whom He wills, and whom He wills He hardens. The law of faith is sovereign election. Election is not that there is a distinction in man. But all distinction is in the sovereign election of God. This is humiliating, so humiliating that we will not even receive the word of this text. But if we will receive it, if we will really hear and believe that there is in God's plan of salvation no room for boasting, then two things result. First, we rejoice in the truth that God justifies the ungodly. Though our sins be as scarlet, they will not trouble us. We may daily confess our sins, but they will not rob us of our peace. We say, "Being justified by faith, we have peace with God."

The other result will be that we say God is God, and to Him belong glory, honor, and praise forever.

Chapter Twenty

Faith Reckoned for Righteousness

Romans 4:3-5
For what saith the scripture? Abraham believed God, and it was counted unto him for righteousness.
Now to him that worketh is the reward not reckoned of grace, but of debt.
But to him that worketh not, but believeth on him that justifieth the ungodly, his faith is counted for righteousness.

We have in the text one of the chief demonstrations and proofs of the statement that the apostle made in the last verse of the preceding chapter. There he had asked the question, "Do we then make void the law through faith?" The apostle had answered, "God forbid." Affirmatively, he had answered, "Yea, we establish the law."

We must be careful when we read the word *law* in Romans. It does not always mean the same thing. It is evident that *law* in the last verse of the preceding chapter does not refer to the body of precepts that Israel had, but to the entire Old Testament Scriptures. When the apostle asks, "Do we make void the law through faith?" the meaning is, "Do we set aside, do we overthrow, the entire Old Testament revelation by faith?" This is a serious question: "Do I teach something new when I teach that a man is not justified by the law, but by faith?" To this question the apostle answers, "No. We *affirm* the Old Testament Scriptures when we teach that a man is justified by faith."

The apostle proves this by the figure of Abraham. The con-

141

text is plain. This chapter is introduced by a question, a question that amounts to a negative declaration. The question is this: "What shall we say then that Abraham our father, as pertaining to the flesh, hath found?" If anything at all in Abraham himself contributed to his righteousness, he was justified by works. Then we would have whereof to boast, but not *toward God*. It is unfortunate that in the King James translation [of v. 2] we read, "*before* God." This is not the idea of the original. The idea in the Greek is that if Abraham were justified by works, he would have nothing with which to glorify God. But this is not the case with Abraham. Abraham was not justified by works. "For what saith the scripture? Abraham believed God, and it was counted unto him for righteousness" [v. 3].

Then in verses 4 and 5 the apostle says, "Now to him that worketh is the reward not reckoned of grace, but of debt. But to him that worketh not, but believeth on him that justifieth the ungodly, his faith is counted for righteousness." Let us emphasize this last phrase: *to him that worketh not,* that is, who has added nothing to his own righteousness, *but believeth on him that justifieth the ungodly, his faith is counted for righteousness.*

That Which Is So Reckoned

The question "What is reckoned for righteousness?" is answered by the text, as well as by the passage that is quoted [Gen. 15:6]. *Faith* is reckoned for righteousness, faith that is looked at from the point of view not of its faculty, but of its power or activity. Abraham believed God, and this faith was reckoned for righteousness. The same is true of the last part of the text: "To him that . . . believeth on him that justifieth the ungodly, his faith is counted for righteousness." It is the *activity* of faith.

The same is true in the passage quoted by verse 3. The Word of God came to Abraham and said unto him that he would have a seed as the stars of heaven in number. The activity of Abraham's faith was such that he believed God. The activity of his faith was such that he took hold of that Word of God. At that moment in Abraham's life, his faith was reckoned for righteousness.

What is this activity, this power that is called believing? What did Abraham do when he believed on Him that justifieth the ungodly? What do we do when we believe? What is faith—saving faith—from the point of view of its activity?

There is no question that saving faith, from this viewpoint, reveals itself as undoubting certainty. Also, the act of saving faith is an activity of the soul whereby the soul is sure of the impossible. That of which faith is sure is impossible. Finally, you will find that saving faith is sure of the impossible because it is the Word of God that speaks. Saving faith hears and believes the reality of the impossible. The Word to Abraham was, "So shall thy seed be" [Gen. 15:5]. To all human experience that was impossible. That Abraham should have a seed as the stars of heaven and as the sand of the sea was, according to all experience, impossible. It was impossible because of the age of both Abraham and Sarah. Abraham believed God; that is, he was absolutely certain of what was impossible. That is saving faith. Saving faith is to be absolutely sure of what is contrary to all human experience. Abraham believed not the thing, but he believed God.

As it was in the case of Abraham, so it is with the Christian. What does the Christian believe? Of what is he certain? In general, he is certain of this: God justifies the ungodly. This is basic in the life of the Christian. It is absolutely necessary that God justifies the ungodly if there is to be salvation. Yet this is impossible from every point of view. God cannot justify the ungodly. Not only is this impossible from God's point of view, it is also impossible insofar as it comes to be a personal certainty in my mind. Everything in my experience testifies against this statement. My conscience testifies against the fact that I am justified. All the world testifies against me. You testify against me. I testify against you. The whole world stands before God and shouts against one another, "You are damned." The devil testifies against me. All my experience testifies against the fact that I am justified. My suffering, my pain, my troubles, my death: it all testifies against the fact that I am justified. Particularly my *death* testifies against it. One who is justified does not die. Saving faith is that I am certain, against all this testimony, that I am justified. The basis is the Word of God spoken in the resurrection. In the resurrection the Word of God comes to us and says, "I justify the ungodly."

Saving faith is not only that activity by which the soul is certain, but as a result of this certainty it is also that activity of the soul whereby I trust that God will do me no harm and that He will do me all good. This is called *confidence.*

What is *confidence?*

Try to feed a squirrel a nut. You call to that squirrel, and you hold out the nut to him. But that squirrel does not come near you. He does not trust you. He is afraid of you. He likes that nut, but he will not come to you, because he does not trust that you will do him good. He is afraid that you will do him harm. But gradually that squirrel comes a little nearer. He begins to have confidence in you; he begins to trust you. Finally he comes to you. This is the confidence of the squirrel. By coming to you, that squirrel says, "I trust that you will do me good."

Confidence is that we believe that God will do us good. As a result of this confidence, I come to Him. Again, this is an impossibility. He who comes to God must believe that He is and that He is a rewarder of them who seek Him [Heb. 11:6]. This is impossible. We will never come to God. We would rather create a thousand idols than come to God. Why? Because we do not trust Him. We do not trust that He will do us good. Why? Is it because God is not to be trusted? No, but because we are ungodly. And God destroys the ungodly. But now God holds before us the promise of eternal life. And confidence is trusting that when we come to God, He will not destroy us but will do us good and give us eternal life.

We may conclude that faith in the text is the consciousness

that God justifies the ungodly and that when I come to Him, He will not destroy me.

How It Is Reckoned

How is it possible and what does it mean that faith is reckoned for righteousness? Abraham believed God, and it was reckoned unto him for righteousness. The meaning is that this faith is not in itself righteousness. In other words, it is not on the part of the believer a work of righteousness. We must be careful. As soon as we say that God reckoned faith for righteousness, some will say that God cannot reckon anything for righteousness that is not righteousness, and that faith, therefore, must be a work of righteousness. Of course, then you have surrendered the entire body of the truth to religious self-righteousness. Then you are saved by works, even though it be religious work-righteousness.

Others say that faith is the source of good works. Even though we do not do all the works of faith, faith is reckoned as if we do the works themselves. This is the same heresy. Then we are justified by works. But we are justified by faith. This is emphasized in the text: faith is reckoned for righteousness.

Why is faith reckoned for righteousness? Notice that verse 4 speaks of a reckoning of grace. Notice also that verse 5 says, "to him that . . . believeth on him that justifieth the ungodly, his faith is counted for righteousness." Which is first? "[He] that justifieth the ungodly" must be first before you can believe on Him. Your faith has nothing to do with justifying the ungodly. God does not justify the believer. He justifies the ungodly. Faith is not righteousness. Your faith does not make you more perfect.

The apostle says that faith is reckoned for righteousness. This means that what in itself contains no righteousness is nevertheless imputed by God for righteousness to him who believes. Here is the judgment book. In this book are the names. The ungodly stands in this judgment book with a debt against him and wrath upon him. But the ungodly believes. You understand, in God's judgment the ungodly remains ungodly. But now he believes. He believes that God justifies the ungodly. God draws a line through his debt. His faith is reckoned for righteousness. This is marvelous!

The subjective side of this is that if you believe, God reckons your faith for righteousness in your experience. I do not say, if you *have* faith. You have faith; faith is a gift of God. But although you have faith, the *activity* of saving faith is frequently weak. The activity of saving faith, whereby we come to God in the confidence that He will not do us harm and that He will do us good, is often wanting. We are afraid of God when it comes to the point. We are afraid to come to Him. We are afraid to die. Why? Because we do not believe one hundred percent that God justifies the ungodly. Our last word must be *ungodly*. And God's last word is, "I justify the ungodly."

This is the purpose of preaching the truth of justification by faith, that by the activity of saving faith we come to God and say that we are not afraid.

The Ground upon Which It Is Reckoned

On what ground can God reckon for righteousness that which is not righteousness? How is this possible? God cannot reckon for righteousness what is not righteousness. If faith is not righteousness, where then is the ground for this reckoning?

Here God justifies the ungodly. This has nothing to do with your faith. God justifies you in Christ. He justified you when He blotted out your sins on the cross. He justified you when He raised Christ from the dead. When God raised Christ from the dead, He gave the testimony to the head of His people that He is righteous. Otherwise, He could not have been raised. Because He was raised as the head of His people, it is a testimony to that people that they have been justified. In the resurrection we have the revelation, in the face of Christ, of Him who justifies the ungodly.

Faith is belief in Him who justifieth the ungodly. It is belief in the face of Christ. Therefore, faith is that activity whereby the soul cleaves to Christ. It is the adhesive power whereby we are connected with Him, so that out of Christ we draw righteousness. When I say "ungodly," and God says "righteous in the face of Christ," I cleave to this Word of God. By faith I have the righteousness of Christ. By faith I cleave to Him.

This is why God reckons faith for righteousness. It is not because there is anything in the faith, but it is because of everything there is in Christ.

Oh, believe! Believe with all the power of faith! Then in the shelter of Him who sustained the wrath of God, bore away your sin, and merited righteousness, you will have the peace that passeth all understanding.

Chapter Twenty-one

The Blessedness of the Justified

Romans 4:6-8
Even as David also describeth the blessedness of the man, unto whom God imputeth righteousness without works,
Saying, Blessed are they whose iniquities are forgiven, and whose sins are covered.
Blessed is the man to whom the Lord will not impute sin.

In these words we have the second proof for a statement of the apostle in the latter part of the preceding chapter. This is the statement that the doctrine of righteousness by faith, without works, does not make void the law. The *law* in Romans 3:31 refers to the entire Old Testament revelation. Therefore, the apostle means that the doctrine of justification by faith is not a new doctrine.

The first proof for this statement the apostle took from the book of Genesis. Abraham was not justified by works, but by faith. Abraham believed God, and it was counted unto him for righteousness.

The second proof is taken from the Psalms. In Psalm 32[:1, 2] David pronounces the blessedness of the man whose iniquity is forgiven and whose sins are covered up, the man to whom the Lord does not impute sin.

The thing to be demonstrated is that there is a righteousness that is without works, that is free, that is of grace. It is to be demonstrated that such a righteousness is also taught in the

Old Testament. To prove his statement, the apostle refers to David. The argument is that if we are to be righteous by works, there can be no forgiveness of sins. If a man is to be righteous by works, works must be imputed. If works are to be imputed, sin must also be imputed. But then there is no forgiveness of sins. In Psalm 32, however, the poet speaks of the blessedness of the man whose sins are forgiven, unto whom the Lord imputes righteousness without works.

A Marvelous Grace

First of all, the thought expressed in the Romans text, by the very form of it, is that the blessedness of the forgiveness of sins is a wonder of grace. Scripture uses many words for sin because there are many aspects to sin. Sin is related to our whole being. It affects our relation to God, to the world, and to one another. There are as many aspects to sin as there are relations. Therefore, Scripture speaks of transgression, trespasses, iniquity, guilt, et cetera. In the passage we have two aspects. The first is expressed by the word *iniquity*. Iniquity means, literally, "negation of the law." The other word, translated *sin*, literally means "missing the mark."

Iniquity looks at sin from the point of view of its relation to the law. The law is the sphere that God ordained for the life of man. Iniquity pictures the sinner as one who denies the law. He denies the law in two ways. He says *No* to the law with his mind, and he shakes his head at that law. He denies that the law is good, and he says *No* to it. Not only does he deny the law in a theoretical sense, but he also shakes his head against that law and says, "*I* will." This is iniquity. The sinner is lawless. When he brings this lawlessness into practice, he commits iniquity.

The other aspect of the word *sin* looks at sin from the viewpoint of God's purpose with us. This purpose is the glory of God. God wills that this be our purpose: with all that we are and have, we are to acknowledge the glory of God. Sin, as characterized in the passage, looks at corruption from the viewpoint that man misses this purpose. This is not accidental, but deliberate. Man misses this purpose because he aims at the opposite. He aims at self, at his own glory. From this point of view, sin is an attack upon the glory of God.

We must realize this in order to understand what it means when the poet David says, "Blessed is the man whose iniquities are forgiven, and whose sins are covered, to whom the Lord will not impute sin" [Ps. 32:1, 2]. Notice that there we have two descriptions of forgiveness. There are really three words used, but to one of them I will call your attention later. We have two descriptions here. The one is *forgiveness*. The other is *not impute* [sin].

The literal meaning of *forgiveness* is "to dismiss." "Dismiss from what?" we ask. Evidently it means dismiss from the only record that exists, that is, from the mind of God. This is forgiveness. We often say, "I can forgive, but I cannot forget." This is possible in itself. But if that *not* forgetting is that you cannot put it from your mind as an offense, then you have not forgiven. When God forgives, according to this meaning of the word in the text, He puts our sins from His mind as sin. God does not forget the fact of sin, but He dismisses it from His mind as sin. Instead of having a feeling of wrath against the sinner, He is filled with favor toward him.

As a result of this forgiveness, God *does not impute* that sin to the sinner. Not imputing describes forgiveness from the viewpoint of guilt. Sin is debt. Sin causes us to be behind in our obligation. Our obligation is to love God with all our heart, mind, and strength. We are to love Him all the time. Never may we fail. Whenever we sin, that is, whenever we say *No* to this obligation, we fall behind, and it is reckoned against us. When this happens, our obligation to love God is changed into an obligation to suffer. The sinner has to be punished.

The poet says, and Paul quotes him as saying, that God does not reckon this obligation. He gives us a clean sheet, so that there is no sin counted against us. God does not impute or reckon sin against us.

∽ *The Blessedness of the Justified*

This is a marvel!

It is a marvel if you look at it *from the point of view of God.* God, who is holy and righteous and who cannot allow His righteousness to be trampled underfoot, does not reckon sin against the sinner. God, who does not change, puts from His mind all our sins, our iniquities, our corruption.

This is a marvel!

It is a marvel *from the point of view of the law,* for the law is not merely an outward code; it is the living expression of God's will. It is a living power to condemn, to punish all who do not keep its precepts, even as the law of fire is to burn you. Would it not be a marvel if you should put your hand in the fire, and it did not burn you? This is the marvel of forgiveness. You put your hand in the fire, and it does not burn you. You trample underfoot the law, and it does not punish you.

It is a marvel also *from the viewpoint of the sinner.* For it is dangerous business to forgive the criminal. It is dangerous business to forgive the criminal not only for his past sins, but also for all the sins that he will commit in the future. Imagine that the Supreme Court would do this! But the marvel of grace is that before we have finished sinning, our sins are forgiven. So the poet says in Psalm 32.

A Great Blessing

Oh, the blessedness of the man whose iniquities are forgiven, unto whom God does not impute sin!

He is blessed because the forgiveness of sins is the greatest of blessings. It is the key blessing of all blessings. If there is no forgiveness, there is no blessing for any man. The reason is simply that God is righteous. God cannot bless the unrighteous. This is impossible. God cannot even for a moment regard the unrighteous in His mind with the purpose of blessing them. If we are to be blessed by God, we must have a clean sheet, for God is God, and He is righteous.

The objective blessing of forgiveness, therefore, spells the

151

difference between God's everlasting wrath and His everlasting good pleasure. It is the difference between hell and heaven. Without forgiveness, the door of hell is inevitably open. Without forgiveness, the doors of heaven are inevitably shut. Forgiveness is the key that shuts the door to everlasting damnation. Forgiveness opens the door to heaven, to everlasting glory, and to fellowship with God.

Is it any wonder that the poet exclaims, "Oh, the blessedness of the man whose iniquities are forgiven, whose sins are covered, unto whom God does not impute sin"?

Forgiveness is the *blessing*. The passage speaks of the blessedness. It looks at forgiveness from the point of view of our own personal, conscious experience of it. We become conscious of the forgiveness of sins when God gives us faith. When by faith we become conscious of the forgiveness of sins, so that we appropriate the blessedness of forgiveness, the result is joy. This blessing causes the blessedness of peace, which we do not have without forgiveness. The ungodly have no peace. There is no peace with God without forgiveness. But if God instills faith in our heart, so that we appropriate the blessedness of forgiveness, we have peace. We have peace with God and with all things.

On the basis of the consciousness of the forgiveness of sins, we have fellowship with God. We may sometimes, out of custom, go to God without the consciousness of the forgiveness of sins. But there is no fellowship with God unless there is consciousness of the forgiveness of sins. There is no fellowship with God unless there is the blessed consciousness that without fear we shall stand in the judgment.

Oh the blessedness of that faith, that God forgives our sins and that we shall stand in judgment without fear!

A Sure Ground

But you say, "How is this possible? Can God forgive sin? Can He reckon what is not? Can He fail to impute what must be imputed? Can He take the name of the sinner from His judgment book? Does He change His mind when He forgives sin?"

This is impossible. He cannot fail to impute what must be imputed. He cannot change His mind. Therefore, the text is careful to add *whose sins are covered.* This is the ground of forgiveness.

Do not misunderstand this. The meaning is not that there is something that covers up our sins so that God does not see them. It is not the case that they are really there, but God does not see them because they are covered up. *Covered* does not even mean that one's sins are hid under Christ, as is often said. The fact is that God looks right through Christ.

Covered refers, as far as the word is concerned, to the cover of the ark of the covenant. Our sins are covered in the sense that insurance covers the damage. You have nothing with which to pay the damage, but there is something to cover, to pay for, the damage. There is an insurance agency. It is God's own insurance agency. The rule of that agency is that you can be a member of it only on condition of full coverage.

You trample God's law underfoot, and God does not impute your sin. He forgives you because you are a member of a corporation. This corporation was established in eternity. God's people are the members. The coverage is the blood of Christ. It is God's own coverage. We became members of this corporation when God engrafts us into it by a living faith. By this we acknowledge the damage. The coverage is Christ. The corporation is the elect body. The policy is God's own Word. Then we exclaim, "Oh, the blessedness of the man whose iniquities are forgiven, whose sins are covered up, and unto whom God does not impute sin!"

We are justified freely, through grace, by faith in Christ Jesus our Lord.

Chapter Twenty-two

The Sign of Circumcision

Romans 4:11
And he received the sign of circumcision, a seal of the righteousness of the faith which he had yet being uncircumcised: that he might be the father of all them that believe, though they be not circumcised; that righteousness might be imputed unto them also.

The apostle emphasizes the point that faith-righteousness is not limited to circumcision. Also, when he teaches that God justifies both those of the circumcision by faith, and those of the uncircumcision by faith, he does not thereby make void the law. That is, he does not teach anything that is contrary to the Old Testament revelation; he does not bring in anything new.

The apostle had shown this in the context. Abraham was not justified by works, for the Scripture says, "Abraham believed God, and it was counted unto him for righteousness" [v. 3]. Not only was this the testimony of the law concerning Abraham, but it was also the testimony of David in Psalm 32. There David calls the man blessed whose iniquities are forgiven and whose sins are covered. That man is blessed to whom the Lord will not impute sin. Plainly the law teaches that a man is not justified by works, but by faith. Thus the apostle had proved that when he teaches that a man is justified by faith without the works of the law, he does not make void the law.

But the question still remains open whether that righteousness was limited to the circumcision (to the Jews), or whether it included the uncircumcision (the Gentiles). The apostle had been teaching that both the Jews and the Gentiles are justified by faith. The objection might be made that although it is true that Scripture teaches a justification without the law, this justification concerns Abraham, but that when Paul teaches both the circumcision and the uncircumcision are justified by faith, he brings in a new doctrine. This question the apostle raises in the context [v. 9].

He responds with another question: when we say that Abraham believed God and it was imputed unto him for righteousness, *how* was it imputed unto him? *When* was that faith imputed unto him for righteousness? Was it imputed unto him when he was in circumcision, or in uncircumcision? Abraham was not always circumcised. How, then, was that faith imputed unto him—before or after circumcision?

The apostle answers his own question: "not in circumcision, but in uncircumcision" [v. 10]. This shows that the righteousness that is by faith has nothing to do with circumcision. Circumcision is not the essential thing. It is true that Abraham was circumcised, but Abraham received the sign of circumcision as a seal of the righteousness of the faith that he had when he was still uncircumcised. That sign, which served as a seal of the righteousness of Abraham's faith, was at the same time a sign that served as a seal that he should be the father of all who believe, though they be not circumcised.

The Seal of
Faith-Righteousness

The heart of the verse is that righteousness, also in the case of Abraham, was in no way to be identified with circumcision. Righteousness is not dependent upon circumcision. It is not dependent upon anything we have. It is not dependent upon any relation. We are not righteous because of our relation to our parents. We are not righteous because our name is on the church roll. We are not righteous because we are born in a certain generation. Righteousness is independent of anything we may see, of anything we may do, of any position we may occupy. Righteousness has nothing to do with anything except faith. This is the general thought of the verse.

This was also the case with Abraham. Abraham was circumcised. But that circumcision was not his righteousness, nor did that circumcision make him more or less righteous. Abraham's circumcision was a sign that he received as a seal of the righteousness of the faith he had when he was yet uncircumcised. Not the seal, but faith-righteousness is the essential thing. When you seal something, not the seal but the thing it seals is essential. Likewise, circumcision is not the essential thing, but that which it seals. What circumcision seals is faith-righteousness.

If we believe in the God who justifies the ungodly, we are righteous. Outside of this faith, there is no righteousness. Faith consists of a certain knowledge, so that we know God in the face of Christ as the God who justifies the ungodly. For this reason faith is at the same time a hearty confidence that this God has blotted out all our sins and has counted us righteous.

It must be understood that faith-righteousness is impossible from every aspect. Everything testifies against our being righteous. Faith that lays hold on the impossibility that God justifies the ungodly—this faith is imputed for righteousness. Faith is not imputed for righteousness because faith *is* righteousness, nor is it imputed because faith *leads to* righteousness.

The essence of Christianity is not in service. The essence of Christianity is not even in faith. But the essence of Christianity is in Christ. God prepares righteousness in Christ. Because God prepares righteousness in Christ, our works do not make us more righteous. Righteousness is in Christ. The fact that faith is reckoned as righteousness is because faith makes us members of the corporation in which sins have been blotted out. Because by faith we are in that corporation in which sins have been blotted out, faith is imputed for righteousness. This is faith-righteousness.

In the case of Abraham, circumcision was given as a *sign* to seal unto him the righteousness of faith. In this respect, circumcision was no different from baptism. Circumcision was a sign. It was a visible manifestation of what in itself is invisible, that is, of faith-righteousness. The cutting away of the foreskin of the flesh was a sign of the cutting away of sin. Circumcision was a sign that one was separated from the sinful organism of the human race, separated from the sinful "old man." Similarly, baptism is now the sign of our separation from the sinful old man.

That sign of circumcision was also a *seal*. It was God's oath that He does what He pictures in the sign, namely, that He justifies the ungodly.

"What is really sealed?" is therefore an important question. Abraham received the sign of circumcision for himself and for his seed when the seed was eight days old. In this respect the Baptist is absolutely wrong. Abraham received the sign for himself *and for his seed*. For himself and his seed he received the sign of the righteousness that is by faith. The question then arises, "If that sign, which is the seal of faith-righteousness, is received by Abraham and his seed when the seed is eight days old, what is sealed?"

To what did God swear?

Of what was circumcision a sign? Was it a sign or a testimony that God justifies the Jews?

Circumcision was a testimony that God justifies the *believer*. This is what was sealed. The unbeliever had nothing in circumcision, even though he tried to have something in it. But that God reckons faith for righteousness—this was sealed to the believer.

This is also true of baptism. We must not throw the *seal* of baptism away. For whatever we see and experience testifies against our righteousness, even when we believe. God's Word that we are righteous needs God's seal. This is baptism. Baptism is the divine assurance to the believer that God counts his faith for righteousness. This was sealed in circumcision and is now sealed in baptism. It is sealed to the believer.

The Sign of a Spiritual Fatherhood

This is why the text says that Abraham became the *father* of believers. It is important that we see this, especially in our day among many errors concerning the Jews. Basically, the error is the teaching that the Jews are the children of Abraham. Many teach that Abraham is the father of the Jews, but this is not true. Abraham is not the father of the Jews at all, not scripturally. This is not Abraham's distinction. Scripturally, the Jews are not the children of Abraham at all. To be sure, Abraham brought them forth, although this was nothing to be proud of. But Abraham did not have to be circumcised to be the father of the Jews. He could bring forth Jews without being circumcised. This is not what Scripture means. Scripture does not teach that Abraham's distinction is that he is the father of the Jews.

What then? Abraham became the father of *believers*, of *believers only*. That is all. That this is mentioned in Scripture with respect to Abraham is not because he is the only father of believers. There are other fathers of believers. Enoch was a father of believers, too. Noah also was a father of believers. There are many fathers of believers. But that Abraham is called the father of believers is because with him God distinguished the line of the generations in which He would establish His covenant. In this sense Abraham is a father of believers. From his loins, in his generations, believers should come.

How is this possible? How could Abraham bring forth believers? Because he was a believer? This is impossible. Abraham was by nature dead in sin. A man who is dead in sin can only bring forth dead children. We can never bring forth anything but dead children. Abraham could never bring forth children of God. God taught Abraham that he could not bring forth children with Sarah. Sarah was the mother of the covenant. Abraham could not bring forth children with Sarah. He could bring forth children with Hagar, but not with Sarah until both he and Sarah were *dead* [Rom. 4:19]. In this, God meant to teach Abraham that it was impossible for him to bring forth children of God. When the Jews later say to Jesus that they are children of Abraham, Christ tells them that God could just as well bring forth children unto Abraham out of the stones.

Abraham could bring forth children of God only by a wonder of God's grace. This is what happened centrally in Christ. The epistle to the Galatians emphasizes that the seed promised to Abraham is centrally Christ. *The* seed of Abraham is Christ. That Abraham could bring forth the Christ is because Christ comes down and unites Himself with the seed of Abraham and becomes Immanuel.

Don't say that in a certain sense the Jews are children of Abraham. The Jews are not children of Abraham at all, not scripturally. Abraham is the father of believers. Abraham received the sign of circumcision, a seal of the righteousness of the faith he had while yet uncircumcised. This was so that he might be the father of all them that believe: of the circumcision, but also of the uncircumcision, that righteousness might be imputed unto them also.

The Promise of Spiritual Children

Abraham, therefore, is the father of believing Jews and Gentiles. This is important. He is the father of a *spiritual* seed. All the promises of God are for that spiritual seed only. Thus, this law remains: righteousness is imputed to Abraham. Centrally the seed of Abraham is Christ. In a larger sense, the seed is all those who are in Christ. They are righteous not because they are born of Abraham according to the flesh, but because they are of the faith of Abraham. Or to put it in New Testament language, we are not righteous because we are born of believing parents and because we are baptized. It is an imputed righteousness. This imputed righteousness can be ours only by spiritual means and in the way of a living faith in Christ.

If we are to come to a clear understanding of this faith, it is necessary to throw everything else away. Not because these things are not precious! It is precious to be born in the covenant, of believing parents, and to be a member of the church. It reveals a terrible profanity when we trample these things underfoot. It is unspeakably precious to live and grow up in the covenant. However, this does not remove the fact that when it comes to the righteousness that is valid before God, all must be put away. Then we will cast ourselves unconditionally upon God, who justifies the ungodly. The more we do so, as undone sinners, the more we will grow in the consciousness of the faith expressed by the apostle Paul: "Therefore being justified by faith, we have peace with God through our Lord Jesus Christ."

Chapter Twenty-three

Believing the Living God

Romans 4:17b
...before him whom he believed, even God, who quickeneth the dead, and calleth those things which be not as though they were.

Of all texts, Romans 4:17b is one of the most fundamental. This will be plain if we consider for a moment the immediate connection. The text belongs to the latter part of verse 16. There we read once again that Abraham is the father of us all. The present text adds to this: ". . . before him whom he believed, even God, who quickeneth the dead, and calleth those things which be not as though they were." Abraham, therefore, is the father of us all before God—not as he looks, not as he appears, not as he sees it, not as he experiences it, but before God. The word *before*, which introduces the text, means "before the face of." He is the father of us all before the face of God. As God sees him, Abraham is the father of believers.

This means, in the first place, that God beheld Abraham eternally and sovereignly, for God does not look at things as they appear but as they really are in His counsel. Abraham is the father of us all before God. That is his significance. That is his position. For this reason his name is changed to Abraham, that is, "father of many nations." This is the name that he has before God in the economy of salvation.

That Abraham is the father of us all before God means, in the second place, that by his faith Abraham was such a father

161

in his own consciousness. He lived as such. It was before God his conviction and his experience that he was the father of believers. It is only from this viewpoint that we can explain Abraham. It is only from this viewpoint that we can explain his departure from Ur of the Chaldees. It is only from this viewpoint that we can explain his willingness to be a sojourner in a strange land. We can explain Abraham only from the fact that he was, before God and in his own consciousness, the father of believers.

This state of Abraham before God, and this conception that Abraham had of himself, was contrary to all experience. What Abraham believed went against all the testimony of the things seen at that time. Abraham was not a father at all at that time. While still childless, he looked upon himself as the father of many nations, as the father of believers. His very name, "father of many," was mockery while he was childless.

How is this possible? The text gives the explanation not only with regard to Abraham's faith, but also in regard to our faith. God is the expectation of the believer's faith. Although all things are contrary to what the Christian believes, he conceives of God as the one who quickeneth the dead and calleth those things that are not as though they were. This is the explanation of the seeming impossibility of what the Christian believes.

Him Whom We Believe

Abraham believed the living God, the God whom he knew and in whom he had all his confidence. He knew the living God in distinction from all that is called God and in distinction from the creature. We must remember, when speaking of God, that He is God. As God He is entirely *other*. We cannot comprehend Him; we cannot conceive of Him; we cannot find Him out. We cannot construe God in our own mind. What we say of Him is always the lie. If we are to know Him, He must say who He is. God is infinitely removed from us, and we cannot reach him.

Therefore, we must not say that God is the first cause, that He is the cause of all causes. As long as God is a cause, we can still reach Him. But God is beyond us.

Therefore, we cannot say, either, that God is ultimate. God is not ultimate.

If we say anything about God, we must say that He is *other*. This is plainly expressed in the text. The text says that God is, in the first place, the one who calls the things that are not as though they were. This means that He is before all things, that He conceives of all things sovereignly, that He sovereignly wills all things that are not, and that then He speaks them. Because God conceives of all things sovereignly, wills all things sovereignly, and speaks them, therefore they *are*. God calls the things that are not as though they were.

This is not true of the creature. This is distinctively true of God. If we are to call a thing, the thing must be there first, but God calls the things that are not as though they were. He calls the things out of Himself. He calls them because He wills them.

The text does not merely refer to creation. The text does not mean simply that God is *able* to call the things that are not as though they were. The text does not mean that Abraham believed that God is able to call the things that are not as though they were, nor does the text mean that God in creation called the things that are not as though they were. Of course, this is true; in creation, God spoke and called the things that are not as though they were. But this is not the thought of the text. The idea is, first, that this is *characteristic* of God, that God *always* works this way. God never calls the things that are. He always calls the things that are not. As the living God, He does this in distinction from the creature. Deny this, and you lose the living God. Evolutionism is atheism. God calls the things that are not as though they were. Note well: the text says that ". . . before him whom he believed, namely God, who . . . calleth the things that are not as though they were," Abraham was the father of all believers.

Second, the text tells us that God *quickeneth the dead*. The relation is this: in quickening the dead, God emphatically calls the things that are not as though they were. He did so in creation. He did so more emphatically in the work of re-creation. God quickens the dead. The verse says that God does so. It does not say that God is *able* to do this, but that He *does* this. He quickens the dead.

The dead are the damned. We must understand this, or we lose the point of the text. The dead are the damned. That is, the dead are they who are dead in themselves. Death is their sentence. When God said, "The day that you eat of that tree you shall die," He did not merely offer a prophecy; He did not simply foretell what would happen; but He meant, "The day you eat thereof, I will execute the sentence of death upon you." The dead, therefore, are the sentenced, the damned. They are those concerning whom God declares that they are unworthy of life, devoid of life, and in a condition of death.

To quicken the dead, therefore, must mean two things. It means that God justifies them. God gives those who are unworthy of life the right to life. This is justification. God calls the things that are not as though they were, and He shows that He does so by giving righteousness in unrighteousness. And it means that God gives life. Again, the text does not say that God is *willing* to quicken the dead. God reveals Himself as the living God in that He *does* quicken the dead.

This is the living God. *Him* Abraham believed. And *Him* the Christian believes. This is the Christian's conception of God, in whom he has all his confidence. He believes in God who quickens the dead. Take this away, and you take the Christian's faith away. That God quickens the dead is the very basis of his faith. It becomes impossible for the Christian to believe what he believes if God is not exactly this, namely, the God who quickens the dead.

That Which We Believe

What did Abraham believe? He believed the promise of God. This promise is essentially always the same. It is the promise that God first gave in paradise when He said, "I will set enmity between thy seed and the seed of the woman" [Gen. 3:15]. It is the promise that He gave to Noah when He established the covenant with him [Gen. 9:8–17]. It is the promise that He revealed more definitely to Abraham when He said to him, "So shall thy seed be" and promised the land of Canaan to him and to his seed [Gen. 15].

Therefore, we must never say that Abraham and his seed shall not possess the land of Canaan. Abraham and his seed shall surely possess the land of Canaan. This is the promise. Not only his seed, but also Abraham himself, shall surely possess the land of Canaan. However, we must understand that Abraham's seed is not the Jews. Abraham is the father of believers. Abraham's seed is the believers. In addition, the land of Canaan is not that strip of land on the Mediterranean Sea but is the whole world, the new heavens and the new earth.

Therefore, the question is not what becomes of the Jews. And the question is not what becomes of that strip of land on the Mediterranean Sea. That is only part of the world. If you ask, "What is the promise to Abraham?" the apostle Paul answers in this same chapter that the promise to Abraham is that he should be an heir of the world [v. 13]. This is why Abraham stayed there. It was not because he wanted that strip of country. Instead, the apostle tells us that the promise to Abraham was that he should be heir of the world.

But if Abraham is to be heir of the world, he must have seed. That was the significance of having seed. This is true also of us. If we are to be heirs of the world, we must have seed. But that was especially true in the old dispensation. How could Abraham become heir of the world without a seed? He could not be heir of the world alone. He must have seed. But he did not have seed, and he had become too old to have seed. He was one hundred years old. Besides, the mother in Sarah was dead.

All things testified that the dead would never be raised. God was not to raise the dead through Abraham personally. He was

165

to raise the dead through Abraham's seed. Abraham longed to see that seed. He longed to see the day of Christ, and he did see it. It all depended on this: if Abraham did not have seed, Christ could not come, and if Christ did not come, the promise would not be realized.

God said, "So shall thy seed be" [Gen. 15:5]. And Abraham said, "I am the father of many." He believed God.

The Reason Why We Believe It

Why did Abraham believe the promise? Because he believed God who quickeneth the dead and calleth the things that are not as though they were. He saw the day of Christ. He saw Christ in Isaac. In his son, Abraham saw the beginning of the realization of the promise.

We are in a better position, but not essentially different. Abraham's faith was this: the things he believed were contrary to all experience. So it is with the Christian. The things we believe are contrary to all that we see and to all that we experience. For we say that we are heirs of the world, that we are righteous, that we are justified, that we are without sin. This is still the promise. But this faith of the Christian is just as impossible as was the faith of Abraham when God said to him, "So shall thy seed be." All that we see, within us and without, testifies against what we believe. All within us testifies that we are not righteous, that we are not justified, that we are not heirs of the world. All the testimony of the conscience is that we are damned. Not only is this the testimony of the conscience, but it is also our life's experience. Even the world about us testifies that we are not righteous, but damned and dying. We are dying now. Our life is a continual death. That is the end. The testimony of all experience is that we are damned, that we are dead, and that we are going to die.

In the midst of this experience, God takes us to Abraham's seed. He tells us that all our sins have been removed and that they have been blotted out. He tells us that we are righteous before Him, before God who quickeneth the dead.

For God did quicken the dead. The resurrection has become a fact. In the resurrection God was revealed as the God who quickeneth the dead. The dead are quickened. *That* Abraham did not see. Abraham longed to see the day of Christ, and he did see it in Isaac. But he did not see God as He quickened the dead. We do see God as He quickens the dead. We believe in Him who quickens the dead. Therefore, we always turn to Him who quickens the dead as He is manifest in Christ.

The tendency of the faith that God has implanted in our heart is to turn to Him, turning away from everything else. There is no hope in anything else. The Christian's hope is only in God who quickens the dead. There you have the reason why the Christian believes.

The reason why Abraham believed was that he had the Word of God, although he did not have much of a Word. He had but a fleeting revelation. See what we have by contrast! We have the complete Word of God as it was given us by means of the prophets and apostles. This Word of God is the reason why our faith triumphs over all. As God realized His Word to Abraham, and as He realized it in Christ in the resurrection, so He will realize it once more when He shall raise the dead and create the new heavens and the new earth.

This God is our salvation. Turn to this God who quickens the dead, and you will be saved.

Chapter Twenty-four

Imputed to All

Romans 4:23, 24
Now it was not written for his sake alone, that it was imputed to him;
But for us also, to whom it shall be imputed, if we believe on him that raised up Jesus our Lord from the dead.

It was not written for his, that is, for Abraham's sake alone, that his faith was imputed to him for righteousness. That faith of Abraham the apostle had described in verse 17 and pictured in the verses following. Abraham believed in God "who quickeneth the dead, and calleth those things which be not as though they were." Only that faith could cause Abraham to hope for the promise God had given him, which is nothing but the Old Testament form of the gospel. The promise was "so shall thy seed be," which seed was centrally Christ. Implied was that Abraham would be father of a spiritual nation of believers.

But this promise seemed to be impossible of realization. Abraham had to hope against hope for the realization of that promise. All things testified against the possibility of the realization of this promise. At the time the promise was given to him, Abraham was dead as far as the possibility of having seed is concerned. Abraham was one hundred years old. Sarah had been barren. She was now beyond the age of having a child. According to all things that are seen and experienced, the realization of the promise was impossible.

That it was possible for Abraham to believe what seemingly

was impossible was because he believed in God who quickeneth the dead and calleth the things which be not as though they were. Believing on Him, "he staggered not at the promise of God through unbelief; but was strong in faith, giving glory to God" [v. 20]. This faith is imputed for righteousness. In brief, this is the content of the chapter thus far.

In the text the apostle returns to the question he had asked in verse 9. The argument might be raised that although faith was imputed to Abraham for righteousness, there is no proof that this same principle of imputing faith for righteousness includes us in the new dispensation. Therefore, the apostle asked, "Was faith imputed to Abraham while he was in circumcision, or in uncircumcision?" He answered that it was while Abraham was still in uncircumcision. In verse 16 the apostle made the remark that *faith* is imputed, not the work of the law. If the work of the law was imputed, only those would be included who are under the law. But it is out of faith. Faith is not Jewish. Faith is universal in the sense that it includes believers out of all nations. Therefore, the promise is not only to those who are under the law, but to all who are of the same faith of Abraham.

To this question the apostle returns when he says, "Now it was not written for Abraham's sake alone, that is, on account of him, but it was written also for us, that is, on account of us, on account of all those who believe on Him that raised up Jesus our Lord from the dead."

We will see that this faith is the same faith as that of Abraham but from the point of view of its new dispensational character. Abraham believed on God who *would* quicken the dead, that is, who would raise up Jesus from the dead. The Christian believes on God who *did* quicken the dead, that is, who did raise Jesus our Lord from the dead. The Christian believes, and this faith is imputed to him for righteousness.

We consider the central thought of the epistle to the Romans. And we have need of considering this, for it is very difficult for the Christian to believe that his faith is imputed to him for righteousness.

169

The Righteousness Imputed

The subject is imputed righteousness. To this the apostle refers when he says, "Now it was not written for his sake alone, that it was imputed to him." Righteousness is imputed. It is imputed to them who believe on Him who raised up Jesus our Lord from the dead. Righteousness, taken all by itself, is moral integrity. It is that state and condition which, according to God's judgment, is in harmony with God's own goodness and God's own will over us.

Righteousness implies, first, that we continually stand before the face of God and are judged by Him. It is an actual fact that we always stand in judgment before God. God always judges us. There is never a moment that we do not stand before God's judgment bar. If we will but consult our conscience, we will find that in our own conscience we carry the testimony that we stand before God in judgment.

Second, the term *righteousness* [v. 22] implies that in this judgment God applies the standard of His own perfect will concerning us. There is only one thing that is righteous. That is God's perfect will. God therefore applies that standard to all that is of me. He applies that standard to my willing, my thinking, my desiring, my walking, my talking—to all my actions.

Third, righteousness implies that God, so applying that standard of His own perfect will concerning me, expresses the verdict of perfect harmony with that standard.

Finally, righteousness implies that God, expressing this verdict of perfect harmony with His will concerning me, calls me His child, blesses me with His favor, and gives me eternal life. This is righteousness.

Righteousness, therefore, is not concerned with what *I* think of myself. Nor do I ask what *you* think of me. I stand before the face of God and ask what *God* thinks of me. This righteousness we must have. In order to have peace, we must know that we have this righteousness. Outside of the knowledge that I am righteous in this way, I have no peace.

The text speaks of righteousness being imputed. You understand that this word *imputed* implies that I am not righteous in myself. Otherwise, imputation would not be necessary. Imputed righteousness implies that the one to whom it is imputed is not righteous. We must understand this. He to whom righteousness is imputed is not righteous. If he is not righteous, he is unrighteous. There is no third possibility. We are either righteous or unrighteous. At the moment when God accredits righteousness to me, I am really unrighteous. I am unrighteous in myself. When God imputes righteousness unto me, I am a sinner, I am corrupt, I am unrighteous. Otherwise righteousness would not have to be imputed. Imputed righteousness looks at the one to whom it is imputed as a sinner.

We must understand this. It is just the fact that we are sinners that makes it so difficult for us to believe that God imputes righteousness to us. Imputation involves three aspects. First, the fact that you are sinful does not cast doubt on your imputed righteousness. Though your sins be as scarlet, this has nothing to do with denying your imputed righteousness, which is imputed to you by God.

Second, imputation implies that there is a righteousness that can be imputed to us, even though it is not ours. When God imputes or accredits righteousness to His people, this righteousness actually exists. It exists in a real sense in Jesus our Lord.

Third, the imputing of righteousness must be an act of perfect justice.

The Faith That Is Reckoned

How is this possible?

To whom does God impute righteousness? The text says those who *believe on him that raised up Jesus our Lord from the dead.* Every word in the sentence has significance. Briefly, therefore, righteousness is imputed to them who believe, not to them who work.

Faith is a spiritual faculty, not a natural faculty. Believing is the activity of this spiritual faculty. Faith is a spiritual faculty that affects the whole soul. If a man is an unbeliever, he is an unbeliever with his mind, with his will, with his desires, with his whole being. If a man is a believer, he is a believer with his whole being. Faith, therefore, is that faculty that affects the whole soul-life of the believer. It is the faculty by which the soul cleaves to God. This the natural man does not do. The natural man turns away from God, but the believing soul cleaves to God. For this reason, insofar as faith affects the mind, it is a certain knowledge of God. Insofar as it affects the heart, it is the letting down of one's self on this God. This is confidence. Believing on God is that act of the believing soul whereby the soul lets itself down on the God of salvation, believing that God will do us nothing but good.

Now notice, the object of this faith is not simply God, but it is God as He has revealed Himself in the raising up of Jesus our Lord from the dead. Saving faith does not merely believe that God is and that he controls all things. The devil believes this. The fact that God *is* makes us afraid. But saving faith is faith in God who raised up Jesus our Lord from the dead. The Scriptures say that if this is the case with us, if we have this assured knowledge of God who raised up Jesus our Lord from the dead, and if we have this confidence whereby we rest on God, faith is imputed to us for righteousness.

Why?

Not because God imputes something that is not. Not because faith is righteousness. Not because of the fruits of faith. Not because by faith we become better men and women before God. The fruits of faith do not make us better before God. If a man comes to saving faith one second before his death, he will be just as righteous before God as any. When the apostle Paul wrote [in II Tim. 4:7, 8], "I have fought a good fight, I have finished my course, I have kept the faith: Henceforth there is laid up for me a crown of righteousness," he was not more righteous than he was when he was on the way to Damascus. Faith and the fruit of faith are not righteousness.

Faith is imputed for righteousness because it lays hold on the only perfect righteousness that exists, namely, Christ Jesus. That the Christian, living from this faith, receives the assurance that God imputes righteousness to him is due to the fact that he lays hold of the only righteous one, Christ Jesus.

This is expressed when the text says, ". . . if we believe on him that raised up Jesus." God raised up Jesus. This means that God killed Jesus. Otherwise His being raised would have no significance. God killed Jesus; He caused Jesus to sink away into our death. That God caused Jesus to sink away into death implies the verdict of God that Jesus was worthy of death. Jesus Himself was not worthy of death. But Jesus our Lord was worthy of death. God caused Him to sink away into death with our sin. That was God's judgment of Jesus. While Jesus sank away into death, He performed the act of perfect obedience in the sacrifice of Himself. God gave His verdict upon that sacrifice. This we have in the resurrection. When God killed Jesus, He said that Jesus was worthy of death. When He raised Jesus, God said that Jesus was worthy of life. Because faith is the tie that binds us to Christ, and because faith is the act whereby we cleave to God, faith has the testimony that we are righteous before God.

We are righteous in Jesus our Lord. We are not righteous in *Jesus*. We are righteous in *Jesus our Lord*. If you say, "I believe on God that raised up *Jesus my Lord* from the dead," you have the assured knowledge of saving faith.

The Christian does not simply believe the *fact* that God raised Jesus. But he believes *on* God that raised Jesus our Lord. He *knows* God that raised Jesus our Lord. Knowing that God, he clings to Him. As soon as the soul does this, faith has the testimony, "I am righteous before God." It is necessary that we see this point. This righteousness comes to us while we are sinners. We die as sinners. But while we die as sinners, we live as righteous.

The Certainty of Faith

How do we know?

This faith is so impossible that it is very difficult for the sinner to believe that he is righteous before God. It is more impossible than the faith of Abraham that he would be the father of many nations. That seemed so impossible. But from the point of view of our righteousness before God, we are in the same case. Everything testifies that we are not righteous, but unrighteous. Everything tells us that we are damned. Your conscience tells you that. Your experience tells you that. Your way testifies against the fact that you are righteous. The world tells you that you are a sinner. The devil tells you that you are unrighteous. Your suffering testifies against your being righteous. When you die, your death tells you that you are unrighteous. And in the midst of all that experience to the contrary, the Christian says, "I am righteous before the face of God."

Where is the certainty?

The apostle says, "It is written." It is written that God accounts the faith of Abraham for righteousness. Abraham had the promise. Abraham believed the promise, and that faith was imputed to him for righteousness. It was written that it was imputed to him.

But it was not written for him alone. It was written for all who are of that same faith of Abraham. "It is written!" But in the new dispensation it is written that it is written. It is written double. By whom? By God. And God cannot lie. The certainty of the truth, therefore, that He justifies him who believes on God who raised up Jesus our Lord from the dead rests on the unchangeable Word of God.

The conclusion is, away with all that is of self! Away with our good works! Away with our religion as a basis of righteousness. Then we will have the assurance that we are righteous before God.

Chapter Twenty-five

Jesus Raised for Our Justification

Romans 4:25
Who was delivered for our offences, and was raised again for our justification.

In order to see the purpose of this text, it is necessary that we keep in mind the context in which it stands. The connection is with the immediately preceding verses, where the apostle had written, "It was not written for his [Abraham's] sake alone, that it [faith] was imputed to him [for righteousness]; But for us also, to whom it shall be imputed, if we believe on him that raised up Jesus our Lord from the dead" [vv. 23, 24]. The apostle then continues, "Who was delivered for our offences, and was raised again for our justification."

It is evident that the text is an explanation, a further justification, of what the apostle had written, namely, that if we believe on Him who raised up Jesus our Lord from the dead, faith is reckoned to us for righteousness. This is an essential thing to know. The apostle had assured the Christian and the church that if we find ourselves as believing on God who raised up Jesus our Lord from the dead, we have the testimony in our hearts and minds, through this faith, that God justifies us. No matter how things may testify against it, if we believe on God who raised up Jesus from the dead, we have the testimony that we are righteous before God.

Why is this? The question is not only why faith should be reck-

175

oned for righteousness, but also why such a faith should be necessary that has for its object God who raised up Jesus our Lord from the dead. It is the faith about this fact that inspires us with the confidence that we are justified. The apostle explains this in the text: "[Christ] was raised again for our justification."

The little preposition *for* in *for our justification* has the meaning "because of, on account of, on the ground of." It is essential that we see this from the outset and keep it in mind. Christ was raised *for* (that is, on account of, on the ground of) our justification. This is the heart of the text. The text does not so much stress the point that Christ was delivered for our offenses; it is the fact that He was raised again for our justification that stands in the foreground.

That Jesus was raised for our justification means that Jesus was raised *because we had been declared righteous by God*. Jesus could not have been raised if we had not been justified. Our justification *precedes* the resurrection. The resurrection cannot be understood unless it is viewed in the light of His deliverance over unto death. This is why the apostle mentions that Jesus was delivered for our offenses.

The Resurrection

We must notice that the apostle says Jesus was *delivered*. It is essential that the apostle puts it just this way. He might have said that Jesus *died* for our offenses, or that He *offered up Himself* for our offenses. But he does not. What Christ did is not the issue here. The issue is what *God* did.

What God did was to deliver Jesus unto death. Deliverance, as used here, presupposes a legal act. Deliverance presupposes, in the first place, that there is one who is accused. It presupposes, in the second place, that there is one who judges the accused. In the third place, it presupposes that this judge finds the one who is accused guilty. In the fourth place, it presupposes that the judge, having found the accused guilty, delivers him to the executioner to be punished.

One is delivered to death, as a legal act. In this manner Jesus was delivered.

The question is, by whom?

The answer is, not by men. It is true that men also delivered Him. Men delivered Him to the Jewish Sanhedrin. The Sanhedrin delivered Him to Pilate. Pilate delivered Him to the executioners. But this is not the point of the text.

The point of the text is, first, that *God* delivered Jesus to death. This is evident because the text says He was delivered for our transgressions. Men did not deliver Jesus for our transgressions. Second, it is evident that He who delivered Jesus is the same as He who raised Him up from the dead. It is also evident from all Scripture that God delivered Jesus to death. So we read in John 3:16: "For God so loved the world, that he gave his only begotten Son." There you have the same idea of deliverance. We read it literally in Romans 8:32: "He that spared not his own Son, but delivered him up for us all."

God *delivered* Jesus. This means that Christ stood before the tribunal of God as the accused. The law was His accuser. The accuser demanded that justice be done. God, as it were, having considered the accusation, found Christ guilty. That is, He found Christ worthy of that which the law demanded, namely, death. Having found Christ guilty, God delivered Him to the executioner, that is, to death. He delivered Him to the death of the cross, which is but an expression of bearing the full wrath of God.

The question is not so much "What did Christ do?" but "What did *God* do? The apostle says, "God delivered Christ."

But here is the strange thing: God also raised Him. First God declares Christ worthy of death; then He lifts Him up. Here again, the question is not what Christ did. We do not read in the text that Christ lived again, or that He arose again. The verse says that He *was raised*.

Jesus was not raised again to the level on which He stood before He was delivered to death. Jesus did not return. This is

177

not the resurrection. Jesus was raised. He was raised above the level on which He stood before He was delivered.

Nor is it so that Christ was raised to the level on which man stood before he fell. That is another level. Man before the fall stood on a certain level. From that level he fell to his present level. When Christ came, He came to our present level. From this level He descended into the lower parts of the earth. To this descension into the lower parts of the earth, Christ was delivered over by God. From this level He was raised. But He was not raised to the original level of man. Rather, He was raised to heavenly glory. I mention these things only in passing.

What the text emphasizes is that also the raising of Jesus was an act of God, another legal act. When Jesus was delivered to death, God sentenced Him. When He was raised, God sentenced Him again, and the final sentence of God is that Jesus is worthy of eternal glory.

What had happened? Did God change? We have the indisputable fact that God condemns Jesus and then raises Him again. Did God change? Did God take pity upon Jesus at the last moment and say, "Although I have found you guilty and have condemned you, I will overlook your sin and raise you again?" This is impossible. God did not change. He still judges Jesus according to the same strict righteousness.

Therefore, the conclusion must be that by Jesus' descension into death, Jesus changed His state before God. He changed His state from a state of guilt to a state of righteousness. On Good Friday, Jesus was actually guilty before God. On Easter morning, He was actually righteous before God. In between lay the act that changed His state before God: the act of perfect obedience.

The Ground of the Resurrection

But if this is all that is to be said, the text would have no significance for the argument of the apostle. The apostle is explaining that faith is imputed for righteousness and that the ground is the resurrection of Christ. The question here is, what is the ground of Christ's resurrection? The text answers, "Who was delivered for our offences, and was raised for our justification."

That Christ was raised *for our justification* is commonly explained as meaning that He was raised for the purpose of justifying us. Then Christ's justification would be first, and He would make us partakers of that justification *after* His resurrection. The Roman Catholics explain justification as meaning sanctification. Then the text would teach that He was raised for our sanctification.

Against these commonly believed explanations is the fact that the same construction in the original Greek is used in both parts of the text. This construction does not mean "for the purpose of" or "on behalf of." This construction always means "because of," "on account of," "on the ground of." So it is here. This is plain from the first part of the text, "Who was delivered *for* our offences." The meaning is that we have sinned. Our sin is God's ground for sentencing Jesus. Jesus is delivered; He is the security. We are the debtors. God takes the security and shuts Him up in the prison of hell. Jesus is delivered into prison as security for the debt of the debtors. But He pays the debt. Having paid the debt, He is set at liberty.

Why? What is the ground of His being liberated? The ground is that the debtors are no more in debt. Jesus paid their debt. This became the ground of His deliverance. Jesus is set free. Because Jesus is set free, it is evident that the debtors are also free from debt. This is the sense of the text. Jesus was delivered on account of our offenses, and He was raised on account of our justification. In other words, the debt has been paid. If we see Jesus, we say, "Those for whom He was security are justified; their debt has been paid."

Implied is the underlying idea that there is an unbreakable union between Christ and His people. There is such a union that Christ and His people are before God a corporation. Christ represents the whole corporation before God; otherwise the death and resurrection of Christ would never have happened. Because of this relation, the offenses of His people are the offenses of Christ.

This union was not established by us. This union is not established when we believe. This union was established before Christ was delivered to death. It was established before Christ was raised. The union could not be established by us. In one word, this text also refers us to God's sovereign election. Without election, you may as well scratch this text from Scripture. God gave a people unto Christ whom He might represent. God gave Him a people whom He might represent before the law so that He might enter into their death and be raised for them. In the death and resurrection of Christ, God passed sentence upon the whole church.

**The Significance of
This Resurrection for Us**

If you ask, "What is the significance, objectively, of the death and resurrection of Christ?" the answer is that the judgment day has passed for the church. This judgment will be revealed. But the revelation of this judgment can never be any different from the judgment in the resurrection. The judgment day is past, and the judgment upon the church is that the church, in Christ, is righteous and worthy of eternal life.

This objective point of view is not the point of the text, however. The idea of the text is how we can live in the freedom of the consciousness that the judgment is past. How is this possible? This question is essential. From everything around us, it is impossible to believe that we are righteous. The apostle in this chapter had called attention to Abraham. Abraham believed in God who quickens the dead. Only in this faith could he live in the consciousness that he would be the father of many nations. The moment he looked at himself, it became impossible.

This is true of us. As soon as we look at ourselves, at reality, what do we say? Do you say, "I am righteous"? Impossible! This would be possible only if we are willingly blind. How can a Christian know that he is righteous before God? Not when he looks at himself! When he looks at himself, there is nothing but sin, corruption, and unrighteousness. We are corrupt, and we deserve to die.

How, then, can we be conscious that we are righteous before God? By looking away from self! By looking away from the things that are seen! By looking to God who raised up Jesus from the dead! The moment I may look away from self and may look to God as He shows His face in the resurrection of Christ, I can say, "I am righteous."

There are two conclusions. Faith is the justifying bond because it binds us to Christ. And faith is the justifying consciousness because it causes us to look away from self and to look to God, who raised up Jesus from the dead.

Therefore, let us more and more look away from self. Abraham considered not his own deadness, nor the deadness of Sarah. Similarly, you must not consider your own sin and unrighteousness; you must look above your own sin, corruption, and unrighteousness to God who raised up Jesus from the dead for our justification.

Chapter Twenty-six

The Believer's Peace with God

Romans 5:1
Therefore being justified by faith, we have peace with God through our Lord Jesus Christ.

There is another reading of this verse that has been accepted by the Revised Version and that makes of the text an admonition rather than a declaration. The difference between the two readings is only a matter of half a letter. According to this other reading, the text would say, "Therefore being justified by faith, let us have peace with God." It cannot be determined whether the Revised Version or the King James Version is correct. Nor does it make much difference. The two readings are not mutually exclusive. We can easily combine the two readings into one: "Therefore being justified by faith, we have peace with God; let us then have peace with God."

As far as the meaning of the text is concerned, the main thought is in the last part. The apostle does not so much mean to call our attention to the fact that we have been justified by faith as he does to the fact that we have peace with God. Our justification by faith is the objective basis of this peace. Subjectively, justification by faith is the way to this peace. In order to have this peace with God, we must be justified. There is no peace for the wicked—not with God. Therefore, in order to have peace with God before our consciousness, it is absolutely necessary that we be aware of our justification by faith. True

182

peace with God is rooted in, and flows from, the consciousness of our being justified before God.

We must not overlook that the text comes to us in the first person. The text does not say that the people of God have peace, but it comes to us and demands that we take these words upon our lips as a personal confession: *we*, being justified by faith, have peace with God.

What It Means

Peace with God means, primarily, that in God there is peace towards us. This is fundamental. Peace with God is not a contract, nor the result of a contract that we have with God. It is not a treaty. You cannot make a treaty with God. Peace with God does not mean that I laid my enmity aside. It does not mean that I made peace with God. Especially does it not mean this in the text.

As to its fundamental idea, peace is agreement. It is not agreement on paper. It is real, fundamental, moral, ethical agreement. It is a really existing harmony among various parties. As a result of this really existing harmony, peace implies the good will of the various parties towards each other.

In the supreme sense, peace is in God. God is good. He is good in the sense of perfection. He is good in essence; He is good in all His being. He is righteous, holy, and perfect in all His essence, and the fountain of all goodness. On the level of this divine essence live the three persons of the Godhead in perfect agreement. This is not because of an agreement among the three persons, but it is because they are of one mind, of one will, and of one heart to seek but one object, and this object is God. This is the peace of God. Fundamentally, therefore, peace always presupposes goodness and righteousness.

But this is peace *in* God. The text speaks of peace *with* God. Peace with God means that attitude of God with relation to us that causes Him to treat us as being in harmony with Him, with His will, and with His law. Accordingly, He shows His good will towards us. This is peace with God.

But this is not all that is implied in the text. The text does not say merely that there is peace with God, but it also says that *we have it*. We have peace with God. In the original we read that we have peace *towards* God. This means that if we place ourselves before God with our whole being, in the consciousness of who and what He is, then there is no fear in our heart. There is peace in our heart as the reflection of the peace that is in God towards us. We have peace.

This is possible because of what the apostle mentions in the first part of the text: *being justified by faith*. The same faith by which we are justified carries with it this peace because it brings to us the consciousness of the peace of God towards us. By this faith I lay hold on the peace that is in God's heart towards me. For faith is, first of all, a certain or assured knowledge of the things not seen. In the second place, faith is a hearty confidence. With regard to peace, therefore, faith is an assured knowledge that there is in God's mind peace towards me. In connection with this knowledge, and based upon it, faith is the confidence that God will fill me with all the blessings of His good will towards me.

What a blessed reality to be able to say we have peace with God! Do you know it?

There is a positive happiness in this knowledge. What a blessed reality, also, if we compare it with the alternative, which is that we have war with God. To have war with God is terrible. If we have war with man, it does not mean much. Over against a man, you may defend yourself. But what can a man do over against God? If God is at war with you, you must utterly despair. If we have war with God, not with an idol but with God, it is absolutely hopeless. Many make peace with their own god because they have no peace with God. Idolatry, mental or otherwise, is easily explained. When we have no peace with God, it is natural that we make peace with a god of our own creation.

To have peace with the living God implies that we have peace with all things. We cannot have peace with God unless we have peace with everything. At the same time, we cannot have peace with anything unless we have peace with God.

What a blessing to have this peace!

Upon What It Rests

How is peace with God possible? The apostle says that it rests on the testimony that we are justified by faith. We do not need to be reminded of the meaning of justification by faith. The apostle has emphasized this in the preceding chapter. But we must briefly consider this justification by faith as a basis for peace. The underlying idea of the text is this: God can have peace only with the righteous. The root, the basis, of the text is that the living God can assume an attitude of peace only with the righteous.

That God assumes an attitude of peace only with the righteous and not with the wicked is due to the fact that the peace of God with us is an expression of the peace God has with Himself. And God cannot deny Himself. The peace of God with Himself is such that He seeks Himself as the highest good. When He assumes an attitude of peace towards us, it is necessary that we be righteous. To be righteous, we must be justified. Justification is that we stand in God's judgment. As we stand in God's judgment, He compares us with the perfect criterion of Himself, with the perfect criterion of His will. Comparing us with the perfect criterion of His will, He finds us to be in harmony with this will. Finding us to be in harmony with His will, He declares as the verdict that we are righteous. Therefore, He assumes an attitude of peace and good will towards us.

But the apostle speaks of justification *by faith*. Justification is the only possible basis of peace for the sinner with God. Justification by faith is the opposite of justification by works. In the original, the text states that we are justified "out of" faith. Justification has its source in faith. The apostle is not so much speaking of the objective reality of justification by faith as he is of our being conscious of it. Out of the consciousness that we are justified arises the consciousness that we have peace with God.

The consciousness that we are justified is the ground for the consciousness that we have peace with God. This is true for three reasons. In the first place, justification by faith is a *sure* justification. Its certainty rests on nothing else but the Word of God, revealed in the resurrection of Christ from the dead. Justification by faith means that I lay hold on the resurrection of Christ. The resurrection of Christ has been certified by God. Justification by faith means that in Christ I stood before the tribunal of God and that God declared me righteous in Christ, that is, in His resurrection. My justification is as sure as if the judgment were already past. In fact, it *is* already past. In the day of Christ there will be only a revelation of the judgment that is past.

Because our justification is sure, our peace with God is sure. Our peace with God is rooted in the consciousness that we are justified by faith. If we try to justify ourselves, our peace is baseless. If we try to have peace with God on the basis of our works, we are never sure, because the uncertainty of our works takes away any peace. But the peace of God is sure.

In the second place, justification is *perfect*. There is nothing lacking in it. There can be no lack in justification. We are either justified or condemned. But as far as our consciousness is concerned, justification by faith carries in itself the testimony that it is perfect. Because there is nothing lacking in justification, there is nothing lacking in peace. It is a perfect peace because in this peace there remains no fear. This peace is perfect because our righteousness in Christ is perfect.

Thirdly, the peace of God is *unchangeable* because justification is unchangeable and because the consciousness of this justification by faith is unchangeable. That is, as long as I look only at Christ, there is an undisturbed consciousness in my soul that I am righteous. The moment I look at myself, this consciousness is gone. But as long as I look at Christ, there is an undisturbed consciousness of justification, and therefore of peace.

How It Can Be Attained

Therefore, the text says, "through Christ." Through Him, and in Him, we have peace.

Let us look at reality. Let us look at the reality of the people of God as they exist in the world. Would you be able to say, "Being justified by faith, I have peace with God"? Would you be able to take this Word, as the Word of God, upon your lips with application to yourself? Would you be able to take this confession upon your lips *always*? When we live before the face of God, do we feel that God blesses us in an attitude of peace? I know you will say that there is in your heart and life but a small beginning of this confession.

There are so many things that disturb our peace in this world. It takes so little to disturb our peace. If you stand at a lake at night, and the lake is quiet and smooth, you can see the reflection of the firmament in the water. But a little wind comes up, and although the beauty of the firmament remains, a little ripple comes upon the water, and you see the reflection no more. This is often the case with our peace. When everything is quiet and smooth, there is a reflection of peace with God in our soul. But a little wind comes, and our peace is disturbed. There are so many things that seem to be against our having peace with God. Often it seems as if God is at war with us. Jacob cries out, "All these things are against me" [Gen. 42:36]. When the storm moves over our life and soul, we are inclined to say that God is against us. Our peace disappears. It is easy, when all is quiet, to say that we have peace with God. But let the storms come; then to keep on saying I have peace with God is a different matter.

But there are also reasons from within that cause us to lose our peace. These reasons from within are primary. The chief reason is that we try to justify ourselves by our works, losing

187

sight of the fact that we are justified by faith in Christ. Therefore, we must read and reread this word: "We, being justified by faith, have peace with God; let us then have peace."

There is an eternal attitude of peace in the heart and mind of God towards us. Looking at Him first, and not at things, we have peace with all things. Let us lay aside all self-righteousness, and let us hope in the justification that rests on the Word of God as revealed in the resurrection of Christ. In other words, let us have our eye on the captain of our salvation and seek all our righteousness in Him.

Chapter Twenty-seven

Standing in Grace

Romans 5:2
By whom also we have access by faith into this grace wherein we stand, and rejoice in hope of the glory of God.

The complete thought of the text is to be understood in connection with the first verse of this chapter. "Therefore being justified by faith, we have peace with God through our Lord Jesus Christ: By whom also we have access by faith into this grace wherein we stand."

To obtain the peculiar blessing implied in the text, it is necessary that we not lose sight of the fact that this entire part of the Word of God is cast into a personal, subjective confession. The text does not say that the people of God have access into this grace. The text requires us to assume that attitude in which we ask the question, "How far is this true of us?" It is in the form of a personal, subjective confession that this Word of God comes to us. *We* have peace with God; *we* have access into this grace in which we stand; and *we* rejoice in the hope of the glory of God.

Is this true? This Word loses all of its significance if we look at it merely as a statement that the apostle made. But is this Word of God true of us? The point of the text is not that God's people have access into this grace, which is true; not that God's people stand in this grace, which is true; and not that God's people rejoice in hope, which is true. But the question

189

is, "Do *we* have access into this grace? Do *we* stand in this grace? Do *we* rejoice in hope?"

There are three closely related elements in the text. It speaks of a *present* reality: we stand in this grace. This is the position of the Christian in this world. In close connection with this position of the Christian, the apostle makes us look *backward,* with a view to the question "How did I come to stand in this grace?" I stand in this grace, but the question is how? How did I come to stand here? The apostle answers that we have had access, or more correctly, we have been introduced, we have been led, into this grace by the same Lord by whom we have been justified. Standing in this position, in this grace, the Christian looks *forward* and finds reason to boast, for the apostle says that we stand in this grace and boast in hope of the glory of God. These, therefore, will also be the three elements in our confession in the measure that we stand in this grace.

A Blessed Position

The apostle says that we stand in this grace—*this* grace. *Grace,* in Scripture, is the general word for salvation from the viewpoint of its divine nature. All the work of salvation in Scripture is called grace. There are two reasons for this. In the first place, salvation is called grace because it is the work of a gracious God; we are saved by a gracious God. In the second place, salvation is called grace because grace is the spiritual power by which we are actually saved. To be saved by grace means not only that we are saved by a gracious God, but also that grace becomes the spiritual power by which we are actually saved.

Grace is one. But although grace is one, it is manifold. To the one grace of God belong many aspects. The one grace of God assumes many different forms. There is, for instance, the power by which we are delivered from the power of death and are made partakers of eternal life. This is called grace. There is also the grace by which we are delivered from a state of sin and guilt and are transformed into a state of righteousness. This is called the grace of justification. Besides, we are delivered from the corruption of sin and made holy. This is called the grace of sanctification. These are not completely different graces; instead, they are aspects of the one grace of God. From this point of view, Scripture calls the grace of God manifold. So the text speaks of *this* grace. It calls attention to a certain manifestation of grace. The question as to which particular aspect of grace the text refers must be answered by the context. The answer here is to be found in verse 1. It is the grace of *peace with God*. This is the grace in which we stand.

Peace is agreement among different parties, the result of which is inward harmony and good will. Peace is the opposite of war. This is why there is no peace in the world: in the world is war. Also in the peace conferences of the world there is war. The opposite is peace. Peace is inner harmony and good will.

Verse 1 speaks of peace with God. We stand in the grace of peace with God. This does not refer to mutual agreement between us and God. It does not suggest that we changed our attitude toward God, so that whereas formerly we stood in an attitude of enmity toward Him, now we assume an attitude of peace. Rather, there is peace in God towards us. It is a relation that originated in God, not in us.

To stand in this grace of peace means two things. It means, first, that we have a living part with this peace of God. We stand in this sphere, in this space, that is the platform of God's peace. The fact that there is peace with God has become my personal possession. I am assured that God is filled with peace towards me and that I am the object of His favor and good will. This peace has become a principle in me that controls my whole life. I am perfectly tranquil; I have perfect rest. The knowledge that God is a God of peace to me affords perfect rest to my heart. I have peace with respect to all things. If I have peace with God, I must have peace with all things, for there is nothing apart from God. If I stand in this grace of peace with God, I am perfectly tranquil in the midst of whatever may happen. Implied is that in the measure that I do not have rest, I am not standing in this

191

grace. Since I enjoy peace with God, I also walk from the principle of peace with God. I walk in the way of peace.

Standing in this grace of peace has, second, the idea of immovability. There is no falling away from this peace with God. The reason is that not we, but God, established this peace.

A Divine Introduction

If it is true that we stand in this grace, not in the objective sense but in the spiritual sense, we must ask the question, "How did I get there?" Do we stand in this grace? Is this a spiritual reality in my life? How did I come to this?

The apostle says, "By whom we have access into this grace." The word *access* is not a good translation of the original. The Dutch word is better. The Dutch has the word *toeleiding*. There is a difference between *access* and *toeleiding*. *Toeleiding* means "the act of leading one into something." The text must be read this way: ". . . by whom also we have had introduction to, have been led, into this grace wherein we stand." *Access* means that the door is open and that, the door being open, you can enter if you want. *Access* really leaves you outside, with the possibility of entering. You stand outside, but the door is open, and now it is up to you to enter if you want. This translation contradicts the statement of the apostle that we stand in this grace. The apostle teaches that you are in. The question is, how did you get in?

In the text, the apostle adds something to what he has declared in verse 1. In verse 1 he says that we have access into peace with God through Christ. There we have access. Jesus is the open door. We have access through Him. But in the text, the apostle adds something else. For he says, "by whom we have been introduced, have been led, into this grace wherein we stand." The apostle does not say [in v. 1] that through Christ we have access into peace with God and then repeat it in the next verse, "by whom we have access into this grace." No, the apostle teaches this: "by whom we have been introduced, led, into this grace."

Jesus is not only the open door. He is also the "Introducer," through that door, into peace with God. If we are to enter into peace with God, we must be introduced into it.

By nature we are outside this peace. The reason is that we know that God is our enemy. The natural man knows this. If you ask the natural man, "Do you feel in your heart that there is peace towards you in the mind of God?" he will say, "No." If he is honest and does not make his own god, the natural man will admit that he knows there is no peace in God's mind towards him. The natural man knows that God is his enemy, but he also knows that he is God's enemy. He does not want peace with God. This is the folly of sin: the natural man does not want peace with God. This is our state of mind by nature also. If we examine what is left of this natural state of heart and mind, we will find that we do not want peace with God. By virtue of this knowledge, the natural man flees from God. By virtue of this knowledge, he stands opposed to God.

You can give this man access, but he will never enter. If it is true that we stand in this peace with God, we stand in it as a grace. If we stand in this grace and know it, we will never say, in answer to the question "How did I get in?" that we *accepted* Christ. Rather, we know that Christ led us into this peace by His Spirit and Word.

The text says that Christ did it *by faith*. The meaning is not that He introduced us into this place, but that we come with our faith. If this were the case, salvation would be impossible. If it were so that Christ is the open door and that He will do it all but that we must *will* it, salvation would be impossible. The meaning of the text is not that Christ has led us into this peace with God by a faith with which we came. Rather, the meaning is that Christ led us into this peace by means of the faith that He gave us. We must read verses 1 and 2 this way: "Christ led us, through the faith that He gave, into peace with God."

Let Jesus come, and let Him implant into our hearts saving faith. In this saving faith we know two things. In the first place, we know that there is in God peace towards us. We come to

193

the consciousness that we who were enemies have become friends of God. This is the confession of all God's people.

In the second place, we know that Christ led us into this peace. Many professing Christians make a serious mistake. They say that they come into this peace by their own free will. But if they say this, they never knew what it means to stand in grace. If one does know what it means to stand in grace, his confession will be that he has been led into this grace by Christ.

A Glorious Fruit

The result of standing in this grace will be that we rejoice in hope of the glory of God. Literally, the text says, "We *boast* in hope of the glory of God." The glory of God is His own glory. It is the radiation of His goodness. But the text does not simply refer to the glory of God. Rather, it refers to the glory of God as we will share in it. It is the glory of God as it will be reflected in us in the state of glory. The apostle John says that we shall be like Him. We shall be like Him in the sense that He will reflect all His glory, His covenant glory, in His people. Not an objective glory, but a glory reflected from within, is the glory of God in the text.

The hope of it is that we expect it, that it is certain, and that we long for it. If we stand in this grace, if this is the sphere in which we live, then this hope is in us. If we stand in this grace, we hope for the time when all that is of sin and that is not of the glory of God shall be removed, and we shall perfectly radiate the glory of God.

In this hope we boast. There is in the heart an inner rejoicing, and we think of it often. Rejoicing in this hope, and thinking of it often, we speak of it. We boast of it, not because of anything that is of us but because we have been led into this grace.

Shall we say, "Into this peace I have been introduced"? Then let us realize this final profession and boast in hope of the glory of God. It is God's purpose that His people shall boast of the hope of the glory of God. Standing in this grace, let us so boast.

Chapter Twenty-eight

Glorying in Tribulations

Romans 5:3, 4
And not only so, but we glory in tribulations also: knowing that tribulation worketh patience;
And patience, experience; and experience, hope.

***And** not only so, but we glory in tribulations also*. Thus the apostle introduces this mighty and, from a worldly point of view, strange confession. To what he has already said, he now adds something. In the preceding verse, the apostle has said that we *rejoice* in hope of the glory of God. In the original Greek, *rejoice* is the same word translated *glory* in the text. We stand in the grace of peace with God. Standing in this grace of peace with God, we *glory* in the hope of the glory of God. The glory of God will be reflected in His people, but not only that; there is more to be said. We glory in tribulations also.

This is strong meat in the form in which it comes to us. Probably we can hardly digest it. It would be much easier for us if this word of the apostle were cast into the form of a doctrine, or if it would come to us in the form of an admonition. For example, in James [1:2] we read, "Count it all joy when ye fall into divers temptations."

In the text the apostle places us on such heights that it would seem that we would have to let it go, for we do not easily do what the apostle speaks of in the text. Perhaps in the fullest sense we never do it. Oh, it is easy, when all is sunshine and prosperity and when there is no sorrow, affliction, and trouble, then in the abstract to say, "We glory in tribulations also." But when the enemy comes—when adversity, sorrow, trouble, affliction, and tribulation come—then to say, "We glory in tribulations" is an altogether different matter.

Still it stands to reason that the text must be true in this very form. Although it may be true that in our conscious life we do not experience it, the people of God, in their deepest heart, glory in tribulations. We must look at the text in this light.

If we read this passage [vv. 2–4] carefully, we see that the apostle points out to us a way from hope to hope. He starts by saying, "We glory in hope of the glory of God." He continues, "We glory in tribulations also: knowing that tribulation worketh patience; And patience, experience." Finally, he lands at hope again when he says, "Experience worketh hope." The apostle starts at hope, and he finishes at hope. That which lies between the two is the way of tribulation. In picturing this way, the apostle points to two stages. The first stage is a way that leads to *patience*. The second stage is a way that works *experience*.

What It Is

Tribulation is suffering. Tribulation is a word that frequently occurs in Scripture and signifies "to distress, to oppress, to press upon someone from all sides, so that his place in life gradually becomes narrower." Tribulation is so to press upon someone that he cannot find a place in life anymore. This suffering includes all kinds of affliction, none of which may be minimized, for this suffering is as deep as human life. All that is implied in the suffering of this present time is of such a nature that it oppresses us.

This oppression may be caused by many things. It may be a suffering for Christ's sake directly. Most probably this is the suffering that the apostle has in mind, for in the original we read, "We glory in *the* tribulations." We suffer for Christ's sake because Christ becomes manifest in our lives, and the world hates Him. This direct suffering for Christ's sake is a suffering that, from a human point of view, can be avoided. You can avoid this suffering by covering up Christ in you. You can avoid it by becoming unfaithful. By covering up Christ in your life, you become too abominable for the devil even to trouble you. But the more Christ becomes manifest in your life, the more you will suffer. This suffering may manifest itself in that you are mocked. Or it may manifest itself in losing a job, or gaining one. But it is a suffering for Christ's sake. With a view to this suffering, the apostle says, "We glory in *tribulations.*"

There is no reason, however, why we should limit this word to direct suffering for Christ's sake. There is also an indirect suffering for Christ's sake. In a sense, all suffering is for Christ's sake. When judgments, war, oppression, famine, afflictions, and sickness enter into the world, the child of God suffers too. Always his suffering is a suffering for the kingdom of God's sake. The kingdom of God must come through these things. When there is suffering of the body, when there is war, affliction, trouble, and tribulation, the apostle places this confession on our lips: "We glory in tribulation."

Don't you think that it makes us ashamed to read this word of the apostle?

The apostle has in mind all the suffering of this present time. With a view to all the suffering of this present time, he says that we glory in it.

Do not misunderstand this. The apostle does not say that the relation of this suffering to glorying is merely a matter of circumstances, as though he says here that even though there is suffering, trouble, and affliction, we nevertheless glory in hope. Even this is beautiful to see. We do not see even this so much. We see this more in stories. We do see sometimes that people, in the midst of suffering, glory in hope, but it takes a long time to learn it. However, this is not the meaning. As long as we do not say more than this, we have not reached the height on which the apostle stands.

For the apostle literally says that we glory *because of* these tribulations. There can be no mistake about this interpretation. We read often in Scripture of glorying. The apostle speaks of glorying in God. He speaks of glorying in Christ. He speaks of glorying in the cross. When we read of glorying in God, of glorying in Christ, and of glorying in the cross, the meaning is that we glory *because of* God, *because of* Christ, *because of* the cross. Our glory is in God; it is in Christ; it is in the cross.

So it is in the text. We glory *because of* tribulations. The reason for our glorying, our rejoicing, is the tribulations themselves. We have something good to say about these tribulations. We not only rejoice in hope of the glory of God, but there is also something else for us to glory in. Our glorying is not only in the future. We glory also in the present. We glory, too, in tribulations.

Why We Do It

How is this possible? Is the Christian morbid? Has he a morbid mind so that he rejoices in what grieves others, so that he loves suffering? God forbid! The child of God does not love suffering. He is afraid of it. The Christian feels suffering far more keenly than anyone else, for he has been reborn. The principle of the life he has received is resurrection life. It is a living life. The world cannot receive it. But the Christian has received resurrection life. Because the life he has received is resurrection life, the Christian dreads suffering. Resurrection life wants glory. The result is that the Christian feels suffering more keenly. No, the Christian does not want suffering.

Does the Christian then set his face like a flint and assume the attitude of one who does not care? Does he challenge suffering? Does he harden himself to it? God forbid! This is sinful. God does not want His child to harden himself against suffering. God wants him to *feel* it. The Christian is no Stoic.

Is he then a Christian Scientist? Does he try to convince himself that suffering is just imaginary? God forbid! The apostle tells us that these tribulations are so real that they work something. They have an effect.

The meaning, then, is not that the Christian loves suffering for suffering's sake, not that the Christian is indifferent to suffering, and not that he hardens himself to it or calls it imaginary. The Christian loves suffering for the sake of its fruits. Suffering bears fruit. This fruit outweighs the tribulations by far. This fruit is heavenly; the tribulations are earthly. The fruit is eternal; the tribulations are temporal.

This fruit is only for the spiritually minded. Tribulation works patience for those who are spiritually minded. If you would rather have earthly treasures and pleasures than patience, you do not understand the apostle. If you would rather have earthly treasures than patience, you do not glory in tribulation. But for the Christian who is spiritually minded, tribulation worketh patience. Tribulation is to him like a bitter medicine, bad to the taste but very necessary to health. It is an operation that is necessary for spiritual and heavenly health.

The spiritual health worked by tribulation is *patience*. There is a certain natural patience. We see it among the people of the world. But we must not confuse this natural patience with the patience of the people of God. The man of the world can sometimes be patient in suffering; there are certain natures in the world that can stand much suffering. But we must not confuse this natural patience with spiritual patience.

Spiritual patience is different. Spiritual patience is a grace. It is that grace by the power of which the soul becomes willing with the will of God to walk in the way of suffering, knowing that it all must work for his good. A spiritually patient person is one who is strong enough to say, "No matter what the way may be, Thy will is my will, and with pleasure I walk in it." This is patience.

Patience is worked by tribulations, but it is not so that tribulation works grace. Tribulation does not work patience if there is not a principle of this patience in the heart. The text does not speak of the work of tribulation as such. Tribulation also works rebellion. But the apostle is speaking of the experience of the Christian. The Christian learns patience through tribulation. He *learns* patience. When he first comes into tribulation, he does not feel patient, but as he continues on that way of tribulation, he gradually learns to be patient. "Tribulation *worketh* patience." When God leads His people into tribulation, He chastens them with one hand while strengthening them with the other. In this way tribulation worketh patience.

And patience worketh *experience*. A better translation, if there were such a word, would be *triedness*. The Dutch has the word *bevinding*, which means "triedness, to be tried." The apostle means that you have been through the fire. Now you have a *tried* nature. You were a child of God before, but you had never been tried. Now you have been put to the test. You had never been though the fire of tribulation. But God brought you into tribulation. In this tribulation you were patient. In this patience you were tried. You were found to be genuine. It is an unspeakable joy to be tried by the fire of tribulation and to come out victorious. The Christian has a *tried* character.

Experience, or *triedness,* worketh hope. The apostle began with hope, and he closes with hope: hope, tribulation, patience, experience, hope. There are different stages of hope. We go through tribulations, patience, and experience in order to come to the highest stage of hope.

The Christian's hope is a looking forward, a certainty, and a longing. It is a looking forward: the Christian looks for his hope in the future. It is certainty: the Christian is certain that he will reach it. It is a longing: the Christian reaches out for it.

The *triedness* of the Christian strengthens him in the assurance that he will certainly reach his hope. In the midst of tribulation, the principle of the Christian's life cries out for the hope of the glory of God, and he is strengthened by tribulation. It is not good to have prosperity. You cannot say of prosperity that it worketh patience. The Christian's hope is strengthened by tribulation.

∾ Glorying in Tribulations

What Its Ground Is

Upon what ground does this glorying Christian stand? Where must one stand in order to say, "I glory in tribulation"? The apostle says that we know it: we are assured that tribulation worketh patience; and patience, experience; and experience, hope. Because we know it, we glory in tribulation.

Here you have a ladder. It reaches up to heaven. At the top you have the highest stage of hope. Below that highest stage of hope, you have experience, then patience, then tribulation, then peace with God, then justification by faith in Christ Jesus, crucified and risen as our righteousness. Therefore, the ground for the Christian's glorying is the death and resurrection of Jesus. Being justified by faith, we have peace with God, and we glory both in hope of the glory of God, and in tribulation. Our glorying in tribulation is rooted in our justification by faith. Say it, and you will glory. Stand on your own righteousness, and you cannot follow the apostle in this confession. But stand in the grace of the peace with God, and you will have peace with all things—with tribulations also.

Chapter Twenty-nine

The Proof of a Marvelous Love

Romans 5:6-8
For when we were yet without strength, in due time Christ died for the ungodly.
For scarcely for a righteous man will one die: yet peradventure for a good man some would even dare to die.
But God commendeth his love toward us, in that, while we were yet sinners, Christ died for us.

We must bear in mind that the apostle is still pursuing the same subject he has mentioned in verse 5. This subject is that the hope of the Christian maketh not ashamed because the love of God has been shed abroad in his heart. The hope of the believer is a marvelous hope. It is not anything common. It is not anything easy to be believed or to be assured of. The object of this hope is nothing short of the glory of God. The Christian looks forward to the time when God will make him partaker of His own glory. He will be righteous with God's own righteousness and holy with God's own holiness. This is the object of the Christian's hope.

The apostle has written that hope does not make ashamed and that the Christian is positively assured that hope does not make ashamed. The Christian is assured that, with a view to this present life, that hope for which he denies himself, for which he suffers and for which he is ready to die, maketh not ashamed. He is assured that hope maketh not ashamed, so that at the end he will never say that hope is not worth all that suffering. Of this, the Christian bears the testimony in his heart.

The ground of this assurance, that hope maketh not ashamed, is that the love of God has been shed abroad in his heart. The apostle is speaking of the love of God to us. He is not speaking of our love to God. Our love to God can never be the basis of our assurance, in the first place, because it is not the basis and is not intended to be the basis. In the second place, our love cannot be the basis, because our love is weak and changeable. Rather, God spread abroad His love towards us in our hearts, so that we know God loves us and so that we act upon the assurance that God loves us. The basis of all religious activity is the assurance that God loves me. This love of God has been shed abroad in our hearts. This love of God is the basis for the assurance that hope maketh not ashamed. How marvelous, then, is hope!

But the love of God is not less marvelous. To this marvelous love the apostle now calls our attention. He does not call our attention to the love of God directly, but he calls our attention to the marvelousness of this love. This is the point in the text. "For when we were yet without strength, in due time Christ died for the ungodly ... But God commendeth his love toward us, in that while we were yet sinners, Christ died for us." Verse 7 is an added illustration of this love of God.

The Proof

The historic proof of the love of God is the cross. If you take the cross away, if you lift the cross out of the history of the world, there is no proof of the love of God. There is no proof anywhere in this world if you take the cross away. This is expressed by the apostle when he says that Christ died for us and that He died in due time. The meaning is that Christ died on behalf of us. He died for our benefit. Negatively, He died in order that we should not die. Positively, He died in order that we might have life—eternal life.

Although this is true, the underlying thought of the text is that Christ died as our substitute. The thought of the text is that Christ died on behalf of us by taking our death upon Himself.

How is it possible that one can die for another? Or, if this is possible, how is it possible that one can die for many? Or, if it is possible that one can die for many, how is it possible that whereas the many must suffer eternal death, He in a few moments can suffer that eternal punishment and obtain life for the many?

As to the first question, we may answer that Christ is not *another*. Christ is not some third party who stepped in between God and the sinner in order to save the sinner. This is impossible. It is also contrary to the meaning of the text. Notice, "God commendeth his love towards us, in that, while we were yet sinners, Christ died for us." In other words, Christ is not *another*, because He Himself is God. Also, He is not *another*, because in the judicial sense He identified with His people; He is so identified with His people that He represents them all. Christ is not *another*. Christ *is* His church.

Regarding the second question, namely, how it is possible that Christ could so represent His people, how He could so die, that in a few moments He could free His own from eternal death and merit for them eternal life, the answer of Scripture is, "God was in Christ, reconciling the world unto himself" (II Cor. 5:19). The text puts it this way: "God commendeth his love toward us, in that, while we were yet sinners, Christ died for us." God was in Christ. This is why His death has eternal value. It was God Himself who tasted death. That death has eternal value because it is the Son of God who died.

This also answers the question why His death could be atoning. The answer is that Christ entered into that death as an act on His own part. His death was not a mere suffering. Christ willed to die. That act of the cross was the counterpart of the sinful act of Adam in paradise. The act of Christ on the cross was an active entering into death for God's sake. On the cross, Christ brought the act of perfect obedience as the counterpart of the act of sin.

He did that *in due time,* the text says. He did that at the proper moment. We read of this frequently in Scripture. The Lord speaks often of "my hour." The meaning is that His death could not be a year sooner or later than that particular moment when Christ gave His life on the cross. It was not merely necessary that Christ die, but if His death had been postponed one hour, it would have been impossible.

If you ask why, the answer of Scripture is that it was the hour of the execution of judgment. "Now is the judgment of this world" [John 12:31], Christ says. The idea of Scripture is that nineteen hundred years ago, in that hour, God sent His judgment into the world, and it could not be postponed. It was the hour of judgment. At the same time, while He judged the world, He came Himself to receive the outpouring of that wrath and to shelter His people. The two are coincidental. Nineteen hundred years ago was the time of judgment. And nineteen hundred years ago God received that judgment in the Head of His people.

This is the proof of the love of God. "God commendeth his love toward us, in that, while we were yet sinners, Christ died for us." God showed, God recommended, His love to us. You understand, then, that the death of Christ cannot be the cause of the love of God. Christ is no third party. It is not that God is on one side, and His people are on the other side, and that Christ steps between the two and reconciles God to us and us to God. In this case, the love of God would be the fruit of the work of Christ. It is often presented this way. But this is not true. Christ did not reconcile God to us. This is a heathen notion. It is not the scriptural notion. The scriptural idea is that the cross is the outflow of the love of God. This lies at the bottom of the text.

The Circumstances under Which This Love Is Given

The text emphasizes that this love of God is marvelous. It does so by pointing to the circumstances under which this love is manifested. It says that Christ died for us when we were yet without strength—when we were yet weak—and while we were yet sinners. To show what this means, the apostle refers to a possible conception when he says, "Scarcely for a righteous man will one die: yet peradventure for a good man some would even dare to die" [v. 7]. In the original we read, "for the good." The righteous and the good must be taken in the strict sense. *For the good* does not mean "for a good cause." The apostle refers to a man. The objection has been raised that there is no such man. This is true, but it is not the point. The apostle means, "It can be conceived that for a good man one would die." That is, supposing that there is such a man, supposing that there are two such righteous and good men, it can be conceived that the one righteous man would die for the other righteous man. This can be conceived because there is fellowship of love between the two. The one loves the other because of his righteousness. There is nothing marvelous about this. Scripture also teaches us that we must be willing to die for each other. We do not find this happening much; still, it is conceivable.

But God commendeth His love toward us *while we were yet sinners*. This is something else. The apostle expresses that this is marvelous in a threefold way. First, he says, we were *weak*. The word that the apostle uses here means "to be morally impeded, without strength to do good." Second, the apostle emphasizes the marvelousness of God's love by saying that Christ died for the *ungodly*. The ungodly are those in whom there is no fear of God. They are those who shook their head and said *No* to God. While we were shaking our head and saying *No* to God, Christ died for us. Third, the apostle says that Christ died for us while we were yet *sinners*, that is, when we refused to glorify God and were completely missing the mark.

Notice once more the phrase *in due time*. When we stood there as weak, ungodly sinners, this *due time* came. And what did God do? Did He hesitate? When the due time came, God did not hesitate a moment. This is the marvel of the love of God.

That Which It Proves

We may emphasize once more that Christ died for those whom God loved. This is the sole basis of the text. If you deny election, you must leave this text alone. The underlying thought of the text is that Christ died for those whom God loved. The apostle emphasizes also that the love of God is unchangeable and will surely save His people to the very end. Christ died for the ungodly whom God loved and whom He will surely bring to glory. This is the basis for our assurance, for this love has been shed abroad in our hearts. This same love that He proved in the cross, He sheds abroad in our hearts.

What is characteristic of this love? First, this love in no way has its source in the ungodly. It is sovereign. Its source is only in God. You do not need anything on your part to support this love of God. Second, this love of God is immovably strong. Nothing can change it. To the contrary, this love changes all. Though your sins be as scarlet, they do not affect this love. Your sins cannot change it. This love, God has shown. Nineteen hundred years ago God showed this love, which is superior to all the sins of His people. Third, this love of God, so manifested, has been attested to be a love that stops at nothing to glorify its object. It stops at nothing to save His people. This has been historically attested. This love of God has been spread abroad in our hearts [v. 5].

This love, spread abroad in our hearts, is never an Arminian love. For a time one may profess the Arminian doctrine, but if you ask him how he experiences the love of God in his heart, he will let go of his Arminianism. Otherwise, he is no Christian. No one will say, "God loved me because I came halfway."

No one will say, "God loved me because I accepted Him." Why not? Because this is not the love of God. Because God loved us while we were yet sinners. The love of God is experienced as sovereign. It is always first. This is the way we experience it. If we analyze the love of God spread abroad in our hearts, we find that it is the love of God, that it is sovereign, and that it is the love that saves us.

Is not the conclusion plain? Hope maketh not ashamed, because the love of God is shed abroad in our hearts. And God commendeth this love to us. Verse 8 does not say that God *commended* His love to us, but *commendeth* [commends], meaning He continues to commend His love to us. If this is so, we have the testimony in our heart that hope maketh not ashamed. Hope maketh not ashamed, because Christ died for us when we were yet weak, when we were yet sinners. And God commendeth His love to us and has shed this love abroad in our hearts.

Chapter Thirty

Saved by His Life

Romans 5:10
For if, when we were enemies, we were reconciled to God by the death of his Son, much more, being reconciled, we shall be saved by his life.

The apostle writes these words as a further elucidation of the theme of which he is still thinking. This theme is, "Hope maketh not ashamed; because the love of God is shed abroad in our hearts" [Rom. 5:5]. The love of God is the guarantee that the object of our hope will surely be attained and that in glory it will not disappoint us. This love of God is spread abroad in our hearts; that is, it has become a matter of our experience, so that we taste it. The assurance that God loves us is the basis of the assurance that hope maketh not ashamed. The reason is that the love of God is sovereign and unfathomably great. God loved us while we were yet sinners. The love of God, therefore, is not supported by anything that is in us. It is not changed by our sin. It has its motive only in God. The love of God is great because while we were yet sinners, God manifested it in the fact that Christ died for us. It is a love that stops at nothing. Therefore, it is the guarantee that hope maketh not ashamed.

Of this the apostle is still speaking. He is still showing and emphasizing that the love of God must be the guarantee of our hope. Of this he speaks in verse 9. There the apostle says, "Much more then, being now justified by his blood, we shall be saved from wrath through him." In the text he gives another reason why verse 9 is true. The reason is, "For if, when we were enemies, we were reconciled to God by the death of his Son, much more, being reconciled, we shall be saved by His life."

Notice the contrast of the two parts of the verse. We were enemies; we are reconciled. When we were enemies, God reconciled us; now that we are reconciled, we shall be saved. When we were enemies, we were reconciled by the death of His Son; much more, being reconciled, we shall be saved by His life. We shall much more be saved than we are reconciled. The sense is not that our salvation will be greater than our reconciliation. Salvation is not greater than reconciliation. Nor is the meaning that our salvation is more sure than our reconciliation. But the apostle teaches that for our faith it is easier to understand, it is more reasonable to say, that we shall be saved, being reconciled, than it is to say that we were reconciled when we were enemies. But our reconciliation is a fact. Is it, then, not much easier to understand, is it not much more reasonable to say, that being reconciled, we shall be saved by His life? Shall we not say, if such is the love of God, it is a guarantee that hope maketh not ashamed?

The Meaning

It is evident that the apostle is speaking of salvation in the final sense, in which it will be realized in the day of Christ. In this sense, salvation, negatively, is to be saved out of death. It is to be snatched out of death, that is, out of physical death. We are in death. We are not yet out of death. As we are here, we are sitting in death. We are not really in life in this present world. We are in death. Out of that death we shall be saved. "Shall be saved," in the text, means that we shall be snatched out of this present, physical death. It also means that we shall be saved from wrath. There is still wrath coming. The final wrath is still to be poured out on this world of which we are a part. When the text says, "We shall be saved," the meaning is that we shall be snatched out of this present death and that we shall be saved from the wrath that is still to come upon the world. We shall not be touched by it.

Positively, by the word *salvation* the apostle means the glory of which he has been speaking. We shall be saved out of death into life, that is, the life of the resurrection. And we shall be clothed with the glory that is the object of our hope, namely, the glory of God.

Of this glory the apostle is speaking. This is evident from the future tense. We shall be saved. We are also saved now. We are saved from sin, guilt, and corruption and are made partakers of the righteousness of Christ. But the apostle is speaking here of future salvation. This is evident also from the context. The apostle is speaking of our hope. This hope receives a further proof. Being enemies, we were reconciled by the death of God's Son; being reconciled, we shall be saved by His life.

We more readily believe this than we believe we are reconciled. It is easier to believe that we are saved, when reconciled, than it is to believe that we were reconciled when we were enemies. We would say that reconciliation is almost unbelievable. It is contrary to all human experience to say, "When we were enemies, we were reconciled." In comparison, it is easier to believe that we shall be saved, when reconciled, than to believe that we were reconciled when enemies.

But even salvation is not easy to believe. It is not so easy to say, "We shall be saved by His life." This is contrary to all that we see. The children of God sink away in death, as do others. Seemingly, they also are swallowed up by it. The pangs of death also torture their frame. They cannot escape it. That they will be saved is not a thing that is seen. Therefore, it is a tremendous thing to say, "We shall be saved."

By his life, the apostle says. *His life* here refers to the life of Christ. As is evident from the contrast, we are saved by the life of His human nature. His death accomplished our reconciliation, and it was the death of His human nature. We are saved by His life, which is the life of His human nature.

211

We are saved by the *resurrection life* of Jesus. To this the apostle refers when he says, "We shall be saved by his life."

In the original there is a sharp distinction made that has been lost somewhat in our translation, which uses the word *by* in both parts of the comparison: "*by* the death of his Son" and "*by* his life." But according to the original, the text should be translated this way: "We were reconciled *through* the death of His Son, and we are saved *in* His life." We were not reconciled *in* but *through* the death of Jesus. Christ died just once, and by His one death reconciliation was accomplished. Reconciliation is an accomplished fact. Christ has finished reconciling us.

But in this sense we cannot say that we are saved *through* His life. Christ lives. Christ is not done with His life. And we shall never be finished living *in* or *by* the life of Christ. Our living *in* the life of Christ will never be an accomplished fact. We will always live *in* the life of Christ.

Two truths about life are taught. First, as risen, Christ Himself lives. Second, He receives the power to impart His life to us. He receives the power to make us live. This is His power as Mediator. If my child is dead, I still live, but my child cannot live by my life. I cannot impart my life to that child. I receive life only for myself and cannot impart it to anyone else. But this is not so with the Mediator. The Mediator not only receives life, but He also receives the power to impart life to His brethren. They are dead, but the risen Lord receives power to impart His life to them. For this reason they live *in*, and therefore *by*, Christ. The Christian has his life only in connection with the life of Christ.

By virtue of the fact that the life of Christ is poured out in the brethren, they shall be saved by the power of this life. The life of Christ can never die. This is the sense of the last part of the text. We are saved out of death because Christ lives in us. And because the life of Christ is in us, we live right through death: "He that believeth in me, though he were dead, yet shall he live" [John 11:25]. We live right through death. Death will never swallow us up. We pass right through physical death. In addition, when the wrath of God shall presently destroy all, there will be those who are saved by the life of Christ. That wrath of God shall not touch them. We are saved by His life.

The Ground

The apostle suggests that this is so because of the fact, on the ground of the fact, that we are reconciled. If we are not reconciled, we cannot be saved.

Reconciliation presupposes a certain relationship. Only they who stand in a certain relation can be reconciled to one another. It may be the relation of man and wife, of parent and child, of master and servant, of teacher and pupil, or of friend and friend. But reconciliation presupposes a certain relationship. In this case, it is the covenant relationship. The covenant relation is the original relation of God to man. It is a relation of friendship. This lies at the basis of the idea of reconciliation. Reconciliation presupposes that this relation has been disturbed; otherwise, reconciliation would not be necessary. There is something in the way that prevents this covenant relation from functioning. Reconciliation also presupposes that the relation is restored by the removal of that which prevents this relation from functioning. In this case, it is sin.

For this reason, it is impossible to speak of a reconciliation of God to us. It is often put this way. Those who put it this way understand reconciliation in the sense of appeasing. But this is impossible. For one thing, this is impossible because the cause of the separation—our sin—lies with *us*. For another thing, if God is to be reconciled, a third party is required. What the text emphasizes is that God did the reconciling, but if God is *to be* reconciled, how can reconciliation go out from Him? Nor is this scriptural. God is not reconciled. We are reconciled to God. That is, we are placed in such a relation to Him that we can again be the objects of His covenant friendship. This God did for us.

We were reconciled by the death of His Son. The death of

His Son is actually the death of God in the human nature. When Scripture speaks of the death of His Son, it teaches that God, through the Son in the human nature, died our death. The Son of God cannot die, but for this purpose He assumed our nature. To express it very forcibly, God became man in order to be able to die. This is the covenant. God took upon Himself our nature in order to taste all the suffering of our death. God did this in the Son.

The Son's death is reconciliation because it is the removal of all that stood in the way on the side of His people, namely, their sin. It is reconciliation because it is the removal of that which hinders God's friendship from reaching us. It is the removal of what stood between the love of God and us, preventing it from reaching us. Because the death of Christ was a voluntary act of His will, it was satisfaction. Christ died by willing to die for God's sake. And because it was the death of the Son, it was able to take away, in a moment, the sin and death of His people.

This death of the Son is the ground for the statement *We shall be saved by His life*. We cannot live except through the death of the Son. We cannot say that we shall be saved if we cannot say that we were reconciled. The reason lies in God and in our sin. If we are not the object of God's favor, we are the objects of His wrath. But we cannot be the objects of His favor while we are sinners. When we are justified, however, we are the proper objects of His favor. Salvation is based on reconciliation.

The Certainty

The apostle says that it is sure: *we shall be saved*. That it is sure is emphasized when the apostle says we *were* enemies. When we were enemies, we were reconciled. It has been asked what that phrase *when we were enemies* means. It may mean when we were the objects of God's enmity. In this passive meaning, God hated us. But the phrase may also have an active meaning. Then it means that we were the enemies of God in the sense that we hated Him.

What is the meaning in the text? It is usually explained that when God was our enemy, we were reconciled by the death of His Son. I don't believe that this is possible, for then we would have to read the text this way: "When we were yet the objects of God's hatred, we were reconciled by the death of His Son." *If* this were true, *if* it might be said that God hates us, *if* there might ever be a moment in which God becomes our enemy—at that moment reconciliation would become impossible. But God is never our enemy. Hatred and love do not exist in God at the same time and with a view to the same objects. Love and wrath may exist together, but not love and hatred—not with a view to the same objects. This is impossible. Especially is this impossible in the text. Hence, the statement there does not mean that we were reconciled when *God* was our enemy. Instead, the meaning is that we were reconciled when *we* were the enemies of God. God tells us that He loved His enemies. He loved them to the extent that He died for them. When we were enemies, we creatures rising up in rebellion against the living God, He died for us. This is the Scripture. This is reconciliation. If the love of God had not been so great, we never would have been saved.

Now do you understand the *much more* of the text? Is it possible, do you believe, that you were reconciled by the death of His Son? Is this true? Do you believe that when you were an enemy, standing before God in sin, God loved you sufficiently to enter into death for you? Is this a matter of your faith? *Much more,* then, shall we be saved by His life! For salvation is nothing compared to reconciliation. Reconciliation is the ground of salvation. Reconciliation is *much more,* because it required the death of God.

Therefore, having been reconciled, we glory in hope. Having been reconciled by the death of His Son, we say that we shall certainly be saved. Though all things seem to testify against it, we shall yet say, "We shall be saved by His life." In the midst of the suffering of this present time, when all things seem to testify that we shall not be saved, we say, "We shall be saved." When we sink away into death, we shall say, "We shall be saved." Nothing can separate us from the love of God that is in Christ Jesus our Lord. Hope maketh not ashamed.

Chapter Thirty-one

All Have Sinned

Romans 5:12-14
Wherefore, as by one man sin entered into the world, and death by sin; and so death passed upon all men, for that all have sinned:
(For until the law sin was in the world: but sin is not imputed when there is no law.
Nevertheless death reigned from Adam to Moses, even over them that had not sinned after the similitude of Adam's transgression, who is the figure of him that was to come.

The rest of this fifth chapter of the epistle to the Romans, from verse 12 to the end, is a parallel between Adam and Christ, between the first and the second Adam. This parallel is drawn by the apostle for the sake of confirming, establishing, and making plain the truth that he has been developing, the truth, namely, that our righteousness is in Christ by faith, without the works of the law. This is the theme of all that precedes.

Strictly speaking, the development of this theme the apostle finishes in verse 11. But he adds this parallel between Adam and Christ to forestall a possible objection that might arise in the minds of some. The objection is that it is an unheard of thing that we should be righteous because of the righteousness of another, without any works on our own part. By drawing this parallel, the apostle shows that there is nothing strange in this, because all our life is constituted just this way. As all are in Adam, so all are in Christ. As Adam is the head and all are represented in him as a legal body, so the elect are in Christ because they are a legal body, represented by Him.

The apostle does not really finish his sentence in the first verse of the text. He says, "Wherefore, as by one man sin entered into the world, and death by sin; and so death passed upon all men, for that all have sinned." We would expect that he would finish by saying, "so righteousness and life came upon all by one man." But the apostle does not do this. The reason is that as he writes, thoughts begin to accumulate in his mind, and he explains what he has just written. Yet at the end of verse 14, the apostle, in a sense, finishes the sentence when he says, referring to Adam, "who is the figure of him that was to come." The complete sentence would then read, "Wherefore, as by one man sin entered into the world, and death by sin; and so death passed upon all men, for that all have sinned: [so that one man] is the figure of him that was to come."

In this one respect Adam was a figure of Him who was to come. In this one particular relation, that is, in his relation to those who are in him, Adam was a figure of Christ. Therefore, the theme of the text is expressed in these words from verse 12: *all have sinned*.

An Amazing Fact

The amazing fact is expressed in the words *death reigns, and reigns universally* [v. 14]. This is an indisputable fact. And now the apostle calls attention to it as a proof that all have sinned. Death is an indisputable fact. That death reigns over all cannot be denied. Nor can it be disputed that death is the punishment of sin. Therefore, somehow it must be admitted that all have sinned.

When the apostle speaks of death in this connection, he refers not merely to physical death, to death of the body, but to death without limitation. He refers to all that is the result of God withholding His grace and favor from man. To this death certainly belongs physical death. To it belongs also all the suffering, sorrow, pain, agony, and corruption that is connected with physical death. To this death belongs not only physical corruption but all the spiritual corruption as well. As physical death is corruption, so spiritual death is corruption. This is the reign of death over our soul, our spirit, our heart. Finally, to this death belongs the swallowing up of a man's being in outer darkness.

The apostle says that death reigns. He makes mention of the period from Adam to Moses because this is the most amazing part of the reign of death, as we shall see presently. But the apostle means that death reigns over all. Death reigns. Death has power over us, so that we are subject to it and so that we cannot escape its influence, its sway. In addition, death is the rightful lord over us. Death is not a matter of fatalism. It is not merely a law of existence. In this case we would have to accept the theory of the world that it is essential to life to die. Then we would have to accept death as an inevitable fact. This is not the explanation. Death is punishment. Death has received the right to rule over us. The one who gave death the right to rule is God.

Death reigns. It reigns over all life. This cannot be disputed. All attempts of man to combat and overcome this ruling power of death are futile and hopeless.

For this reign of death as punishment, you do not find sufficient ground and explanation in the actual transgressions of man. If you ask how you explain the universal reign of death, the Pelagian answers, "Death reigns because every man has individually sinned." Man, so the Pelagian teaches, comes into the world free from the corruption of death, but he sins. Everybody sins, individually and actually. Because everybody sins, everybody dies.

This explanation does not fit the facts, however. We do not die because of our own individual transgressions. You and I are not under the reign of death because of our own individual, actual sins. We were under the power of death before we sinned. To show that this is true, the apostle points to the period from Adam to Moses. If you tell me that everyone is under the power of death because of his own individual transgression of the law, I point you to the fact that death reigned before the law. I admit, the apostle says, that where there is no law, sin is not imputed. Where there is no law, there is no transgression of the law and, therefore, no imputation of sin. If there is no law, sin is a mistake, an error, and therefore cannot be imputed. This principle must certainly be maintained. In this connection the apostle calls attention to that period when there was no law, when there was no code of outward precepts, when the law had not yet been revealed. Death reigned when there was no law. Death reigned before the law had been revealed.

There is still another objection that might be raised. You ask, "Did not man have the work of the law written in his heart, even apart from the law of Moses?" Before the law of Moses, man had no need of an outward code, of an outward set of precepts. He had the work of the law written in his heart. And man knew that he transgressed that law. Paul has taught this [Rom. 2]. Man, therefore, is punished because of that transgression of the law, the work of which he has in his heart.

Against this objection, the apostle makes another statement. He says, "Death reigned even over them who had not sinned after the similitude of Adam's transgression." That is, death reigned over them who had not transgressed as did Adam. Throughout the ages there are those who have not sinned after the similitude of Adam's transgression. Adam transgressed the commandment of God wantonly, consciously, willingly. But there are always those who have not sinned like Adam. And the apostle teaches that long before man sins wantonly, willingly, and consciously, death reigns over him after the similitude of Adam's transgression. When a babe comes into the world, death reigns over it. Does death wait until that babe sins after the similitude of Adam's transgression? You know better. When a babe is born, death is waiting for that babe, and it rules over that babe from the very beginning of its entrance into the world. Death takes hold of us and corrupts our bodies and our souls from the beginning. That this is true of physical death is evident. But it is just as evident that this is true of spiritual death. Why is a child subject to death? Did it sin after the likeness of Adam? Of course not. Therefore, the explanation is this: death reigns over all.

An Only Solution

How is death's reign over all to be explained? Death is the punishment of sin. Therefore, if death rules over all, all must have sinned. What the apostle means when he says, "All have sinned," he expresses when he says, "as by one man sin entered into the world." The gate was opened by one man. When that one man opened the gate, sin entered into the world. And when sin entered into the world, death slipped in with it as the inevitable companion of sin. With sin, death entered into the world as the inevitable infliction of punishment.

Death entered by sin. And so death passed upon all men by that one man, because all have sinned. When? When did all sin? When that one man sinned. When the apostle says, "Death passed upon all men, for that all have sinned," he does not mean that all repeat the sin of Adam. He means that in that one man, all have sinned.

How? How did all men sin in that one man? Does the apostle mean that all have sinned because all are in Adam? This cannot be. Our nature is in Adam, but not our person. And sin is imputed to the person. But the explanation is that the human race is not a mass of individuals, but a corporation. Adam was the legal head of this corporation. As our representative, Adam put out a hand to the forbidden tree. As our representative, he ate of that tree. In this sense all have sinned, not after their birth, but before their birth. All have sinned in that one man who was the legal, covenant head of all.

A Significant Figure

In this respect, Adam is the *figure* of Him who was to come. In the original, the apostle uses the word *type:* "who is the *type* of him that was to come." When the apostle says that Adam was a type—not of Christ, but *of him who was to come*—he refers not only to the coming of Christ in the flesh, but to His entire coming. That he uses this expression is because he looks at Adam as God created him, as a figure of Him who was to come. When God created Adam, He had Christ in mind. God created Adam in such a way that He who was to come *could* come. In others words, if God had created the human race as a mass of individuals, all the gospel of righteousness in Christ would be forever impossible. When God created Adam, He had in mind Him who was to come; therefore, we have this parallel between Christ and Adam. The latter is a figure of the former. Adam was the head of the *entire human race;* Christ is the head of the *elect human race.*

Because of this relation, we have a typical effect: that as in Adam all sin, so in Christ all obey. Even as we are guilty in Adam before we ever committed any actual sin, so we are righteous in Christ before we ever commit one act of righteousness. We are damned before we actually sin. The works of sin proceed from our damnation. We are also justified before we are righteous. The works of righteousness proceed from our justification. As we die before we sin, so we live before we do any works of righteousness. Life is first; works follow.

The gospel of Paul still stands; wherefore, we are justified without works through faith in Jesus Christ. Christ is the only reason why we are righteous.

The practical, spiritual result of our appropriating this Word of God is a broken heart and a contrite spirit. This must become our confession. We must appropriate the sin of Adam. If we do not, we can never understand that God killed all. Our confession must be this, that even if I did not commit one, personal, actual sin, yet I am worthy of death and damnation.

Death reigns. It reigns justly. Therefore, we must cease speaking of innocent children.

The positive result of appropriating this Word is that we realize that our righteousness has nothing to do with our works. Thus, we are confident that our righteousness is complete, is perfect, in Him who is our atonement and all our righteousness. And we have peace with God.

Chapter Thirty-two

The Abounding Gift

Romans 5:15
But not as the offence, so also is the free gift. For if through the offence of one many be dead, much more the grace of God, and the gift by grace, which is by one man, Jesus Christ, hath abounded unto many.

In these words we have a comparison. In the last part of the preceding verse, the apostle had stated that Adam was the figure of Him who was to come. Adam was a figure of Christ. He was intended to be such. He actually appeared as such. There is, therefore, as always, a certain similarity between the type and the antitype. There is a likeness between Adam and Christ. This thought the apostle stated in verse 14. As is always the case, however, the figure is not entirely like that of which it is a figure. Adam was not wholly like Christ, or else he could not be a figure. The apostle draws a comparison between Adam and Christ from the viewpoint of this dissimilarity. He shows in what Adam was unlike Christ. As far as the text is concerned, there is one point of dissimilarity.

What is compared is the offense and the gift of grace. The offense is the fall into sin, the first offense of Adam. The text speaks of that. The gift of grace is all the work of Christ. The offense and the gift are put in the balance. They are compared from the viewpoint of what each effects. Both abound. They overflow to the many. The many, in the one case, are all men. By the offense of Adam, all men are dead because all were in him. As the offense of the one overflows to the many, so the gift by grace, which is by one man, overflows to the many, that is, to all who are in Him. The one overflows unto evil. The other overflows unto grace. The comparison elicits several questions. Which of the two is the greater in its abundance? Or are they both alike? Does the offense of Adam overflow to the many unto evil in the same measure that the gift overflows to the many unto grace?

The apostle answers that the gift overflows in a greater measure than the offense. In other words, there is much more good, much more life, flowing out of the gift than there is evil, or death, flowing out of the offense. Thus, we have an answer to the question, "Is it worthwhile to die?" Or is it vain to die? Is it worthwhile to die, or would it have been preferable if the offense had never come? Would it have been better if the offense and all that flows from it had never come? Or is that which flows out of Christ so rich that it is worthwhile to die? The answer of the apostle is that it is worthwhile.

We can put it in a theological way and ask, "Is God justified in choosing this way of sin and death instead of leaving us in paradise?" The apostle says that He is, because the offense is not like the free gift: "For if through the offence of one many be dead, much more the grace of God, and the gift by grace, which is by one man, Jesus Christ, hath abounded unto many."

The Gift That Abounds

It is the gift of grace that abounds. The text distinguishes between the gift and the grace. Grace is the source; the gift is the result. The grace of God is the source of all that the Christian receives.

God is gracious. This is one of the most fundamental teachings of Scripture. God is this in Himself, apart from any relation to His creature. Grace is one of God's virtues. It is one of the virtues of God's being. It is a virtue in God. God does not *become* gracious. He *is* gracious. Even if there were no people to be the object of that grace, God would still be gracious. When we say that God is gracious in this sense, the meaning is that God, in His divine essence, is beautiful. God is pleasant. And God knows Himself as a pleasant God. God beholds Himself as pleasant. God is a living God. He sees Himself in all the beauty of His divine grace in His Son. In the Son, who is the express image of His being, God beholds His own beauty. And He loves His beauty as He beholds it in His Son.

Beholding His own beauty in His Son, God has eternally willed to make a people that should look like His Son. This is His church. This church He has had eternally with Him. He has this church engraven in the palms of His hands. This is His counsel of election. Having this church in Christ eternally before Him, He is eternally gracious to the church. This grace is the source from which everything else flows. From this grace flow all the blessings that the Christian will ever receive. It is this grace to which the apostle is referring: the grace, and the gift by grace.

Centrally, the gift is Christ. It is Christ as He now is. It is Christ as He became through the incarnation, through His death, through His resurrection, through His ascension, through His exaltation at the right hand of God, and through His reception of the Spirit.

It is not that Christ makes God gracious unto us. The opposite is true. Out of the eternal grace of God came the gift. It was in this grace that God sent His Son. It was in this grace that He gave Him. When all through the three years of His public ministry Christ spoke and revealed God, it was the gift of grace. When He was lifted up on the cross and paid the price of redemption, it was a price paid out of God's grace. Out of the grace of God came the cross. The cross is a gift that flows from grace. When Christ was raised, ascended, was exalted, and was filled with the Spirit, the gift was complete.

The apostle speaks of the overflow of this gift to the many. Jesus must not stay alone. The gift must overflow. We can look at the overflow of the gift from a twofold point of view. If we look at it from the point of view of its central significance, the gift is righteousness. When the gift overflows to us, we receive righteousness. Righteousness is the greatest blessing we can possibly receive. From its legal side, righteousness is the forgiveness of our sins and adoption unto children while we had no right to anything but eternal death. In the midst of death, we receive the right to eternal life. Can you conceive of anything greater than to receive forgiveness of sins, eternal life, and heavenly glory? You may have all the world, but let me have righteousness. For what does it profit a man if he gain the whole world and lose his soul? And he will surely lose his soul if he does not have this righteousness.

From the spiritual and ethical side, righteousness is deliverance from the power of sin and death. In the ultimate sense, Christ overflows in us until we shall be wholly like Him. He will overflow in us when we die, so that the soul will be like Him. He will overflow when our bodies shall be raised from the grave, so that our bodies will be like Him. He will also overflow in all creation.

This is the gift.

That in Comparison with Which the Abounding Gift Abounds

The gift is compared with the offense. Do not underestimate the offense; it was bad enough. Adam was in the state of righteousness in paradise. He offended, and he fell. That one offense of his overflowed to the many. It overflowed unto physical death. It overflowed unto spiritual death. It overflowed unto eternal death.

This is not an accidental overflow. When God said, "The day you eat thereof you shall die," He did not mean that death would be the inevitable result. Rather, God said, "If you eat of that tree, I will surely kill you." This is God's wrath. This is God's justice. This is God's proof that you cannot mock Him. Being the head of the many, Adam represented the many. Therefore, in that first offense of Adam, God killed us all. Every hour is a living testimony of this. It is sometimes said that the Bible has so little regard for life. This is true because of the overflow of the offense.

We must not take the offense lightly. It is an awful thing with which the verse compares the gift. Because of that offense, we are in the death-house. Death holds us in its power. It tortures us. It casts us into all kinds of sins and corruption and into all kinds of suffering and misery. It kills us. After it has killed us, it casts us into everlasting damnation. This is what the text means when it says that by the offense of one, all died.

If all the suffering of the death-house, through which also the receivers of the gift must pass, is put on the one side and the gift is put on the other side, the gift abounds more. The meaning is not that the gift abounds unto more *people*. The offense abounds unto all. The grace does not, but abounds only to the many that are in Christ.

Neither does the apostle mean that the gift abounds more in kind than the sin of Adam. Some have explained that sin abounds unto death, but that the gift abounds much more unto righteousness and life. But the apostle does not say this. He says, "Much more the grace of God, and the gift by grace, . . . hath abounded unto many." The meaning is that out of the grace of God came Christ. And Christ abounds with blessings. The blessings that flow out of Christ are more than there is evil flowing out of Adam.

The Effect of the Abounding Gift

When we shall have received the fulness that is in Christ, what will be the result? Shall we have returned to the same place where Adam stood? This would indeed be the result if the gift were like the offense. Then sin brought death, and Christ removed it. God would have done a repair job. This is not the case. The grace of God does not bring us back where we were. If this were the case, salvation would be a foolish piece of work. God would be the loser. In this case, all the suffering, pain, sorrow, and death of this present time would be for nothing.

Others say that the grace of God brings us where Adam would have brought us if he had obeyed. This is a popular teaching. But neither is this the case. For in this also, God's work would be foolish. If God could have obtained the same purpose through Adam, Christ would never have come. The fact is that Adam could never have brought us to heaven. Adam was a figure. At best, Adam would have remained in paradise.

On the contrary, the result of the abounding gift is that God brings us to a glory that is as far above the original glory in paradise as Christ is above Adam. It is God's purpose to lead His people to this glory. For that purpose, the grace of God much more abounds.

Do you know what will happen? God will wipe away all tears from our eyes. This could never have happened if we had not passed through this death. The glory to which God leads us is so great that it far surpasses our imagination. When we shall have reached this glory, we will say, "I would rather pass through a thousand death-houses than to miss this glory."

Chapter Thirty-three

Our Justification of Life

Romans 5:18
Therefore as by the offence of one judgment came upon all men to condemnation; even so by the righteousness of one the free gift came upon all men unto justification of life.

A close look at the text as it is in the Authorized Version will show that the words *judgment came*, in the first half of the verse, and the words *the free gift came*, in the second half, were inserted by the translators. A literal translation of the original Greek is this: "Therefore, as by the offence of one, upon all men to condemnation, even so by the righteousness of one, upon all men unto justification of life." Because this did not seem to give a full sentence, words were inserted. But they are a commentary. We do better to leave them out. We should understand the text this way: "As on the one hand, the rule is, by one offense, upon all men to condemnation, so on the other hand, the rule is, by one righteousness, upon all men unto justification of life."

Once more the apostle compares Adam and Christ, but now in a conclusion. He compares them from the viewpoint of what is effected by each. Adam was a figure of Christ. Both were the legal, representative head of a corporate body. In that sense, Adam was a figure of Christ. There is also dissimilarity. The dissimilarity consists in this: Christ overflows, or abounds, more unto life than Adam overflows, or abounds, unto death.

230

In the verse the apostle draws a conclusion. This is indicated by the word *Therefore*. Compressing the thought that he has been discussing into one sentence, the apostle says, "As on the one hand, the rule is, one offense upon all to condemnation (and this is a matter of experience), even so, on the other hand, the rule is, through one, righteousness upon all unto justification of life."

Justification of life is the heart of the text. The text gives an answer to the question, "How do I obtain justification of life?"

What It Means

About the meaning of justification of life we can be brief. *Justification* in Scripture is a thoroughly forensic, or legal, term. It has nothing to do with what we are in ourselves. It has nothing to do with our condition. It has to do with what God says of us when we stand before His bar of judgment.

Justification is not an abstract matter. It is not that we shall stand before the bar of God's judgment some day in the distant future. If we would understand the text, we must be conscious of our standing before the judgment seat of God daily. God never stops judging us.

Justification implies a judge. The judge is God. It presumes defendants. We are the defendants—before the judgment seat all the time. It implies a standard according to which we are judged, which is the law of God. It requires a sentence. Justification is a favorable verdict. God says, "Yes, I approve of you. You are righteous. You have a right to be in My house."

Justification stands opposed to the other verdict in the text, implied in the phrase *as by the offence of one upon all men to condemnation*. Condemnation is that God says, *No!* He continues to say *No!* until man finds himself in hell. God says, "No! I do not approve of you. You are not righteous. I do not want you in My house." For this reason condemnation is a verdict of death. In contrast with this, when God justifies us, He says, "Yes! I approve of you. You are righteous. I want you to be in My house."

Justification is not the favorable sentence of God upon those who are righteous. Rather, it is the favorable sentence of God upon them who are not righteous. The justification of God concerns sinners. They who are justified have been condemned. From a certain point of view, we are all condemned. We are already in the death-house. When God expresses a verdict, His Word immediately executes what it expresses. The result is that we are in the death-house. It is while in the death-house that we become justified.

For this reason justification includes several blessings of grace. It includes the forgiveness of sins. It includes our adoption as children. It includes a positive righteousness, which gives us right to more than we lost, that is, right to eternal life. It is a justification to life. The expression *justification to life* means that God declares we are so righteous that we have a right to life. We are justified in condemnation; we have life in death. Between these two sentences of life or death is no third possibility. When God condemns, He condemns to death. Death is the only punishment that God knows. God is the God of life. He cannot allow any creature to curse Him and live.

Life in the text is eternal life. Justification does not lead us back to the life we had. It is not, as some would have it, the life we might have had if Adam had obeyed. There was no eternal life for Adam in God's mind, nor could Adam ever have attained eternal life. Adam was "of the earth, earthy" [I Cor. 15:47]. But even apart from all this, the life in our verse is the messianic life.

Justification, then, is that verdict of God by which they who are naturally under condemnation are now declared worthy of life.

How It Is Realized

How does this happen? This is an important question. This is the question raised by the text. How is the sentence of God, whereby we are declared righteous and worthy of eternal life, effected by God? The text says, *even so*. In the same way in which the one offense redounded unto all to condemnation, so the one righteousness redounded unto all to justification of life. There is a comparison in the text. It is very instructive. Just as the sentence of condemnation comes upon us, so the sentence of justification to life comes upon us. Just as, on the one hand, the rule is, one offense unto all to condemnation, so on the other hand, the rule is, one righteousness unto all to justification of life.

The fact that condemnation came upon all through one offense means that condemnation came upon all as a corporate body in one man. We are all in the death-house. In this death-house we die. There is no mercy. In this death-house die the little child, the young man in the prime of life, and the old man. And death is a matter of condemnation. But the question is, how did we get there? Did we get in this death-house one by one? This is really Pelagianism. Pelagianism is an awful doctrine. It teaches that all are born free. Somehow all follow a bad example and run into the death-house. But this is not Scripture, and this is not the text.

The text says that we all entered into the death-house six thousand years ago. We entered into the death-house by one man. The Bible knows no individualism. The Bible teaches that God created man as a body. This body was represented by one man. That one man committed one offense. That one offense landed us all in the death-house. The moment Adam committed the offense of eating of the fruit of the forbidden tree, God passed sentence upon him. Adam stood before the bar of God's judgment when he took the fruit of the forbidden tree. The moment he ate the fruit, Adam was sentenced to the death-house. And in him we all were sentenced to death.

Our condemnation was not through all the offenses of Adam but through that one offense. Adam did not commit all the offenses of his life in that legal capacity. But through that one offense, we all entered into the death-house. The reason is that Adam represented us in that one offense, and not in his other offenses. Adam stood at the head of the body. As he stood at the head of the body, he committed one offense. For that one offense God sentenced him to the death-house, and us with him.

Even as a corporate body, through one deed, by one man, we were all condemned to death, so as a corporate body, through one deed, by one man, we are justified to life. Just as we are not fundamentally *condemned* by an individual act on our part, so we are not *justified* by an individual act on our part. As we were condemned by a deed of the one head of the body, so we are justified by the deed of the one head of the body. Of the one body Adam was the head; of the other body Christ is the head.

The one deed of righteousness by which we are justified is the cross. It is the atonement. It is that act whereby Christ went freely, willingly, obediently, lovingly, into death. Again, as was the case with Adam's other sins, Jesus did many good deeds that are not imputed to us. When Jesus, for example, raised Lazarus, that deed is not imputed to us. But one act of Jesus *is* imputed to us because in that one act He represented us. In that one act He obtained justification of life. And the verdict of God is immediately expressed in the resurrection. This is a historic fact. There are two basic historic facts. The one is that we are all under condemnation because of the one offense of the one man, Adam. The other historic fact is the death of Christ. When God raised Christ, He justified Him as the head of the body. And we were justified to life at the same time.

The judgment day is past. There will be a public revelation of it, but the judgment is past. Golgotha was the hour of judgment. In that hour, God poured out His judgment. One received it as an act on His part, as a deed of righteousness that He performed. The damned in hell do not do that. They also receive the judgment of God, but they do not receive it as an act. Christ stood in the judgment, in the love of God. The offense was that Adam did not love God in the state of righteousness, but Christ did love God, even in hell. Therefore, as on the one hand, the rule is, one offense upon all to condemnation, so on the other hand, the rule is, one righteousness upon all unto justification of life.

Who the Participants Are

Upon all men, the text says. There are some who, regardless of anything Scripture teaches elsewhere, insist that *all men* means every individual of the human race. According to them, the verse teaches that as every individual is under condemnation because of the one offense, so justification of life comes upon every individual of the human race because of one righteousness. There are two distinct theories about this. One theory teaches that every individual is saved. This is consistent. The other theory recognizes that not all are saved. It teaches that all men are justified in Christ as far as God's *intention* is concerned, there being a condition upon which the fulfillment of God's intention depends. The question to every man then becomes, "Do you want it? Do you want to be justified?" In other words, this theory explains it in such a way that the justification of Christ was not a justification after all.

The truth is that those who according to God's verdict are justified are also saved, even as those who are condemned according to God's verdict must die. Scripture says, "Whom He justified, them He also glorified" [Rom. 8:30]. The simple meaning is this: all men in the one man, and all men in the other man. Just as, on the one hand, the rule is, through one man condemnation upon all who are in him (and this is all men), so through one man justification of life upon all who are in him (and this is the elect church). Christ did not make of justification a *chance.* The judgment took place nineteen hundred years ago. Even as all in Adam die, so all in Christ are justified.

There is no "But I must believe." The *but* must be an *and:* "All in Christ are justified, *and* I must believe." In the midst of our darkness comes the Word of God. It reaches out to you (and this is the gospel) and says, "I have justified you." God says this. When God says this, you believe. It is not, "God justifies you, *but* you must believe." Rather, it is, "God justifies you, *and* you believe." Believing, in the midst of our darkness we will shout, "I, then, being justified by faith, have peace with God through Jesus Christ our Lord."

Chapter Thirty-four

The Reign of Grace

Romans 5:21
That as sin hath reigned unto death, even so might grace reign through righteousness unto eternal life by Jesus Christ our Lord.

The text is immediately connected with the preceding verse as a purpose clause. There we read, "Moreover the law entered, that the offence might abound. But where sin abounded, grace did much more abound." Then come the words of the text: "That (that is, that this purpose might be reached) as sin hath reigned unto death, even so might grace reign through righteousness unto eternal life by Jesus Christ our Lord." The context, then, is this: sin, that is, that *one* sin—the *offense* to which the context refers repeatedly—must abound. It must not be checked. It is not God's purpose to cover up the real, hideous nature of that one offense in paradise and to check its development. The offense must abound. Or if you please, it is God's will that all that is in that one sin of Adam must come out of it. God's purpose with Adam's sin is the very opposite of the doctrine that God would keep that sin in bounds.[1] The purpose of God is that the first sin develop in all its hideousness and contents. This is one thing.

---

1. Hoeksema refers particularly to the doctrine of "common grace," which posits a work of grace in all humans after the fall that has as a purpose the restraint of sin.

But this is not all. In order that everything that is in that one sin might come out, God gave His law. That is, God gave His law to Israel. The law was not given as a check upon sin. Far less was the law given that through it Israel should be saved. But the law was given as a poultice. Just as a poultice serves to break open the sore and draw out the poison, so the purpose of the law was to draw out sin. The reaction to the law by the natural man always is that he says "*I* will" to the law that expressed *God's* will. The law does not serve as a restraint. It serves as a poultice to draw out sin.

The result of the giving of the law to Israel was that there was no nation so ungodly as was Israel. Can you conceive of a nation more ungodly than Israel? There was none. Tyrus and Sidon would have converted themselves, the Lord says, if the works had been done in them that were done in Israel. Can you imagine another city besides Jerusalem that would crucify the Lord of glory?

But this is only the negative side of God's purpose. God's positive purpose was that *grace* might abound. Suppose that first offense of Adam had remained as it was, had not developed, and God had then given His Son and His grace. Would it have become manifest that the gift of His Son was necessary? But now, "Where sin abounded, grace did much more abound."

"As sin hath reigned unto death, even so grace reigns through righteousness unto eternal life by Jesus Christ our Lord." The last part of verse 21 is the victorious conclusion of this entire passage.

A Blessed Reign

Once more the text draws a comparison, this time between the reign of sin and the reign of grace. There is a figure. Sin is personified. Sin is pictured as a person who reigns. The explanation of the reign of sin requires that we answer four questions. First, what does it mean that sin reigns? Second, where does sin reign? Third, how is it possible that sin reigns? What is its right and power to reign? Fourth, how does this reign of sin come to manifestation?

In answer to the first question, the reign of sin means that sin has the *right* to reign, and that it has the actual *power* to reign.

In answer to the second question, as to where sin reigns, it reigns universally in the world. The world is the domain of sin. But this vitally important stipulation must be added: the reign of sin has its seat, its throne, in the heart of man. Therefore, it is impossible that the reign of sin be broken by external means. You can do nothing to break this reign of sin by means of reformation or education. Sin is enthroned in the heart of man. From this seat it rules over the will, over the mind, over the desires, indeed over man's entire life.

Sin rules from the heart of man over the entire life of man, also in its outward manifestation. It becomes manifest, therefore, in every aspect of life: in malice, in envy, in backbiting, in hatred, in slander, in covetousness. It is manifest in every relation: in that of husband and wife, in that of parents and children, in that of master and servant, in that of lord and subject. No one can do anything about it. I am speaking now of the reign of sin apart from the grace of God. Sin reigns supremely and unconquerably.

The nature of the reign of sin is not such that it rules as a tyrant over an unwilling servant. Rather, man in the service of sin is free: man serves sin willingly. As a result, man never acknowledges that sin rules over him.

In answer to the third question—how sin has a right to reign—its right is found in this: man is guilty. This is the basis for sin to rule, for it is the law of God that sin reign over him who commits it.

In answer to the fourth question, the manifestation of the reign of sin is death. You see it everywhere. You see it in the individual. You see it in every relation. You see it in the home, in society, in the state, in war, in destruction. You see it from epoch to epoch. No matter what form of political state or economy the world may adopt, sin reigns unto death. Sin reigns in the world. All that we see in the devastation of war, revolution, and crime is due to this reign of sin.

Just as sin reigns, so grace reigns. Grace reigns in the same way, in a formal sense. It reigns according to the same fundamental rule of God. It reigns on the same fundamental basis. Only now there is a blessed reign. It is a reign of grace. We need not now go into the different connotations of grace. In the text, grace means two things. Grace is the attitude or disposition that God assumes towards His people. Grace is also a reigning power. Regeneration is grace. Calling is grace. Faith is grace. Conversion is grace. Sanctification is grace. All these blessings of salvation together are called grace. Grace reigns as the favor of God and the power of this favor upon His people.

The reign of grace takes its inception in the heart of man, in the heart of the elect. Also grace does not come by reformation. It does not even come by preaching. It comes about by the Spirit of Christ taking hold of the heart. In this heart the Spirit pours the power of grace. From the heart this reign of grace controls the will, the mind, and the desires. Grace takes hold of the heart of the individual, and from the heart it takes hold of all the issues of life proceeding from that heart. As is the case with sin, so grace cannot rest until it has taken hold of all the life of man, all the relations of life.

A Righteous Reign

The question is, does the reign of grace have a basis? Does the Bible also give an answer to the question whether grace has the right to take the condemned sinner and transform him? Does grace have a right to reign? In the Authorized Version, the same preposition is used both with regard to the reign of sin and with regard to the reign of grace: "As sin reigned *unto* death, so grace reigns *unto* eternal life." But in the original a different word is used for the reign of sin. We read in the original, "as sin hath reigned *in* death."

Sin reigns *in* death. The meaning is that sin has the right to reign only in the realm of death. Death is God's curse. This is not a matter of our experience. We never interpret death as the sentence of God—not if we set aside what the Bible says about death. But in Scripture death means that God kills us. Because God kills us, death is so terrible. This is why we need such a clear insight into Scripture. We must believe that when God kills us, He brings us to life. But death as such is the manifestation of the wrath of God. It is the manifestation of the wrath of God over sin. That wrath of God on us causes all to turn away from Him. In this sphere sin has a right to reign. Not only has it a right to reign there, but only sin has the power to rule there.

Is there also such a thing for grace? The text says, ". . . even so might grace reign through righteousness." Notice the distinction. The text says that sin reigned *in* death, but grace reigns *through* righteousness. Grace does not find righteousness. Righteousness is already a matter of grace. Righteousness here is imputed righteousness. This righteousness is a gift of grace. It must be, because we have no right to be righteous. Before we can be righteous, God must say that we are righteous. This is why grace reigns through Jesus Christ. He died as we never could die. He died in the consciousness of God's sentence upon Him. That was dying. That was dying as an act. This is why the death of Christ takes away the sin of the world.

Do you believe this? You must believe this. This is your only salvation. Jesus died. And that He died an atoning death is plain from the resurrection. Jesus so died that God said in the resurrection, "I make you to live." Do you believe it? If you do, you are saved. I do not mean that you merely believe the *fact*. Rather, you let yourself sink on Him. Do you believe it? Then you are saved. "Believe on the Lord Jesus Christ, and thou shalt be saved" [Acts 16:31]. As soon as this is the case, and you have become righteous and your sin has been forgiven, God says, "Now grace shall reign over you." This grace quickens you.

A Victorious Reign

Let us go back to the beginning. Grace reigns unto eternal life. Sin reigned unto death. Death is the wages of sin. This did not have to be stated, because the context states that sin abounds. Where sin abounds, the end is death. This is the goal of the reign of sin. God wants this to be plain. This is why sin must abound. But while the reign of sin is unto death, the reign of grace is unto life.

Grace so reigns in you that you obtain life. Life is the fruit of this grace in you that ever turns you toward God. This is life. Grace reigns unto life. It does so when it first takes hold of you and you cry out, "O God, be merciful to me!" It does so when it takes you out of darkness into the light. It reigns unto life when death comes. When death comes, grace reigns and leads you through the valley of death. It lands you into the house of many mansions. Still it goes on. It reigns over your body in the grave. It brings your body, with your soul, into the new order of things. Oh the glorious power of the grace of Christ, who died and rose again for our justification!

Chapter Thirty-five

The Christian and the Sin-life

Romans 6:1, 2
What shall we say then? Shall we continue in sin, that grace may abound? God forbid. How shall we, that are dead to sin, live any longer therein?

There is a very intimate, indeed inseparable relation between doctrine and life. There is an inseparable relation between the truth and practice. The relation is mutual. There is an influence of doctrine upon life, when doctrine is applied, but there is also an influence of life upon doctrine.

It is a question to me which of the two is the more important. A certain inclination toward a certain direction and walk in life tends toward a certain form of doctrine. In other words, if it is our inmost desire to walk in ways of sin, corruption, and the world, it is impossible for us to maintain the truth. For the sake of a sinful life, for the sake of a life in the world, we will forsake and corrupt the truth.

People sometimes say that we must have practical preaching. But there is nothing more corrupt than the practical preaching they have in mind. It is not often that anyone will reject a piece of doctrine as long as it is just a piece of doctrine. It is not very likely that anyone will hate me just for preaching a certain doctrine. He may not like it, but he will not hate me for it. But as soon as doctrine becomes practical, we will never tolerate doctrine, unless we depart from the way of sin. As soon as doctrine is applied, the test comes. Jesus says that he who will do the will of His Father will say that His doctrine is true [John 7:17].

Ultimately the church does not consist of people who believe doctrine, but of people who adorn doctrine with a godly life. Therefore, we can test doctrine by its fruit. If a certain doctrine leads to a corrupt life, to a life in sin, there is something wrong with that doctrine. If, on the other hand, a doctrine leads to a godly life, you can depend upon it that it is the truth.

This is also the underlying thought in the text. The apostle begins a new section here. He does not yet speak on the matter of practical life. He does not here begin the practical part of his epistle. But the apostle stands before a question: "What is the relation between the doctrine I have taught thus far and its application to the life of the Christian before God? What *follows* from my doctrine, or what shall we say then?"

The apostle intends to speak about the question "Can my doctrine be applied so that it can stand the test?" This he does in chapters six and seven in order to take up again the thread of his doctrine of justification by faith in chapter 8. This is the connection.

What shall we say then? Shall we say this: "We will continue in sin, that grace may abound"? If we shall say this, if this follows from my doctrine, then the doctrine I have been teaching would have been a corrupt doctrine. Therefore, the apostle immediately answers, "God forbid." God forbid that we should say, "Let us continue in sin." To the contrary, we will say, in answer to this question, "Impossible!" The reason why we say that it is impossible is because we are dead to sin.

The justified Christian and the sin-life: this is the theme here. We must consider, first, the reason for this question. The question is apparently justified. Second, we must consider that when this question comes to the Christian, he immediately responds. He does not first reason it out. He immediately, spontaneously responds. Third, we must see that the Christian conceives of the sin-life as impossible for him because he is dead to sin.

The Reason for the Question

Apparently the doctrine of the apostle gives the Christian freedom to sin. The question the apostle asks here is a question that he knew some might and will ask. Sinful men, after hearing a certain doctrine, will often say, "All right, we will suppose that what you have said is true. Let us see what follows." Then they will proceed to make your doctrine look absurd. They do this, for example, with the doctrine of sovereign election. They cannot deny this doctrine. The teaching of Scripture is too plain for that. But if they do not like this doctrine, they will try to make it look absurd. They will say that God is the author of sin. No Reformed man ever taught this. It is wicked man's, it is the devil's, conclusion from the doctrine of sovereign election.

So it is here. You must remember that the church, already in the apostle Paul's time, was attacked. It was attacked exactly on this point. The enemies of the church said, "Those Christians will not have anything to do with good and decent people. They preach a gospel that gathers all kinds of crooks and sinners. They say that the gospel they preach is not for good, for righteous, for decent people, but it is only for sinners. And they gather all kinds of sinners."

They had said this already to Jesus. They had told him, "You eat with publicans and sinners."

They said the same thing in Paul's time. They said, "He preaches a gospel concerning sinners, and he gathers sinners."

This is also characteristic of the church today. The church deals not with good, decent, and righteous people, but with sinners.

Still more, the apostle had plainly taught these things. He had taught that there is absolutely no value in good works as far as our righteousness before God is concerned. He had been teaching that all are under sin. On the other hand, the apostle had taught that a man becomes righteous exactly by doing nothing. God justifies not the righteous, but the ungodly. The Christian testifies that God justifies him for nothing.

In addition, Paul had taught that the righteousness they receive is perfect, and it is a righteousness forever. The righteousness that the Christian receives is perfect, not only in the sense that he receives a clean slate, but also in the sense that it is a righteousness unto eternal life. God does not make a man righteous in the sense that he receives a clean slate and then is told, "Now you must see to it that you remain righteous." No. The righteousness that the Christian receives is perfect and forever.

The apostle had taught, "Your works do not detract from your righteousness, no matter how sinful they are. And your good works do not add to your righteousness, no matter how good they are." This is our doctrine today.

Don't you see how the enemy would come and say, "Let us see. What shall we say then? We will say, 'Let us continue in sin, that grace may abound.'"

There is one more important element in what the apostle had taught. He had taught that sin must serve to glorify God's grace. This is why it is God's purpose that sin shall abound. He gave His law in order to bring out how corrupt sin is. Is it not logical that we say then, "Let us sin that grace may abound"? This is the apparent license to sin that the sinner sees in the doctrine of sovereign grace.

The Spontaneous Response of the Christian

What does the Christian say? Abhorring the very thought, the Christian spontaneously answers the question "Shall we continue in sin?" by saying, "God forbid." The Christian also says, "How shall we?"

What is there in this question that the Christian so abhors? What does the apostle express in this question of the enemy? Does he say, "Shall the Christian still sin?" He does not. We all sin. This is not the intent of the question. Instead, the apostle asks, "Shall we *continue,* that is, shall we *abide* in sin?" This is quite different from asking whether the Christian still sins.

That the intent of the question is *abiding* in sin is evident from what the apostle asks next [v. 2]: "How shall we live any longer in sin?" That is, how shall we dwell with sin, how shall we feel at home in sin, how shall we find pleasure in sin, how shall we love sin, how shall we have peace with sin? And how shall we live in the sphere of sin, as fish live in the sphere of the water, and feel at home in sin?

The enemy's intent by asking, "Shall we continue in sin?" is to prove that it follows from the doctrine of grace taught by Paul that we live in sin, that we dwell in sin, that we seek sin, that we feel at home in sin. But the answer of the apostle and of the church is, "God forbid." That this is the answer of the church and that, therefore, this is a test question is plain from the plural: "How shall *we* live in sin?" In answer to this question, every Christian will say, "God forbid." The answer comes spontaneously from the Christian.

Is this so with us? This is a test question. Can we really say, "I abhor the idea of dwelling in sin"? Can we say this?

The Christian does this. He does so in principle. But he says this. He says with all his heart, "God forbid." Not only does he say this, but he also expresses it more strongly. He says that it is impossible. It is spiritually impossible for the Christian that he answer in the affirmative to this question. He will say, "I admit that I sin, but it is impossible that I should ever say I will dwell in sin and take sin to my bosom. That is impossible."

This is an important statement. This is reality. This is the reality of the gospel, reflected in our life. This is so true that if for some reason we cannot say this, we cannot say that we are saved, either. We can sin and still say that we are a Christian. We can sin daily and say that we are a Christian. We can sin repeatedly, and truthfully say that we are a Christian. We can sin the same sin repeatedly, and say that we are a Christian. We can even curse and swear and say that we would rather be damned than belong to Christ, and still be a Christian. This is what Peter did. We can go a step further. We can for a time walk in sin and be a Christian. But if we do, whether we fall or for a time walk in sin, when the Word of God comes to us, that Word reveals to us that in that sin we have no peace. And if the Word does this, we have never lived in sin.

One other thing is sure. If we are Christians and we fall into sin, we will come to repentance. The end of our falling into sin will then be proof of the statement "God forbid."

If this is *not* so with you—if you say about sin, "Yes, I live in it, I dwell in it, I love it, I feel at home in it"—you are not a Christian. If this is the case with you, then you are a stranger to Christ. Sin and grace do not dwell together with God, not even in His counsel. They are there, but in antithesis, so that the one is overcome by the other.

The Christian does not say, "I will abide in sin." If he should fall into sin, he will come to repentance.

The Sin-life Impossible for the Christian Because He Is Dead

Why is it impossible for the Christian to say this? Why can he not say, "Let us continue in sin?" The reason is that the Christian is dead to sin. This is the subject of Romans 6.

Literally, the apostle says here, "We have died to sin." This is somewhat different than being dead to sin. A stock or block is also dead to sin, but it has not died to sin. The Christian died to sin. He was once alive to sin, but he died. This means two things. First, the legal relationship between us and sin has ceased. This is always the case. You cannot hold anyone responsible after he has died. This is true, for example, in the marriage relationship. After death the marriage relationship ceases. The same is true if we have died to sin. The expression implies that there was a time when we were legally bound to sin. God cursed us and gave sin the right to rule over us. But now we have died to sin. Sin has no more right over us. The legal relationship between us and sin has been broken.

Second, when we have died to sin, the actual relation of fellowship ceases. We have nothing to do with sin, legally or actually. Don't make a mistake. The apostle does not say that sin is dead. Sin is not dead in the Christian. Sin is very much alive in the Christian, and sin is alive in the world in which he lives. He must walk even with sin alive in him and in the world about him. Sin is not dead. But I am dead. I am dead to sin.

To be alive to sin means that there is agreement between me and sin. I am alive to sin by nature. As a result, when sin commands, I obey. When sin comes to me, I say, "I am glad to meet you."

But I died to sin. Sin may be alive, but I died. "Old things are passed away; behold, all things are become new" [II Cor. 5:17]. This does not mean that we are never attracted by sin, but when we are attracted by sin, the end is always that we fall down upon our knees and say, "O God, be merciful to me a sinner." Formerly the Christian loved sin. Now he abhors it, he flees it, he desires to be rid of it.

Is this true of you and me? If I should say to you, "Shall we continue in sin, that grace may abound?" would this be your spontaneous, enthusiastic response: "God forbid! How shall we, that are dead to sin, live any longer therein"?

Chapter Thirty-six

Buried with Christ

Romans 6:4
Therefore we are buried with him by baptism into death: that like as Christ was raised up from the dead by the glory of the Father, even so we also should walk in newness of life.

This fourth verse must be understood in connection with the main subject of the entire chapter: the kind of life that follows from justification by faith. This is expressed in verses 1 and 2. We must remember that the subject in this chapter is not yet what must we do. The epistle does not as yet take a practical turn. It does not turn to practical subjects until chapter 12, when the apostle applies his doctrine to practical life.

What we have in chapters 6 and 7 is an answer to the question, "What kind of theory follows from the doctrine of justification by faith with a view to practical life?" The apostle introduced that question by saying that it is possible from the doctrine of justification by faith, or if you wish, the doctrine of righteousness without works, that we might draw the conclusion, "Let us abide in sin, that grace may abound." To the question in verse 1 about abiding in sin, the apostle gives a twofold answer. The first answer is the one that naturally, spontaneously arises from the hearts of God's people, namely, "God forbid." Abiding in sin is spiritually impossible. If anyone should say to him, "Let us continue in sin," the Christian spontaneously answers, "God forbid!"

The question remains, how must it be explained that the Christian spontaneously says, "God forbid that I should live in sin"? And the apostle answers that we are dead to sin. A man who is dead to sin does not say, "Let us live in sin."

In the verses immediately following, the apostle explains how we are dead to sin. [In v. 3] the apostle says, "Know ye not (that is, has it not been your experience; is not this the way you have experienced it) that so many of us as were baptized into Jesus Christ were baptized into His death?" By this the apostle means, "Can I not appeal to your experience, that as you were baptized into Jesus Christ, you were baptized into His death? Is this not true?"

In the text the apostle goes a step further. He goes one step beyond having died with Christ when he says that we have been buried with Him. "Therefore we are buried with him by baptism into death." We must not read it, as is often done, "buried with Him, by baptism, into death." Instead, we must read, "buried with Him, *by baptism into death.*" By baptism into death, we have been buried with Christ. Not only have we been buried with Him, but we have also been raised with Him. And we have been raised with Him with the purpose that we should walk in newness of life.

Buried with Christ: this is the theme in the verse. What does this mean? This is the first question. Notice that the apostle places these words on our lips. Therefore, we must know what it means. We must know what it means when we say we are buried with Christ, by baptism into death. The second question we must ask is how this burial with Christ is accomplished. The apostle says, "by baptism into death." Third, we must ask what is the ultimate purpose of this burial with Christ.

The Meaning

There are three elements involved in the question "What does it mean to be buried with Christ?" The first is the meaning of *burial*. The second is the meaning of *Christ's burial*. The third is the meaning of *our burial with Christ*.

Burial is the absolute end. From burial there is no return. It is the end of all that goes before. When a man is buried, it is the end of all that goes before that burial, never to return. Even though that man is raised, all that goes before his burial is gone, never to return. In this sense, burial is the end. And it is decidedly burial that is the end. When a man lies in state, it is not yet the end. Then there are still friends and tears and sermons and flowers. But when he is let down into the grave and the coffin is covered up with earth, he is gone. That is the end of all earthly life. It is the end of all that this earthly life ever meant. It is the end of all earthly relations. It is the end of all earthly responsibility.

That is the end to which we are all hurrying. As the cradle is the beginning, so the grave is the end.

This was also the case with Christ. Our question is, what is the meaning of *Christ's burial*? The answer is that it was the end of Christ. It was the end of Christ as He sojourned among us for thirty-three years. All that was connected with that earthly sojourn of Jesus ended when He was buried. That is the idea of Christ's burial.

To understand the significance and power of Christ's burial, we must ask about the significance of the life of Christ that was buried. The answer, expressed in one phrase, is *for sin*. We read in Romans 8:3, "For what the law could not do, in that it was weak through the flesh, God sending His own Son in the likeness of sinful flesh, and *for sin,* condemned sin in the flesh." *For sin*. This phrase we must remember. Take this away, and the burial of Christ loses all its significance. For sin He came. For sin He suffered. For sin He died. For sin He descended into hell. This is the significance of the life of Christ: *for sin*.

Mark you well, not for His own sin did He live and die, but for sin. He stood in such a connection with sin that all sin was on Him. He stood so connected with sin that the Bible tells us, in II Corinthians 5:21, that He was made sin for us. Upon Jesus' whole life was written *for sin*. Jesus came for the special purpose of taking all the sin of His elect upon Himself, and then removing it. The sin of all His people was on Him. It was concentrated on Him. He contracted it.

Then He was buried—He who from the moment of His birth to the moment of His death contracted all the sin of His people. That was the end of that man. Sin had no more claim on Him. The relation between Him and sin was gone. He died for and unto sin so that it is gone. Every last connection of the saints with sin is gone. That man who walked with all the sins of His people upon Him and died has gone forever, never to return. This is the meaning of Christ's burial. The man of sin is gone.

Our burial with Christ means that there is a judicial, a legal relation between Christ and us. Christ and we are a corporation, a unity before the face of God. It could not have been written that we are buried with Christ, by baptism into death, if this were not true. If we were no legal corporation in Christ, we could never say this.

That we are buried with Christ also means that because of that legal relation, the church is buried with Christ at the moment Christ is buried, and in the same sense. When Christ is buried, the church is buried with Him. In this legal sense, the church, including you and me, was buried nineteen hundred years ago.

Burial with Christ is applied to us when we are regenerated and when God gives us faith. The moment we receive the gift of faith, we say, "Because Christ died, the old man of mine is dead. My relation to sin and the dominion of sin over me are broken."

Do you think that we can say it? Do you think that we can take these words upon our lips and say, "Our relation to Christ is such that the dominion of sin is no more"? It is not true that we do not sin anymore. We are not perfect, although this will be the case in heaven. In heaven it will not be hard to say, "Sin has no more dominion over me." Now it is a matter of faith.

Now the matter stands that we lie in the midst of sin. Now it looks as if we are still in the midst of death. We do not look like saints who are holy.

We must understand these things. They must become real to our consciousness. The faith of the Christian means that while he is in the midst of death, he says, "I live"; while in the midst of unrighteousness, "I am righteous." But then we must look at Christ and say, "Buried with Him!" If we are not buried with Him, we will be buried without Him. We *will* be buried. We *must* be buried *with Him*.

How It Is Accomplished

The apostle says that burial with Christ takes place *by baptism into death*. We must leave the phrase in this form. The meaning is that we are buried with Christ, by baptism into death. To make it plain, the meaning is that we are killed by baptism. It is a baptism into death.

An aspect of this baptism into death is that we are baptized into fellowship with Christ. We are incorporated into Him. As the apostle expresses it, we have become "planted together" with Him [v. 5]. Just as by nature we are one plant with Adam, so we have become one plant with Christ. How do we become one plant with Christ? Again, in the moment of regeneration. Regeneration is that the glorified Lord reaches down from heaven into your heart and never lets you go again. It is regeneration, regardless of age, that is meant by baptism here.

When we are so incorporated into Christ, we are baptized into fellowship with all that He is. And this means that we become partakers of His death. Again, this is a matter of faith. Christ implants faith into the heart of the Christian, and by this faith he takes hold of Christ and of all that Christ is. He says, "I have died with Christ, and I have been buried with Him by baptism into death"—not the death of Christ, but our own death. By this baptism into death, we are buried with Christ, so that His death becomes our death. His death was the death of sin. We are baptized into death so that we die to sin. By baptism into death, that is, our own death, we are buried with Christ.

Again, this is a matter of faith. But let me ask, is this a reality that you possess by faith? Is this what your life is? Is this what you say? Notice that the apostle says later in this chapter, "Reckon yourself to be dead to sin" [v. 11]. This reckoning is the reckoning of faith. We are buried with Christ, by baptism into death, and this death is the death unto sin.

The apostle is not speaking of the outward form of baptism. Of course, our baptism is the sign and seal of this. But the apostle is not speaking of the outward form. He is speaking of the reality of baptism. We are a baptized church. Do you reckon it to be so?

What Its Purpose Is

The purpose of burial with Christ is that we should walk in newness of life. We are dead, and now we must walk. This sounds strange: we are dead, and now we must walk. We are buried with Christ in order that we should walk in newness of life. We always walk. We walk before and after we are buried with Christ, but there is a difference. Before our burial we walk in oldness of death. We are under the dominion of sin. We are a slave to sin, and we walk in oldness of death. We walk with a walk that has its source in death. But after our burial, that walk in oldness of death is gone. That man who was under the dominion of sin is dead. And now we walk with another walk. We walk with another life. What is the difference? That now we walk with a walk that has its source in newness of life.

The text says that Christ was raised up from the dead by the glory of the Father. Christ was raised by glory. This glory by which Christ was raised is the glory of the Father. The glory of the Father is His infinite majesty manifested. Never did the infinite majesty of the Father become more manifest than in the resurrection. Far greater than creation is the act of the resurrection. Far more than in creation did the glory of the Father shine forth when Christ was raised from the dead.

What was the resurrection? That when the old Christ was buried and gone, God opened up the grave on the other side and raised the new Christ. God raised Christ because He died for sin. Christ was raised by the glory of the Father. This resurrection life was implanted in the heart of the church. As we are buried with Christ, so we are raised with Him, and out of this resurrection life comes this newness of life. Then we speak in the light of the resurrection of Jesus. Then we walk in the light of the resurrection of Jesus. Then we do all things in the light of the resurrection of Jesus.

What shall we say then? If this is true (and it is true), if this is true of you and me, what shall we say then? Shall we say, "Let us abide in sin"? God forbid.

We will rather say, "buried with Christ, by baptism into death, that like as Christ was raised up from the dead by the glory of the Father, even so we also should walk in newness of life."

Chapter Thirty-seven

The Christian's Self-esteem

Romans 6:11
Likewise reckon ye also yourselves to be dead indeed unto sin, but alive unto God through Jesus Christ our Lord.

It must be remembered that in the ultimate sense of the word, Romans 6 does not yet belong to the practical part of the epistle. We have not reached the actual practical application of the doctrine of justification to life. The question before us now is whether that doctrine of the apostle can be applied at all. The question is whether the doctrine of licentiousness does not follow from the doctrine of justification by faith without works. And the apostle answers no, for we are dead to sin. To this he adds that those who are dead are also alive.

He bases this truth on the truth concerning Jesus Himself. That Christ died and was raised is the fundamental reality on which the apostle bases the truth that we died and are alive. Christ came in the likeness of sinful flesh. He had the claim of sin upon Him. He satisfied the claim sin had upon Him in that He died; therefore, sin has no more claim on Him. Therefore, He was raised. Otherwise He could not have been raised. If He had not so died—that through His death He satisfied the claim of sin upon Him—He could not have been raised. Because sin had no more claim upon Him, Jesus was raised. Since He so arose, He lives forever, and He lives to God only. "In that he died, he died unto sin once: but in that he liveth, he liveth unto

God" [v. 10]. This is the basis of all that the apostle teaches in the first eleven verses of this chapter.

What he teaches is this: we died with Him and are raised with Him. Because of our relation to Him, we died when He died, and we were raised when He was raised. We died as He died. That is, we died to sin. But since we died with Him and because of our relation to Him, we believe that we shall also live with Him, and even now live with Him.

On this basis the apostle comes to us with the admonition in the text: "Likewise reckon ye also yourselves to be dead indeed unto sin, but alive unto God through Jesus Christ our Lord." Thus, we have in the text an admonition concerning the proper Christian self-esteem.

The Content

The content of this self-esteem of the Christian is expressed in the words *dead unto sin* and *alive unto God*. To understand what this means, it is necessary that we keep before our mind the figure of a lord and his servant, or rather his slave. For according to Scripture, and according to the underlying thought of this passage, the sinner is a slave of sin. Sin is his lord.

In this lordship of sin over the sinner are two notions. First, there is the notion that sin has a claim upon the sinner. When Scripture says that the sinner is a slave to sin, the underlying thought is that sin has a claim upon us. Having a claim upon us, sin demands that we obey. Second, there is the notion that the sinner obeys the dictates of sin. The sinner willingly serves sin. He is willing in the sense that he is not compelled from without, but is impelled from within to serve sin. Sin rules over the heart, the mind, the will, the thoughts, the desires, and all the actions of the sinner. The result is that the sinner thinks for sin, wills for sin, desires for sin, and does all things for sin. He is alive to sin. All his life is determined by sin.

Now this servant dies. He dies to his lord. What takes place when the servant dies? Two things again. First, that lord loses his claim over the servant. Second, when that servant dies, he renders no more service to his master.

Accordingly, when we read in the text that we are dead to sin, the idea is that we have died to sin as our master, as our lord. Sin has lost its claim upon us. We have died to the service of sin. Where formerly we thought for sin, we now no more think for sin. Where formerly we willed for sin, we now no more will for sin. Where formerly we desired for sin, we now no more desire for sin. We are dead. Sin tries to speak to us, but we pay no attention to it. And we may as well add that where formerly we loved sin, we now hate it. When you *reckon* yourself dead to sin, you reckon that sin has lost its claim upon you. "Reckon yourselves to be dead unto sin." This is the negative element of the self-esteem of the Christian.

The positive element of this self-esteem is expressed in the words *alive unto God*. Also here we must keep in mind the figure of a servant and his lord. God is our Lord. He has a claim upon us.

When we say that the sinner is by nature dead unto God, the meaning is not that God relinquishes His divine claim upon the sinner, nor does it mean that God relinquishes His right to kill the sinner if he does not serve Him. Rather, God deprives the sinner of the *right* to serve Him. This is fundamental. To serve God is not merely a duty, but it is also the greatest possible privilege. It is a right to serve God, but the sinner does not have this right. He must serve God, but he does not have the right. God has discharged him from His service. He has relinquished the sinner to the service of sin. Therefore, to be dead to God means that we have no right to serve God. In the spiritual, ethical sense, to be dead unto God means that God does not get any service out of us. God demands that we serve Him, and we do not heed His demand. We are dead to God.

To be alive to God means just the opposite. To be alive to God means that we again have received the right to be God's servants. This is a gift bestowed upon us. As we have received the right to again be God's servants, so God also quickens us to His service, so that we are alive again. When we are alive, we hear His Word, not only intellectually, not only with the natural understanding, but as God's Word *to us*. Hearing this Word of God as the Word of God to us, we understand it and hide it in our heart. This Word of God brings us His promises. It brings us Christ and salvation, and we take hold of it. We are alive. When we are so alive, the result is that God determines the direction of our life. This is what it means to be alive to God.

Of course, we are one or the other. We are either alive to sin and dead to God, or we are dead to sin and alive to God.

The apostle is not addressing sinners here. He is addressing the church. He tells the church that the first practical result of his doctrine is that we are dead unto sin, but alive unto God. The apostle appeals to the self-consciousness of the church and says, "Reckon yourselves to be dead indeed unto sin, but alive unto God." Really, the apostle says to the church, "You must have before your mind an answer to the question 'What are you?' If anyone asks you, 'What do you say of yourself?' you must be able to say, 'I reckon myself to be dead unto sin, and alive unto God.'"

The idea is not that although we are *not* really dead to sin, nevertheless we must *reckon* ourselves to be dead unto sin. This interpretation is rising again in our day. This interpretation comes down to this: in this world we are not really *alive*, but we must *reckon* ourselves to be alive. We will only be alive *in the future*. We are not alive, but should reckon ourselves to be.

However, the apostle does not exhort us to reckon ourselves to be what we are *not*. He exhorts us to reckon ourselves to be what we *are*. We are dead to sin and alive to God. This is a fact. Because we *are* dead to sin and alive to God, we must reckon ourselves to be so. It is the reckoning of faith.

The Ground

This *reckoning* is a reckoning that cannot rest on experience. I would be ashamed to make this confession that I am dead to sin if it had to be based on experience. If we understand what this word means, we would be ashamed to repeat this confession after the apostle if it is based on our experience. According to our experience we are not dead to sin. We are not alive to God. Sin still seems to have sway over us, and we follow its dictates.

No, the apostle bases this reckoning on *Christ*. "Through Jesus Christ our Lord," the apostle says. This is the ground of the reckoning. In myself I am in the midst of death, but through Jesus Christ our Lord I can make this reckoning. As Christ died and is raised, so I also reckon myself to be dead and to be alive.

In other words, I make this self-estimation in Christ. Christ died. This is a fact. In a certain sense He is the only one who ever died. He is the only one who completely died. He is the only one who finished dying. Do you believe it? Let this be impressed upon your heart and mind. Christ died. He died as no other man ever died—as an act. This is why He arose again. He had finished dying from His relation to sin. He arose because He had so died. If we all could so die, we would all have to rise. If we could only die as a deed, and finish dying, we would not have to go to hell. This Christ did. He had to rise, and He did arise. He is now alive to God. He is the only one who is alive to God. There is no one alive to God outside of Him. And we are in Him.

When the apostle says, "through Jesus Christ our Lord," this means that we belong to a legal corporation of which Christ is the head. We belong to this corporation because of election. We do not determine this. We are in Christ because of election. To be in Christ means that in the legal sense we are before God in this corporation. And the reckoning of ourselves is through faith. We reckon that we belong to this corporation by faith. If this is the case, when Jesus died nineteen hundred years ago, we also died. By faith I say, "I have died. I will die no more." This is the testimony of faith. This is our confession. Therefore, when sin comes, we say, "No, I am dead to you." This is the gospel.

To be in Christ also means that there is a spiritual body in which the Spirit of Christ dwells and rules. This is the mystical body of Christ. When I believe that I am so in Christ, His death and resurrection are realized in me. His death actually becomes my death. His resurrection becomes my resurrection. The ground of my reckoning, then, is the crucified and risen Christ.

The Significance

There is one question that remains. Why does the apostle say, "Reckon yourselves"? Why does he not say, "You *are* dead to sin and alive to God"?

Let me use an illustration. Suppose there is a crown prince whose father dies when he is still very young. That crown prince is heir to the throne, but he is too young to rule. A king-regent is appointed temporarily, to rule in his stead. That king-regent is of a strong character and overbearing personality. When the crown prince becomes of age, he is crowned. But because he has been under the rule of that king-regent, and because that king-regent is of an overbearing personality who loves to rule, the crown prince allows him to continue to rule. The friends of that crown prince come to him and say, "You are king. Now reckon yourself to be king!"

The Christian has only a small beginning of the new obedience. Sin still wants to rule over him, and the Christian often gives in to sin. Therefore, the Word of God comes to him and says, "You are dead to sin. Now reckon yourself to be so."

The heeding of this admonition is significant from a practical point of view. If we hear this Word, and our heart and mind respond so that we really reckon ourselves to be dead to sin, we will say to sin, "Be dismissed." Not just once will we say this: while we sit in church. Say it tomorrow, and the next day, and all the time. Say, "I reckon myself to be dead to sin and alive to God." And walk as being dead to sin and alive to God.

Chapter Thirty-eight

The Justified Christian Liberated from the Dominion of Sin

Romans 6:14
For sin shall not have dominion over you: for ye are not under the law, but under grace.

It will be evident that in Romans 6:14 the apostle has reached a conclusion that is the very opposite of the contention expressed by those who objected to his doctrine of justification by faith. That contention was expressed in the first verse of this chapter. Although it was put in the form of a question, it was meant to contradict the doctrine of the apostle that a man must be justified by faith without any works on his part. The question was, "What shall we say then? Shall we continue in sin, that grace may abound?" Very simply, this is the charge that the doctrine of justification by faith alone inevitably leads to the teaching that it does not matter how the Christian lives. The conclusion of the objector is that if we are saved by grace, then the more we sin, the more grace will abound.

In this fourteenth verse the apostle reaches the very opposite conclusion from that of the objector. The objector says, "Your doctrine leads to a life of sin." To this the apostle raises a twofold counterargument. In the first place, he declares that as long as you are under the law, sin shall have dominion over you. In the second place, the apostle argues that instead of the doctrine of grace leading to a life of sin, the Christian, by this grace, is liberated from sin. For you are under grace, not under the law. If you are under the law, sin will have dominion over you, but you are under grace.

Therefore, says the apostle, let not sin reign in your mortal body [v. 12]. The reference is to the physical body, not because the body is the seat of sin, but because it is through the body—the eyes, the ears, the mouth, the hands, the feet—that sin expresses itself and becomes manifest. "Neither yield your members as instruments of unrighteousness unto sin: but yield yourselves (that is, your person, your mind, your will, your heart) unto God, as those that are alive from the dead, and your members as instruments of righteousness unto God" [v. 13].

What This Means

With emphasis, and in opposition to what the objector had stated in verse 1, the apostle attacks here the question, "Shall we continue in sin?" That was a proud question. It was a question rooted in the pride of the sinful heart, as if it were for man to decide whether he will continue in sin or not. The old Pelagian pride was expressed in that question. It is pride when the sinner assumes the attitude that he is the master of sin. He looks upon himself and acts in that delusion, as if at any time he can decide not to sin. And we must not forget, this lives also in our natural hearts. The sinner says, "I decided to sin; I wanted to sin. And although I know that I am playing with fire when I sin and that sin will lead me to destruction, I have sin in my own hand. And I can drop the fire whenever I want to and say, 'I will serve sin no longer.'" That is the Pelagian pride expressed in the question in the first verse: "What shall we say then? Shall we continue in sin?"

That attitude the apostle attacks when he says, "Sin shall not have dominion over you." It is implied in this statement that by nature sin does have dominion over us. It is impossible, therefore, for the sinner to say that sin shall or shall not have dominion over him. The sinner cannot say, "I can quit sinning whenever I want to." Why? Because he is under the dominion of sin.

It is easy to see how the sinner has the delusion that he can quit sinning if he wants to. This would not be the case if sin forced the sinner from without, forced him to sin against his will. It is true that, in a certain sense, the sinner is free to sin. But this is his only freedom. When we say that the sinner is free to sin, we mean that he never sins contrary to the dictates of his own heart. The sinner certainly decides upon every sinful act. He always stands before the alternative: what is according to God's law and what is contrary to that law. He stands with a subjective freedom before this alternative. He is like one born in a prison who does not know of a freedom beyond the prison walls. When he sins, he follows the dictates of his own heart and says, "I am free." However, it is nothing but imagination.

The apostle is speaking of the dominion of sin. Sin binds the sinner from within, not from without. It binds the sinner in his heart. This is the deepest aspect of his being. If sin were a question merely of the mind, or of the will, there would be conflict between the heart and the mind of the sinner. But there is no conflict. Sin is enthroned in the deepest depths of man's being. From the heart, sin rules over the mind, the will, and the desires. Sin has dominion over the sinner from the very root of his being to his entire life.

Sin has dominion over him. He can never say, "Sin shall not have dominion over me." And yet the fool says, "I am free." It is only in certain cases that the sinner becomes conscious that he is under the dominion of sin, that he cannot break away from the dominion of sin.

We must see that sin not only has dominion over the sinner, but sin is also his legal lord. We read in Romans 8:3, "God sending his own Son in the likeness of sinful flesh, and for sin, condemned sin in the flesh." That is, He condemned the right of sin to lord it over His people. Sin has a legal right to lord it over the sinner. The right of sin to lord it over the sinner is rooted in the guilt of the sinner. He is born under the sentence of death. This sentence includes what Scripture calls spiritual death. As he comes into the world, the guilty sinner is consigned to the service of sin. God has consigned him to the service of sin. The sinner has no right to be free from sin as long as his guilt is there. He is a legal slave of sin.

The apostle says to the church (remember, the apostle writes to the *church*), sin shall not have dominion over you. This is no admonition, no possibility, no exhortation. It is a fact. It is nonsense to come with the admonition *Let not sin have dominion over you* unless the fact is stated first. That would be like coming to a man locked up behind closed doors and barred windows in prison and calling to him, "Come out of your prison; don't sit there any longer." This is not any more foolish than it is to come to the sinner, who is under the dominion of sin, and to say to him, "You must quit sinning." It is not less foolish to go to the cemetery and call to the dead, "Come out of your graves; don't lie there any longer," than it is to say to the sinner, "Don't let sin have dominion over you any longer."

The apostle does not do this. The apostle comes with the fact. He says, "Sin shall not have dominion over you." The dominion of sin has been broken. The church must understand this as a matter of fact. The dominion of sin is broken as to its legal right and as to its actual dominion.

Impossible for the Law to Liberate Him

Inasmuch as the reason why sin shall not rule the Christian is that he is not under the law, it is evident that the Christian cannot be under the law and be freed from the dominion of sin. The law here does not refer to the ceremonial laws. The term *law* in Scripture does not always have the same meaning. In the text the apostle has reference to what we call the moral law. It is the law that is comprehended in this one expression:

love God. Not to be under the law means that one is not under the law's obligation. To be under the law means that one must do it himself. To be under the law means that in order to be free from sin, one must work.

This is impossible. The law can never free from sin. If you are under the law, you die in your sin. This is evident. The law can never do anything else but demand. It can never do anything but bless and curse. The law can demand, and it does. The law can say, "Love me with all the heart and mind and soul." This is all that the law can say. It makes no difference where you are. Even if you are in hell, the law will still say, "Love me." And if you do, the law will say, "I bless you." If you do, you shall live by that law. And if you don't, the law says, "Cursed." Cursed is everyone who does not keep the words of this law [Deut. 27:26]. This is all the law can do.

Suppose that from now on you could keep the law, loving God perfectly. The law would still say, "Satisfy me for the past." We can go a step further. Suppose that from the moment of your birth you had kept the law perfectly. Even then the law would condemn you because of your guilt. It condemns you because of the guilt in which you are born.

Of course, I have been supposing the impossible. We cannot keep the law. The sinner is under the dominion of sin. The law stands before him and says, "Cursed." The law says, "I agree with sin, and I give sin the right to continue its dominion over the sinner." If we are under the law, we are by the law consigned to sin's dominion.

This implies that all our darkness, all our troubles as a people of God, is due to the fact that we still consider ourselves to be under the law. It is not easy to say, "I am free from the law." This is because we cannot get rid of the notion that our works have something to do with our justification.

We are righteous by faith. As sin cannot detract from our righteousness, so our works do not add to our righteousness. As soon as we yield to the inclination that our works have something to do with our righteousness before God, we are not saved.

Liberated by Grace

We are saved by grace. Sin shall not have dominion over us, for we are under grace.

Do you believe this? This is the fundamental word of your life. It is the last word when you die. When you stand before God, you cannot do anything with your works. You cannot do anything with your works as a basis of righteousness. As a basis of righteousness, your works mean nothing. Sin shall have no dominion over you, for you are *under grace*.

Grace here has a twofold meaning. First, it is an attitude of favor that God assumes toward His people, from everlasting to everlasting. It is the attitude of favor that becomes manifest in the cross. It is the attitude of favor that became manifest in the blotting out of the sin and guilt of His people through the death of Christ. By that act of God, the dominion of sin is taken away. By looking at Christ we can say the dominion of sin is taken away. When He died, we all died. Sin can have no more dominion over me. And sin cannot appeal to the law anymore. The law does not agree with sin anymore. The law says to sin, "I am satisfied." This is grace.

Second, grace is also a power, for on the basis of that blotting out of your sins, God, by Christ, also delivers you from the power and dominion of sin. He breaks the shackles and leads you out of your prison. He says to you, through the gospel, "Sin shall not have dominion over you, for you are not under the law, but under grace."

Is this true? Of course, this is true. It is true of the church. This is the truth we receive by the faith God has planted in our hearts by that same grace. [In v. 11] the apostle has said, "Reckon yourselves to be dead unto sin," but in verse 14 he says, as a basis for that admonition, "Sin shall not have dominion over you, for you are under grace." If this is not so, it is hopeless. But if this is so, we can also say, "Let not sin therefore reign in your mortal body, that ye should obey it in the lusts thereof" [v. 12].

Chapter Thirty-nine

The Grace-gift of God

Romans 6:23
For the wages of sin is death; but the gift of God is eternal life through Jesus Christ our Lord.

The remoter context of this last verse of Romans 6 must be found in verse 17, for there we find the viewpoint from which the apostle considers those to whom he writes. We read in verse 17, "But God be thanked, that ye were the servants of sin, but ye have obeyed from the heart that form of doctrine which was delivered you." This is the viewpoint. He is addressing the church. He is addressing free men. He is, therefore, not admonishing people to become free. When the apostle writes to them, "The wages of sin is death; but the gift of God is eternal life," he is addressing those who have been liberated from the service of sin. He is addressing those who are heirs of eternal life. That remoter context shows that even as they had yielded their members servants to uncleanness and to iniquity, so they shall now yield their members servants to righteousness, unto holiness [v. 19].

In a closer context, the apostle is comparing the misery of the service of sin with the blessedness of the service of righteousness. The service of sin means misery, and the service of righteousness means blessedness because of the fruit each yields. The service of sin yields corruption and iniquity unto iniquity. The end of it is death. The apostle says that they who are in the service of righteousness yield fruit unto holiness [v. 22]. In verse 23 he comprehends this fruit into a general truth. When you were the servants of unrighteousness, you yielded fruit unto iniquity, for the wages of sin is death. But now that you are free, you yield fruit unto holiness, for the gift of God is eternal life.

The text teaches two contrasting truths, but the chief, the positive thought of the text, is that the gift of God is eternal life.

What It Is

The grace-gift of God is the opposite of that which the apostle mentions in the first part of the text: "The wages of sin is death." Death is not *nonbeing*.[1] This is what is so terrible about the nature of man. Man cannot *not* be. In this sense, man is immortal. Man is not immortal in the sense that he cannot die. In this sense, man is mortal. But if you mean immortality in the sense that man cannot *cease* to be, it is applicable. We read in this sense, in Revelation [9:6], that men shall seek death, and shall not find it. Men seek death. The suicide seeks death to escape from his own existence, but this is not possible.

Death in relation to God is that in a negative way the sinner tastes that God is good and that God maintains Himself as good—good in the sense of perfection. When God maintains His own goodness by causing the sinner to taste that He is good, the result is death for the sinner. The sinner seeks his good outside of God. But God maintains His goodness in the sinner by causing him to die. When the sinner turns against God, God turns against him in His wrath and makes him miserable. This is death. The wages of sin is death.

Here the apostle is speaking of final death. We have learned to speak of three stages of death. One is temporal death. Temporal death is the dissolution of the body. At the same time it

---

1. Swart's manuscript reads, "Death is not *not to be*."

is the preparation of the body for its eternal state, whether that be in glory or in damnation.

A second stage of death we call spiritual death. This is not merely death of the soul. Spiritual death is a moral, ethical reality. It is a turning about of the image of God as the punishment for sin. It is the turning about of original righteousness into unrighteousness. It is the turning about of original holiness into unholiness.

Eternal death, of which the apostle speaks in the text, is the third stage, in which the whole being will never have anything to do but suffer the wrath of God, by which he tastes, nevertheless, that God is good. That misery—the suffering that results when God causes the sinner to feel all His wrath so that he can never get away from it—that is hell. That is death in all its fulness.

The opposite of that death is eternal life. As death is not non-being, so life is not mere being.[2] Life is not merely that we exist, that we are. This is not life for man who is made after the image of God. The fact that we eat, walk, talk, and move about is no proof that we are living. For man who is made after the image of God, life is that state of the whole being in which the operation of that whole being is in the direction of God. To live is also to taste that God is good, but now positively. Death is to taste that God is good, negatively. Life is to taste, positively, that God is good. Life is to know, to have fellowship with, God.

Eternal life is not merely endless life. When the Bible speaks of eternal life, it does not have in mind life that is endless. Of course, it is true that eternal life is life without end. And what glory it will be that the moment of death will not even be in it! The moment of our death is in all our living now. Death follows us every step of the way. We live with that moment of death in all our existence. Living eternal life, we will never

---

2. Swart manuscript reads, "As death is not *not to be*, so life is not *to be*."

think of the end anymore. We will never be chased by death anymore. We will never say, "It is time; I must hurry."

Yet this is not the fundamental idea of eternal life in Scripture. Eternal life is *other* life. There never was such life. It is the life that became manifest in the resurrection of Christ. It is the resurrection life. It is a life on a higher plane that will be characterized by a higher revelation. Eternal life is to see God face-to-face. It is also evermore to respond to the sight of God.

Its Nature

Of this eternal life, the apostle says it is the gift of God. Again, there is contrast with death, which is *the wages of sin*. In this expression is a threefold idea. The first idea is that sin is the master, and the sinner is the servant. The sinner is the servant who voluntarily serves his master for wages. It is true that the sinner is bound to sin and can never be liberated from sin by his own power. Nevertheless, he is a willing servant. The sinner is bound from within. He is a voluntary servant. As such, the sinner receives wages, although not in the sense that sin naturally results in death. Death is punishment. When sin is presented as paying wages, it is only because God inflicts death upon the sinner. Because God has determined that death should be the punishment of sin, sin is presented as paying wages.

The second idea in *the wages of sin* is that of merit. The sinner merits something: death. Death is the only thing that the sinner can merit before God.

The third idea of these wages is that sinners receive what they agreed upon. There is in the expression *the wages of sin* the idea of agreement. The sinner receives what he agreed upon with his master. He receives his due wages. The wages he receives is death. And he agreed on those wages. So it was in paradise. Sin did not overtake man. Adam, although he did not say it, in his heart agreed to what God had said: "The day I eat thereof, I shall die." So it is always. We read in Romans

1:32 that they who do such things know that the result is death. The sinner knows that death is his wages. If he serves sin, the sinner knows that he must die. And he agrees that if he serves sin, he will die. This is the way it is now. This is the way it will be in hell. In hell all will agree that they received what they had agreed upon.

The apostle does not say this to scare the sinner out of the service of sin and into the service of righteousness. He is speaking to free men. But he writes this so that they who have been made free from sin should rejoice. "What shall we say? Shall we say, 'Let us continue in sin'? God forbid." It would be foolish that the heirs of life should say, "Let us continue in sin" when the wages of sin is death.

But the gift of God is eternal life. In the original we read, "the grace-gift." The Dutch has *de genadegifte*. Eternal life is a grace-gift. This means three things. If you ask, "Where does this gift come from, what is its ground, and why is it bestowed on me?" the answer is *grace*. Grace is the only source of this gift of eternal life. Grace is the only condition, motive, and source of this gift. If you ask, "How can it be bestowed on me? Is it not a contradiction to say, 'The wages of sin is death, but the gift of God is eternal life'?" If you ask, "How can this gift be bestowed on me?" the answer is, again, *grace*. Grace is the ground for this gift. If you ask how it is possible that one who is dead in sin can receive this gift, how he can become a partaker of it, the answer is, again, *grace*. Grace is the source, the ground, and the cause of our becoming partakers of the gift of eternal life.

It is a *grace-gift*. This excludes all merit. The gift of eternal life is a grace-gift. There is nothing of us in it. It is free grace. You must not mix the *source* of that gift with something of your own; you must say, "Grace." You must not mix the *ground* of that gift with something of your own; you must say, "Grace." You must not mix the *application* of that gift with something of your own; you must say, "Grace."

It is all of grace. There is in eternal life no work of man. You cannot merit eternal life. You can never merit anything with God. We are unprofitable servants. Suppose that God gave us the privilege of serving Him for one hundred years and then dropped us into nothingness. Would He be unrighteous? If we had served God for one hundred years, would we be able then to say to God, "Give me my wages"? No, it is a privilege to serve God. And the service of God is already the beginning of eternal life. God bestows the grace-gift first. When God bestows the grace-gift, we become active in His service.

Although eternal life is a gift, it is nevertheless in harmony with the righteousness of God. The unrighteous can never have eternal life. Eternal life is based on righteousness, but it is a righteousness of grace. This righteousness is itself a gift of grace.

How It Is Bestowed

This is why the grace-gift is in Christ. "The gift of God is eternal life through Jesus Christ our Lord." God made us one with Christ before the foundation of the world. He did so not because He saw anything in us. It was grace. Grace moved Him, not we. It was grace that caused Him to send Christ. It was grace that He sent Christ into death. And Jesus tasted death in all its fulness. Because He was the Son of God, His death had value to merit eternal life. It is grace that this righteousness of God in Christ is imputed unto us. It is grace that we receive it. This is why it remains of grace, even though it is based on Christ's righteousness.

But there is more. The gift is in Christ. Christ was raised from the dead. The Spirit is given Him to impart this gift unto His people. This is why the only way in which we can receive the gift is by faith. "Believe on the Lord Jesus Christ, and thou shalt be saved" [Acts 16:31]. The moment you believe, you shall be saved. Faith in Christ is the content of all the gospel whereby we have eternal life.

The apostle also connects the gift with the service of righteousness: "being made free from sin, and become servants to God, ye have your fruit unto holiness, and the end everlasting life" [v. 22]. This is the connection between holiness and eternal life. It is never of wages, but it is *the way*. The service of righteousness is the way in which we become heirs of eternal life. As the gift is of grace, so the way is also of grace.

The conclusion is this: thanks be to God that "ye were the servants of sin, but ye have obeyed from the heart that form of doctrine which was delivered you" [v. 17]. Therefore, you have been made free. This is the starting point.

What shall we say then? Shall we live in sin? God forbid. In the first place, we are dead to sin. In the second place, we have become servants of righteousness. Rejoice, therefore, in the liberty with which Christ has made you free. And yield not your members to be servants of sin, "but yield yourselves unto God, as those who are alive from the dead" [v. 13].

Chapter Forty

Our Marriage to the Risen Lord

Romans 7:4
Wherefore, my brethren, ye also are become dead to the law by the body of Christ; that ye should be married to another, even to him who is raised from the dead, that we should bring forth fruit unto God.

In chapter seven the apostle continues the discussion of his main theme as announced in verse 1 of the preceding chapter: "What shall we say, then, if we teach that justification is without the works of the law and that the law has nothing to do with our righteousness before God? What shall we say if we teach that righteousness is freely given us without our works? Shall we say, 'Let us continue in sin, that grace may abound the more abundantly'? God forbid."

More specifically, chapter 7 connects itself with the question asked in verse 15 of Romans 6. There the apostle had asked, "What then? shall we sin because we are not under the law, but under grace?" Is this the indication of the Christian's freedom from the law? Is this the practical conclusion: since the Christian has nothing to do with the law, he can sin freely? To elaborate upon this question, the apostle connects Romans 7 with the statement he made in Romans 6, namely, that the Christian is not under the law. That he is not under the law means that he has been united to someone else. This freedom from the law has been accomplished by the body, that is, by the death of Christ. Therefore, the apostle introduces this chapter by the general statement, "The law hath dominion over a man as long as he liveth" [v. 1]. He illustrates this general statement in verses 2 and 3. The woman is bound by the law to her husband as long as the husband lives.

This illustration the apostle applies in the text. The church used to be the wife of the law. As long as she was under that law, she was bound by that law, but she has been legally divorced from that law due to the fact that death came in. The death that came in was the death of Christ. By the death of Christ, the church was legally divorced from the law, so that the law is no more her husband. Therefore, the church is no more under the *law* of the law. Instead, she has been married to another. That other is Christ. And the purpose of this new marriage is that we should bring forth fruit unto God. We are united with Christ for this purpose.

A Legal Union

The text uses a figure. We used to be married to the law. Now we are married to Christ. What does this figure mean? First, what does it mean that by nature all men are *married* to the law?

The law in the text is not merely the Jewish ceremonial law. The attempt has been made to show that the apostle is referring to the law in the Old Testament sense, that is, to the ceremonial law. But this is not the case. This is plain from the entire chapter. The apostle says, for example, in verse 7, "I had not known lust, except the law had said, Thou shalt not covet." There the apostle evidently refers to the law of the ten commandments. He also says that the law is holy, just, good, and spiritual [vv. 12, 14]. He could never say this of the law of the Old Testament church. The apostle, therefore, does not mean that we are married to the law of shadows. He refers, rather, to the entire law.

From this law the Christian is made free. The meaning is not that he is free to violate the law. This is not freedom. When the apostle speaks of the Christian being free from the law, he does not mean that formerly he was obliged to keep the law, but that now he has been freed from this obligation. If we understand the law as the requirement to love God above all, and the neighbor as ourselves, the law is not abolished.

Instead, the apostle teaches that we were under the *law* of the law, or the yoke of the law. The *law* of the law is that the law says, "Keep me, and you shall live." The negative *law* of the law is this: "Cursed be everyone who does not keep me." If when we are married to the law, we are ever to become righteous before God, we must never fail to observe the law perfectly. If we fail to observe the law perfectly, even for a second, we will be immediately under the curse of the law. This was our former relation to the law.

Under the law there is no mercy, no pardon, no way out. The law can never say anything but "Keep me, and live." The law does not say, "If you keep me, I will give you the eternal life that is in Christ." The law cannot give the higher, perfect life that we have in Christ. It is often presented so, but this is a mistake. The law cannot say anything but "Observe me, and live; break me, and die." The law does not say, "Keep me, and I will give you life." The law says, "If you keep me, I will not kill you. But speak one word against me, and I will kill you."

Under this law we were held. This is the law under which we all are by nature. Let us remember this. If we want to be saved by works—if, for example, we want to be saved by our faithful worship on the Lord's Day—we must sit perfectly. We must be able to say, "Lord, Thou canst not lay a finger on me." We must be able to say, "I have kept thy law perfectly." But this is impossible. Under this law we were formerly. That was a hopeless case.

Under this law Adam was placed. With Adam it seemed a little better. It did not seem quite so hopeless with him. The Lord said to Adam, "If you keep My law, I will not kill you." The Lord did not say, "If you keep My law, I will give you life," but He said, "If you don't keep My law, I will kill you." Adam failed. The result was that the law cursed him, and he died.

Also Adam became corrupt and could never keep the law again. In Adam we are a people who cannot keep the law. In fact, the more the law says, "Do this," the more we say, "I will not." The result is that the law can only curse us. It is absolutely hopeless.

The apostle says that we are become *dead* to the law. In other words, we are divorced from the law. The sense is not that we have nothing to do with the keeping of the law anymore, as some wrongly teach. Rather, we are free from the *law* of the law. The law can never say to me anymore, "Do this, and you shall live." It can never say to me anymore, "Fail, and I will curse you." In this respect the Christian is free.

We must assume this attitude over against the law. This is difficult because there is the tendency in our nature to suppose that we must do something to be righteous before God. The more we are frightened by our old attitude to the law, the more we stand in jeopardy every day. If you allow the law to come to you and say, "Do this, and live," and you don't say to the law, "We are divorced"; if you allow the law to say to you, "Do this, and live," and you don't cut it off; if you allow the law to say to you, "Do this, or I will curse you," and you don't cut it off—in each case you will lose your faith. You must tell the law, "I am righteous. Do you tell me, 'Do this, and become righteous'? I *am* righteous. Do you tell me, 'Do this, and live'? I *do* live. I am *free.*"

We are divorced from the law through the body of Christ, through the cross of Christ, through the death of Christ—they all mean the same thing. Christ died in the body. He lay down His life in the body. He did so under the law. The law came and said to Christ, "Do this." And Christ said, "I will." The law said, "Remember that Thou must stand at the head of a cursed people and that Thou must satisfy me." And Christ said, "I will." He bore the curse voluntarily, obediently, satisfying the demands of the law. In His body, that is, by His death, Christ became free from the law under which He came.

Because He died not for Himself but for His church, the

church is divorced from the law. No more than the law can say to Christ, "Do this, and live," can it say to the church, "Do this, and live." God's people must say, "We are free from the law."

A Glorious Union

This is of practical significance for our life of faith. This is the faith by which we live. This faith we must have in death. When we die, it must be so with us that we are righteous without the law.

And we must be married to Christ. The church is not divorced to remain a widow. No, she is divorced to become another's. That other is Christ. The church has become the wife of Christ. This means two things. First, our marriage to Christ has the legal significance that He is our Lord. We belong to Him, He owns us, we are His property, and He is responsible for us. Second, there is a real, organic union between Christ and us, a union symbolized in the natural marriage relationship between man and wife.

Our marriage with Christ is a *union of life*. We are bone of His bone and flesh of His flesh. Out of Him flows a stream of life into the church. There is in this marriage relationship a *union of love,* based on the union of life. This union is an *exclusive relationship*. Just as the marriage relation between man and wife is exclusive, so the relation between Christ and His people is exclusive. Christ belongs to the church, and the church belongs to Christ and to no one else. If she flirts, she becomes an adulteress. Finally, it is a *union for life*. The union cannot be broken, even as the marriage relation cannot be broken. The marriage relation is a union for life.[1] In this case, the marriage is eternal, for Christ can never die. The reason He cannot die is because He is raised. We must not simply say that

---

1. Already in the late 1930s, Hoeksema had come to believe and was teaching his congregation that marriage is an unbreakable bond for life. This is demanded by the unbreakable nature of the covenant relation between Christ and the church, of which marriage is the symbol.

we have been married to Christ. We must say that we have been married to Him who was raised from the dead. The church has become the wife of the risen Lord.

That Christ is raised means two things. It means, first, that He is righteous and that we are righteous in Him. Second, the resurrection of Christ means that He is possessor of the glorious life the Father gave Him. He is possessor of the life that the law could not give. That Jesus is risen does not mean that He came down from the level of our life and was then raised back to the same level. He arose to a higher life. That we have been married to Christ who was raised from the dead means that we have become partakers of that higher life.

When the law says, "Do this, and live," we must say, "We have a life that you could never give. We have been married to Christ. We are righteous with a righteousness that you cannot give."

God realized this union. It is not our work. It is God's work because He conceived of this marriage in His counsel. He conceived of Christ as the bridegroom and of the church as the bride. Also, He realized this counsel in time. By faith alone we live in this union, and we are righteous.

A Fruitful Union

The purpose is that we should bring forth fruit unto God. What shall we say then? Shall we say, "Let us continue in sin, that grace may abound"? How absurd! The purpose of our relation to Christ is that we should bring forth fruit.

We always bring forth fruit, either to sin unto death, or to God unto righteousness. When the apostle speaks of bringing forth fruit, he uses figurative language. He compares the church to a tree. We bring forth fruit by the constant activity of our body and of our soul; by our willing, thinking, and desiring; by our walking and talking; and by all our actions. Always we bring forth fruit. By nature we bring forth fruit unto the devil. That we did under the law. Therefore, the emphasis falls on the phrase *we should bring forth fruit unto God*.

The meaning is not that we do something for God so that we can say to God, "See what I have done." Nor is the reference to certain actions, such as preaching or teaching. Not at all. The expression refers to our whole life. To bring forth fruit unto God is to be motivated by the love of God and to praise Him in all our life. The church does this. Because she has been divorced from the law and has been married to Christ, the church brings forth fruit unto God. Bringing forth fruit, therefore, is due to our marriage with Christ. Christ is the vine; we are the branches. Christ brings forth fruit, but in the branches. Therefore, we have nothing of which to boast.

In this respect we differ from the tree. The tree does not know that it brings forth fruit. God brings forth fruit in the tree, but the tree does not know it and therefore is not blessed in bringing forth fruit. But we do know. God brings forth fruit through our will, our mind, and our heart. God's purpose becomes our purpose. And this is our chief reward. This is our true blessedness: we bring forth fruit unto God. This is the glory and the blessedness of the heavenly life.

What shall we say then? As a church we shall say that we are redeemed. We shall say that we are free from the law. We shall forbid the law to condemn us. We shall say that we have righteousness to begin with. We shall forbid the law to say to us, "I will give you life." We shall say to the law, "I have life to begin with."

What shall we say then? Shall we say, "Let us live in sin"? God forbid. It was God's purpose in making us free from the law and in uniting us to Christ that we should bring forth fruit unto God. And God's purpose has become our purpose.

Chapter Forty-one

Serving in Newness of Spirit

Romans 7:5, 6

For when we were in the flesh, the motions of sins, which were by the law, did work in our members to bring forth fruit unto death.

But now we are delivered from the law, that being dead wherein we were held; that we should serve in newness of spirit, and not in the oldness of the letter.

*E*specially the last part of the text constitutes a new element to which the apostle calls attention, in distinction from what he has taught in the immediately preceding verses. The new element is that we should serve in newness of Spirit and not in the oldness of the letter. In verse 4 the apostle has called attention to the fact that formerly we were joined to the law, as in a marriage relationship. Therefore, we were under the *law* of the law. The *law* of the law is that we must obtain righteousness and life by performing all that is prescribed in the law. That was our former union. That union was hopeless.

But we have been made free from that obligation of the law. We have become dead to the law. That we have become dead to the law is due to the fact that Christ died. The death of Christ is our death. The death of Christ is of such a nature that He fulfilled the obligation of the law, removed the curse of the law, and merited life. The result is that we have righteousness and life to begin with. This is our new marriage relation, for we are joined to Him. Being joined to Him, we bring forth fruit unto God.

This is in answer to the question [of Rom. 6:1]: "What then? Shall we sin because we are not under the law?"

The apostle is still busy with that question. [In the text] he answers that question in a twofold way, negatively and positively. This is plain from the word *For*. We bring forth fruit unto God when we are joined to Christ, and not when we are under the law, *for* when we were under the law, we served the flesh. The result is that the motions of sin, which were by the law, did work in our members to bring forth fruit unto death. Therefore, when we are under the law, we cannot bring forth fruit unto God. But now, delivered from the obligation of the law, we serve in newness of Spirit and not in the oldness of the letter.

What This Means

We must pay attention to the fact that the apostle is speaking of serving in newness of Spirit in contrast with serving in the oldness of the letter. Serving in the oldness of the letter refers to our work under the obligation of the law. Why does the apostle call this the *service* of the letter? What does this mean? It is usually explained as meaning the external keeping of the law. This is true, but this is not the fullest explanation of the term. Notice that the apostle speaks of the *letter* of the law. The letter of the law is the law as it is written. We must distinguish between the letter of the law and the law itself. The law is the living will of God concerning us. This is the essence of the law. When this law is written in our hearts, it becomes a power. When it is written in our hearts, it produces the knowledge of sin and brings us to our knees. Then it becomes a power. When man was created, he did not have the letter of the law. He had the law. But the apostle is speaking of the letter of the law. In other words, he is speaking of merely the written copy of the law. That written copy of the law he calls the *letter* of the law. What does that letter of the law do? It is a means to convey the will of God to us. This is all that the letter of the law can do. It cannot change us. It can do nothing but convey to us the will of God concerning us. This is what the letter of the law did in Israel. It came to Israel and said, "Don't do that; go this way." This is all that the letter of the law could do. The *service* of the letter, therefore, is the service that we can do when we have nothing but the external letter of the law.

The question is, what becomes of us if we have this? The apostle says that when we were under the law, we were in the flesh. And when we were in the flesh, the motions of sin, which were by the law, did work in our members. *Flesh* has more than one meaning in Scripture. It can refer to the soft substance of our bodies. So we read in I Corinthians 15[:50]: "Flesh and blood cannot inherit the kingdom of God." Sometimes Scripture refers to flesh as the body of sin because it is in the body that sin comes to manifestation. Because it is the body through which sin expresses itself, flesh is also used for the sinful nature, as in Romans 8:3: "For what the law could not do, in that it was weak through the flesh, God sending his own Son in the likeness of sinful flesh, and for sin, condemned sin in the flesh." When *flesh* is used in contrast with the *Spirit,* it refers to our nature as it is under the power of sin.

It is in this last sense that the apostle uses *flesh* in the text. We are no more in the flesh; that is, we are no more under the dominion of the sinful nature. We were in the flesh; hence, we were incapable of doing any good. We were all under the influence of the sinful flesh. We were inclined unto all evil in the sense that we had fallen flat into evil, so that the heart, the mind, and the will always tended in the direction of evil. We did not love God, but we hated Him. We could have no delight in the will of God, but had to have a delight in what is contrary to His will. This is what it means to be *in the flesh.*

The letter of the law came to us when we were in the flesh. It was not the law that came to us, but the letter of the law. What was the result? It came to us and said, "Do this, and don't do that. Go in this way." What was the result? The apostle says,

"The motions of sin, which were by the law, did work in our members."

When the letter of the law, when the written law, comes to sinful man, what is the effect? Does it improve him? Does it strike his will? And when it does, does he say, "I am sorry that I did not keep the letter of the law"? Is the influence of the letter of the law that it checks sin in man so that he does not become quite so sinful? So it is sometimes said. But this is not true. This is not even true of the political laws. This is not true of the municipal laws. If you do not put a policeman by a stop sign, man will not stop for it. Man will not stop unless he is afraid for his hide. This is not the effect of the law.

When the law says, "Do not do this, and do this," the flesh reacts. When the law says, "Don't do this," the flesh says, "I will." When the law says, "Do this," the flesh says, "I won't." The law tickles sin into action. The law incites the flesh into sinful actions. This was the case with Israel. There was never a more corrupt nation than Israel. Why? Because the law, working upon the sinful flesh, wrought death.

Don't you see how hopeless it is? The more you know of the law, the more you will go against it. Do not say, then—if you understand the letter of the *gospel* and come to humiliation and confession—that it was yourself. By nature you don't want the gospel.

In contrast with the service of the letter of the law, the apostle introduces the service in newness of Spirit. Service in newness of Spirit is the opposite of the service in the oldness of the letter. When the apostle speaks of the *spirit,* he does not mean your spirit. He means the Holy Spirit. You must read the text this way: in newness of the Holy Spirit. *Newness of spirit* is newness that the Spirit has wrought in us. Instead of the old mind, there is wrought in that same mind a new principle. The old mind is not taken away, but in that old mind the Spirit works something new, so that the mind works in the direction of God. So it is with all our nature. In the old will, the Spirit works a new tendency: to will the will of God. When He works this newness, the Spirit gives the Christian a new heart. From the heart are the issues of life, so that the Christian has a new mind, a new will, and new desires.

Do you see the difference? Under the old relation, in which we were under the law, we had to work our own righteousness and life. When the law said, "Do!" we said, "Don't." Now the Spirit comes. He works newness in the heart, in the mind, and in the will.

What is the result? Does the Christian become perfect? It might seem so, but if you read the rest of this chapter, you will see that this is not the case. If you want to know whether you serve in newness of Spirit, you must not ask, "Am I perfect?" But you must ask, "Do I find in myself the prayer that I may be pleasing to God?" Do not deceive yourself. We are in the midst of death. Don't try to gauge yourself by perfection. But if you want to know whether you serve in newness of Spirit, you must ask, "Do I find in me the prayer 'O God, be merciful to me, a sinner'?" This is the same as the prayer "Deliver me from sin." Is this your desire? This is not of the flesh, for the direction of the flesh is exactly the opposite.

How This Service Is Realized

Do you find this? If so, this is wrought in you by the new union with the resurrected Lord. The apostle says that we are *delivered* from the law. He uses a strong word. The word really means that the law has been put to nought. It means that all our connection with the law has ceased. We may read, "But now, having no connection with the law anymore, we serve in newness of Spirit." The meaning is not that we have nothing to do with the law anymore. But we are free from the *law* of the law. We have righteousness to begin with. This righteousness we have, the apostle says, because "we are dead to that wherein we were held." That *wherein we were held* is the law. But we died in that bondage. And the law can never more say, "Do this and live." We died to the law.

How? Christ died. This is the foundation of all that has been said. We must believe in this Christ, crucified and raised, and then we shall be saved. Christ died and thus removed the curse of the law and merited eternal life. We must believe. Nothing else! We must believe. By this faith in the Lord who was crucified so, who died so, and who was raised so—in this faith we say, "I am righteous." No matter how corrupt we may seem, no matter how sinful, by faith in the risen Lord we say, "I am righteous."

What the Fruit Is

United with Christ, we bring forth fruit. In the old service, we brought forth fruit unto death. Our fruit is our actions. That we bring forth fruit unto death means that under the law we did nothing but what was worthy of death. Being worthy of death, all that we did tended to death.

Being delivered from that obligation of the law and starting out with righteousness, we bring forth fruit unto God. Hallelujah! For bringing forth fruit unto God is to bring forth fruit unto eternal life through Jesus Christ our Lord.

Chapter Forty-two

The State of Imperfect Perfection of the Christian

Romans 7:15-17
For that which I do I allow not: for what I would, that do I not; but what I hate, that do I.
If then I do that which I would not, I consent unto the law that it is good.
Now then it is no more I that do it, but sin that dwelleth in me.

The main question that must be answered before all things is this: "Who is speaking in these verses?" In what capacity, in what state, is the apostle speaking in the text? Does he speak as a natural man? Does he say this of himself as he was before his conversion? Or does he speak as a converted Christian? This question must be answered first.

Pelagianism always answers this question in such a way that it is the natural man who is speaking. According to this view of the chapter, in verse 9, where the apostle says that he was alive without the law once, he refers to the time of his childhood. "When I was a little child," the apostle means, "I was without the law. And then I was alive, that is, I did not feel myself to be under the sentence of death. But as soon as I began to know the law, then I began to know that I was under the sentence of death." Throughout this chapter, according to this Pelagian interpretation, the apostle is speaking of himself as a natural man. So also does he speak in the text. As a natural man, the apostle says, "For that which I do I allow not: for what I would, that do I not; but what I hate, that do I."

But this interpretation is impossible. In the first place, when the apostle says, "I was alive without the law once," he could not refer to his childhood, for in that sense the apostle never was without the law, not even in his childhood. He always had the law. From his childhood he had known the law. The apostle could not speak of a time when he was without the law.

In the second place, this interpretation is impossible because of what we read in verse 20: "If I do that I would not, it is no more I that do it, but sin that dwelleth in me." This is not the language of a natural man. Again, in verse 19, "For the good that I would I do not: but the evil which I would not, that I do" cannot be said by the natural man. Nor can that which is said in verse 18: "For I know that in me (that is, in my flesh) dwelleth no good thing: for to will is present with me; but how to perform that which is good I find not." The natural man does not speak this way. According to the context, therefore, the apostle does not speak of himself in his natural state.

Besides, this would be contrary to the teaching of Scripture. It would be contrary especially to the teaching of Paul. Paul does not teach that the natural man says, "For that which I do I allow not: for what I would, that do I not; but what I hate, that do I." To the contrary, he speaks of the natural man as being dead in sin and misery. The apostle, therefore, does not refer to the natural man.

Instead, he refers to the Christian. When he says, "I was alive once without the law," he refers to his pharisaical state. Then he was without the law. It was not that he did not have the law in the *external* sense. Rather, he did not have the law in the *spiritual* sense. He did not have the law in his heart. Then the apostle was alive; he looked upon himself as righteous. In other words, he did not consider himself to be under the sentence of death.

But the law came to him in the spiritual sense. Then two

things happened. First, sin began to work. Second, the apostle began to see himself as being under the sentence of death. He began to see himself as unrighteous. Thus, the apostle begins to describe the Christian as he is in this world.

A Strange Experience

Although Paul is speaking of his own experience, his purpose is not that we should make a study of the apostle. The purpose is that we should find *ourselves* in this picture. The apostle is examining himself. He asks himself the question, "Am I really righteous? Am I really dead to sin?" He expresses the answer in strange language, in terms of his own experience.

Our English translation is not exact. Throughout the passage we find, in the King James, the word *do*. Three times in verse 15 we read the word *do,* but in the original, the text uses three different words. The basic meaning of all three is expressed in our word *do,* but they have different meanings. In the first phrase, where we read in our translation, "For that which I *do* I allow not," we read in the original, "What I *have accomplished,* what I *have finished,* that I allow not." In the second phrase, we ought to read, "For what I would, that I *practice* not;" that is, "I do not *do it habitually;* I do not *do it all the time.*" And in the last phrase—"What I hate, that *do* I"—the translation "do" is correct.

There is one more correction. We read, "For that which I do I *allow* not." That *allow not* should be, "I *know* not, I don't *recognize* it."

We must read Romans 7:15 this way: "What I have accomplished, what I have finished, I know not, I don't recognize, for what I would, that I practice not; but what I hate, that I do." The meaning of the first phrase is this: "What I have accomplished, I know not; I don't recognize it. I thought I was doing something good, but now when it is finished, I don't know it; I don't recognize it. It is so polluted with sin that I don't recognize it." Is not this the experience of us all? When we look back on our work, is it not true that so much corruption and so many sinful thoughts crept in that we say of our work, I don't know it anymore. If we examine our work, we find that it is polluted with sin. We don't recognize it; at least we don't approve of it anymore.

[In the second part of v. 15] the apostle means, "What I would, that is, that in which I have a delight, I do not *practice.*" The apostle is not saying, "I never do it," but he is saying, "I do not *practice* it; I don't do it *habitually;* I don't *always* do it."

[In the third part of the verse] the apostle says that what he hates, he does. That is, he often does it: "I often do that which I hate."

There is in this word of the apostle an expression of love for that which is good. There is also an expression of hatred for that which is evil. But while the apostle loves what is good and hates what is evil, he does what he hates, and what he loves, he does not.

We must remember that it is the same person who is speaking here. The Christian is not a dual person. This one and the same person speaks of himself in the most contradictory terms. In the natural sense, it is possible to do what we hate. But this is not what the apostle is speaking of. He is speaking of the same person with respect to the same thing: "What I would, I do not; but what I hate, that I do." This is a paradox. The apostle says that he loves that which he does not do, and he hates that which he does. He thinks what he does not want to think, and what he wants to think, he does not think. He desires what he does not want to desire, and what he wants to desire, he does not desire. He wills what he does not want to will, and what he wants to will, he does not will.

You say this is dark language? But this is experience. This is exactly what the Christian does.

A Perfect Man Speaking

How must this dark language be explained?

The one who is speaking is a perfect man. This must be understood. He may be an imperfect perfect man, but he is certainly a perfect man. This becomes evident when he says, "What I would, that do I not." What is it that the apostle would, or wills? He wills to keep the law of God. This is his delight. And he who has his delight in the law of God is a perfect man. The same is evident when he says, "What I hate, that I do." He may do it, but he hates it. And one who hates evil is a perfect man. This is evident also when the apostle says, "It is no more I that do it, but sin that dwelleth in me." This is a perfect man.

Scripture speaks of the *perfect* man time and time again. II Corinthians 5:17 says, "If any man be in Christ, he is a new creature: old things are passed away; behold, all things are become new." There you have the perfect man. In I John 3:9 the apostle John says, "Whosoever is born of God doth not commit sin; for his seed remaineth in him: and he cannot sin, because he is born of God." This is the perfect man.

So here the perfect man speaks. "If then," the apostle says, "I do that which I would not, I consent to the law that it is good. That is, I consent to the law, I agree with the law, I delight in doing what is in the law." This is the perfect man speaking.

What is the perfect man? The Christian is perfect in principle, spiritually. He is regenerated and called. What happens when a man is regenerated and called? Not this: he is reformed, so that he says, "I used to drink and curse, but I don't anymore." That is reformation, not regeneration. But when a man is regenerated, Christ Himself, through the Spirit, takes hold of his heart. What does He do with that heart? He turns that heart around. With the fall of man, what happened? His heart was attached to the world of the lie. When a man is regenerated, Christ takes hold of his heart and turns his heart around. This is why I say that a Christian is a perfect man, in a spiritual, ethical sense.

The Christian is not a man with two hearts. He is a man with a new heart. And this heart is perfect. The Christian never sins from the heart. His heart, from a spiritual, ethical point of view, is perfect. This is what the apostle means when he says, "It is no more I that do it, but sin that dwelleth in me." This is why he says, "What I hate, that do I." From the heart he says, "I hate sin." And from the heart he says, "I have a delight in the law of God, after the inward man."

This is one-half of the Christian.

The Indwelling of Sin

But it is not all of the Christian. The other half is this: "Sin . . . dwelleth in me." Where is this sin? Not in the heart. The heart is regenerated. And if only there were no outside influences, the Christian would be able to say, "I do what I would, and I don't do what I hate." This will be the case in heaven, but this is not the case here. Why not? It is because a regenerated man is perfect only *in principle*. He is perfect only in beginning, not in full. Sin dwelleth in him.

Where does sin dwell? Not in the heart. Where then? In the body, for one thing. The body is not regenerated until the resurrection. And this body has been in the service of sin for six thousand years. We do not get our body new. Our body was old when it was born. We got our body from our parents, and our parents got their body from their parents, and so on. And the ruts of sin are in this body. The ruts of sin are also in our soul-life. And there are ruts of sin in the life of our spirit, outside the heart. There are ruts of sin in our body, in our soul-life, and in the life of our spirit, all outside the heart.

What happens in the experience of the Christian? From the regenerated heart come motions of righteousness, of love of God, of hatred of sin, of love for God's law. And when these motions issue from the heart, they often get into the ruts in our nature. Therefore, the Christian can say, "It is not I that do it, but sin that dwelleth in me." Remember, too, the motions of sin are around us. This is why it is so nice that we have services in church. Then we are separated from the world. But with the old nature, with its ruts of sin, the Christian lives in the world of sin. Therefore, he says, "My work is finished, but it is so corrupt that I do not know it; I do not recognize it. What I would, I do not; but what I hate, that I do."

Notice the attitude. The Christian does not say, "I sin, but I can't help it, and therefore I need not worry. To the contrary, the Christian hates sin. He turns to the cross. He fights the battle of faith to the very end.

Then this language will change. Then he will say, "I have a delight in the law of God, and I will forever live out that delight perfectly."

Chapter Forty-three

The Wretched Christian

Romans 7:24, 25a
O wretched man that I am! who shall deliver me from the body of this death? I thank God through Jesus Christ our Lord.

A personal note characterizes both the context and this final exclamation of the apostle. When the Bible uses language of this kind, the purpose is not that we should make a psychological study of the apostle Paul, but that we should join in his confession. This expression of the apostle is the expression of all the people of God.

If we are to receive this Word of God, we must therefore assume the attitude expressed in the question [v. 24]. Are we able to take this confession on our lips? Is what the apostle expresses here our experience? Can we say, "O wretched man that I am"? Have we learned to say this? This is an extremely important and practical question.

If we have learned to say this, do we then also say, "Who shall deliver me from the body of this death?" The apostle does not merely say that he is a miserable man. He follows it up with the question "Who shall deliver me?" Do we ask this question? Is this question in our souls?

If this exclamation of the apostle—"O wretched man that I am!"—lives in our souls, and the question follows, "Who shall deliver me from the body of this death?" do we then also find the answer: "through Jesus Christ our Lord"?

If we say that we have found this answer, do we bear the seal of the genuineness of it in what the apostle says: "I thank God"?

This is the general significance of this Word of God. We find here the same line that we have in our Heidelberg Catechism, namely, knowledge of misery, of deliverance, and of gratitude. "O wretched man that I am"—there is your misery. "Through Jesus Christ our Lord"—there is your deliverance. "I thank God"—there is your gratitude.

The context shows that this exclamation of the apostle is the result of a self-examination. He found a conflict in his life. There were two laws in him. There was a law in him according to which he had a delight in the law of God, but there was also a law in his members that brought him into captivity to the law of sin. These two laws warred against each other. The result of that twofold law was that what he loved to do, he did not do, and he often found that he did what he hated. That was the conflict.

With a view to that conflict in his nature, the apostle came to the exclamation in the text: "O wretched man that I am! who shall deliver me from the body of this death? I thank God through Jesus Christ our Lord."

Who He Was

The exclamation *O wretched man that I am!* shows a consciousness of a deep misery. There is something in the man's life that is a burden to him and that he would like to cast off. The question is, what is the cause of this misery? Why is the man so miserable?

Some people feel miserable because of all kinds of natural suffering. They are in trouble, in distress, in suffering. They are inclined to cry out, "O wretched man that I am!" This does not mean very much. There are others who would cry out, "O wretched man that I am" with respect to the results of sin. They are going to die. With a view to their death, they are inclined to cry out, "O wretched man that I am!" This does not mean much. There are even people who are miserable because they feel that they are not saved. That is, they are afraid that when they die, they will not go to heaven. There is nothing distinctively Christian in this. There is nothing of all this in the text.

The apostle is not thinking of natural misery; he conceives of this as of little significance. Nor is he afraid of death; in fact, he longs for it—not for death as such, but for what death will bring him. Nor is it that the apostle is afraid that he is not saved; he *is* saved. It makes a difference what is the cause of our misery.

In this case, the cause of the misery of the people of God is *the body of this death*. What is the body of this death? In the first place, the apostle refers to his body. Some would take the expression in a figurative sense. They say that the apostle conceives of sin as a body. And he calls it the body of his death. But Scripture presents the body as the instrument of sin and, therefore, as representative of the old nature. Sin is accomplished by the body.

In the second place, by the word *body* Scripture covers all that is elsewhere called "the old nature." Note well, the apostle does not say, "the body of death," but he says, "the body of this kind of death." Sin reveals itself in the body. This is why the apostle calls it the body of this death. It is of this body of sin and death that the apostle would like to be delivered. In the original his words are, "Who shall deliver me *out of the body of this death*?" He is now *in* this body. According to the inward man, he is in this body. And he cries out, "O wretched man that I am! who shall deliver me from the body of this death?"

This is why we speak of a wretched Christian. There is no natural man who will take this language on his lips. The natural man may find himself miserable for many reasons. He may be miserable as the result of his sin. By the result of sin, I mean every form of death. Because of the result of sin, the natural man feels remorse. But if this is the character of one's misery, he will always find in the knowledge of misery this testimony: "If only I could sin safely, I would not mind it. If only I could sin safely without suffering the results, I would sin." This is characteristic of the natural man. Why? Because he is not miserable on account of his sins, but on account of the results of his sins. He never exclaims with the apostle, "O wretched man that I am!"

Back of this exclamation is the desire after perfection, which is rooted in the love of God. In principle the Christian, if he examines himself, will find in his heart a longing after perfection. It is this longing after perfection that causes him to look at the other part of himself and to cry out, "O wretched man that I am!"

What He Seeks

Another mark of this unique knowledge of misery is that the wretched Christian seeks deliverance. This does not mean that there is in man a period in which he seeks, and another period in which he finds, and another period in which he is thankful. These three are simultaneous. These three are always present in the life of the Christian. The Christian is always a seeking, finding, and thankful person. Therefore, if we say this with the apostle, we cannot stop there. If we say, "O wretched man that I am," we must also say, "Who shall deliver me?" The Christian must seek deliverance. From what? From the body of this death. This implies that he seeks legal deliverance from the body of this death. But this is not all. He also seeks deliverance from its power.

Also, the Christian always seeks a deliverer because in the midst of this knowledge of his misery, he knows that he cannot deliver himself. This is why the apostle does not say, "How must I be delivered?" He says, "Who shall deliver me?"

The man who comes to the knowledge of his misery surely seeks. The man who has only dogmatic knowledge of his misery does not seek. There is also another type of people who do not seek. They are a sickly kind of people. They are people who have a certain sickly knowledge of sin. They are people who leave the impression that they rejoice in the fact that they are able to say that they are so miserable. You can recognize these people by the fact that they always stop there. They say, "O wretched man that I am!" And there they stop. They do not seek. This is not the apostle. If one knows his misery, he seeks spontaneously.

What He Finds

And he finds. This is just as true as that first element. The outcry *O wretched man that I am* is surely followed by the question *Who shall deliver me?* And the question *Who shall deliver me?* is surely followed by the answer: *through Jesus Christ our Lord.* A man once said to me that he had been seeking all his life. I told him that was not true. Scripture says that he who seeks shall surely find. This man said, "Yes, but in God's time." I answered, "Yes, and God's time is, 'Before they call, I will answer them.'" This surely follows. You cannot ask the question without the answer being there. If you seek, you shall surely find.

Why are there so many who seem to seek and never find? There may be three reasons for this. In the first place, it may be that they are not really seeking after all. This is possible. Our hearts are so deceitful. It is possible that while we exclaim, "Who shall deliver me?" there is something in our hearts that says, "I hope the Lord doesn't hear me." This is possible because of a certain sin we don't want to be rid of.

In the second place, it may be that we don't seek the right thing. If you ask some people what is the object of their search, they will have to confess that what they seek is the assurance that when they die, they will go to heaven. For this the Christian does not seek. This is of minor importance. This is a secondary concern. The main object of the search of the Christian is that he may be delivered from the body of this death. And if you really seek deliverance, you will find the answer.

The third possibility is that we do not seek in the right way. How do you seek? There is only one way: in the Word of God. Some people would like to have an angel come down from heaven to tell them. That cannot be. Others would like to have a certain word, or a certain experience. But it is a seeking outside of the Word of God. These people do not find. You cannot find God outside of the Word. But if you seek the answer to the question "Who shall deliver me?" in the Bible, you will find the answer.

This will never fail, because the answer is there. God gives the answer, but He gives it through His Word. And God's answer is, "I will deliver, through Jesus Christ." Another reason the answer can never fail is because the seeking is already the fruit of grace. God never leaves His work unfinished. Also, this answer cannot fail, because God says so in His Word, and He does not lie: "Seek, and ye shall find" [Matt. 7:7]. Even as the question is God's question, wrought by Him in your heart, so the answer is God's answer. Through His Son, by His Spirit, and through His Word, God gives the answer.

What He Does

If this is your experience, you will conclude by saying, "I thank God." The Christian who seeks and finds is finally characterized by this: he thanks God. The Christian acknowledges God as his deliverer. God through Christ is the deliverer. Christ is God's Mediator. He is the Mediator through whom God works and accomplishes salvation.

If you understand that this God of salvation has reached you, has spoken to you, and has given the answer to your question through Jesus Christ, what do you say? You say, "I thank God." The original word for thanks is *grace:* "*Grace* be to God." The fundamental meaning is that he who has found the answer— and daily finds the answer to the question "Who shall deliver me?"—will attribute it to the grace of God. Let us all say it. Having found the answer to the question, let us say, "Grace be to God."

Chapter Forty-four

The Blessedness of Freedom from Condemnation

Romans 8:1
There is therefore now no condemnation to them which are in Christ Jesus, who walk not after the flesh, but after the Spirit.

The connection between the first verse of Romans 8 and the preceding chapters is expressed in the two little words *therefore now*. "There is *therefore now* no condemnation to them which are in Christ Jesus." With regard to this connection, it is important that we understand two things. First, the word *now* does not have a temporal sense. The apostle does not mean to say that there used to be condemnation, but now there is no condemnation anymore. The word does not have a *temporal*, but a *logical* sense. The apostle means this: "Since the case is as I have set forth in the preceding, it follows, the conclusion is, that there is therefore now no condemnation to them which are in Christ Jesus."

Second, we must bear in mind that the word *therefore*, which connects this verse with the preceding, and connects it as a conclusion, does not refer merely to the last part of the preceding chapter. [In v. 25] the apostle had written, "So then with the mind I myself serve the law of God; but with the flesh the law of sin." There are those who would like to connect this first

302

verse [of Rom. 8] with that last part of chapter 7. Then we would have to read it as follows: "With the mind I myself serve the law of God; but with the flesh the law of sin; therefore, there is now no condemnation." But this is not the meaning.

The word *therefore* refers to the entire section in which the apostle centrally expresses the truth that we are not under the law but under grace. Therefore, because we are not under the law but under grace, there is now no condemnation to them who are in Christ Jesus. Understanding this connection, we are ready to enter into this eighth chapter.

The Blessing

The blessing is expressed in the words *There is now no condemnation*. The blessed are "them which are in Christ Jesus." The way of this blessedness is, "Walk not after the flesh, but after the Spirit."

The assertion *There is no condemnation* places us all in judgment. That there is no condemnation presupposes that there is a judgment and that there is a judge. It presupposes also that the judge judges. He judges always, and He judges righteously. When we speak of judgment, we are always inclined to think of the future. We are inclined to think of this judgment as a day of judgment that is coming. There is such a day coming, but that will be a day of the *revelation* of the continual judgment of God. We must not think that the judgment then begins. It is true that there is a day coming when there will be a revelation of this judgment of God. This judgment does not become evident now. Therefore, there will be a day when it will be revealed. But remember, although there is a day coming when this judgment shall be revealed, God judges always, He judges continually. He is the Judge. This is His essential relation to us and to the world. God judges every moment. He judges the heart and the secret thoughts of the heart. If we understand this, we will understand the present tense used in the text. "There *is* therefore now no condemnation."

This is significant to remember because God also always *acts* according to His judgment over us. This also we are inclined to put in the future, but God judges now, and He acts now according to His judgment over us. God now judges the wicked, and He acts accordingly. There will be a day of the revelation of this judgment, but God judges now and acts accordingly. It is important that we see that the apostle uses the present tense. "There *is* no condemnation." This is the background on which we must read the text.

Therefore, we must change the negative form of the text into the positive notion: God declares us righteous and acts accordingly.

However, the apostle does not say that God declares us to be righteous and that He acts accordingly. He puts it in the negative form and says, "There is therefore now no condemnation." If we say, "There is therefore now no condemnation," the idea is that there is good reason why we should be condemned. The expression *There is no condemnation* also implies that everything I see makes me believe that there *is* condemnation for me. There is plenty of reason why I should say, "There *is* condemnation." Everything testifies that there is. There is my connection with the sinful human race. I am a member of a condemned race, and my relation to this condemned race testifies against the fact that there is no condemnation. There is the testimony of my conscience. If I consult my conscience, there is only one conclusion: condemnation. My conscience testifies loudly that God ought to condemn me. We run along in the world of condemnation. The testimony that comes to us out of the world and out of our conscience is that we ought to be condemned. There is, in addition, the suffering of this present time and the fact that we die. I die. And that I die means that God kills me. The fact that I die is a loud testimony that God condemns me. Here I stand, in the midst of the testimony of a condemned race, the testimony of my conscience, and the testimony of the suffering and death of this present time, and I say, "There is no condemnation." Is it not evident that the text must remain in this negative form?

But there is more. The apostle literally means that there is nothing in which we can be condemned. I may be condemned in many relations. I may be condemned in my relation to the head of the human race. But with a view to this relation I say, "There is no condemnation." I may be condemned in my relation to the corrupt human nature. But with a view to that relation I say, "There is no condemnation." There are my actual sins. There are many relations in which I may be condemned. But the apostle says, "There is no condemnation."

There *never* was condemnation. As I said, the word *now* does not have a temporal meaning. It is not as if the apostle meant, "There is now no longer condemnation." The apostle does not mean that there used to be condemnation. He does not mean that up to the year A.D. 33, before Christ died, there was condemnation, but now this condemnation has been removed. No, the word has a logical meaning, and the apostle merely says, "There is no condemnation." There never was any condemnation. God does not change. It is not so that He first condemned, but now He condemns no more. There is no condemnation to them which are in Christ Jesus *from all eternity*.

In the deepest sense of the word, the matter does not stand this way: God for a certain time condemned His people in His counsel and then gave them to Christ in His counsel. No, in God's counsel Christ is first. God determined to glorify Himself. He determined to glorify Himself in His Son. He determined to glorify Himself in Christ and His church. He determined to glorify Himself in the way of sin and grace. God glorifies Himself in Christ and His church. There never was any condemnation for them which are in Christ Jesus. It is true that God realizes this *no condemnation* through the cross. Still, there never was any condemnation.

The Blessed

This is true for them who are in Christ Jesus. To be "in Christ" is a common expression. We usually read over it because we have become so used to it. What does it mean to be in Christ? Christ Jesus is the one who came down from heaven. He is the one who was with us for a short time, flesh of our flesh and blood of our blood. He is the one who died for us on the cross. This man is Christ Jesus. Historically speaking, this is Christ Jesus. It is He who was raised, who ascended into heaven, who was exalted to the right hand of God. He is the Son of God, who came down from heaven in our nature and who returned to the Father.

What does it mean to be *in* Him? We can be *in* a thing in more than one sense. We can be in something in a local sense. For example, we can be in a church building. We cannot be in Christ in this sense. We can be *in* something in the sense that we are covered by something. For example, we are in an insurance company so that we are covered by its policy and benefits. Or we can be in a corporation and thus be within the scope of the power and benefits of the corporation. There is still another sense in which we can be *in* something. We can speak of a branch being in the vine. There is a vital connection between the branch and the vine.

To be in Christ has, in the first place, a legal meaning. God has ordained a legal corporation. Of this corporation Christ is the head. The corporation is represented, in all its obligations and benefits, by Christ. All the benefits of the corporation are bestowed by Him. To be in Christ is to be a member of this corporation.

In the second place, to be in Christ means that there is a vital relation between us and Him, even as the relation between the branch and the vine is a vital relation. There is such a connection between us and Christ that we can live out of Him. There is such a connection that we appropriate Him, that we draw Him into us.

Both of these relationships work through faith. By faith, we are a member of the corporation of which Christ is the head. And as soon as I consciously become a member of this corporation, I discover that I am connected with the sinful human race.[1] By faith I also live out of Christ. Put the living Christian in connection with Christ, and he says, "He is mine."

The apostle emphasizes the first idea, the legal meaning. He does not emphasize the vital relationship. He does not mean, "I live out of Christ, and therefore there is now no condemnation for me." Our sanctification can never be the ground of our assurance that there is no condemnation for us. We can never reason like this: I am a Christian; I am in Christ, and therefore there is no condemnation for me. Remember all the sins that testify against you and that still testify against you! That there is no condemnation means that there is no imputation of sin. And that there is no imputation of sin means that there is forgiveness of sins. But there is no good work on the basis of which God can forgive one sin. Therefore, it is not because of that vital relationship to Christ that we say, "There is now no condemnation for me." Rather, it is because of the legal corporation, the head of which is Christ, who came in our world, flesh of our flesh and blood of our blood; and who died, was raised, ascended into heaven, and was exalted to the right hand of God. They who are in Christ say, "There is no condemnation for me." No matter what their conscience may say, there is no condemnation for them who are in Christ Jesus.

The Way of This Blessedness

It is not as if our works have nothing to do with this assurance, for the apostle adds, "who walk not after the flesh, but after the Spirit." As far as our justification is concerned, these words could be omitted. They are not the ground that there is no condemnation, but they mark those who are in Christ. The flesh refers to our sinful nature. This is not because the substance of our body is the seat of sin. But sin must necessarily reveal itself, become active, and become real in the body. Sin

---

1. In this sentence Hoeksema makes an intriguing observation that he does not develop further.

becomes active; it becomes a fleshly matter in my speaking, in my walking, in my actions, and even in my thinking and desiring. This body is not regenerated until the day of the Lord. As Christians we have a regenerated heart, but unregenerated flesh.

By *walk after the Spirit* the apostle means the new principle of life in conflict with that old sinful nature. Our walk refers to our whole life. If I walk after the flesh, my whole life is inspired to be in harmony with the principle of sin. But if I walk after the Spirit, my whole life, outward and inward, is inspired by the desire and motive to walk after the Spirit of Christ, who works in my spirit.

They who are in Christ are the same as they who walk after the Spirit. They do not walk after sin. This is impossible. The Christian is not a man who is motivated by the desire to live in sin. He has no delight in sin, but in the law of God. Against his own sin he cries out, "O miserable man that I am!"

Walking after the Spirit is the necessary characteristic of them who are in Christ Jesus. Why? Because we cannot be in Christ in the legal sense without being in Him in the vital sense. We cannot be justified without being sanctified. Therefore, he who is in Christ also walks after the Spirit. Nor can we have peace and say that we are in Christ unless we walk after the Spirit. The assurance of our being in Christ is in the way of sanctification. The way of our being blessed is that we walk in sanctification. And the fruit of this walk in sanctification is that we say, "There is no condemnation for me."

Chapter Forty-five

Spiritual Liberation

Romans 8:2
For the law of the Spirit of life in Christ Jesus hath made me free from the law of sin and death.

In the first verse of this chapter, the Word of God speaks of our freedom in a legal sense. It expresses the truth concerning this freedom in the form of a negation: "There is therefore now no condemnation to them which are in Christ Jesus." That this truth was expressed in a negative form was due to the fact that this testimony of faith must be a contradiction of all we see and experience in this world of sin, of suffering, and of death. If we look at life as we see and experience it, there can be but one conclusion: there *is* condemnation. There are our sins, our suffering, and our death—all testifying that there is condemnation. This is such a reality that we can hardly get rid of it. It is not easy to live in the contradiction of this reality. It is no wonder that the Christian frequently is in darkness and doubt. He carries in his system the testimony that there is condemnation. It is because of this condition that the apostle puts it in the negative form and says, "There is no condemnation to them which are in Christ Jesus."

God, who is constantly judging us, does not condemn us. This is the victory of the child of God. His salvation is that he can say, "There is no condemnation." In verse 2 the apostle gives a reason for this statement: "*For* the law of the Spirit of life in Christ Jesus hath made me free from the law of sin and death."

In this second verse the apostle turns to the personal form when he says, "hath made *me* free." This was not the case in the first verse when the apostle said, "There is no condemnation to them which are in Christ Jesus." This is a doctrinal statement. But the second verse is a personal confession.

What kind of reason for the statement in verse 1 does the apostle give [in the text]? Suppose you make a statement, "He is not here, for the door is locked." Then you have given a reason *not* for his *not being here,* but for your *statement* that he is not here. Does the apostle mean, "The fact that the law of the Spirit of life in Christ Jesus hath made me free from the law of sin and death is the reason, the basis, for the fact that there is no condemnation?" This cannot be, for then our sanctification would be the ground of our freedom from condemnation. Rather, the apostle intends to give a reason for the *assurance,* for the *knowledge,* of that statement. The apostle means, "I know that there is no condemnation, for I have already been made free."

Let me illustrate again. A man is in jail, locked behind the prison doors, bound with chains. An official comes to him and says, "There is no condemnation for you." The man believes this word of the official, but he is still bound and locked behind the prison doors. Presently, however, the jailer comes and opens the doors and sets the man free. Then that man says, "I know that there is no condemnation, for I have been set free."

This is what the apostle means in these two verses. The sinner is a prisoner, bound in the shackles of sin and death with the sentence of condemnation upon him. Now the prison door is opened, and an official comes to him with an official document, namely, the gospel. In the gospel he is declared free from condemnation. The sinner believes the gospel. If he had nothing more, he could say, "I know that I am free from condemnation." But the jailer comes to him, cuts the shackles of sin and death, and sets him free. Now he says, "I know that there is no condemnation, for I have been set free." He has not escaped; he did not break jail. But he has been set free. In other words, it is the reason of *evidence*. This is the connection.

What It Means

The text speaks of *law* twice: "The *law* of the Spirit of life in Christ Jesus hath made me free from the *law* of sin and death." Some say that *law* in the last phrase must be taken in the regular sense of a code of legal precepts. It is simply the law of God. The law of the Spirit of life, according to them, is the gospel. The meaning would then be that the gospel has made us free from the law.

There are three reasons why this cannot be the meaning. In the first place, we may not call the law of God the law of sin and death. I know that the law cannot free from sin, but this is not because the law is the law of sin and death, but because of our sinful flesh. Second, it is a very strange designation of the gospel to call it "the law of the Spirit of life." The gospel is never called this in Scripture. Third, it must be recognized that when the same word occurs twice in the same text, and in the same connection, the word must have the same sense. Therefore, the interpretation—that the gospel made us free from the law—is not correct.

The apostle uses *law* here in the same sense in which he used it in the preceding chapter. There the apostle said, "I see another *law* in my members, warring against the *law* of my mind, and bringing me into captivity to the *law* of sin which is in my members" (v. 23). It is evident that the apostle used the word *law* there, not in the sense of a code of legal precepts but in the sense of a spiritual principle, a spiritual "directing power."

In this sense the apostle uses the word *law* in the text. It is used in the same sense as we use it sometimes when we speak of the law of gravitation. This is not a code, but a principle. Similarly, we speak of the law of expanding and contracting. This is not a code of precepts, but a principle. This is the idea of *law* in the text. Let us read the text like this: "For the principle, the spiritual 'directing power' of the Spirit of life in Christ Jesus hath made me free from the principle, the spiritual 'directing power' of sin and death."

There is a spiritual "directing power" of sin and death. The sinner is not compelled to sin from without. He is directed from within by the power of sin and death. That the apostle speaks of sin and death is because the one always accompanies the other. The relation is this. Death is the condition for sin. Because the sinner is dead, there is in him the direction of sin. Because the sinner is dead, he sins. And because he sins, he is dead. He is bound in the power of sin and death. This is not a physical slavery, but a spiritual slavery. His will is bound; his mind is bound; his desires are bound. The motivation comes from within. Sin and death are in the heart. They direct the will, the mind, and the desires. This is the condition of the sinner, of the natural man.

From this we have been made free. Of course, this freedom is not the same as that of verse 1. It is true that we are declared free in the gospel. But this is not what we have in the text. The text speaks of a moral freedom, a moral liberation. And this moral freedom consists in this: I do as I please, providing I do the will of God.

We can speak of freedom in a threefold sense. We can speak of a *limited freedom*. That was the freedom of Adam. Adam was free in the sense that he could will to do good or evil. There is the *freedom of slavery*. This is the freedom of the sinner. The sinner is free to sin. Finally, there is the highest freedom. The highest freedom is that we are *free from all sin*. It is the freedom wherein we do as we please, and we always please to do the will of God. This is the freedom of which the text speaks: liberated from the law of sin and death.

How It Is Accomplished

How is this accomplished?

It is by *the law of the Spirit of life in Christ Jesus,* that is, the Holy Spirit.

We can connect the phrase *in Christ Jesus* in more than one way with the rest of the text. We can connect it with the word *law*. In this case, it is the law that is in Christ Jesus. Or we can connect it with the word *Spirit*. In this case, it is the Spirit who is in Christ Jesus. Or we can connect it with the word *life*. In this case, it is the life that is in Christ Jesus. Or we can connect it with the phrase *hath made me free*. In this case, it is the liberty that is in Christ Jesus.

I prefer the first way: connecting *in Christ Jesus* to the word *law*. The apostle means that this new spiritual "directing power" is in Christ Jesus. Life is the opposite of death in the text. Therefore, it must be taken in the spiritual, ethical sense. Death is movement away from God. Life is movement toward God. It is to think in the direction of God, to will in the direction of God, to desire in the direction of God. Life is to be in harmony with God in all our life. The apostle speaks of the Spirit of life, who is the Holy Spirit because this life is in the Spirit. Also, the Spirit is the author of this life. He is the worker of this life. Just as the Spirit is the author of life in nature, so the Spirit is also the author of eternal life.

This Spirit is in Christ. *In Christ* means "in the sphere of Christ," that is, in the sphere where Christ is head, in the sphere in which He rules. This implies that He is also in the church, for the church is also in Christ. The Spirit of life is in the sphere of Christ and His church. In this sphere the Spirit unleashes the directing power that delivers us from the law of sin and death. The spiritual directing power of the Spirit of life in Christ Jesus delivers us from the spiritual directing power of sin and death.

The Spirit does this. Man never delivers us from the prison of sin and death. A man may reform to a certain extent. He may be a drinker and not drink anymore. But man cannot reach that inner center from which are the issues of life. Man is not lord of the heart. The heart is lord of him. Man cannot change it. The liberation process is from beginning to end the work of the Spirit. The Spirit does it. The Holy Spirit, that new directing power, takes hold of the center. He takes hold of the heart of man. He puts the heart of man in reverse. He changes that heart. When the Spirit has changed the heart, He comes with the Word of Christ and changes the willing, the thinking, the desiring, and all the conscious life of man to the will of God. This is conversion. The Spirit abides in him. He stays at the controls. He continues to be the "directing power" in the heart of the Christian.

The Christian is free, not in the sense that he never sins, but in the sense that even over against his own sin he is free. He never delights in sin anymore. He hates sin. Is this not freedom? Therefore, the Christian takes these words on his lips: "The law of the Spirit of life in Christ Jesus hath made me free from the law of sin and death."

Of What, and Why, It Is an Evidence

I call your attention to that little word, that connecting word *For:* "*For* the law of the Spirit of life in Christ Jesus hath made me free from the law of sin and death." My freedom from sin is the evidence of my freedom from condemnation.

Oh, when the Word of God, when the gospel, declares that there is no condemnation for me, I believe it, but there is so much that testifies against it. The only evidence I have is the fact that I have been set free. I have been set free! If I had escaped from prison, I could never say, "There is no condemnation for me." Then condemnation would still be there, and the law would continue to pursue me. But now it is different. God sent from heaven, through Christ, and set me free. It was God who did it. Because God liberated me, I know that He first justified me. For God liberates only those whom He justifies. Because God has liberated us, we say, "There is no condemnation for me."

Hallelujah!

Chapter Forty-six

The Certainty of the Resurrection of the Saints

Romans 8:11
But if the Spirit of him that raised up Jesus from the dead dwell in you, he that raised up Christ from the dead shall also quicken your mortal bodies by his Spirit that dwelleth in you.

The context of Romans 8:11, in general, is verse 9. There the apostle wrote to the church of Rome and to the church of all ages: "But ye are not in the flesh, but in the Spirit, if so be that the Spirit of God dwell in you. Now if any man have not the Spirit of Christ, he is none of his." The church of Jesus Christ is in the Spirit. This Spirit is the Spirit of God. The Spirit of God is also the same as the Spirit of Christ, as is evident from the context. This Spirit of God and Spirit of Christ is the same as Christ who became the quickening Spirit. This is also plain from the context.

The fact that we are in this Spirit, in this Spirit of God and of Christ, or in Christ, means that we have a living connection with the sphere in which the Spirit of God and of Christ has dominion. In this sphere is all. In this sphere all the benefits of Christ are imputed. In this sphere all the merits of Christ are bestowed. If we are in this sphere in which the Spirit of God and of Christ, that is, Christ, has dominion, we are partakers of all the benefits and blessings that Christ has merited. Since, in fact, the church is in this sphere, it follows that now already we are already partakers of the benefits that the Spirit bestows on the church. And we *shall be* partakers forever of the benefits that the Spirit bestows on the church.

Verse 11 really completes the sentence in verse 10. There the apostle says, "If Christ be in you, the body is dead because of sin; but the Spirit is life because of righteousness." The spirit here is our spirit. It is sometimes called "soul" in Scripture. If Christ is in us, the spirit is life. If Christ is in us, our spirit becomes a living spirit. But the body is still dead. This cannot possibly be the end. Our body cannot remain dead. Verse 11, therefore, completes the sentence and truth of verse 10. It speaks of the certainty of the resurrection of the saints.

The Resurrection

The apostle denotes what will be resurrected as our mortal bodies. Our body is that physical organism in and through which our spiritual substance functions. It is in and through the body that we live. We cannot conceive of living without the body. We are living, certainly, as a spiritual "soul-creature." But this spirit, which God created in the beginning by breathing into man's nostrils the breath of life so that man became a living soul, lives only through the body. It is through the body that the spirit sees, hears, talks, thinks, wills, and desires. It is in the body that the spirit rejoices and is made sorrowful.

It is through the body that we stand in connection with this world, and with *this world only*. If I am to have, with this body, connection with any other world, it must be through revelation and by means of faith. I must *believe* that heaven is. I must *believe* that God is. But I stand connected with *this* world. It is in this world that I have my relationships. It is in this world that I see, hear, touch, smell, and taste. It is in this world that I eat and drink, that I walk and talk, that I have all my activity.

The body is mortal. It is subject to death. That our bodies

are mortal does not mean that they are liable to cease to exist, but it means that they are subject to death. This body is "die-able." It is born die-able. When the body dies, all our present life is lost. This is the mortality of the body.

This is also physical death. When we die, the body dies. I want to emphasize this because it is often said that death is caused by, and consists in, the spirit leaving the body. This is not so. It is the other way around. The body dies. Because the body dies, the spirit cannot function in the body anymore. It cannot function without the body. This is why spiritism is nonsense. The spirit needs the living body to function. When the body dies, the spirit leaves the body.

The body dies. All that pertains to this body is taken away. This eye can see no more. This ear can hear no more. This mouth can talk no more. The heart stops. The organism of this body functions no more. Also, all the relations that this body now sustains will be broken. When we die, all the ties of husband and wife, of parents and children, and of brother and sister, are broken. From this point of view, too, spiritism is nonsense.

That we have a mortal body means also that we die when we are still living. We are born dying. This is the meaning of our Baptism Form when it says that this life is nothing but a continual death. It is well for us to remember, from a practical point of view, that this life is a mortal life. Scripture tells us that if we shall save this life, we shall lose it, but if we shall lose it, we shall save it. It is poor business to contend for this mortal life. And yet this is all that the world contends for. The world contends for nothing but this life. This is also a practical thing for the Christian to remember. The question is sometimes asked, "Must we not live? What if I can't find a job unless I join the union?" But Scripture emphasizes that the time will come when we will not be able to buy or sell unless we are willing to ally ourselves with Antichrist. Therefore, it is well that we remind ourselves that all we can lose is a few years of this mortal life. We must die. This body is mortal. We must learn to die.

That our body is mortal also means that from the point of view of the life of our spirit, this body is dead. In verse 10 the apostle says, "The body is dead because of sin; but the spirit is life because of righteousness." This body cannot partake in the new life in Christ. This is the conflict in the Christian: a living spirit in a dead body.

This mortal body will be quickened. To quicken is to make alive. Making alive is not the same as making alive again, as if this same body were to be returned to us. The apostle does not say that God will make us alive *again*. He says that God will make us *alive*. He will give to this body of ours the same life that we now have in the spirit. When God shall make our present body alive, He will give to this body a life that is in harmony with our regenerated spirit. Our regenerated spirit will be able to function in our new body.

With this new body we will be able to be in heaven. With this present mortal body we cannot be in heaven. With our mortal body we cannot see the heavenly things. With this present body we cannot see Christ. We can never enjoy and possess the eternal kingdom of God in this mortal body. But God will give to our mortal body the same life that we now possess in our spirit. We will receive new eyes so that we can see the heavenly things. We will receive new ears so that we can hear the heavenly things. He that raised up Christ from the dead shall also quicken our mortal bodies with an immortal, heavenly life. The glorified spirit will function in the glorified body in the new heavens and the new earth, which God will create.

How It Is Accomplished

God will do this. He that raised up Christ is God. The triune God raised up Jesus according to His human nature. It is not so that the Father, the First Person in the Trinity, raised up Jesus. The triune God raised Him. This is a historical fact. It is this fact to which we cling. The *Father* raised the Son; the *Son* arose; the *Spirit* quickened Him. The raising of Jesus was thus the work of the triune God.

This same God will also raise us. There is abundant testimony in Scripture that the triune God is the author of our resurrection. But He will raise us *as the God of salvation*. This is why the apostle describes God in the words that he uses. The apostle does not merely say, "*God* will raise you," but he says, "*He that raised up Jesus* will also raise you." On the basis of what Christ did, and through His Spirit that dwells in you, He will quicken your mortal bodies.

The Spirit who dwells in you is the Spirit of God, but as the Spirit of Christ. The Spirit of God was given to Christ as the Mediator in His human nature. What happened is this. He who was raised was highly exalted. But He possesses this glory not for Himself only, but that He might impart this glory to His own. Christ must impart Himself. This is His mediatorial work. Therefore, we cannot *accept* Christ. We *receive* Him. He must impart Himself to us. The blessings that He received He must also bestow on us, so that we become like Him. This, however, does not proceed from us, but from Christ.

For this reason the Spirit is also bestowed on Christ according to His human nature. The first Adam was made a living soul, we read in I Corinthians 15:45, so that he could transmit this soul-life to his posterity. But Christ must do more than this. He must also quicken us. This is why He became a quickening spirit. That is, He received the Spirit in such a way that He could send out this Spirit, so that He should dwell in us until we become like Him. This is why the text says that God will quicken your mortal bodies by His Spirit that dwelleth in you. The Spirit was poured out on the day of Pentecost. In this Spirit, Christ returned to His church. He dwells in us. He makes in us a fitting home in which He can dwell.

This implies that He will abide in us. He will abide in us forever. He will never leave us. No matter what becomes of us, He never leaves us. Through this Spirit, God in Christ spiritually quickens us already now. He regenerates us. He calls us out of darkness. He makes us inwardly like Christ. He gives us the new life whereby we cry, "Abba, Father." Therefore, the apostle says in verse 10, "If Christ be in you, . . . the Spirit is life because of righteousness." But the body is still dead. And the same Spirit who dwells in us will not rest until He has quickened our mortal bodies.

Why It Is Certain

This is the assurance of the resurrection. Subjectively, we rest in the assurance of our personal resurrection. Objectively, the resurrection is certain because God raised Jesus. It is certain for two reasons. First, the resurrection of Jesus is a testimony that He merited eternal life. God could never have raised Jesus if the cross had not effected that righteousness on the basis of which we can live. But God did that to Jesus. And Jesus is the head of the corporation. He died because of our sins. When He was raised, it was not because His sins had been blotted out, but ours. There is a second reason why our resurrection is objectively certain. Jesus is not only the head of the corporation. He is also the head of the body. The resurrection of Jesus is the beginning of the resurrection of the body. The head is raised; the resurrection of the body must follow. There is no question, therefore, that if you are in Christ, your mortal body will be quickened.

What the apostle wishes to impress upon us is that the saints must be subjectively sure of their personal resurrection. This subjective assurance is guaranteed by the gift of the Spirit: "If the Spirit . . . dwell in you." If the Spirit of Him who raised Jesus from the dead dwell in us, we are also sure of our own resurrection. If the Spirit *of Christ* dwell in you, you are sure of your own resurrection. Of course, if the Spirit of Christ does not dwell in you, you are none of His. But if the Spirit of Christ dwell in you, you have in Him the earnest of your own resurrection. Why is this Spirit given to you? It is because He wants to quicken you. Therefore, if the Spirit dwell in you, your mortal bodies will be quickened. And you will shout with the apostle, "O death, where is thy sting? O grave, where is thy victory?" [I Cor. 15:55].

If the Spirit of Christ dwells in you! This Spirit dwells in you if you walk not after the flesh, but after the Spirit. If you mind the things of the flesh, if you walk in sin, you are without the comfort of all that I have said with regard to the resurrection. If the Spirit is not in you, you walk after the flesh. And if you walk after the flesh, you cannot enjoy the things of the Spirit. If the Spirit of Christ does not dwell in you, you are none of His. In the way of the flesh, there is no comfort for you in this word. There is no comfort in this word for the ungodly, and there is no comfort in it for the child of God if he walks in the way of sin.

But if we are in the Spirit and walk after the Spirit, we will have this comfort. If we shall save our life, we will lose it, but if we lose our life, we will save it. "Therefore, my beloved brethren, be ye steadfast, unmoveable, always abounding in the work of the Lord, forasmuch as ye know that your labour is not in vain in the Lord" [I Cor. 15:58].

Chapter Forty-seven

Sons of God Led by the Spirit

Romans 8:14
For as many as are led by the Spirit of God, they are the sons of God.

Repeatedly we find in verses 12–15, and throughout Romans 8, the short but significant connecting word *For:* "We are debtors, not to the flesh, to live after the flesh. *For* if ye live after the flesh, ye shall die: but if ye through the Spirit do mortify the deeds of the body, ye shall live. *For* as many as are led by the Spirit of God, they are the sons of God. *For* ye have not received the spirit of bondage again to fear." It is important for the right understanding of Scripture that we pay attention to these little connecting words and follow the line of thought.

By the little conjunction *For* in verse 14, we are referred to the preceding verse: "If ye . . . through the Spirit do mortify the deeds of the body, ye shall live." The practical effect of being led by the Spirit of God is that we mortify the deeds of the body. Or, putting it the other way, if we mortify the deeds of the body, we are led by the Spirit. It follows that if we mortify the deeds of the body, we shall live, for then we are led by the Spirit. And if we are led by the Spirit, we shall live, for then we are sons of God. This is the line. If we mortify the deeds of the body, we are led by the Spirit. And if we are led by the Spirit, we are sons of God. And if we are sons of God, we shall live.

Who Are They?

Sons of God is a phrase that occurs often in Scripture in a twofold connotation. It is used frequently in the legal sense. Two Greek words are used in Scripture to express the sonship of the people of God. The one word emphasizes the legal aspect of this sonship. The other word emphasizes the spiritual, moral, ethical aspect of sonship. Paul emphasizes the legal aspect. John almost exclusively emphasizes the spiritual, moral, ethical aspect of sonship.

The legal aspect of sonship emphasizes the *right* to sonship. It emphasizes the right to be in God's house. It emphasizes the right to be heirs of God. In the legal sense, we have a right to all these things. We do not have this right in ourselves, but God established the basis on which He makes us heirs, on which He makes us sons, and on which He gives us the right to be in His house. By nature, we have not the right to sonship. There is no universal Fatherhood of God. There is no universal sonship. By nature, we have no right to sonship. Adam had a right to sonship. He lived in God's house. Paradise was God's house. But Adam lost this right to be in God's house. He was expelled from it. He became an exile. By nature, we are not sons; however, we become children of God in the legal sense by adoption. God adopts us to be His sons and gives us a right to be in His house. When we adopt a child, we give to the child the legal status of a child. Similarly, God bestows upon us the legal right to be His child in adoption.

There are in this adoption four different stages. First, there is the eternal adoption in God's counsel. God eternally adopts us as His children. God eternally calls us His sons and daughters, but eternally we are His children *by adoption*.

Second, adoption is realized in the death and resurrection of Christ, for in Christ God establishes the basis upon which He can bestow the right to sonship. Therefore, there is no chance, no free will, with respect to the adoption of the children of

God. God adopts His elect. This cannot be changed. You cannot add to the number, nor take any away.

Third, God gives us adoption when He works faith in our hearts. He gives us the assurance of our adoption when He gives us faith. He gives us this assurance through the Spirit of adoption. This is why He is called the Spirit of adoption. By the Spirit of adoption, through faith, we receive the assurance of our sonship. Thus, we receive the confidence to call God our Father.

Finally, there is still another stage of the adoption that is coming. Of this the apostle speaks in verse 23, where he says, "We ourselves groan within ourselves, waiting for the adoption, to wit, the redemption of our body." There is a public adoption coming. This public adoption is coming at the redemption of our bodies.

All of these meanings of adoption emphasize the legal aspect.

Another aspect to sonship is the spiritual, moral aspect. When we adopt children, we can never *make* them our children. An adopted child never becomes our own. We cannot change an adopted child so that he or she will have our flesh and blood. However, God does this. The legal adoption is first. On the basis of the legal adoption, He makes us children. There are three elements in our becoming children of God: the element of life, the element of likeness, and the element of love.

When we are born again, we become partakers of God's own life. When we become children of God in this sense, we also show His likeness. And on the basis of this likeness, there is a relation of love. We are partakers of the life of God! On the basis of this life of God, we have a likeness of God! And on the basis of this likeness, we experience a relation of love!

All of this was lost through sin. By nature, there is in us no life of God. By nature, there is in us no likeness of God. The image of God in us was changed, so that we now show the likeness of the devil. The image was changed, so that we became children of the devil. We make no apology for this statement!

By nature, we are children of the devil, and we show his likeness.

But by grace and by the Spirit of Christ, we become partakers of the life of Christ. Our life is again the life of God, but now in a higher sense. It is the life of the resurrected Lord. Then we become sons of God. When God so makes us partakers of life, we again show His likeness. Upon the basis of life and likeness, there is again a new love relation.

These sons of God are led by the Spirit. "As many as are led by the Spirit of God, they are the sons of God." Implied is that as many as are sons of God are so led.

How Are They Led?

To be led, or guided, means that we walk in a certain way, a way we cannot find of ourselves. And even if we did find it, we would not be able to keep to it to reach a certain destination. Therefore, we are guided by someone. If a man travels in an unknown, mountainous country, he needs a guide. He does not know the way. Besides, there are many dangers and pitfalls, so that it is not safe. Therefore, he has a guide. The guide leads him safely along the way.

If we apply this illustration, it means that the child of God is called to walk in the way everlasting. The way everlasting is the way of God's precepts. This is the way in which the child of God is called to walk and in which he wants to walk. The difficulty is that the way leads through this world. In this world there are many other ways—ways that lead away from the way everlasting. These side roads sometimes look more like the way everlasting than the way everlasting itself does. It is not always easy to distinguish the way everlasting. Especially under the influence of the devil and the world, these side roads appear as the way. All the world says, "This is the way."

Through this world the Christian must walk in the way everlasting. It is not an easy way. It is a way of cross-bearing. This is one difficulty. The other difficulty comes from within. If only we were perfect, it would not be so bad, but this is not so. We have only a small beginning of the new obedience. There is in our body still the working of the old nature. According to this old nature, we walk in the byways.

God wants His sons to go in the one way; therefore, they are led by the Spirit.

How is this done?

We must emphasize that God leads His children by the Spirit always through His Word. He does not lead them by His Spirit as blind men. The guidance is never such that we are entirely passive. It is not that the Spirit does something, and we do something, too. We are led by the Spirit as moral, conscious children who want to walk in the way.

With regard to this leading, or guidance, we can say three things. First, the Spirit guides us by the Word of God. The Word of God is our road map. This road map is designed by the Spirit. In this Word we find the way everlasting. Therefore, this guidance by the Spirit implies that we study the Word.

Second, the guidance of the Spirit leads from within. It is not that the Spirit gives us the road map and says, "Now go ahead and walk in the way." Rather, the guidance of the Spirit also consists of the opening of our eyes so that we can read the road map. It is the opening of the heart, so that we want this way. No matter what sacrifice it may call for, the Spirit urges us from within to walk in the way.

This does not imply that we are never out of the way. The Spirit does not so guide us that we never depart from the way. Sometimes the Spirit intentionally lets us go out of the way, especially if we become conceited and want to walk in our own way. This is why we have such grave sins as the sins of David and of Peter. Peter was conceited, and the Spirit said to Peter, "Go ahead, Peter, in your own conceited way." But if we are sons of God, this is true also: the Spirit will never leave us alone and will always lead us back.

Third, this guidance of the Spirit is an organic guidance. By this I mean that the Spirit guides the church. The Spirit dwells not in the individual, but in the church. He dwells in the whole church, the church of the past, of the present, and of the future. He guides the church in all the truth. He guides you and me only as members of the church. This is also the way we experience the guidance of the Spirit. We are instructed by the church. We are kept by the church. We are embraced by the church.

The practical implication is that we must not become conceited and leave the church. The eye must not become conceited and say, "I have nothing to do with the body." We have here another reason why we must not easily leave the church. We must seek the church in her purest manifestation. This is the guidance of the Spirit.

As many as are so guided by the Spirit, they are the sons of God. And they shall live.

How Does This Leading Become Manifest?

Is it possible to know that we are so guided?

The apostle gives the answer in the context. He says that the guidance of the Spirit becomes manifest in the mortification of the deeds of the body. If we mortify the deeds of the body, we can say that we are led by the Spirit. On the other hand, if we do not mortify the deeds of the body, we are not guided by the Spirit. Then we live after the flesh, and we shall die. But if we, through the Spirit, mortify the deeds of the body, we have in this mortification the proof that we are led by the Spirit. If you ask, "Can we know that we are led by the Spirit?" the answer is that we can know it by this: whether we mortify the deeds of the body.

The body is our sinful nature. Our sinful nature is called the body because it is the body that is the instrument through which sin comes to manifestation. The body is the seat of the operation of sin. By the deeds of the body is meant that part of our nature that is not regenerated. The heart is born again.

From the heart we do not sin. But around the heart is the old nature of sin, which the apostle calls the deeds of the body. There is, therefore, a conflict in our being.

Verses 12 and 13 teach that if you are led by the Spirit, you mortify the deeds of the body. To *mortify* literally means "to kill." To mortify is to kill the operation of sin. We do not kill the old nature. Our old nature remains with us to the grave. But we fight these old operations of sin. We overcome them. In spite of the old operations of sin that we put down and kill, we have a delight in the law of God.

For as many as are led by the Spirit, they are the sons of God. If we walk in sin, we shall die. But if we are led by the Spirit, we are the sons of God. And if we are sons, we shall live, and live forever.

Chapter Forty-eight

Assurance of Our Sonship

Romans 8:15, 16
For ye have not received the spirit of bondage again to fear; but ye have received the Spirit of adoption, whereby we cry, Abba, Father.
The Spirit itself beareth witness with our spirit, that we are the children of God.

Verse 15 of Romans 8 is connected with the preceding verse by the significant word *For*. "*For* ye have not received the spirit of bondage again to fear." The word *For* makes what follows the ground for that which the apostle had stated in the preceding verse: "As many as are led by the Spirit of God, they are the sons of God." The ground is an appeal to our consciousness. The apostle teaches this: "In your consciousness, you have the witness that you are children of God, for you cry, 'Abba, Father.' And this cry arises spontaneously from your consciousness."

The cry "Abba, Father" would not prove anything if *you* originated the cry. But this is not the case. The cry is originated by the Spirit whom you have received. The church has received the Spirit. The Spirit whom the church has received is not the spirit of bondage again to fear, but it is the Spirit of adoption. It is the Spirit whereby we cry, "Abba, Father."

Therefore, says the apostle, I may appeal to your consciousness for the statement that you are children of God. And because you are children of God, you live. For children of God

329

do not die. You live because you are children of God. And you have the assurance of this fact in your own consciousness, for you cry, "Abba, Father."

The Evidence of Assurance in Our Consciousness

Assurance of sonship is evidenced in the cry "Abba, Father." This cry is the evidence that we are children of God. If you leave the child of God alone, he will cry, "Abba, Father." If you approach him, if you ask him, he will most probably shrug his shoulders. But leave him alone, and he will cry, "Abba, Father."

Abba, Father is really a repetition of the same word: *abba* also means "Father." Since *abba* is the Chaldean for "Father," the words are nothing but a repetition.

The question is, how did the phrase originate? The phrase *Abba, Father* occurs three times in Scripture. The first time is in Mark [14:36], where we find it on the lips of the Lord. There Jesus, in the garden of Gethsemane, says, "Abba, Father, all things are possible unto thee; take away this cup from me." The second time it occurs in Galatians 4:6, where it is said that the Spirit cries, "Abba, Father." And it is found in our passage. Here the believers use it.

Most probably there are two reasons why the church used this phrase, which evidently was a standing phrase at that time. The first reason is that the church found that the Lord used it. The second reason is that the church consisted of both Gentile and Jewish people. However this may be, it is a most intense expression of the word *Father*.

What the apostle points out is that the church spontaneously, without any effort, manifests the Spirit of sonship. It is a son who cries, "Abba, Father." By saying *Father*, thereby you say that in your heart you have the assurance that God loves you. Thereby you also say that in your heart you have the confidence that God forgives your sins. You cannot say and feel that God loves you unless you can say that He forgives your sins.

This is implied in the cry "Abba, Father." Thereby you show, too, that there is in you the consciousness that you love God. And if you say, "Abba, Father," thereby you also say that you love the brethren. The assurance that God loves you, the confidence that He forgives your sins, and the consciousness that you love God and the brethren—this is all expressed in the cry "Abba, Father."

The passage comes to us as a statement of fact. It does not say that you *must* cry, "Abba, Father." But it comes to us personally and says, "You *do* cry, 'Abba, Father.'" This is a fact. If this is not a fact, the text means nothing to us. Therefore, the text brings us face-to-face with the question, is this so? Do we say this? Only then can we appropriate the rest of this text. Is this so?

In answering this question, we must beware of two errors. In the first place, do not answer this question too superficially. The question is, do we cry, "Abba, Father?" This is a question of the heart. It is not a question whether we belong to the church. It is not a question whether we are baptized. It is not a question of religion. It is a heart-question. Do you find in your heart the assurance that God loves you? Is this really true? Do you find in your heart the confidence that your sins are forgiven? This is implied in the cry "Abba, Father." I have reference to the spontaneous life of the child of God. You ask him if he is a child of God, and he may say, "I don't know," but the next moment you will find him on his knees, crying, "Abba, Father."

The other error is this: you must not overemphasize your experience. There are children of God who complain that they do not love God as they ought, but there is no one of us that does. We all have but a small beginning. We have a small beginning of the cry "Abba, Father" in the midst of sin and death. This is why the apostle says that we *cry*. In heaven, we shall not cry. There, we shall *sing!* The question is, therefore, do you find a small principle in your heart of the assurance that God loves you? Do you ever find in your heart the confidence that

God forgives your sin? Do you find that you love the brethren? Then you will find that you have in your consciousness the evidence for saying, "Yes, I cry, 'Abba, Father.'"

The Author of Assurance

How does the child of God get this assurance? If *he* must appropriate it, it means nothing. But the apostle says that this assurance is worked by the Spirit of adoption. The church has received the Spirit. This Spirit whom she has received is not the spirit of bondage again to fear. He is the Spirit of adoption whereby we cry, "Abba, Father."

By nature, we are under the spirit of bondage again to fear. Sooner or later we find ourselves trying to do something for God, not because we love Him but because we are afraid of Him. We are afraid of God. We are afraid of death. Therefore, we try to work for God. This is not the relation of love. This is the attempt to go to some kind of heaven. We find this attempt from the very beginning. We find it in the heathen world. The heathen are afraid of their god, and they work for him in order that they may go to some kind of heaven. That is the spirit of bondage. And we never get out of it. We stay under it.

We have not received the spirit of bondage again to fear, but we have received the Spirit of adoption. The adoption is that God makes those who are no children *His* children. God adopted us in His counsel. He realized this adoption in the cross and resurrection. He bestows the spiritual blessing of adoption by faith. Final adoption will come in the day of the Lord, when we shall be publicly adopted.

The Spirit is called the Spirit of adoption because He is the Spirit who effects adoption. By nature, we do not believe that we are adopted children. The Spirit works in us the assurance that we are children of God. The Spirit causes us to cry, "Abba, Father."

We *receive* the Spirit. This is the point of the text. We received the Spirit of God. God gave us the Spirit through Christ. He poured the Spirit out in the church. Why? What is the mission of the Spirit? The mission of the Spirit is to tell us that we are children of God and to make us children. God sends His Spirit, through Christ, into the church to assure His children that they *are* children.

How the Author Works Assurance in Us

The apostle expresses the way the Spirit does this when he says, "The Spirit beareth witness with our spirit, that we are the children of God." To bear witness means "to say something" and "to be surety for it." Back of the cry "Abba, Father" is the assurance of the Spirit that we are children of God.

How does the Spirit do this? He does not do it in a fanatical way, nor does He do it in a mystical way. Some teach that the Spirit directly, mystically, audibly, tells every child of God, outside of the Word, that he is a child of God. But there is no such thing. I never heard such whisperings of the Spirit in my heart. And if I did hear such whisperings, I would not trust them. I could not be sure that these whisperings were not the testimony of some other spirit. The Spirit never says anything outside the Word. He does not speak of Himself, the Lord says, but "of mine" and declares it unto you [John 16:13–15]. Not directly, but through the Word, this testimony comes to us.

But even then we must be careful. Some people, when they say that this testimony comes to us through the Word, mean that the Spirit at a certain time comes with a certain text. This is not true. I do not mean to say that the Spirit never comes with a certain text, at a certain time, and under certain circumstances. But I mean this: your assurance cannot rest on that. The Spirit does not work through a certain text, but He works through the *whole* Word of God. It is through the whole of Scripture that the Spirit bears this testimony.

There is another side to the matter. Some say that all you

have to do is believe the Bible in order to come to the assurance that you are a child of God. Neither is this true. The Bible does not mention us by name. It says only that God saves His people. The question always asked is, does this mean *me,* so that I can say the Lord has told me in His Word that I am His son? This is effected by the Spirit. The Spirit takes the content of the Word of God. He applies it to our hearts. The content of what the Spirit witnesses always comes from Scripture, but the personal assurance is wrought by the Spirit. The practical implication, all things being equal, is that the closer we live to Scripture, the more we will have the assurance that we are sons of God. We will have less assurance according as we live further away from this Word. If we are rich in the Bible, we will be rich in assurance.

There is one more thing. The Spirit works assurance in the fellowship of the church and in the way of sanctification. There is no one who has the Spirit all by himself. The Spirit is given to the church. The Spirit witnesses in the church. When the Word of God is preached, there is an organic testimony of the Spirit through the church. There is an organic testimony of the Spirit in the church in which we and our children grow up. Thus, the Spirit teaches us to say, "Abba, Father."

Do we say it? We are sons of God. If we are sons, we are heirs. There is no question about this. And if we are sons, we shall live.

Chapter Forty-nine

The Suffering of This Present Time

Romans 8:17b, 18
If so be that we suffer with him, that we may be also glorified together.
For I reckon that the sufferings of this present time are not worthy to be compared with the glory which shall be revealed in us.

In these words is a significant limitation of what the apostle had written in the immediately preceding context. These words are also a comfort to them to whom this comfort still applies after the limitation is made.

The apostle had written that we are the children of God. We mortify the deeds of the body. We do this only through the Spirit. If we mortify the deeds of the body, we must be children of God. Besides, the Spirit who leads God's children is not the spirit of bondage again to fear, but the Spirit of adoption, whereby we cry, "Abba, Father." Thus, we have the testimony in ourselves that we are children of God. This testimony spontaneously characterizes the life of the child of God, for he cries, "Abba, Father." Nevertheless, this testimony is not the Christian's own, but it is the testimony of the Spirit, for "the Spirit beareth witness with our spirit, that we are the children of God" [v. 16].

The purpose of the apostle, however, is not to assure us that we are children of God. It is to show that we shall live. Therefore, he continues: ". . . if children, then heirs; heirs of God, and joint-heirs with Christ" [v. 17a]. And if we want to know what the children of God will receive, we must look at what Christ received. We are heirs of God, and joint-heirs with Christ.

But now comes the limitation. Some might think that these things applied to them when really they did not. Some might take these things a little too lightly. When we see how little some people value the eternal glory, how unwilling they are to suffer and sacrifice anything for the inheritance, there is reason to fear. Therefore, the apostle makes a limitation. We are heirs of God, and joint-heirs with Christ, *"if so be that we suffer with him,* that we may be also glorified together." This is serious, because the implication is that if we do not suffer with Him, we will not be glorified with Him. This is the limitation.

The comfort is this: "For I reckon that the sufferings of this present time are not worthy to be compared with the glory which shall be revealed in us."

A Suffering with Christ

The suffering of this present time is the suffering that characterizes the entire dispensation of this world. This present time is necessarily characterized by suffering. The reason is that this present time is the time of death. We live in death, paradoxical as this may sound. We are in the death-house. That we are in the death-house is due to God's curse, and the curse is due to sin. Sin, God's curse, death, and therefore suffering characterize this present time. This is why, in a general sense, all men suffer. This is why we have sighs, groans, and tears. Suffering is *essentially* connected with this present time.

However, the apostle restricts the suffering of this present time to a suffering with Christ. The apostle is not speaking of general suffering. He speaks of a suffering that is limited to this present time, but the suffering of the world never ends. Also, it is evident that the apostle is speaking of a suffering of the people of God: he is speaking of a suffering with Christ. In addition, he is speaking of a suffering of our own choice. The apostle does not have in mind the general suffering of all. Even that suffering is not worthy to be compared with the glory that shall be revealed in us, but the apostle has in mind the suffering with Christ.

Somehow we suffer with Christ, but this suffering that we suffer with Christ is not the suffering of Christ in the atoning sense. It is not the suffering that Christ suffered for us; it is not the suffering by which He atoned for us. That atoning suffering is complete; it is finished. We cannot suffer that suffering of Christ, and we need not suffer that suffering, because it is complete. But there is another aspect to the suffering of Christ. It is not another suffering. Rather, it is another aspect of Christ's suffering.

This is the suffering of Christ that the *world* caused Him to suffer. It caused Him to suffer because it hated Him. The world never loved Christ, from the beginning to the end. It could not bear Christ. The world hated Christ because Christ gave testimony, uncompromisingly, of God and of God's cause. Christ did not go along with the world. Uncompromisingly representing God, He stood alone. The world walked in darkness, and Christ condemned the darkness. And they hated, reproached, persecuted, and finally killed Him on the accursed tree. To *this* suffering, the text refers.

Our suffering, then, is a suffering with Christ because Christ is in us and becomes manifest in us. Christ is in us, and they hate Christ. As soon as the world sees that Christ appears in someone, they hate that someone, just as they hated Christ. They have hated Me, Christ said, and they will hate you also [John 15:18]. The manifestation of Christ that they see in us is in the form of confession. The confession is that we always speak as Christ. That manifestation of Christ in our walk is that we always walk as Christ.

Therefore, we may really say that Jesus Christ still suffers. This is thoroughly scriptural. In this sense, Christ suffers from the beginning of the world to the end of it. The measure of the suffering of Christ must be made full. Of this the apostle Paul speaks when he says that he suffers the remains of the suffering of Christ in his body [Col. 1:24]. Christ suffers in His people, in His body, until the measure of His suffering shall be full.

This suffering of Christ has always been. From Abel to Christ, the saints and the prophets were killed. They were stoned, sawn asunder, tempted, slain by the sword, chased about, afflicted, and tormented. Of them "the world was not worthy" [Heb. 11:37, 38].

This was the case when the apostle wrote this epistle. The people of God were hated. They suffered. They were persecuted. They were burned at the stake. Nero used them for torches to illuminate his gardens, just for amusement. That was reality. When the apostle wrote these things, he was not writing something he knew nothing about. You must not suppose that people were always put before a stark proposition. Often the authorities merely said to them, "You may keep your Christ, but you must say that Caesar is Lord, too. You may bow before Christ if you will only bow before our image, just once." Could they not do that? Those people said no.

How about us? No, I do not mean that we should go out and seek martyrdom. But the same alternative always finds us. When we stand before the question of losing our honor, our position, our money, our job, our freedom, or our life—or of denying Christ—what do we do? There is no compromise in the text: *If so be that we suffer with him.* And notice: in order that we may be also glorified together. This implies that if we do not suffer with Him, we will not be glorified with Him, either. It is either/or. If we are confronted with a choice between earthly life, honor, position, and money on the one side, and shame, reproach, suffering, and persecution on the other side; and if connected with life, honor, position, and money is the denial of Christ, and connected with shame, reproach, and persecution is prison and death—I say, if we stand before this choice, and we choose not to suffer with Christ, we will not be glorified with Christ. *If so be that we suffer with him:* this is the limitation. We cannot get around it. We must choose.

But the text also gives comfort to those who fall within the circle of the limitation. The one is the purpose of the other. It is God's purpose that His people shall be filled with shame, reproach, and suffering in order that presently He may show that they who were so despised by the world are heirs of life and glory. This is God's glory. Because it is God's glory, it is also our glory. Our glory is inseparably connected with God's glory. We read of Christ that for the glory set before Him, He endured reproach and shame [Heb. 12:2]. We may do this, too. Moses despised the riches of Egypt and chose the affliction of the people of God because he had respect unto the recompense of reward [Heb. 11:24–26].

An Inevitable Suffering

But why the limitation? Why is this suffering inevitable? The reason is not because the suffering is the ground upon which we receive the glory. Christ is the only ground for the glory. Our suffering is not the ground for our entering into glory. But it is the inevitable *way*.

In a certain sense, the suffering with Christ is not inevitable. You can avoid it in the sense that you must choose it. This is not the case with the suffering that God brings upon you. That is not of your own choice, and you cannot avoid it. But the suffering of Christ you can avoid. You must choose it. God places you before the choice. He places you before the choice repeatedly. Repeatedly you are called upon to say what you want: Christ or your honor, Christ or your position, Christ or your wealth, Christ or your job, Christ or your freedom. And then we must choose the suffering.

We can avoid it; that is, we can avoid this suffering if Christ is not in us. If we persistently avoid it, we are not of Christ. This is not to say that a child of God never sinfully avoids the suffering of Christ. Peter did. Peter chose the honor of men rather than the reproach of Christ. But Peter did not walk in his avoiding of the suffering of Christ. When Peter had fallen, he repented. Later he chose the way of suffering. Who of us has never been unfaithful? But if we persistently walk in our avoiding of the suffering of Christ, we choose it. If we choose it, we are not of Christ. And if we are not of Him, we will not be glorified with Him.

A Comparatively Insignificant Suffering

If we suffer with Him and are glorified with Him, then, says the apostle, the sufferings of this present time are not worthy to be compared with the glory that shall be revealed in us. There is a comparison. On the one hand is all the suffering of this present time with Christ in the center. On the other hand is the glory that shall be revealed in us. The glory is ours. We possess it, but it must be revealed. We cannot now see the glory. It is hid behind our sin and suffering by this present life. But it shall be revealed. It shall be revealed in us. The glory of the children of God is not merely that they will go to a glorious heaven with glorious streets and gates. This, too. To a glorious people belongs a glorious heaven. But this glory shall be revealed in *us*. God reveals His glory in His people. They shall be glorious. And this glory is about to be revealed. This is really the expression in the original. The apostle places that suffering and glory over against each other.

Then he says, "I reckon." The apostle comes to a conclusion. What is the conclusion? "*I reckon* that the sufferings of this present time are not worthy to be compared with the glory which shall be revealed in us." However great that suffering may be, it can never be compared with the glory that shall be revealed in us.

The apostle reckons it so. Can we see a little of it? Yes, we can. The suffering is temporal; the glory, eternal. Time cannot be compared with eternity. Shall we then hesitate to sacrifice that little span of time for a never ending eternity? The suffering of this present time is extremely limited because of our limited capacity. We can suffer but a little. If they make us suffer too much, we die. But the capacity for glory is so great that we shall forever be able to receive more glory. The suffering of this present time can only make us lose perishable things. Let me take an extreme form of suffering. It can only take away your present life. But if it does, it only takes away that which you will lose anyway. The loss of perishable things is all that the suffering of this present time can take away. But we shall receive imperishable things. Finally, the suffering of this present time is never unmixed. In fact, it is an unspeakable joy to receive grace to suffer with Christ. This is why the people of God, in the midst of the flames, are able to sing psalms. Besides, God uses the suffering unto their sanctification.

Although the suffering of this present time is never unmixed, the glory is unmixed. There is in this glory no mixture of sorrow. It is an unspeakable joy.

The suffering of this present time is not worthy to be compared with the glory that shall be revealed in us. Be not afraid! "In the world ye shall have tribulation: but be of good cheer; I have overcome the world" [John 16:33].

Chapter Fifty

The Waiting Creature

Romans 8:19-22

For the earnest expectation of the creature waiteth for the manifestation of the sons of God.

For the creature was made subject to vanity, not willingly, but by reason of him who hath subjected the same in hope,

Because the creature itself also shall be delivered from the bondage of corruption into the glorious liberty of the children of God.

For we know that the whole creation groaneth and travaileth in pain together until now.

Verses 19–22 are related closely to verses 17 and 18. There the apostle speaks of the suffering of this present time. He characterizes this suffering as a suffering with Christ, that is, a suffering in fellowship with Christ and for the sake of Christ. He characterizes it also as a suffering that is unavoidable on the way to glory. Another way to glory there is not. The apostle expresses this plainly when he says that we are heirs of God, and joint-heirs with Christ "if so be that we suffer with him, that we may be also glorified together" [v. 17b]. There is no glory for the one who does not want this suffering.

The passage is connected especially with verse 18. The apostle characterizes the glory that shall be revealed in the children of God as exceedingly great. The suffering is not worthy to be compared with this glory which shall be revealed in us. No matter how great this suffering may be, all the suffering of the children of God throughout the history of the world, with Christ at the center, is not worthy to be compared with the glory that awaits them. So great is this glory.

In connection with this glory, the apostle introduces the first of three groanings [spoken of in Rom. 8]. There is the groaning of the whole creation [vv. 19–22]. There is the groaning of the children of God [v. 23]. And there is the groaning of the Spirit [v. 26].

The first groaning is evidence that the glory awaiting the children of God is so great that the sufferings of this present time are not worthy to be compared with it. The whole creation groans, waits, and longs for the glory that shall become manifest in the children of God. The glory that is to be revealed in the sons of God, therefore, will be all-comprehensive; it will include the whole of creation.

What It Is

To the question what or who is the *creature* spoken of in the text, there are many answers. Some answer that it is the whole creation, including all men, the angels, and even the devils. The whole creation shall be restored, so they say. No creature will ultimately be lost. There is no hell. Others say that it is the whole of creation, excluding the angels. Also these people teach that there will be a universal salvation of mankind. There are those who say that the apostle again refers to the world, excluding the rational creature. Others say that he refers only to men. Others say that the apostle refers only to the believers. Still others say that he refers to the heathen world in distinction from those who had been brought into the church.

It is peculiar that so many minds should find so many interpretations of a passage that is rather definite as to what this *creature* is. The apostle says that it is the "whole creation" [v. 22]. If we are to make limitations to this expression, these limitations must be made by the text itself. The apostle says that it is the whole creation. If there is nothing more, we will have to understand that this creature is the whole of creation, including men and angels. If we are to exclude anything, we must exclude only what the text excludes.

The text does, in fact, eliminate several creatures. In the first place, the text excludes the sons of God themselves, for in verse 23 the apostle distinguishes the children of God from this creature. In verse 23 we read, "And not only they, but ourselves also, which have the firstfruits of the Spirit, even we ourselves groan within ourselves." The apostle distinguishes between the believers and the rest of creation. This leaves the whole creation, except the children of God.

But the text excludes more. It also excludes the good angels. This is evident from the fact that they were never made "subject to vanity" [v. 20]. Besides, they were never in the "bondage of corruption" [v. 21]. It is true that the angels are interested in the final glory of the sons of God, but they are not made subject to vanity and they are not in the bondage of corruption. This leaves the whole creation, minus the children of God and minus the good angels.

Excluded also by the text are wicked, ungodly men. The reason is that the wicked do not long for the manifestation of the sons of God. The apostle says that "the earnest expectation of the creature waiteth for the manifestation of the sons of God" [v. 19]. This leaves the whole creation, except the children of God, the good angels, and the wicked. To this we may add the wicked angels, for they also do not long for the manifestation of the sons of God. What is left, finally, is this: the whole creation, excluding all the angels, both good and bad, and excluding all men, both good and wicked.

This *creature* of which the passage speaks, therefore, is all of the irrational, brute creation in its organic existence. It includes sun, moon, and stars. It includes the firmament. It includes the atmosphere. It includes the soil and all that it contains. It includes trees, plants, and all the world of vegetation. And it includes all the living souls that are irrational.

What It Hopes For

Of this creature the apostle says that it waits: "The earnest expectation of the creature waiteth for the manifestation of the sons of God." The apostle expresses the object of the hope of the creature in a twofold way. First, the object is "the manifestation of the sons of God." Second, the object is "the glorious liberty of the children of God."

When the apostle speaks of the manifestation of the sons of God, the presupposition is that they are now already sons of God, but that they have not yet been revealed as such. The meaning is not that in this world we are ignorant as to who the children of God are. It certainly must become manifest who the children of God are. The children of God confess it. This is their calling. It is the calling of the children of God to confess that they are children of God through His grace. Not only is it their calling to confess this, but it is also their calling to manifest this in their walk. Because it is their confession and their walk, they certainly become manifest as children of God.

But in this world they do not become revealed in their character as sons of God. You cannot see that they are children of God. They look just like anyone else. The fact that you cannot see has a fourfold reason. In the first place, they are not manifest in their character of perfection. Sons of God are perfect, but because of their sinful nature, they do not yet shine forth in their final perfection.

In the second place, they do not yet become manifest in their character of glory. Sons of God are glorious; they possess a heavenly glory. But in this world this heavenly glory is hid by the image of the earthy. They look earthy as long as they are in this world.

In the third place, the sons of God are hid in this world from the viewpoint that they die as other men. Sons of God live. Sons of God cannot die. No more than God can die, can the sons of God die. They live. They have eternal life. But this eternal life they have is hid. When you see two men lying side by side in coffins, the one a son of God and the other a son of the devil, you cannot tell the difference.

Finally, the sons of God are hid from the viewpoint of their position, power, and riches. Sons of God have power; they have riches; they have dominion. Sons of God have all things. They must possess all things, and they must reach the position in which they rule over all things. But in this world, with few exceptions, the children of God possess nothing. Usually they occupy no position of power. The things, the positions, and the power of this world are in the hands of the wicked. They cause all the trouble in this world. By contrast, the children of God have nothing. They do not look like sons of God. This is true of all the sons of God with Christ in their midst.

Therefore, the passage says that they *shall become manifest* as the sons of God. God will lift the cover. When God lifts the cover, they will become manifest in their perfection. The image of the earthy will be removed, and the image of the heavenly will appear. They will look like Christ. The appearance of death will be removed. It will become manifest that they have eternal life. It will also become manifest that they possess all things and rule over all things. This will be their glory.

This same glory is what the apostle also calls *the glorious liberty of the children of God.* Literally we read in the original, "the liberty of the glory of the children of God." The children of God shall be glorious. According to verse 18, this glory will be a glory that shall be revealed *in them.* It will be a glory that shall become manifest from *within.* This glory is the very glory of God. It pleased God to make children who would be the reflection of His own glory. It will be a glory in our own nature, consisting in this: we will be righteous as He is righteous, we will be holy as He is holy, we will be perfect as He is perfect, and we will look like Him.

The character of this glory will be liberty. Liberty is that we do as we please, providing that we do the will of God. Liberty is that condition of the heart, of the will, and of the mind in which we submit ourselves to the will of God and serve Him. This is the liberty that will be characteristic of the glory that God will bestow upon His children.

Why It Is Waiting

For this liberty and for this glory, the creature waits. Remember now, the creature is the organic, brute creation. This creature waits for the manifestation of the sons of God. In the original Greek, this creation is pictured as a living creature. The creature is said to wait for the manifestation of the sons of God with "uplifted head," with "stretched out neck." This does not mean that sun, moon, stars, trees, and plants do so consciously. But neither do we have in the text a mere poetical representation. Two truths explain creation's waiting. First, the creature is made subject to vanity and is in the bondage of corruption. Second, the creature is to be delivered from this vanity and bondage of corruption.

The creature is subject to vanity. The one who subjected the creature to vanity is God. By an act of man's will, God made the creature subject to vanity. Vanity is vain labor, vain toil. To such vain labor, such vain toil, God subjected the creature. How could it be any different? The purpose of the creature could not be reached except through man. The purpose of the creature was that it should serve man in order that man should serve God. The sun, the moon, the stars, the animals, the trees, the plants, and the world of vegetation had this for their purpose. But since man does not serve his God, the labor and toil of the creature are vain. The creature does not reach its purpose. Likewise, the liberty of the creature is inseparably connected with the manifestation of the children of God.

Not only is the creature made subject to vanity, but the creature is also made subject to corruption. It serves a man who dies. When the tree throws its fruit into the lap of man, it serves corruption and death. Death is written on all creatures. The creature serves corruption and death. It is in the bondage of corruption.

In this bondage it groans. It groans! "We know that the whole creation groaneth and travaileth in pain together until now" [v. 22]. In this travailing is hope, for the creature is to be delivered. It is to be delivered from the bondage of vanity and corruption. The creature is to be delivered from bondage into the glorious liberty of the children of God. When God's children shall shine forth in all their liberty and shall occupy their position as prophets, priests, and kings, God will give to these sons of God the new creature—the new heaven and the new earth with new trees, new plants, and new vegetation. He will submit the whole new creation to the sons of God. The new creation will serve the sons of God. And the sons of God will serve God.

This is the teaching of Scripture. This is the all-comprehensive idea of God's covenant as symbolized in the rainbow. This is the meaning of the promise to Abraham and his seed. They will possess the land; they will possess Canaan in its heavenly form. This is why all creation rejoices. This is the picture we have in the book of Revelation.

You probably ask, how will this be? My answer is, I don't know. I don't have to know. You ask, will the animals have a place in the new creation? I believe not that the individual animal shall have a place there, but that there will be a heavenly representation of what is now the animal kingdom. You ask, will there be trees and plants? I believe that there will be a heavenly representation of all that we have here.

The point of the text, however, is this: do not be afraid when the suffering of this present time comes. The suffering of this present time is not worthy to be compared with the glory which shall be revealed in us, and for which the whole creation waits. Do not be dismayed. Without shall be the unrighteous, the wicked, the unfaithful. Within shall be the righteous, the faithful. Be faithful, therefore, and God will give you the crown of life.

Chapter Fifty-one

The Groanings of the Spirit

Romans 8:26, 27
Likewise the Spirit also helpeth our infirmities: for we know not what we should pray for as we ought: but the Spirit itself maketh intercession for us with groanings which cannot be uttered.

And he that searcheth the hearts knoweth what is the mind of the Spirit, because he maketh intercession for the saints according to the will of God.

This is the third of the three groanings in Romans 8. There was the groaning of the creature, then the groaning of the children of God. Here we have the groaning of the Spirit. The threefold groan, better translated as a threefold sigh, is related to the glory of which the apostle is speaking as his main subject. It is a sigh caused by the longing for this glory. It is a sigh caused by the longing for the manifestation of the children of God. It is caused by the glorious liberty of the children of God [v. 21], better translated as *by the liberty of the glory of the children of God*. For this glory, the creature sighs. For this glory, we sigh. With a view to this glory, the Spirit sighs.

The text is connected to the immediately preceding by the word *likewise*. The connection is this. If we "hope for that we see not," that is, if we really hope for the invisible things, then we wait for them with patience [v. 25]. "Likewise the Spirit also helpeth our infirmities: for we know not what we should pray for as we ought: but the Spirit itself maketh intercession for us with groanings which cannot be uttered."

A Perfect Prayer

The text speaks of the prayer of the Spirit. There can be no question of this. Some have tried to generalize and make of *the Spirit* the spirit of the church. But it is evident that the apostle is speaking of the Holy Spirit. However, He refers to the Holy Spirit not as the Third Person in the Godhead, but as the Spirit of Christ as He dwells in the church. This indwelling Spirit is here presented as praying.

The question is, how must we conceive of this praying of the Spirit? Is it a prayer that the Spirit prays in us and through us, so that we become conscious of it? Or is it a prayer that the Spirit prays without us, a prayer that the Spirit prays from our heart, but of which we do not become conscious?

The latter is the case. The text teaches that from the heart of the believers arise more prayers than we consciously know. That there arise more prayers from the church and from the heart of the believers than those of which we are conscious is due to the prayers of the Spirit from our heart. This is evident, first, from the fact that the apostle refers to something special. After all, the Spirit works *all* prayer in us. Every prayer of the church is prayer of the Spirit in the church and through the church, but here the apostle has reference to something special. Second, the apostle speaks of this prayer of the Spirit as intercession. Third, he speaks of these prayers of the Spirit as groanings that cannot be uttered, that is, groanings that *we* cannot utter. They are sighs. Somehow, when we have prayed, we feel as if we would like to say more. We feel oppressed about it, and we sigh. These sighs are prayers of the Spirit. They are prayers that the Holy Spirit prays from our heart, but without our speaking, without our knowing it.

There is, then, the prayer of the people of God. There is also the prayer of Christ. And there is the prayer of the Spirit. However, these are not three prayers. They are one prayer. In this one prayer we have only a small part. Insofar as we do not have a part in this one prayer, we sigh.

~ *The Groanings of the Spirit*

The prayer of the Spirit is a prayer for saints. It is not for *the* saints, but for *saints*. "He maketh intercession for saints."[1] The Spirit does not pray for anything else, but only for saints. The Spirit prays for saints in their capacity as saints. He does not pray for them as men. He prays for them from the viewpoint of their being saints. This makes a difference. It spoils our prayers that we do not look upon ourselves as saints. We go to work and do things as men. We forget that we are saints. Then we bring these things before the throne of God. Thus, we pray as men, not as saints. The Spirit never does this. He prays for saints.

Implied is that the Spirit knows just what we need. He knows just how everything must be done in order that the kingdom of God and His glory may come. And He makes intercession "according to God." That is, He prays for saints with the glory of God in mind. He never asks for anything that does not tend to the glory of God.

It is a perfect prayer.

A Much-needed Intercession

This prayer of the Spirit is a much-needed intercession for two reasons. It is much needed, first, because of our infirmity. The correct reading of the text is not "infirmities," but "infirmity." The reference is not to the infirmity of our prayers. The reference, rather, is to our infirmity in connection with our waiting for the things for which we hope. If we are really waiting for the realization of our hope, then we wait patiently. But as regards our patience, we are imperfect. That we are not perfect in patience is due to several things. For one thing, we are still carnal. If we were perfect, we could patiently wait for what we hope. But this is not the case. We are sinful. There-

---

1. According to the original Greek text, the correct translation of verse 27 should be *for saints*. There is no textual basis for the insertion of the definite article by the King James Version.

fore, our waiting is characterized by infirmity. Second, we are still earthy. Because we are earthy, we like the things that can be seen. We *may* like them. I like my body; I like my home; I like my position. This has nothing to do with my hope. But I like these things, and I may like them. But when we are placed before the choice *my home or the hope*, we hesitate. This is our infirmity. And, third, we do not always understand the way of the Lord. It seems to us sometimes that the things God does are wrong. We become impatient.

Now the Spirit prays, makes intercession for us, with a view to helping our infirmity. He prays, "Make My people patient." The result of this prayer is that we believe all God does, works for our good. Also, we grow in the confidence that all things work together for our good. In addition, we have peace with all things.

The other reason why the prayer of the Spirit is much needed is that we know not what we should pray for as we ought. We do not know what we should pray for in detail. We know how to pray in a general way. With this we have no difficulty. Did you ever notice that this is the way the Lord taught us to pray: "Hallowed be thy name"? As long as we pray in this general way, we have no trouble. But as soon as we apply this general principle to our actual life and pray in detail, we come into trouble. As soon as I tell the Lord how He should hallow His name, I am off the track. As soon as I tell the Lord that I would like to fill the pulpit in Fuller Avenue [First Protestant Reformed] Church for a long time to come, I am off the track. I may not tell the Lord how He must do things. This is not so bad as long as one does not know that he *knows not* what he should pray for. Some people are not carnal, but they do not know that they *know not* what they should pray for. Therefore, they pray for anything and everything. To a certain extent this is the trouble with us all.

This was even the trouble with the apostle Paul. Paul had been given a thorn in the flesh. He prayed that it might be taken from him, but the Spirit prayed that it be *not* taken away from him lest Paul should exalt himself. The answer that Paul received upon the prayer of the Spirit was, "My grace is sufficient for thee" [II Cor 12:7–9].

The more we understand things, the more we will refrain from telling the Lord what He should do. We must pray for things in general. This is our share in the prayer of the Spirit. Then there is the prayer of the Spirit for the details. The Spirit brings to the attention of Christ, and Christ brings to the attention of God, all the needs of His people. And all things work together for their good.

Therefore, there is much that we cannot utter. If we do, it comes into conflict with the prayer of the Spirit. Then the Spirit says, "My grace is sufficient for thee."

A Prayer That Is Always Heard

Isn't this nice? I think it is. For the prayer of the Spirit is always heard. God gives to His people exactly what the Spirit prays for. The prayer of the Spirit is always heard because it is a prayer for God and a prayer on behalf of saints. When the text says, "He that searcheth the hearts knoweth what is the mind of the Spirit," it distinguishes the mind of the Spirit from the foolish prayers we utter, as well as the prayers we cannot utter, but only sigh. God grants the prayer of the Spirit. He makes His people patient, so that this becomes true: "If we hope for that we see not, then do we with patience wait for it" [v. 25].

What a glorious assurance is ours! We are assured that in the way of the prayers rising from our hearts through the Spirit, God gives us what we ask for. And we know that all things will work together for our good.

Chapter Fifty-two

The Assurance That All Things Work for Good

Romans 8:28
And we know that all things work together for good to them that love God, to them who are the called according to his purpose.

In the preceding verses, the apostle has spoken of the greatness of the glory of the children of God. He now gives an answer to the question, is it possible that this glory will never be realized? Or, with a view to our personal part in this glory, the question arises, is it possible that we will be disappointed and that evil powers will cause this glory to be taken away from us? Is it possible that evil powers will frustrate God's works? Is it possible that through these evil powers the manifestation of this glory of the children of God will never be seen? In other words, from the greatness of the glory of which the apostle has been speaking—the glory for which the creature groans, for which the children of God themselves groan, and for which the Spirit groans—Paul now passes to the *certainty* of this glory.

To the question whether it is possible that evil powers might frustrate this glory, the apostle answers that there are no such powers for God. He does not say that no power can frustrate, can hinder, the manifestation of the glory, but most positively he declares that there *are* no such powers. To the contrary, all things must work together with God. All things must work for good to them that love God.

The connection with the preceding context is this. The apostle had said that the Spirit makes intercession for us according to the will of God. This prayer of the Spirit is always heard. Therefore, all things must work together for our good.

It is a marvelous thing to say, "All things work together for good to them that love God." Nevertheless, the ultimate purpose is not merely that we should say this, but the purpose is that we include ourselves in this group and that we say, "All things work together for good for *us*." This is the practical purpose of the text. If we appropriate this word, the practical fruit will be that we will commit our way unto the Lord in the assurance that all things do work together for our good.

The Content of This Assurance

When the apostle says that all things work together for our good, he means that all things are beneficial for us, all things work for our well-being. Accordingly, all things lead to a good end. However, the apostle does not speak of earthly good. This is not the *real* good. Good is not that we are successful, that we prosper in earthly goods. The mere fact that a man prospers and is successful is not the real good. To the contrary, death hangs over all the earthly good. It is not possible that all things work for good in this world. Instead, the apostle is speaking of the good of which he had been speaking in the preceding context. He is speaking of the glory of the people of God, of the glory that shall be revealed in them. He is speaking of their glorious liberty. This final glory, when the people of God will become heirs of all things, is the good that is in view.

What we must notice is that the apostle says *all things*: "*All things* work together for good." This is all-comprehensive. Included are all things that God has made from the beginning, in heaven and on earth. The angels in heaven, principalities, and powers are included. The angels that have fallen are included in the statement. When we turn to the earthly creation, we can take *all things* in the widest sense: the stars in the heavens, sun and moon, the brute creature, trees and plants, and also the living creature.

Although having all these things in mind, so that he means sickness or health, sorrow or joy, prosperity or depression, nevertheless, the apostle wishes to emphasize the evil things. He wishes to emphasize those things that appear evil to us. This is evident from the fact that it is not so much a question in our mind that good things work for our good, but the question is whether evil things work for our good. That *all things* refer especially to evil things is also evident from the context, in which the apostle speaks of the sufferings of this present time. He says especially these sufferings work for good.

We notice that the apostle says that all things work, and that they work together. Did you ever notice that everything in God's creation *works?* It is not only the rational creatures who work. Everything works. Things have never stood still since God made them. Sun, moon, and stars are working agents. Trees, plants, rivers, and streams are working agents. The clouds in the heavens are working agents. The soil itself works. It produces something. So it is with the rational creatures. Men always work. All things work. Nothing is at a standstill. If we could look even into a grain of sand, we would find that in it things are working.

Not only do all things work, but all things work so that they accomplish something. Things are not simply moving in space, but they are going somewhere. Things work together, that is, things do not work to gain their own end. Each thing does not do its own work. They work together. They all work one work. They all have the same object in view. Every one of God's creatures, each one in its own place, works together to one purpose. That one purpose is the glory of God. The roaring lion in the forest and the little germ that creeps into your lungs work together. Sun, moon, and stars—all things work, and they work together. In many cases, they do not know this. Sometimes they do not want this. It is not the devil's purpose to work for the good of God's people. Nevertheless, he does.

All things work because God works through them. If God would stop working, nothing would work. But God works. He works in everything. God works for His own purpose, which is the glory of His people. Therefore, all things work for the glorious manifestation of the children of God.

We do not see this. We sometimes see little snapshots of it. We see it when the devil went to paradise. He did not go there for the purpose of bringing to manifestation the glory of Christ and His church, but this is what he did. So it is frequently. When the sons of Jacob sold Joseph into Egypt, it was not their purpose to seek the glory of Joseph and to keep a large number of people alive, but they worked together. We see this especially in the cross. When Pilate, the Jewish Sanhedrin, and the wicked world conspired against Jesus to crucify Him, it was not their purpose to bring about the salvation of God's people, but this is what they did. So it is with the things that affect us. The way sometimes seems dark and gloomy. God does things we think are foolish. And yet, how often do we not see it, when God leads His people in dark ways, that His people strike the roots of faith deeper into the Lord.

The Ground of This Assurance

With the phrase *to them who are the called according to his purpose,* the apostle points to the ground by which we are assured of the truth that all things work together for good to them who love God. He points to God's counsel. God's counsel is not simply a plan, a drawing, on a piece of paper. But it is that which God has eternally set before Himself to realize. God's counsel is as old as God is Himself. God's counsel consists of the things God has in mind and that He purposes to realize. This counsel is all-comprehensive. Nothing is excluded from it. That we sit in worship is due to the fact that God set us in worship in His counsel. We can carry it further. The hairs of our heads have been eternally counted. Each hair has been determined in God's counsel. There is nothing excluded from that counsel. Because everything must work together, God has included all things in His counsel. God forgot nothing.

According to His counsel, we are called. We are called according to God's purpose. God's purpose is that He should have a people like unto His Son. Therefore, to take a step back, God purposed to glorify Himself in His Son. God has a Son. This Son reflects His glory. God wanted to expand His glory. Therefore, He determined to reflect His glory in His people. God determined to glorify Himself in Christ. To do this, He gave Christ many brethren. Around that one purpose, God arranged all things in His counsel so that they must serve that one purpose. Things do not happen by accident. Everything has a place in God's counsel. Everything must serve the one purpose of God, the glorious manifestation of the children of God. According to this purpose, we are called. This is why everything must work together for good to them who are so called. God has so arranged things that they must all work together for the salvation of God's people.

God's people must be assured of this for themselves personally. When the apostle says that we know that all things work together for good to them that love God, the meaning is not merely that we know all things work together for good to God's people. This is not sufficient. For remember, the opposite is also true. All things work together for evil to them who do not love God. All things work together for evil to them who are not called according to God's purpose. The one is inseparably connected with the other. This is terrible, but it is true. And it is as it should be. Things never work together for good to them who do not love God. Just as there is a working of all things to bring those who love God to glory, so there is a working of all things to bring those who do not love God to desolation. All the more serious, therefore, is the question, "How can I know that all things work together for good *to me*?"

The Participants of This Assurance

To this question, the answer is that the comfort of the text is for them who are called. All things work for good to them who are called efficaciously. The calling is that work of God whereby He changes a man and makes him a child of God. This takes place, indeed, through the Word of God. But it is itself the work of the Holy Spirit. This calling may take place suddenly or gradually, but we can know it. How can we know that we are called? Is it that in order to know this we must be able to say, "Ten or twenty years ago I was converted"? This is possible. But this is the exception. By far the largest majority have no such experience to point to. But this is sure: if we are called, we will love God. They who are called are the same as they who love God. The love of God is the fruit of the calling.

Therefore, the question is this: do we love God? The love of God is not a certain sentiment. The love of God does not express itself in a smile, or a tear, or a good deed. The love of God is a matter of the heart. From the heart, it is a matter of the will. It reveals itself in this: we love His commandments, His Word, His people. It reveals itself in this: we are sorry for sin, hate it, and flee from it. We cannot love sin and love God too. We must not say that we love God while we walk in sin. Antithetically, the love of God means that we hate sin and flee from it. It is not that we never sin, but we never sin with our heart.

The implication is that we do not experience the Word of the text—that all things work for our good—unless we walk in the love of God. It is possible to say, "All things work for our good" and still not experience it when it comes to the point.

Why? Because it is only as we walk in the love of God that we appropriate the words of the text and say, "Nothing can separate us from the love of God, which is in Christ Jesus our Lord" [v. 39]. Thus, the peace of God, which passes all understanding, will fill our hearts [Phil. 4:7].

Chapter Fifty-three

God for Us

Romans 8:31, 32

What shall we then say to these things? If God be for us, who can be against us?

He that spared not his own Son, but delivered him up for us all, how shall he not with him also freely give us all things?

In this section of Romans 8, the apostle begins a new thought. There are in this chapter different passages in which the apostle looks at new phases, new aspects of his theme, which is the security and glory of the children of God. Not in verse 29, as is sometimes said, but in verse 31, the apostle starts a new section. He asks the question, "What shall we then say to these things?" With this question he is referring to the things he has written in the preceding context. The apostle asks, "Seeing that these things I have written are so, what must be our final conclusion? What must be the practical conclusion with regard to the people of God in this world?" The question is not whether we have understood these things, but the question is, what has been the practical significance for us? What shall we say with a view to these things? The answer to this question we have in what follows. We will say this: "If God be for us, who can be against us?"

A warning is necessary. We must not compare ourselves with this Word of God from the viewpoint of the question whether we are really Christians. This would be rash. In these words the standpoint is not really that of the actual level on which the Christian usually lives, for then we would draw the conclusion that we are not Christian. In principle the Christian lives on this level, and it is possible to live on this high level. But it is also true that you and I in our actual life live on the level indicated by the old patriarch Jacob when he expressed the very opposite of the thought of Romans 8:31: "All these things are against me" [Gen. 42:36]. Therefore, we must remember that under the guidance of the Holy Spirit the apostle in the text ascends the dizzy heights of an absolutely victorious faith. The purpose of the text is not to give us a picture of how we usually live, but to draw us thither. The purpose is to draw us out of the depths in which we say, "All these things are against me." The purpose is to draw us up to the height in which we say, "All things are for me."

Meaning

It is not necessary to give an extended exposition of the phrase *If God be for us*. We all know, in a general way, what it means that God is for us. It means two things especially. It means, first, that God is for us in His heart. And, second, it means that all His work is for us. We are the objects of His love, of His favor, of His loving-kindness, and of His mercy. God works for us.

There is also something else. There is in the question "Who can be against us?" the suggestion of powers that *are* against us. The apostle definitely has in mind powers that are opposed to us, powers that work against us and seek our destruction. We meet with these powers. There is the power of the devil and his host. There is the power of the world in an evil sense: the power of temptation; the power of the lust of the flesh, the lust of the eyes, and the pride of life. There is the power also of persecution, of reproach, of affliction. We come into contact with these powers, if we are faithful. We cannot avoid them. There is in this world the power of sin and corruption. Even our nature is part of this world. The power of sin is within us. Besides, there is in the world the power of death. We cannot escape death, because we are still in the world upon which

God's curse is operating. With a view to all these powers, the apostle says that God is for us. Other powers may be against us, but God is for us.

When we say in such a setting that someone is for us, the strength of the assertion depends on who it is that is for us. Who is he? What is he? What is his character? What is his relation to me? What is his relation to the powers that are against me? The one answer here is *God*. That He is God means, first, that He is the supreme and final Judge. He passes sentence. He executes the verdict. From His verdict there is no appeal. If this Judge is for us, He justified us; otherwise, He could not be for us. And He will justify us in the future. That He is God means, second, that He is the eternal Architect of the entire universe. He planned it all, and He planned it all alone. There was no one who helped or advised Him. If God is for us, He was for us then. When He made His counsel, He did so in that attitude of favor. He so arranged all things in His counsel that they must all be for us. That He is God also means that He made all things. This is creation. If God is for us, He was for us when He made all things. He made the world with a view to our salvation. Finally, that He is God means that He is the supreme King. He is the supreme King who holds all things in His hand from moment to moment. He rules over all things. He does all He wills, and He always did. Nothing ever happened that He did not will.

Remember, I am speaking of His counsel, and of the execution of His will. There is no dualism. There is no God plus something else. There is no God plus some other power. The history of the world is nothing but the execution of His counsel. The history of the world is not a duel between God and the devil. The devil executes God's will even though he does not intend to.

As to the character of God, Scripture tells us that He is almighty, unchangeable, and all-wise. The question might be asked whether there is not something that slipped out of God's hands. Scripture answers that God is almighty. That God is almighty does not mean that He is very strong, but it means that there is no power outside Him. There is no power that opposes Him and that He must fight. God does not fight the devil. If God did not want the devil to work, all He would have to do is drop him, and the devil would be no more. If God does not want sickness to attack your frame, all He has to do is drop it, and the sickness is no more. But might it be that there was a mistake? Scripture answers that God is all-wise. He never is mistaken in anything. But might it not be possible that we lose the favor of God? Scripture answers that God is unchangeable. Nothing can separate us from His love.

Therefore, if we can really say that God is for us, we have no need of anything else. All we need to know is this one thing: whether God is for us. If God is for us, we can have peace.

Manifestation

How do I know this? How do I know two things? How do I know that God is for *us*? And how do I know that God is for *me*? The first question the apostle answers by saying, "He that spared not his own Son, but delivered him up for us all, how shall he not with him also freely give us all things?" Verse 32 distinguishes God's eternal and natural Son from us, His adopted sons. But this doctrinal distinction is not the purpose of the expression in the text. The purpose is to point out that this Son is the object of God's love. Jesus was God's most beloved Son and therefore more precious than all else to Him.

That God delivered Him up refers, of course, to the cross. God actually gave that Son up, actually delivered Him up. We must not think of it by imagining that the First Person of the Trinity delivered up the Second Person. No, the triune God delivered up the only begotten Son of the Father in the human flesh. This is of dogmatic interest, but, again, this is not the purpose of the text. The purpose is to reveal something that I tremble to say. The purpose of the text is—I say it with all reverence—to point to the tragedy of God's own suffering when He delivered up His Son to the cross. If the text does not mean this, it means nothing.

Don't you see that the text teaches that it cost God something to be for us? Don't you see that this is the point? Don't you see that this is exactly the proof that God is *for* us? The phrase is something like what we read in Genesis [22:2], where God says to Abraham, "Offer unto Me your only son Isaac." With a believing heart, Abraham must give all that he has. If Romans 8:32 does not mean that through the flesh of His Son there was in God that which corresponds to what we feel when we nail our only son to the cross, the text means nothing. How this is I do not know. God gave something. He gave His own Son. He spared Him not. Rather than to let His children go to hell, He let His Son go there. In this sense, we can speak of the divine tragedy of the cross.

The fact that God spared not His own Son but delivered Him up for us all is the evidence that God is for us. Paul is not teaching that God is for all. And yet the text does not say, either, that He is for the elect. This is not its purpose. The text does not say, "God delivered up His Son for the *elect*." But it says, "God delivered up His Son for *us*." The question is, how is it possible for me to say that I am included in that *us*? The answer is, He was delivered up for *me* if I am in Christ. He was delivered up for *me* if I am ingrafted into Him by faith. If I have been delivered from sin and death, then I can say that He was delivered up for *me*. He was delivered up for *us* if we mortify the deeds of the body and walk in newness of life. Then God is for us. In other words, God is for *us* if we are for *God*, because God was for us *first*.

Result

The result is twofold. One result is indicated in the words of verse 32: "How shall he not with him also freely give us all things?" *All things* are not merely the whole universe, although this is true. All things are all that God purposes to give us, all the blessings of salvation that He will surely give us. He will surely give us the eternal inheritance in glory. As to this present time, He will surely give us all the spiritual blessings that are in Christ. He will also give us in this life all things necessary for our salvation. Also, He will give us all the necessary temporal things. They may be suffering, affliction, persecution, sickness, and death, but He gives them. In his first epistle to the Corinthians, Paul says, "All things are yours." Summing up certain things, he also mentions death. "All things are yours . . . And ye are Christ's; and Christ is God's" [I Cor. 3:21–23]. Is it not enough that God gives us all things that tend to our salvation?

How could it be any different? "How shall he not with him also freely give us all things?" If God gave the greatest that He had, shall He not give the smaller things? This is the argument of the apostle. If God gave His own Son, can you doubt that He will give you all things? God really gave us all things already. For all things are in Christ. If we are in Christ, God has already given us all things to the glory of Christ.

Another result of God's being for us is that nothing can be against us. It is not that there is nothing that *seems* to be against us. There are many powers that seem to be against us. Our comfort concerning these powers is not merely that they will all finally be overcome, but there is also no power that at any moment can do us any harm. There is no power that can at any moment be against us. All things must work together for our good.

Of course, the important question is this: "Is God for *me*?" This is different from the question whether you are a Christian, for this question asks whether we walk with Christ so that we suffer with Him. In this way of suffering, we receive the testimony, "Yes, God is for me." And then the purpose of the text is that we say it; that we say it today, tomorrow, and all the days of our life: "Nothing can be against us, for God is for us." Hallelujah!

Chapter Fifty-four

No One to Condemn Us

Romans 8:34
Who is he that condemneth? It is Christ that died, yea rather, that is risen again, who is even at the right hand of God, who also maketh intercession for us.

"Who is he that condemneth?"
This is one of the questions that make up the specific content of the general question that the apostle had asked before: "If God be for us, who can be against us?" [8:31]. The answer implied in this question is, "Nothing can be against us." But there are several questions that follow from this question. Especially three questions make the general question specific and concrete. The first is, "Who shall lay any thing to the charge of God's elect?" The answer is, "It is God that justifieth" [v. 33]. The second question is found in the text: "Who is he that condemneth?" That is, who can be against us in judgment? The answer to this question reads, "It is Christ that died, yea rather, that is risen again, who is even at the right hand of God, who also maketh intercession for us." The third question is this: can there be any power that is able to separate us from the love of God? [v. 35]. The answer is, "I am persuaded, that neither death, nor life, nor angels, nor principalities, nor powers, nor things present, nor things to come, Nor height, nor depth, nor any other creature, shall be able to separate us from the love of God, which is in Christ Jesus our Lord" [vv. 38, 39].

With regard to the question in verse 33, as contrasted with

the question in verse 34, there are two points of difference. The question in verse 33 deals with the *accusers*. But the question in verse 34 deals with the *judge*. There might be many accusers to bring accusations against us. The question may well be asked, "Who shall succeed in laying any charge against us?" The answer is, "It is God that justifieth." If He justifies us, no one can successfully lay any charge against us. But verse 34 deals with the judge. It deals with the condemner.

The second point of difference is that in the text the question is in the singular. The former question deals with the accusers. There might be many accusers; many accusations might be brought against us. But verse 34 deals with the condemner. Therefore, the singular is used. The question is asked, "Who is he that condemneth?" The answer is, "It is Christ that died, yea rather, that is risen again, who is even at the right hand of God, who also maketh intercession for us."

We must read the text just this way. The answer is, "No one condemns us." But the text expresses this by declaring that Christ died, is raised again, is at the right hand of God, and makes intercession for us. Christ is with the judge who is for us. Therefore, Christ is for us.

The text leads us to the heights of faith. We do not always live on this height of faith in which we say, "Who is he that condemneth?" But this Word comes to us in order that we might be lifted up out of the depths and brought to a higher level of faith. Let us look at the text in this personal light.

Because Christ Is the Only Judge

"Who is he that condemneth?" is a way of saying that there is no one who condemns us. A condemner is one who is judge. That is, a condemner is one who has the right to judge and who, when he judges, expresses a negative verdict. He also has the power to execute the sentence upon us.

The thought of the text is that there is no one in all the universe who has this power. There may be many things that seem to condemn me. The devil condemns me; the world condemns me; even my own conscience condemns me. It seems that this condemnation will be realized. Nevertheless, I say, "No one can condemn me." The reason is this: Christ sits at the right hand of God. "Who is he that condemneth? It is Christ that died, yea rather, that is risen again, who is even at the right hand of God, who also maketh intercession for us."

The death of Christ, the resurrection of Christ, Christ's being at the right hand of God, and Christ's intercession for us are not four different things. There is unity in the text. The unity is this: it is Christ who died, or rather who is risen again, who sits at the right hand of God, and who makes intercession for us. This is why there is no one who can condemn us. Christ is at the right hand of God. The right hand is the symbol of power and authority. To sit at the right hand of a king is to be raised to the highest position in the kingdom. The fact that Christ sits at the right hand of God means, therefore, that He occupies the highest position in the universe. God rules through Christ. This implies two things. First, because God has clothed Christ with all authority to rule over all things, Christ has the authority, the right, to impose His will upon all. Second, God endowed Christ with power to maintain this position so that He is able to exercise His authority.

The conclusion is that Christ occupies the position of Judge. This is the implication of His sitting at the right hand of God. Christ is our Judge. He judges us, and He will judge us in the final day. We read repeatedly in Scripture that we must all appear before the judgment seat of Christ and that Christ will judge all things [II Cor. 5:10; John 5:22]. Christ will be seen again. When we see Him again, He will be the Judge.

If God placed Christ at His right hand as Judge, it follows that He is the *only* Judge. If we are to be condemned, He must do it. There is no one else to condemn us. There may be many who try it. The devil may condemn us; the world may condemn us; our conscience may condemn us. But regarding all these attempts to condemn us, we ought to appeal to Christ, to the Judge. The only question of importance in the matter is, will *Christ* condemn me?

Because the Only Judge Is Our Advocate

Will He?

He maketh intercession for us, the apostle says. The one who is to be the manifestation of the righteous judgment of God makes intercession for us. He prays for us. The intercessory prayer of Christ is not that He appears before the Father once in a while and prays for us. Rather, His intercessory prayer is a constant and perfect prayer. Strictly speaking, this intercessory prayer of Jesus is the only intercessory prayer that can be made. There is only one who can make this intercessory prayer. That one is Christ. In the sense that Christ prays for us, we cannot pray for one another. Therefore, we should be careful in asking someone to pray for us. You must not ask someone to pray for you too quickly. This is all right if one is spiritually weak and sick, but not otherwise. Even then, our prayer for one another must not be compared with this prayer of Christ. The only intercessory prayer is this prayer of Christ.

For Christ is our Mediator. He is not only the Mediator in the sense that He came in the likeness of our sinful flesh, died for us, was raised again, ascended into heaven, is seated at the right hand of God, and pours out His Spirit; but He is also the Mediator in the sense that salvation is *through* Him. He is our Mediator not only in the judicial sense, but also in the organic sense. We receive the blessings of salvation through Christ. They are bestowed upon Christ first, and the church receives these blessings through Him. Because this is the case, Christ stands before the Father in an attitude of prayer. Christ constantly stands before the Father in an attitude of prayer in order that He may receive the power to bestow the blessings of salvation upon the church.

I know that there are some special intercessory prayers. As there are some special cases, so there are special intercessory prayers. One example of this we have in the case of Peter. The Lord says to Peter, "I have prayed for thee, that thy faith fail not" [Luke 22:32]. However this may be, the intercessory prayer of which the apostle speaks is the prayer of Christ that He may receive the blessings of salvation and that He may receive the power to bestow these blessings upon the church.

In this consciousness—the consciousness that He makes intercession for us—we must look at Jesus as Judge. His intercession for us reveals that He loves us. Jesus always loves us. The one who judges us loves us. To pray for someone is an act of love. Therefore, do you think Christ will condemn us if He can avoid doing so? It is another question whether He can avoid it. But do you think that if Christ can possibly avoid it, He will condemn us? Not if He can help it!

The fact that Christ makes intercession for us also reveals that He is our advocate. Jesus is our Attorney. He pleads for us. He pleads! He insists! He says, "I will that My people receive the blessings of salvation." Jesus is a strong lawyer, pleading for our justification. He says, "I will, Father, that Thou give Me power to justify My people." In addition He says, "I will that Thou give Me the power to give them the blessing of eternal life." If Jesus can at all accomplish it, He will win His plea.

He who makes intercession for us receives these blessings of salvation. The Father fills Him with them. What does Jesus do with these blessings? Condemn us? Don't you believe it! Is it not evident that we can say, "Who is he that condemneth?" Is it not evident, in other words, that we can say, "There is no one to condemn us"? Is it not evident that the apostle John was right when he said, "Herein is our love made perfect, that we may have boldness in the day of judgment"? [I John 4:17]. We can say, "We will not be afraid in the day of judgment, for He who is Judge is my Advocate."

Because This Advocate Has the Right to Be Our Advocate

Still, we may hesitate to make this confession. We may say, "I believe that Christ sits on the right hand of God and that He is the sole Judge. And I believe that this Judge makes intercession. But I doubt that He makes intercession for *me*." After all, the one for whom Christ pleads cannot be a sinner. If Christ is to plead for someone successfully before God, this person must be righteous. But we are sinners.

In this reasoning there is an element of truth, for it is true that Christ can plead only for the righteous. He cannot plead for sinners. This is because He must plead before God, and God cannot excuse the sinner. Christ can plead only for the righteous. But the righteous for whom this Advocate pleads *are* righteous as sinners. They are not righteous because of anything in themselves, but they are righteous with a righteousness that He merited for them. He pleads for the righteous whom He justified.

This is why verse 34 says, "It is Christ that died, yea rather, that is risen again." This Advocate has the right to be the Advocate of sinners. He has this right because of what the apostle says so beautifully: He died and was raised again. This is how we should read the verse [according to the Greek original]: "He *was* raised," not "He is risen." There is a difference. The difference is as follows. That He *was raised* means that the resurrection of Jesus was an act of the Father. If the words had said, "He *arose*," that would mean that it was an act of Christ's own divinity. But it is stated that He *was raised*. Emphatically, the apostle says, "yea rather, who was raised again." If Christ had merely died and stayed in the grave, his death would have meant nothing. But that was not the case. He died and was raised. When He was raised, that resurrection was God's answer to His death. In the resurrection God said to Christ, "You have the right to live; you are justified."

All the emphasis is on Christ. It is Christ who died. It is Christ who was raised again. It is Christ who sits at the right hand of God. It is Christ who intercedes for us. It is Christ whom God appointed to die and to be raised again. It is Christ who took the sin of His church upon Himself. When He was raised, He was free from the sin of the church. This Christ is our Advocate. He pleads for us. On the basis of that atoning work of His, He says, "I will that where I am, they whom Thou hast given me shall also be" [John 17:24]. I will that My people be justified. I will that they receive all the blessings of salvation. I will that Thou give them eternal life, for I died for them, and in the resurrection I have Thy Word that I was successful.

Is there any reason why we should not say, "Who is he that condemneth?" There is no reason why we should not say it if we are in Christ. If we are not in Christ, the text has nothing for us. It speaks of them who are in Christ. Why should there be anything in the text for you if you are not in Christ? If you are not in Christ, you don't care. But there is no condemnation for them who are in Christ Jesus, who walk not after the flesh, but after the Spirit [Rom. 8:1]. There is no reason why we should not say, "Who is he that condemneth?" The world, the devil, my own conscience—I bring all of that to Christ.

Therefore, the end of it all is, "Believe on the Lord Jesus Christ, and thou shalt be saved" [Acts 16:31].

Chapter Fifty-five

Separation Impossible

Romans 8:35-39
Who shall separate us from the love of Christ? shall tribulation, or distress, or persecution, or famine, or nakedness, or peril, or sword?
As it is written, For thy sake we are killed all the day long; we are accounted as sheep for the slaughter.
Nay, in all these things we are more than conquerers through him that loved us.
For I am persuaded, that neither death, nor life, nor angels, nor principalities, nor powers, nor things present, nor things to come,
Nor height, nor depth, nor any other creature, shall be able to separate us from the love of God, which is in Christ Jesus our Lord.

"Who shall separate us from the love of Christ?" is the only question that remains [in Rom. 8]. After this question is answered, there is no other question that can possibly be asked as to the security of the people of God. Of the security of their salvation, the apostle has been speaking throughout this chapter. He had finally asked the question, "Who can be against us?" Concerning this question, the apostle found that there are no accusers who can accuse us; there is no charge that can be laid against us. The accusers were put to silence. Looking from the accusers to the Judge, the apostle then asked, "Who is he that condemneth?" Also this question is answered in the negative. No one has the power and authority to condemn us, for there is only one Judge. He is Christ. And Christ died, or rather,

He was raised again. He sits at the right hand of God. He also makes intercession for us. There is no one who can condemn us.

But there is one more possibility: in spite of the fact that the accusers have been silenced, and in spite of the fact that no one has the power and authority to condemn us, somehow some evil power may separate us from the love of God and consequently from our salvation. Is this possible? You may be perfectly safe in a courtroom under the protection of the police. You may be able to look up to the judge and say, "You have nothing against me." But around the courtroom there may be a wild mob that does not care about the decision of the judge, and that mob may take you and lynch you. Now is it possible for us to be separated from the love of God? There is no one who can lay a charge against us. There is no one to condemn us. But can we be separated from the love of God? This is the question. And the question has the force of a denial: no one shall separate us from the love of God.

The passage must be treated in its entirety. There is abundant material for several discussions. We must not go into details in a passage like this, however, for it constitutes a unity. It has a purpose. The purpose is to make us say, "Who shall separate us from the love of Christ?" If this is not, in a certain measure, the fruit of the exposition of the passage, either the exposition has failed, or the reader has not heard the Word of God in the passage. The purpose of this portion of the Word of God is to lift us up out of what is the real condition of you and me. Our daily life is not such that we do not fear. We do fear. I do; you do. We fear life, and we fear death. We fear hunger, and we fear nakedness. Our real life is considerably removed from the level of the text. We always ask, "What shall we eat, and what shall we drink, and wherewith shall we be clothed?" [Matt. 6:31]. We do not ordinarily stand on the level where we say, "For thy sake we are killed all the day long." Therefore, the purpose of the text is to lift us up so that in all circumstances and experiences we may feel safe in Christ. The purpose is that we may be persuaded that it is impossible to separate us from the love of Christ.

What Is Impossible

It is impossible that we should be separated from the love of Christ. And it is impossible that we should be separated from the love of God that is in Christ Jesus our Lord. Two expressions are used to denote that love from which we cannot be separated. The one expression is *the love of Christ*. The other expression is *the love of God, which is in Christ Jesus our Lord*. This is one and the same love. In the latter phrase, the apostle explains love in more detail. It is the love of God. But it is the love of God in Christ. It is the love with which God loved us from eternity. This love He cannot realize outside of Christ. We are not to suppose that there is the love of God plus the love of Christ. Still less are we to suppose this: God hated us, but Christ moves God to love us. Instead, it is the love of God as He manifested that love in Christ, especially in the cross. For this reason, when the Word of God speaks of the love of God, it does not mean our love to God and to Christ. When Scripture speaks of the love of God, it usually refers to the love of God to us. So it is in the text. The question in the text is not, "Can our love to God be extinguished?" but, "Can anything separate us from the love of God to us?"

What is the meaning of being separated from God's love? Does it mean the same as if the apostle had written that we cannot become estranged from the love of God? We can become estranged from the love of someone. This can happen in two ways. One way is that my love for him dies. The other is that his love for me grows cold. Evidently this is not the meaning of the apostle, for Paul does not say, "Who shall kill the love of God in my heart?" This is possible—if not to kill this love, nevertheless to become so estranged from this love for a time that we are not conscious of it. It is possible in certain circumstances that we are not conscious of the love of God in our heart. It is possible that our physical suffering is so severe that we can think of nothing else. Our physical suffering may be so intense that it is possible only by a special miracle of grace to sing of the love of God. We read of this in stories, but usually this is not the case. Usually when we are in severe suffering, we can think of nothing else. For a time we seem to be estranged from the love of God as far as our consciousness is concerned. But this is not the meaning. Nor is the meaning that nothing can cause God to stop loving us.

The question is, "Who can separate us from the love of God?" The love of God is His eternal desire to save His people. This love of God sent Christ into the likeness of our sinful flesh. This love of God caused the cross, the blotting out of the sins of His people, their justification, their deliverance from the power of sin and death. This has already been effected. But this love of God must also *preserve us*. The question might be asked, "Is it not possible that something might step in between us and this love of God?" In this case, the love of God could no more reach us. God, then, could not save us to the end. Something would come between us and our salvation. The love of God must save us, but it must also preserve us. Is there anything anywhere that can cut us off from this saving love of God?

The apostle says, "*Who* can separate us from the love of Christ?" Although in the list that he enumerates Paul does not mention a *who*, but circumstances and experiences, he is thinking of a *who*. He is thinking of the devil and his host. He is thinking of the power of the world, in the midst of which the church exists.

Then the apostle begins to enumerate. As he enumerates, he is thinking of the suffering inflicted upon the church for Christ's sake. Shall the enemy, by any suffering inflicted upon the church, separate the church from the love of God? That this is the idea is evident from the fact that the apostle mentions persecution. This is also evident from the quotation from Psalm 44: "For thy sake we are killed all the day long; we are counted as sheep for the slaughter" [v. 22]. Shall anything separate us from the love of God?

The things that the apostle enumerates come in pairs. Tribulation and distress are a pair; they come together. Famine and nakedness are a pair. Peril and sword are a pair.

Tribulation and distress always come together. Tribulation consists of making our place very narrow, of leaving us no room anywhere, or pressing us out of the world. There is room for business, but there is no room for a job, let us say, by means of a closed [union] shop. This may come very soon. We still have an open shop, and you can still get a job, but this may change, and you may be forced out of a job. Tribulation makes your place narrow, so that finally you have no place left in the world. Don't think that these things are not really so. Things change very fast. Don't think that you are safer here than in Germany or Italy or Russia.[1] In our day we can conceive that these things may be upon us next year. Things change fast in our day. This tribulation may come before we know it. Then our place will be made very narrow, and the enemy will leave us no room in the world. Of course, this causes distress. Tribulation and distress are related as cause and effect. When the enemy comes with tribulation, we become distressed.

The second pair and the third pair also belong together. Hunger and nakedness go together. Hunger and nakedness are not due to a scarcity of things, but the thought is that we can't get things because we belong to Christ. There is plenty, but we cannot get at this plenty because we belong to Christ. Peril and sword refer to the political power, which is used by the enemy. If you belong to Christ, you are subject to the sword. This is the case even today in other parts of the old world where the servants of God are persecuted by those who carry the sword, by those who are in authority.

The apostle emphasizes that these dangers are real. This is why he appeals to Scripture. He means, "Don't think that this

---

1. Hoeksema preached this series at the time of the dominance of the totalitarian, anti-Christian governments in the countries he names.

is just philosophy; don't think that I am just saying things. These things are real." He quotes Psalm 44, which belongs to the period after the captivity. It was composed, perhaps, at the time of the Maccabees when that mad beast Antiochus Epiphanes slaughtered the people of God. "For thy sake we are killed all the day." All the day they were never safe. This is always the condition of the church in this world. This will be the condition of the church when the man of sin shall come. Will we then be willing to sing, "For thy sake we are killed all the day long"?

Shall these things separate us from the love of God? This is the question. This is the only question. The question is not whether we shall eat or drink. The question is whether *anything* shall separate us from the love of God.

In Spite of What It Is Impossible

The answer of the apostle is that this is impossible. He answers with another list. No state or condition can separate us from that love of God. There is no power, rational or irrational, that can separate us. There is nothing that we can think of in space that can make separation possible. Life with all that belongs to it, and death with all that it implies, are the only states there are. But they cannot separate us from the love of God. There are no "powers" that can separate us. No devils or angels can separate us. I maintain, in spite of what others say, that the reference is to evil angels. The good angels surely do not try to separate us from the love of God. Neither is there a principality anywhere that can separate us. Nor can world powers separate us. They can kill us. But they cannot separate us from Christ's love. Is there anything in time—things present, or things to come? Is there anything in the universe—heights or depths? Is there anything in space between us, or is there anything in the depths of hell? "No, nothing," the apostle answers.

Indeed, in all these things "we are more than conquerors through him that loved us." We fight because we *have* overcome, not *to* overcome. We fight in the consciousness that we have the victory, not in doubt whether we shall have it. We are more than conquerors because even the enemies fight for us. Is there anything that can separate us from the love of God? Can death, life, angels, principalities, powers, things present, things to come, height or depth, separate us from His love? No, they only serve the church to bring about their salvation.

Still more, in all these things is the love of God. In His love He sends the devil. In His love He sends the sword. The devil and the sword only serve to purify the church. They serve to separate the good from the bad and to bring out the beauty of the people of God. And when suffering comes, the church clings closer together to Christ. Through suffering, Christ causes His church to cling closer to His love. Nothing can separate us. We are more than conquerors. It is impossible that we should be separated from the love of God.

Why It Is Impossible

"I am persuaded." The church should take this upon her lips. The church should say this. This must be her song of victory over all things. The church can say this, because it is the love of God upon which everything depends. If it depended upon you and me, together with God, whether anything should separate us from His love, it would be hopeless. If it depended upon a *mutual* bond of love between us and God, it would be hopeless. If you have a chain of strong links, but there is in that chain one link of silk, that chain is no stronger than the silk link. If the love of God depended upon our love to Him, it would not mean anything. Don't misunderstand me. I do not mean to say that you must be indifferent as to whether you love God. In fact, I am talking to people who *do* love God. But I mean this: the fact that you shall not be separated from the love of God depends only upon the love of God. All things are arranged by the love of God; therefore, they must all work for our good.

"We are more than conquerors," the text says, "through him that loved us." The apostle does not say, "Who *loves* us." He says, "Who *loved* us." There was once upon a time one who loved us. That one fought for us. He fought for us on the accursed tree. He loved us to the end. He became victorious over these powers. Therefore, He could say, "In the world ye shall have tribulation: but be of good cheer; I have overcome the world" [John 16:33]. Jesus overcame the world, and having overcome the world, He is seated at the right hand of God. He rules over all things. No one can separate us from His love, and from the love of God.

What shall we say, then, to these things? Who can be against us? We will say to them who are against us as accusers, "It is God that justifieth. Who is he that condemneth? It is Christ that died, that is raised, who sits at the right hand of God, who makes intercession for us" [vv. 33, 34].

"Who shall separate us from the love of Christ? . . . I am persuaded, that neither death, nor life, nor angels, nor principalities, nor powers, nor things present, nor things to come, Nor height, nor depth, nor any other creature, shall be able to separate us from the love of God, which is in Christ Jesus our Lord."

Chapter Fifty-six

The True Children of Abraham[1]

Romans 9:6-8
Not as though the word of God hath taken none effect. For they are not all Israel, which are of Israel:
Neither, because they are the seed of Abraham, are they all children: but, In Isaac shall thy seed be called.
That is, They which are the children of the flesh, these are not the children of God: but the children of the promise are counted for the seed.

The viewpoint in this chapter is that Israel of the old dispensation, the Jews as a nation, had apparently not received the salvation promised to them. Salvation was promised them. In the fulness of time, it was realized. Christ had come. The long expected Messiah had come. But Israel, who had been the object of the promise and who would be expected to enter into salvation, did not enter. Rather, they were rejected. This is the historic fact from which the apostle proceeds.

---

1. The sermons on Romans 9–11 in Hoeksema's series on the book of Romans were published in 1940 under the title *God's Eternal Good Pleasure*. This book was reprinted by the Reformed Free Publishing Association in 1979. The reprint added the sermon on Romans 9:17, 18, "God's Raising Up of Pharaoh," which had been omitted from the original edition of 1940. Chapters 56–80 of the present volume, therefore, are substantially the content of the 1979 edition of *God's Eternal Good Pleasure*. There are also significant differences, which are noted in the introduction to *Righteous by Faith Alone*.

This subject the apostle approaches from his own psychological point of view and therefore in great heaviness and sorrow of heart [Rom. 9:1–5]. We are to imitate the apostle in this. When we speak of election and reprobation, we must not rejoice in the damnation of the reprobate. The apostle did not. Paul assumed an attitude of great sorrow and heaviness of heart. He meant, "If I stand before the choice of being accursed from Christ and my brethren saved, or I saved and my brethren accursed, I could wish to be accursed from Christ for my brethren according to the flesh, whom I now see accursed."

The apostle assumed this attitude for two reasons. First, there was his own relation to them: "my brethren, my kinsmen according to the flesh." The second reason was that Israel was so greatly privileged: ". . . who are Israelites," the apostle says, that is, the people of God "to whom pertaineth the adoption," that is, the adoption unto children; "and the glory," represented by the cloud in the holy of holies; "and the covenants." Concerning this last, the apostle speaks in the plural because there are many different manifestations of the one covenant, such as the covenant with the house of Aaron, the covenant with the Levites, and the covenant with the house of David. The privilege of the Israelites included the giving of the law—not the law, but the *giving* of the law. The law had been entrusted to them. In addition, theirs was the service of God, the service in the temple. They also had the promises, that is, the promises of salvation in Christ. Besides, theirs were the fathers: Abraham, Isaac, and Jacob. And from them was Christ according to the flesh. This is why the apostle is so heavy.

The question is, did God's Word fail? When all these Jews are lost, did the Word of God fail?

In the text the apostle says, "No, the Word of God did not fail, for the Word of God did not pertain to all. They were not all children of the promise."

What They Are

The true children of Abraham are called by different names. One name is *Israelites*. For a true understanding of this and the following two chapters, it is of interest to us to notice the peculiar signification of the term *Israel* in the text. It has been stated by some that when the apostle in this and the following two chapters speaks of the children of Israel, the term always means the nation of Israel, the Jews. In verse 6 we already have a plain proof that this is not correct. We read, "They are not all Israel, which are of Israel." Try reading it this way: "They are not all *Jews,* which are of Israel." That would be absurd. Of course they were all Jews. Already in the text, therefore, we have the proof that the apostle is not speaking of the nation of Israel. He is speaking of the true Israel, that is, spiritual Israel, the people of God. He is speaking of the true children of God, of Israel in the true, spiritual sense of the word.

The true children of Abraham are also called the *seed.* They are called the seed of Abraham. We read that not the children of the flesh are the children of God, but the children of the promise are counted for the seed. The children of the promise are designated as the seed of Abraham. The true seed of Abraham is Christ. The true children of Abraham, therefore, are they who are in Christ.

Abraham's seed are also called *children of the promise.* The promise in Scripture is always the same. It takes on different forms, but the promise, as to its content, is always the messianic salvation. As to the form of the promise, it is the Word of God, who cannot lie and who is faithful, true, and powerful to realize the promise. God will surely realize His promise. Nothing can resist His will. When God promises something, He does what He promises, for He is faithful, true, and mighty.

When we read *children of the promise* [in v. 8], we must not understand "children to whom the promise was made." Nor does the expression mean "the promised children." The phrase *children of the promise* must be interpreted the same way as the phrase *children of the flesh*. Children of the flesh are children that are born of the flesh, that are born through the instrumentality of the flesh. Likewise, children of the promise are children that are born through the power of the promise. They are children in whom God works with almighty power so that they are, as it were, brought forth by the promise. God brings them forth through the power of the promise by realizing His Word of promise in them. The promise is their mother. They are the children of the promise. That was Isaac, and Isaac was a type of all children of the promise.

Therefore, the true children of Abraham are also called *the children of God*. Children of God are children to whom God gives the right to be His children through the adoption. They are children, too, in the sense that they are born of God. They have received of Him His own divine life. They are the true children of Abraham.

In the old dispensation all the children of God were for a time Israelites. Don't turn this around. Not all Israelites were children of God, but all the children of God were for a time Israelites. All horses are animals, but all animals are not horses. All the children of God were for a time Israelites because they came in the line of the generations of Israel. This is the one truth. The other truth is that Abraham could not bring forth children of the promise; he could not bring forth children of God.

The same is true today. All the children of God are the seed of believers. I do not say that other believers cannot come in, but the children of God come in the line of the generations of believers. The Word of God to Abraham, "I will be thy God, and the God of thy seed," is true today. This is why we have our Baptism Form. This is why we are proud of our seed. This is why we have as many children as possible. This is why we have nothing to do with the damnable practice of birth control.

But we cannot bring forth children of God. Abraham could not. Abraham could bring forth only children of Abraham.

And Abraham was a child of Adam. Abraham could bring forth only children of damnation. He could not bring forth children of God any more than he could bring forth Isaac. Abraham could only bring forth Ishmael. But the almighty promise of God works in the line of the generations of His people, and they bring forth children of God.

Who They Are

The question is, does God do this in every one of Abraham's natural children? Is every one born of Abraham adopted by God? Is every one of Abraham's natural children also made a child of God? Or, if we apply it to the new dispensation, can we bring every baby to baptism and say, "There is a child of God"? Does the promise of God concern every child of Abraham? And does the promise of God concern every child of believers?

Some say that it does. Even among Reformed people we find this notion. We read and hear this view of the covenant often. It is said that the promise concerns every one in the church. And it would seem so. God said to Abraham, "I will be thy God, and the God of thy seed," seemingly without distinction. So also was it said to Noah. At the very dawn of the new dispensation, the apostle Peter says, "The promise is unto you, and to your children" [Acts 2:39]. It would seem that the promise of God concerns all the children of believers. Accordingly, some people say that as far as God is concerned, the promise concerns all the children of believers. Parents, then, are instructed to plead on this. They are told that they must say to God, "You promised to save my children; now you must do it; I plead upon your promise." Or they say, "We must presuppose that all our children belong to the children of the promise until they come to years of discretion and of their own free will reject the promise."

But there is one thing that they cannot avoid in Scripture, and in this text, that utterly refutes their view. It is this: the apostle, seeing his brethren according to the flesh perish in unbelief, says that the Word of God has not failed. Though thousands upon thousands of Jews are not saved, the Word of God has not failed. This can mean but one thing. If you say that all the children of believers are also children of the promise, and if later some of these children perish, it can mean only one thing, and that is that the Word of God has failed in them. You say that they rejected the promise? That makes no difference. The Word of God failed in them. If God does not work the promise in them to make them children of the promise, then the Word of God failed. If you say that man did not want the promise, then you make man stronger than God. The apostle says that the Word of God has not failed. It is effective in all who are covered by the promise.

But the apostle says, "They are not all Israel, which are of Israel." That is, not all those who are born of Jacob, or Israel, are true children of Israel. The children of the flesh, namely, of Abraham, are not the true seed of Abraham, but the children of the promise are counted for the seed. "In Isaac shall thy seed be called." Abraham had many children. Not in Ishmael, but in Isaac shall thy seed be called.

What Their Connection with Abraham's Carnal Children Is

So it is today. This is a very practical message, also for our day. Let us look at the old dispensation. There were children of the promise, and there were children of the flesh. They formed one nation, one people. All received the same treatment. All were led out of Egypt, all were witnesses of God's terrible wonders, all passed through the sea, all were baptized into Moses, all ate of the spiritual bread, all drank out of the spiritual rock that followed them, and they were led into Canaan. They were all called by the same name. Yet from that one people always arose a carnal seed.

So it is today. Again, there is always one church, one congregation. They are all called the church of Christ. As such they are known. All have the same treatment from their infancy. There is a difference of degree, but there is no essential difference. All receive the same instruction. And yet there arises out of this church a carnal seed. And you and I bring them forth.

What does this mean? What does it mean practically? In the first place it means a great heaviness and sorrow of heart. No, I do not want to compare myself to the apostle Paul. God forbid. But we can understand the apostle a little. There is in the church a great sorrow and heaviness of heart for the minister when he sees the children of the church go the way of destruction. This is especially the case if he is in a congregation a long time. These children grow up with him, and he learns to know them. What would he like to do? I would like to take them all along to heaven. So would you. I instruct them. I preach to them. I admonish them. And what do they do? They trample it underfoot. The result is great sorrow and heaviness of heart for the minister, but he cannot change it.

Is there anything more grievous than to see your own children walk in the way of destruction? You pray for them. You instruct them. You plead with them. But if God does not work in their heart by the power of the promise, they trample it underfoot.

That carnal seed is also the cause of contention and trouble in the church. So it was in Israel. At the very time when the covenant was given to them, they danced around the golden calf. And they carried that golden calf with them all the way. They persecuted the true seed, killed the prophets, and finally killed Christ. The trouble with Israel was that they were one nation and could not separate themselves. Otherwise, there would have been a new denomination every twenty or twenty-five years.

So it is in the new dispensation. The carnal seed is the cause of much trouble. This is why it is necessary every now and then to separate and form little churches. Finally, this carnal seed forms the false church. It is these carnal children that cause the false church to come into existence. And it is the false church that finally gives birth to the Antichrist.

But God realizes His promise in the children of the promise. At the end of time we will say that the Word of God has not fallen out.

Chapter Fifty-seven

Jacob's Election

Romans 9:10-13
And not only this; but when Rebecca also had conceived by one, even by our father Isaac;
(For the children being not yet born, neither having done any good or evil, that the purpose of God according to election might stand, not of works, but of him that calleth;)
It was said unto her, The elder shall serve the younger.
As it is written, Jacob have I loved, but Esau have I hated.

We must remember the question and the answer that the apostle treats according to the context. The question is whether the Word of God has become of none effect, or, as we read literally, whether the Word of God has "fallen out" [v. 6]. This question the apostle faced with reference to a definite historic fact. The historic fact is the rejection of Israel as a nation and the evident rejection of thousands of Israelites with respect to the kingdom of heaven. It had become evident that thousands of the people to whom the promise had come did not receive the promise, the salvation, but were lost.

Over against this fact, the apostle assumed a very humble attitude. This attitude must also be ours. We may not assume a haughty attitude toward those who are lost as if we were better than they. Instead, we must assume the humble attitude that the apostle expressed when he said, "I have great heaviness and continual sorrow in my heart. For I could wish that myself were accursed from Christ for my brethren, my kinsmen according to the flesh" [vv. 2, 3].

In this attitude the apostle faced the question of whether the Word of God has fallen out.

To this question, the apostle answered, "No, the Word of God has not fallen out." But the Word of God, the Word of promise—"I will establish my covenant between me and thee and thy seed after thee in their generations for an everlasting covenant, to be a God unto thee, and thy seed after thee"—did not pertain to all the children of Abraham according to the flesh. It referred only to the children of the promise. Not all the natural children of Abraham were also children of the promise, and therefore not all are Israel, which are of Israel.

The apostle demonstrated that the promise did not pertain to all the natural children of Abraham. Quoting from an example in the Old Testament, he said, "In Isaac shall thy seed be called." Abraham had other children; not in Ishmael, but "in Isaac shall thy seed be called." That is, the promise is not to run in the line of Ishmael and his generations, but in the line of Isaac and his generations.

Now the apostle points to another example in the Old Testament. He points to another illustration to corroborate the fact that not all the children of Abraham are also children of the promise; or, to apply it to the new dispensation, not all the children of believers in the New Testament are also children of the promise. There is a twofold seed. And as this already became evident at the time of Isaac, it becomes evident more clearly, more forcefully, in Esau and Jacob. This second illustration, as dealt with in the text, points to the reason or the ground for the distinction that God makes in the seed of Abraham. That ground is the purpose of God according to election.

A Personal Election

This second illustration, which the apostle quotes from the Old Testament to prove that the Word of God has not fallen out when all the children of Israel are not saved, is stronger, is more forceful, than the first illustration. Esau and Jacob were both of the same parents. With regard to the first illustration, the objection might be made that Ishmael could hardly be called the seed of Abraham, because he was not of Sarah, the mother of the promise. But that cannot be said of the second illustration. Esau and Jacob were both of the same parents, and both parents were parents of the promise.

The second illustration is also more forceful because Esau and Jacob were twins. They were intimately related. They were born under the same conditions. Both received the same care and training. Both had the same covenant privileges. There was no difference between them from a natural point of view.

More powerful is the second illustration, too, because strictly speaking, Esau should have had the preference over Jacob, since Esau was the firstborn.

Finally, this second illustration is an advance over the preceding because the apostle refers to the sovereign purpose of God in distinguishing between Esau and Jacob: "(The children being not yet born, neither having done any good or evil, that the purpose of God according to election might stand, not of works, but of him that calleth); It was said unto her, The elder shall serve the younger." Rebekah was told that the older would serve the younger. Rebekah was a beautiful example of a covenant mother. When she found herself in a peculiar condition, she went to the Lord. She asked the Lord, "If it be so, why am I thus?" The answer that she received from the Lord was, "Two nations are in thy womb, and two manner of people shall be separated from thy bowels; and the one people shall be stronger than the other people; and the elder shall serve the younger" [Gen. 25:22, 23]. The apostle quotes only the last part, that the elder shall serve the younger. This cannot possibly mean that the elder *nation* shall serve the younger *nation*. It can only mean that the elder *child* shall serve the younger *child*. To the one who had the firstborn's right, the right was not granted. God would establish His covenant, not with the elder but with the younger. It belonged to the birthright that he who was the firstborn might rule over the younger brothers. Therefore, when God said to Rebekah, "The elder shall serve the younger," He meant that the elder would take the place of the younger, that the younger would take the place of the elder, and that God would grant His promise to the younger.

This was said to Rebekah, the apostle explains, in order that the purpose of God according to election might stand. The purpose of God is that which He has had in mind forever. And His mind never changes. It is what God has in mind with the purpose of realizing it. That which God has in mind in this case is the promise. That promise God purposed to realize not in Esau, but in Jacob. When, therefore, the apostle says that the elder shall serve the younger in order that the purpose of God according to election might stand, the meaning is that God had in mind to realize this promise according to the rule of election. When it is said to Rebekah, "The elder shall serve the younger," the meaning is that the promise is to be realized in Jacob because this is God's purpose.

This is strengthened by the quotation from Malachi [1:2, 3]: "Jacob have I loved, but Esau have I hated." It is often said that this love and hatred with regard to Jacob and Esau do not refer to the sovereign love and hatred of God, but the meaning is evident. When God told Rebekah that the elder would serve the younger, He revealed His purpose to her. Again, this purpose is in harmony with the fact that God loved Jacob and hated Esau. Commentators have tried to weaken this Word of God. One commentator made it mean, "Jacob have I loved, and Esau have I loved also, only in a different way and in a smaller measure." Such an interpretation is not worthy of refutation.

The popular interpretation is this: "Jacob have I loved, and Esau have I loved a little less." These interpreters appeal to Scripture. They say that the word *hatred* occurs with this meaning in Scripture. They argue that when Christ says, "If you do not hate father, or mother, or brother for my sake, you cannot be my disciple" [Luke 14:26], the meaning is, "If you do not love them less than me."

But this understanding of Christ's teaching is mistaken. The Lord plainly taught that if one cannot *hate* father, mother, or brother for His sake, he cannot be His disciple. The situation may well arise that one will be rejected by father, mother, and brother, and will be delivered up by them. If then he tries to keep their love, if then he cannot hate them, he cannot be Jesus' disciple. There is no relation a professing Christian may keep that is in conflict with his relation to Jesus Christ. "Hate" does not mean "love less," but "hate."

This is the meaning of *hate* in Romans 9:13. The meaning is, "Jacob have I loved with a love that causes me to accept him. And Esau have I hated with a hatred that causes me to reject him." I emphasize this because these truths are the heart of the church.

This election is a *personal* election of Jacob and a *personal* rejection of Esau. Many who like to evade the doctrine of election and reprobation contend that the love of Jacob and the hatred of Esau is not an election and rejection of *persons,* but of *nations.* God chose the nation of Israel and rejected Edom. It would make no difference if this were the correct interpretation. Suppose that the text did teach that God accepted the nation of Jacob and rejected the nation of Edom. What difference would it make? Edom is all the citizens of Edom, and all are outside God's salvation. It is plain that this interpretation does not exclude the persons, for verse 11 states that God spoke His Word of love and hatred before the *persons* were born.

The interpretation that by Jacob and Esau are meant *nations* does not hold. The apostle is not dealing with nations. He is dealing with individuals. He is asking the question, "Why is it that thousands of Israelites do not receive God's salvation? Has the Word of God fallen out?" The answer is not that God made distinction between nation and nation, but that God gave preference between persons and persons in the seed of Israel. It is a *personal* election.

This does not imply that God chose an arbitrary number and rejected an arbitrary number. Rather, God had before His mind a church, the body of Christ. He had before His mind a body in which Christ should become manifest. As God ordained the body, so He ordained how many members should be in this body. Every member of this body has been determined. Just as I do not determine how many members my body shall have, so man does not determine how many members shall be in the body of Christ.

But this is not all there is to the election of the church. God not only determined the number, but He also determined the position of every member in the body. Every Christian does not have the same position.

Still more, God not only determined the number and the position of the members, but He also ordained who among the children of men should enter into that body, and who should not. It has been God's eternal purpose that not everyone should be a member of the body of Christ.

All of this is the meaning of "Jacob have I loved, but Esau have I hated." To Jacob, God will realize His promise according to His purpose, and to Esau He will not.

An Election unto Salvation

Others object that the election of Romans 9 is not an election to salvation. You must remember that to man, to the sinful flesh, this is a hard doctrine. The reason is that we always think wrongly of God. That is no wonder, is it? Remember, man always lies about God. Whenever a man begins to talk about God, he begins to lie about Him. When we do not let God say what He is and who He is, we lie about Him, because man is a sinner and does not want God. This is why he objects to the doctrine of election and reprobation. There is no doctrine in which it becomes more manifest that God is God.

Accordingly, some say that the apostle is speaking not of an election unto salvation, but of an election with respect to certain temporal privileges. They will not accept the doctrine of election and reprobation with respect to salvation.

Suppose that this interpretation were correct. Would it make any difference? Would it make any difference that God according to His sovereign purpose determined to give to one, and not to another, all the theocratic privileges? This would mean that God would establish His covenant with, that He would give His Word to, and that He would bestow all the covenant blessings upon Jacob, not Esau. Or, if you wish, it would mean that God would establish His church with Jacob, not Esau. It would mean that God determined Esau to live and die without the Word of God. If Esau is excluded from the theocratic privileges, he is excluded from salvation.

But the apostle is not speaking of theocratic privileges. He is not sorry that so many did not receive the theocratic privileges. Rather, he is filled with sorrow because so many are lost. He is dealing with the fact that so many are accursed from Christ.

How must this be explained?

Has the Word of God fallen out?

No. This is the explanation: "Jacob have I loved, but Esau have I hated." And if we turn to Malachi [1:4], we find that God's hatred of Esau means that the Edomites are the people against whom the Lord has indignation forever. God determines His own people.

A Sovereign Election

God does this sovereignly. Also against this, objections have been raised. It is difficult to eliminate the doctrine of election and reprobation from Scripture. Therefore, they say that God chose some and rejected others because He foresaw who would, and who would not, love Him. This is the doctrine of the adherents of free-will.

Once again, what difference would it make if this were so? Suppose that I would preach that Esau was known by God from eternity as a fornicator, and Jacob as one who would love Him? What difference would it make? If God saw Esau eternally as a wicked person, did He then not eternally see him in hell? And if God eternally saw Esau as a wicked person, and therefore as lost, did God then intend the promise for him? Did God then intend Christ to die for those whom He knew would be lost?

The free-will doctrine is false, however. With this view you do not save Esau, but you do lose your God. Listen to Scripture: "Before the children were born, and before they had done either good or evil, it was said of them, The elder shall serve the younger. As it is written, Jacob have I loved, but Esau have I hated." The apostle adds, "not of works, but of him that calleth" [9:11–13].

Sovereignly, with a reason that is only in God, without respect to works, without respect to the question who they are, God places all men before Himself, some as vessels fitted unto destruction and others as vessels fitted unto salvation. Then He conceives of all the means to realize this purpose.

As far as the practical aspect is concerned, some charge that if God determined who should be saved and who should not, we have nothing for the ungodly. My response is, Has *anyone* anything for the ungodly? They say, "Yes, if he repents." I say, "If he repents, I have much more for him. If he repents, he has been elected, and then he shall surely be saved. But if he does not repent, who has anything for the ungodly?"

Practically, this doctrine teaches us to humble ourselves. "It is not of him that willeth, nor of him that runneth, but of God that sheweth mercy [Rom. 9:16]. The conclusion is this: "Let him who glories, glory in the Lord" [I Cor. 1:31].

Chapter Fifty-eight

The Righteousness of God's Sovereign Mercy

Romans 9:14-16
What shall we say then? Is there unrighteousness with God? God forbid.
For he saith to Moses, I will have mercy on whom I will have mercy, and I will have compassion on whom I will have compassion.
So then it is not of him that willeth, nor of him that runneth, but of God that sheweth mercy.

The particular subject of Romans 9 is occasioned not only by the fact that the nation of Israel was rejected, but also by the fact that so many of the children of Israel did not receive the promise. The promise has been fulfilled in Jesus Christ, but thousands upon thousands of Jews rejected the gospel and did not enter into the kingdom of heaven. This gives rise to the implied question: "Has the Word of God taken none effect?" [v. 6]. Should not that Israel, to whom the promise had come, enter into the kingdom of God? The promise has been fulfilled, but it is evident that many of the people of Israel were not partakers of the promise.

The apostle answers this question by saying that the promise did not pertain to all the natural seed of Abraham. All are not Israel, which are of Israel. All are not children of the promise who are the natural children of Abraham. Still more, the apostle plainly teaches that the ultimate cause of this distinction between the children of the promise and those who were not children of the promise was the sovereign good pleasure of

God. God's determination, and God's determination alone, made that separation between the children of the promise and those who were not.

In proof, the apostle gave two illustrations from the Old Testament. First, he pointed to the fact that Isaac was the child of the promise, although there were more children of Abraham. Second, he pointed to the history of Jacob and Esau. That history proved that the determination separating between the children was due to the purpose of God according to election. Before the children were born and before they had done either good or evil, God told Rebekah, "The elder shall serve the younger." Here is the deepest source of the distinction between the children of the promise and those who are not.

The text is really a third illustration from the Old Testament. It answers a question that might arise: "Is there unrighteousness with God?" For the answer to this question, the apostle appeals to what God had told Moses: "I will have mercy on whom I will have mercy, and I will have compassion on whom I will have compassion" [Exod. 33:19].

Then the apostle draws the conclusion of this entire section: "So then it is not of him that willeth, nor of him that runneth, but of God that sheweth mercy." The main thought, therefore, is the righteousness of God's sovereign mercy.

How This Sovereign Mercy Is Asserted

The important question is, *what* is not of him that willeth, nor of him that runneth? In answering this question, many twist the Word of God and corrupt it. They contend that mercy in the text is not the mercy that is unto salvation. It is rather a mercy that refers to national privileges and temporal prerogatives.

How foolish this interpretation really is! It is impossible to maintain it. In the context Paul is not speaking of temporal blessings. He is speaking of the promise. He is speaking of the fact that so many are excluded from the kingdom of God. This holds with double force in verses 14–16. Why else should the apostle ask [in v. 14], "Is there unrighteousness with God?" In the text there is a quotation from Exodus 33:[19]. Certainly Moses was not speaking there of temporal privileges. Moses had before him the entire nation of Israel. All had the same temporal privileges. This was not the question. The question was, who shall be blotted out of the book of life? This is why Moses said, "If thou canst forgive the sin of this people, blot me out of thy book" [Exod. 32:32]. This question is answered in the statement in Exodus to Moses: "I will be gracious to whom I will be gracious, and will shew mercy on whom I will shew mercy." The question is one of salvation. The mercy of which the apostle speaks in verse 16, therefore, is the mercy according to which God saves sinners. The plain meaning is this: salvation is not of him that willeth, nor of him that runneth, but of God that sheweth mercy.

He that willeth is one who wills salvation. He wants it. He desires it. He seeks it. And *he that runneth* is he who is already on the way. It is the one who runs after it, who strives after it. The figure is that of a race in which the runner strives to obtain the prize. The text teaches that salvation is not of him who wills salvation, nor of him who runs after it, who strives after it.

Does this mean, then, that salvation is not for him who wills, so that the one who wills salvation shall not be saved? Will not the one who strives after salvation be saved? Certainly, he who so wills shall be saved. "Whosoever will" may come. It is impossible that anyone should stand in the judgment and say, "I willed; I strove after salvation; and I still find that I am lost." He who wills is saved already. This is exactly what we teach in distinction from those who teach the free-will doctrine. They cannot say this. They must say that a man may will to be saved today, but be lost tomorrow. They cannot say, "He who wills shall be saved." We do say this: he who wills shall be saved. In fact, he is saved already. On the other hand, he who is lost never willed to be saved.

Nor is it the intention of the apostle to teach that we do not have to will and strive, as though our attitude may be a passive one. No one is saved who takes this attitude. One who is saved does not talk this way. God does not let him talk this way.

Rather, the apostle is declaring that the cause, the fount, the deepest reason, why the distinction exists between people who will and who do not will, between people who run and who do not run in the same nation, in the same church, from the same family, with the same surroundings and the same training, is not that one wills whereas the other does not, or that one runs whereas the other does not. But the reason is in God who shows mercy. When you see two people from the same family, receiving the same training, living under the same conditions, and the one wills salvation whereas the other does not, and the one runs and endeavors to obtain salvation whereas the other does not, you must not say that the reason for this distinction lies in the fact that the one man willed and ran, whereas the other did not. But you must say that the cause of this distinction is that God shows mercy to the one, but does not show mercy to the other. A man wills because God shows him mercy. God does not show mercy *because* a man wills. But when God shows mercy to a man, the result is that he wills, he runs. His willing is not the cause, but the effect. God's mercy is first. And although it is true that one cannot enter into the kingdom of God unless he wills, the cause of this willing is not in man, but in God. God's mercy is sovereign.

Compare this plain teaching of Paul with the teaching of the free-will preacher. Ask whether the free-will preacher stands foursquare upon the truth, or whether he corrupts the truth.

How It Is Proved from Scripture

Yet another Old Testament passage is quoted to support and illustrate the doctrine that God's mercy is sovereign [Exod. 32–34]. God had led His people to Sinai. There He had given them His law. They had received the covenant, as a nation. At the same moment they received the covenant, they revolted against the Lord and danced around the golden calf. And I am convinced that the sin of Sinai followed them throughout their entire history. Sinai was the beginning of the rejection of Israel. However this may be, Moses came down from the mount and was indignant. When the sons of Levi responded to the call of Moses, three thousand of the people were slain. Moses then told the people that he would intercede for them. He went to the mountain and asked, "If thou wilt, forgive the sin of thy people; but if thou canst not forgive, blot me out of thy book." But God answered Moses, "I will not blot thee out of my book. But him that sinneth will I blot out of my book" [Exod. 32:32, 33]. The Lord told Moses to go up and carry the people to the land that God had promised them. And the Lord told him, "I will not go with thee, because if I did, I might consume the people" [Exod. 33:3]. The Lord had also said, "I will certainly visit their sin upon them" [Exod. 32:34].

Moses did not understand, because to him that people *were* God's people. They were the people whom God had led out of Egypt. They were the people of the promise. Moses could not understand how these people could perish in the desert. So he went to the Lord again. He said, "If thy presence go not with us, I cannot carry this people up" [Exod. 33:15]. He pleaded with the Lord until the Lord promised to go with him: "My presence, which is the same as my face, shall go with thee" [v. 14]. But Moses did not feel safe even then. He remembered that God had said, "If I go up with this people, I may consume them." So Moses said, "Show me thy glory. Show me thy goodness. Show me thy face, that I may see thy goodness and mercy." That is what Moses wanted to see. He wanted to see God's face. In that face he wanted to see God's goodness and mercy.

God answered Moses, "I will grant you this request. But remember, when I show you my goodness and mercy, even then I will have mercy on whom I will have mercy."

Similarly, when we pray for our children, as we do, the answer to us is, "Certainly I will let all my goodness come upon you. Yet remember, I will have mercy on whom I will have mercy." And if one of your children who has the same upbringing as your other children, who receives the same instruction, goes astray so that you can see that he is going astray, you must not say that the reason is that your other children willed, whereas this one did not. Nor may you say, "It was because I gave my other children a better education." That has nothing to do with this matter. If this happens, you must rather say, "It is of God that showeth mercy."

Oh, I know that God can bring back a straying child, but this is not God's usual way. It is not God's usual way to let His covenant children walk in sin for a while. These are exceptions when God brings them back. Usually, when they start on the way of sin, they gradually fall away until they are completely lost.

On the basis of the Old Testament, then, the apostle teaches that God alone determines who shall be saved and who shall not be saved.

How Its Righteousness Is Maintained

"What shall we say then?" the apostle asks in the text. Implied by this question is the fact that when one has met the opponent of the doctrine taught here and has led him through these verses, so that it is impossible for him to deny the truth that they teach, the opponent then comes with other arguments. He comes with arguments of his own. Man does not want the doctrine of God's sovereign mercy. There has never been a preacher who cut the Word of God straight on this point who has not been attacked. Some argue this way: "If this is so, God is a cruel God," or they say, "Your God is a tyrant," or, "Man is not responsible," or, "Then there is unrighteousness with God."

This was the case already at the time of the apostle Paul. When the apostle asks, "Is there unrighteousness with God?" he does not ask in the abstract. He knows that there are people who will come with this question. And the question is, "What shall we say then?"

This question comes to *us*. We must say something. What shall we say then? Shall we say, "Is there unrighteousness with God?" One point about this question that must be noted is this: when the question "Is there unrighteousness with God?" is asked, who will answer the question? Will we? Will you and I? Will man? Shall we summon God before the bar of judgment and ask Him whether there is unrighteousness with Him? This is the question that must be answered.

There are people who have tried to answer this question. Their answer is this: God might righteously have condemned all, because all have sinned and forfeited all right to salvation; therefore, God is not unrighteous when He does not save all. This is a well-meaning answer, but it fails. From the one question others arise: "Why did not God prevent the fall? And if He did not want to prevent the fall, why does He not save all?"

But we must not answer at all the question whether God is unrighteous. This is the point of the text. You might just as well ask whether a plumb line is perpendicular as to ask whether there is unrighteousness with God. God is God. To put it very paradoxically, if there is unrighteousness with God, this same unrighteousness is righteousness. Man cannot ask that question, because God is the highest standard of measurement. Shall we call God before the bar of judgment? Where is our standard of measurement? Besides, what we say about God is always corrupt. We cannot answer the question.

God must answer it, and He does. This is what Paul does. He allows God to answer the question. Notice: "What shall we say then? Is there unrighteousness with God? God forbid. Is this because I, Paul, say it? No, but *God* says to Moses, "I will have mercy on whom I will have mercy, and I will have compassion on whom I will have compassion." God says that He has the sovereign prerogative to decide who shall be saved and who shall not. The implication is that we must get the answer to the question from Scripture.

When the day of judgment comes, God will justify Himself. He will justify Himself not according to the doctrine of free-will. But by His Word and Spirit, He will justify Himself in the consciousness of them who are lost and in the consciousness of them who are saved.

They who are lost will not say in hell, "We are here because we did not want to go to heaven," but they will say, "God brought us here." And they will forever confess that there is no unrighteousness with God in bringing them there.

And the righteous in heaven will say, "It is not because of us that we are here, but it is because of God who showed us His mercy."

Chapter Fifty-nine

God's Raising Up of Pharaoh

Romans 9:17, 18
For the scripture saith unto Pharaoh, Even for this same purpose have I raised thee up, that I might shew my power in thee, and that my name might be declared throughout all the earth.

Therefore hath he mercy on whom he will have mercy, and whom he will he hardeneth.

This passage is the second part of the answer to the question [in v. 14]: "What shall we say then? Is there unrighteousness with God?" If the matter stands as the apostle has written in the preceding context—so that salvation is not of him that willeth, nor of him that runneth, but of God that sheweth mercy; and so that God loves one and hates another—shall we say, then, that there is unrighteousness with God?

To this question the apostle has answered, "God forbid." By implication, the answer is that we will say nothing. We will certainly not call God before the bar of our judgment to determine whether there is unrighteousness with Him. Instead, we will turn with the question to God Himself; that is, we will turn to Scripture and let God say whether He has the sovereign right to have mercy on whom He will. Thus, the apostle turns to Exodus 33:19, where God Himself declares that He has the sovereign right to have mercy on whom He will. God said to Moses, "I will shew mercy on whom I will shew mercy, and I will have compassion on whom I will have compassion."

But this is only one-half of the question, the part concerning God's love and salvation of elect men and women. Now the other half of the same question comes to the foreground. Is there unrighteousness with God when He *hates* some and when He does *not* save some? Is there unrighteousness with God when He prepares some as vessels of wrath fitted to destruction? To this second half of the question, we have the answer in the text. Again the apostle turns to Scripture where God said to Pharaoh, "Even for this same purpose have I raised thee up, that I might shew my power in thee, and that my name might be declared throughout all the earth" [Exod. 9:16]. In the text the apostle identifies Scripture with the Word of God itself: Scripture said to Pharaoh, that is, God said to Pharaoh, "for this same purpose have I raised thee up." Then the apostle draws the conclusion that applies to both sides of the question, the question about God's love and the question about God's hatred: "Therefore hath he mercy on whom he will have mercy, and whom he will he hardeneth."

It is hard for some people to believe especially this last half of the question, for sinful man is always inclined to say the wrong thing about God. If it is hard for him to believe the doctrine of sovereign election, it is far harder for him to believe the doctrine of sovereign reprobation. Therefore, it behooves us to humble ourselves; otherwise we will not receive this Word of God.

The Meaning

Unto what did God raise Pharaoh up? And how far does this raising up apply to Pharaoh? Did God raise up Pharaoh only from a natural point of view? Is the meaning only that God raised him up as a man, so that God gave him his power, his talents, his position, and his honor; and that God raised him up as king, so that He gave him his throne, his kingdom, his dominion? Or does God also mean that He raised up Pharaoh in his wickedness?

Usually the answer given to this question is that only the former is meant. The phrase *for this purpose have I raised thee up* is interpreted as meaning that God gave to Pharaoh only his position, his honor, his greatness, his power, his talents, and his kingdom. But surely, these interpreters say, it does not mean that God raised him up in his wickedness, so that Pharaoh in his wickedness, in his rebellion against God, was put there by God.

Yet there can be no question that all these things are included. This is true not only with regard to Pharaoh, but also with regard to all the wicked. Pharaoh is mentioned as a type of all the wicked. From a natural point of view, God gives to every wicked person his position, talents, place, and power. But this is not all of the truth. Certainly this is not the meaning in the text. In the first place, the context makes this plain. What is the apostle speaking about in Romans 9? He is speaking about sovereign election and reprobation. The apostle quotes the Word from Exodus 9:[16] in Romans 9:17 and in connection with the explanation that he gives in verse 18: "Therefore hath he mercy on whom he will, and whom he will he hardeneth." This is a double conclusion from a double example. The meaning necessarily is that Pharaoh was hardened for this purpose.

In the second place, this is also the meaning of the Word in Exodus. Repeatedly we read that God hardened Pharaoh's heart. I know that this is usually interpreted as meaning that God hardened Pharaoh's heart after Pharaoh had rebelled and had refused to obey the Word of the Lord. But this is a bold interpretation, because already at Mount Horeb, long before Moses came to Pharaoh, God had said to him, "I will harden his [Pharaoh's] heart [Exod. 4:21]. Also in Exodus 9, this hardening of Pharaoh's heart is attributed to God.

God hardens the heart of all the wicked. We must know this. The wicked must know this, too. If we walk in ways of wickedness, we must not imagine that we do as we please. It is not salutary to tell the wicked man that he can do as he pleases. Then he will not tremble before God. The sinner will not tremble before a God with whom he can do as he pleases. But he will tremble before a God who has him in His power and who predestinated him to do the very things that he does.

Besides, the text says that this was God's purpose: "For this same purpose have I raised thee up." The text does not say that God raised up Pharaoh from a natural point of view, so that He gave him position, honor, and greatness. No, the text says in the original Greek, "for this very thing I have raised thee up." This very thing was that Pharaoh should rebel against God. This is the purpose. God says to Pharaoh, "You must not imagine, when you rebel against Me, that you do anything contrary to My counsel. For this purpose have I raised thee up."

Therefore, the text does not merely mean that God raised up Pharaoh from a natural point of view. But it means, first, that God predestinated Pharaoh in His counsel to do the very thing that he does. Second, it means that God says to Pharaoh, "The fact that you stand there, Pharaoh, in your wicked rebellion against Me is not apart from My work, but is because I give you the power to stand there. You stand there only by My strength." If this is not the meaning, the context has no significance. Therefore, the meaning is that God predestinated Pharaoh to do the very things that he did and that He put Pharaoh there in his wicked rebellion.

It is especially here that the doctrine of predestination has been designated as a hard doctrine. As long as you speak of God's sovereign election, the opposition is not so strong. But when you also maintain the doctrine of sovereign reprobation and say that God also sovereignly determined the works of the wicked, people say that predestination is a hard doctrine. We must understand this because we must have something to answer. The question is not whether we will defend God. The question is not whether we will judge that there is unrighteousness with God when He determines the wicked in his wickedness. Instead, the question is whether God says that He has this right. Then all the context teaches that God predestinated Pharaoh as a vessel of wrath fitted unto destruction and that as such, Pharaoh must do His work.

Do not say that this is a hard doctrine. If God says that this doctrine is truth, we must be humble and believe it.

Let us see whether this is a hard doctrine, or whether the alternative is a hard doctrine. We must choose between the two: either the wicked do their wickedness by their own power and in their own strength, or God put them there. Remember, Pharaoh oppressed the people of God. He sought to destroy the church. We can look upon the reprobate merely as men, and then our attitude should be one of humble pity. But they do not appear merely as men, but as wicked. And then the question is, do they stand there in their own power, or does God put them there? When Israel had passed through the Red Sea, they sang a song. Why? Because God had destroyed their enemies. Is it a hard doctrine to say that all our enemies are in the hand of God? Or is it a hard doctrine to say that these enemies stand there in their own power? I say, let us put them where God puts them: in the hand of God.

The Realization

God executes His counsel of reprobation as well as His counsel of election. When God executes His counsel of election, he says, "I will have mercy on whom I will have mercy." In other words, He says that He will make whomever He pleases the object of His mercy. And when God makes anyone the object of His mercy, He causes His grace to enter into his heart. He humbles and breaks that heart and causes that heart to turn to Christ.

But does Scripture merely teach that the elect go to heaven because God showed them mercy and that the reprobate do not go to heaven because God does not show them mercy? Is this the teaching of Scripture? Or does Scripture go a step further and teach that there is always an operation of God upon His creatures, in this case His moral creatures?

We must understand the question. People say that the elect go to heaven because God shows them mercy and that the reprobate do not go to heaven because God does not show them mercy. In other words, the reprobate go to destruction by themselves. Some even say that in time God shows grace to the reprobate. This is the theory of common grace. God shows grace to the reprobate, and they go to destruction by themselves.

Is it true that there is a gracious operation of God upon the elect, and that there is no operation of God upon the reprobate? The text says, "Therefore hath He mercy on whom He will have mercy, *and whom He will He hardeneth.*"

There is a twofold working and influence of God upon men. There is a saving influence of God upon men by the preaching of the gospel, an influence upon their mind and will, but there is also another influence: that expressed in the words *whom He will He hardeneth.*

What is this work of God whereby He hardens the heart of the wicked? We must notice, first, that God brought His Word to Pharaoh. The Word of God to Pharaoh was that he should let God's people go. Pharaoh understood that Word of God. Likewise, the Word of God comes today, not only to the elect but also to the reprobate. This Word simply means, "Repent!" The Word of God to Pharaoh was, "Repent!"

Second, God gave Pharaoh the strength to stand there. That was good strength that God gave to Pharaoh. He gave him strength of will. God strengthened Pharaoh by His good strength. Otherwise, Pharaoh might have become afraid. Becoming afraid, he might have said, without coming to repentance, "I will let the people go." Since that was not God's purpose, God strengthened Pharaoh. You may be driving your car toward a precipice. You can do two things. You can give your car more gas (and it is good gas), so that you hasten to destruction, or you can apply the brakes and bring the car to a stop. If you give a locomotive that is running toward a broken rail more good steam, it will hasten to destruction. God gave Pharaoh more steam. He gave him more will power. In that good power, Pharaoh said, "No!"

This is what God does to all the wicked. In other words, God realizes His sovereign reprobation in harmony with man's responsibility. Therefore, the conclusion of the apostle stands: He has mercy on whom He will have mercy, and whom He will He hardens.

The Purpose

Why? What is the purpose? Verse 17 says, "that I might shew my power in thee." God wanted to show His power in Pharaoh; that is, Pharaoh must serve God's purpose in order that God's power might become manifest.

What is this power? What does God mean when He tells Pharaoh, "that I may show my power in you"? Does God merely mean, "that I may show that I am stronger than you are?" This does not show God's power. God over against little Pharaoh? This does not reveal divine power. Divine power is not a stronger power. God does not show that He is stronger. God does not have to fight. A god that has to fight is no god. If this is our conception, we have a little and a wrong conception of God. God does not want to show that He is stronger. There might be some man who could do this. There might be some other king who could show Pharaoh that he was stronger than Pharaoh.

When God says, "I will show my power in you," He means that He will show His divine power. And God's divine power is that He is God, that He is God alone, that there is no power outside Him, and that He does all His good pleasure. "I have raised you up, Pharaoh, and I will show you that I am God, that I am God alone, and that you and all the wicked only serve me." This is the idea. This is God's purpose.

Thus, the purpose becomes that God's name may be declared throughout all the earth. This is God's purpose with regard to all the powers of wickedness. The wicked may not say,

"We have power, too." This was promised in paradise: "You shall be as God" [Gen. 3:5]. That voice must be silenced. God's name must be declared throughout the earth.

The righteous must declare this name of God in a twofold way. For one thing, they must say to the wicked, when they rage against God, "I want you to understand that for this purpose God raised you up." This is the practical calling of the church. Remember, this was not said to Pharaoh *after* his destruction. This was said to him while he stood in his rebellion. Moses must say to Pharaoh, *while Pharaoh stands there in his rebellion against God,* "For this purpose God has raised thee up." The church must never say anything else to the powers of wickedness. It is a shame to the name of God that churches say to the wicked, "Oh, how God would like to have you come to Him. Won't you please come?" The true church must say to the wicked, as he raves against God and His church, "For this purpose God has raised you up." The time will come when the wicked will do the same to the church that Pharaoh did to Israel. What shall we say then? We must say, "For this purpose God raised you up." Thus, by faith, we will have the victory.

For another thing, the people of God themselves must always confess, "Thou hast been merciful unto us; this is why we are saved." This is why this doctrine is not contrary to "whosoever will may come." Granted, this is a hard doctrine, but for whom? For the wicked who do not repent. But it is not hard for him who repents. However, when we repent, we must not say, "It was of me. Rather, we must say, "It was of God that showeth mercy. His be the glory and the praise for ever." And then His name will be declared throughout the earth.

Chapter Sixty

God's Absolute Sovereignty

Romans 9:19–21
Thou wilt say then unto me, Why doth he yet find fault? For who hath resisted his will?
Nay but, O man, who art thou that repliest against God? Shall the thing formed say to him that formed it, Why hast thou made me thus?
Hath not the potter power over the clay, of the same lump to make one vessel unto honour, and another unto dishonour?

"Thou wilt say then unto me . . ." In this manner the apostle introduced the second objection that he knew the objector would raise against the doctrine he had been teaching. The first objection concerned God's righteousness. For the right understanding of this second objection, we must understand that the question concerning God's righteousness is now settled. That question the apostle has answered by quoting two Old Testament passages: "[God] saith to Moses, I will have mercy on whom I will have mercy, and I will have compassion on whom I will have compassion" [Rom. 9:15]; and "[God] saith unto Pharaoh, Even for this same purpose have I raised thee up" [v. 17]. Since God said this, predestination must be righteous, for God is righteous. That question is settled.

Now the objector comes with a second objection. The second objection is this: "Thou wilt say then unto me, Why doth he yet find fault? For who hath resisted his will?" This is the second objection against the doctrine that God determines who shall be children of the promise and who shall not, against the doctrine that God will have mercy on whom He will have mercy and compassion on whom He will have compassion, and against the doctrine that God hardens whom He will. "Why doth He yet find fault?" This is the objection. In this objection, the objector refers to the last clause of verse 18: ". . . whom he will he hardeneth." The argument is that if God hardens a man, He cannot find fault.

I am glad that this objection is found here and that the apostle deals with it, for it is a check on the interpretation that we have given of this entire passage of Scripture. This objection is a common one. It is as old as the truth of God's sovereign predestination and as modern as our present day. When all other objections have been exhausted, the objector comes with this one. And I am glad, for the truth's sake, that the objection is found in this chapter. It is proof that our interpretation of what the apostle has been teaching is the right one. You will never hear this objection raised against the Arminian interpretation of these words. The simple reason is that the Arminian comes with this objection himself. It is against our interpretation that this objection is raised.

The objection is, "Why doth he yet find fault? For who hath resisted His will?" The answer is, "Who art thou, O man, that repliest against God?" The answer is a confession of God's absolute sovereignty. For sinful man and for sinful human nature, this is the clearest revelation of God and therefore the hardest to accept.

How Expressed

The sovereignty of God is expressed in a figurative way in the text. The apostle uses the figure of the potter and the clay. There is a potter. He has a lump of clay from which he makes different kinds of vessels. He makes vessels of honor, that is, vessels of beauty that you put in your living room or place on the mantel. He also makes vessels of dishonor, that is, vessels that you use for ash cans and garbage containers. The main idea expressed in this figure is that the potter has power over the clay, to do as he pleases with it. When the text speaks of "power," you must not think of brute power, of strength, but you must think of power in the sense of authority. The potter has absolute authority over the clay, and the vessel may not complain.

This is a familiar figure in Scripture. We find it also in Jeremiah 18 [:1–4], which is sometimes quoted in connection with Romans 9. There we read, "The word which came to Jeremiah from the LORD, saying, Arise, and go down to the potter's house, and there I will cause thee to hear my words. Then I went down to the potter's house, and, behold, he wrought a work on the wheels. And the vessel that he made of clay was marred in the hand of the potter: so he made it again another vessel, as seemed good to the potter to make it." Jeremiah is told to go down to the potter's house. When he comes there, the potter is making a vessel from clay, and the vessel was marred in his hands. The potter made the vessel, and it was spoiled. It was spoiled while he was busy with it. Therefore, he made it again. "Then the word of the LORD came to me, saying, O house of Israel, cannot I do with you as this potter? saith the LORD. Behold, as the clay is in the potter's hand, so are ye in mine hand, O house of Israel" [vv. 5, 6].

There is a threefold difference between Jeremiah 18 and Romans 9, however. First, Romans 9 refers to individuals. In Jeremiah the reference is to the nation of Israel. Second, in Jeremiah the potter makes one vessel after the other. He makes one vessel, and when it becomes marred, he makes it into another vessel. In Romans, however, the potter makes several vessels of different kinds from one lump of clay. Third, the purpose of Romans 9 is to show that the potter sovereignly makes vessels of honor and vessels of dishonor. The purpose of Jeremiah, on the other hand, is to show God's sovereignty with regard to vessels that have become marred.

In Isaiah 64:8 we read, "But now, O LORD, thou art our father; we are the clay, and thou our potter; and we all are the work of thy hand." Here the people acknowledge God as their sovereign.

In Romans 9 the figure is applied in this way: when the potter has made several vessels—vessels of honor and vessels of dishonor—the vessels may not complain. They may not protest. The vessels may not protest to the potter and say, "We had some rights that Thou hast violated." The reason is that the vessels, when they were in the clay, had no rights.

The meaning of the figure is plain. God is the potter. The vessels unto honor and unto dishonor are the finished work of God with men—their final, eternal state. The vessels unto honor are the saved. The vessels unto dishonor are the damned. The final state of the saved and of the damned are the vessels. The purpose is to teach that God has a right to do as He pleases. No more than the clay may complain to the potter may the damned say to God, "Why hast thou made me so?" The damned may never say to God, "I had certain rights that Thou hast violated." Although they say it here, in hell they will never say it again. This objection will then have come to an end.

Let us look at the figure in more detail. The main question is what is really meant by the lump of clay? What does this lump of clay represent? The Arminian view is that this lump of clay represents men as God finds them at any moment of history. Then Romans 9:21 means that when God finds the wicked and the righteous, He has the right to use them for His purpose. But this cannot be the interpretation. For one thing, if this were the interpretation, men could never come with the objection, "Why doth he yet find fault?" In addition, the text speaks of one lump of clay from which different kinds of vessels are made, both vessels of honor and vessels of dishonor.

The common interpretation is that this lump of clay represents fallen humanity. In this case, the text means that God has the right, out of fallen humanity, to show His mercy to some and to determine who shall be saved and who shall not be saved. The objection to this interpretation lies in the figure itself. The text does not say that God has the right to make vessels of honor out of the clay of dishonor. But it says, "Hath not the potter power over the clay, of the same lump to make one vessel unto honor, and another unto dishonor?" God makes both out of the same lump. He does not begin with vessels, but with clay. But fallen humanity are vessels. And the text says that God, with sovereign right, makes vessels of honor and vessels of dishonor.

Concerning the historical process of forming man, God did not start with man but literally with clay—red clay. This is the meaning of the name *Adam*. God took a lump of red clay. Out of that lump of clay, God made the human race. That was the beginning of the process of making vessels of honor and vessels of dishonor. God made the vessels in Adam. But in Adam the vessels were divided. God also saw to it that these vessels were produced. He caused them to be produced by the fall of Adam into sin. Then, having so cast His clay into the shape of the human race and having so made that human race a vessel of dishonor through sin, He sovereignly formed vessels unto honor and vessels unto dishonor.

We must not suppose that God first decided to make the human race, then permitted the human race to fall into sin, and finally decided to choose some to make them vessels of honor and to leave others as vessels of dishonor. In such a case, God *permits* the vessels to *become* vessels of dishonor. However, the text says that God *makes* them vessels of dishonor. This must stand. God is God. The potter has power over the clay.

Therefore, we must present it this way. For His own name's sake, God wanted vessels unto honor and vessels unto dishonor. This is what you do, too. You do not first get a lump of clay, and then say, "I wonder what I can do with it." First you plan the thing you want to make, and then you get your material to carry out your plan. God wanted vessels of honor and vessels of dishonor to show His grace and His wrath. God then decided that these vessels would be created. He then decided that through the will of man sin should come. God did not *permit* sin to come. God does not *permit* things. One denies the divinity of God when he has God permit things. God *makes* things.

How Opposed

Only on this interpretation does the objection [in Rom. 9:19] make sense. Beware that you do not fall into the error of objector! When people come with this objection, it is proof that I am preaching the Word of God correctly. If people do not come with this objection, it is a sign that I have not divided the Word of God aright. When Paul preached these things, the objector came with his objection.

The objector says, "No one can resist God's will. If it pleased God to make me a vessel of dishonor, if it pleased God to harden me, can I resist Him? Is He not stronger than I? And if I cannot resist God's will, then (to put it in modern form) I am not responsible. Then God cannot complain, because I am exactly what He made me."

Let me say a few things about this objection. In the first place, it is common to all who oppose the truth of predestination. If you will study history as it runs from Augustine, over Calvin, and through the Reformed churches, you will find that when all other objections have been exhausted, the opponents will come with this censure: "You make God the author of sin; you deny the responsibility of man."

In the second place, even from the viewpoint of the objector, this objection is a lie. Why? Because the objector presents it as if God hardens a man who is trying to *resist* the hardening process. This never happens. The will of the wicked, shaped into a vessel of dishonor, always cooperates with God's will to harden him. When God hardens and shapes a man into a vessel of dishonor, that man is in perfect harmony with the form into which God shapes him. If one says, "I wish that I were a child of God," he is not a vessel of dishonor. Therefore, this doctrine is not contrary to the teaching that "whosoever will" may come. It never happens, when God shapes a man into a vessel of dishonor, that the will of that man struggles against this process. Therefore, this objector lies when he says that he resists this shaping process, but that God is stronger than he.

How Maintained

What does the apostle answer? Does he say, "You misunderstood me"? (This would have been the place for the apostle to make himself plain if he thought he had been misunderstood.) On the contrary, the apostle says nothing of the kind. He lets the doctrine stand.

Does he say, "There is also another line"? There are Reformed people who maintain the doctrine of predestination up to a certain point, but then they get scared. When they meet the objector, they draw back. They say that our line of thought must run along two tracks. The one track is that of sovereign predestination; the other track is that God desires all men to be saved. The result of such reasoning is that they run along the track of common grace, while the track of particular grace is forgotten. This is the death of the church. In principle it is an attempt to get away from the sovereignty of God.

Paul does not do this. He leaves the truth as it is. He says this: "Who art thou, O man, that repliest against God?" The apostle puts man where he belongs. He says to the objector, "You answer against God." In the original this means two things: you contradict God, and you rebel against God.

Because the objector's opposition to the doctrine of God's sovereignty is not one of understanding but of the spirit, the apostle says, "Who art thou, O man?" We are small and insignificant before God. We are not as much as a fly before Him. Does not God say that if you take all the nations together, they are but a dust speck on the balance and a drop on the bucket? The nations are not a drop *in* the bucket, but a drop *of* the bucket, that is, a drop on the outside of the pail that presently falls off and means just nothing. Who art thou, O man? You are nothing but a speck of dust. Shall, then, that speck of dust say to the great God, whom he cannot understand, "What doest Thou?" We have no rights over against God.

God forbid that this objection should ever come upon our lips. We may not understand, and I am glad of it. We are small and cannot comprehend God, but when God puts us where we ought to be, that is, in the dust, and when He takes the perverseness out of our hearts, we do not say, "What doest Thou?" Rather, we say that God is the absolute sovereign, and He does all His good pleasure.

Chapter Sixty-one

God's Sovereign Dealings

Romans 9:22, 23
What if God, willing to shew his wrath, and to make his power known, endured with much longsuffering the vessels of wrath fitted to destruction:
And that he might make known the riches of his glory on the vessels of mercy, which he had afore prepared unto glory.

This text is the second part of the answer to the second objection raised against the apostle's development of the truth of God's sovereign predestination: election and reprobation. Two objections had been raised against this doctrine as the apostle had written about it in the context. The first objection was, "Is there unrighteousness with God?" [v. 14]. The apostle had answered that objection with a twofold example from Scripture, showing that God Himself claimed the sovereign right to have mercy on whom He will have mercy and to harden whom He will harden.

The second objection raised against the apostle's doctrine was, "Why doth he yet find fault? For who hath resisted his will?" [v. 19]. If God not only shows His mercy to whom He will, but also hardens whom He will, God has no right to find fault with man. This latter objection the apostle answered with the figure of the potter and the clay, showing that God is absolutely sovereign with His work: "Hath not the potter power over the clay, of the same lump to make one vessel unto honour, and another unto dishonour?" The answer of the apostle to the second objection also included that man should know his position in relation to the living God: "O man, who art thou that repliest against God? Shall the thing formed say to him that formed it, Why hast thou made me thus?" This was the first part of the answer to the second objection: God has no right to find fault if He shows mercy to whom He will and hardens whom He will.

In the text the apostle now continues his answer to the second objection. The answer is still that God is sovereign to do as He pleases, and that we may not be critics of God. What the apostle says is this: what if it pleased God to show His wrath and to make His power known in the vessels of dishonor? Would you say that God has no right to so reveal His wrath? And what if it pleased God to make known the riches of His glory on the vessels of honor? Would you say that God has no right to so reveal His mercy?

But in this second part of the answer to the objection, the viewpoint is slightly different from that in the first part of the answer. In the first part the apostle asked whether God does not have the right to *make* vessels of honor and dishonor. In this second part of his answer, the apostle is speaking rather of God's dealing with the vessels of honor and dishonor *in time.* The apostle tells us that God bears, or endures, these vessels of wrath with much long-suffering in time. Has God no right to do this? What if God, willing to show His wrath and to make His power known, endured with much long-suffering the vessels of wrath fitted to destruction?" This is the subject.

This dealing of God with the vessels of wrath in time has a twofold purpose. The first purpose of God, enduring with much long-suffering the vessels of wrath fitted to destruction, is to make known His wrath and power. The second purpose is to make known the riches of His glory on the vessels of mercy.

With Whom

The question "With whom are God's sovereign dealings?" is answered by the words *vessels of wrath,* on the one hand, and the words *vessels of mercy,* on the other hand. With both of these God deals sovereignly. Who the *vessels of wrath* are is plain. They are the same as the vessel made unto dishonor in verse 21, that is, the reprobate. But the viewpoint of the description is slightly different. *Vessels . . . unto dishonour* looks at the reprobate from the viewpoint of their final destiny. There are vessels that are vessels of honor, and you place them on the shelf or on your table. But there are other vessels that are vessels of dishonor, and you use them, let us say, for garbage cans. The sovereign potter makes vessels of honor and vessels of dishonor. In Romans 9:22 the vessels of dishonor are called *vessels of wrath.*

Does the expression *vessels of wrath* refer to men as they are actually found in the world who *become the object* of God's wrath in time? Or does the expression *vessels of wrath* mean that certain people *are the product* of wrath? In the latter case God conceived of them in eternal wrath and in that wrath formed them to be the bearers of His wrath.

It is plain both from the context and from similar expressions in Scripture that the latter is the meaning. *Vessels of wrath* does not mean vessels that become the object of wrath in time, but they are vessels that God forms to be the bearers of His wrath. The entire context teaches that God is doing something. God is merciful, and God hardens. In harmony with the context, vessels of wrath are vessels that God has conceived of in wrath in His counsel. According to this counsel, God, in time, forms these vessels to be the bearers of His wrath.

This is also plain from similar passages in Scripture. We read more than once in Scripture of children of wrath. The meaning is not children who are the object of wrath, but children who are brought forth by wrath. They are born of wrath; wrath is their mother. Similarly, we read of children of the promise. These are not children who are the object of the promise, but children who are brought forth by the promise; the promise is their mother.

This is also plain from what is added: *fitted to destruction.*

To be fitted to destruction is to be so constituted and instituted that the end must necessarily be destruction. The entire constitution and institution of the vessels of wrath are such that everything must serve to reach this end. Dropping the figure, there are men so constituted that everything serves to lead them to destruction. This destruction is not temporal destruction, but eternal destruction. To this they are fitted.

Fitted by whom? The Arminian says that these vessels of wrath fit themselves, but this is so contrary to the context that we need not waste words on it. The text plainly teaches that God fitted them to reach this end. Unto the service of this end, God uses them. This is the purpose of all the wicked, as we read in Psalm 92:7: "When the wicked spring as the grass, . . . it is that they shall be destroyed for ever."

The other vessels are the *vessels of mercy*. Also this expression must be interpreted according to the same method as applied to the vessels of wrath. Vessels of mercy are not merely vessels that are the objects of mercy, but they are vessels that God eternally conceived of as such. God eternally conceived of vessels that should be formed as vessels of mercy and be bearers of mercy.

These vessels of mercy are fitted unto glory, the glory of God. God is good and the overflowing fountain of all goodness. The radiation of this goodness is God's glory. As the radiation of the light of the sun may be called the glory of the sun, so the radiation of the goodness of God is the glory of God. It pleased God to cause His glory to reflect in His people. God wanted His glory to be reflected in His people in a creaturely way.

We read in Romans 8:29, "For whom he did foreknow, he also did predestinate to be conformed to the image of his Son, that he might be the firstborn among many brethren." This is His glory. When the apostle speaks of *vessels of mercy . . . prepared unto glory*, the meaning is that God determined a people to be the bearers of the glory of His Son. God determined that the one glory of His Son should be reflected in the individual vessels of mercy, so that ultimately that glory might shine forth a thousandfold in the church. Nevertheless, that glory is one. In the millions of vessels of mercy, the one glory of Christ will shine, so that each one gives his own little reflection.

Unto that glory they are fitted. This is the idea of the phrase *afore prepared*. The vessels of mercy are prepared beforehand; they are fitted to that glory. In addition, everything has been so arranged—everything that takes place in time has been afore so fitted—that it must serve that glory for which the vessels of mercy have been prepared.

What They Are

With these two kinds of people, God deals sovereignly in time. He endures, or forbears, the vessels of wrath fitted unto destruction, and He endures these vessels of wrath in connection with His long-suffering over the vessels of mercy afore prepared to glory. Forbearance and long-suffering do not mean the same thing in Scripture. Endurance, or forbearance, is suspended and sustained wrath. Long-suffering, in contrast, is suspended or sustained love. Forbearance says to its object, "I long to destroy you now, but I forbear, I endure, I tolerate you, until you have served My purpose." But long-suffering says to its object, "I long to glorify you now, but I forbear until I have reached My purpose."

A couple of illustrations will make the difference plain. Suppose that for a certain purpose it is necessary for you to take a stranger into your home. You support him and supply him with all his needs. You supply him with bread to eat, water to drink, clothes to wear, and a bed to sleep in. But while he is in your home eating your bread, drinking your water, wearing your clothes, and sleeping in your bed, he ignores you and behaves as though you were not there. He even abuses your children, mistreats them, and persecutes them. But you keep him in your house for the purpose you have with him. You say of him,

"I forbear, I endure, I tolerate you, until I have reached my purpose with you. Then I will throw you out."

The other illustration is that of a surgeon who finds it necessary to operate upon his own child. The operation is of such a nature that no anesthetic can be administered, but he must operate. He cuts into the flesh of his child, and the child cries, begging him to stop. But the doctor keeps on, although his heart bleeds, until the operation is finished. This is long-suffering.

The first is an illustration of God's dealings with the wicked: forbearance. The wicked are in God's house. If God did not want them there, all He would have to do is drop them out of existence. If God did not want them there, all He would have to do is to fail to supply them with power, strength, and talents. But God supplies them with power, talents, food, drink, and clothing, and they flourish. While these wicked are in God's house, they ignore Him or curse Him to His face. They persecute and kill His children. Yet God keeps on sustaining them. He says to them, "I tolerate you until My purpose with you has been reached."

The other is an illustration of God's dealings with His people. These people are in the midst of suffering. They cry unto God, but God does not deliver them. Why not? Because He is long-suffering to them, and He says to them, "I cannot deliver you until My purpose has been reached." God endures with much long-suffering, that is, long-suffering to His people. If you ask why God sovereignly determined the way of sin and death, the answer is, God is long-suffering to the vessels of mercy *in connection with* His endurance of the vessels of wrath.

When Adam plunged the human race into sin, the elect also plunged into sin. They suffer and die with the human race. Not only do they suffer and die with the human race, but as they live in the same world, they also suffer through the instrumentality of the vessels of wrath. This was the case with Pharaoh and the people of God in Egypt. Pharaoh used his power to crush the people of God. They cried unto God. And God endured Pharaoh in order that He might reach His purpose with him.

When the vessels of wrath laid hands on the Son of God, abused Him, beat Him, and killed Him, it was because God endured, with pent-up wrath, the vessels of wrath fitted to destruction; and he was long-suffering over His people in order that the blood of atonement might be shed. Because the blood of atonement must be shed, God endured the vessels of wrath with much long-suffering over His people.

Their Purpose

The purpose of God's sovereign dealings is twofold. "What," so the text says, "if God, willing to shew his wrath, and to make his power known, endured with much longsuffering the vessels of wrath fitted to destruction?" God's wrath is the reaction of His holiness against sin. From before the foundation of the world it pleased God, who is a light and in whom there is no darkness, that the fact that He hates darkness and sin should become known. This is His purpose. This must become known.

Has God not the right to do this? Would you dispute the fact that God has the right to reveal His wrath against sin and the sinner? But if God is to reveal His wrath against sin and the wicked, if He is to reveal the antithesis of His holiness, sin and the wicked must be there. It pleased God eternally to determine in His counsel that sin and the wicked should be there in order that He might show that He hates them. To show that God hates sin, the wicked must be there. This is the only purpose they ever serve.

With the showing of wrath, God's purpose is to make known His power. God's power is not a superior power. God is the *only* one who has power. God does not manifest that He is strong, but He wants it to become known that He is the only one who has strength. The power of the devil and his host and of all the wicked also is God's power.

God makes known His power by causing the wicked to serve in bringing the riches of His glory on the vessels of mercy. Are not the vessels of wrath fitted to destruction, on the one hand, and the vessels of mercy fitted unto glory, on the other hand? Still the vessels of wrath must *serve* the vessels of mercy. The devil and all the wicked powers must serve to make known the riches of God's glory on the vessels of mercy. Reprobation serves election according to God's purpose. If sin had not come, grace could not have been revealed. If death had not come, and the resurrection, the final glory of the vessels of mercy could not have come. The suffering of this present time is not worthy to be compared with the glory that shall be revealed in us.

Just look at the cross. There you find the vessels of wrath shedding the blood of atonement in order that the vessels of mercy might be glorified.

What shall we say then? We shall say, "O the depth of the riches both of the wisdom and knowledge of God! how unsearchable are his judgments, and his ways past finding out! . . . For of him, and through him, and to him, are all things: to whom be glory for ever. Amen" [Rom. 11:33, 36].

Chapter Sixty-two

The Calling of the Vessels of Mercy

Romans 9:24–29
Even us, whom he hath called, not of the Jews only, but also of the Gentiles?

As he saith also in Osee, I will call them my people, which were not my people; and her beloved, which was not beloved.

And it shall come to pass, that in the place where it was said unto them, Ye are not my people; there shall they be called the children of the living God.

Esaias also crieth concerning Israel, Though the number of the children of Israel be as the sand of the sea, a remnant shall be saved:

For he will finish the work, and cut it short in righteousness: because a short work will the Lord make upon the earth.

And as Esaias said before, Except the Lord of Sabaoth had left us a seed, we had been as Sodoma, and been made like unto Gomorrha.

Verses 24–29 belong together and cannot very well be separated. Strictly speaking, verse 24 is yet a part, the second part, of the answer to the question [in v. 19]: "Why doth he yet find fault?" If God has mercy on whom He will and hardens whom He will, why doth He yet find fault? God's answer to that question was that He bore the vessels of wrath with much long-suffering over His people, whom they persecuted. He endured the vessels of wrath in order to make known His glory unto the vessels of mercy, which He had afore prepared unto glory.

In verse 24, the apostle continues this answer and says, "Even us, whom he hath called, not of the Jews only, but also of the Gentiles."

At the same time, there is in verse 24 a conclusion to this entire section. Verse 24 is the final answer to the question posed in verse 6: "Is the Word of God fallen out? Has the Word of God taken none effect?" To this question, the apostle answers here finally, "Not at all! The Word of God is not fallen out, but has been realized, for He calls us not only of the Jews, but also of the Gentiles." This is the connection of the text to this entire section.

In verses 25–29 we have quotations in which the apostle proves that this calling of God's people out of Jews and Gentiles had already been prophesied in Scripture. In other words, the apostle proves in these quotations that Israel, as a nation, has been utterly rejected by God. Finally, he proves from these quotations that the Word of God has not fallen out, even though not a majority of the individual Jews are saved but only the remnant according to election. Therefore, already here, the apostle begins to instruct us with regard to what must be expected of the future of the Jews and what is to become of them. We must pay special attention to this because it will help us to understand what the apostle teaches in chapter 11. But the apostle here is speaking on the calling of the vessels of mercy.

The Calling

When the apostle Paul speaks of the calling, he uses the term in the broadest sense. In verses 24–29 he uses the term *calling* repeatedly. He uses it in verse 24: "Even us, whom he hath *called,* not of the Jews only, but also of the Gentiles." He uses it in his quotation from Hosea [2:23]: "I will *call* them my people, which were not my people." He uses it also in another quotation from Hosea [1:10]: "In the place where it was said unto them, Ye are not my people, there shall they be *called* the children of the living God." *Calling* does not always have the same meaning in Scripture. But Paul uses the word in the sense of that act of God whereby the sinner, dead in sin and misery, is translated from darkness into light.

In dogmatics we usually distinguish between regeneration and calling. God regenerates a man first. When He has regenerated a man, God calls him. In a dogmatic sense, therefore, we often use the word *calling* in a restricted sense. This is perfectly scriptural. The apostle John speaks of regeneration, but the apostle Paul speaks very little of regeneration. Paul usually speaks only of the calling, but in such a way that regeneration is included. This is evident from the eighth chapter of Romans, where Paul writes, "Whom he did predestinate, them he also called: and whom he called, them he also justified: and whom he justified, them he also glorified" [v. 30]. He includes regeneration in calling. When Paul speaks of the calling, he includes all the work of God whereby we become conscious children of God. That the apostle Paul speaks of the calling, and not of regeneration, is perhaps due to the fact that he was the apostle to the Gentiles. He saw that God called His people out of these Gentiles. He saw the calling, and he loves to speak of this calling of God.

This calling is efficacious. When God calls, He does not send forth an invitation. I do not say that we cannot speak, in a restricted sense, of the form in which the calling comes to us through the gospel as a kind of invitation. But this refers only to the form in which the calling comes to us. God, however, does not invite when He calls. An invitation differs from the calling. It differs from the calling of God in two respects. First, an invitation you may decline, but when God calls, you may not decline. God calls with authority. To decline the calling of God is an act of disobedience. Second, not only *may* we decline an invitation, but we *can* decline it. But when God calls, we cannot decline. It is true that there is a certain outward side to the calling that we not only can decline, but in fact can *only* decline. But the apostle is speaking of the calling in its complete reality. This calling is efficacious. When it comes to us, we cannot decline. Just as surely as the light came in creation when God said, "Let there be light," so surely, when God calls a man, that man comes. God did not send out an invitation to the light. When God said, "Let there be light," the light was bound to come. No more than God sent out an invitation to the light does He send out an invitation to the sinner to make Him alive. God does not invite. God calls. When God calls, He sends His creative, regenerating Word into the heart of the sinner. And when God sends His regenerating Word into the heart of the sinner, the sinner is changed into what God calls him. Of this calling the apostle speaks.

God brings the calling through His Word in the Scriptures; otherwise, the calling would have no content. It is true that there is a certain universal calling through nature. God did not leave Himself without witness. But this is not the saving calling. It is the calling that man shall glorify and praise God, but it is not the calling that makes known that God is merciful. In Scripture it is different. God does not simply call in Scripture that man shall glorify Him, but He calls man to come unto Him and see that He is merciful. The call in the text is the saving, efficacious calling through the Word in Scripture.

Unto What the Calling Is

Unto what God calls men is indicated in the quotations from Hosea 1 and 2. There God said, "I will call them my people, which were not my people; I will call her beloved, which was not beloved. And it shall come to pass, that in the place where it was said unto them, Ye are not my people, there shall they be called the children of the living God" [Hos. 2:23; Hos. 1:10].

In the prophecy of Hosea, the prophet is told to take him a wife of adultery, a wife of whoredoms [Hos. 1]. He must have children of adultery. Hosea does this, and his wife bears him three children, whom he must name *Jezreel, Lo-ruhamah,* and *Lo-ammi.* Here we only have to do with the last two: *Lo-ruhama,* which means "not beloved" or "not an object of mercy," and *Lo-ammi,* which means "not my people." This adulterous woman, in her relation to Hosea, is a picture of Israel in her relation to Jehovah. She is a picture of Israel as Israel has become an adulteress. As an adulteress, Israel brings forth adulterous children. These children represent the individual Jews. To them God says *Lo-ruhamah* (not beloved) and *Lo-ammi* (not my people). The prophet is speaking to Israel, to the ten tribes. He addresses them as *Lo-ruhamah* and *Lo-ammi*—not beloved and not my people. It is also to Israel that the word of restoration is spoken. To Israel it is said that they who are "not my people" shall be called "my people." The apostle explains this prophecy as describing the calling of God's people out of Jews and Gentiles. In other words, the prophecy is applied to the calling of the church of the new dispensation from Jews and Gentiles.

Thus, Israel is placed here on a par with the Gentiles. Of Israel is said what had always been said of the Gentiles: *Lo-ruhammah* and *Lo-ammi*—not beloved and not my people. The apostle teaches that there is no difference. It holds for both that by nature they are *Lo-ammi*—not God's people. God says to the Jews, as well as to the Gentiles, "not my people." This is something to be remembered when we labor among the Jews. Some still like to look upon the Jews as a favorite people of God. When they establish Jewish missions, they give to the Jews the names *Ruhamma* (beloved) and *Ammi* (my people). But God calls the Jews *Lo-ruhamah* and *Lo-ammi,* and we have no business to call them *Ruhamah* and *Ammi.* God says that the Jews are no more His people. The text also teaches that God calls His people out of Jews and Gentiles. Only by this calling do they become *Ruhamah* and *Ammi.* Out of Jews and Gentiles, God calls *Ruhamah* and *Ammi.* Thus, the text teaches plainly that there is no difference between Jews and Gentiles.

According to the context in Hosea, Jews and Gentiles are called into God's covenant. God enters into a covenant relation with them. Also in the new dispensation, God establishes

His own covenant, and He does it alone. There is a man, dead as a stone. He belongs to those of whom it was said, "not my people." And God comes to this man. What does He do? Does He invite the sinner to come into His covenant? And does the sinner have the power to reject this invitation? If this popular presentation is right, this whole chapter is a lie. No. Instead, God says, in an efficacious way, "Beloved," and this sinner becomes beloved. God says, "my people," and they become His people. Just as surely as when God said, "Let there be light," that light came, so surely when God says, "my people," they become His people. It is just as foolish to say that God invited Lazarus to come out of the grave as it is to say that God invites the dead sinner to come into His covenant. The establishment of the covenant is one-sided. God does not say, "Let us get married." God says, "I am going to marry you."

When God says, "I am going to marry you," the result is that you love Him. The result is that you say, "I want to be married to you." But this is the result of the calling.

Who the Called Are

As concerns the identity of those whom God calls, we must still keep in mind the connection with the question in verse 6: "Has the Word of God fallen out?" With this question in mind, the apostle proves two things. First, that which God calls is not the nation of Israel. The relation between God and Israel as a nation is gone. This is the meaning of the quotation from Isaiah 10:22, 23: "He will finish the work, and cut it short in righteousness: because a short work will the Lord make upon the earth" [Rom. 9:28]. The Holy Spirit led the apostle to quote from the Greek translation of the Old Testament, the Septuagint. This Greek translation is an explanation of the Hebrew. It throws light upon the meaning of the original Hebrew. The meaning is plainly this. The work that God will finish is His relation to Israel. The text declares that God will send destruction on the nation of Israel. That He will cut it short means that

He will cut off His relation to Israel. It will be terminated forever. God never returns. When God cut off His relation with the nation of Israel, it was a final act. God never returns to them again to deal with them as a nation. Verse 28 adds that God will do it quickly. How quickly God did it we know from history. It is the teaching of the text, therefore, that God will never again call Israel, as a nation, into His fellowship.

The second thing that the apostle proves is that it is not the case that the Word of God has taken none effect, even when a majority of the Jews do not enter into the kingdom. Even then, the Word of God has not fallen out but has been fulfilled, for [in v. 27] the apostle quotes Isaiah as saying, "Though the number of the children of Israel be as the sand of the sea, a remnant shall be saved" [Isa. 10:22]. In another place Isaiah said, "Except the Lord of Sabaoth had left us a seed, we had been as Sodom, and been made like unto Gomorrah" [Isa. 1:9]. The meaning is that when God calls His people out of Jews and Gentiles, it is the realization of His promise to Abraham. Whom does God call out of Jews and Gentiles? The true, spiritual children of Abraham. The Word of God has not fallen out, for "They are not all Israel, which are of Israel" and "the children of the flesh . . . are not the children of God: but the children of the promise are counted for the seed" [Rom. 9:6, 8]. God calls His elect out of Jews and Gentiles, and this calling of the elect is the calling of the true Israel of God in all the ages.

Surely there is a calling of God that is not unto salvation, for God is merciful to whom He will, and whom He will He hardens. When the calling in the outward sense comes to man, man will always refuse to obey, but in the full sense of the call, they who are called will come.

Therefore, the question is, can we join in with the confession in verses 24 and following? The apostle says, "Even us, whom he hath called." Can we join in saying with the apostle, "Even us"? We can, if in response to God's "my people," we say, "my God."

Chapter Sixty-three

The Realization of God's Sovereign Purpose

Romans 9:30-33
What shall we say then? That the Gentiles, which followed not after righteousness, have attained to righteousness, even the righteousness which is of faith.

But Israel, which followed after the law of righteousness, hath not attained to the law of righteousness.

Wherefore? Because they sought it not by faith, but as it were by the works of the law. For they stumbled at that stumblingstone;

As it is written, Behold, I lay in Sion a stumblingstone and rock of offence: and whosoever believeth on him shall not be ashamed.

When you maintain the truth of sovereign, free election and reprobation—the truth that God shows mercy to whom He will and hardens whom He will—you must expect opposition from various quarters. But it is also true that you will meet with opposition if you maintain that there is no special future to be expected for the Jews. You will meet with opposition if you maintain that there is no special salvation to be expected, either for the nation of the Jews or for the individual Israelites. You will meet with opposition if you maintain that in the new dispensation there is no difference between Jews and Gentiles. You will meet with opposition if you maintain that from a natural point of view both Jews and Gentiles are *Lo-ruhamah* (not beloved) and *Lo-ammi* (not my people) and that there is only one way of salvation for both. The only way of salvation for Jew and Gentile is that they are called into the fellowship of Christ. Many oppose this idea. Many cherish the idea of a special future for the Jews. They maintain that there will be a special dispensation, either for the nation of Israel as a whole or for individual Jews. This idea is based on a wrong conception of Old Testament prophecy and a failure to interpret it in the light of the New Testament.

It is not my intention to go into this error, but I want to be understood correctly. We do not hold that all God's curses are for Jews, whereas all God's blessings are for the Gentiles. Our view is not that only the Jews are objects of God's wrath, whereas only the Gentiles are objects of mercy. Our view is that both Jew and Gentile are under God's curse by nature and are the objects of wrath. Neither the one nor the other can get from under this curse, except by the gracious calling of God. Salvation is not for the Jews or for the Gentiles, but for the vessels of mercy out of Jews and Gentiles. By nature both Jews and Gentiles are *Lo-ruhamah* and *Lo-ammi* (not beloved and not my people). Both are saved only by the gracious calling of God.

The apostle introduces the words of the text by the question *What shall we say then?* The meaning of the question is, "What is to be the final conclusion of our discussion of the theme of the entire passage?" This theme is that the Word of God had not fallen out, had not become of none effect, not even when the nation of Israel as a whole and a great majority of the individual Jews did not enter into God's salvation. The line of discussion went like this. Not all are children of the promise. Not all are Israel, which are of Israel. But the vessels of mercy are the objects of the promise. Therefore, the Word of God has not fallen out.

What shall we say then?

We shall say that the historical result corresponds with the truth expounded in this chapter, for the Gentiles, although they pursued not after righteousness, have attained to righteousness, even the righteousness which is of faith. And the mass of the Jews, which followed after the law of righteousness, have not attained to the law of righteousness. Therefore, it is as I have taught: the vessels of mercy from Jews and Gentiles are saved, and the vessels of wrath from Jews and Gentiles are hardened.

Through What This Purpose Is Realized

Through what is this purpose of God realized? The answer is given in verse 33: "As it is written, Behold, I lay in Sion a stumblingstone and rock of offence: and whosoever believeth on him shall not be ashamed." In this verse, the apostle quotes from two different verses [of Isaiah]. That is, he takes a part from each of two verses and combines them in one. We may not do this, but we must remember that when the apostle quotes Scripture, it is really the Holy Spirit who is quoting His own Word. Surely the Holy Spirit has the right and the ability to quote His own Word in whatever connection pleases Him.

One of these quotations is from Isaiah 8:14: "He shall be for . . . a stone of stumbling and for a rock of offence to both the houses of Israel." The context deals especially with the wicked Israelites. There were Jews who refused to put their trust in the Lord. They put their trust in Rezin, rather than in Jehovah. They rejected the Word of the prophet. When the prophet came to them, they laughed at him and mocked him. Against these wicked Israelites, the Lord says, through His prophet, "I lay in Sion a stumblingstone and rock of offence." The meaning is that God lays this stone there for the wicked Jews to stumble over and break their necks.

The rest of the last verse [of Rom. 9] is quoted from Isaiah 28:16: "He that believeth shall not make haste," with reference to "a stone" that is described as "a tried stone, a precious corner stone, a sure foundation."

The apostle is speaking of this stone. This stone becomes the means through which God realizes His twofold purpose.

The idea of this stone is plain. The stone is mentioned often in Scripture. In Psalm 118:22 we read, "The stone which the builders refused is become the head stone of the corner." We read of it also in I Peter 2:4, 6–8. First of all, this stone has positive significance. The figure is that of a building of which Christ is the cornerstone. Christ is the cornerstone of the church. He is the foundation stone of the church. The church rests on this stone. The stone also determines the shape and size of the building. Of this stone the apostle is speaking in the text. It is evident that this stone is Christ. It is evident from I Peter 2:3, 4: "If so be that ye have tasted that the Lord is gracious. To whom coming, as unto a living stone, disallowed indeed of men, but chosen of God, and precious."

Christ is a stone, laid by God. In Isaiah 28:16, we read, "Therefore thus saith the Lord God, Behold, I lay in Zion for a foundation a stone, a tried stone, a precious corner stone, a sure foundation." As the foundation stone of the church, Christ is elect and precious. In laying this stone, God ordained in His counsel that Christ would be this stone. He lays this stone throughout the ages. The sacrifices and ceremonies of the dispensation of shadows were a laying of the stone. But the laying of the stone is realized especially in the fulness of time. It is realized when God sends His Son in the flesh, when He died, when He was raised, when He ascended into heaven, when He received the Spirit, when He poured out the Spirit into the church, and when God calls men into the fellowship of the church.

The stone has a second purpose. We find that negatively the stone is a rock of offense and a stumblingstone. Christ is a stone of stumbling and a rock of offense for the wicked. In verse 33 this even has the emphasis because the apostle has in mind especially the fact that through Christ, the Jewish nation stumbles and falls. God laid that stone in Sion in order that it might also serve the purpose of being such a stumblingstone.

When people stumble over this stone, they realize God's purpose just as much as when people put their trust in Christ. We are familiar with a stumblingstone. You lay a stone in someone's way. He stumbles over it. You put it there with the purpose that that person should stumble over it. God put a stone in the way of the carnal Jews in order that they should stumble and break their necks over it. He did so in order that the wickedness of that carnal Israel might become manifest.

This same stone also serves the purpose of salvation. Therefore, the apostle says, "Whosoever believeth on him shall not be ashamed." To believe on Christ is to acknowledge Him. To believe on Christ is to know Him. It is to know Him in His power of salvation and to put our trust in Him. When we put away everything else (when we do not seek a way out of our own devising) and in confidence come to Christ and know Him with a certain knowledge and put our trust in Him, then we believe on this stone. Of those who believe on this stone, the apostle says they "shall not be ashamed." Isaiah says, "They shall not hasten," which does not mean that they shall not hasten with a view to their salvation, but that they shall not fly away, shall not flee. That will not happen if they believe in Christ. No matter what may happen, they will not run away, will not be disappointed, will not be ashamed, when they believe in Christ.

Through this stone, therefore, God works out His twofold purpose, His purpose of election and of reprobation, His purpose of showing mercy to some and hardening others. God does not show His mercy through Christ, but harden through some other means. No, through the same stone God works out His twofold purpose.

This is why one cannot be a preacher if his only purpose is to save souls. God does not use a preacher only to save souls. He also uses him as a means to harden people. This is a comfort for the preacher. I am sure, when preaching, that God will save His people, but I am also sure that by my preaching God will harden the reprobate. Therefore, the comfort of the preacher is that God accomplishes His purposes through him. On the one hand, He saves His people; on the other hand, He hardens the reprobate.

However, God does not harden the reprobate merely as reprobate, but as wicked, as sinners. The reprobate do not go to hell as reprobate, but as wicked. In order that this may become manifest, God throws this stumblingstone in their way. This is what God did to the wicked Jews.

In What Way This Purpose Is Realized

This twofold purpose is reached in the way of faith and unbelief. The apostle says, "The Gentiles, which followed not after righteousness, have attained to righteousness," but it is "the righteousness which is of faith." Righteousness is that God declares man to be right with Him. Here it is a righteousness that is by faith, because righteousness is in that stone. Righteousness is in Christ. When God declares us righteous, He imputes unto us the righteousness of that stone. We receive this sentence of God by faith. When God gives us faith, we receive in our hearts the assurance that He declares us to be right with Him. This righteousness in Christ implies more than the righteousness in Adam. The righteousness in Christ implies not only the forgiveness of sins, but also the right to eternal life. This was not so with the righteousness in Adam.

The wicked also come into contact with that stone. They reject and despise Him and cast Him out. This is always the case. On the one hand, there are those who put their trust in that stone; others stumble over it and reveal their wickedness. Thus, the basis is laid for their damnation.

Some say that the realities of salvation and damnation are only matters of faith and unbelief and, therefore, of the free-will of man. They say that a man is saved because he believes and that another is lost because of his unbelief. The issue between the free-will teachers and us is not that salvation is a matter of believing in Christ and damnation is a matter of unbelief. All believe this. "Whosoever will" may come. There is no limitation to this "whosoever." I will add, "whosoever will" *is* saved. There is no doubt that whosoever believes in Christ is saved. Neither is it the question whether he who rejects Christ will be damned. Rather, the question is this: "Who determines whether a man shall believe in Christ or whether he shall be hardened?" The free-will teacher says that man determines this. We say that God determines it. And we say that if a man wills to come to Christ, he is already touched by grace.

It would be curious, indeed, if at the end of this extended teaching of the sovereign grace of God, the apostle would say, "Now it is up to man." God forbid! For faith is a gift of God. That the Gentiles believed was not the work of the Gentiles, but of God. When the Gentiles, which followed not after righteousness, attained to righteousness, it was only because God worked out His purpose of election in them. And that the reprobate did not attain to righteousness was due, negatively, to the fact that God did not give them faith, and positively, to the fact that God put that stone in their way. There is no general, well-meant offer of salvation. God places that stone. Through that stone His twofold purpose is realized. In Peter we read that some are appointed to stumble at the Word [I Pet. 2:8].

In Whom
This Purpose Is Realized

God works out His sovereign purpose, on the one hand, in the vessels of mercy, and, on the other hand, in the vessels of wrath. The apostle does not teach that God works the purpose of reprobation in all the Jews. We might receive this impression. Instead, the apostle means that God laid the stumblingstone before all but the remnant.

We read [vv. 31, 32] that "Israel, which followed after the law of righteousness, hath not attained to the law of righteousness . . . because they sought it not by faith, but as it were by the works of the law." This is not to be read as though it said that Israel, which followed after the righteousness of the law, did not attain to the righteousness of the law. It is true that God did not give faith to the Jews, but they did have a revelation of the law of righteousness. They had a revelation of the justifying law in the law of shadows. That law of shadows was the justifying law. What did the Jews do? They followed after that justifying law. But they followed after it as though it were a law of works. They had the revelation of the justifying law, if only they had followed it by faith. The believing Jews did that. They put their trust in the stone. But the carnal Jews made of the sacrifices and ceremonies a work. They reasoned this way: "If we give a lamb to God, He has to justify us." That was wicked. God had said, "The cattle on a thousand hills are mine" [Ps. 50:10]. The Jews made of the law of righteousness a law of works. And when Christ came—the revelation of grace—they hated Him because they were wicked.

But the Gentiles attained to righteousness. Why? Because they were better? Because they were more receptive? Because they were more fit? Hear the answer of the text: the Gentiles, who followed after righteousness not at all, attained to righteousness by faith. Through whom? Through God, who said, "I lay in Sion a stumblingstone and rock of offence."

What shall we say then? We shall say this. All boasting is excluded, even the boasting of the reprobate. God works out His will, even through the wicked, and He does as He pleases. If you believe, your boasting is excluded. And the conclusion is this: "He that glories, let him glory in the Lord" [I Cor. 1:31].

Chapter Sixty-four

Christ the End of the Law

Romans 10:4
For Christ is the end of the law for righteousness to every one that believeth.

It is essential for the right understanding of this verse that we clearly see the connection in which it occurs. The apostle introduces this verse by the conjunction *For*. "*For* Christ is the end of the law for righteousness to every one that believeth." *For* expresses that the apostle gives a reason for that which he said in the preceding verse. There the apostle wrote, "For they being ignorant of God's righteousness, and going about to establish their own righteousness, have not submitted themselves unto the righteousness of God." The connection is as follows. In verse 3 the apostle speaks of the possibility of the righteousness of God for the Jews of the old dispensation. He is speaking of the righteousness that God prepares for His people in Christ and that they receive by faith. Carnal Israel did not want this righteousness, or rather, they did not submit to it. They went in a different direction. They went about to establish a righteousness of their own by the works of the law.

This gives rise to the question, could they do anything else? Could the Jews in the old dispensation have done anything else but go about to establish their own righteousness by keeping the law? Or was there no way for the Jews to submit themselves to righteousness but in Christ? The apostle answers that

445

there was such a way, for also in the old dispensation, Christ was the end of the law.

Of What Christ Is the End

When the apostle speaks of the law, he has in mind the entire Mosaic code of ordinances, precepts, and statutes. He has in mind all the old dispensational institutions. He has in mind the law as it was given to Israel from Mount Horeb. We must keep this in mind. Otherwise we will carry an idea into the verse that the apostle did not mean. We must distinguish between the moral law (the decalogue, the law of the ten commandments) and all the other ordinances and precepts. Certainly the apostle includes the moral law. The decalogue is included. In fact, the law of the ten commandments was given from Mount Sinai *first*. Not only was it given first, but it was also given in a distinctive way—on two stones. Thus it was emphatically declared to Israel that the decalogue was the basic law. The decalogue was the heart of the Mosaic law-giving. Without it, the other laws could not be kept. If that law of the ten commandments was not kept, but one would try to keep the other ordinances, he became an abomination to the Lord. If one would kill, commit adultery, and steal, but would come to the temple and bring sacrifices and keep the sabbaths, the feast days, and the new moons, he became an abomination to the Lord. This is still the case today. If we walk in sin, lie, steal, kill, and commit adultery, but at the same time are very diligent in coming to church, in bringing our gifts, in adhering to the Reformed truth, we are abominable to the Lord. Then we are hypocrites.

However, the apostle is not thinking of the law of the ten commandments only. He is also thinking of all the other ordinances and precepts of Israel. He is thinking of the temple, of the offerings, of the sacrifices, of the washings, of all the ceremonies. Israel's life was limited by precepts in all that it did. Israel was told in detail how it should serve the Lord. Israel was told what to bring, how to bring it, when to bring it, and where to bring it. Step-by-step the way was mapped out for Israel.

That is not the case with us. We are free. We are not told how often we must come to church. That is left to the discretion of the people of God. We are free when it comes to the question as to how often we shall come to church—not that we come once, but that we come as often as possible. But the way is not mapped out for us. In the old dispensation they could not do as they pleased. In the new dispensation we can do as we please, providing that we please God.

What was the meaning of the law for Israel? The law demanded strict obedience. If you ask, "Could the Jews be saved if they did not keep the *law*?" the answer is no. In the new dispensation we cannot be saved if we do not heed the *gospel*. Likewise, the Jews could not be saved if they did not go to the temple. That is why it was so terrible when that temple was destroyed. The Jews had to go to the temple. They had to go to the priest and ask him to bring a sacrifice for them. That is why it was so terrible if the priests were carnal men. That was just as terrible as—no, *more* terrible than—our having a modern preacher on the pulpit. A modern preacher we can get rid of, but they could not get rid of the priest, even though he was carnal. They did not appoint him, and they could not get rid of him. Still the child of God in the Old Testament had to keep the law.

The law demanded strict obedience. The law would say to all who kept it, "You are righteous." The law said, "Do this, and you shall live." This meant, "Keep me, and you are righteous." This is all the law could do. That did not mean that they should keep the outward precepts, so that they would keep the law only in the external sense. Then, too, the law demanded, "Thou shalt love the Lord thy God with all thy heart, and mind, and soul, and strength." On this the law and the prophets depended. The law said, "Do this, and live." On the other hand, it said, "Fail to do this, and thou art cursed."

Was there any hope for the Jews in the Old Testament? The answer is that there was no salvation by keeping the law and, in that way, perfecting it. In that way there was for Israel no salvation, any more than there is for us. Suppose that one kept the law. This was, of course, impossible. But just suppose for the moment that it were possible and one did keep the law, not merely outwardly, but *really*. If he kept the law, would he be saved? No, for the law could not atone for his sinful nature or for any sinful deed he may have committed. There was no salvation in the law.

Nor could the purpose of that law be that if the Jew kept the ceremonial law, he would be saved. This was just the mistake he made. He looked upon the law as a means to work himself into righteousness, but that could not be done. The blood of bulls and goats could not atone. If the Jews would come to the Lord with their sacrifice, the Lord would say, "That bull is mine."

Was there, then, any way of salvation for the Jews in the law? The apostle answers yes, for Christ was also then "the end of the law for righteousness to every one that believeth."

In What Sense Christ Is the End

The usual interpretation of "end" is that Christ terminated the law. According to this explanation, given by almost all commentators, there is a sharp difference between the old dispensation and the new dispensation. In the old dispensation the law was the basis of righteousness; in the new dispensation, the basis of righteousness is the gospel. In the old dispensation the Word of God was, "Do, and be righteous." When Christ came, He brought an end to the dispensation in which the law was the basis of righteousness. He ushered in the dispensation of righteousness by faith.

This explanation, however, is not according to the context. Also in the old dispensation, men and woman were righteous by faith. The difference is not that in the Old Testament they were saved by works, whereas in the New Testament we are saved by faith. This is not Scripture, especially not in the context. The meaning of the text, therefore, is not that Christ made an end to the dispensation in which the law was the basis of righteousness. The law never was the basis of righteousness. Besides, was not Abraham saved by faith? Was not circumcision the seal of the righteousness of faith?

Nor does the text mean that Christ fulfilled the law. This is not the meaning of the word *end*. To be sure, Christ fulfilled the law. Christ fulfilled the law in such a way that we are righteous before we begin to do anything as to our righteousness. We are righteous to begin with. Christ fulfilled the law, but He did not terminate it. How could He terminate this: "Thou shalt love the Lord thy God with all your heart, and your neighbor as yourself"?

The meaning of *end* is different. *End* here has the same meaning as when we speak of the end we have in view. The end is the object, the aim, that we have in view. When we say we do something with an end in view, we mean that all we do aims at that object. The apostle teaches that the object that the law had in view was Christ. The ceremonies, the temple, the altar, the priest, the sacrifices—all had Christ in view.

That was plain to the Jews, especially when the prophets interpreted the law. When the Jews brought their sacrifices to the temple but did not do so by faith, they did not obtain the righteousness of the law. But when they brought their sacrifices and looked at the end, they were saved. They were saved not by works, but by faith in Him who was the end of the law. Verse 3 tells us that the Jews, "being ignorant of God's righteousness, and going about to establish their own righteousness, have not submitted themselves unto the righteousness of God." Why? "For Christ is the end of the law for righteousness to every one that believeth." There never was a dispensation of law without the gospel. The law of the Old Testament was also gospel. The law pointed to Christ. When the end was attained, the law dropped away. In this sense, there is no more law. In the Old Testament law, the gospel pointed forward and made the people look forward in hope. In the New Testament, we look back to the realization. But this we must understand: the saved, both in the Old Testament and in the New Testament, are righteous by faith.

"Righteous" means that in all our being, nature, and walk we are in harmony with God according to God's judgment. God always judges us. We are not *going to be* in the judgment. We *are* in the judgment. We are judged every day, constantly. God is the Judge. We are righteous when God declares us to be in harmony with His precepts. But when we read of righteousness in the gospel, it means more. Righteousness in the gospel also means that God deems us worthy of something more. It means that God deems us worthy of eternal life. This is the righteousness of the gospel. God said to Adam, "As long as you stay righteous, you can remain in paradise." But in Christ there is another righteousness. In Christ is a righteousness according to which we are deemed worthy of eternal life. It is this righteousness that is intended when the apostle says that Christ is the *end* of the law for righteousness.

Unto What
Christ Is the End

Righteousness in the statement "Christ is the end of the law unto *righteousness*" is connected with Christ. Righteousness is not connected with law. The text does not mean that Christ is the end of the law of righteousness. Christ is righteousness. Christ is the end, the aim to which all the law points as our righteousness.

~ *Christ the End of the Law*

The reason why God declares us righteous is Christ. We know this. And still I think we do not. We can stand a constant repeating of this fact. Christ is our righteousness, and Christ only. If you ask, in this sense, "What must we do to be righteous?" the answer is, "Nothing!"

Can we do *nothing* that is pleasing to God, that will make us righteous?" The answer is no.

"Does it not make us more righteous if we do good works?" The answer is no.

Our righteousness is perfect. Christ is our righteousness. Our own righteousness is nothing but unrighteousness. Christ is our righteousness. When the End of the Law came, He fulfilled it all for every one who believes.

If you ask, "Must I do nothing to be righteous?" I say that you must believe. On the one hand, the apostle limits those who are righteous. It was not the case that in the old dispensation all the Jews were righteous. They had to believe. At the same time, the apostle expands the sphere of the righteous. The same righteousness extends to all nations. It extends to all those who believe.

Faith is the power by which we strike our root into Christ and by which we draw out of Him all the blessings of salvation. Then we confess, "There is nothing in me. Christ is the only ground; all other ground is sinking sand." And by faith we confess that Christ is the end of the law for *me*.

Chapter Sixty-five

The Confession of the Righteousness by Faith

Romans 10:5-8
For Moses describeth the righteousness which is of the law, That the man which doeth those things shall live by them.

But the righteousness which is of faith speaketh on this wise, Say not in thine heart, Who shall ascend into heaven? (that is, to bring Christ down from above:)

Or, Who shall descend into the deep? (that is, to bring up Christ again from the dead.)

But what saith it? The word is nigh thee, even in thy mouth, and in thy heart: that is, the word of faith, which we preach.

In these words is a proof of the statement in verse 4 that Christ is the end of the law. This statement the apostle proves in the text from the Old Testament Scriptures. As we have seen, this statement that Jesus is the end of the law must not be explained as meaning that Christ terminated the law. Nor does it mean that Christ is the end of the period in which the law was the basis of righteousness in distinction from the dispensation of faith. Rather, the meaning is that the law had Christ in view. Christ is the end of the law in the sense that He was the object, the aim, the goal, to which the law pointed. The Jews might look at that end of the law and be saved. Now the apostle proceeds to prove this statement from Scripture. There is no difference of opinion about the passage containing the apostle's proof. All explain that it contains a proof of the statement that Christ is the end of the law.

However, there is quite a difference as to the sense of this proof. Interpreters differ according as they differ in their explanation of verse 4. There are those who explain that Christ ended the period in which the law served as the basis of righteousness and inaugurated the dispensation of righteousness by faith. They read the text this way: "Christ terminated the dispensation in which the law was the basis of righteousness. For Moses describeth the righteousness which is of the law, that the man which doeth those things shall live by them." That was the rule in the old dispensation, they say, but in the new dispensation the righteousness of faith speaks. It says, "The Word is nigh thee, and all you have to do is believe." According to this interpretation, we have a sharp contrast between the old dispensation, in which the law was the basis of righteousness, and the new dispensation, which is the dispensation of righteousness by faith.

But this interpretation is already in conflict with the context, as well as with the words of the text. When the apostle says, "The righteousness which is of faith speaketh on this wise, Say not in thine heart, Who shall ascend into heaven? . . . Or, Who shall descend into the deep?" it is evident that he is quoting Moses. Therefore, he is not speaking of a righteousness of faith in the new dispensation, but of a righteousness of faith in the old dispensation. The contrast, therefore, is not between the old dispensation and the new dispensation. The contrast is not between a righteousness of the law in the old dispensation and a righteousness of faith in the new dispensation.

Instead, the contrast is between the righteousness of the law and the righteousness of faith, both in the old dispensation *and* in the new dispensation. In the old dispensation there was a righteousness of the law [Lev. 18:5], but also a righteousness of faith [Deut. 30:10–14]. This contrast is the point of the quotation.

The language used here is rather difficult to grasp. I would paraphrase it as follows. Christ is the end that the law had in view. It is true that Moses described the righteousness of the law as consisting in this, that a man shall live if he perfectly obey that law, but remember, Moses also spoke of a righteousness of faith. The doctrine of righteousness by faith in Moses speaks in this way: "Do not say that it is impossible to become righteous! Do not say, 'Who shall ascend into heaven?' Or, 'Who shall descend into the deep?' as if it were impossible to be righteous, for the Word, that is, the Word of faith, is near. And that Word in the old dispensation is plainly preached: believe in the Lord Jesus Christ, and thou shalt be saved!" [10:4–9].

The One Who Confesses

"The righteousness which is of faith speaketh on this wise," the apostle says. It is, therefore, the righteousness of faith that speaks here, in distinction from the righteousness that is of the law. The apostle opposes these two sharply. On the one hand, there is *the righteousness of the law*; on the other hand, there is *the righteousness of faith*. There is a difference in presentation. The righteousness of faith is presented as speaking. But of the righteousness of the law Moses said something. Moses described what is required of a man who would be righteous by the law.

A man must be righteous to be saved. An unrighteous man cannot be saved. If a man is to be saved, he must be righteous. This cannot be changed. To be righteous, negatively speaking, is to be without sin. Positively, righteousness is to be in harmony with the will of God concerning us, which is the same as to be in harmony with God Himself. Righteousness is to be in harmony with God's precepts. It is not merely a formal, external harmony with the law; it is also an inward harmony with the law. The state of the heart is in harmony with the law of God.

What is *the righteousness of the law* in the text? *Law* here is the entire body of the Mosaic law. The text does not merely have reference to the moral law, the law of the ten commandments, although this is included, but it refers to the entire body of the Mosaic law as it was revealed to Israel through Moses.

The principle of the law was this: "Thou shalt love the Lord thy God with all thy heart, and with all thy mind, and with all thy soul, and with all thy strength, and thou shalt love thy neighbor as thyself." This is not the New Testament's interpretation of the law. Rather, this had been plainly revealed to the Jews in the Old Testament. The connection between this righteousness and the law is that the law is for us the source of that state in which God pronounces us righteous. The law, then, is the sole standard by which God judges us and pronounces us to be without sin. This is the righteousness of the law. It is the same as the righteousness of works.

Against this righteousness of the law stands *the righteousness of faith*. There is a difference here. The righteousness of faith speaks; the righteousness of the law does not speak. Moses says something about the righteousness of the law, whereas the righteousness of faith itself speaks. The question is, what is the righteousness of faith in contrast to the righteousness of the law?

Faith here, of course, is saving faith. This faith is always meant when Scripture speaks of the righteousness of faith. The righteousness of faith is the same righteousness as the righteousness of the law. It is that God judges us to be without sin. Faith is the power whereby the soul clings to Christ. It is that spiritual power, that gift of grace, whereby we cling to Christ so that we become one body with Him. We know Christ with the certain knowledge of faith, and we put all our confidence in Him as the God of our salvation. We know that He died for us and was raised again from the dead. We know that because of His death and resurrection we are righteous. This is the righteousness by faith.

The relation between righteousness and faith is important. First, faith is not the ground upon which God judges us to be righteous, for the ground of our righteousness is Christ. Remember, faith receives. It does nothing else but receive. Faith has nothing in itself. Faith looks always at Christ. We are not righteous because we believe. Second, in the expression *righteousness of faith,* faith must not be regarded as a power by which we can do good works and therefore become righteous. That is the Roman Catholic view. According to this view, Christ merited the right for us to do good works, and because of these good works we become righteous. But this cannot be, for then the comfort of the expression is gone. We must have in the expression *righteousness of faith* a perfect comfort, but if we must be saved by works, we cannot have a moment's rest.

The relation of faith and righteousness is this: faith is the source of righteousness because it takes righteousness out of Christ. The righteousness of faith is the righteousness of Christ for me.

The righteousness of faith speaks. The righteousness of the law says nothing. Moses says something about the righteousness of the law. What he says about the righteousness of the law makes it impossible for the righteousness of the law to say anything at all. If we must become righteous by the law, either salvation is hopeless, or we become Pharisees. Why? Because Moses describes the righteousness that is of the law in this way: the man who does those things shall live by them. The man who would become righteous by the law must do something. That which he must do must be perfect. He cannot say, "I went to church on Sunday, and therefore God will declare me righteous" if he does not serve God on Monday. He cannot say, "I never killed and therefore God will declare me righteous" if he commits adultery. If a man would become righteous by the law, he must keep the law perfectly. The law speaks on this wise: "Cursed is every one that continueth not in all things which are written in the book of the law to do them" [Gal. 3:10; Deut. 27:26]. But it is impossible to keep the law perfectly. We come into the world as violators of the law in that we are guilty of the disobedience of Adam. We are guilty to start with. Even if it were possible that we could keep the law perfectly all our life, the law could not wipe out that original guilt. The fact is that perfect obedience is impossible for us. Because of our corrupt nature, we can only increase our guilt. Moses' description of the righteousness of the law—that the man who doeth those things shall live by them—is at the same time the description of the impossibility of anyone's ever becoming righteous by the law.

This is not all that Moses had to say, however; there is also the speech of the righteousness of faith.

The Confession

The righteousness of faith says two things. Negatively, it confesses this: "Do not say, 'Who shall ascend into heaven?' Or, 'Who shall descend into the deep.'" Positively, it confesses this: "The word is nigh thee, even in thy mouth, and in thy heart." The language here brings to us what were stock expressions at that time. Every language has such stock expressions. If the Jews wanted to express that something was impossible, they would say, "Who shall ascend into heaven for us?" Or they would say, "Who shall descend into the deep?"—again expressing that something was impossible. That which is conceived as impossible is righteousness. It is impossible to be righteous. It is impossible to live.

The righteousness of faith, both in Moses' day and in the New Testament, speaks on this wise: "Say not in your heart, 'Who shall ascend into heaven?' Or, 'Who shall descend into the deep?' But say this: 'The Word is nigh thee, even in thy mouth, and in thy heart.'" The Word of God is the Word that brings a righteousness prepared for us, for Christ is its righteousness. This Word is near. How near? To whom is this righteousness of faith speaking? It is speaking to the believer. It says to the believer, "Do not say, 'Who shall ascend into heaven?' Or, 'Who shall descend into the deep?' But say, 'The Word is in thy mouth.'"

You say it, don't you? The church speaks; she confesses this.

But this Word is still nearer. It is in your heart. If you have this Word in your heart, do not say that it is impossible to be righteous. The Word is nigh, and this is sufficient.

This is significant not only for the Jews, but also for us, although it is true that the apostle is speaking specifically to the Jews. For their mistake was that they sought to become righteous with the righteousness of the law. But the *believing Jews* brought their sacrifices by faith in Christ.

The Ground of This Confession

Christ becomes the ground for this righteousness. The apostle gives two explanatory notes in verses 6 and 7 that make this plain. "Do not say, 'Who shall ascend into heaven?' for this," explains the apostle, "amounts to a *denial* of the ascension of Christ. And do not say, 'Who shall descend into the deep?' for this," explains the apostle, "amounts to a *denial* of Christ's descension." The fact is that Christ *did* descend. He *did* die. He *was* raised. He *did* ascend. And this is the Word of righteousness that we preach.

I know, when we look at ourselves, it is hard to believe. It is difficult to believe that we are righteous without works. We are inclined to look at ourselves, at our works. We are inclined to ask, "What have I done that is pleasing to God?" The answer is, "Nothing." Day by day, moment by moment, we are sinners. And then we begin to be afraid. And then we hear the righteousness of the law say, "Thou shalt love the Lord thy God with all thy mind, and heart, and soul, and strength." Then we tremble. And we say, "Who shall ascend into heaven or descend into the deep? Righteousness is impossible."

But then the Word comes, the Word of faith that is preached to you and to me. And this Word of faith says, "Do not talk this way; stop condemning yourselves; stop looking at the law. Do not say, 'Who shall ascend into heaven?' *Christ* did. Do not say, 'Who shall descend into the deep?' *Christ* did. Though your sins be as scarlet, they shall be white as snow."

Chapter Sixty-six

The Certain Salvation of the Confessing Believer

Romans 10:9
That if thou shalt confess with thy mouth the Lord Jesus, and shalt believe in thine heart that God hath raised him from the dead, thou shalt be saved.

The text gives the contents of the Word of faith of which the apostle had spoken in the immediately preceding verses. The Word of faith is the Word to which the righteousness of faith appeals and on the basis of which, righteousness of faith is established. The righteousness that is of the law had been described by Moses when he said that the man which doeth those things shall live by them. But the righteousness that is of faith speaks to the believer and says, "Do not say in your heart that it is a very remote possibility, or even an impossibility, to attain righteousness and life. Do not say in your heart, 'Who shall ascend into heaven?' Or, 'Who shall descend into the deep?' For that virtually would be to deny that Christ died, arose, and ascended into glory. But say this: 'The Word is nigh thee, even in thy mouth, and in thy heart.' This Word of faith that is in your heart is the realization of thy righteousness."

In the text we have the contents of this Word. The contents of the Word of faith is this: "If thou shalt confess with thy mouth the Lord Jesus, and shalt believe in thine heart that God hath raised him from the dead, thou shalt be saved."

His Faith

The object of the faith of the believer, which is described in the text as a way to salvation, is a fact. The text does not say that he who believes *in Christ* shall be saved, but the text mentions a fact: something took place. Our Christian belief is belief in a historic fact. That historic fact is presented as an act of God. Upon what God did, on that act of God, the faith of the believer relies. That act of God he believes. By believing that act of God, he is saved. That fact, which is the object of the believer's faith, is the resurrection of Christ. "If thou shalt believe in thine heart that God hath raised Jesus from the dead, thou shalt be saved." He who believes that fact, the apostle says, shall be saved. This is the Word of faith.

If you ask what this implies and what it means to believe in the heart that God raised Jesus from the dead, we must remember that the apostle is speaking of the Lord whom we confess. "If thou shalt confess with thy mouth the *Lord* Jesus," the apostle says. The confession that Jesus is Lord implies that you belong to Him. We may say, therefore, that he who believes in his heart that God raised Jesus from the dead confesses that He is Lord.

The emphasis falls on the resurrection of the Lord. This is also the heart of the apostles' preaching. They preached the resurrection of Christ. This is even far more the center of their preaching than the cross. If you will study the Acts of the Apostles, you will find that the heart of the apostles' preaching was the resurrection. But the resurrection does not stand alone, as an isolated fact, so that you can believe the resurrection, but not the rest of Christ. To believe the resurrection, you must believe the coming of Christ in the flesh. To believe the resurrection presupposes that we believe His death. It presupposes that we believe His death as the death of atonement. If one does not believe the atoning death of Christ, he cannot believe in the resurrection. If one does not believe the resurrection, he cannot believe that Christ is glorified. But the resurrection is mentioned as the object of our faith, inasmuch as it is the central act of God.

The resurrection was an act of God. The text does not say, "If you believe that Christ is risen." Emphatically, the apostle states, "He who believes that *God raised* Jesus from the dead." It was an act of God. God did something. And our faith clings ultimately to that act of God. The faith that saves clings to God, to His work. That act of God whereby He raised Jesus from the dead was the act by which He declared us righteous. It was an act of judgment. Christ and His church stood before God in the cross and in the resurrection. Standing before God, Christ and His church were justified. In this sense, the resurrection means that the judgment is past. Therefore, the apostle mentions the resurrection. "Say not in thine heart, 'Who shall ascend into heaven?' Or, 'Who shall descend into the deep?'" It is accomplished. The Word of faith in thy heart is the Word of righteousness. It is the righteousness that God prepared for you when He raised Jesus from the dead. "If you believe that God raised Jesus from the dead, you shall be saved."

The faith that believes the resurrection is faith of the heart. There is such a thing as mere intellectual faith. There is such a thing as mere head faith. It might easily happen that the apostle is understood as saying that if we have mere intellectual faith, the mere assent that God raised Jesus from the dead, we will be saved. There is such a thing. A man may believe, intellectually, that God created the world. That intellectual assent is possible. It is possible that a man believes intellectually, as he believes that Lincoln was assassinated. It is likewise possible, intellectually, to assent to the fact that Christ was raised. But that intellectual faith differs from saving faith in three respects. In the first place, the object of that intellectual faith is not "*my* Lord." Intellectual faith does not say, "God raised *my* Lord from the dead." It does not contain the *personal* element. The Word of the apostle contains a personal element.

In the second place, that mere assent to the truth does not contain the element of *confidence*. He who simply assents to the fact of the resurrection does not rely on the risen Lord. If one really believes, he relies on what he believes. If in a saving sense you believe that God raised Christ from the dead, you rely on that act of God as your righteousness. You say, "I rely on nothing else. I rely only on the fact that when God raised Christ from the dead, He justified me."

In the third place, intellectual faith differs from saving faith in this respect: intellectual faith has no effect on a man's life. In other words, he who has that mere intellectual assent to the truth does not *confess* the Lord Jesus.

To guard against mere intellectual faith, the text speaks of faith *in the heart*. The heart of man is the spiritual, ethical life-pump. Just as in a physical sense the heart is the life-pump, pumping the blood through the body, so in a spiritual sense the heart is the center of life from a spiritual, ethical point of view. Out of it are the issues of life in a certain direction. If your heart is worldly, your thinking is worldly, your willing is worldly, and your desiring is worldly. If your heart is worldly, all your life will be worldly. All your life is as your heart is. If the Word is near, if God brings the Word of faith into the heart, that heart believes. There are in this faith the elements of a certain knowledge and of heartfelt trust. Our heart believes; our whole being believes. With the heart we are certain and trust that God raised Jesus. Then He is our Lord. Then God justifies us. One believes in his heart, and that one will say, "Don't say in your heart, 'Who shall ascend into heaven?' Or, 'Who shall descend into the deep?' The Word is nigh you. He who believes shall be saved."

His Confession

There is something else that characterizes the way of salvation. One confesses with the mouth the Lord Jesus. Faith and confession are not two things. To confess with the mouth the Lord Jesus and to believe that God raised Him from the dead are not two separate elements of the way of salvation. These two belong together. They are inseparable. That which we confess, the apostle designates as the Lord Jesus. By this is meant that he who confesses Jesus is Lord shall be saved.

That Jesus is Lord must be understood in the widest sense. That Jesus is Lord means that He has power and authority over all things. He is Lord without any further limitations. When God raised Jesus from the dead, He gave Him power and authority over all things, so that He is Lord over heaven and earth. Jesus, the Savior, is Lord. He has power over angels, principalities, devils, men, and all powers in this world. He has power over life and death.

In a more specific sense, the fact that Jesus is Lord implies that there exists between Him and us a lordship of love. The church belongs to Him because He purchased it. He rules over it by the power of grace. By grace He makes the church ready to do His will, and the church delights to do His will.

To narrow it down to the personal aspect of saving faith, the confession that Jesus is Lord implies that Jesus has become *my* Lord. I acknowledge Him as my Lord. I say that I am not my own, but that I belong to my faithful Savior. I acknowledge that He has the right to lord it over me and to execute His will over me. I delight in doing His will. On His part, He is responsible for me. He will save me to the full.

If the Word is nigh you, the apostle says, you will confess this. You will confess this with the mouth. This is simple, you say. How shall we confess except with the mouth? But notice that the apostle emphasizes that this confession with the mouth is the expression of what lives in the heart. You say, "It is not necessary to say everywhere that Jesus is Lord, is it?" The apostle says, "If thou shalt confess with the mouth the Lord Jesus." You do not always have to say it in exactly that form, but you must confess this truth. The implication is that if we do not confess it, we must not imagine that the last part of the text is applicable to us. He who does not confess this denies it. There are only two alternatives: either we confess that Jesus is Lord, or we deny that He is Lord.

The apostle does not mean, of course, a mere "mouth-confession." There is a mere mouth-confession, but it disappears as soon as trouble comes. As soon as it will cost us our position, our job, our name, our honor, or our wealth, such a mouth-confession vanishes. Plainly, the apostle does not refer to this, because he brings that confession into connection with the second part of the text, namely, "he who believes that God raised Jesus from the dead." Confession that Jesus is Lord arises from faith in the heart.

To confess that Jesus is Lord is to insist that Christ shall be Lord over us in our whole life. In our whole life we acknowledge Him as Lord. When we pray, we say that Jesus is Lord. We confess this when we stand in the midst of the church and make confession of faith. When we make confession of faith, we really say, "Jesus is Lord." We say that Jesus is Lord in our home life. But also in our public life we confess Jesus as our Lord. We say it in labor, in business, in our profession, in our associations, in every relation into which we may enter. This is very serious. This implies that we never sign a contract, an agreement, that does not have in it that Jesus is Lord. We sometimes join a certain organization and mention that it is a neutral thing so that joining is not wrong. That is not the question. You must say in that organization that Jesus is Lord. The Christian must not go to places where it would sound crazy to say that Jesus is Lord. People sometimes ask, "May I do this, or may I go there?" You may go anywhere where you can confess that Jesus is Lord. But you must insist that Jesus be Lord there. If it is a place where you cannot say it, where it would sound crazy to say it, you don't belong there. You must insist that Jesus is Lord everywhere.

The meaning is not that you never fail to say it. The text means that if you do not confess, but knowingly and willingly deny that Jesus is Lord, you are on your way to hell. "If thou shalt confess with thy mouth the Lord Jesus, . . . thou shalt be saved" implies this: "If thou shalt *not* confess the Lord Jesus, thou shalt be damned." Of course it implies this!

His Salvation

In light of the text, the reality of salvation is plain. There is nothing sentimental about it. It does not consist of yielding to the plea, "Please accept Jesus." No. But if God brings the Word of faith in our heart, we believe. And if God brings the Word of faith in our mouth, we must speak. Therefore, the text is really the criterion for the Christian. If we want to know whether we shall be saved, we must be able to say, "Yes, I believe that God raised Jesus from the dead, and I confess that Jesus is Lord." Then we may say, "Although my conscience testifies against me, I shall be saved." He who believes that God raised Jesus, and confesses that He is Lord, is saved. He is justified. He has been regenerated, and in that regeneration he received all the blessings of salvation in principle.

But the apostle is not looking at salvation from this point of view. The question that he answers is this: who shall inherit eternal life? The righteousness of the law says, "The man which doeth those things shall live by them." But the righteousness that is of faith says, "If thou shalt confess with thy mouth the Lord Jesus, and shalt believe in thine heart that God hath raised him from the dead, thou shalt be saved." In other words, the apostle is looking at the future salvation. He is looking at the salvation in the day of the righteous judgment of God. He is looking at our salvation when we shall be snatched from death into life, and when we shall be glorified with Christ. We shall be saved. This is absolutely certain. If we believe that God raised Jesus from the dead, and if we confess the Lord Jesus, we shall be saved.

Why? Because we believe and confess? Not at all! It is not the case that faith becomes another work and confession another righteousness. There is no work in faith. There is no righteousness in confessing. But we become righteous in Christ. And we can have no access to Christ other than by the faith by which we cling to Him for righteousness.

Chapter Sixty-seven

The Universality of Salvation

Romans 10:11-13
For the scripture saith, Whosoever believeth on him shall not be ashamed.
For there is no difference between the Jew and the Greek: for the same Lord over all is rich unto all that call upon him.
For whosoever shall call upon the name of the Lord shall be saved.

The difference between the old and the new dispensations from the viewpoint of salvation is not that in the old dispensation righteousness was attainable through the works of the law, or even that the law was intended as a basis for righteousness. In the new dispensation, of course, righteousness is attainable by faith. The truth is that also in the old dispensation there was the revelation of the righteousness that is by faith. There was the righteousness that speaks on this wise: "Say not in thine heart, 'Who shall ascend into heaven?' Or, 'Who shall descend into the deep?'" There was the righteousness of which the content is, "He who believes in the Lord Jesus shall be saved." That righteousness was known in the old dispensation under the law as well as in the new dispensation, for Christ was the end of the law for righteousness in the old dispensation to every one who believed.

The difference between old and new dispensation lies in this: in the old dispensation, the truth of righteousness by faith was inseparably connected with the law, that is, the entire ceremonial law. Outside of that law, there was no revelation of the righteousness that is by faith. In that law of shadows, the righteousness of faith was foreshadowed. Outside of it, the righteousness of faith was not known. In the new dispensation, by contrast, the righteousness of faith has been revealed without the law. Let me put it this way. In the old dispensation they had the righteousness of faith wrapped up in the package of the law. And that package of the law, containing the righteousness of faith, was addressed to the Jews. Apart from that package of the law, there was no revelation of the righteousness of faith. But in the new dispensation, the package is opened; it is unwrapped, and the law fell away. What remained was the righteousness of faith. Because of this, the righteousness of faith became universal. It is no longer bound to the law. Because it is no longer bound to the law, it is no longer addressed to the Jews; it is addressed to men of every nation.

Universal in What Sense

It ought to be evident that universality is the point the apostle wants to stress [in the text]. Twice he uses the word *whosoever*. "*Whosoever* believeth on him shall not be ashamed," and "*Whosoever* shall call upon the name of the Lord shall be saved." *Whosoever* means everybody: everyone who believes on Him shall be saved. There is also the word *all*. The apostle uses *all* twice: "for the same Lord over *all* is rich unto *all*." There can be no question, therefore, that universality is the central thought of the text.

But the question is what is meant by that *whosoever* and by that *all*? What do we mean when we say that the text teaches that salvation has become universal? This can be determined only from the text and from its context. In Scripture *whosoever* and *all* do not always have the same context. We must ask what is the scope, the extent, of that *whosoever* and of that *all*? What is the distinction here? *All* in distinction from whom?

We find that the text does not teach that all men—everyone—will be saved. This is evident from the text. It says everyone who believes shall be saved. Everyone who calls on the name of the Lord shall be saved. This is also evident from the context. Verses 9 and 10 have taught that God promises salvation to everyone who believes and confesses.

Nor does the text mean to convey the idea that in the new dispensation salvation has become a matter of a certain "well-meant offer." In this case, it would teach that God offers salvation to all, with the gracious desire to save all, but that it is now up to man. This is contrary to all that the apostle has been teaching.

Rather, it is evident that by *whosoever* and *all* the apostle has in mind a distinction between the Jews and all other nations. The reference is to everyone from every nation in distinction from the Jews alone. This is plain from what the apostle says in verse 12: "There is no difference between the Jew and the Greek." Whosoever believes in Christ shall be saved, for there is no difference between the Jew and the Greek. *The Greek* stands for the entire Gentile world. The meaning is that there is no difference between the Jew and any other nation. If you ask what is the way of salvation, there is no difference between Jew and Greek. There is no difference in the new dispensation as to the way of their obtaining righteousness. In the old dispensation, there was a difference. Then it could *not* be said, "Whosoever believes shall be saved." Salvation at that time was distinctly Jewish. Salvation was wrapped up in the law. It was addressed to the Jews. Not that the Jews as a whole were saved. The Jews never were the people of God. Salvation for the Jews was not national. But the children of the promise were limited to the Jewish nation. Now this has changed. When the law fell away, when Christ, the end of the law, came, this was changed. Now we can say, "Whosoever believes in Christ shall be saved." In this sense salvation has become universal.

There is another limitation in the text. As in the old dispensation all Jews were not saved, so today all in the nations of the Gentile world are not saved. Salvation was certainly meant to be universal. And this was known. The people in the old dispensation could know that salvation was to be universal. "For the scripture saith, Whosoever believeth on him shall not be ashamed." Again, at the end of the text, "Whosoever shall call upon the name of the Lord shall be saved." At the same time, this *whosoever* contains a limitation. Salvation has become universal, but among the nations it is limited to those who believe and call upon the name of the Lord.

When the apostle says, "Whosoever believeth on him shall not be ashamed," he is quoting Isaiah [28:16]. *Him* in the text is not God but Christ. *Him* is the same as *Lord*. It is noteworthy that the apostle speaks of believing "*on* Him." We also read in Scripture of believing "*in* Him," or "*into* Him." But here we read of believing *on* Him. There is a difference. Essentially the meaning is the same, but there is a definite, important difference in connotation. Believing *in* Christ has the idea that we are united with Christ. To believe is to strike our roots into Christ. We believe *into* Christ as a tree strikes its roots deep into the soil and draws out of that soil its life-sap. As a tree draws its life-sap out of the soil, so the believer draws his life-sap out of Christ. To believe *on* Christ emphasizes the idea of confidence. Faith is also confidence. Faith is not only a certain knowledge, but it is also a hearty confidence. When we read in verse 11, "believeth *on* him," the idea is that Christ became the basis of that act of faith whereby we trust that we are righteous and shall be saved. This is confidence: believe *on* Him, and believing on Him, trust that you shall be saved. This is the emphasis in the verse: he who puts his trust on Christ shall be saved.

The apostle says more. In verse 13 we read, "Whosoever shall call upon the name of the Lord shall be saved." Also here the Lord is Christ. The *name* of Christ is Christ as He has been revealed to us. It is Christ as we know Him. It is Christ as we have contact with Him. Only in the name do we have contact with Christ. We cannot see Christ. We can only know Him in His name.

"Call on the name of the Lord" is a phrase frequently used in Scripture. The phrase is usually interpreted as worship. However, the phrase means something more specific. The meaning is that we cry out of the midst of trouble. This is the meaning in Joel [2:32], the passage that is quoted [in v. 13]. In Joel the day of the Lord is at hand, a day of fear, terror, and destruction. And then the prophet says, "Whosoever shall call on the name of the LORD shall be delivered." To call on the name of the Lord presupposes trouble. It presupposes sin, guilt, and the fear of death and hell. But the one who, out of trouble—out of sin, guilt, and death—shall call on Christ shall be saved.

There is no question about it: if we believe on Christ, we shall be saved. We have heard this often, but I wonder how real this central and fundamental truth is for us. If we believe on Him, if we trust on Christ for our salvation, we shall never be ashamed.

Do you say, "But if I consider myself, I can't believe that I can have a living part with this gospel"? There is no "but" to this gospel.

Do you say, "My sins are as scarlet"? That makes no difference to this gospel.

Do you say, "I would like to see a little more love, a little more zeal in my life"? That makes no difference to this gospel. That is not the question.

Do you say, "I sin over and over again"? That is not the question. He who puts his trust for his righteousness on Christ shall be saved. *That* is the sole question. If when you and I shall presently put our head on the death-pillow, and we shall have before us a long list of our sins and shall see that even our best works abounded with sins, then there is but one question that can remove all fear. That question is this: "Do I for my righteousness trust on Christ?" That is the question. Your works do not enter in. The apostle John was no more righteous when he died than the murderer on the cross.

What Is Universal

What is universal is expressed in the words *shall be saved*. Negatively, to be saved is to be delivered from our greatest evil.

Our greatest evil is our sin: our guilt, our corruption, and our fear of death and hell. To be saved is to be delivered from that guilt, from that death, from that hell. Positively, salvation is to become partakers of perfect righteousness, righteousness in both the legal and the moral sense, and heirs of eternal glory.

When one believes and calls on the name of the Lord, he is already saved. If we believe on Christ, we are already saved. If we believe, we are delivered from sin, death, and corruption. This is a present reality. This cannot fail, because the grace of God is always first. If we believe and call on the name of the Lord, grace preceded this faith. But the apostle has in mind the final salvation. When he says, "shall be saved," he has in mind the end. He has in mind the judgment. In that judgment we shall be justified and shall inherit the heavenly glory. He who believes in Christ *shall be* saved.

What is universal is also indicated, negatively, by the words *shall not be ashamed*. This is beautiful. If we put our confidence on Christ, we shall not be ashamed. If we put our confidence on anything else, we shall be ashamed, but if we put our confidence on Christ, we shall never be ashamed. When we expect something and the time comes when we should receive it, but we find that what we expected is not there, or that it is not for us, or that it is so insignificant that it is not worthwhile, we are put to shame. The Christian puts his confidence on Christ. Doing this, he expects righteousness, holiness, eternal life, and heavenly glory. And he finds, first, that it is there. Second, he finds that it is for him. Third, when he receives it, he will not say, "How insignificant!" Rather, he will say, "I had not imagined the half of it!" We shall not be ashamed!

Why It Is Universal

The apostle points out why salvation is universal in the new dispensation when he writes, "The same is Lord over all, and He is rich unto all." Isn't this beautiful? The same Lord over all is rich unto all. Also here, the Lord who is over all is Christ, not God. Commentators are divided as to whether *Lord* refers to God. I do not think so, because this could never be the ground for the universality of salvation. If the reference is to God, the expression simply means that the Lord is God of all creatures. But it would not mean that He is Savior of all nations. Besides, also in the old dispensation it was true that the Lord was God over all. But the apostle means to teach here that because He is Lord over all, salvation is become universal. Therefore, the text means that *Christ* is Lord over all. He was not Lord over all, but He *became* Lord over all. The seed was cast into the ground, died, and was raised. Thus, He was made Lord over all. He is Lord of us. He is Lord of His own because He purchased us. Christ is over all in His present state. He was out of the Jews. He was out of the seed of Abraham, the tribe of Judah, the house of David. When He lay in the manger, He was a Jew. He died. He died for His own. And He was raised, exalted to the right hand of God. And when He is at the right hand of God, He is no more a Jew. He is Lord of all. Don't let anyone tell you that He is Lord of the Jews. He never was, and He never will be. He is Lord over all. He is the universal Lord. You must not make Christ a Jew. You must not make Him a Jewish king. There is no difference between Jew and Gentile. Christ is Lord over all.

He is also *rich* unto all. Christ is rich. He is a rich Lord. He merited riches through His death. He received these riches in the resurrection. His riches consist of righteousness, forgiveness of sin, deliverance from death, and heavenly glory. He is rich unto all who call upon His name. He is not rich unto all, however. Some like to say that Christ's riches are sufficient for all men. I don't believe it. Christ is not rich to everyone. He is rich unto all who call upon His name. This is sufficient. They who call on the name of Christ are the same as those who believe on Him. They are presented here as coming out of trouble and asking for something. They ask for forgiveness of sin, for righteousness, for life, for heavenly glory. And the Lord is rich. His riches are sufficient for all who call upon His name.

~ The Universality of Salvation

In addition, He actually realizes these riches in all who call upon Him.

The conclusion is that no one calls upon the name of the Lord in vain. This is enough. Ask, and it shall be given unto you. "Him that cometh to me I will in no wise cast out" [John 6:37]. You will never come empty-handed to Christ and be sent empty-handed away. Blessed is he who puts his trust in Christ for righteousness.

Chapter Sixty-eight

The Mission of the Preacher

Romans 10:14, 15

How then shall they call on him in whom they have not believed? and how shall they believe in him of whom they have not heard? and how shall they hear without a preacher?

And how shall they preach, except they be sent? as it is written, How beautiful are the feet of them that preach the gospel of peace, and bring glad tidings of good things!

There are in the text especially two main elements. Ultimately they can be reduced to one truth. In the first place, the apostle shows that in the new dispensation the preaching of the gospel must be as universal as is salvation itself. In the old dispensation there was no need of universal preaching, and in a sense there was no preaching. Insofar as there was preaching, it was limited to the Jews. Salvation in the old dispensation came in a wrapper; it was wrapped up in a package. The wrapper was the Mosaic law, and the wrapper had an address on it. It was addressed to the Jews. Israel could know what was in that package. The content of the package was transparent through the wrapper. Israel could look through the wrapper and see the righteousness which is by faith inside the package.

But when Christ came, who was the end of the law, to whom the law pointed, and who could therefore be seen in that law, the wrapper was torn off; the package was then thrown away. All that was left was the righteousness that is by faith. It no longer contained an address; that is, it no longer contained a national address. But whosoever calls upon the name of the Lord shall be saved. There is no difference between Jew and Greek.

In the text the apostle continues, and he proves that for this reason also, the preaching of the gospel must be universal. "How then shall they call on him in whom they have not believed?" Faith is first. "How shall they believe in him of whom they have not heard?" Hearing is essential to believing. "How shall they hear without a preacher?" Preaching is essential to hearing.

We have in verse 15 the second element, namely, that there is no preaching without sending: "How shall they preach, except they be sent?"

The Preacher

It is certainly not superfluous to have our attention called to the scriptural teaching as to what constitutes a preacher. Today everybody preaches, except those who should. Today women and children preach. Almost anybody preaches in our day. When people want someone to play on the emotions, they call in some preacher. It makes no difference whether the preacher is a woman or a child if only she can play upon the emotions.

But this is impossible. In the first part of the text, Paul says, "How shall they call on him in whom they have not believed?" Then he adds, in our translation, "How shall they believe in him of whom they have not heard?" This translation is incorrect, however. It is only an error of a little word of two letters, but this little error makes a world of difference as to the meaning. In the original, the text does not read, "*of* whom they have not heard." Very differently it reads, "*whom* they have not heard." You can hear *of* someone. This implies that the one of whom you hear is not there. You do not hear that person. You hear about him. But when you hear *him,* you hear that person himself. This is quite different. As the hymn has it, "I heard the voice of Jesus say, 'Come unto Me and rest.'" This is something quite different than saying, "I know that the voice of Jesus says, 'Come unto Me and rest.'"

A preacher is not one who speaks about Christ. Anyone can do that. Anyone can speak about Christ. A preacher is a man through whom it pleases *Christ* to speak. This is quite different. Therefore, when Christ speaks through the preacher, you do not say, "I have heard a nice sermon." That is not the point. If you want entertainment, you might as well go to a movie theater. It is no more pious to hear a nice sermon for entertainment than it is to go to a movie theater. But when you have really been under the preaching, and have heard it, you say, "I heard the voice of Jesus say, 'Come unto Me and rest.'"

This is why not just anybody can say, "I want to be a preacher." If Scripture teaches that Christ does not speak through a woman, a woman can never preach. If Christ does not speak through a man, he cannot preach. "How shall they believe in him *whom* they have not heard?" This is Scripture throughout.

Christ is officebearer in the church. His is that work, committed to Him by the Father, to gather His own. It never becomes our work. To gather Christ's flock is not the work of man. It is absolutely the work of Christ. Jesus says, "I, if I be lifted up from the earth, will draw all men unto me" [John 12:32]. When it pleases Christ to gather His flock, when He causes His voice to be heard through a man, then you have a preacher. The apostle says in II Corinthians 5[:20], "We are ambassadors for Christ, as though God did beseech you by us: we pray you in Christ's stead, be ye reconciled to God."

From this it follows, first, as to the content of the preaching, that it must be nothing else but the Word of Christ. Christ does not speak through anything else but His own Word. We read in II Corinthians 5[:18, 19] that Christ has put the Word in the apostles, and they take it with them. Just as when the government sends a messenger to a foreign country with a message, that messenger takes that word with him, so Christ gives His Word to the preacher, and he takes it with him. The preacher has no message of his own. As soon as he comes with a word of his own, he is no longer a preacher. Just as when a messenger is sent to a foreign country, he may bring nothing else but the message from his government, so a preacher must not preach anything outside of the Word of Christ. If he comes with anything outside of the Word of Christ, he is no preacher. And if he does so under the cloak of a preacher, he is a liar, too. A preacher who brings anything but the Word of Christ is a liar and a fake. Christ speaks only through His own Word.

It follows, second, that the content of the preaching must be nothing but the Word concerning *Christ.* The apostle writes in the text that the preacher brings the gospel of peace; he brings glad tidings of good things. He preaches the *word of faith,* as the apostle describes it in the context [v. 8]. The word of faith is that a man is justified by the righteousness of God in Christ, without works. The gospel of peace is that God has blotted out our sins. And the glad tidings are all those things that have for their contents all the blessings of salvation.

This is all that the preacher has to bring: glad tidings of good things. He may bring these glad tidings, that gospel of peace, in different forms. But he may not preach about other things. He may look at other things. He may look at social problems, he may look at economic depression when he brings these good tidings, but he may not preach about depression. He is a preacher only when he brings good tidings.

For the same reason, the preacher must *preach.* The word for preaching in the Greek means "to speak as a herald, as a messenger." As far as the form is concerned, this means that the preacher must simply bring his message. He must bring his message with the authority of the Word of Christ. He must not come with this message and say, "Won't you please accept it?" This is contrary to the idea of preaching. The preacher must say, "Thus saith the Lord." That is all. Just as an ambassador has no business explaining his message and saying, "Won't you please accept it?" so anyone who claims to be a preacher may not say anything but "This is the Word of Christ!"

As to the power of the preaching, it all depends on Christ's speaking through the preacher. The preacher must not try to play on the emotions of his hearers. The so-called "altar call" is no preaching. When a preacher calls people to come to the altar and says, "Won't you please come?" he is no preacher. He must bring good tidings; he must bring the gospel of peace, and that is the end of it. The power of the preaching depends on the power of the exalted Christ speaking through the Word.

People sometimes say that the preacher was too doctrinal, or that it was a nice sermon. But this is not the question. The question is, "Did you hear in the preaching the Word of Christ?" No preaching has any power unless Christ at that same moment takes hold of your heart and says, "I speak to you."

His Mission

This is why it is necessary that the preacher be *sent*. Preaching without sending is impossible. That this is so is evident if we consider that preaching is nothing but the authoritative bringing of the gospel of peace. Let me use the illustration of an ambassador once more. Suppose that two men know of a message from the government to a foreign power. Let us say that it is a declaration of war. One is delegated to bring that message to the foreign government, but the other one gets there ahead of him and informs the foreign government of that message. Would not the foreign government ask him if he had authority to say what he did? So it is with the preaching. One who would be a preacher must be sent. Again, because Christ pleases to speak through the Word of the preacher, it stands to reason that only through him whom He sends will He speak His own Word.

To be sent is, first, to receive the official commission to speak the Word of Christ. Second, it means that the preacher receives the promise that Christ will speak through him. Third, the meaning is that the preacher must speak where Christ sends him. How shall they preach unless they receive the commission? How shall they preach unless they have the promise that Christ will speak His own Word through them? How shall they preach unless they serve in the station where Christ puts them?

Unless Christ speaks though the preacher, there is no preaching. This is why our fathers distinguished between preaching and speaking "an edifying word."[1] This is why the apostle always emphasized that he was sent to preach. Christ sent him. He had the promise that Christ would speak His Word through him. And Christ sent him wherever He would.

Today the sending of the preacher differs in form, but not essentially. The preacher today is not sent directly by Christ, as were the apostles. Today Christ does not call the preacher directly. But the truth of verse 15 applies to preachers today: "How shall they preach, except they be sent?" When He ascended into heaven, Christ gave this commission: "Go ye to all nations and preach the gospel, and I will be with you unto the end of the world" [Compare Matt. 28:18–20 and Mark 16:14–18]. It is evident that Christ gave this commission to the apostles. But it is also evident that in the apostles Christ gave this commission to the church. Christ could not have told the apostles to go to every nation and preach the gospel. He could not have told them that He would be with them to the end of the world. Christ gave that commission to the church, in the apostles. He did not give it to everybody. He gave it to the church. Christ gave to the church the ministry of the Word. He did this in order that the church might have the commission to preach through the ministry. It is not the minister who preaches. The church preaches. Only when he is called though the church has the preacher the right to occupy his place as a minister. We must understand this. If the church does not have the promise that Christ will speak His Word

---

1. In the Reformed tradition, seminarians speak only "an edifying word."

though the preacher, there is no preaching. Therefore, if anyone should be inwardly persuaded that he is called to be a preacher, he should bear in mind that he can never be certain that he is called until the church has called him outwardly. Only when Christ calls though the church do we have the calling and the sending. Only in this way do we have preaching. "How shall they preach, except they be sent?"

His Importance

"And how shall they hear without a preacher?" In these words, Scripture makes salvation dependent upon the preaching. There is no doubt about this. The apostle shows the importance of the preaching in a threefold way. In the first place, he says, "How then shall they call on him in whom they have not believed?" To call on Him is not merely to worship Him, but according to the prophet Joel, whom the apostle quotes here, it is to call on Christ for help out of the midst of trouble [Joel 2:32]. Our trouble is our sin, our corruption, our death. To call on Him is to cry for help. And the apostle says that those who call on Him shall be saved. But this calling on Christ is impossible unless they believe. Faith is first. By faith we see our trouble. Seeing our trouble, we call on Christ for help.

In the second place, the apostle says, "How shall they believe in him whom they have not heard?" To believe is to trust, to confide in. To believe on Him is to rely on Him for righteousness. But how can anyone so believe on Christ if he has not heard Him? Hearing is not to hear something *about* Him. It is to hear *Him,* to hear Him in the personal sense that He has spoken to you. The question is, did you hear Him speak to you? Your righteousness, your justification, your salvation do not depend upon the word of man. You must be able to say, "I heard Christ speak to me." It is this calling that causes faith.

In the third place, we cannot hear unless there be preaching. "How shall they hear without a preacher?" Without a preacher it is impossible to hear Christ. Perhaps you say, "Yes, that may have been true at the time of the apostles, for the heathen world. But that is no longer true for us. We have our Bibles. At the time of the apostles, they did not have Bibles. We have all kinds of tracts. It is not necessary anymore to have a preacher in order to hear Christ."

If you mean that it is not necessary to have a preacher to know *about* Christ, what you say is true. But if you are really saying, "I can just as well stay at home on Sunday and read my Bible and have my own spiritual gatherings," you contradict Christ. You can baptize your child at home and eat bread and drink wine at home, but if your child does not receive more than water, and if you receive no more than bread and wine, you do not receive Christ. And if you have edifying gatherings, you do not hear the Word of Christ. You hear *about* Him, but you do not hear *Him*.

Therefore, let us rather hear the Word of the text and say, "How beautiful are the feet of them that preach the gospel of peace, and bring glad tidings of good things!" How beautiful are the feet; that is, how welcome are they who preach the gospel of peace, not because of what they are personally, but because Christ speaks through them.

Chapter Sixty-nine

The Hearing of the Preaching

Romans 10:16-18

But they have not all obeyed the gospel. For Esaias saith, Lord, who hath believed our report?

So then faith cometh by hearing, and hearing by the word of God.

But I say, Have they not heard? Yes verily, their sound went into all the earth, and their words unto the ends of the world.

In these words the apostle returns once more to the main theme of this section of the epistle to the Romans, that is, to the question why many of the Jews are not saved. This subject had been introduced in the beginning of chapter 9, and its discussion is continued in this chapter from a slightly different point of view. When the text states that "they have not all obeyed the gospel," the reference is once more chiefly to the Jews. In the new dispensation there is no difference between Jew and Gentile. The same Lord is rich unto all that call upon Him. In that sense of the word, salvation is not particularistic but universal, and so is the preaching. But even though this is all true, very many of the Jews are not saved. They have not all obeyed the gospel. The apostle expresses himself mildly, euphemistically, for there were *many* who had not obeyed the gospel. In fact, the majority of them who heard the report of the preaching had not believed, as is evident, too, from the quotation from Isaiah's prophecy that appears in this passage.

~ *The Hearing of the Preaching*

Of course, this is true with respect to the Gentiles who hear the glad tidings of salvation proclaimed by the preacher as well as of the Jews. Always it is true, wherever and whenever the gospel is preached, that "they have not all obeyed" it. Yet the apostle is, no doubt, thinking especially of the effect of the preaching of the gospel upon the Jews and therefore returns to the main theme of this whole section once more.

The text is somewhat difficult to understand, even though on the surface it may appear rather lucid. Even the translation is not easy, and the rendering we have in our English Bible does not really do justice to the original text. The same Greek word occurs three times in this passage but is translated by two different English words, once by *report* and twice by *hearing*. In English *report* and *hearing* are closely related but do not have the same denotation. The relation is that a *report* is *heard,* or is at least audible. But the term *report* looks at the matter from the viewpoint of the speaker, the *reporter,* in this case the preacher; while *hearing* denotes the same thing from the viewpoint of the activity of the listeners. The root of this difficulty must be found in the fact that in Isaiah 53:1 the word that is translated *report* in our English Bible, in the Hebrew is derived from the verb "to hear." In the Hebrew, therefore, a report or sermon is "a thing that is heard." It looks at the *report* both from the viewpoint of the speaker and of the hearer. When the same word occurs three times in such close connection as it does here, it ought to be rendered by the same term in English, if at all possible. This is possible if we use the term *the thing that is heard* every time, meaning "the word, or preaching that is heard." This includes both the speaking and the hearing and combines them into one whole. They supplement each other. Without the speaking, there is nothing to be heard; without the hearing, the speaking is vain. Therefore, we render the text as follows: "But they have not all obeyed the gospel. For Esaias saith, Lord, *who* hath believed *the thing that is heard* from us? So then, faith cometh out of *the thing that is heard,* and *the*

483

thing that is heard through the word of God." Only when the preaching is heard can belief be the result, but preaching is heard only through the Word of God.

What Is Heard

The apostle is still speaking of the preaching as an indispensable requisite unto salvation. That the preaching and the preacher are necessary unto salvation he had emphasized in the immediate context. For all they, and they only, who call upon Him shall be saved. But how shall they call upon Him in whom they have not believed? And how shall they believe on Him whom they have not heard? And how shall they hear without a preacher? And how shall they preach except they be sent? In order, therefore, to believe on Him, one must hear Him. One must not merely hear all about Him, but he must hear *Him,* His own Word, the Word of God, the Word of Christ.

In the present passage the apostle positively asserts that the fruit of this hearing of the Word of God, or of Christ, is faith. Faith is out of the Word that is heard. The apostle does not say that this *may be* the result, while it may also fail to produce this result. He does not represent the matter as contingent upon the attitude of man, as if it depended upon the choice of his will whether or not he will meet "the Word that is heard" with faith. He does not say that faith is the indispensable condition unto hearing the Word of God. No, he very definitely declares here that faith is the result, the fruit. The inevitable effect is belief. The thing heard is the cause; belief is the effect. Wherever there is "the thing heard," faith is produced, for faith is out of the thing that is heard, and the thing heard is through the Word of God.

What the thing is that is heard and that so surely produces faith as its fruit, verse 15 plainly identifies as the gospel. "How beautiful are the feet of them that preach the gospel of peace, that bring glad tidings of good things" [quoted from Isa. 52:7]. This gospel is the subject in verse 16: "But they have not all obeyed the gospel." The gospel had been *reported* by Isaiah, and the sound and words of them that preach that gospel had gone out into all the earth and unto the ends of the world (v. 18). The gospel had been preached from the beginning. God had revealed it in paradise when He promised that He would put enmity between the serpent and the woman, and between his and her seed, and that the seed of the woman, though it would be in the way of suffering, would have the victory [Gen. 3:15]. In the fulness of time He had spoken to His people through the Son, who in His incarnation, His cross and resurrection, His exaltation and pouring out of the Holy Spirit, is at the same time the realization of the gospel of peace. Now the feet of them that bring the glad tidings of good things move swiftly in every direction to carry that gospel into every land and to all the nations of the world.

The gospel is a wonderful message, for its contents is the promise. It is a Word of God concerning His Son, a Word that contradicts and overcomes all our experience in this present world. In this world the wrath of God is revealed from heaven over all ungodliness and unrighteousness of men. All our experience loudly speaks of sin and corruption, of damnation and death. But the gospel is the light in this darkness. It is the Word of God that speaks of righteousness in the midst of unrighteousness, that brings to us the assurance of the forgiveness of sin, of the adoption unto children, of joy and hope. It conveys to us the message of life in the midst of this present death, of the resurrection to overcome all mortality and corruption, of beauty for ashes and glory for shame. It is, indeed, the glad tidings of good things!

This gospel is the *report,* the thing that is heard.

The thing that is heard, and the fruit of which is faith, is not the report by men, but the Word of God. The "preaching that is heard" is not merely the external preaching of the gospel, not even the Scriptures that are the infallible record of that Word of God, but emphatically the Word of God Himself. The Scriptures are, indeed, the Word of God in the sense that they are the infallible record of the revelation of God concerning His Son, and all preaching must have these Scriptures for its contents. But without anything further, there is no *preaching that is heard* in the saving sense of the word, nor can it be said that a report of men and by men, even though it derived its contents from the Scriptures, could ever produce faith. The apostle writes that faith is out of the thing that is heard, but he adds, "and hearing," or rather, "the thing that is heard [is] *through the Word of God.*" By this last phrase the apostle is not referring to the Scriptures, nor to the mere external proclamation of the gospel by men, but to the living and mighty Word that God Himself speaks through the Spirit of our Lord Jesus Christ. Without this almighty and quickening Word of God, speaking to us through the gospel and dogmatically known among us as the efficacious calling, there is no "preaching that is heard" that produces in us the activity of lively and saving faith. The thing that is heard is through the Word of God.

God speaks His own Word. He does so in creation. Through the Word of God the things that are not, are called as if they were. Similarly, God speaks His Word of salvation in Christ— a Word of life, of righteousness, of forgiveness, of eternal glory. He spoke that Word centrally in Christ, and through Christ in His prophets and servants of the old dispensation, and in His apostles of the new dispensation. He sent them, and they preached. They *reported* that Word. God preserved the contents of that Word of salvation through infallible inspiration in the Scriptures. Still today there are preachers who are sent. These preachers are absolutely bound to the Scriptures. The contents of their *report* they can and may derive from that infallible Word of God only.

But if nothing more took place, would there be *preaching that is heard?* Would there be repentance and faith? Never! Through the Scriptures, through the report of the preacher, God must speak His own Word of grace and mercy, of forgiveness and righteousness, of adoption unto children and eternal life, of repentance and faith, through His Spirit, in your and my heart. Then, and then only, is there a report that is heard. Then, and then only, the result is faith; for faith is out of the preaching that is heard, and preaching that is heard is through the almighty, irresistible, efficacious Word of God!

An instance is Peter's marvelous report on the day of Pentecost [Acts 2]. He preached a sermon that even a few moments earlier he would not have been able to preach. God made a preacher out of him. Through the Spirit of Christ that had been poured out that very hour, God had spoken His Word to Peter. He filled him with His Word of salvation. God said to him, "Preach, Peter," and he preached. He could not have resisted that Word of God. It became an overpowering impulse in Him. The report that issued from Peter's mouth at that moment came through the Word of God.

What must be noted is that the report of Peter became preaching that is heard. Men were "pricked in their hearts." They were amazed. They saw their sin. They looked for a way of escape. They asked, "Men and brethren, what shall we do?" They repented. They saw the light of salvation. Three thousand believed and were baptized. There was preaching that is heard.

Is the explanation that Peter was such a mighty revivalist? Was he powerful to move the hearts and consciences of men, so that they repented and were saved? Or was it, perhaps, the mere content of his word—the fact that he reported the Word of God—that produced this amazing effect? It was neither one. God through the Spirit of Christ spoke His own Word through the preaching of Peter. The audience heard the Word *of God!* God said to them, "You have crucified the Lord of glory, and I have made Him Lord and Christ! Repent! Believe! Be baptized. And I will forgive you all your iniquities!" And that Word of God they heard.

God speaks His Word through the preaching still today. The preacher who is sent brings the good tidings of the gospel. He preaches the Word of God as it is found in the holy Scriptures. Through the preaching it pleases God by the Spirit of the Lord

Jesus Christ to speak His own Word, to call efficaciously whom He will. Because He does this also among us, we have preaching that is heard.

Suppose this were not true. Suppose that when the congregation gathered for worship, God Himself would not speak His efficacious Word to us. What would our assembly and what would our ministry amount to? We would not hear the Word of God unto salvation. We would hear the sound of the minister's voice. We would judge his word—like it or dislike it, be entertained or annoyed, agree or disagree, be pleased or filled with disgust, or assume an attitude of indifference. But we would not fear and tremble. We would not repent and believe. We would not hear the *Word of God* addressed to our inmost heart.

Such is not the ministry of the Word, however. Through the preaching God speaks. When God speaks, all criticism ceases, and with fear and trembling we bow before the Word of Him who calleth the things that are not, as if they were. When He says, "Repent," we do repent. When He says, "Believe," we do believe. When He speaks through the preaching, there is the report that is heard, for through the living Word of God is the preaching that is heard.

How It Is Heard

Thus is explained the fact that while the preaching of the Word is promiscuous and the gospel is proclaimed by the preacher to all who are within his reach, yet through the preaching, God is merciful to whom He will be merciful, and whom He will He hardens. Thus is explained that while the gospel is preached universally, so that the same sound of the same Word of God reaches all, some do not obey the gospel. The apostle is still considering this matter, especially as it concerns Israel: "But they have not all obeyed the gospel." This refers primarily to the unbelieving Jews. They had not attained to the righteousness that is by faith under the old dispensation, when Christ was revealed through the shadows, when the blessing of righteousness was wrapped up in the law and addressed to the Jew only. Also many of them had not obeyed the gospel when it was preached openly and universally to all nations. But this is always and everywhere applicable. Wherever the gospel is preached, these words are a correct summary of the fruit of the preaching: "But they have not all obeyed the gospel." This is a very sad and bitter experience for any preacher.

Why do not all obey the gospel?

Have they not heard?

One might answer, "Yes and no." There is a twofold hearing, even as there is a twofold fruit of the preaching of the gospel. There is a hearing of obedience, and there is a hearing of disobedience. There is a hearing unto salvation, and there is a hearing unto damnation. There is a hearing unto conversion, and there is a hearing unto hardening. Even the latter is a hearing of the gospel. The apostle speaks of this in verse 18: "But I say, Have they not heard? Yes verily, their sound went into all the earth, and their words unto the ends of the world." In these words there is a reference to Psalm 19. The words of that psalm are here applied to the preaching of the gospel. The apostle does not really quote the words, as if he intended to say that in the psalm they refer to the Word of the gospel. In the psalm the reference is to the Word of God in creation, for we read, "The heavens declare the glory of God; and the firmament sheweth his handiwork. Day unto day uttereth speech, and night unto night sheweth knowledge. There is no speech nor language, where their voice is not heard. Their line is gone out through all the earth, and their words to the end of the world. In them hath he set a tabernacle for the sun" (vv. 1–4). But the apostle applies those words to the universal preaching of the gospel. Just as the Word of God in creation is heard everywhere, so that one cannot escape its sound, so in the new dispensation the sound of the gospel is heard everywhere, among all nations and in every tongue. No one can escape its sound. One may attend church or refuse to attend, but he cannot escape the sound of the preaching.

It may not be overlooked that the apostle here writes, "their *sound*" and "their *words.*" It is the sound and the words that all hear. The hearing of verse 18 is different from that mentioned in verse 17. The passage does not teach that the preaching that is heard, out of which faith cometh, is universal. God does not speak His almighty Word of grace and salvation to all who hear the sound of the gospel. In this case, God would speak His efficacious Word unto salvation to *all* who hear the sound of the gospel, but this Word of God produces the fruit of faith only in some, while in others it remains barren. The well-known "first point" of common grace adopted by the Christian Reformed Church in 1924 presents a view very similar to this. It teaches that through the preaching, God is gracious to all who hear the gospel.[1] If one who believes this still wants to keep up the pretension of being Reformed, maintaining that God efficaciously calls unto salvation whomever He will, he is confronted with an insoluble problem. How could God in grace direct His Word to any sinner without causing it to be efficacious unto repentance and faith? How then could that efficacious Word of God

---

1. The first point, as translated by the author from the Christian Reformed Church's *Acta der Synode 1924*, Art. 132 in his book *The Protestant Reformed Churches in America: Their Origin, Early History and Doctrine* (Grand Rapids: First Protestant Reformed Church of Grand Rapids, [1936]), 84, reads as follows: "Regarding the first point, touching the favorable attitude of God toward mankind in general and not only toward the elect, synod declares that according to Scripture and the Confession it is established, that besides the saving grace of God shown only to the elect unto eternal life, there is also a certain favor or grace of God which He shows to His creatures in general. This is evident from the Scripture passages that were quoted and from the Canons of Dordt, II, 5 and III/IV, 8, 9, where the general offer of the gospel is set forth; while it also is evident from the citations made from Reformed writers belonging to the most flourishing period of Reformed theology that our fathers from of old maintained this view."

fail to effect the fruit of faith in the sinner who is so called? Small wonder that they who try to maintain this dilemma seek refuge in the theory that two contradictory statements constitute a "mystery," readily accepted by faith!

The apostle teaches no such thing. He merely explains that there are two kinds of hearing: the one saving, the other not. The one is the hearing of the gospel through the Word of God unto salvation, the thing that is heard and that produces faith. The other is the hearing of the sound of the gospel as it comes by the mouth of man, the hearing of the *words* of the gospel as they are proclaimed by the preacher. To be sure, that sound of the gospel, that word of the preacher, conveys to all hearers the content of the Word of God. It brings to them the demand to repent and to believe. The natural man hears the sound and understands the word, but he does not receive it, heed it, or obey it, for he is by nature in darkness, dead in sin, foolish, disobedient. He minds the things of the flesh. He is not subject to the law of God, neither indeed can be. He hears in the preaching of the gospel the word of a man. And when a man brings to him the Word of God, he does not tremble, humble himself, or repent. The sound may disturb his peace of mind for a moment, but sorrow after God he knows not. When Isaiah brought his report, they hated him for it. When Christ preached the gospel to them, they crucified Him. When the gospel was preached to all nations, they persecuted the apostles. But their sound went out into all the earth, nevertheless, and their words to the ends of the world.

In this sense of the word, the listeners all heard, but they did not all obey the gospel. Even this is no accident. That they did not obey the gospel did not defeat the purpose of God. The apostle quotes from the prophecy of Isaiah [53:1] and thus places the fact that some did not obey the gospel in the light of God's purpose: "For Esaias saith, Lord, who hath believed our report?" Long before the coming of Christ, centuries before the new dispensation when the gospel would be preached to all nations, Isaiah saw the suffering of Christ and also "the glory that should follow" [I Pet. 1:11], but he also prophesied that many would not believe the report of these things. God's purpose is never defeated. It is realized when the preaching that is heard bears fruit in repentance and faith, but it is realized as well when the sound of the gospel goes forth into all the earth, and the words of the preachers unto the ends of the world, and when some, even many, do *not* obey the gospel. Whether the gospel shall be obeyed or not, does not, in the last instance, depend upon the will of man. By nature and of himself, no man can hear and obey the Word of God. When the sound of the gospel goes forth into the earth, there is a twofold operation of God upon them that hear this sound. On the one hand, there is an operation of the Almighty upon the heart and mind of sinful man whereby he becomes hardened and blinded; on the other hand, there is the operation of God's irresistible grace, so that His Word is heard unto salvation, and faith is the fruit.

The Result of the Hearing

This does not change the fact that man is a rational and moral being, nor does it violate his responsibility over against the Word of God that comes to him even through the sound of the gospel. The fact remains that the natural man disobeys the gospel. This is emphasized in the text. It does not say that they have not all accepted Christ, or that they have not all received the gospel, or that they have not all been saved through the gospel. No, they "have not all *obeyed* the gospel."

The word *obey* shows how the Scriptures look upon the gospel of God concerning His Son. In our day it is in vogue to present the gospel as an offer of God, as a kind invitation. Such a presentation of the gospel pleases the flesh of sinful man. It flatters him. He likes to hear that God comes to him with an offer that he may accept or reject. It pleases him to hear that it is up to him, that it depends on the choice of his own mind and will whether he will accept or decline that kind invitation.

But the text puts the gospel in a different light when it speaks of disobedience. Surely you cannot be disobedient to an invitation. No one thinks of accusing you of disobedience when you are offered something and you refuse the offer. An offer is not binding. It leaves you free. It cannot possibly oblige you to accept.

When, therefore, the text speaks of disobedience to the gospel of God, it implies that the gospel is more than an offer, more than a kind invitation; it is a *demand*. This stands to reason, for it is the gospel of *God*. God always demands, just because He is God. In the way of obedience to what He demands, He blesses us with life and glory. When any man, therefore, hears the sound of the gospel, this demand of God is conveyed to his consciousness: the demand to repent, to mourn over sin in sorrow after God, to turn away from unrighteousness and corruption and rebellion against the Most High, to seek righteousness, to turn back to God.

To disobey the gospel is to say *No* and to act it out to the end. When the sound of the gospel, the word of the preacher, reaches a man's ears, enters into his natural understanding, and he disobeys the gospel, he deliberately, intelligently, and consciously declares that he, above all things, loves sin and does not want righteousness, and he so delights in iniquity that he would rather go to hell than be delivered from it. Thus the sound of the gospel serves to bring to clear manifestation the horrible character of his sin, the damnableness of his unrighteousness. And God is justified. On the other hand, the result of the preaching that is heard through the living and powerful Word of God is faith. Faith is out of the preaching that is heard. This is always the result. The apostle does not say that the preaching that is heard *sometimes* produces this fruit. No, faith is always out of the hearing, that is, out of the thing that is truly heard when God speaks through the preaching, to our soul, unto salvation. This can never fail.

When the apostle speaks here of faith as the fruit of the preaching that is heard, he refers to the act of faith, to the activity of believing. We can speak of faith as a faculty, as a spiritual power, in distinction from its conscious activity. This power or faculty of faith is wrought in the sinner's inmost heart when he is regenerated by the Spirit of Christ. But the apostle is not speaking of this faculty or power of faith, for this power is wrought in the heart of the elect immediately, and not through the preaching of the gospel. The smallest infant, on whom the preaching of the Word has as yet no hold whatsoever, may possess this faith-faculty as well as the adult believer. The text, however, speaks of faith as it is wrought by the living Word of God through the preaching of the gospel. It has its source in the preaching that is heard. The reference is to the *conscious* act of faith, the act of believing.

This faith or belief is an act of the entire soul whereby the soul clings to God in Christ as the God of our salvation. It is not the mere superficial stir of the emotions that characterizes so-called temporary faith and that is frequently the result of revival preaching. It is not a mere intellectual assent to the truth without personal interest. Saving faith is a matter of the heart, and from the heart it becomes a spiritual, ethical activity of the mind and of the will. It fixes itself upon the gospel as revealed in Holy Scripture, because the gospel is the revelation of the God of our salvation in Christ Jesus our Lord, crucified and raised. By faith the believer knows this gospel, not with a mere natural, intellectual knowledge and interest, but with a profound spiritual discernment and with personal certainty. By it he is personally assured of all that is promised in that gospel: righteousness and the forgiveness of sin, adoption unto children, and eternal life. Even though all his experience from within, and all he perceives round about him in the world, may testify to the contrary, loudly witnessing of sin and guilt, of corruption and death, of condemnation and damnation, yet by his faith the believer knows that he is righteous before God and that he is an heir of eternal life. Faith is an act of the will whereby the believer wholly surrenders himself in life and in death to Christ Jesus crucified and raised as the revelation of the God of his salvation, completely trusting in the eternal love of God, so that fear is driven out of his soul.

Faith is the means, the God-given means, whereby we are saved. It is not a *condition* of salvation. Salvation is never conditional. There are no conditions we must fulfill in order to be saved. It is all of grace. It is not a *ground* of our salvation, whether you think of faith as such or of the works of faith. There are no grounds of salvation within us. The only ground is Jesus Christ and His righteousness. It is not even the hand that we extend in order to accept the offer of salvation and grace God brings to us in the gospel. Salvation is no offer. And if it were, we would have no hands to accept it. Faith is *means*. It is the God-given means, wrought in us by the Spirit of Christ, called into conscious activity by the Word of God through the gospel, whereby we receive Christ and embrace Him and all His benefits.

What a caricature is often made of saving faith! Persuaded by a would-be preacher, often under an emotional strain, a man repeats, "I accept Jesus Christ as my personal Savior"—and he is said to be saved! Therefore, it should never be forgotten that faith is out of the preaching that is heard, and preaching that is heard is only through the Word of God. If you merely hear me assure you that your sins are forgiven and that you are righteous before God, or if one would rise from the dead and say these things to you, or if tonight an angel from heaven would stand at your bedside and proclaim to you that you are saved, it would be of no avail. To no word of man or of any other creature can faith ever cling. By no mere word of man can it be evoked. Upon no word of man can it rest for righteousness and salvation in life and in death. But when the Word of God resounds in your soul, when you hear that Word as the Word of God to you, your heart will cling to that Word, receive it, embrace it, lay a firm hold upon it, and you will say, "I heard God speak unto my soul; whatever may testify against me, I am righteous forever!"

Chapter Seventy

God Found by a Strange People

Romans 10:20, 21

But Esaias is very bold, and saith, I was found of them that sought me not; I was made manifest unto them that asked not after me.

But to Israel he saith, All day long I have stretched forth my hands unto a disobedient and gainsaying people.

The words of the text are a part of the answer to the question we find in verse 19: "But I say, Did not Israel know." The meaning of that question is not, did not Israel know the gospel, did she not know the Word of faith, the Word of truth. The apostle had clearly shown that they did know. In verse 18 Paul had said that they had heard, for "their sound went into all the earth, and their words unto the ends of the world." Therefore, when the apostle asks in verse 19, "Did not Israel know?" he again refers to the main theme not only of this chapter, but also of the previous one. The meaning of the question is, did not Israel know that God would reject her as a nation and that He would turn to the Gentiles?

In answer to this question, the apostle, as he does so frequently in this chapter, quotes Scripture. He refers first to a quotation from Moses [Deut. 32:21]. Moses had said, "I will provoke you to jealousy by them that are no people." The apostle points out that long before, Moses had prophesied that God would make His name known to the Gentiles and thereby provoke Israel to jealousy. The apostle goes on to say that

"Esaias is very bold"; that is, the prophet expresses himself very plainly, very definitely. Isaiah had said [65:1] that God was found of them that sought Him not and was made manifest unto them that asked not after Him. The Gentile world has come to the knowledge of the name of the Lord. "But to Israel he saith, All day long have I stretched forth my hands unto a disobedient and gainsaying people" [Isa. 65:2].

Did not Israel know? They did. It had been plainly revealed to them that as a nation they would be rejected and that God would go to the Gentile world.

If we read the passage in Isaiah from which the apostle quotes, we will notice that we have in it an answer to the prayer of Israel at the time of the captivity. Israel was in captivity. Jerusalem and the temple had been destroyed. The covenant appeared to have been forgotten. It seemed that Israel was rejected even then. And the prophet ideally (for in reality Isaiah never was in captivity) stood at the head of the people of Israel and prayed that God might have mercy on them to deliver them. The Lord answered that prayer. In this quotation we have the answer to the prayer of the true Israel. The answer was that God will certainly remember His covenant, but He will not remember it as they expected. They looked upon the covenant as being inseparably bound up with the nation of Israel, but the Lord will remember His covenant by making Himself known to a people that did not seek Him and that asked not after Him, whereas Israel will be rejected as a nation.

Who Is Found

The "I," of course, is God. Both in Isaiah and in the Romans text, it is God who is speaking and who says concerning Himself that He is found. But God is here presenting Himself not merely as God without further definition. Surely as God He is known and revealed in all the works of His hands. His eternal Godhead and power are clearly revealed in the works of His hands. We can know God in His divinity, power, and wisdom from the creation of the world. The Gentiles in the old dispensation knew God as God. They knew Him as He must be served. As regards this knowledge and revelation, we cannot say that anyone has found God.

To find God has a more favorable meaning. It is to find Him so that we have communion, fellowship, with Him. This is not true of God as He is revealed to all in creation. As we are in our sins, there is nothing in God as He is revealed in creation for us to desire. Whatever we may see of God and whatever the revelation of God may speak to us in nature, it never speaks forgiveness. If we have no more than the revelation of God in nature, we will never seek Him. The reason is that there is no forgiveness in nature. It is not possible to violate an ordinance of God in nature and be forgiven. Even if one repents of his sins, such as drunkenness or fornication, he never receives a word of forgiveness in nature.

But when God says, "I was found of them that sought me not," it is plain both from the contexts in Isaiah and in Romans 10, as well as from the words of the text itself, that it is God as the God of salvation who speaks. It is God as He has revealed Himself in the face of Christ Jesus. This is the revelation of God. This is plain from Isaiah. Isaiah prayed for the restoration of the covenant. God answered that prayer in the words of Isaiah 65 quoted by the apostle in the text. The same is clear also from the context in Romans 10, where the apostle has been speaking of the righteousness of God in Christ.

This is especially plain from the words of the text itself when we consider the expression *All day long* (meaning "continually") *I have stretched forth my hands unto a disobedient and gainsaying people*. God presents Himself here as standing before His people with outstretched hands. This is a figure. The figure makes us think of a parent teaching his child to walk by stretching out his hands to the child, telling it to come to him and ready to catch the child in case it should fall. God presents Himself as a parent, ready to receive His child into His arms when the child is about to fall. The meaning of the figure is also plain. When God says, "All day long I have stretched forth my hands," He means, "All day long have I assumed the attitude of one who is ready to receive and save." All day long God reveals Himself this way.

Therefore, in the concrete sense, these outstretched hands refer to all the abundance of the revelation of God to Israel. God had revealed Himself to Israel as a God who is ready to receive and save them. This was true in all God's work. This was true when He led them out of Egypt, when He led them through the Red Sea, when He led them through the wilderness, and when He led them into Canaan. In all these things God became manifest as a God who is ready to receive and save. In all these things God became manifest as a God who stood with outstretched arms. This was true also of the revelation of God in His Word. In all His Word God revealed Himself as a God who is merciful and kind, ready to receive and to save. This was true also in the ceremonies and sacrifices. In all this work God revealed Himself as a God ready to receive and save. This was true, finally, in the supreme sense when Christ came. Christ came to the Jews first. In Christ God stood before the Jews as a God who was ready to receive and to save them. That is, He was ready to receive all who sought Him. God stood before Israel and said, "I am ready to receive and save all who flee to Me."

God says the same thing to us in Scripture today. In Scripture God says that all day long He has stretched forth His hands to us.

And God has been found. To find God is not a theological activity. Finding God does not consist of receiving and understanding some instruction about God. To find God in Christ is something different. It is, in the first place, that we feel the need of this God and that we hunger and thirst after Him. When you say that you have found something, you do not mean that you have seen it, or heard about it, but that you have it in your possession. When you say that you have found happiness, you do not mean that you have heard about happiness, but that you have it. When you say that you have found peace, you do not mean that you read about it; you mean that you have it in your heart. So when you say that you have found God, you do not mean that you read about Him. You mean that you found in your heart a longing after Him. You have found a vacancy in your heart that can be filled only by God in Christ.

In the second place, finding God is that you have seen and heard Him stretching out His arms to you personally. You have seen Him in the gospel, and you have heard Him say, "All day long I have stretched forth my hands," and you said, "That means me."

In the third place, finding God is rushing into those arms. You have gone with your sins into those outstretched arms, in Christ. You said, "I take Thee at Thy Word, and I believe Thee."

You found Him. And you found forgiveness, righteousness, justification, and peace. And those arms embraced you. And the Word of God said to you, "You are My son. You are My daughter." And you said, "I have found God."

By Whom He Is Found

Who found Him? The people before whom God stood with outstretched arms did not find Him. "All day long I have stretched forth my hands," God Himself says, "unto *a disobedient and gainsaying people.*" That was the Jews in the old dispensation. God was not found by them.

We must consider this part of the text very carefully, because these words are used to overthrow all that the apostle has been teaching. The explanation goes like this. God stood before a rebellious and gainsaying people with outstretched arms. Those arms are a symbol of God's general will to save everyone, including the gainsaying and rebellious people. And if that is so, some argue, there is no doctrine of election and reprobation. Similarly, there are Reformed people who confess the doctrine of election, but this text, they say, shows that there is also a general will in God to a save all, and we must accept both. They call this a "mystery." But we reject a general will of God to save all. We cannot overthrow all that we have learned in Romans 9 and 10 and all that we will be taught in Romans 11.

Let us look at the text. Does it teach anything like a general will of God to save all? It does if the outstretched arms mean that God says to these rebellious and gainsaying people, "I sincerely desire to save you all." But this is contrary to the gospel. Nowhere does Scripture teach that the outstretched arms symbolize God's readiness to save all. The meaning of the outstretched arms is that God is willing to receive and save *all who come to Him.*

Does this contradict the other fundamental truth that we will never repent and come into the outstretched arms unless God gives us the heart and the will to come? Scripture says *No.* There is no contradiction. If any man is to come into the outstretched arms of God, God must give him the will.

Surely God stood before the entire nation of Israel, just as today He stands before the entire congregation with outstretched arms, saying, "I am ready to receive and save all who come to Me." The preaching is general. But in that nation of Israel there were many who would not have Him. There were many who showed themselves, over against the outstretched arms, as gainsaying and disobedient. They rebelled against the Word of God. They were gainsaying. They opposed that Word of God. That was Israel. Why? Because God is merciful to whom He wills. When Christ came, the outstretched arms of God became manifest to all, but they rebelled against these outstretched arms. They rejected them.

We must not overlook the positive aspect of these words. The positive aspect is that some Jews believed, found God, and were saved, even though they, too, were rebellious by nature. Although the reference of the text is to the Jews in the old dispensation, its teaching applies as well to the Gentiles in the new dispensation. God does not say, "I first stretched out My arms to disobedient and gainsaying Israel, and then I went to a different nation that did not disobey and gainsay My Word." The notion that the Gentile world was seeking after God is simply nonsense. There were no such Gentiles. The Gentiles were no better than the Jews. The text says, "I was found of them *that sought me not.*" This is forever true. The Gentile world in the old dispensation was hostile to God. By nature, we are all gainsaying.

The Way in Which He Is Found

How then did the Gentiles come to find God? Christ came. He died, atoned for sin, was raised, and was glorified. Salvation had now become universal. The gospel was preached among the Gentiles. When the text says, "I was found of them that sought me not," the meaning is that hitherto the Gentiles did not have that revelation of God's outstretched arms. But now God manifested Himself to them through the gospel.

When the gospel was preached to the Gentiles, did they find God of themselves? God forbid! If nothing else had taken place, neither would the Gentiles ever have found God. But the preaching is through the Word of God. It is not the word of man. When the apostles preached, God spoke through them. God said to the Gentiles, "Behold Me. Behold Me as I stand with outstretched arms." When God says, "Behold Me," we cannot help looking. And God said this. He said this to the Gentiles.

This, then, is the situation. We of ourselves will never seek God in Christ. But when, through the Word that is preached, God says, "Behold Me in My outstretched arms, ready to receive and to save," we begin to seek and to long after Him. We find peace through the righteousness of God in Christ.

Chapter Seventy-one

The Ever Abiding Remnant

Romans 11:1-5

I say then, Hath God cast away his people? God forbid. For I also am an Israelite, of the seed of Abraham, of the tribe of Benjamin.

God hath not cast away his people which he foreknew. Wot ye not what the scripture saith of Elias? how he maketh intercession to God against Israel, saying,

Lord, they have killed thy prophets, and digged down thine altars; and I am left alone, and they seek my life.

But what saith the answer of God unto him? I have reserved to myself seven thousand men, who have not bowed the knee to the image of Baal.

Even so then at this present time also there is a remnant according to the election of grace.

This part of his epistle to the Romans, the apostle introduces by the word that we find frequently in the epistle and with which we have become somewhat familiar. It is the little word *then:* "I say *then*." By this introductory word, the apostle indicates that he is going to consider a conclusion that might possibly be drawn from what he had written in the preceding verses. This conclusion, which might be drawn by some from what he had written in chapter 10, the apostle states in the question in the first verse of chapter 11: "Hath God cast away His people?" These words are connected especially with the last part of chapter 10. There the apostle had stated that although the Jews had heard, they had not believed; neither had they received the Word of God. They had rebelled against this Word. Indeed, it had been foretold them that the time would come when God would put an end to His dealings with them and would turn to the Gentiles. Moses had said, "I will provoke you to jealousy by them that are no people, and by a foolish nation I will anger you." Isaiah had stated very boldly, "I was found of them that sought me not; I was made manifest unto them that asked not after me."

Considering these things, the apostle asks, "Must we say now that God has cast away His people?" When we say that in the new dispensation God has put an end to His dealings with Israel and has put Jew and Gentile on a par, does it follow that God has cast away His people?

Let me briefly give the meaning of what the apostle states in this section of his epistle. The apostle asks the question, "Has God, now that in the new dispensation He has finished His work with Israel and has turned to the Gentiles, utterly and finally cast away His people, so that now there is for them no salvation?" The answer of the apostle is, "God forbid." This is impossible, because God has among the Jews, as well as among the Gentiles, a remnant according to the election of grace. This remnant God has foreknown.

That God has not cast away His people is evident from the fact that Paul himself was saved. Paul also was a Jew, "an Israelite, of the seed of Abraham, of the tribe of Benjamin." The apostle adds this last designation because he was of Tarsus. He means, "I am not a proselyte, but a born Jew of the tribe of Benjamin. Therefore, I am a living proof that God has not cast away the remnant according to the election of grace."

Then the apostle illustrates the fact that God has not cast away His people from the history of Israel. It does, indeed, seem as if God had finally and utterly cast away His people. But, says the apostle, this was often the case in Israel's history. Especially was this the case at the time of Elijah. Elijah accused Israel of being very wicked and made intercession against her.

~ *The Ever Abiding Remnant*

But what was the answer of God? "I have reserved to myself seven thousand men, who have not bowed the knee to the image of Baal." So it is always. There always is a remnant according to the election of grace.

The Remnant

Even though the contents are rather doctrinal, it is essential that we have a correct understanding of this eleventh chapter of Romans and that we go through it very carefully. For we will find considerable opposition to the truth revealed in this chapter with regard to the question as to what is to become of the Jews in the national sense of the word. This chapter has been interpreted as referring to the Jews as Jews. It is explained as referring to the Jews as a nation. There are many who teach that we must expect a special, glorious future for the Jews in a national sense. For this view they appeal also to Romans 11. According to this view, we must suppose that the apostle is speaking of the Jews as though they were still the peculiar children of the promise, still the peculiar nation of God as it was in the Old Testament. Therefore, they say, the apostle teaches here that we must expect a special dispensation for the Jews in the future. According to some, God will restore the nation as such. He will restore the land of Canaan, and the Jews will return to the land of Canaan. They point to the fact that many are returning today.[1] When they shall have returned to Canaan, they will receive the Messiah, repenting for having rejected Him. The nation of Israel, so some say, is to be restored in the land of Canaan.

There are also others who do not go as far as this, but who believe that somehow God will deal with the nation of Israel in a special way in the future. They say that sometime in the future all the Jews will be converted. Although they do not return to Canaan, they will be converted and turn to the Lord.

---

1. In 1938, when the sermon was preached.

Let us see how those who hold these views of the Jews interpret this passage. The question "Has God cast away His people?" they interpret as meaning, has God cast away His people *finally*? It is plain, they say, that the Jews are cast away *now*. But is it final, or will God return to the Jews and receive them again? They interpret the words *God hath not cast away His people which He foreknew* as referring to the nation of Israel. They do not see any limitation in the word *foreknew*. They explain it as meaning that God has foreknown Israel nationally. When they come to the fifth verse, where the apostle says, "Even so then at this present time also there is a remnant according to the election of grace," they interpret the *remnant according to the election of grace* as the remnant of the nation of Israel. There is a remnant of the Jews left, and there always will be until God shall restore them. Finally, as regards Paul's reference to himself as an example, they understand this as though he said, "I am also a Jew. Do you think that I would be so unpatriotic as to teach that God has cast away the Jews?"

I have reviewed these things repeatedly, and it is my conviction that the apostle does not teach anything of the kind. Let me begin with the last argument. That the apostle should say "I am not so unpatriotic as to teach that God has rejected the Jews" is contrary to all Scripture. Paul would never turn to his own person to determine what God will do. Rather, the apostle points to his own example to prove that God did not utterly cast away His people. The apostle argues that his own personal salvation proves the negative answer to the question, "Has God cast away His people?" But in this case, the question is not simply, "Has God cast away His people?" but "Has He cast them away *utterly*?" That God cast away His people does not mean that He cast away every Jew. He did not cast away all the Jews, for He did not cast Paul away. The question is this: "When God cast away those who were His peculiar people, Israel, did He cast away all of them?" The answer is, "God forbid."

Therefore, we conclude that the remnant of which the passage speaks is the elect remnant of the Jews. Of them only can we say that they are the people whom God foreknew.

God's foreknowledge is a divine foreknowledge. God does not foreknow as we sometimes foreknow. We sometimes foreknow in the sense that we predict the weather by means of certain instruments, or by observing certain signs. God does not know in this sense at all. God does not come to knowledge by observing things. God's foreknowledge, rather, is the *cause* of all that exists. It is causative. It is creative.

Let me use an illustration. When an artist designs a painting and has finished it, he will say, "I foreknew this painting." This means that he had the painting in mind before he started it. This somewhat illustrates God's foreknowledge. When Scripture tells us that God foreknew His people, it does not mean that He saw beforehand what they would do (for example, believe and accept Christ). No. It means that God had them in His mind, that He conceived of them sovereignly just as the artist conceives of his picture. And when Scripture adds that God elected His people, it means that He also willed and desired them to be His people.

His people which he foreknew is that section of the church brought into the church from the Jewish nation. The *election of grace* means the same as gracious election. Therefore, we can say that the distinction of the Jews is this: there will always be among the Jews a remnant according to the election of grace. There is such a remnant according to the election of grace among them now, and there always will be.

Its Abiding Character

This remnant according to the election of grace will never be cast away. It will forever abide. At times this seems not to be the case. This is why the apostle points to the history of Elijah [I Kings 19:1–18]. That was a pathetic moment in the history of Israel. Is it not pathetic when a prophet of Israel intercedes *against* Israel? Don't you think it would be pathetic if our church was in such a condition that I would feel constrained to say in my prayers, "O God, they are all wicked!"

The history is familiar. It was after the incident on Carmel. Queen Jezebel threatened Elijah's life. Elijah fled into the desert and came to Mount Horeb. There he interceded against Israel. The Lord asked Elijah, "What doest thou here?" Elijah answered, "They have killed thy prophets, and digged down thine altars; and I am left alone, and they seek my life." Elijah exaggerated, of course, but it appeared that way to him. And this is often the case. This was especially the case when the nation of Israel rejected the Messiah.

This is often the case also in the church in the new dispensation. You may ask how it is possible that the church appears so hopeless that the prophet is constrained to intercede against her. The explanation is that the church is never unmixed. There is always the reprobate shell. There are periods in the history of the church when this reprobate shell multiplies and gets into power. Things are all right as long as the elect remnant is in power. And we must see to it, as much as possible, that the remnant remains in power.

But they could not do this in the old dispensation. The reprobate shell could make it impossible for the people of God to serve Him. As long as there was a wicked king on the throne and wicked priests to minister in the temple, the people could not bring their sacrifices; they could not perform the ceremonies. Then it appeared as if there was no one left who served God. Elijah said that he alone was left. This is often the case in the church also.

But although it appears this way, it is really never the case. The Lord rebuked Elijah. He declared, "I have reserved to myself seven thousand." This is always the case. And this seven thousand can never perish. No matter how the church may appear, the Lord will have His seven thousand. The remnant according to the election of grace can never perish.

The Reason Why It Abides

There are two reasons why the remnant abides. One reason why the remnant according to the election of grace can never perish from the Jews is the general reason that holds for all the church: they are foreknown. The other is that they are preserved. The apostle mentions both reasons. "God has not cast away His people which He foreknew." And, "I have reserved to myself seven thousand."

That God does not cast the elect remnant of Jews away is due to the fact that if He did, His ultimate work would be marred, so that it could not be the manifestation of the glory of His grace. Let me use the illustration of the artist once more. Is it possible that the artist, who foreknew his picture, should refuse to put a part in it when painting it? No, for if he did, the picture would be spoiled. Is it possible that God should cast away a part of His people whom He foreknew? No, because the church is a whole. The church is not a mob. It is a whole. When the church is finished, it must reveal the glory of the Son. If a part were missing, the glory of God would be marred. Therefore, He preserves them. He regenerates them, calls them, justifies them, and glorifies them. No matter how the church may appear to us, God always preserves His seven thousand. God always saves His people. Praise to His holy name!

Chapter Seventy-two

By Pure Grace

Romans 11:6
And if by grace, then is it no more of works: otherwise grace is no more grace. But if it be of works, then is it no more grace: otherwise work is no more work.

In verses 1–5 the apostle is speaking of the actual existence of the remnant according to the election of grace from the Jews in the new dispensation. He is not speaking of the fulness of the election from the Jews, but he is speaking of those elect Jews who had actually been called into the church. Of the other part of elect Jewry, the apostle speaks later in the chapter.

Verse 6 is connected with the last phrase in verse 5: "... a remnant according to the election of grace." With reference to the truth expressed in this phrase, Paul says, "And if by grace, then is it no more of works." If it is of works, it cannot possibly be of grace. Grace and works are mutually excluded. We must not try to mix the two. We reject the reading of the Revised Version, which omits the last part of the text.[1] It is true that essentially it makes no difference whether the last part of the text is omitted. The main thought remains the same. Nevertheless, that last part of the text looks at the truth from the opposite viewpoint. The first part of the text warns us that if we believe we are saved by grace, we must not carry into this faith the element of works. If it is by grace, then it is not of works. The second half of the text looks at it from the view-

---

1. The Revised Version omits the words *But if it be of works, then is it no more grace: otherwise work is no more work.* The New International Version and other modern translations also omit these words.

point of him who maintains that somehow, in some measure, salvation is by works. If it is of works, it is no more of grace. We must choose, therefore. If we say that it is by grace, we must stop talking of works. If one says that it is of works, he must stop talking of grace.

If someone asks why the apostle lays the emphasis on the fact that salvation is by grace, the answer is found in the next three verses in which the apostle says that Israel has not obtained what it was looking for. The reason for this we have in verse 6: it is not of works, but of grace.

The text teaches that "it" is by pure grace. When we connect the text with the preceding context, we learn what it is that is of grace. First, by grace without works we are elected. Second, the context tells us that by grace without works we are saved. Third, by grace without works we are preserved.

By Pure Grace Elected

That election is in view is plain from the context. [In v. 5] the apostle says, "[There is] at this present time also . . . a remnant according to the election of grace." *Election of grace* is gracious election, and gracious election is election that is motivated by grace. It is evident, therefore, that verse 6 ought to be read this way: "If election is by grace, election is no more of works. But if election is of works, we must stop talking of grace."

According to the scriptural meaning, election is materially the same as God's foreknowledge. Election is the eternal foreordination of God's people to glory and salvation. Election is personal. That is, every single one of the elect is foreordained and foreknown. In this sense, it is a personal election. It is not national; it is not a group election. It is a personal election.

This does not imply that election is arbitrary, as though God could just as well have chosen more or fewer than He did. The number of the elect is not arbitrary. God did not choose some and reject others arbitrarily. This is why Scripture speaks of the foreknowledge of God. An illustration will help to make this clear. A work of art is not a certain arbitrary number of trees or houses, but it is a unified scene. Every part belongs in it. So the church is not a crowd, anymore than a church building is merely a pile of bricks. The church is a whole. And this whole church is foreordained. God foreordained a church that should reflect the glory of His grace.

Election means, first of all, that God foreknew a church that should be a reflection of the glory of grace. In the second place, God foreordained a definite number that should fit in this whole. The number is not arbitrary; it is determined by the foreknowledge of God concerning His church. In the third place, election means not only that God determined the number, but also that He determined what position each one should occupy in the whole of the church.

When Scripture has in mind the foreordination of the church as a whole, it sometimes speaks of the *foreknowledge* of God. But if Scripture thinks of the foreordination of them who are to be saved, in distinction from those who are to be lost, it speaks of *election*.

The apostle says that election is not of works; it is of grace. You ask, "Are there then people who believe that election is of works?" Yes, indeed there are, and there always have been. That was already the case with the Jews. That is why the apostle includes verse 6 in the discussion of the election of the Jews. The Jews said that they were the chosen people of God because they served the Lord, because they kept the law, because they brought their sacrifices, because they observed the ceremonies, the sabbaths, and the feast days. "This is why we are better than the heathen," they said. "This is why God has chosen us."

However, the remnant according to the election must not have this conception. This is why the apostle says, "If it is of grace, it is no more of works." That you are chosen, and others are not chosen, is not because of works.

In our day the Arminians say that election is of works. They admit that there is such a thing as election. They cannot very well deny election outright, for it is taught too plainly in Scripture. But they explain election this way: God chose those whose good works he foresaw. The good works were not their keeping of the law, or their serving the Lord, but He foresaw who would perform the good work of accepting Christ.

If the Arminian doctrine is the truth, election is not of grace. Then it is not an election unto *becoming* the best, but it is an election *of* the best. Then the motive of election is not in God, but in those who are elected. The apostle declares that the Arminian doctrine is not true. But he adds that if it were true, they must never talk of grace anymore, for if they do, they are double-tongued. Arminians should stop talking about grace. If election is of works, it is not of grace. In such a case *we* determine whom God shall choose.

The truth is that election is of grace. We have nothing to do with our election. Our works have nothing to do with it, either. The motive of election is in God only. If we go into it a little more deeply, we must say that God is gracious. He is not gracious because of any relation to us. God does not become gracious. He is gracious in Himself. Grace is an attribute of God. As an attribute of God, the grace of God is His beauty. God is a beautiful God. He is pleasant, gracious, good. There is nothing repulsive in Him. God knows that He is beautiful. He sees His own beauty eternally, for He is the triune God. He forever beholds His own beauty in His Son. God sees Himself eternally. Seeing Himself, He is gracious to Himself. He favors Himself; He loves Himself. Since His own beauty is His Son, He determined to make a people as beautiful, in a creative way, as that Son. God wanted a people whom He could make as beautiful as Himself, whom He could favor as Himself, whom He could love as Himself. This is the motive of election.

Don't you see that there is no work in it. All that we shall ever be and become is of grace. If you say that election is of works, never speak of grace anymore.

By Pure Grace Saved

From this it already follows that when the text says that "it" is of grace, salvation is included. This is also plain from the context [v. 5], which makes plain that the apostle is teaching that there is now, at this time, a remnant that is already saved by grace. At the time when Paul wrote the book of Romans, a remnant believed in Christ. There were the disciples; there were the women who followed Him; there were the five hundred to whom Jesus appeared after His resurrection; there were the three thousand who were converted on the day of Pentecost. They believed in Christ; they trusted in Him; they were the church. When the Spirit was poured out, He was poured out in that church. The New Testament church was not added alongside the Old Testament church. It was a *continuation* of the church of the Old Testament. This church is the subject of the apostle's discussion in the context. The apostle is asking, "Why are you saved and the rest hardened? Is it because you were better? Is it because you were more faithful, because you kept the law, because you observed the ordinances of God?" Not at all! That there is such a remnant according to the election of grace today is of grace.

This means that salvation is also of pure grace. Salvation may be distinguished, both in the objective act and the subjective application. But both are of grace. Why did God send His Son? It was of grace. Why did He commission Him to reveal the full counsel of God to you and me? Why did He let Christ die so that we might be delivered? It is of grace.

You ask whether there are people who teach and believe that Christ came because of our works. Well, they do not put it in exactly these words, but this is really the basis of their conception. The Arminian will confess that Christ died for all. This is not what he really means, though. If he would express what he really believes, the Arminian would say that Christ died, as to His intention, for those He knew would accept Him. This means that Christ died "of works." Because God knew that there would be some people who are good enough to accept Him, God caused Christ to die. But then Christ died "of works."

The apostle denies that it is of works. It is of grace. Grace is the basis of our reconciliation to God. Nor may this be turned around into the statement that Christ reconciled God to us. God did not have to be reconciled. God does not love us because Christ came; Christ came because God loved us. Grace is the basis of our salvation as regards the objective act.

The same is true of the subjective application of salvation. We do not regenerate, justify, sanctify, and glorify ourselves. It is of grace that there is a remnant according to the election of grace. If you ask, "Why am I regenerated, whereas others are not?" the answer is, "It is of grace." The Arminian, however, boasts that God saves him, and not his neighbor, because he was willing to accept and believe in Christ, whereas his neighbor was not. If this is the case, salvation is of works. It is not of grace. And the apostle commands, "If this is the case, don't talk of grace anymore!"

Contrariwise, if we confess that salvation is of grace, let us no more talk of works. Don't we see that if we carry works into the basis of our salvation, we lose our assurance. Don't misunderstand me. The question now is not whether the Christian does good works out of gratitude. I am speaking of works, as is the text, as the basis of salvation. We are not saved because of works. This means that there is no devil, no power of darkness, that can take this salvation away from us. I pray you, let your faith take hold of this grace without works.

By Pure Grace Preserved

That which is true of our election and of our salvation is also true of our preservation. "I have reserved to myself seven thousand," we read [v. 4]. In the critical time of Elijah, God had preserved seven thousand unto Himself. So it was at the time of Paul. So it is always. God always preserves a remnant.

Why?

Once more, the answer of the Arminian is, "because of works." He may babble on about grace, but what the Arminian really is saying is, "God will preserve you if you let Him. God helps him who helps himself." This is Arminianism in all its forms. And if this is so, don't talk of grace anymore.

The apostle teaches that the remnant is preserved by grace. We must be preserved to the end. There is our old nature that seeks to draw us away from salvation. There is the world that seeks to turn us in the direction of that old nature. There are days of persecution. And these days may be upon us soon.

Are you not afraid when you think of those days? I do not refer to fear of wars, or of persecution. But are you not afraid that when you shall be put before the choice of your life or Christ, you will not receive grace to stand? According to the Arminian, you will receive grace if you want it. According to Scripture, you will receive grace whether you want it or not. God will certainly preserve the remnant according to the election of grace.

Therefore, he who glories, let him glory in the Lord.

Chapter Seventy-three

Obtained by the Election Only

Romans 11:7-10
What then? Israel hath not obtained that which he seeketh for; but the election hath obtained it, and the rest were blinded
(According as it is written, God hath given them the spirit of slumber, eyes that they should not see, and ears that they should not hear;) unto this day.
And David saith, Let their table be made a snare, and a trap, and a stumblingblock, and a recompence unto them:
Let their eyes be darkened that they may not see, and bow down their back alway.

These verses are the conclusion and summary of the contents of this first section of chapter 11. The section was introduced by the question "Hath God cast away his people? Did God utterly and entirely reject the Jews, so that in the new dispensation there is no salvation for the Jews at all?" The negative answer to this question, "God forbid," was discussed in verses 1–5. After the discussion of this question and its answer—having said, "No, God did not cast away His people"—the apostle asks [v. 7], "What then is the positive answer?" It is this: the election hath obtained it, and the rest were blinded.

The connection with the teaching in the preceding context is this. [In v. 6] the apostle had written that righteousness, or salvation, was purely of grace and not of works. Works do not enter into the matter of our salvation. In the text the apostle

517

explains why Israel did not obtain that for which it was seeking. The thing to be sought was a thing of grace, and the things of grace cannot be obtained by works. Israel did not obtain, because it sought by works, not by grace.

When we read the text, we may receive the impression that the main subject is the hardening of "the rest." But if we read the text in light of the context, we find that hardening is not the main subject. The main subject is that the Word of God has not fallen out, for *the election hath obtained it.*

A Twofold Seeking

The text plainly speaks of a twofold element in the Israelitish people. The apostle says, "Israel hath not obtained [it]." This means that the Jewish nation as a whole has not obtained righteousness and salvation. Then the apostle makes a distinction. In that Israel "the election" hath obtained it. The *election,* the apostle says, and not the *elect,* because he wants to consider them not as individuals, but as a whole. *The election* is one group in the Israelitish nation, and *the rest,* that is, in distinction from the election, were blinded. *The rest* is the other group.

Also the rest had been seeking. Israel as a whole has not obtained that which it seeketh for, the apostle says. This implies that Israel had been seeking. The word used for *seeking* indicates an intensive searching, together with a striving for the object sought. It must be said, therefore, that also the ungodly Jews had been seeking. They had been seeking righteousness with God. There is a seeking that is not unto finding and unto salvation. We may not simply distinguish between those who seek and those who do not seek. Christ says, "Seek, and ye shall find" [Matt. 7:7]. But the apostle here states that Israel hath not obtained that for which he seeketh. Rather than distinguish between those who seek and those who do not seek, we must distinguish a twofold seeking. There is a seeking that is not unto salvation. That seeking is a seeking of the things of God's grace in the wrong way. Therefore, it is a seeking of the wrong object. It is a seeking of a righteousness that is, after all, not the righteousness of God, and that cannot be valid in the day of judgment. It is the seeking of a righteousness according to man's judgment. Because it is the seeking of a righteousness according to man's judgment, it is a seeking in the wrong way—the way of the law.

This the Jews did. They were earnestly seeking. They went to the temple, they brought their sacrifices, they paid their tithes, they said their prayers. When they had done so, they said to God, "Because we have done these things, we expect that Thou wilt declare us righteous and that Thou wilt give us the reward of the righteous, namely, salvation." They did not do this by honest error, as if they did not know any better, but they did this in order to maintain their sinful pride before God and man. This was their motive.

It is possible to be faithful in works, but never come to repentance. It was possible for the Jews to perform all their religious duties—and they were duties—without being brokenhearted over sin. Still more, it was possible in that way of living to keep the whole law, in the external sense, while ignoring the weightier things of the law, namely, mercy, truth, and justice. This is still possible. It is possible to be faithful in church attendance, in giving to the poor, and in all kinds of good works, and to be an abomination in the sight of God. We are an abomination as soon as we live and act on the imagination that these external works have anything to do with our righteousness before God. If we do seek righteousness in this way, it will be said of us, as it was said of Israel, "You seek for that which you do not find."

There is another side to seeking and finding, which, although it is not mentioned in the text, is plainly implied. It is that the election obtained righteousness in the way of seeking. We must not understand the text this way: Israel did not obtain what it was seeking, but the election did obtain it, even though the election did not seek it. Verse 7 says that the election hath obtained. To obtain is to attain to the object of our seeking and striving. It is not so that they who obtain do not seek. If we obtain, we have been seeking.

To be sure, this seeking by the election that ended in their obtaining was not the *ground* of their obtaining. We do not obtain because we seek. We obtain only on the ground of election. It is of grace, not of works. The truth is that God, by the power of His grace and Spirit, works in the election the spiritual urge to seek. This seeking to obtain is the fruit of the election.

When God's election touches us, we see our own emptiness and the fulness of Christ. We see our own unrighteousness and the righteousness that is in Christ. Seeing it, we hunger and thirst after that righteousness of Christ. Hungering and thirsting after that righteousness of Christ, we go after it, and we go after it in the right way. We seek it in the sense that we turn to the cross. Coming to the cross, we take all our works and put them at the foot of the cross, confessing that they are sins and asking God to blot them out and to give us the righteousness of the cross.

A Twofold Divine Operation

Not only was there a wrong seeking on the part of the Jews; there was also an operation of God upon these Jews. This was an operation of God unto damnation. The text says, "The rest were blinded." More literally, the translation is, "The rest were hardened." If we take this expression by itself, it might merely teach the fact of their hardening without any indication as to the worker of the hardening. But when we look at the context, it is plain that the expression does not merely teach that they were hardened. Rather, it teaches that God hardened them. In verse 8 we read, "God hath given them the spirit of slumber, eyes that they should not see, and ears that they should not hear." This work of hardening is a work of divine operation proceeding upon these Jews and because of which they kept on seeking in the wrong way. God hardened them.

Negatively, hardening is that work of God by which man becomes insensible to the things of the gospel. It is not so that at first he is sensible to the gospel and that then he becomes insensible to the gospel. The starting point is that he is insensible to the gospel, but there are differences in degree in this hardening. There is in natural man a certain fear, a trembling, to touch the sacred things. This fear was in the Pharisees. We find this fear in the devils. The devils tremble at the Word of God. Hardening is that all the natural sensibility to the gospel is removed.

The example of a young man born and raised in the church illustrates this hardening process. At first that youth comes to church and to catechism. Gradually he begins to neglect his lessons. Then he stays away once, twice, until finally he does not come any more at all. The consistory goes after him, talks to him, and admonishes him. He promises to mend his ways, and for a time it seems as if he will. But it is not long before he becomes negligent again, and finally you see him no more. When the consistory goes after him again, they find that he has become entirely indifferent. He refuses to listen to them, and he does not care to see them. That young man has become hardened. This is one side of hardening.

The other side is that they become hardened to walk in the way of sin. This happens to the natural man. It is the operation of God upon him. This should make us fear and tremble. This operation of God is always present under the preaching.

How God hardens is described in the passage. God gave them the spirit of slumber. God sent them into a stupor, so that they became insensible to the gospel. God gave them eyes that they should not see, and ears that they should not hear. They understood the gospel intellectually. God gave them eyes. He gave them ears. But He gave them such ears that the moment they heard the gospel, they hated it. He gave them eyes to see the things of the gospel, but such eyes that the moment they saw the things of the gospel, they hated them. He gave them eyes that saw Christ, but they hated Him and nailed Him to the cross.

We must not say that only because of their sins God gave them the spirit of slumber, for then we must come to the conclusion that He did not give us that spirit of slumber, because we were worthy. This is not the case, however. That God did not give us the spirit of slumber is because of election. God finds us dead in sin, no different from those whom He hardens. By grace He changes our heart and gives us eyes, so that we see the gospel. This softening and saving operation of God is because of election. God's hardening of the rest ultimately proceeds from His eternal decree of reprobation.

A Twofold Prayer

Back of this twofold operation, there has been a twofold prayer. The apostle calls attention to this in the last part of the text, in the quotation from Psalm 69 [:22, 23]. The hardening took place in answer to a certain prayer. David prayed a remarkable prayer: "Let their table be made a snare, and a trap, and a stumblingblock, and a recompence unto them: Let their eyes be darkened that they may not see, and bow down their back alway." It is a petition that men's welfare, their prosperity, their earthly peace and abundance, become a curse. David prays this against the ungodly enemies of God. David is the one who prays thus, to be sure, but David is, after all, only the typical subject of Psalm 69. Centrally, it is Christ who prays this remarkable petition. The preceding verse, in Psalm 69 verse 21, puts this beyond all doubt: "They gave me also gall for my meat; and in my thirst they gave me vinegar to drink." Then follows the prayer that Paul quotes: "Let their table become a snare before them." It is Christ who is praying here.

The question arises, "Can we also pray this?" The answer is that we can and do, provided that this prayer against the enemies of God is a prayer that is sanctified by the Spirit of Christ. We may never pray this prayer against our enemies. We may only pray this prayer against the enemies of God. For this reason, it is impossible to direct this prayer against any individual. We can only direct it against the ungodly reprobate in general.

But it is upon this prayer of Christ that reprobate, ungodly persons are hardened.

Do you say, "Christ prayed something else, too"? He did. At the cross He prayed, "Father, forgive them; for they know not what they do" [Luke 23:34]. But this does not exclude the other prayer. Those for whom Christ prayed at the cross are certainly not the same as those against whom He prayed in Psalm 69. They are not the same group. When Jesus said, "Father, forgive them; for they know not what they do," He had reference to His own who had not yet been brought in and who had helped to crucify Him. For these elect Jesus prayed, "Father, forgive them."

The conclusion is that the election hath obtained, and the rest were hardened. The election obtained, not because of themselves, but because of sovereign, gracious election. They obtained because Christ prayed for them and because He bestowed the blessings of salvation on them. Because Christ bestows these blessings upon them, they seek righteousness and salvation and obtain it. Praise be to His grace.

Chapter Seventy-four

The Divine Purpose of Israel's Stumbling

Romans 11:11
I say then, Have they stumbled that they should fall? God forbid: but rather through their fall salvation is come unto the Gentiles, for to provoke them to jealousy.

Here the apostle begins a new section in the chapter. He indicates this by introducing this section with the same phrase with which he began the chapter: *I say then.* In the first verse he said, "*I say then,* Hath God cast away his people?" There he asked a question with regard to the nation of Israel as a whole. The answer was, "No, God hath not cast Israel away utterly and completely so that no Jew can be saved." Although many Jews are lost and do not obtain salvation, the Jews as such are not excluded from the salvation that is in Christ. The conclusion the apostle drew was that the election had obtained it, and the rest were hardened according to the prediction of the Old Testament.

In the text the apostle really asks the same question, but now with a more limited scope. "I say then, Have they of whom I have been speaking, the Jews that were hardened, have they stumbled that they should fall?" Once more the answer is, "God forbid." I think it best to treat this one verse. We could, of course, take this section as a whole, but it is best that we proceed slowly here. For here it is that the false view is developed, either that God will restore the nation of Israel as such, or that the salvation of all the Jews will be effected at some future date.

Verse 11 does not present any difficulty in this regard. When the apostle says, "Have they stumbled that they should fall?" he is not thinking of any future restoration of the nation of Israel. Nor is he thinking of any future salvation of the Jews. He is thinking of the salvation of the Jews who lived at his own time, for he says that in preaching the gospel, his aim is to provoke the Jews to jealousy.

But the text does raise important questions. What is meant by the *stumbling* of these Jews? Also, how was that particular stumbling of the Jews the salvation of the Gentiles? In this lies the practical purpose of the text. After all, the apostle is not writing to the Jews; he is writing to the Gentiles. This word concerning the Jews is addressed to *us*. And the question is, "How can the stumbling of the Jews be our salvation?" The text speaks of the divine purpose of the stumbling of Israel.

The Stumbling

Although the text does not present a difficulty regarding a future restoration of the nation of Israel, there is a difficulty here. The difficulty is not so easy to solve. The apostle begins to speak of *the rest* of whom he had been speaking in the context. In the preceding verses, he had spoken of the elect remnant that had received salvation. He had stated that *the rest* had been hardened [v. 7]. The apostle continues to speak of the hardening of the rest. In the text he turns to that *rest* that had been hardened. The elect had been taken out of them. *The rest*, therefore, are the reprobate. The apostle asks, "Have this *rest*—these Jews who had not received salvation, who had been hardened—have they stumbled that they should fall?" The answer is, "God forbid." Rather, God intends to provoke them to jealousy. This is to say that they will be saved. When God provokes people to jealousy, they are saved. Now you see the difficulty.

The question is this: is it possible that the reprobate Jews—those who have been hardened and who have stumbled—will return and be saved? This is impossible. God never does this, either with Jew or Gentile. Scripture teaches that there is a state of hardness from which it is impossible to return. This is plain, for example, from such a passage as Hebrews 6[:4–6]: "It is impossible for those who were once enlightened, and have tasted of the heavenly gift, and were made partakers of the Holy Ghost, And have tasted the good word of God, and the powers of the world to come, If they shall fall away, to renew them again unto repentance." This was the case with those Jews who had been hardened. This is the case with people today who are so hardened by God. Besides, it stands to reason that this *rest,* inasmuch as it refers to the reprobate, cannot be provoked to jealousy and be saved. Therefore, we understand that the apostle is not speaking of those individual Jews who had stumbled, who fell, and who were hardened. If you ask the question whether those Jews could be saved, the answer is no.

Instead, the apostle is speaking of *the rest,* that is, of the reprobate Jews *in their generations.* We must bear this in mind. The reference is to those Jews who at the time of Christ stumbled at the stone, crucified Christ, and did not enter into the kingdom in their generations. The apostle is thinking of the Jew in the ages to come. Or, to put it differently, he is thinking of the Jew as we know him today. He is thinking of the children of those Jews who stumbled.

The question that brings out the meaning of the text is this: "Are you saying, Paul, that there was in your day a remnant that was saved, and that the rest are rejected *forever,* so that there is no salvation for *any* Jew anymore?" Apart from the Jews, we would say yes to this question. The falling away of people is the end of them, also in their generations. I believe that God never returns to save a generation that has once been the generation of the children of God and has fallen away—except in the case of the Jews. I do not say that there may not be an individual out of such a generation that is brought back and is saved. But he is an exception. On the whole, it is not true that God returns to save a certain generation that has stumbled and has fallen away.

We can see this in our own country. We can see this even in our own city.[1] Our country, and even our city, are full of people who used to belong to the church, even as we do now. Our country is full of people who came to this country in order that they might serve God according to their conscience. Where are they today? They are modern. They have forsaken God. They have forsaken His Word. This has happened according to God's operation of hardening: they stumbled that they should fall. God never returns to them to save them.

By the way, this is not true only with regard to the slums. Some people regard it their special calling to do mission work among the slums because of a wrong conception of the Word of Jesus to go into the highways and byways [Matt. 22:9]. But people who have departed from the church do not live only in the slums. They live in the high-class districts as well. You might just as well go there to do mission work.

The point I want to make is this. To my mind, God makes an exception in the case of the Jews. God never returns to the generations of those who stumble and fall away from the church, but with the Jews this is different. "Have they stumbled that they should fall?" as is generally the case. God forbid.

The usual interpretation of the words *Have they stumbled?* is that the apostle refers to the fact that the Jews did not receive the gospel, but rejected it. There are objections to this interpretation. First, it is evident that the apostle refers to a definite event that was already finished in his day, whereas the preaching of the gospel was still going on. Second, it is difficult to see how the rejection of the gospel by the Jews could be the salvation of the Gentiles. The mere fact that the Jews rejected the gospel does not explain the salvation of the Gen-

---

1. Grand Rapids, Michigan. Hoeksema was not impressed with the godliness of the city—not even in the late 1930s.

tiles. Third, there were always Jews who accepted the gospel. The early church consisted of Jews as well as Gentiles.

The apostle speaks of a stumbling that is the cause of the salvation of the Gentiles. He refers to the fact that they crucified Christ. Scripture always refers to this fact when it speaks of the stumbling of the Jews. Thus it is in the parable of the husbandmen in Matthew 21[:33ff.]. The lord of the vineyard sends his servants to these husbandmen to receive the fruit of the vineyard, but the husbandmen take the servants, beat some of them, and kill others. Finally the lord sends his son, and they take him and kill him. Then Jesus turns to the Jews and asks, "What will he [the lord] do unto those husbandmen?" They say to Jesus, "He will destroy them, and give the vineyard to others." Jesus responds: "Did ye never read in the scriptures, The stone which the builders rejected, the same is become the head of the corner . . . Therefore say I unto you, The kingdom of God shall be taken from you, and given to a nation bringing forth the fruits thereof." In other words, salvation shall be taken from the Jews and given to others.

The same is found in Romans 11. Israel hath not obtained salvation. Why not? Because they stumbled at the stumblingstone. Therefore, when the apostle asks the question, "Have they stumbled that they should fall?" he is referring to the crucifixion of the Son of God. And the question is this: "Is the fact that the Jews crucified Christ sufficient reason that they should be rejected forever? Did they stumble *that they should fall?*" There is a difference between *stumbling* and *falling*. To stumble is temporarily to be offended at Christ. Stumbling is not necessarily final. Stumbling does not always end in falling. I do not say this in order to give anyone an excuse temporarily to be offended at Christ. This chapter exactly warns us against such stumbling. We stumble when we walk in the world. We stumble when we walk in sin. But this is not what the text means. The apostle is speaking of a particular event of stumbling: the crucifying of Christ. And the apostle asks whether that stumbling does not necessarily mean their fall, so that there is no salvation for these Jews forever. Was this God's purpose with their stumbling? The apostle answers, "God forbid. This is not the case."

Its Immediate Purpose

What then? Their fall is the occasion of the salvation of the Gentiles. In the original, a different word for *fall* occurs than was used in the opening of the text. The word the apostle used in the second sentence of the text should be translated *transgression*. Their transgression, the apostle says, is the salvation of the Gentiles. Through the transgression of the Jews, salvation is come unto the Gentiles.

How this can be is plain. First, if the Jews had not crucified Christ, there would have been no kingdom of God at all. This stumbling—the crucifixion of Christ—was necessary to shed the blood of atonement. The purpose of God in having reprobate Jews who were hardened at that time was the cross.

Second, by the fall of those Jews, salvation came unto the Gentiles, because that act of the Jews was the basis of God's rejection of the nation of Israel. Thereupon, God turned to the Gentiles.

Third, that nation was entirely Jewish. Consequently, salvation was Jewish. There could be no salvation for the Gentiles as long as salvation was wrapped up in the shadows of the law. But when Christ is crucified, the wrapper is taken off. Salvation is no longer Jewish, but international.

Fourth, by the crucifixion, Christ Himself became international. Before the crucifixion, Christ was a Jew. But He died and rose again. After His resurrection, Christ was no longer an individual Jew. When He ascended into heaven, was seated at the right hand of God, and received the Spirit, He became international. The Spirit He received was not Jewish. That Spirit was international. To receive that Spirit, Christ had to die. And so that Christ might die, the Jews had to stumble and be hardened.

This is the practical element in the text. What shall we say with regard to the Jews? Shall we despise them? Shall we hate them? Shall we help along with Hitler and the rest of the world in despising the Jews and casting them out?[2] It is true that from a natural point of view the Jews today give cause for this hatred. They provoke this persecution themselves. But the question is, shall we assume the same attitude of the world? The text answers, "God forbid." To the contrary, we shall pity them. Shall we not sympathize with them who bore the brunt of the battle all though the old dispensation in order to be the bearer of the Word of God? Shall we not sympathize with them who had to be hardened so that Christ might be crucified, so that salvation might be the inheritance of the Gentiles?

Its Ultimate Design

The ultimate purpose of God is not that we should say that there are no more elect among the Jews and that we should despise them; instead, the text adds, "for to provoke them to jealousy." Jealousy presupposes that you have something you love, which is precious to you, and which you consider as exclusively your own. An example is your wife. You love your wife. She is precious to you, and you consider her as exclusively your own. Jealousy is the painful suspicion that what you consider exclusively your own is also partaken of by another. Then you have the feeling of jealousy.

The text says that salvation is come unto the Gentiles "for to provoke them [the Jews] to jealousy." Salvation for years and years had been exclusively of the Jews. If you asked them, "Whose God is Jehovah?" they would have said, "He is our husband, and we are His wife." They looked upon the Gentiles as a strange woman. Now God takes His love and gives it

---

2. This sermon was preached in 1938. It was common knowledge that Nazi Germany was bent on the destruction of the Jews. By no means, however, was hatred of the Jews limited to Nazi Germany.

to the Gentiles also. And the Jews despised His love. When the apostle says that God will provoke the Jews to jealousy, he means that the children of those Jews who were hardened in his time will be saved.

The meaning is not that the Jews will be converted merely by seeing that the Gentiles are saved. Rather, God will convert them. But when God converts them, their conversion will take on the form of a holy jealousy. The converted Jew will say to the Gentiles, "That love you have is mine. That Christ you have is mine, and He always has been mine." The Jewish convert will talk just as the prodigal son did. When he came to himself, that is, when he was converted, what did he say? He said, "The servants of my father have plenty, and I suffer want" [Luke 15:17]. In other words, he became jealous. So it will be with the Jews. God will receive these Jews, in their generations, even though they were hardened and crucified Jesus. God will receive them, not to make them Jews again. He will receive them to bring them into the fold in order that there may be one flock and one shepherd [John 10:16].

What then is our calling? Our calling is to manifest to the Jews the love of Christ in order to make them jealous. And God will provoke them to jealousy in order that they may be saved.

Chapter Seventy-five

The Greater Glory of Israel's Reception

Romans 11:15
For if the casting away of them be the reconciling of the world, what shall the receiving of them be, but life from the dead?

The connection of the text with the preceding is indicated by the word *For:* "*For* if the casting away of them be the reconciling of the world." The text offers a reason for what the apostle had stated in the immediately preceding verses. There he had written that the stumbling and falling of the Jews who had been hardened had become the salvation of the world, according to God's purpose. But that was not the sole and final purpose. With that stumbling of the Jews who had been hardened, God also purposed to provoke those Jews to jealousy in order to save them. It is of the salvation of those Jews that the apostle continues to write.

The apostle had written that if the fall of the Jews is of such great benefit and riches to the Gentile world, then we may expect that the salvation of those Jews will have a far more glorious effect. It is to this effect that the apostle writes in verses 11–15. The riches that will come upon the world through the salvation of the Jews will be far greater than the riches that have already come upon the world through the fall of the Jews.

He writes this to the Gentiles because they are interested. In this way he magnifies his office. When he preaches the gospel to the Gentiles, he seeks to provoke the Jews to jealousy in order that he might save some of them. "For if the casting away of them be the reconciling of the world, what shall the receiving of them be, but life from the dead?"

The Reception

When the apostle speaks of the *receiving of them,* he is referring to the same Jews of whom he has spoken in the preceding verses. He had said of these Jews that they had been hardened, that they had stumbled, and that they had fallen. But God had purposed that through their fall, salvation should come unto the Gentiles. God's purpose also was to provoke the Jews to jealousy, and thus to save them. The apostle says of those same Jews that they will be received. He is not speaking of the generation that lived in his day, but he is speaking of those Jews in their generations from the time of the apostle Paul until the end of this dispensation. He is speaking of the children of those Jews who crucified Christ. Of their reception into the kingdom, and therefore of their salvation, the apostle is speaking.

The question arises, "Which Jews are in view?" when verse 15 asks, "What shall the receiving of them be, but life from the dead?" Does it have in view *all* the Jews? This explanation is impossible. All those Jews will not be saved. All the generations of the Jews from the time of Paul until the end of this dispensation will not be saved. Thousands of them have been lost already. The apostle does not teach that all the children of those Jews who had been hardened will be saved.

Does the text, then, perhaps teach that at some future time all the Jews will be saved? This is the conception of many. Many expect that at some future time the Jews who are then alive will all be saved. The Jews now still belong to the castaways, but at some future time God will come and save every single one of them. However, verse 15 does not say this. It simply says that the receiving of them will be life from the dead. To find in the text a prophecy that God will save all the Jews at some future time, one must first insert this notion into the text, which does not speak of any future salvation of all the Jews. Neither does it speak of a future restoration of Israel as God's special nation. The text does not teach anything of the kind. Against such an interpretation stands the very evident attempt of the apostle, already in his day, to work on behalf of provoking the Jews to jealousy. He says, "I magnify mine office: If by any means I may provoke to emulation [jealousy] them which are my flesh" [vv. 13, 14].

In order to determine what is meant by the *receiving* of the Jews, we must notice that in verse 12 the apostle speaks of the "fulness" of the Jews who shall be saved. Verse 12 reads, "If the fall of them be the riches of the world, and the diminishing of them the riches of the Gentiles; how much more their fulness?" By the *receiving of them* in verse 15, the apostle refers to that same fulness. We may read the text this way: "If the casting away of them be the reconciling of the world, what shall the receiving of the fulness of the Jews be?" Therefore, the text teaches that the receiving of the fulness of the Jews will be life from the dead.

What is the "fulness" of the Jews? In Scripture we read often of the fulness of something. We read of the fulness of Christ [Eph 4:13]. We read of the fulness of time [Gal 4:4]. Here it is the fulness of the Jews. By *fulness* is always meant that which is filled with something. The church is the fulness of Christ, that is, the church is filled with Christ. The fulness of time is that which is filled with time. Think of a glass of water. The last drop that goes into the glass is the fulness of water. That which fills it is the *fulness*. The fulness of the Jews, therefore, is that which is filled with the last Jew.

Fulness implies a certain measure. What is the measure of the Jews? Does it mean all the Jews without exception? This cannot be, for it is always the case that "they are not all Israel, which are of Israel" [Rom. 9:6]. Besides, the apostle also speaks of the fulness of the Gentiles that must come in before Christ can come [11:25]. Even as the measure of the fulness of the Gentiles cannot mean the salvation of all Gentiles without exception, so the measure of the fulness of the Jews is not the salvation of every Jew. The measure of the fulness of the Jews is God's election. Just as the last drop of water that goes into a glass is the fulness of water, so the last Jew who goes into the measure of God's election is the fulness of the Jews. The teaching of the text is that the receiving of the last of the Jews, which will be the fulness of the Jews, will be life from the dead.

The question begs to be asked whether this fulness of the Jews will take place all of a sudden, or gradually throughout this dispensation. Think again of a glass of water. One can pour it full all at once, or one can fill it drop by drop. Similarly, as regards the fulness of the Jews, will God leave the measure empty for years, and then in the future suddenly fill it with Jews? There is nothing against this interpretation as such. It is not in itself objectionable to hold that there will be a marked conversion of many Jews at some future time, but the text says nothing about it. Also the context is against it, for the apostle says that he is already laboring to fill the fulness of the Jews. In light of the context, the text teaches that from the time of the apostle until the end of this dispensation—all through the New Testament dispensation—God is engrafting Jews into their own olive tree, and they are saved.

The Comparison

When the last Jew will have been received into the kingdom, this reception will be greater glory than the reconciliation of the world. There is a comparison in the text between the casting away of the Jews and their fulness. The comparison is between what God worked on the occasion of their fall and what He will work on the occasion of their fulness. This is plain from verse 12: "If the fall of them be the riches of the world, and the diminishing of them the riches of the Gentiles; how much more their fulness?" What is meant by the *riches of the world* is evident from verse 15. It is the reconciliation of the world. What the apostle is saying, therefore, is this: if God worked on the occasion of the fall of Israel, much more will He work on the occasion of their fulness.

The reception of the Jews will be greater glory than the reconciliation of the world. The word *world* has different meanings in Scripture. Contrary to the popular notion, *world* does not mean all men without exception. In fact, the word *world* never means simply men. But *world* in Scripture sometimes means all the works of God as He knew them in His counsel. God beholds the world. We do not behold the world. We don't see the world. All we see of the world is a snapshot of a part of the world as it passes by. The world passes by. We see a little part of it, and it has passed. But God sees the world as it will eternally be. This world God loves. And this world is going to come. The new world in Christ is the world that God loves.

World in Scripture sometimes means the whole of present existence as it is under the influence of sinful men. Men do not live by themselves; they must have a world to live in. Through this world men sin. They make a wicked world of it. This is the world to which the apostle John refers when he says, "Love not the world" [I John 2:15]. This is the world concerning which Christ says, "I pray not for the world" [John 17:9]. We must be careful not to love this world. People sometimes ask, "May I do this, or may I do that?" Of course, you can, if you want to. But remember, then you are in the world for which Christ did not pray. Christ did not pray for the world of movies, theaters, and dancing.

Sometimes in Scripture *world* means all the organism of God's elect church, not only of the Gentiles, but also of the Jews. This is the meaning of *world* in the text. God purposed that all the world should be reconciled to God.

Reconciliation is a beautiful term. It presupposes the covenant relation. Reconciliation does not make the covenant relation. It presupposes the covenant relation. God eternally placed the world in covenant relation to Himself in His counsel. Because of this relation, God reconciles them.

We must not turn this around. We must not say that God reconciles Himself to the world. This is a heathen conception. If this were the case, there would be no reconciliation. Reconciliation is an act of love. God was not reconciled; *we* were reconciled.

Reconciliation is that God removes the obstacle that prevented the covenant relation from functioning. This is glorious! Oh that the gospel be preached to the world: be ye reconciled to God! This is glorious. And this was effected through means on the occasion of the fall of the Jews. God hardened the Jews in order that they should crucify Christ. He hardened the Jews in order that the blood of reconciliation might be shed.

The apostle says that the *receiving* of the last of the Jews will be more glorious than the reconciliation. On the occasion of the fall of the Jews, the world received reconciliation. On the occasion of their reception, it receives life from the dead.

The Glory

The last part of the text, which describes the greater glory, is explained in many ways. There are three possible interpretations. The first is very commonly held. This is the explanation that the receiving of the Jews will be the awakening of the Gentile church. But how lame this interpretation is! The objection to this interpretation is that it ignores the expression *life from the dead.* An even weightier objection is that it is impossible to see how the awakening of the Gentile church can be more glorious than the reconciliation of the world.

A second interpretation is that somehow the conversion of the Jews will bring about a glorious state for the church in the world. But again, this interpretation ignores the expression *life from the dead.* In addition, the earthly glory of the church would not be a greater glory than the reconciliation of the world.

The correct interpretation consists of the literal understanding of the apostle's words. The glory of Israel's reception is *life from the dead,* that is, the resurrection life. That will be more glorious. There is one thing that is greater than the reconciliation. It is greater because life out of the dead is the ultimate fruit of the reconciliation. The objection has been made that then the apostle would have said "the resurrection." The reason why he does not use the word *resurrection* is that the apostle does not have in mind the moment of the resurrection, but the glorious state into which the church is to be resurrected.

That will be glorious! We *are* reconciled—are we not? Being reconciled and having the new life in us, we are strange creatures. In the midst of death, we have a little bit of life. We have but a little bit of life until the moment of the resurrection. We have just a little bit of life to cling to Christ. All the rest is death. But we shall receive life out of the dead. That is the life for which we are looking. Then all this death will stay behind. And when this life shall be in all the church, that will be glorious.

Does someone ask what this has to do with the fulness of the Jews? It has everything to do with it. That glory cannot come until the fulness of the church has come. The church is not a crowd. It is one body, one whole. Every one of God's elect must first be called into the fellowship of Christ. There may not be one lacking. Just as a building would be marred if one brick is missing, so God's church would be marred if there were one Jew missing. This does not hold true only of the Jews. The fulness of the Gentiles must be there, too. But when the fulness of the Jews shall be there, that will be life from the dead. The resurrection will come as the glorious state in the new creation. Then there will be one shepherd and one fold, in which God will be all and in all.

Chapter Seventy-six

Humility toward the Old Branches[1]

Romans 11:16–21

For if the firstfruit be holy, the lump is also holy: and if the root be holy, so are the branches.

And if some of the branches be broken off, and thou, being a wild olive tree, wert grafted in among them, and with them partakest of the root and fatness of the olive tree;

Boast not against the branches. But if thou boast, thou bearest not the root, but the root thee.

Thou wilt say then, The branches were broken off, that I might be grafted in.

Well; because of unbelief they were broken off, and thou standest by faith. Be not highminded, but fear:

For if God spared not the natural branches, take heed lest he also spare not thee.

This section of Romans 11 forms a unity. We must not separate the different elements that make up this section. In the Authorized Version these verses are introduced by the conjunction *For*, but there is no reason for this conjunction, either in the original or in the context. The text should simply be translated, "And if the firstfruit be holy, the lump is also holy." By the introductory word *And*, the apostle not only continues

---

1. In the publication of this chapter in the book *God's Eternal Good Pleasure*, Hoeksema gave it the title "Holy Branches."

his discussion concerning the Jews and their conversion, but also adds a new thought. The new thought we have in the words *Boast not*.

The apostle has been dealing with the salvation of the generations of the hardened Jews of his day. From verse 11 on, he has dealt with the hardened Jews. He has been teaching, on the one hand, that through the fall and hardening of the Jews, salvation has come to the world, to the Gentiles. He explains in verse 15 that this salvation was nothing less than the reconciliation of the world. But the apostle also states that the reception of the fulness of the Jews would be of greater glory than the reconciliation. It would be life from the dead. The apostle continues to speak concerning the Jews and their conversion. But in the text he adds the thought that the children of the new dispensation must not boast against the still unconverted Jews. This is the main thought of this section. The passage teaches that we must not exalt ourselves against the Jews, even though they are still unconverted and rebellious. Rather, we should assume an attitude that is characterized by humility.

These Branches Still Holy

The apostle uses two figures, one of which he quickly abandons. He uses the figure of an olive tree. This olive tree represents the church of God as the church develops in the line of the people of God throughout history, both in the old and in the new dispensations. But he also speaks of the firstfruit and of the lump. Israel in the old dispensation had to bring the firstfruit of the dough to the temple after the harvest. The firstfruit of the dough of that harvest had to be brought as a heave offering [Num. 15:17–21]. To that ceremony the apostle refers when he says, "If the firstfruit be holy, the lump is also holy." That firstfruit of the dough was considered holy by being consecrated to the Lord. That firstfruit represented the entire lump. Therefore, he says, "If the firstfruit be holy, the lump is also holy."

The apostle saw that the figure of the olive tree would suit his purpose better. Upon it, therefore, he elaborates. He can better use the figure of the olive tree, because the figure of the lump does not represent the people of God as they develop throughout history. The idea of development is conveyed by the figure of the olive tree. In addition the apostle speaks not only of the old branches, but also of the new branches grafted into the olive tree. The figure of the olive tree is suited to the apostle's doctrinal purposes.

The branches of the olive tree represent not the individual people of God, but generations. It is essential that we bear this in mind in order to understand how branches are broken off. The breaking off of branches would be impossible if these branches represent the individual people of God. But what is not possible with respect to the individual people of God is possible in their generations.

It is also evident that the text distinguishes three kinds of branches. There are, first, the branches that the apostle calls the natural branches. They are the Jews. The Jews are the natural branches because the very root was Jewish and also because for a time the church was Jewish. Among these natural branches the apostle makes a distinction. There are natural branches that are still in the tree and that are not broken off. When Christ came, He continued His church in the Jews. They never are broken off. They are the natural branches that remain in the tree and in which Christ continues His church. But there were also natural branches that were broken off. And then the apostle speaks of branches from the wild olive tree that are grafted in. The branches from the wild olive tree, grafted into the tree that is by nature Jewish, are the Gentiles.

It has been said that the apostle here reverses what is done in nature. In nature a cultivated branch is grafted into a wild tree. But the apostle speaks of a wild branch being grafted into a cultivated tree. However, the apostle simply means that the Gentiles are made partakers of Christ and His body.

What is meant by the *root* of the olive tree is more difficult to determine. There are several explanations. The most common explanation is that by the *root* the apostle refers to the patriarchs Abraham, Isaac, and Jacob. It is said that they are the root because they are the root of Israel's natural existence. The text then means that if the patriarchs are holy, the rest of the nation is holy. A second explanation is that the apostle refers to the early church, to the firstfruit of the Jews into the church. In this case the meaning is that if the firstfruit be holy, their generations are holy. A third explanation is that the root is Christ.

Against the first two explanations there are many objections. First, if by the root the apostle refers to the patriarchs Abraham, Isaac, and Jacob, this is the only place in Scripture where the patriarchs are so described. Second, the apostle is not speaking in this section of Israel's national existence, but of the olive tree. The patriarchs might be called root of Israel's national existence, but they cannot be called the root of the spiritual existence of the church. Third, we simply cannot say that if Abraham, Isaac, and Jacob are holy, their generations are holy. Fourth, we can hardly apply the text to Abraham, Isaac, and Jacob in light of the relation of the branches to the root [according to vv. 17 and 18]. [In v. 18] the apostle says that the Gentiles must not boast against the branches. If they do boast, they do not bear the root, but the root them. However, it cannot be said that Abraham bears the Gentiles. On the view that the root is the patriarchs, verse 17 would have to be teaching that the Jews are the natural branches of the natural root. However, verse 17 is speaking of the spiritual olive tree. Besides, the apostle says, "Thou partakest of the root and fatness of the olive tree." This does not apply to Abraham, Isaac, and Jacob. We are not partakers of the fatness of Abraham, Isaac, and Jacob.

The same objections against taking the root as the patriarchs hold against the explanation that the root is the early church.

But there is good reason for understanding the root to be Christ. Christ is called the root more than once in Scripture. In Isaiah 11[:10], Christ is called the *root of Jesse*. This root was in the loins of Jesse at that time. In chapter 15 of this very epistle, the apostle refers to the root of Jesse and identifies it as Jesus Christ [v. 12]. Scripture also calls Christ the *root of David* [Rev. 5:5; Rev. 22:16]. The same is true regarding the *firstfruit*. Christ is called the *firstfruits* in Scripture [I Cor. 15:20, 23]. We have Scripture on our side, therefore, when we say that this root is Christ. He is the root of the family of God throughout history.

If the root is holy, the branches are holy. By these branches the apostle still refers to the same generations of the unconverted Jews. He reminds the Gentile Christians that the root did not come from their generations. The Jews carried that root in their loins. Christ took on the seed of Abraham. If the root, which is in the Jews, is holy, these branches, too, are still holy. Holiness here has its full, rich, spiritual sense. The branches borne by the holy root are spiritually clean, redeemed, and—in this spiritual sense—consecrated to the Lord. However, the holy branches are not individuals. Nor are they every generation of Jews. Rather, the meaning is that there is still holy seed among the generations of Jews.

Boasting against the Branches Is Probable

Against these branches, Gentile Christians are forbidden to boast: "Boast not!" It is evident that we must not boast against the branches that are broken off. The apostle is not forbidding us to boast against the Jewish branches still in the tree, but we must not boast against the Jewish branches that are broken off. This is evident from verse 19: "Thou wilt say then, The branches were broken off, that I might be grafted in." Against the Jewish branches that are broken off from the olive tree, whose root is Christ, "Boast not."

It is easy to boast against these branches. From a natural point of view, there is sometimes occasion to boast against the Jews. Often the Jew gives occasion to nominal Christians to say, "We will have nothing to do with Jews." This is what Hitler says. This is the attitude that we also sometimes assume, speaking with scorn of the Jews.

From a religious point of view, there is much in the Jew that would make us despise him. The Jew is a bitter enemy of our Christ. He is a bitter enemy of the church. The Jew early revealed his enmity by persecuting the church, or if he could not persecute the church himself, he instigated this persecution. Even today if you speak to the Jew about Christ, he is filled with hatred. If a Jew is converted to Christ, he is cast out from his own family. How easy, then, to assume an attitude of boasting over against the Jew. That Jew is cut off; he is dead; he lies under the tree as a dead branch. Yet the apostle of Christ says, "Boast not against the branches."

The other side of the prohibition is that we must not boast about ourselves. The Gentile Christian is presented as saying that the Jewish branches were broken off "that I might be grafted in." In itself, that is "well," says the apostle. They were broken off. (I want to emphasize again that these branches are generations; individuals cannot be cut off.) When the Gentile Christian says that these branches were cut off to make room for him, he is boasting that he is much better than they. But the Gentiles are not better. Did the Gentiles do any better than the Jews? The history of the Jews is one continual history of apostasy, but is the history of the Gentiles better? You have but to look around in our own city to answer this question. Half of what was once the olive tree is dead. They lie under the tree with the dead Jews. The only difference is that they still call themselves branches. What is the difference? Has not the modern church despised Christ just as much as the Jews—although in a more civilized manner, more decently, more scientifically?

Let us look at our own congregation. We are loaded down with the blessings of salvation. Do we care about it? We don't! We would like to have God feed grace and salvation to us with a spoon, and then we are too lazy to swallow it. Every once in a while, we need a poke; otherwise, we go to sleep. We can't wake up unless we get a poke once in a while.²

Reason for Humility

The apostle says, "Don't boast. Don't sit there so piously. Rather, be filled with humility." If God would deal with us according to our boasting, He would cut us off too. We have no reason to boast. In the first place, we have no reason to boast, because the branches that have been cut off are still children of God in their generations.

In the second place, we have no reason to boast, considering that these branches were cut off "because of unbelief." By this is not meant that it was their own fault that they were broken off; rather, he reminds us that the unbelief of the Jews is all that we Gentiles have by nature. We have nothing of ourselves to boast about. If God would leave us as we are by nature, we have nothing but unbelief. In our generations we would rot off the tree. This has happened in many generations. They have rotted off the tree and lie as dead branches at the foot of the tree. If God gives us faith, we remain in the tree. But if not, we will do nothing but rot off. If you place a dead pole in fertilizer, it will rot.

Therefore, "Be not highminded, but fear." We stand by faith, and faith is the gift of God. We have nothing to boast about. If we do boast (and we may boast), then let us boast in the root. Let Christ be the object of all our boasting. He that glorieth, let him glory in the Lord.

---

2. Not all was well in First Protestant Reformed Church of Grand Rapids in the late 1930s, and Hoeksema knew it. As a good minister, he sharply warned his congregation of the sin. Although he did not know it at the time, he was speaking prophetically here. The "poke" for First Church, and for the denomination, was the schism of 1953. God "woke up" the congregation and denomination. In his edited version of this sermon in *God's Eternal Good Pleasure,* Hoeksema noticeably softened these statements.

Chapter Seventy-seven

The Goodness and Severity of God

Romans 11:22–24

Behold therefore the goodness and severity of God: on them which fell, severity; but toward thee, goodness, if thou continue in his goodness: otherwise thou also shalt be cut off.

And they also, if they abide not still in unbelief, shall be grafted in: for God is able to graft them in again.

For if thou wert cut out of the olive tree which is wild by nature, and wert grafted contrary to nature into a good olive tree: how much more shall these, which be the natural branches, be grafted into their own olive tree?

The verses that precede the text had the practical purpose of admonishing the converts from the Gentiles that they should not boast against the branches that had been cut off from the olive tree of God's covenant. The Gentile converts should not boast against the Jews who at the beginning of the new dispensation had not entered into the kingdom of God. If they might be inclined to boast, they should remember that those Jews were cut off because of unbelief. We ourselves have nothing but unbelief. "Because of unbelief they were broken off, and thou standest by faith" [v. 20], that is, by grace.

In verses 22–24 the apostle is still elaborating upon the figure of the olive tree. He concludes this figure by connecting the text with the preceding by the word *Behold*. The apostle is still writing to the Gentile Christians. He wants them to behold: "*Behold* therefore the goodness and severity of God," he says, "that you may not be highminded, that you may not boast, that you may not exalt yourselves" [vv. 22, 20, 18].

There are three distinct instances in the text that illustrate the goodness and severity of God. First, there is an instance of the goodness of God in the branches from the wild olive tree that have been grafted into the family of God. This is the conversion and calling of the Gentiles into the church. Second, there is the cutting off of branches as an instance of the severity of God. Not only does the text speak of branches that have been cut off, but also of branches that may possibly be cut off. Third, there is the engrafting again of branches that have been cut off. We must look at the goodness and severity of God from the viewpoint of these three instances.

With a View to the Converted Gentiles

Goodness in Scripture has a variety of related meanings. With respect to God, the word *good* in Scripture means His moral, ethical perfection. God is holy, righteous, and just; He is without imperfection. In this sense, God is good. But goodness in Scripture may also mean benevolence. The word *goodness* is used regarding God's goodness to us. In this sense, goodness is the will of God to do us good, which is the way the word is used in the text. When we read, "Behold therefore the goodness of God," the meaning is God's benevolence, so that God's goodness includes His mercy, His love, and His long-suffering.

Severity, on the other hand, is "justice applied to the limit." This is how we use the word in our daily talk. When we say that a man is severe, we mean that he is just, without mercy. When the text speaks of the severity of God, it describes God's justice applied to the limit. Severity is His justice without mercy.

Does someone object that these two cannot be harmonized?

Does someone ask, "How can God be good, that is, benevolent, and still be severe?" We must understand that God's benevolence is not separate from His goodness in the moral, ethical sense of the word. God is never benevolent in conflict with His righteousness, because God cannot deny Himself. His benevolence cannot be in conflict with his moral perfection. God's goodness is always a righteous goodness. There is no unjust goodness with God. Therefore, the two harmonize. God is good to and blesses only the righteous. In other words, God is good only over those who are in Christ Jesus.

Concerning this goodness the apostle mentions the conversion of the Gentiles: "Behold the goodness . . . of God . . . toward thee." Speaking to the Gentile Christians, the apostle says, "Behold the goodness of God over you." In what? How was this goodness revealed in these Gentile Christians? In that they had been taken out of the wild olive tree and had been grafted into the good, the cultivated olive tree. That was a manifestation of God's goodness. We used to be branches of a wild olive tree. We were growing wild. We had not been cultivated. We had not been cultivated by grace. We had not been cultivated by the Word of God. That we were wild branches had become evident from our wild fruits. We had borne wild fruit such as the apostle mentions in the first chapter of this epistle: fruits of envy, hatred, backbiting, murder, and deceit. It was a wild tree, and it bore wild fruit. God had taken *some* of those branches. He did not take the tree. The tree is still there. Contrary to nature (for it is contrary to nature to graft a wild branch into a cultivated tree; according to nature, it should be just the opposite), God had taken these Gentile generations and grafted them into the cultivated tree of Israel. We Gentiles have become one with the family of God. We have become partakers of the root and fatness of the olive tree, namely, of all the promises of God. The fact that this was done was God's goodness toward us.

How is this possible? If God is good only to the righteous,

how could He be good to the Gentiles? Were these Gentiles better than the Jews? God forbid! They were not. How then, if God is good only to the righteous, could He reveal Himself in His goodness over these Gentiles by taking them and engrafting them into the good olive tree?

The answer is that God's goodness is sovereign. It is first. It is eternal. Only because God conceived of these branches in His counsel as in Christ are they grafted into the tree. God did not see them as unrighteous. He saw them as righteous. He saw them as righteous because He chose them. God says to these Gentile Christians, "When you behold My goodness, you must understand that it is nothing but sovereign goodness."

With a View to Rejected Jews or Gentiles

Not only must these Gentile Christians note the goodness of God, but they must also pay attention to His severity. They must also pay attention to the instance of God's justice to the uttermost. This instance of God's justice to the uttermost was, in the first place, His cutting off of the natural branches, that is, His cutting off of the Jews who fell. "On them which fell, severity," we read. This severity is shown by cutting them off. By *them which fell,* the text refers to the Jews who had always manifested their enmity to the truth and who had finally crucified Christ. That was their fall. God had taken them, cut them off, and thrown them under the tree.

The other instance of severity is a *possible* one: the possible cutting off of the Gentiles in the same way as the Jews. The text states, "toward thee, goodness, if thou continue in his goodness: otherwise thou also shalt be cut off." An important, controversial question is what is meant by the words *if thou continue in his goodness.* Is the meaning this: "If you continue to make yourselves worthy of goodness"? Are we to explain the expression this way: "If you make yourselves constantly worthy of goodness, you will remain in the olive tree, and if not, you will be cut off"? This interpretation is common. Some even like to read the text this way: "If thou continue in (thy) goodness," but this reading is mistaken. The text refers to the goodness *of God*. The question remains whether the apostle teaches here that God's goodness grafted the Gentiles into the tree, but that their remaining in the olive tree depends upon their *continuing* in God's goodness. This is not the meaning. The expression means, "If God continues to be good to you." It was God's goodness that grafted them into the olive tree, and the text teaches that their continuing in the tree always depends on the same goodness of God.

Let us apply this truth to our own congregation. God made us partakers of the tree. To us, too, the Word of God says that our continuing to be a church depends upon God's continuing to be good to us. It depends upon whether God will continue to be gracious, merciful, and long-suffering to us. *If thou continue in goodness* means, "if God continues to be good to you."

We ask, is it possible, then, that God can discontinue His goodness over those to whom He has once shown His goodness? The answer is yes. There is no falling away from grace of the individual Christian. God's election and calling are without repentance. No saint in Christ can fail to continue in the grace of God, because God chose him in His goodness and because this same goodness preserves him. But the apostle is speaking of *generations*. The branches in the text are not individuals, but generations. They are you and your children in your generations. And what is not possible with individuals is not only possible, but also a patent fact, with generations.

All history is a proof of this. When Paul preached, there were but a few branches under the tree. But now there is a great pile of branches under the tree, not only of the Jews but of the Gentiles as well. If you would trace some of the most recent generations under the tree, you would find that two or three generations back, they were grafted into the tree. The same is true of the false church, the church that still bears the name of church but is a church no more. There are many such churches. They are dead branches, and there is a pile of them under the tree.

Why are those dead branches under the tree while we are still in the tree? This is the issue for the apostle in the text. What shall we say? Shall we boast? What shall we say in answer to why we are still in the tree whereas there are many dead branches under the tree. Perhaps we will say, "It is because we stick to the truth; we hold to sound doctrine." The apostle replies, "Don't boast. This is the fruit of God's goodness. That you are still in the tree is God's goodness." As soon as His goodness leaves us, the truth, sound preaching, our Christian schools—all will go. In their place will come modernism. If we continue in goodness, all is well. But if not, we will be the object of God's severity. And we will also be cut off in your and my generations. We will be added to the pile of dead branches.

With a View to the Jews Received Again

Finally, God's goodness will become manifest again in the regrafting into the olive tree of the branches that have been cut off. Verse 24 reads, "If thou wert cut out of the olive tree which is wild by nature, and wert grafted contrary to nature into a good olive tree: how much more shall these, which be the natural branches, be grafted into their own olive tree?" The apostle calls the Jews *natural branches.* Implied is that this is more than can be said about us Gentiles. The meaning is not that the Jew has greater adaptation for grace than the Gentile. We must remember that for century after century, the olive tree had been limited to the generations of the Jews. If we start with Abraham, the olive tree belonged to the Hebrews longer than it has belonged to the Gentiles. The olive tree was Jewish. The form of salvation was Jewish. God spoke Jewish. He revealed Himself in the Jewish language. The Bible was Jewish. The prophets were theirs. The promises were theirs. Christ was theirs. Christ was a Jew. He was a Hebrew. He is not a Jew now, but He was a Jew. In light of this history, it is easier to graft a Jew back into the family of God than it is to graft a heathen into this family.

The explanation is not that it is easier to make a Jew believe. It is no easier to make a Jew believe than a Gentile. This is why the apostle says, "if they abide not still in unbelief," and "God is able to graft them in again." If a Jew is to be grafted in again, God must do it.

But it is easier to make a conscious, confessing Christian of the Jew than of the Gentile. It is hard to make a Christian of a Gentile. It sometimes takes years of instruction before he can be made a living, confessing Christian. But it is easy to make a conscious Christian of the Jew if once he has faith. Give a Jew faith, and what does he say? Does he say, "Instruct me"? No. Give a Jew faith, and he will say, "That is my Bible; that is my Christ; that is my gospel; that is my salvation." In this sense, it is easier to graft a Jew into the tree than it is a Gentile.

Being grafted in again is the special privilege of the Jew. The privilege is not that the Jews again become a special people. Rather, they become one with the family of God. It is one tree, one organism.

Did you ever notice that in a few generations a Jew disappears as a Jew if he becomes a Christian? Let a Jew become a Christian, and in a few generations you cannot tell that he is a Jew anymore. There may be many of us who are of Jewish descent, but you cannot see it anymore. If he does not become a Christian, he will always remain a Jew. Let him become a German, and he will remain a Jew, and you can see that he is a Jew. Let him become an American, and he will remain a Jew. But let him become a Christian, and in a few generations the Jew is a Jew no more.

Behold the goodness and severity of God—goodness in grafting you into the olive tree, goodness in keeping you in that tree in the line of generations, and severity in cutting you off if you do not continue in this sovereign goodness.

And why *behold* it? In order that we may not boast. Boast not against the branches, but boast in the goodness of God. He that glorieth, let him glory in the Lord.

Chapter Seventy-eight

The Mystery of the Salvation of All Israel

Romans 11:25, 26a
For I would not, brethren, that ye should be ignorant of this mystery, lest ye should be wise in your own conceits; that blindness in part is happened to Israel, until the fulness of the Gentiles be come in.
And so all Israel shall be saved.

It is, of course, to this part of Romans 11 that we have been looking forward. In a way, this entire chapter has been anticipating this passage, which is its climax. Therefore, we must bear in mind the immediate context. This section of the chapter was introduced by the figure of the olive tree, of which the root is Christ and the branches are the people of God in their generations. The olive tree is a figure of the one people of God. The apostle has called attention to the dead branches under the tree. These dead branches are the Jews who had been cut off, the Jews who fell. There is mention also of branches that had been grafted into the tree. These are the converted Gentiles. In addition, verses 23 and 24 spoke of branches that would be regrafted into the tree, that is, the Jews who had been cut off and whom God would graft again into the tree in their generations. This conversion of the Jews must be considered easier than the conversion of the Gentiles. This is not because the

~ *The Mystery of the Salvation of All Israel*

Jews have more spiritual receptivity than the Gentiles, but it is because the line of the covenant ran for years in the generations of the Jews. The line of the covenant is not strange to them. The promises were theirs. The Scriptures were theirs. Christ was theirs. The result is that, provided God give them faith, it is easier to graft Jews into the tree than Gentiles.

Verses 25 and 26a pursue the same subject. The passage begins with the word *For:* "*For* I would not, brethren, that ye should be ignorant of this mystery . . . that blindness in part is happened to Israel, until the fulness of the Gentiles be come in." The text is a reason why the apostle writes about the conversion of the Jews. He does not want the Gentile Christians to be ignorant of the mystery of the salvation of all Israel. They must know this mystery. They must know that blindness in part is happened to Israel until the fulness of the Gentiles be come in. They must know that "so all Israel shall be saved."

What Is Meant by "All Israel"

It would be easy simply to state what is meant by "all Israel." But it will be more beneficial to consider the main explanations that have been given. These may be classified in two groups. First, there is the group that would refer the expression *so all Israel shall be saved* to some future time. This group interprets the word *so* as meaning "then." They read the text this way: "Blindness in part is happened to Israel, until the fulness of the Gentiles be come in. And after this, all Israel shall be saved." On the other hand, there is the group that looks upon this salvation of all Israel as taking place now. They read the text this way: "Blindness in part is happened to Israel, until the fulness of the Gentiles be come in. And so, that is, in this way, all Israel shall be saved."

Each of these two main explanations of *all Israel* includes two distinct views. Among those who refer the salvation of all Israel to the future, some explain *all Israel* as consisting of every Jew then living. They read the text, "And then every Jew then living will be saved." But there are also those who interpret the phrase as teaching that the nation as a whole will be converted. They read the text this way: "Blindness in part is happened to Israel, until the fulness of the Gentiles be come in. And then the greater part of Israel as a whole will be saved as a nation."

The other group, which interprets this salvation of all Israel as taking place now, also contains two distinct views. Some of them interpret the expression *all Israel* as meaning "all the elect Jews." These elect Jews are saved all through this dispensation until the fulness of the Gentiles be come in. The others interpret the phrase *all Israel* as meaning "all Israel out of Jews and Gentiles." They read the text this way: "Blindness in part has happened to Israel, until the fulness of the Gentiles be come in, and so, in this way, all Israel out of Jews and Gentiles shall be saved."

Examining these views, it is plain, in the first place, that when the apostle speaks of all Israel that is to be saved, he cannot mean every Jew without exception, either now or in the future, for in the beginning of his discussion of the "Jewish question," the apostle has said that they are not all Israel, which are of Israel [Rom. 9:6]. The apostle would not now teach something that is in direct conflict with that former statement. It is the children of the promise who are counted for the seed. There can be no question that also in the text the apostle means the children of the promise.

In the second place, it may also be regarded as an established fact that we must not expect a special restoration of the Jews as a nation, or a special salvation for the nation as a whole. What we have learned thus far clearly contradicts this view. The figure of the olive tree contradicts this view. The fall of the Jews became the salvation of the Gentiles. But the Jews are again to be grafted into the same olive tree with the Gentiles. They, with the Gentiles, will become one people. There will be one Lord, one fold, and one shepherd. God does not form two peoples, but one people.

There is still another fact that has become established at this point. When the apostle is speaking of the salvation of the Jews, he is not speaking of some future time. This would contradict what the apostle has been teaching: that the Jews can be grafted in at any time. In verse 26 we read, "And so all Israel shall be saved." This word *so* is conveniently overlooked by those who would refer the salvation of all Israel to a future restoration of the Jews. Nevertheless, the word in the text is *so,* not *then.*

In the light of these facts, the first group of interpretations must be eliminated as contradicting the apostle's teaching. The text does not teach that God will restore the nation of Israel. It does not teach that after the fulness of the Gentiles be come in, every Jew shall be saved.

This leaves the two views of the second group. The first interpretation is that by all Israel is meant all the elect Jews. This interpretation is possible. The second possible interpretation is that all Israel means all Israel out of Jews and Gentiles. It is easy to come to the conclusion that these are the only two possible interpretations, but it is not easy to choose between them. Besides, doctrinally there is no difference between the two. Whether we understand that all the elect Jews shall be saved with the fulness of the Gentiles, or whether we understand that all the elect from Jews and Gentiles shall be saved makes no difference doctrinally.

In the past I thought that the expression *all Israel* referred to spiritual Israel from Jews and Gentiles. But I have changed my mind. It is now my view that by *all Israel* the apostle means all the elect Jews. My reason is that throughout this chapter the apostle has been speaking of Israel in distinction from the Gentiles. It is dangerous when a term has one meaning in a passage, suddenly to give it another meaning. This is also substantiated by what follows. We read in verse 28, "As concerning the gospel, they are enemies for your sakes: but as touching the election, they are beloved for the fathers' sakes." There the apostle is again speaking of the Jews. This would indicate that also verse 26 is speaking of the Jews. All the elect Jews—all true Israel—will be saved.

How All Israel Is Saved

All Israel will be saved *thus*, says verse 26. *Thus* refers back to verse 25: "Blindness in part is happened to Israel, until the fulness of the Gentiles be come in. And *so* (or *thus*) all Israel shall be saved." By the fulness of the Gentiles, of course, is not meant every Gentile without exception. Many explain that the time will come when all the Gentiles will be saved. When all the Gentiles shall be saved, then also will all the Jews be saved. And then Christ will come to a saved and righteous and peaceful world.

This interpretation we must not adopt. The Word of God gives us an entirely different picture of the future. That there will be a gradual conversion of all, Scripture does not teach. What we must expect is that there will be a falling away from the faith in the generations of them who were once in the olive tree. We must expect an increase in wickedness, not a gradual improvement of mankind. So much is this the case that Christ asked the question, "When the Son of man cometh, shall he find faith on the earth?" [Luke 18:8]. We must expect the Antichrist. We must not expect a bright future. It is pleasing to see the church increase. People like to hear that there will be gradual increase of the church, but this is contrary even to experience. There is always a falling away. We must not expect a great increase in the church. We must not even expect that all nations will be nominally Christianized. Such nations as China and Japan will never become Christian, not even nominally.

Therefore, we must explain the fulness of the Gentiles in the same way as the fulness of the Jews. The fulness of something is the full measure of that thing. The fulness of the Gentiles is that which is filled with Gentiles. But the question is, what is the measure? The answer is that the measure is God's election. When you put the last drop of water in a glass, you have the *fulness*. Likewise, when the last of the elect Gentiles is brought in, you have the *fulness* of the Gentiles.

Until then, hardness in part is happened to Israel. The meaning is not that the Jews have been hardened to a certain extent. Rather, it means that this hardening does not extend to every Jew. Only part of them are hardened. And when the apostle says that "blindness in part has happened to Israel, until the fulness of the Gentiles be come in," the meaning is plainly that this hardness will last until the fulness of the Gentiles be come in. To infer that after the fulness of the Gentiles has come in, all the Jews will be saved is a mistake. This is not implied by the word *until*. *Until* simply points to the end that is in view without any implication that after the end is reached, all or even many Jews will be saved. Similarly, for example, we read in I Corinthians 15[:25] that Christ must reign as king "till he hath put all enemies under his feet." The meaning is not that then He will reign no more. So here the apostle teaches that this hardening of the Jews in part must last until the fulness of the Gentiles be come in, and then will be the end. If the apostle had intended to teach that after the fulness of the Gentiles has come in, all the Jews will be saved, he would have written, "And *then* all Israel shall be saved." In fact, he wrote, "And *so* all Israel shall be saved.

Throughout the new dispensation the Jews are hardened in part; the others are saved. And thousands of Jews have already been brought in. The hardening in part must remain until the end. And the glory of the plan of God is that when the last Gentile shall have been brought in, the last of the Jews shall also have been brought in. In this way—*so*—all of the elect Jews shall be saved.

Why We Must Know This Mystery

The apostle begins verse 25 by saying, "I would not . . . that ye should be ignorant of this mystery." A mystery in Scripture is not something we do not understand. First, it is something that concerns the plan of salvation. Second, it is something that cannot be understood except by revelation. A mystery is something that we receive by revelation.

The apostle would not have us to be ignorant of the mystery of the salvation of all Israel. Why not? "Lest ye should be wise in your own conceits," that is, lest you pretend to know anything outside of revelation. We can apply this in general. Never be wise in your own conceits, because in your own conceits you know nothing. All that you know must be bound to the Word of God. You must always ask of everything, "What does the Word of God say about it?" Here the apostle applies the warning to the Jewish question. The warning is, "Don't say anything about the Jews as if you could solve the problem of the Jews in your own wisdom." People are trying to do this today. We try to answer the Jewish question in our conceits. This is what they are doing in Germany, and this has frequently been the case. Remember, though, there is woe upon the people who answer the question of the Jews in their own conceits, for there are people of God among them. Although they are enemies for the gospel's sake, we must not assume an attitude of pride over against them, for they are beloved for the fathers' sakes [v. 28]. Be not wise in your own conceits. Do not say, "They were cut off that I might be grafted in." Then you are wise in your own conceits.

Be not ignorant of this mystery: hardness has happened in part to Israel until the other part be saved and the fulness of the Gentiles be come in. And they will all be one people with this one confession: he that glorieth, let him glory in the Lord.

Chapter Seventy-nine

Hated yet Beloved

Romans 11:28-31
As concerning the gospel, they are enemies for your sakes: but as touching the election, they are beloved for the fathers' sakes.

For the gifts and calling of God are without repentance.

For as ye in times past have not believed God, yet have now obtained mercy through their unbelief:

Even so have these also now not believed, that through your mercy they also may obtain mercy.

The apostle is still speaking of the branches of the olive tree that had been cut off and that may and will be grafted into the tree again. I want to call special attention, once more, to what may be called the heart of this eleventh chapter, namely, the expression *and so all Israel shall be saved* [v. 26]. The words *all Israel* cannot possibly mean every Jew that shall live at a certain future time, as it is often explained; nor does it refer to the nation of Israel as a whole, a restored nation of Israel, as others interpret it. Neither does it mean all the spiritual children of the promise from both Jews and Gentiles, for whenever the apostle speaks of Israel in this chapter, he is referring to the Jews. Therefore, there is only one possible interpretation of the expression. By *all Israel* is meant the same thing as *the fulness* of the Jews spoken of in verse 12. When the fulness of the Gentiles shall have come in, then all Israel shall have been saved, too.

Chapter 11 of Romans is opposed to the idea of a special salvation for the Jews. It is also opposed to the idea of a certain mass conversion of the Jews. If this were the idea, the apostle would have written [in v. 26], "after that, or then, all Israel shall be saved." Instead, he wrote, "And *so* (that is, *thus*) all Israel shall be saved." The salvation of all Israel takes place throughout this entire dispensation. This is also evident from the quotation [from Isa. 59:20] that follows: "There shall come out of Sion the Deliverer, and shall turn away ungodliness from Jacob." This certainly refers to the coming of Christ in the flesh.

The mystery of which the passage speaks is this: the fulness of the Gentiles must be brought in. For this reason some of the Jewish branches were cut off. At the same time, while the fulness of the Gentiles is brought in, the Jews are grafted into the tree again.

Of this same fact the apostle is still speaking. He says that not only does Scripture show it, but it is also in harmony with the idea of election: "Although concerning the gospel they are enemies for your sakes, as touching the election, they are beloved for the fathers' sakes."

An Unchangeable Love

As concerning the gospel, the Jews are hated for the sake of the Gentiles. The Jews are *enemies,* as concerning the gospel, for your sakes. The term *enemies* may have an active or a passive sense. In the active sense, enemies are they who hate. In the passive sense, enemies are they who are hated. In the text the word *enemies* occurs in the passive sense. The meaning is not that the Jews hate God, Christ, the gospel, and God's people. Rather, the Jews are hated of God. They are the object of God's wrath. That this is true is evident from what follows. The apostle goes on to say that they are beloved for the fathers' sakes. Just as *beloved* is to be taken in the passive sense as beloved of God, so *enemies* must be taken in this same sense. With a view to the gospel, the Jews are hated for the sake of the Gentiles; but with a view to the election, they are beloved for the sake of the fathers. This is the contrast in the text.

That the Jews are hated "as concerning the gospel" means that they are hated according to the standard of the gospel. If you measure them according to the standard of the gospel, you can see that they are enemies. The gospel is this: "Believe in the Lord Jesus Christ, and you will have life; reject Him, and you will not see life, but the wrath of God will abide on you." The Jews had always hated the gospel. They hated the gospel to the extent that they killed Christ. If, therefore, you apply the gospel to them, they are hated. The wrath of God is on them.

But verse 28 explains that they are hated *for your sakes*. They are put in that place of hatred for your sakes. The apostle is speaking from the point of view of God's purpose. Suppose that the Jews had not rejected the gospel. What would have happened? Then they would not have crucified Christ, and there would have been no salvation. Those things had to happen. Salvation had to become universal. In the old dispensation, salvation was wrapped up in a package, and the package was addressed to the Jews. That package had to be unwrapped. It had to get a new address. If this was to be done, all that was Jewish had to be taken away, but if it was to be taken away, it had to be done in righteousness. Salvation had to be worked out so that it could come to the Gentiles. Therefore, all that was Jewish had to be taken away. They are enemies for your sakes.

But according to the election, they are beloved for the fathers' sakes. The expression *according to the election* does not refer to the remnant according to election mentioned in verse 5. Some interpret it this way, but this is not the meaning, as is plain from the context. It is also plain from the word *election* itself. The apostle is referring to God's counsel. He is referring to God's eternal mind concerning His people. When we speak of God's counsel, we mean that which God eternally had in mind concerning His people. Election means that God determined to save some, in distinction from others, whom He determined not to save. This does not mean that God at some moment back in eternity determined this. This is not the correct understanding of eternal election. God's counsel is that which is as eternal as God is eternal. It has no time. Election is God's eternal mind concerning His people. According to this election, the same people are beloved. This is possible, is it not? Not only is this possible, but if this were not the case with salvation, there would be no salvation. In God's counsel these same fallen Jews still appear as beloved. God sees His people in Christ. He loves them eternally. He does not see them as enemies. He never did. He never will. He chose them in Christ. He justified them in Christ. He sanctified them in Christ. He glorified them in Christ. As such they are the objects of His love. God does not love sinners. But He does not see His people as sinners. He sees them as beloved in Christ. If we look at the Jews according to the standard of election, they are beloved. This presupposes that the line of election never leaves the Jews. This is why the apostle says that they are beloved for the fathers' sakes. It is evident that the line of election is to continue with the Jews until the very end.

For the fathers' sakes does not refer to what the fathers were and did. It regards the fathers as fathers in the covenant, because God established His covenant with these fathers in the line of their generations. Therefore, the line of election continues with the Jews until the end. God said to Abraham that He would be the God of Abraham and of Abraham's seed forever. Although the covenant takes on a new form, yet that covenant cannot fail. "I will establish my covenant between me and thee and thy seed after thee in their generations" [Gen. 17:17] is a promise that we Gentiles also appropriate and that we have a right to appropriate, but this is only because we have been grafted into the trunk of the old olive tree. This does not alter the fact, however, that for the sake of the promises made unto the fathers, the promise continues to be fulfilled in the line of the generations of the Jews forever.

According to the standard of the gospel, the Jews are enemies for your sakes, but according to the standard of the election, they are beloved for the fathers' sakes. See the Jew in the light of what he did to Christ, and you say, "The Jew has no right to the fellowship of God's covenant." And we hate him, even as God also hates him. This is certainly not the motive of the political hatred of the Jew in our day.[1] Politically the Jew makes himself hated. When you read in the newspapers about the sympathy for the poor Jews, you must take it with a grain of salt. People talk about how sorry they are for the poor Jews, although no one wants to open their country to them. They are now talking about sending them to a place in South America where even a mosquito can hardly live. When people say that they are sorry for the poor Jews, you must not take them too seriously. They did not feel sorry for those poor people in Russia. When the Jews are hated today politically, and people tell you how sorry they are for them, I think that money is behind it. The Jews have some money. This hypocritical sympathy for the Jews has nothing in common with the love for the Jews of verse 28. The Jews are beloved for the fathers' sakes, and we must not despise them.

An Irrevocable Gift of Grace

Why are the Jews beloved of God? "For the gifts and calling of God are without repentance" [v. 29]. By *gifts* is meant the gifts of grace—those that in Christ God bestows upon His people to save and to glorify them. They are the objective gifts of atonement, reconciliation, forgiveness, justification, and the adoption to children. They are also the subjective gifts as we receive them by the Spirit—the gifts of regeneration, faith, hope, love, sanctification, and the final resurrection.

When the apostle uses the term *calling*, he does not use the

---

1. The late 1930s. In what follows, Hoeksema exposes the hypocrisy of the Western nations, who knew what Nazi Germany was doing to the Jews.

term as we use it in dogmatics. In dogmatics we usually make a distinction between regeneration and calling. But the apostle does not make any distinction between regeneration and calling. As the apostle Paul uses the term, calling includes regeneration. Calling, therefore, is the regenerating, creative, life-giving power of God in the heart. He says to the sinner, "Rise from the dead." This calling does not come through preaching. But there is a calling that is God's address of the sinner's consciousness through the preaching of the Word. God translates him from darkness to light so that he becomes a fellow citizen of the household of God.

These gifts and this calling of God are without repentance. Why is *calling* mentioned in distinction from the *gifts?* The calling is certainly one of the gifts of grace. Why, then, is there mention of the gifts *and* of the calling? The reason is plain: it is through the calling that all the gifts of grace are bestowed upon the elect sinner. The calling is the *means;* the gifts of grace are the *fruit.* Since the Jews are beloved, the gifts of grace belong to them; therefore, God will surely call them.

The gifts and the calling are without repentance; that is, they are without repentance in God's counsel. God determined upon whom He should bestow the gifts of grace and the gift of the calling, and upon whom He should not bestow them. In this determination God never changes His mind, because this determination of God to bestow His grace upon His people is sovereign, is free. It has nothing to do with our works, whether good or bad. God never changes. We do. We make a will and leave our goods to someone. But we live a few years longer, and we see that the person whom we named in our will is unworthy. We say that we are sorry that we named that person in our will. We change our mind; we change our will; we make what is called our *last* will. But there is no *last* will in God. God never says that He is sorry, because the people upon whom He determined to bestow His grace are themselves the products of that grace. He beholds them as beloved. Therefore, He never changes His mind.

The Jews are beloved because of the election.

Election is the most beautiful comfort we have. Take election away, and we lose our comfort. Do you believe in Christ? Listen! The gifts and calling of God are *without repentance.* If God gives you the gifts of grace once, He never repents. If you fall into sin, you may repent and plead that grace, for the gifts and calling of God are without repentance.

A Sure Mercy

What is true of the people who have been called is true also of them who have not yet been called. Since the gifts and calling are without repentance, it follows that the elect Jews obtain mercy. Against this, there is one more possible objection. The Jews once were possessors of mercy in their generations, but they despised that mercy; therefore, God is finished with them. What does the apostle say to this? He says that the same thing is true of us Gentiles. "As ye in times past have not believed God, yet have now obtained mercy through their unbelief: Even so have these also now not believed, that through your mercy they also may obtain mercy." The apostle concludes that when it comes to the principle of the matter, the position of the Jews who have been cut off is no different from that of the Gentiles. They have not believed; neither have we Gentiles. We have obtained mercy; they will obtain mercy. The unbelief and breaking off of the Gentiles is a reality in the fall of Adam. If you look back to Adam, all are covenant breakers. Also the Gentiles were beloved in their generations, but they fell. They believed not in God in times past, even as the Jews now have not believed.[2] Our English version says that we

---

2. In *God's Eternal Good Pleasure* Hoeksema declines to find the unbelief and breaking off of the Gentiles in the fall of Adam. He chooses, rather, to find the breaking off of the Gentile branches from the olive tree in the history subsequent to Noah. The Swart manuscript definitely appeals to Adam and says nothing about Noah.

Gentiles did not *believe*. The Dutch version says that we were *disobedient*. The word in the original really means neither "believe" nor "obey" but includes both. The original says that we were not *persuaded*. If one is persuaded by the Word of God, he will believe and obey.

In times past, we Gentiles were not persuaded by the Word. In the new dispensation, even though we did not look for it, we obtained mercy. Why? Because according to the election we are beloved. This is why we obtained mercy. Mercy is God's will to bless His people. It is His will to make them happy as He is happy, that is, blessed as He is blessed.

Where is the objection then? It is true that the Jews have now not believed. In fact, they have always opposed the gospel. But they are beloved according to the election. We obtained mercy through their unbelief. Their unbelief became the occasion that we obtained mercy. As in times past we have not believed, yet have now obtained mercy through their unbelief; even so have they now not believed, that through our mercy they also may obtain mercy.

We must not misunderstand this as though the Jews will be saved by our showing mercy to them. Rather, through the mercy that we have received from God, the Jews must obtain mercy. Implied is that we must not despise them. We must walk, in our confession and conduct, as those who have obtained mercy. We must glory in the mercy of God in Jesus Christ. We must manifest the mercy that we have received. The Jews will become jealous. This is not because our mercy makes them jealous. Rather, God will awaken that old love through our mercy.

The conclusion is this: if you boast, boast in the Lord. Our salvation is not because of what we are. It is according to the election that we are beloved. He that glorieth, let him glory in the Lord.

Chapter Eighty

The Only Adorable God

Romans 11:33-36
O the depth of the riches both of the wisdom and knowledge of God! how unsearchable are his judgments, and his ways past finding out!
For who hath known the mind of the Lord? or who hath been his counsellor?
Or who hath first given to him, and it shall be recompensed unto him again?
For of him, and through him, and to him, are all things: to whom be glory for ever. Amen.

These are the closing verses of this entire section. As to the connection with what precedes, they might be considered merely to follow upon the immediately preceding verses, especially verse 32. They might also be viewed as the closing verses of chapter 11. But we might extend the scope and consider them to be the doxology upon chapters 9-11. In a still broader sense, we might consider them to be the closing verses of all that precedes in the book of Romans. It seems to me that the last is the most proper. First, there is nothing in the context limiting these verses to the immediately preceding. This doxology is applicable to all that precedes. Second, chapter 11 is the closing chapter of the doctrinal part of the epistle, so that this doxology closes the doctrinal section. But the verses do so in such a way that all that precedes them gradually leads up to this song of praise, especially the last three chapters, chapters 9-11.

It is not necessary to discuss in detail all the material found in this doxology. This would also be impossible in just one brief exposition. However, we must notice that there is a certain order in these verses and their subject material. We discover that the number three prevails. There are especially three sets of conceptions corresponding with each other. There is, in the first place, the riches, the wisdom, and the knowledge of God. Corresponding to them, there is a second set of three, namely, that no one gave God anything, no one counseled Him, and no one knew His mind. These two sets correspond. Because there is in God a depth of riches, no one gave anything to Him. Because there is in Him a depth of wisdom, no one has been His counselor. And because there is in Him a depth of knowledge, no one has known His mind.

To this again correspond the last set of three. Because God is infinite in riches, so that no one gave anything to Him, all things are *out of* Him. Because He is infinite in wisdom, so that no one counseled Him, all things are *to* Him. And because He is infinite in knowledge, so that no one has known His mind, all things are *through* Him.

We must remember these three sets. O the depth of the riches, the wisdom, and the knowledge of God. No one gave anything to Him; no one counseled Him; no one has known His mind. Out of Him, to Him, and *through* Him are all things. The conclusion is that God is God alone. Therefore, glory be to Him forever.

An Inexhaustible Fountain

Verse 33 should be read a little differently than our translation suggests. Our English translation would have wisdom and knowledge modifying the riches. The meaning then beomes, "O the depth of the riches, that is, of the wisdom and knowledge of God." But in the original Greek there is no reason for reading it this way. The original Greek reads, "O the depth of the riches, and of the wisdom, and of the knowledge." The riches, wisdom, and knowledge modify the word *depth*.

When we speak of the riches of God, we must not think of what we usually consider to be riches. When Scripture speaks of the riches of God, these riches are entirely spiritual. God's riches are not riches that He possesses outside of Himself. God's riches are His adorable virtues, His perfections. At the same time we must remember that the riches of God are the only riches there are. Riches never consist in things we possess. Material things are never riches in themselves. In God, riches are His grace, His love, His mercy, His justice, His holiness, His righteousness, and His long-suffering. God is rich in virtues. God is rich in light and therefore in virtues. Because these virtues are really riches, man can never have riches apart from these virtues.

The idea of the depth of these riches is that the apostle stands at the edge of the fountain. From the top, he looks down at the riches of the content of the fountain. He sees but a little of it. He just sees the top. But the little that he sees is a suggestion of the infinite riches of God. The question is, how do we receive this knowledge of the infinite depth of the riches of God? The answer is that we can know it only by seeing and knowing that which comes out of Him, just as we know a fountain by the water that sparkles out of it.

This is why the expression O *the depth of the riches of God* corresponds to the expression *for out of Him are all things*. To see the depth of the riches of God, one must know that all things are out of Him. The things that come from Him indicate the riches that are in Him. All things in creation, all things in the history of the world, all things in the work of redemption—all things are out of God. The earth and its fulness are out of God. All that ever happens in history is out of God. So it is with redemption. Christ is out of God. All the blessings in Christ are out of God. Regeneration, calling, faith, justification, sanctification—all are out of God.

All things are not out of God in the sense that what is now outside of Him is now no more in Him. God is not emptied out.

Nor is the meaning that all things emanate from God.

That all things are out of Him refers to God's counsel. God conceives of all these things. He has them eternally in His mind. He eternally wills them. Therefore, they have their origin nowhere else. There is no other source of anything besides God.

The inescapable question arises: do the *all things* that are out of God also include evil? Do they include the devil? Do they include the reprobate? Do they include hell? Today many have forgotten these truths. Many would rather give a negative answer to these questions. Would we really rather have another source for hell than for heaven? Would we really rather have another source for evil than for good? God is the source of all things. He is the source of evil, not in the sense that there is any evil in Him, but in the sense that He decreed the devil, the wicked, and the evil. There is no other source. There is no other explanation of things. It is impossible to find another explanation in which the heart can rest. The church fathers always said that the heart can find no rest until it finds rest in God. Come what may, I know one thing: all things are out of God. Knowing that all things are out of God, I also know this: all things work for good, and I rest in Him.

From this follows what the apostle says in verse 35: "Who hath first given to him, and it shall be recompensed unto him again?" We have never given anything to God whereby He became obliged to us. A man would be an utter fool—should some millionaire give him ten dollars—if he would give a penny back to that millionaire and then imagine that he had done something for the millionaire. This is a weak illustration of the attempt of man to give God something, or to do something whereby God would become obliged to him, supposing that we do something first. God has all the riches. We have nothing. We have nothing in the natural sense or in the spiritual sense unless God gives it first. God is the source. We always receive out of Him. We can never come to God and say, "I have done this for you; now you must do something for me." All things are out of God. If we would serve and glorify God, we must never take our little cup and pour a drop into the fountain. O the depth of the riches of God! Out of Him are all things. Who can ever give anything to Him? The result is that we get down in the dust and say, "I thank Thee."

An Infallible Executive

God is not only the fountain; He is also the executive head of all things. The text teaches this: "O the depth of the knowledge of God, of His judgments, and of His ways; all things are through Him." All that takes place in history and all that takes place in redemption are through Him. There is a difference between the expression "all things are *out of* God" and the expression "all things are *through* God." The former refers to things as they are in His counsel. This counsel is realized in history. It is not realized by the creature outside of God. God is not only the source of all things, but He is also the sole executive, the one who works out His counsel in history. He works through Himself. *Through Him* all things are made, sustained, governed, and controlled. *Through Him* is Christ. *Through Him* is redemption. *Through Him* is the church. All things are not through Him in such a way that what is accomplished is now independent of Him. But *through Him* all things continue to be. All things exist and continue to be through God.

O the depth of the knowledge of God! This is our conviction, especially when we look at all things from the viewpoint of God's judgments and ways. God's judgments must be understood in the wider sense of decisions. The ways of God are His advance in history. God goes right on in history. How untraceable are His ways!

There is a difference between *knowledge* and *wisdom*. To know things is to penetrate into the nature and purpose of things. The knowledge of God is, primarily, His knowledge of Himself. He knows things out of Himself. God has in mind everything that takes place in history. He has all things in His mind eternally. Things that are past, present, and future to us are all in God's mind. They are in His mind in such a way that He has them always before Him. This is not so with us. Even the knowledge we have, we do not always have before us. But God has all things always before Him. This is God's eternal knowledge. This is why God always knows what to do and how to decide. This is why He never retraces His steps. God always goes on. His ways are ways of knowledge and of perfect wisdom. And they are His ways alone, for no one gave anything to Him, no one counseled Him, no one has known His mind.

It is the same with the depth of *wisdom*. We see a little of it when we see that sin must serve righteousness, when we see that corruption must serve holiness, when we see that death must serve life. We see a little of it when we see that the fall of the Jews must serve the reconciliation of the world. The outcome of the little that we see is that we cry out, "O the depth of the wisdom and knowledge of God! How unsearchable are His judgments, and His ways past finding out!"

The Sole End and Purpose of All

The end and purpose of all things are expressed this way in the text: "All things are to (*unto*) Him." All things are unto God. Nothing is excepted. This is not a wish or an ideal but a fact: all things are unto Him. They always will be. Heaven and hell, the devil and his hosts, reprobate and saint, good and evil—all things are unto God. They all point to Him. He is the end they all have in view. This is the scheme of things in time and eternity. If we look at them rightly, all things say, "There, in God, is the source of all riches, wisdom, and knowledge." As all the sunbeams point to the sun and say, "There is the sun," so all things in time and in eternity point to God and say, "There He is." Not only do they say, "There He is," but they also say, "O the depth of the riches, wisdom, and knowledge of God!" The reason is that all things are a manifestation of His riches, and this is so because of the depth of wisdom.

Wisdom differs from *knowledge*. Wisdom is knowing how to adapt things to a certain purpose, to a certain end. Because the depth of wisdom is in God, because no one counseled Him, because no one has known His mind, and because no one gave anything to Him, there is but one proper position for us to take. That is to say what the apostle says: "To Him be glory forever"!

It makes no difference whether you say it or deny it: still all things are *unto Him*. The difference is in this: it is the folly of sin to stand in the midst of all things and say, "I will not confess, 'To Him be glory.'" This is the pride of the devil. The devil says, "I will have all things point to me." He refuses to point to God. This is the pride of sin. It is also the folly of sin, for all things do and will point to Him. The question is this: will you point to God willingly, and be blessed, or will you point to God unwillingly, and be damned?

The scheme of all things is that all things are unto Him. Blessed is the man who will find his place in this scheme and will join in with the closing words of the apostle. It is grace when we delight in saying, "Glory be to Him for ever!" In saying it, we will be eternally blessed.

Chapter Eighty-one

Transformation from Within

Romans 12:2
And be not conformed to this world: but be ye transformed by the renewing of your mind, that ye may prove what is that good, and acceptable, and perfect, will of God.

Practice and doctrine are inseparably connected. They cannot be divorced from each other. This is indicated in what the apostle writes in verse 1 of Romans 12: "I beseech you therefore, brethren, by the mercies of God, that ye present your bodies a living sacrifice, holy, acceptable unto God, which is your reasonable service." The meaning is that we have understood these mercies of God of which the apostle has been speaking in the preceding chapters of Romans, and by faith we have received them. The implication is that if this is not the case—if he cannot address us as possessors of the mercies of God—he cannot even begin his practical admonition.

The mercies of God are a prerequisite for a Christian life from a twofold point of view. First, they are the ground, or possibility, for a true Christian life. Second, they are at the same time the ground of the obligation to walk in these mercies of God. If we are not in principle delivered from sin, if we are not children of God, it is impossible to hear and do the Word of God as we have it in Romans 12–16. Some people always call for a practical sermon, but a practical sermon is not less difficult than a doctrinal sermon. While a doctrinal sermon brings to us the mercies of God, a practical sermon comes to us with the admonition, "Do!" In what follows in Romans, we must not expect something easy, but we must prepare ourselves for something to which we may have many objections. For the Word of God is not according to the flesh. Many times when we are inclined to respond to the Word, doing it is impossible. Therefore, the apostle here addresses the church by the mercies of God. It is only by the mercies of God that we do, and *can* do, what the Word admonishes us to do.

According to verse 1, we must present our bodies a living sacrifice, holy, acceptable unto God. Our bodies are mentioned here because all our life becomes manifest through our bodies. By our body is meant our whole life. Our whole life, as it becomes manifest in and through the body, we must present to God as a living sacrifice. But if we are to do this, it is necessary that we hear this other Word of God: "Be not conformed to this world: but be ye transformed by the renewing of your mind, that ye may prove what is that good, and acceptable, and perfect, will of God."

The Meaning

In order to be understood clearly, the apostle first puts this admonition in a negative form, and then in a positive form. The negative form of the admonition is, "Be not conformed to this world." The word *world* in the original literally means "age." It has come to mean *world* from the viewpoint of the development of the world in time. The world has had different ages, different times, different periods. In these different ages or times or periods, the world fills itself with different ideas and things. For example, we speak of our present age as the machine age. The text admonishes us not to be conformed to the world as this world develops in the particular age in which the church lives.

We must not copy the world in our walk and conversation. This is a literal translation of the original Greek. One beautiful word in the original declares that the world of our own day has *forms*. The world has certain schemes. The world lives from the spiritual, ethical principle of sin. The deepest principle from which the world lives is enmity against God. It never lives from any other principle. There is nothing else in the world. Even when the world speaks piously, telling us, for example, that democracy is rooted in religion, the world actually hates God. There is no difference between a pious wickedness and downright wickedness. From this principle of enmity against God, the world creates forms. It creates a certain scheme of life. In its outward walk the world is characterized by this deepest principle of sin. Living from the principle of enmity against God, the world practices a form of life consisting of sinful works, sinful speech, sinful amusements, sinful pleasures, and sinful treasures. This is true of the world in every relation. The form of the home becomes carnal. You can see it before your very eyes. Why is the relation between man and wife being corrupted? It is corrupted in divorce. It is corrupted in the murder of the seed of children that is called birth control. You see it in the pleasures of the world: the dance, the movies, the theaters. You can see the world's sinful form of life in its attitude against all authority. You see it in the relation of employer and employee. Negatively, the admonition is this: let not your life be characterized by copying the form of this world. Do not copy this world. Be not conformed to this world.

Does anyone object that an admonition of this kind is not necessary? The fact is that no admonition is more urgent than this one. There is no admonition more timely. This is because there is oh so much world in the Christian. And there is oh such a small beginning of the new life. We must take this seriously. The Christian is almost all world and only a little Christian. It is easy to brag about a life to the glory of God and a life of sanctification as if we were almost in heaven, but in truth there is much world, much flesh, to the Christian. Our body is all world. And our soul, so intimately connected with our body, is also all world, apart from the new principle of the life of Christ instilled into the soul by the Holy Spirit. Besides, the Christian is surrounded by the forms of the world. When we open our eyes, we see nothing but world. We see nothing of the kingdom of God. If we go the way of least resistance, therefore, and don't fight, we will do what the apostle says we must not do. We will always copy the world. We will copy the world in our dress, in our face, in our speech, in our pleasures, in everything.

We may compare life in the world to people drifting on a strong current in a rowboat. They are drifting just above the falls. On this current are three kinds of people. There are people who help the current along. They row with the current, laughing, singing, and having a good time. There are also people who row desperately upstream. And there are people who let the oars rest and drift downstream. The Word of God says to them, "Don't drift downstream! Row against the stream!" This is the text. Are you going downstream? Don't copy the world! Don't be conformed in your life and walk to the forms of the world! If you do conform your life to this world's forms, you go to destruction.

Instead, be *transformed!* This is the opposite of copying the world. To be *transformed* is to be independent of forms. This is the meaning of the word in the original. To be transformed means that we must be changed, but in the changing we are independent of any forms. We row upstream. This is the admonition. This is practical.

The Possibility

How is it possible to row upstream against the current that is in the world? How is it possible in view of the fact that all that is in the world is inclined to copy the forms of this world? The apostle says that we have a motor. We have motor power so that we can go against the stream. This motor power is the renewing of the mind. If this is not so, it is hopeless. But I beseech you by the mercies of God revealed in Christ Jesus—the mercies of reconciliation, forgiveness of sins, justification, and sanctification—be not conformed to this world, but be transformed by the renewing of your mind.

The mind in Scripture, and especially in the epistle to the Romans, is what we may call the highest faculty of man's spiritual existence. The highest, the noblest part of man's soul is the mind, according to the Word of God. In a formal sense, it is the part of man that makes it possible for him to be religious. It is the mind that makes it possible for man to know God and to determine his own relation to God, consciously and willingly. In this respect, it is man's mind that distinguishes him from other creatures. It is the mind that distinguishes him from the animal. The animal has many characteristics, but it has no mind.

The mind of man is by nature corrupt. It is darkened. Man has not lost his mind. It is not that he has no knowledge of God. But man's mind is darkened in a spiritual, moral sense, so that he cannot see God as one who is to be desired above all. This is who God is: the one to be desired above all. God is good, benevolent, merciful, and the fountain of all goodness, but the natural mind is so darkened that man looks upon God as the cause of all his evil. This is literally expressed by a certain society in Russia that calls itself the "Society of the Godless." They teach that God is the source of all the evil that befalls man. Therefore, they persecute the Christians. But this is only the expression of the darkened mind.[1]

The apostle speaks of the renewing of the mind. This refers to God's calling of us. It refers to our regeneration, to the irresistible calling of God. The result is that we seek Him. The mind of the Christian has been renewed, but the renewing of

---

1. Hoeksema preached this sermon early in 1939. The evil of Nazi Germany did not blind him to the wickedness of the communism of the Soviet Union. Hoeksema's condemnation fell upon the fundamental evil of the communism of Marx, Lenin, and Stalin: its godlessness.

his mind is but a renewing in principle. There is still the old man in the Christian. He has a renewed mind in principle, but he also has much of the world in him. To the Christian with a renewed mind, but also having much of the world in him, the apostle says, "Turn around! Let your new mind determine what should be your walk! Be ye transformed by the renewing of your mind."

Does someone respond, "How can I do this?" First let me ask what you said to the exhortation. Did you say, "Yes, but . . ."? There is no "but." It may be that you said, "Yes, but then I must practically go out of the world." My answer is, go out of the world then. Perhaps, you said, "Then I will lose my name, my position." My answer is, lose your name, then. Or you said, "They will laugh at me." I answer, let them laugh. Did you say, "Then I will provoke the wrath of the world to the extent that I may have to die"? My answer is, die then. There is no other biblical answer. "Whosoever will save his life shall lose it: and whosoever will lose his life for my sake shall find it" [Matt. 16:25]. But for God's sake, for the sake of His mercy, don't copy the world!

Did you say, "I have in my heart the desire to do that, but how can I? How can I obey this admonition?" There are only two ways by which you can do it. You can do it by using your Bible. If you want to row upstream, you can do so only by clinging to your Bible, studying your Bible! Then you will not be conformed to this world. The other means is prayer. You must be instant in prayer. Are we? Is it not true, as we are sliding back, that we have not been a praying people? Oh, we are a religious people. But I speak of a consciousness of wanting to do this Word of God that brings us to our knees in prayer.

The Result

The result will be that we "prove what is that good, and acceptable, and perfect, will of God." God's will here is God's will concerning you and me. His will is good in that it is salutary. Sin is never good for us. Only the will of God is good for us. The will of God is also acceptable. It is well pleasing; that is, it is well pleasing to Him that we do His will. It is also perfect, leading to perfection. It has a good end.

But if we do not go upstream, we do not prove that good, acceptable, and perfect will of God. Proving the will of God is tasting or experiencing that the will of God is good. When we do the will of God, we experience that we lack nothing. To prove, to taste, to experience, what is that good, and acceptable, and perfect will of God is a blessedness that if we know it once, even in part, we will not exchange it for all the world.

Therefore, I beseech you, by the mercies of God that have been bestowed on you, be not conformed to this world, but be transformed by the renewing of your mind, that you may prove what is that good, and acceptable, and perfect will of God.

Chapter Eighty-two

Sober-mindedness with a View to the Gifts of Grace

Romans 12:3-8

For I say, through the grace given unto me, to every man that is among you, not to think of himself more highly than he ought to think; but to think soberly, according as God hath dealt to every man the measure of faith.

For as we have many members in one body, and all members have not the same office:

So we, being many, are one body in Christ, and every one members one of another.

Having then gifts differing according to the grace that is given to us, whether prophecy, let us prophesy according to the proportion of faith;

Or ministry, let us wait on our ministering: or he that teacheth, on teaching;

Or he that exhorteth, on exhortation: he that giveth, let him do it with simplicity; he that ruleth, with diligence; he that sheweth mercy, with cheerfulness.

Verses 3–8 of Romans 12 form a passage that cannot very well be divided. In this section the apostle begins to apply concretely the general exhortation with which he introduced this practical part of his epistle. He applies the exhortation first of all to the church. Specifically, he applies it to the activity and life of the church through her many members.

The general admonition with which the apostle began this part of his epistle was that we should present our body a living sacrifice unto God. Here on earth, in our present body, we should present all our life, in all its relations, to God. This is our reasonable service. Not merely being busy in the outward service, but giving ourselves: this is our reasonable service.

But to do this in the world, it is necessary that we row against the current. We may not allow ourselves to drift downstream with the current. We may not become conformed to this world. We may not copy this world. The world must not tell us how we should live and walk. Instead, we are to be transformed by the renewing of the mind, that we may prove what is that good, and acceptable, and perfect will of God. From the new principle that God has instilled in the heart, we must fight against the current, for we are only a little spiritual, and much worldly. And the little that is spiritual must combat that which is worldly.

The text begins with the little word *For* so frequently used in Scripture. "*For* I say, through the grace given unto me, to every man that is among you, not to think of himself more highly than he ought to think." The text continues: ". . . but to think soberly, according as God hath dealt to every man the measure of faith." The apostle is saying that what he now exhorts, we will never carry out, we will never do, we will rebel against, unless we are transformed by the renewing of the mind.

The apostle emphasizes that he addresses every man in the church of Rome. He comes to every individual among them. It is not as though the entire epistle does not come to all, but the apostle emphasizes that this particular exhortation concerns every member among them. He wants them to understand that one cannot receive this part of the Word of God for his neighbor, but every man must receive it for himself. "I say . . . to every man that is among you . . ."

Each of us must listen attentively to this Word of God, for we are all infected with the disease of highmindedness. Although this is very humiliating, this is the viewpoint that the apostle takes. To every member of the congregation comes the exhortation not to think more highly of himself than he ought to think. This exhortation has in view the gifts that Christ bestows on His church.

The apostle makes plain that he is not exhorting the church merely as a man exhorts other men, for by nature all, including Paul himself, are filled with the same highmindedness and pride. The apostle is exhorting not merely as a man to other men, but through the apostolic grace of God given unto him. He speaks as an apostle. In this grace he says, "Be not highminded. Think not more highly of yourselves than you ought to think, but think soberly, according as God hath dealt to every man the measure of faith."

I once read a fable about an ass and a little dog. The ass was in the stable, but the little dog was in the parlor. Frequently the little dog sat on its mistress' lap. The ass became jealous of the little dog. It broke into the parlor, sat on its mistress' lap, and was shot. The apostle tells us, do not be an ass in the spiritual sense.

The Gifts

The text speaks of *gifts*. In the original Greek, the word in verse 6 translated *gifts* is the word in the New Testament for *grace*. The verse speaks of the gifts of grace. The giving of these gifts is according to the measure of grace that each has received. In this respect also, the apostle addresses each member of the church.

There are gifts that we all have in common. We all have the gift of regeneration, of faith, of hope, of love, of adoption, of justification, and of sanctification. There is no difference as to these general gifts. There is, to be sure, a difference in degree, but essentially there is no difference. The apostle is not speaking of the gifts that all have in common. He is speaking of those gifts that all do not possess in the same sense and that all do not have in common. He is speaking of the gifts of prophecy, of ministry, of teaching, of exhortation, of ruling, and of mercy.

These gifts are really natural capacities sanctified by God and pressed into the service of the church. For example, the gift of teaching is not a gift unique to the church. There is also teaching in the world. The gift of exhortation is not a gift peculiar to the church, either. You also have this gift in the world. But the gifts of which the apostle is speaking are the natural gifts, sanctified by faith. It makes a world of difference whether one has the gift of teaching without faith or has this gift sanctified by the Spirit. The gifts in view in Romans 12 are all sanctified by the Spirit. They have become gifts of grace.

These gifts are distributed among the members of the church according to the measure of grace. Not all are teachers. All do not have the gift, the knack, of teaching. We are not all rulers. Everybody does not know how to rule. We do not all have that gift. We are not all prophets. We are not all ministers. We are not all able to exhort. We are not all givers. We are not all able to show mercy. Blessed be God that we are not! For then there would be no harmony in the body. Some have some of these gifts; others have others of these gifts.

No one man has all of these gifts. There have been great men in the church, men upon whom God bestowed brilliant gifts. There have been greater men in the church than in the world. It is sometimes said that these gifts are more abundantly bestowed upon the world than they are upon the church. It is true that the world has a far wider scope in which to use these gifts. Because of this, it looks as if God bestows more brilliant gifts upon the world. This is not so, however; there have been great and brilliant men in the church, but there is never one man who can claim that he has all the gifts that God bestows upon His church. God never does this.

In addition, God does not bestow these gifts in such a way that one has one gift and the other has another gift. Rather, He bestows the gifts "according to the grace that is given to us." One has more of a particular gift than another has of the same gift. This is the meaning of the phrase in verse 6 that says, "Having then gifts differing according to the grace that is given to us."

Let us look at these gifts. We must keep in mind that the apostle is not speaking exclusively of the special offices. He is thinking of all in the church: "I say . . . to every man that is among you." The elders and deacons have gifts, but also every officebearer in the church has gifts. All of the members are officebearers, for all have the office of believer. The first gift that is mentioned is prophecy. This gift the church has no more. There was a time when the church did not have the entire revelation of the Word of God. Then it had the gift of prophecy. There was an operation of the Spirit upon some by which they revealed certain things that were still hidden. They had this gift of prophecy.

Then there are ministers. The general meaning of the word *minister* is "servant." There are many servants in the church. We ought all to be servants. There are always some special servants in the church. The church has servants in her elders and deacons, but she also has many other servants. The leader of a society for Bible study is a servant. The teacher in the Sunday school is a servant. The janitor is a servant. The organist in the worship service is a servant. The passage refers to anyone who serves in any capacity in the church.

There is also the gift of teaching. Of course, the minister of the Word is a teacher, but there are also others in the congregation who have the gift of teaching. They know how to teach. Others have the gift of exhortation: they know just how to comfort, to exhort, to admonish. There are people who have a knack of exhorting others.

The apostle speaks of the gift of ruling. There are some in the church who have the gift of ruling. The Dutch translation uses the word *voorstander,* "one who stands before others" [v. 8]. The ruler may be an elder, but he may also be a president of a society or anyone who is a leader of some kind. Not everyone has the gift of ruling. Some people are unable to rule.

Some people have the gift or knack of giving. All can give, but the apostle has in mind that gift by which some people have the knack of giving graciously. They know just *how* to give.

Then there is the gift of showing mercy. To be merciful is not everybody's work. It is something that cannot be trusted to everyone.

Three principles must guide us in the use of our gifts. First, one must never pretend that he has more of a certain gift than he really has. That is what is meant by the words *according to the grace that is given to us*. If you have received a certain gift, stick to it, and do not act as if *all* of that gift was received by you. Do not act as if you had all of that gift by yourself. It is dangerous to have gifts. For example, if the Lord gives just a little of a gift to someone, he will be inclined to hide it. You can see this in our societies for Bible study. Some do not speak at all. They do not take part in the discussion. They have only a little of the gift of teaching, and they hide it. You must be active according to the proportion of the gift of grace received. You may not be a great teacher, but this does not imply that you cannot teach at all.

The second principle is that every one must be busy in the office to which his gift calls him. One should not act as if he had all the gifts. If he has the gift of teaching, he should be satisfied with teaching. He should not act as if he had the gift of mercy, too.

The third principle is that we do the work diligently to which our gift calls us. If someone is a ruler who must be pushed all the time, he cannot be a ruler. A ruler must rule *with diligence*. So it is with every member and his gift. He who gives, let him do it *with simplicity*. He who shows mercy must do it *with cheerfulness*. He must not be constrained to do it. He must not do it simply because he is compelled. If one is busy in the work of mercy, he must do it cheerfully.

The Sober-mindedness

If these gifts are to be used in this way, there is one fundamental requirement: we do not think too much of ourselves. The apostle says, "I address this warning to everyone," for it is characteristic of sin that we think too much of ourselves. If we were already in heaven, this admonition would not be necessary, but there is still much flesh in us. The characteristic of sin is that we want to be someone.

We think highly of ourselves on three counts. First, we think that we have something *of ourselves*. However, we have nothing of ourselves. We have nothing that we have not received. If we think we have something of ourselves, we act as if we are somebody, and then we think too highly of ourselves. Sane thinking is that we know we have nothing of ourselves. Sane thinking is that we know what we have is only by grace.

Second, we think too much of ourselves when we imagine that through these gifts we should glorify ourselves. This is dangerous. There are people who like to show off. They are dangerous people. They are dangerous anywhere. They are dangerous in society; they are dangerous in the consistory; they are dangerous in any gathering. They use their gifts to extol themselves.

Third, one thinks too much of himself when he supposes that he has all the gifts. He thinks that he is the only pebble on the beach, or he thinks that his gifts are twice as large as the gifts of others. If such a man gets in office and there is another next to him who also thinks too highly of himself, the church will have trouble.

Thinking too highly of self is one of the main causes of the trouble in the church. Therefore, think soberly; think sanely.

The Ground of Sober-mindedness

The ground is that we are one body. There are many members, but there is only one body. This is the body of Christ, of which Christ is the head. The Spirit of Christ is in the whole body. We are so many members of the one body.

The church is not a mob, is not a crowd, is not a group of individuals. The church is one organic whole. The purpose of this one organic whole is that through the church, now in principle, the glory of God in Christ may shine forth in many forms. This is the true pluriformity of the church. The purpose of the church is that the one glory of God in Christ may shine forth. The church is one grand chorus. The church has only one song to sing. The one song is, "Glory to God in the highest." This is the song of the church. Everyone must sing this song in his own voice, with his own capacity, in his own place, but all sing one song.

Is not this sufficient reason that we think soberly? Is not this sufficient reason that when we have received a gift, we do not say, "Here I am"? Is not this sufficient reason that we rather get on our knees and say, "Thanks for the gift"?

To serve God will be the highest element of our glory in heaven. In the new earth and the new heavens, there will also be gifts, but there will be no more conflict about them.

Don't we see that we are only members, and not the whole body? Don't we see that we must think soberly? Don't we know that we need all the members in order to function ourselves? If my eye should pop out of my head, would it still be an eye? And if we become puffed up, don't we think that we should listen to this Word and not think more highly of ourselves than we ought?

Underlying this admonition lies the general admonition of the apostle in verse 2: "Be not conformed to this world: but be ye transformed by the renewing of your mind." Then the church will be blessed. The members will rejoice. Christ will be praised, and the glory of God will become manifest.

Chapter Eighty-three

Love without Hypocrisy

Romans 12:9
Let love be without dissimulation. Abhor that which is evil; cleave to that which is good.

In the immediately preceding verses, the apostle has been applying the general principle of the Christian's life and walk, which he had announced in the first verse, to the spiritual gifts and their uses in the church. He had said in verse 1 that we should present our bodies, that is, all our earthly life, a living sacrifice unto God. Because our earthly life must be presented a living sacrifice unto God in this world with its sin and imperfections, the apostle added that we must not become conformed to this world. Rather, we must be transformed by the renewing of our mind, meaning we must be transformed from within. This truth the apostle applied to the gifts of grace and to the different positions and offices in the church.

In applying this truth, the apostle held before the church this spiritual principle: they should not think too highly of themselves, but they should think soberly. In the first place, if we think soberly, we will not forget that our various abilities are gifts. We will remember that we have nothing of ourselves. What we have is all a gift. We have nothing to boast of. It is all of Christ. It is all a manifestation of the riches of Christ. In the second place, not to think too highly of self implies that no one must imagine that he has all the gifts. The gifts are distributed so that one has this gift and another has that gift. In the third place, it implies that we do not forget that the gifts we possess, we have only in a measure. We do not possess them beyond the measure of faith. In the fourth place, the implication is that we possess these gifts as members of the body.

Still having in mind the admonition that we must present our bodies a sacrifice unto God, the passage in Romans 12 continues with a series of admonitions concerning the relation of the members to each other. This series is introduced with an admonition that is the most fundamental of them all: "Let love be without dissimulation." But if love is to be without dissimulation, it is necessary that we practice the next two admonitions: "Abhor that which is evil; cleave to that which is good." If we do not obey the last part of the text, we must not expect that our love will be without dissimulation, or hypocrisy.

The Meaning

We are busy with the practical part of the epistle to the Romans. There is plenty of doctrine in these admonitions, of course. But when the apostle speaks of love without dissimulation, he is thinking of love in action. More particularly, he is thinking of the love that the people of God must and do have for one another. The exhortation is that in our practical life we love without dissimulation, without hypocrisy. All that we do in relation to one another is to be motivated by sincere love.

Therefore, in considering the idea of love, we can be brief. It is presupposed that we know now what love is. Love is in God. Love in God is love of Himself. God loves Himself because He is the highest good. For the same reason, when we read that God loves His people, we must remember that He does so for His own sake. He loves them as they are a reflection of Himself. God has revealed His love in Christ, particularly in His death and resurrection. This same love that God revealed in Christ He pours out in the hearts of His people.

The result of God's pouring out His love in our hearts is

threefold. First, when God pours out His love in our hearts, He causes us to know and to taste that He loves us. Second, when God pours out His love in our hearts, He causes us to love Him. This love of God in our hearts is not a mere sentiment; it is a matter of the will. Therefore, this love becomes manifest in that we keep His precepts. Third, when God pours out His love in our hearts, the fruit is that we love one another. We love each other with God's own love. With God's love in us, we know that He loves us, we love Him, and we love one another.

Verse 9 speaks of this last expression of love—that we love one another—and from a practical point of view. The exhortation is this: whatever you may do in relation to one another, let it be done in love and in sincerity.

What such love consists of in the church we may gather from I Corinthians 13. Love is long-suffering; it is kind. Therefore, if there is love, there is kindness in the congregation. Love does not envy. Therefore, if there is love in the congregation, there is no malice, no backbiting, no envy, no jealousy. Love is not puffed up, vaunteth not itself. Therefore, if there is love in the congregation, if love is active, there is no seeking of our own honor. Love does not behave unseemly. The word *unseemly* means that you cannot find your place. Then it is not possible to cooperate with you. If you are motivated by love, this will not be the case in the church. Love is not easily provoked. When there is love, we do not easily become angry; we are not easily offended. If love is active, we can stand a good deal. Love thinketh no evil. It is not filled with distrust. It is not suspicious. It does not think the worst of the brethren. It thinks in a charitable way. Love rejoiceth not in iniquity. You do not find love in the company of evildoers. Nor does it lend itself to iniquity. When love is on company, it is not busy in backbiting and slandering. It rejoiceth not in iniquity, but it rejoiceth in the truth. When there is love, we tell one another the truth. Love beareth all things. It believeth all things. It hopeth all things. It endureth all things. It never faileth. In short, if you have sincere love in action in the church, you will not find malice, envy, hatred, and strife, but you will find peace, joy, and harmony.

It is a shame that the apostle had to write, "Let love be without hypocrisy." The Word of God speaks in like manner in other places. We read in I Peter 1:22: "Love one another with a pure heart fervently." Love is always without hypocrisy, for love is of God. But the reference is to our actual practice. In our walk and conversation, all our life is to be characterized by sincere love, not by hypocritical love.

We can mention four instances in which love is hypocritical. First, love is dissimulated when we perform acts that are properly acts of love while there is no love in our hearts. There are acts of love that the church performs every Sunday. The very act of our sitting together in church is an act of love. We perform an act of love when as a congregation we gather around the table of communion. When on Sunday we sit in church, offer up our prayers, sing psalms, contribute our gifts, and listen to the Word of God, yet there is no love in our hearts, we are hypocrites. Our love is dissimulated. We are not as we seem to be. When there is something sinful that we do not want to put out of the way, we are hypocrites. Love must be without dissimulation. This does not mean that we stay away from church. Rather, what is not of love, cut it out!

A second instance of hypocritical love is the conventional show of love. This is also hypocrisy. People sometimes say that we could be a little more friendly. Well, maybe we could. But it is also true that there creeps into the church a worldly, conventional love. This is sickening. This is hypocritical. It is good to smile, to shake hands, and to be friendly—provided that the love of Christ is in the heart. If it is mere conventionalism, it is love with dissimulation.

Third, love may be dissimulated because of self-interest. We may have personal reasons why we pretend love. This is the most abominable form of dissimulated love.

A fourth kind of dissimulated love is that we love in word

and not in deed. We do love in word. Of course the people of God love in word. This is their confession. The fact that we are members of the church implies the confession that we love God's people. And then if you are rich and your brother is suffering hunger, and you send him away empty, how does the love of God abide in you? Such love is hypocritical.

I know it is a shame that we have to hear the admonition, "Let love be without dissimulation." It is necessary, however, because we are only a little Christian and much flesh. By nature we do not love, but hate one another. Because this hatred is not crushed in us, the general admonition is always in order that we be not conformed to the world. And the specific admonition must always come to us: "Let love be without dissimulation." This is a fight. Remember, we must hear this Word and do it. Then we must humble ourselves, asking for grace to do it.

The Indispensable Condition

If we are to love without hypocrisy, we must also abhor that which is evil and cleave to that which is good. Abhorring evil and cleaving to good is the indispensable condition for heeding the admonition to love without hypocrisy. When the apostle speaks of good and evil, he uses the terms in the most unlimited sense. Some explain that we must abhor evil and do good in relation to one another, but there is no need of this limitation. The apostle is thinking of evil in the most unlimited sense: evil in relation to God, evil in relation to the world, evil in relation to one another. To be concrete, evil includes such things as false doctrine, an unholy walk, and love of the world. Evil includes wickedness that we see every day in the world. We meet it on the street, in pictures, and in paint, powder, and dress. It is the wickedness of the world that the Christian is tempted to copy. It is also the evil we commit in relation to one another. It is untruth, malice, envy, hatred, slander, and backbiting.

Abhor these things. The apostle does not simply say, "Don't do the evil." The exhortation addresses the state of our mind: "*Abhor* it." Then it is repulsive to us. We hate it. We shun it. We run away or fight it. Abhor false doctrine! Abhor an unholy walk! Abhor evil books, literature, and pictures. Don't even cast one eye on them in the lust of the flesh. Hate them. Condemn them.

Cleaving to that which is good is also a state of mind. *Good* refers to spiritual, ethical, and moral good in relation to God, in relation to the world, and in our relation to one another. We are to cleave to the fruits of sanctification, particularly honesty. As we abhor evil, so are we spontaneously to love what is good. When we see it, we love it, set our heart on it, and take hold of it.

The question is, how can this exhortation address our inner life? If the Word commands, "Do it!" I might try to do it. But if I must abhor and cleave, how can I do this? It must be remembered that the apostle is speaking here to the church. One cannot give this exhortation to a worldly crowd. The church has the inner, spiritual principle of the renewal of the mind. If there is not this renewal of the mind, the exhortation is impossible. But the renewal of the mind transforms us from within. To put it concretely, there is a new principle of life in us. And if there is a new principle of life in us, we abhor evil, and we cleave to that which is good.

Still, *means* are necessary. Scripture teaches that there are two means by which we learn, more and more, to do what the text commands. The first means is *the Word of God*. If we want to abhor evil, we must live close to the Word of God. The more that Scripture becomes a living principle in our life, the more we will develop the spiritual principle by which we abhor evil. The second means is *prayer*. And I mean prayer by which we cry unto God. If we really pray, we will become more and more unhypocritical in love.

We might be inclined to read the text this way: "Let love be without dissimulation, and then you will never do evil, but you will always do that which is good." But this is not the meaning. Abhorring the evil and cleaving to the good is the condition for loving without hypocrisy. We cannot love without dissimulation if we do not abhor evil and cleave to that which is good. The reason is that love is the love of God. We cannot love God and one another if we walk in darkness. If we walk in darkness, we cannot be loved as a child of God.

Therefore, this admonition is serious. "Let love be without dissimulation." If this is to be so in our life, we must abhor evil and cleave to that which is good. Then there is the action of love, and the blessing of Christ will be richly manifest in the church.

Chapter Eighty-four

Patient in Tribulation

Romans 12:12
Rejoicing in hope; patient in tribulation; continuing instant in prayer.

The idea of the three phrases in Romans 12:12 is that they should be read as a direct exhortation: "Rejoice in hope; be patient in tribulation; continue in prayer." This chapter applies to our lives the doctrine found in the preceding chapters, particularly in chapters 1–8. Romans 12 begins with the general exhortation that we shall present our bodies a living sacrifice unto God, which is our reasonable, that is, logical, service. In order to accomplish this in the midst of this world in which there is much sin, we shall watch that we be not conformed to this world. This is urgent since we ourselves have in us little that is Christian and much that is world. Rather than be conformed to the world we shall be transformed by the renewing of our mind, that is, inwardly.

This general admonition the apostle applies, first, to the life of the church in the matter of the gifts of grace and the use of these gifts by the members of the church in relation to one another. This application of the general admonition is introduced by an exhortation indicating what our spiritual attitude should be with a view to these gifts of grace, namely, that we be not highminded, but that we think soberly. We must remember that we have not received these gifts as mere presents, but as obligations that we must use to the glory of God.

This admonition is followed by another group of admonitions referring to the relation we must assume toward one another. In this group the fundamental exhortation is, "Let love be without dissimulation." If love is to be without dissimulation, it is necessary that we abhor that which is evil and cleave to that which is good.

There is still another kind of admonition that refers to our personal walk in this world. I wish to single out one of these admonitions, which is fundamental. This is the admonition we find in verse 12: "Rejoicing in hope; patient in tribulation; continuing instant in prayer." On the face of it, we can see at once that these three are one. They are closely related to each other. Rejoicing in hope, having patience in tribulation, and continuing instant in prayer cannot be separated from one another.

To bring out the unity of this group, it is best that we take our stand in the middle one, namely, "Be patient in tribulation." This places us in the midst of reality. From this middle admonition we will look back to the first and see that it is impossible to be patient in tribulation unless we rejoice in hope. Looking forward, we will see that if we are to rejoice in hope so that we may be patient in tribulation, it is necessary to continue instant in prayer.

The Meaning

The word *tribulation* occurs frequently in Scripture. The basic meaning of the word is "pressure." Tribulation puts such pressure on a man that he has no room to live. In tribulation the Christian is pressed from every side, so that his place becomes very narrow until, finally, there is no place for him at all. Tribulation is always suffering of some kind, suffering that makes our earthly existence miserable. There is the suffering of the body: hunger, sickness, pain. There is the suffering of the mind: sorrow, grief, loss of position, loss of honor, loss of name.

There are two causes of the suffering of the children of God. First, our suffering may be the general suffering that no one can escape. We lie in the midst of death. This life is a continual death. Therefore, there is a suffering of death all along our earthly way. This is the suffering of this present time. It carries with it sorrow and grief. It includes suffering of the body and suffering of the mind.

There is also a specific suffering. This is suffering caused by the fact that we are in the world as Christians. This is suffering caused by the fact that the world hates Christ. Since they cannot get at Him, they oppose His people and cause them to suffer. This is what Scripture calls suffering for Christ's sake. This suffering comes upon us because we belong to Christ. It comes upon us because we are righteous, because we are faithful, and because we testify against the world that lies in darkness. There is a difference between the two kinds of suffering. The first kind of suffering, all have in common as humans. The other kind is only for the Christian. The first kind we cannot escape. It is not of our own choosing. We cannot avoid it. When sickness or death comes our way, we have nothing to do with it. But the other kind of suffering we must choose. We can avoid it. We stand before the alternative of confessing Christ and suffering, or denying Him and escaping suffering.

The latter kind of suffering Scripture calls *tribulation*. This is the suffering referred to by verse 12. Tribulation is always, to a certain degree, the lot of the Christian. He must suffer tribulation according as he is faithful. He cannot avoid it. He is always called upon to deny himself and take up his cross. The place of the Christian is always limited. This is not because the things of this world do not belong to his Lord; rather, the wicked world limits his place.

At times tribulation becomes especially intense. Sometimes, as at the time of Nero, tribulation takes on a special form. Then the place of the Christian is made very narrow. The Christian is put before the choice of denying Christ or being put to death. This was the case for the early church. This was also the case for the church of the Reformation. And this will be the case, in the extreme sense, when the power of Antichrist shall be revealed. The time may not be far off when the Christian will again be placed before the choice of denying Christ or dying. Imagine what it will mean for the Christian in the world when he will not be allowed to buy or sell, when he will not be able to find work, when he will not be able to buy his daily bread, unless he denies Christ.

The text admonishes us to be *patient* in tribulation. Patience is literally the power to bear up under suffering. The exercise of patience is that we walk in the way of suffering without rebellion, without murmuring. The apostle is not speaking of a certain natural power to suffer. He is not speaking of a certain insensibility to suffering. There are people who, as is sometimes said, can "take it." They can endure suffering without wincing. They are able to endure the keenest physical suffering without moving a muscle. Sometimes this is called patience, but Scripture does not call this patience. This is, in fact, the very opposite of the patience to which the text refers. This is pride—pride over against the suffering put on him by God. Such a man really means, "God may press me as hard as He wants to, but I will not shed a tear." This is not patience.

Christ's patience was something much different. Christ suffered as no man ever suffered. When He suffered, He was not unmoved. He was sorely afraid of His suffering. He cried unto God. His sweat became as great drops of blood. So sorely afraid was Jesus of the way He had to travel. Yet He was always patient.

Patience is the power of faith to walk in the way of the Lord, no matter what that way may bring. Patience is this. Here is the way of God. I know it. Here is my calling to walk in this way of God. I know it. As I walk straight on, I see tribulation on this way. If I do not take a side way, reproach will be on the way I must travel. I see it. People will laugh at me if I keep on the way. They will pour scorn upon me if I continue on the way. I will lose my job, my position, my freedom. There, on the way, is the scaffold, the stake, death. There are other ways for me, ways that lead off from that straight way of God's precepts. I see them, too. They are ways in which I can keep my name, my honor, my position, my freedom. Patience is that, although there are byways, I go straight ahead, straight through shame, reproach, and suffering—without murmuring.

That we find here an admonition to be patient is because the flesh will never choose suffering. And there is oh so much flesh in us! When we come before the choice of the straight way of obedience with suffering, and of the byways by which we can escape suffering, we have a hundred excuses to take the byways. This we often do. If we are honest, we will admit that for our honor, our name's sake, we often depart from the straight way of God's precepts.

The Requirement

If we are to be patient in tribulation, it is necessary that we listen to the other admonition: rejoice in hope. It is impossible to be patient in tribulation unless we rejoice in hope. The word *hope* in the Bible may mean "the act of hoping," consisting of the assurance of, the expectation of, and the longing for the final salvation, but it also may refer to "that for which we hope, the object of our hope." The second meaning of hope is the one in the text. This is evident from the fact that "the act of hoping" is really expressed in the word *rejoicing,* as well as in the idea of rejoicing.

The object for which we hope is what the apostle in another place indicates as the glory of God. We hope for the glory of God. This glory of God consists of a glory within and a glory without. It has its ultimate beginning in the deliverance from the body of sin, corruption, and death. Its end is our being made perfect. It consists of being delivered from the earthly and being translated to the heavenly. When the glory of God shall have been perfected in us, we shall be holy as He is holy; we shall be righteous as He is righteous; we shall be clothed with heavenly beauty. This glory of God that is ours in body and soul will also be spread over the new heavens and the new earth. This is the incorruptible inheritance that does not fade away. This is the hope of the Christian.

In this hope we are to rejoice. That ultimate glory is to be the ground of our rejoicing. Negatively, we must not be glad on the ground of earthly things. Don't say, always and exclusively, "I am glad that we are all well," for the fact is that we are going to die. Don't always say, "I am glad that we have prosperity." Rejoice, rather, that you are heirs of eternal glory. Let that be the object, the ground, of your rejoicing. If people ask you why you are singing, you must answer, "Because I go to heaven." This means that the act of hoping is active in your life. It means that this hope is with you constantly. It means that you become singing Christians.

This is indispensable for practicing patience in tribulation. This is evident. Tribulation takes away from you everything that is seen. It takes away everything and leaves you nothing. It takes away your bread, your job, your position, your freedom, your life. If that tribulation stares you in the face, and if you find that you are without the joy of hope, you will never be patient in that tribulation. If you rejoice in things, you will never let them go, but if you rejoice in hope, you have something to say to the enemy who causes your tribulation. What the Christian has to say is this: "Take away all that I have, and you take away nothing. I do not rejoice in those things. I rejoice in hope. With my eye on that hope, I go on."

There is another reason. If I rejoice in hope, I know that all things work together to make me possessor of the object of my hope. The enemy can take ten or fifteen years off my life, but when they do, they only help me to come into possession of the eternal glory, which is the object of my hope. All things must work together to bring me into that glory. Therefore, be patient in tribulation. And if you want to be patient in suffering, the object of your rejoicing must be that hope daily.

The Way of Attainment

If this is to be the case, we must walk in the way of prayer. The apostle says, "continuing instant in prayer." The meaning is that we persevere constantly in the exercise of prayer. If we are to be a patient people and a singing people, we must be a praying people.

Prayer is not that we ask God for whatever comes into our mind. I say intentionally that such is not prayer. When we are sick, to say to the Lord, "Please make me well" is not prayer. When we are in prison, to say to the Lord, "Please get me out" is not prayer. When we have economic depression, to call a prayer day is not prayer. The devil can pray all of that.

Prayer is always a seeking of God's kingdom. What does not belong to the seeking of God's kingdom is not prayer. Prayer is always the desire to see the manifestation of the glory of God and the realization of His will. Because this is the case, prayer is always that exercise of faith by which we open the soul to seek the grace of God as a flower opens its bosom to the sun. Prayer is the seeking for, the turning to the fountain for, that grace of God.

Persevere in it! This does not mean that we must always be on our knees, but it does mean that we must let prayer be our daily exercise. We must fight for the exercise of prayer. You know it is a battle to pray. We must exercise ourselves daily in the holy art of prayer. We must open our soul to seek the grace of God, grace to be patient in tribulation and to rejoice in hope. Perseverance in prayer implies that we need grace every moment. God does not give us grace in such a way that we go away with a storehouse of it. We need grace as we need bread—every day. And we receive it in the way of prayer.

There are these three virtues. We need them all. We cannot be patient in tribulation if we do not rejoice in hope. And we cannot rejoice in hope and be patient in tribulation unless we continue instant in prayer. But if we rejoice in hope, are patient in tribulation, and persevere in prayer, we will be strong. Thus, we will be able to stand in the evil day.

Chapter Eighty-five

An Exhortation to Be of One Mind

Romans 12:16
Be of the same mind one toward another. Mind not high things, but condescend to men of low estate. Be not wise in your own conceits.

Following the group of practical exhortations in verse 12, there are several other exhortations enjoining various graces of Christ upon the people of God. We are exhorted to exercise the grace of charitableness when the apostle admonishes us to distribute to the necessity of the saints. Similarly, we are exhorted to the exercise of hospitality. This meant far more in those days than it does now. When the apostle said, "Be given to hospitality," he did not mean that we should take anyone who comes along into our homes, but he meant that the Roman saints should take in the brother who at that time was frequently without home and friends and who was persecuted for the sake of Christ. Because of this, one given to hospitality was frequently in danger himself. Therefore, a special admonition was needed with a view to giving hospitality. The apostle goes on to enjoin upon us the love of our enemies so that when they persecute us, we bless them. Then the apostle exhorts the church to exercise spiritual sympathy. This sympathy reveals itself in our rejoicing with those who rejoice and our weeping with those who weep.

In the admonition of verse 16—that we shall be of the same mind one toward another—the apostle really returns from the viewpoint of the individual members of the church to the church's unity. The church is one body with many members; therefore, it can be admonished from the viewpoint of the individual members. But the church can also be admonished from the viewpoint of the unity of the members. When the apostle says, "Be of the same mind one toward another," he is speaking from the viewpoint of the unity of the church.

The main thought of the group of admonitions in the text is that we all be of one mind. All of the admonitions are grouped around this one thought: "Be of one mind, and therefore mind not high things." Then we read in our translation, "Condescend to men of low estate." This translation is mistaken, however. The original does not mean men of low estate, but lowly things: "Mind not high things, but condescend to lowly things." If we are to practice same-mindedness, it is necessary that we condescend to the lowly things.

The Meaning

Verse 16 calls us to be of the same mind, one toward another. The old Dutch translation is expressive: "Be unanimous of mind among each other." Being of one mind in relation to one another means that in all those activities in which we have a common task, a common work to do, all of us mind the same thing. Because of the unity of the body of Christ, there are things in the church that we have in common, that are common, and that we do in common. If all set their mind on the same thing in this common task, in this common work, in this common calling, there is one-mindedness.

The word *mind* in the text does not refer only to thinking. It has a broader meaning. To mind a thing means, first, that we look on that thing as something that is good. If we do not consider a thing good, we do not mind it. Second, to mind a thing means that we desire it. We desire to possess that thing, or to realize it. Therefore, to mind a thing implies, too, that we set our desire on the thing that we mind. Third, it means that we make the thing the object of our choice. We want it; we seek it. Fourth, to mind something is to pursue it, to strive after it. If, therefore, we mind the things that are above, we call those things that are above good, in distinction from the things that are below. If we mind the things that are above, we desire them, we make them our choice, we strive after them.

We are to be of the same mind. All of us are to consider the same thing as being good. All are to desire the same thing. All are to choose the same thing. All are to pursue after the same thing. We are to do this in relation to one another, that is, in relation to things that all have in common. We have many things in common. This is because we are one body. If we are not a body, we have no common calling. But a body is a unity. Because this is the case, we stand in a certain relation to one another. We have many things and callings in common.

Let us notice concretely what it means that in our common tasks we all mind the same thing. There are things that are individual and personal, such as repentance. Repentance is my personal affair. But there are other things common to us. Preeminent is the one great calling of the church to maintain, defend, and propagate the truth. Where the Word of God is maintained, defended, and propagated, there is the church of Christ. Where this is not the case, there you have no church, no matter how pious the people may appear. This calling of the church with respect to the truth is a common calling. It is not my calling or your calling. It is the calling of the church. Only the church can accomplish this calling. With a view to this calling, we do many things in common. With a view to preserving, defending, and propagating the truth, we call ministers, elect officebearers, choose presidents of societies, and have Sunday school teachers. Why do we call ministers, elect officebearers, and choose presidents of societies? To preserve, defend, and propagate the truth! With a view to the truth, we also instruct the youth of the congregation. We do this in common. Don't think that the consistory or the minister instructs the youth; the congregation does. It is the common calling of the congregation. With a view to preserving the truth, we have societies for Bible study. As organism we have Christian schools. Supporting Christian schools belongs to our common calling to maintain the truth. Because we want to maintain the truth, we not only call ministers and elect officebearers, but we also build churches. Because we want to maintain the truth, we build Christian schools. This is the common calling of all.

Because there are many things that we do together, the apostle exhorts, "Be of the same mind." Being of the same mind is necessary. The church must be unanimous. In fact, the church has only one mind. Your mind and my mind do not belong to the church except insofar as our minds are subject to the mind of Christ. The mind of Christ is the one mind of the church. All, therefore, mind the same thing. This does not mean that we must always have the same opinion. This is impossible. It would be nice. In heaven we will all be of one opinion. However desirable this might be, here it is impossible. There are certain aspects of the common activities of the church that we call "nonessentials." When we call a minister, we differ in our opinion as to who is the best and the most capable to serve us. In this particular nonessential, we differ. But we may never differ in this one thing: all minding the same thing. We may say that the glory of God, the edification of the church, and the propagation of the truth is the one thing that all must mind. We may have different opinions, but the one thing that all must mind is that we seek the glory of God, the edification of the church, and the maintenance of the truth.

There are other things in which we may differ. We may differ as to language. We may differ as to whether we should have four worship services, or only three—having only one service in the morning. This is a nonessential. The one thing we must bear in mind is the glory of God, the edification of the church, and the propagation of the truth. Do not say, "I can have dinner at a better time if we have only one service in the morning." Your dinner has nothing to do with the one thing that all must mind. The one thing that all must mind is the glory of

God, the edification of the church, and the maintenance of the truth.[1] The apostle does not teach that we must all have the same opinion, but we must all look on the one good. We must will it, seek it, choose it, strive after it. What does not belong to this one good is not of the church.

On the truth we may not differ. You may say, "Yes, but there are people who think differently." This may be so, but that is their responsibility. I am convinced that if our only desire is to seek the truth and if no other considerations enter in, the Holy Spirit will lead us in the truth. The Word of God does not support the notion that departure from the truth is honest error. That there are doctrinal errors in the church is due to the fact that this admonition to be of the same mind one toward another is forgotten. All do not mind the same thing with the purpose of having the truth.

The Way to Attain It

If this is to be done, something else must take place. This is why the apostle continues: "Mind not high things, but condescend to the lowly things." This gives a beautiful picture of the church. We do not look at high things, but all of us are drawn to the low things. We must not understand this exhortation in the absolute sense. We must certainly also seek high things. Often Scripture admonishes us to seek the things that are above [Col. 3:1]. The highest that we can seek is the glory of God. We must mind high things. In the objective sense, we must not mind the low things.

When the apostle speaks of *high things,* he adopts the subjective point of view. The reference is to things that we esteem as high for us. These are things that flatter our pride, things

---

1. At the time when Hoeksema was preaching this series on Romans, First Church held four worship services every Sunday, two in English and two in Dutch. Two of the services were in the morning, thus delaying the noon meal for some. Evidently there was some disagreement in the church over the matter.

that result in honor and glory for us. The question "Who shall be the greatest?" is inspired by the desire to seek the high things. We may not *mind* these things. We must not will, desire, choose, and strive after such high things. We must not ask the question "Who shall be the greatest?" But all must be drawn to the lowly things. Lowly things are things that are without glory for you and me. For instance, a lowly thing is that we get on our knees before one another, confess our sins, and ask forgiveness of one another. In other words, the admonition is that we do not all strive to be the greatest in the church. All must not desire to be ministers. All must not desire to be elders. All must not desire to be presidents of societies.

Oh, suppose that we all would seek the lowly things. What a beautiful church we would be! If we would all run to the lowly things, the glory of Christ would become manifest in us. We do not seek the lowly things by nature. The chapter begins with the warning "Be not conformed to this world" [v. 2]. By nature we are proud. This pride is still in the flesh of the church. We still live with the notion that it is great to be masters. But it is not. It is great to be servants because there is only one who is great; He is the one who became the least of all. There is only one mind; this is the mind of Christ, who traveled the way of the lowly things. This mind of Christ is in the church. And God has taken care that in order to be saved, we must become so brokenhearted that we crawl into heaven by the grace of Christ. It is all of the grace of Christ. And shall we now say, "I am it"? Be not high-minded, but condescend to the lowly things.

One more thing is necessary in order to be of one mind. This is that we be not wise in our own conceits. The meaning is not that we must agree with every Tom, Dick, and Harry who comes along with a false doctrine. The meaning is not that we must never say, "I know that this doctrine is the truth." We have to say this. People who go along with every wind of doctrine are not Christians. The true Christian must say, "I know it."

But we must be sure that what we know is not our own wisdom. Literally, the text reads, "Be not wise by yourself." In other words, we must not insist upon our own carnal notions. Positively, all our wisdom must come out of the Word of God. If we let all our wisdom come out of the Word of God, we are not wise in our own conceits. We have been instructed by Him whose is all the wisdom. And if we have been instructed in the Word, it makes no difference that we may stand alone. Then we must say, "I know it." But we may not be wise in our own conceits. The Christian may not be wise "by himself." Our wisdom must be in Scripture.

If we do this, we will be of one mind. If we do not seek the high things, but condescend to the lowly things, and if we are not wise by ourselves, then we will be unanimous. On the other hand, if all seek the high things and are wise in their own conceits, there will be as many minds in the church as there are members. But if all of us together, saved by grace, have humbled ourselves and have received the mind of Jesus so that we seek not high things, then as a church we will set our mind on one thing: the glory of God. We will show forth the praises of Him who called us out of darkness into His marvelous light [I Pet. 2:9]. There will be no more differences. All will be of one mind to sing the praises of Him who redeemed us.

Chapter Eighty-six

Leaving Vengeance to the Lord

Romans 12:19
Dearly beloved, avenge not yourselves, but rather give place unto wrath: for it is written, Vengeance is mine; I will repay, saith the Lord.

In the twelfth chapter of Romans, the apostle has written a series of admonitions to the church. All of these admonitions are based on the fundamental one: that we present our bodies a living sacrifice, holy, acceptable unto God, which is our reasonable service. In order to do so, we must not be conformed to this world, but must be transformed by the renewing of our mind, that we may prove what is that good, and acceptable, and perfect, will of God.

On the basis of this fundamental admonition, the apostle first exhorts the church with a view to the gifts of grace bestowed on them and their use in the church. This admonition is introduced by a warning to the people of God that they should not think too highly of themselves, but that they should think soberly, according as God has dealt to every man the measure of faith. The apostle continues with a series of admonitions setting forth what the relation of the individual members to each another should be. The apostle introduces this series with the words *Let love be without dissimulation.* Therefore, they must abhor evil and cleave to that which is good. The apostle goes on to call the attention of the people of God to their individual walk in the world. He admonishes them to rejoice in hope, to be patient in tribulation, and to continue instant in prayer. Then the apostle changes the viewpoint and considers the church as a unity. He admonishes the church as a unity to be of one mind in the relation of the members to one another. To accomplish this admonition, they must not mind high things, but turn to the lowly things, not being wise in their own conceits.

The apostle closes this chapter with a series of admonitions concerning the relation of the people of God to the world. The underlying supposition of this series of admonitions is that this world is not of Christ. This world is evil; it will persecute the people of God. Therefore, the apostle admonishes the people of God that they must not recompense evil for evil. They shall provide things honest in the sight of all men. As much as is possible, that is, insofar as it is not in conflict with the Word of God, they are to live peacefully with all men.

In the text the apostle exhorts the church that they avenge not themselves. As a ground for this negative admonition, the apostle reminds the church that vengeance belongs to God.

The Idea of True Vengeance

It is noteworthy that the apostle emphatically addresses the church here as "dearly beloved." In connection with the admonition concerning revenge, the address of the church as *beloved* must be understood in the absolute sense. The church is not addressed as the beloved of the apostle, but as the beloved of God. God has loved His people with an eternal love. He manifested this love by giving His Son to redeem them.

When the apostle uses the term *beloved* in connection with vengeance, the meaning is that vengeance presupposes, first, a love relation. Vengeance is a covenant idea. When God established the covenant with Abraham, God said that He would bless them that blessed Abraham and curse them that cursed him. Even among men, vengeance presupposes a relation of love. You avenge those whom you love. You avenge your wife if she is wronged. You avenge yourself. So it is here. The teaching of the text is that God loves us and, in His love, will surely avenge us.

The idea of vengeance has a second presupposition: a wrong has been done us. The implication is that we walk in the world as God's beloved. We know that God loves us. We know that God has realized His covenant with us. He has spread abroad His love in our hearts. Knowing and tasting that God loves us, we now walk as beloved of God. The covenant has two parts. It does not have two *parties,* but two *parts.* When God spreads abroad His love in our hearts and we receive this love of God, our part in the covenant is that we love Him. We must love God with all our heart, with all our mind, with all our soul, and with all our strength. This is our part in the covenant of God. God loves us. He causes us to love Him, and then we love Him.

That we love Him in this world consists of our keeping His Word. This is our sole calling. This is the calling of the church. We have no other calling but to keep the Word of God. We must keep this Word in our hearts. We must keep it in our mouth. We must keep it in our walk. This is the sole calling of the church in the world as the beloved of God. We must remember this. The church is not an institution to save souls. The sole question is not whether we are saved. This is not our question. God will take care of this. The sole question is, Do we keep His Word? This is the calling of God's people. "If you love me, you will keep my commandments," said Jesus [John 14:15].

The third presupposition of true vengeance is that if you keep Christ's Word, you will have to suffer. As long as you soft-soap it, you do not have to suffer. But keep the Word of God, refuse to go along with the world, and the world hates you and persecutes you. You will suffer reproach and shame; you will be called a "back number" and narrow-minded; you will be laughed at. If this hatred becomes more emphatic in its manifestation, they will hurt you; they will take away your freedom; they will kill you. The world will hurt you if you are faithful. And when they hurt you, they hurt the apple of God's eye. Throughout history the church in the world has suffered for Christ's sake. The people of God have been killed all the day long with Christ in the midst of them.

Revenge in the text is something different from what vengeance means among men. Among us, vengeance means that we inflict as great an evil as possible upon the one who has hurt us. This is not the idea of vengeance in the text. The idea of true, biblical vengeance is just retribution. When this vengeance of God shall be inflicted, it will be absolutely just and therefore complete. The time will come when God will dispose of His and our enemies. They are usurpers. All things of creation belong to the people of God, but the enemies of God's people have usurped them. God will take it all away from them. He will give them their just retribution. And He will give everything to His people.

The admonition to the church is, "Avenge not yourselves." By this negative admonition the apostle points to our flesh. We are inclined to avenge ourselves. When someone hurts me and I am not on guard, the first thought that comes into my mind is to hurt him in return. When someone reviles me, my first thought is to revile again. When someone speaks bitter words about me, I am inclined to speak bitter words about him. This is our flesh. We always desire to recompense evil for evil. If we do not fight against it, we will harbor the thought of revenge in our soul.

Yet another element enters in: God seems to be slow to avenge His people. If only every evil inflicted upon us was avenged in a moment, it would be easier to hear this Word. But it appears as if God does not care. This is the way it looked at the cross. When all the world reviled, mocked, and scoffed at the beloved of God, it seemed as if God did not care. This is frequently the case. Therefore, we are inclined to avenge ourselves. When someone slanders us, we are inclined to slander him back. When someone hurts us, we are inclined to hurt him back. This is a grievous sin. We cannot excuse such an attitude by saying, "He did it first." It is a sin to avenge ourselves.

That Vengeance Is a Divine Prerogative

It is a grievous sin to avenge ourselves, because vengeance does not belong to us. It is a divine prerogative. It is a divine prerogative, in the first place, because when the world hurts us, it does not really mean to hurt us, but God, and we can never avenge this. We cannot defend God. God's cause, God's name, God's holiness is at stake. Because it is His cause when we suffer, we have no right to avenge ourselves. We must keep on doing well. When our enemy hungers, we must feed him. If he thirsts, we must give him to drink. We must pray for those who persecute us. We must keep on doing well.

Vengeance is God's prerogative, in the second place, because only He has the right to judge. This is not our right. Suppose we have two children. One hurts the other, and the other seeks to hurt him back. When we intervene and that second child says to us, "He hurt me first," we will say to that child, "Never mind! You come to me with it. I will be the judge." This is supremely true with respect to God. We have no right to judge. That right belongs to God.

In the third place, vengeance is a divine prerogative because we cannot fully avenge ourselves. When someone touches the apple of God's eye, we cannot avenge it by hurting the offender.

What then? The apostle says, "Give place unto wrath." This might mean our wrath. Someone hurts us, and our wrath is provoked. Giving place unto wrath might mean, "Don't execute your wrath." The trouble with this interpretation is that this is never the meaning in Scripture of giving place or not giving place to anything. We read in Ephesians 4:27, "Neither give place to the devil." The meaning is that we not make room for the devil. Likewise when the apostle says here, "Give place unto wrath," the meaning is, "Make room for wrath." Another possible interpretation is that the expression means, "Make room for the wrath of the enemy." But again, this is never the meaning of the expression in Scripture.

Therefore, there is only one possible interpretation. This interpretation explains *wrath* as the *wrath of God*. The admonition is, "Give place to the wrath of God." An illustration will make this clear. When Korah, Dathan, and Abiram sinned, the wrath of God was to strike them. Presently the wrath of God was to swallow them up. But before that could happen, the rest of the people must make room for that wrath. They must depart from the tents of Korah, Dathan, and Abiram. That is the thought of the text: "Make room for the wrath of God so that it will not strike you."

In principle, to make room for wrath is that we separate ourselves from the world and flee to the cross. There is only one place where the wrath of God never strikes. That is at the cross. If you don't stand there, this wrath will strike you, but at the cross you are safe from this wrath. It struck there once. If you stand there now, there is no danger. It will never strike there again. But if you so stand by the cross, it follows, too, that with Jesus you stand in separation from the world. It follows that you will be reviled as He was reviled.

Don't you see that if the enemy hurts you, and you hurt him again, you leave the cross and became the object of wrath. If the enemy hurts you, and you hurt him again, you stand where the wrath of God strikes.

Avenge not yourselves! Make room for wrath by doing well. Make room for wrath by giving bread to the hungry, by giving drink to the thirsty, by praying for them that persecute you. Make room for God's wrath. Depart from the tents of wickedness.

That Vengeance Is Certainly Coming

May we then not long to be avenged? Of course we may. All Scripture testifies that the church and the Spirit in the church cry out for vengeance to God. This is the teaching of the parable of the unjust judge. The widow in that parable is presented as crying continually to the judge for vengeance. The Lord Jesus concludes the parable by saying that the Lord will avenge them speedily that cry to Him day and night [Luke 18:1–8]. In the book of Revelation, the souls under the altar are presented as crying to the Lord for vengeance [Rev. 6:9–11]. All the history of the church cries for a day of avenging. The blood of the saints, from the blood of Abel and the other saints of the old dispensation to the martyrs of the present day, has never been avenged. The prayer of the church is, "How long, Lord, wilt Thou not avenge us?"

The text says that God will surely recompense. In our translation, we read, "Vengeance is mine." The fundamental idea is that vengeance is God's prerogative. But in the Greek, as in the Hebrew passage that is quoted here, we read literally, "Vengeance with me." The meaning is not only that vengeance is God's prerogative, but also that it is actually with Him. This phrase is a quotation from Deuteronomy 32:35. There we read, "To me, vengeance and recompence." This is also emphasized in the last part of the text.

Therefore, beloved of God who are the apple of His eye, avenge not yourselves, for God will do it. The day will come when God will open up the books. He will ask payment for every evil word spoken against His people. He will avenge every drop of blood that the enemy has shed. He will take everything away from them and give it to His people. The enemies will pay for all the suffering that they have caused the people of God. Wiping away all tears from their eyes, God will say to His saints, "Come in, and inherit the kingdom that has been prepared for you" [Matt. 25:34]. Beloved, avenge not yourselves. Vengeance is with God.

Chapter Eighty-seven

Subject to the Higher Powers

Romans 13:1-5

Let every soul be subject unto the higher powers. For there is no power but of God: the powers that be are ordained of God.

Whosoever therefore resisteth the power, resisteth the ordinance of God: and they that resist shall receive to themselves damnation.

For rulers are not a terror to good works, but to the evil. Wilt thou then not be afraid of the power? do that which is good, and thou shalt have praise of the same:

For he is the minister of God to thee for good. But if thou do that which is evil, be afraid; for he beareth not the sword in vain: for he is the minister of God, a revenger to execute wrath upon him that doeth evil.

Wherefore ye must needs be subject, not only for wrath, but also for conscience sake.

At the time when the church of the new dispensation was first called out of the world from every nation, there was special need of an admonition to be subject to the higher powers. The Jews had always been averse to having a foreigner rule over them. Indeed, this was even contrary to the law. This aversion was carried over into their converted state. Also the Gentile Christians might easily assume an attitude of resistance against the powers of the world, for was not Christ their Lord? If Christ was their Lord, was it not the prerogative of Christ alone to rule over them? Was it not in conflict with the dignity of Christ that His citizens were subject to the worldly powers? This aversion was aggravated by the fact that these higher powers were often corrupt. The higher power is often in the hands of men who are evil. Moreover, especially in those days, the higher powers used the sword against the church.

If we bear all this in mind, we can understand that under the heading of presenting our bodies as a living sacrifice unto God, the apostle also admonishes the church that they be subject to the higher powers, remembering that they are ordained of God. As to the connection of the opening verses of chapter 13 with the preceding, it seems that the exhortation concerning the higher powers stands in close connection with the admonition at the end of chapter 12. There the apostle had said that the saints should not avenge themselves. That admonition is to be applied personally, but it receives special significance with a view to their relation to the higher powers. In this connection, the apostle admonishes the church to be subject to the higher powers.

We will not go into all the details of the attitude that the church must assume toward the higher powers. We will lay down only the general principles. The attitude that the church must assume is expressed by the word *subject:* "Be *subject* unto the higher powers."

The Powers

The higher powers are the authorities. Power is not mere strength. A man may be strong enough to subdue another, but that brute strength is something quite different from the power mentioned in verse 1, which is literally *authority*. A man may have the power of wealth, but that power of wealth is something different from the power of authority. A man may be of higher intelligence than others. This may give him a certain influence over others, but this is not the same as authority. It is all very well if authority is combined with strength, with the power of wealth, and with the power of intelligence, but these are not authority.

Authority means that whether a man is strong or weak, whether he has wealth or is poor, whether he is of high intelligence or of low intelligence, he has the right to impose his will on others and the right to expect that the will of others be in subjection to his will. Authority is that a man has the right to tell others what to do and to expect that they obey him. Therefore, when the apostle speaks of higher powers, the implication is that some men are placed over others with the right to command others and to expect that they will obey them.

There are many such powers. There are many spheres in which one has authority over others. There is authority in the social sphere. There is authority in the home. There is the authority of the husband over the wife. There is the authority of the teacher in the schoolroom. There is the authority of the master over the servant. It makes no difference what form of economic system is in place—whether it be the form of master and slave, as in former years, or the form of capitalist and labor, as in our present day—the employer belongs, in his own sphere, to these higher powers. In this sphere he has the right to command and to expect obedience. There is also the large sphere of the church. There is authority in the church. Christ has instituted offices in the church. They are higher powers. It is true that these higher powers in the church are of a spiritual, ethical nature, but they are higher powers.

Then there is the authority of the state. When the apostle speaks of higher powers, he has reference specifically to the authority of the state, to the civil government. That this is true is plain from the fact that the higher powers are said to bear the sword [v. 4]. There is only one power that bears the sword. This is the civil power. The church does not bear it. It is plain, therefore, that the passage refers to the civil government, to the magistrate. It is the magistrate that is the *minister of God*.

The apostle gives us a description not only of these higher powers, but also of their authority. Why should there be higher powers? Why should one have power over others? This is a fundamental question. Since the time of the French Revolution, especially, the principle that has taken root is that authority is vested in the people. Therefore, it is the people who confer their authority upon their officers. But it is a communistic principle that the people are sovereign. This is the principle that the source of authority is in man himself.

That man himself is the source of all authority is contrary to all Scripture. It is contrary to all that Scripture teaches concerning the relation of man to man and concerning the relation of man to God. Man has no authority in himself. Man is not the source of authority. Nor is the majority the source of authority. The mere fact that people have a majority does not give them the right to rule over the minority. There is only one who has authority. That is God. Outside of Him there is no authority. Therefore, if it is not true that it pleased God to confer power upon men, there would be no higher powers. If a man is simply stronger than I am, it is not sin to resist him. But if God has conferred power upon men, I may not resist them but must be subject to them.

Authority has been conferred upon men in civil government as regards *the powers that be*. We must not overlook this. By *the powers that be* is meant that these men are placed in their positions by God. It makes no difference how they got there. Whether they got there by the vote of the people or by force, they are the powers that be, placed in their positions by God. The president of our country is a "power that be." In Germany, Hitler is a "power that be." Mussolini is a "power that be."

These *powers that be* do not only have the source of their power in God; they also have the sword-power. It is often said that government was instituted because of sin, but this is not true. The government has more power than the sword-power. There is also government among the angels. There will be government in the new creation. Government was not instituted because of sin. It developed from the family. But because of sin, to these authorities is also given the power of the sword. This is the power to punish. The higher powers have the right to punish the evildoer and to protect the good. This implies that the civil authorities have the right to inflict capital punishment. In the sword-power is also the right to wage war. We must not go along with those who cry "pacifism." The state has the sword, and though it may not use the sword for aggression, it has the right to use it against the aggressive nations.[1]

Because the authority of the state is a derived authority, it is limited. The American power is limited to America. The higher powers of America have no authority except in America. The authority of the civil government is limited to its own domain.

In addition, the civil government is limited by other spheres of authority. The civil government has no authority in the church. The authority of the church is to preach the Word, to administer the sacraments, and to exercise discipline. The civil government has no authority over this threefold office of the church. If the president of the United States should be a member of our church, he would be subject to our consistory. The same is true of the home. There is an authority in the home, which the civil government must respect. In other words, the authority of the state concerns the life of its citizens in their public manifestation. If I get drunk in my home, the state has nothing to do with it, but if I get drunk on the street, I am in the domain of the state.

Our Attitude toward the Powers

The only proper attitude we may assume toward these higher powers is that of subjection. Subjection is the opposite of re-

---

1. No doubt, this condemnation of pacifism was occasioned in part by the strong sentiment in the United States at the time against involvement in a coming war in Europe caused by Nazi aggression. The sermon was preached early in 1939. Hitler invaded Poland in September 1939. It is worthy of note that, although Hoeksema never made social conditions his text, nor allowed social and political trends to shape his message, he had a keen, observing eye on local, national, and international social and political developments as he brought the gospel to the church *in the world, at a particular time.*

sistance. Resistance is a little different than disobedience. Resistance is that we disobey the authorities and maintain the disobedience. Resistance is that we take the sword in our own hands. Resistance is that when the speed limit is twenty miles per hour, we say, "I don't want that law," and then defiantly go forty miles an hour. The command is that we obey the higher powers and be subject to them, never taking the sword in our own hands and never resisting the authorities.

I do not believe that we can ever justify revolution of any kind. We must be in subjection to the authorities. They are the higher powers. We must remember these principles.

Perhaps someone will say that this is all very well as long as we have a good government, and he may criticize the apostle for not mentioning the bad governments. I reply that at the time of the apostle there were no good governments. "But what," someone asks, "if the government becomes corrupt, as is often the case, and interferes with the church, forbidding us to worship God?" This may happen, also in our own country. This time will come, and it may come soon. Suppose now that these higher powers, instead of being faithful to their calling as the apostle describes them here, become unfaithful and use the sword against the good and for the evildoer? What then? My answer is that the subjection remains, but the positive obedience falls away. Suppose that the authorities should forbid us to worship? What then? Scripture says that we must never cease to do good. We must always obey God rather than men [Acts 5:29]. We must go on with our worship. But if the sword turns against us, what then? We must be subject to the sword. The apostle says, "Be subject to the higher powers." If they turn against us for righteousness' sake, we are to suffer for righteousness' sake.

The Reward

There is a reward in this. The reward is that you shall have praise of them [v. 3]. If you resist the powers, you must be afraid of them, and not merely because of the sword. You must not only obey the law when there is a policeman around. Your attitude must be a spiritual one. You must obey for conscience' sake. If you do evil, you have reason to be afraid of the magistrate, not only because of the sword, but also because he is God's minister. Resist the magistrate, and you resist God's ordinance. Then you have reason to be afraid. But if you do good, you will have praise of the magistrate.

Do you ask, "Will the magistrate praise us? If they kill us, persecute us, and use the sword against us, will they still praise us?" In the first place, you will have in your consciousness the feeling that they *should* praise you. And they, in their consciousness, will have the divine testimony that they *ought* to praise you. When the Antichrist shall come, you will have praise in the deepest heart of Antichrist. In the second place, you must remember that Christ is Lord. Because of His lordship, you shall have praise of the magistrate. Christ will come again. Once He stood before the magistrate and was subject to the magistrate. He committed Himself to Him who judges righteously [I Pet. 2:21–23]. As it was with Him, so it has been with His people in the past. When Christ shall return, all will be justified and have praise of the magistrate. The higher powers will forever say that Christ and His people were the welldoers, and you will be justified.

Chapter Eighty-eight

The Ever Abiding Debt

Romans 13:8
Owe no man any thing, but to love one another: for he that loveth another hath fulfilled the law.

In this part of the book of Romans, we are dealing with the practical part of the epistle. This means that we must assume the attitude expressed in the question "Since we are partakers of so great a salvation, what now follows as to our calling in the world?" It is from this point of view that we must also receive the admonition in the text so that we may be not only hearers of the Word, but doers also.

If we assume this attitude, we will see that the admonition in the text is by no means an easy one. Even the first part of verse 8 is not easy. Here the apostle generalizes what he has enumerated in the preceding verse by stating, "Owe no man any thing." In the preceding verse the apostle has enumerated what each must give to every man: "Render therefore to all their dues: tribute to whom tribute is due; custom to whom custom; fear to whom fear; honour to whom honour." In this light we must also understand the first phrase in the text: "Owe no man any thing."

This is not the most difficult part of the sentence, nor the most fundamental, for the next part of the sentence speaks of a debt that we *do* owe: "Owe no man any thing, *but to love one another.*" By this is expressed that although you pay that debt, it is never paid in full.

What It Is

Let us have the general meaning of the text clearly before us. There are some who think that we have here simply a statement, not an exhortation. They would read the first part of the text this way: "You owe no man anything, except to love one another." It is true that the text can be read this way, but if the text is read in the context, it is evident that it is an exhortation. It is an exhortation to owe no one anything. It is an exhortation to have no debts.

There are various debts that we owe due to the various relationships of life. There are various God-ordained relationships. These relationships entail various debts, or obligations. There is, for example, the relationship of the magistrate and the subjects, of the parent and the child, of the teacher and the pupil. All of these relationships imply the obligation of honor. For example, the subjects in a nation owe to the magistrate the obligation of honor.

There are other relationships. There may be the relationship caused by well-doing. This brings about the obligation of gratitude on the part of him who is the object of the well-doing. There may be the actual debt of money. You may owe someone money. This relationship places you under the obligation to pay the debt.

Some may think that these things are insignificant details of human life, but Scripture does not think so. There are people who take their debts very lightly. They are indifferent with respect to their debts. They try to cover up their indifference by saying that they owe honor only to God. They will say, "We owe fear only to God." They will say, "We owe thanks only to God."

Such an attitude is not to the glory of God. If we honor God, we will honor those whom God has placed over us. For instance, a Christian cartoonist is impossible. It is wrong to make a cartoon, let us say, of the President. We owe honor to those whom God has placed over us. One does not honor the man who has been placed in office by God when he makes a cartoon of him. Those who have no respect for the higher powers do not heed this admonition. They do not pay their debt. And they do have a debt; they owe something to those in office in the state. This is not because of the persons themselves, but it is because of the God-ordained relationship.

The same is true of financial debts. Some people will run up a big bill. After they have run up a bill in one place, they will go somewhere else and run up a bill there. And they do not pay their debts. This is not a matter of money. It is a spiritual matter. We must pay our debts for God's sake. "Owe no man any thing."

When we have paid these debts, they are finished. When we meet someone who has been placed in a position over us and we have paid him the debt of honor that we owe him, it is finished. Our debt is paid. When someone has done us well, and we have shown our gratitude, our debt is paid. But there is one debt that exceeds all other debts. This debt is never fulfilled. "Owe no man any thing, *but to love one another.*" If this debt is paid, the debt remains. This debt always remains. We cannot rid ourselves of this debt.

Keeping in mind that we are dealing with the practical part of this epistle, I want to show the practical side of love. It is not the purpose of the apostle here to say what love is. He does not say, "Let there be love in your heart." The exhortation is, "You must love in deed! You must be actually loving."

Nevertheless, we must ask, "What is love, and what is the activity of love? What do we do when we love one another?" Love in Scripture is not a mere affection or feeling or emotion, such as the feeling of a mother for her child. Certainly Scripture also calls this feeling love, but it is a natural love, rooted in a blood relationship. Such love is a natural love, which is preserved by God's providence. But there is in this natural love no spiritual, moral, ethical love. Such natural love you do not find only among men; you find it also among animals. Besides, this natural love may exist alongside a profound hatred.

When Scripture speaks of love, it refers to a moral, ethical disposition of the heart toward God, or toward one another. Love in Scripture is a spiritual, moral, ethical disposition of the heart. It is of such a nature that it seeks its object in the way of righteousness. Because love seeks its object in the way of righteousness, it seeks the good of its object. Love always does this. Verse 10 of this chapter says, "Love worketh no ill to his neighbour." The meaning is not that love never causes its object to be unhappy in the carnal sense. Rather, love seeks to make its object truly happy. Because there is no happiness possible except in the way of righteousness, love seeks to make its object perfect. This is why love sometimes seems to be so very stern. And this is why hatred sometimes seems so sweet. A mother may love her child, even to the extent of giving her life for the child, and yet if she leads the child into the corruption of the world, into theaters, movies, and dance halls, that mother hates her child. That is hatred. When a man pretends to love a maiden and tries to entice that maiden into the sin of adultery, he hates her. Love does not do that. "Love worketh no ill." Positively, love always works good. It works good both in the temporal sense and in the eternal sense. Although love may seem stern, it never works ill to the neighbor, because it seeks its object in righteousness.

Whom must we love? Must we love all? Of course, when the apostle writes in the text that we must love one another, he is thinking of the church. Reciprocal love is possible only in the church. There is no love in the world. This is why men must have contracts. If there were love in the world, they would need no contracts to insure peace. There is not that disposition, that spiritual quality of love, in the heart of man. Men do not seek the good of one another. They seek ill for one another. In the church, however, there is love of one another. There cannot be love between the unrighteous. Therefore, when the apostle says, "Love one another," he is thinking of the church.

Nevertheless, the apostle is speaking of the life of the Christian in the world. He has been speaking of this in the preceding context. He also speaks of this in the text: "Owe *no man any thing.*" In verse 10 the apostle says, "Love worketh no ill to his neighbour." The implication concerning our love for each other is that when we do not love one another, we do not love the neighbor, yet the debt of love extends to the ungodly neighbor. Our love to the man of the world cannot be a relation of fellowship, but love that consists of never doing ill to the neighbor is an obligation. When the neighbor is hungry, we must give him to eat; when he is thirsty, we must give him to drink; when he is naked, we must clothe him. Love to the neighbor who is ungodly does not mean that we play ball with him and have a good time with him. That is not love. Love seeks the good of the neighbor in the way of righteousness.

Why It Is an Abiding Obligation

Loving one another is our obligation. You must love me, and I must love you. When you do, you have just paid your debt. But the debt remains. You can never be rid of this debt. You always owe this debt of love. Sometimes people say, "I have done so much for that man; I am going to quit now. I wash my hands of him." But this is impossible. You say, "It is of no use; he does not appreciate it anyway." This is not the issue. You must love the neighbor whether he appreciates it or not. You must always love the neighbor. And if you do, you merit nothing. You simply paid your debt.

Why is this an obligation? First, it is an obligation because love is the fulfillment of the law. The text says, "He that loveth another hath fulfilled the law." God requires in His law that we love. It is the will of God that we should love. If one asks, "Why does God will that we shall love?" the answer is, because God loves Himself. He created a creature who should manifest this love. This is why there is the common mandate to love one another.

This is not the only reason. The apostle is not writing to the world. He is writing to the church. The obligation of the Christian to love has been deepened by a far greater love, the love manifested in the cross. God manifested His love in the cross as this love could not be manifested in creation. When we were yet enemies, God manifested His love to us [Rom. 5:8, 10]. As Christians we confess that we know this love of God. We confess that we know and taste that God has loved us. He has loved us so deeply, so highly, so widely, that He gave Himself in His Son to die for us. And Scripture emphasizes repeatedly that if God so loved us, if He performed such an act of love for us, we ought to love one another. Brothers and sisters, owe no man anything, except to love one another.

An ever abiding debt!

How We Can Fulfill It

Loving one another is impossible for us as we are by nature. We feel this when we read this Word of God in light of the fact that it is not a mere moral lesson. We feel that we will never do it by nature. By nature we are filled with the desire for unrighteousness and the desire to lead others into evil. By nature we are corrupt. By nature we speak evil of one another; we do evil to one another.

Therefore, I point us to the first part of this epistle. Then all is well. For this love of God, which He revealed when He gave His Son, He has poured out in our hearts [Rom. 5:5]. We have tasted that God loves us. This must be experienced first. God poured out His love in our hearts so that we taste that He has loved us. When we have tasted this love of God so that we get on our knees and experience that He has blotted out our sins, this same love returns to Him in that we love God. And when we love God, we walk in the light and love one another. Only in this way can we take this Word along in our life: "Owe no man any thing, but to love one another: for he that loveth another hath fulfilled the law."

Chapter Eighty-nine

The Calling of the Dawn

Romans 13:11, 12
And that, knowing the time, that now it is high time to awake out of sleep: for now is our salvation nearer than when we believed.
The night is far spent, the day is at hand: let us therefore cast off the works of darkness, and let us put on the armour of light.

In the text the apostle gives us an added reason for the exhortations and admonitions in the previous verses. He gives an added reason for the admonition with regard to the powers that be and our being in subjection to them. He gives an added reason for the admonition with regard to our giving to every man his due: tribute to whom tribute, custom to whom custom, fear to whom fear, honor to whom honor. He gives an added reason particularly for the admonition that we owe no man anything, except the ever abiding debt to love one another. This is a debt that accumulates as we pay it, a debt that is with us always. The first reason for paying the debt of love is that he who loves the neighbor has fulfilled the law. Now the apostle adds something else. He gives an added reason why we should walk in the practical manifestation of love to the neighbor, a love that we must also manifest in the world.

The added reason is that we know the time. Time is referred to from the viewpoint of the peculiar characteristic that time has in our own day. Time is not always the same. It changes. It is not always characterized by the same thing. What is characteristic of our time is that the night is far spent and the day is at hand. The Christian is to know this. This knowledge ought to live in our consciousness so that it may be an added reason why we should walk as the apostle has said in the preceding verses.

The entire text is really a figure. The figure is that of a sleeper, or rather, it is the figure of one who has just awakened from his sleep but who is still drowsy while the night is far spent and the day is at hand. We would say that he can see the dawn coming. That coming dawn has for the sleeper a calling. The calling is that he awake out of his sleep, take off his nightclothes, and put on his dayclothes.

The Dawn

The important question suggested in verse 12 is, What is meant by *the day?* What is this day that is at hand? This same day is called the day of salvation in verse 11. The salvation that is nearer now than when we believed is the same as the day of verse 12. What is this day?

Different answers are given. Some explain that it is the day of the Lord in the final sense. It is the day when Christ shall come again. It is the day when we will receive the perfection of the salvation that now we possess in principle. It is the day of the resurrection of the body. It is the day when the church will be separated from all sin and from all suffering. It is the day when the old things will pass away and when God will create new heavens and a new earth. But these interpreters go on to charge that when the apostle said that this day is near, he was mistaken. This day was not as near as the early church expected. In the mind of the early church, according to this explanation, the night that is far spent referred to the short period from the time of their conversion to the time in which Paul wrote this epistle. The early church expected the Lord to come in their own day. This expectation the apostle expressed in the words *Now is our salvation nearer than when we believed.*

With the last part of this interpretation—that the apostle

labored under the mistaken notion that the Lord would come in his own day—we cannot agree. In the first place, the apostle did not have a revelation of the time of the day of the Lord. Therefore, he could not speak of the nearness of that day. In the second place, the apostle had no such expectation. He wrote in one of his epistles that he would die and be with Christ [Phil. 1:20–25]. To the church of the Thessalonians, he wrote that they must not suppose that the day of the Lord is at hand [II Thess. 2:2]. The apostle did not labor under the notion that the Lord would come in his own day.

Besides, it is not really the issue whether the apostle labored under the notion that the Lord would come in his own day. This in itself might be possible. But we are dealing with Scripture. If it is not true that the day of salvation is near in the sense that the apostle intended, the whole text is not true. Then the text cannot be an added reason for the admonition to pay the ever abiding debt of love. Therefore, we must maintain that the apostle was not mistaken when he said that the night is far spent and the day is at hand. What he wrote to the Romans comes to us as the Word of God: "The night is far spent, the day is at hand."

In order to avoid the notion that the apostle was mistaken, others explain the text as referring to the destruction of Jerusalem. They argue that the destruction of Jerusalem is called the day of the Lord. *The day of the Lord* in Scripture is a broad concept. The destruction of Jerusalem was a certain relief for the church. The Jews hated the church and persecuted it. Thus, in a sense, the destruction of Jerusalem was a day of salvation for the church. But the apostle does not speak of the destruction of Jerusalem in the text. The destruction of Jerusalem cannot be called *the day of salvation.*

Still others explain that the apostle refers to the day of our death. The day of death is a day of salvation. In the day of death, we are delivered from sin and death, and we enter into glory. Therefore, the day of our death may be regarded as the day of salvation.

When Scripture speaks of *the day of salvation,* or of *the day of the Lord,* it always refers to the day of Christ. To understand verses 11 and 12, we must start from this fundamental truth. The day of the Lord is the day of our ultimate salvation. In what sense can it be said that this day is *near?* And in what sense can it be said that the night is *far spent?* In the first place, as far as the church as a whole is concerned, it can be said of this entire dispensation that the night is far spent and the day is at hand. The night started in the beginning. It is the night of sin, of death, and of the curse that settled upon us in paradise. This is the night. According to Scripture, in this night there have been different periods that can be distinguished by God's wonderwork, and which are called *hours.* There was the hour from paradise to the flood. There was the hour from the flood to the calling of Abraham. There was the hour from the calling of Abraham to the establishing of the covenant on Mount Sinai. There was the hour of Israel's national existence. There was the *hour* of Christ. And now this is the *last* hour. Of this hour the apostle John writes, "Little children, it is the last hour."[1] [I John 2:18]. This is the last hour of the night.

In this last hour, therefore, the only thing we can and may expect is the coming of Christ. In the old dispensation, they could not say this. When Noah preached as the preacher of righteousness, they could expect the flood. They expected different things in the old dispensation. But now the only thing we can expect is the coming of Christ. As the different things that they expected dominated the life of the people of the old dispensation, so the coming of Christ must dominate the life of the people of God today. The night is far spent; the day is at hand. What the text urges is as true for us as it was for the Romans.

There is something else. For the individual believer the day of the Lord is much *nearer.* For the individual believer, the day of the

---

1. The Greek original of I John 2:18 has *hour* where the KJV twice translates it *time.*

Lord comes when we die. This is true because the death of the Christian is his salvation. Salvation is separated from him only for a few years, for it comes when he dies. But there is another reason why death is the coming of the day of the Lord for the believer. I suggest that after we die and enter into eternity, time must be changed. I do not think that the church in heaven still passes through the days, months, and years that the church passes through here. Therefore, it will seem to be but a short stretch of time from the day of our death to the day of the Lord. From this point of view, too, the day of the Lord is at hand. Our salvation is nearer.

It makes no difference whether we call death *the day of death* or *the day of salvation*. We call it the day of death from an earthly point of view. In death we are separated from all earthly ties and relations. But we can also say with respect to death that our salvation is near. This is different. Then we mean that we will be delivered from all sin and corruption and will be with Christ. This is the biblical view of looking at death. When we look at death in this light, there is no fear in death. And there is in this view of death the constant urge to walk in sanctification. This is the central purpose of the text. Don't say, "Death is nearer." You must say, "Salvation is nearer." And you must live in the hope of this salvation.

In comparison with the coming day of salvation, the apostle calls the present state of the Christian *the night*. It is not as though we have no light at all. It is dawn. But if we compare the present state of the Christian with that day, it is still night. It is night because his present state is still earthly, sinful, and characterized by death. It is night because the Christian carries about with him this present nature, which is also earthly and carnal. As long as we are in this present nature, we cannot see the heavenly things as we shall see them in that day. We do not now see face-to-face. We live by faith, not by sight. We cannot see the spiritual things of the kingdom of heaven because we are still in the night. But then we will see face-to-face. We will know as we are known. We will be like Him. We will no more look at a letter from Father to learn a little about Him. Rather, we will see Him, and we will know Him. That is the day—the day of perfect light, the day of perfect righteousness, the day of perfect holiness. In comparison with that day, it is still night, but the day is at hand.

It is a fundamental element in the text that we know the time. Perhaps someone says, "This is not true. We Christians do not often look at the time as the coming of the dawn." This may be the case. When the apostle writes that we know the time, his meaning is that we, the church, are dominated by the hope of the coming day and by the consciousness that the day is near. We long for it. We desire it. We look for it. Probably we respond, "I ought to know the time, but I don't."

I do not think that the church today is characterized by the spiritual knowledge of the time. I do not think that the church today is characterized by looking forward to the time. We like to grope around in the dark. We do our business. We count our money. We amuse ourselves. But it can hardly be said that we live in the consciousness of knowing that it is dawn and that the day is near. Let us humble ourselves! Let us repent! And let us turn away from the night so that we may live in the consciousness of the coming day!

Its Calling for Us

That day has a calling for us. This calling is threefold: that we awake out of our sleep, that we put off our bedclothes, and that we put on our dayclothes. Of course, when the dawn comes, you get up, put off your nightclothes, and put on your dayclothes. When the text speaks of sleep, it does not mean the sleep of death, but the sleep of sin. We awake out of the sleep of death once. This takes place in regeneration. The meaning is that we awake in relation to sin and unrighteousness. We awake to hate sin and to rejoice in the light. If we do this, we will put off our nightclothes. Verse 12 calls these nightclothes *the works of darkness*. These we must put off.

We must put on our dayclothes of light. The original has, "Put on the armor." We are to put on the whole armor of God. We must put on the armor, for it is still dawn, and we walk in the dawn. In other words, we are to let the day of the Lord dominate our whole life, knowing that it is at hand.

Does someone say, "I did awake out of the sleep of sin when I was converted, as well as out of the sleep of death"? This is true, but the difference is this: we must awaken out of the sleep of sin *daily*. Sin is within us. The nightclothes stick to us, and the world likes to put them on us. We ourselves are always inclined to fall back into sleep. Therefore, the admonition is to awake out of sleep, put off the works of darkness, and put on the armor of light. Fight the good fight of faith so that no one takes your crown.

Chapter Ninety

Receiving the Weaker Brother

Romans 14:1-3
Him that is weak in the faith receive ye, but not to doubtful disputations. For one believeth that he may eat all things: another, who is weak, eateth herbs. Let not him that eateth despise him that eateth not; and let not him which eateth not judge him that eateth: for God hath received him.

There is a sharp difference between chapter 14 and what has preceded. The preceding two chapters called attention to things that are in themselves right or wrong. They treated activities that we cannot do or leave undone, as the case may be, and still serve the Lord. The apostle admonished the people of God that they make the proper use of the gifts that each has received, that they love without dissimulation, that they be of the same mind one toward another, and that they avenge not themselves. He admonished them not to resist the higher powers, but to be subject unto them. He admonished them to owe no man anything but the ever abiding debt of love. And he admonished them to walk in the day, not in the night, and therefore not in rioting and drunkenness. Those are acts that must be done, or avoided, if we are to serve the Lord.

Chapter 14 speaks of a different kind of activity. This is an activity that has in itself no moral character. If we do such acts, we do not necessarily serve the Lord by doing them. If we do not do them, we do not necessarily serve the Lord by not doing them. They are acts that are in themselves indifferent, acts that have no moral, ethical content in themselves. I eat, but a dog does, too. There is no moral value in these things in themselves. They are indifferent things. They receive moral content only from the consideration, reason, and motive why we do them, or why we do not do them. To these indifferent things, the apostle calls attention.[1]

We might think that such a subject for preaching is fruitless to the church, but in the first place, nothing is fruitless for the edification of the church. In the second place, history teaches that from these indifferent things often arise strife, wrangling, and hatred that destroy the church. Therefore, we must understand what our attitude toward them should be.

The apostle approaches the subject of these indifferent things from the viewpoint of the weaker brother: "Him that is weak in the faith receive ye." It is from this viewpoint that we must consider the passage.

Who He Is

The text speaks of one who is *weak in the faith*. Weak in the faith does not have the sense of a lack of personal assurance that one belongs to the Lord. The Bible does not sanction weakness in the faith in this sense; to the contrary, the Bible admonishes us to be in the full assurance of faith. Neither does the text refer to a weakness in the faith that reveals itself in a negligent, slothful life. There are people who reveal in life and doctrine that they are weak in the faith in this sense. There are Christians who are weak in the faith with respect to doctrine. They cannot see that it makes much difference whether they belong with us or whether they go to some other church. There are also Christians who are negligent and slothful with respect to life. They do not attend divine services regularly. They live in the world and run after the pleasures and treasures of the

---

1. What Hoeksema calls *indifferent things* are commonly referred to as the "adiaphora." As Hoeksema explains, these are activities that Scripture neither commands nor forbids.

world. Such people are not referred to in the text by the words *weak in the faith*.

The Christian of whom the text speaks is in many ways a model Christian. He is not negligent. He does not live in the world. He is just the opposite. He has a very sensitive conscience. He is a man who could be an example in many ways. But he is weak in the faith; that is, he is weak in the faith with respect to the things indifferent. The original literally states that he is weak *in respect to faith*. He is weak. He is like a child learning to walk with a chair. When the child gets to be about three years old, and the parents want that child to walk without the chair, the child is afraid to do so. That is weakness. The child does not have the confidence to walk without the chair. Similarly, this Christian is weak. He is weak as to his knowledge of what Scripture teaches. Because he is weak as to knowledge, he clings to certain institutions. He does not dare to walk alone. He is not strong enough to walk only by his faith and the Word of God.

Therefore, the Christian of whom the apostle is speaking does not dare to eat; that is, he does not dare to eat everything. As we gather from verse 21, neither does he dare to drink. He does not dare to eat meat. This meat is not meat that has been offered to idols. This is not the reference. This man does not eat meat at all. He is a vegetarian. When you set meat before him, his conscience bothers him, so that he does not dare to eat. The same is true of drink. That this man does not eat or drink is because he is too weak to believe that there is nothing wrong with eating meat or drinking wine. This weak man, of course, is not a man who is afraid of being a drunkard, but he is so delicately construed that he supposes Christians may not eat meat and drink wine *at all*. The subject is things indifferent as far as our serving the Lord is concerned.

There are many such things. We are not today so much concerned about eating and drinking, but there are Christians who have similar notions with regard to things indifferent. There are farmers who are too weak to put lightning rods on their barns. They cannot understand how they can put lightning rods on their barns and serve the Lord. They cannot understand how they can put lightning rods on their barns and thank the Lord for them. There are also people who cannot understand how they can take out fire insurance for their property and serve the Lord. They say that fire insurance shows a lack of faith. These are indifferent things of which life is full, acts which in themselves are not moral or immoral, but into which we put moral content. Such is the weak brother. He does not stand in Christian liberty.

The strong man, in contrast, is not the Christian who does everything. It is probably not out of place to note that in certain circles the category of indifferent things becomes rather rubbery, rather stretchy. In the name of things indifferent, some claim the right to do everything. This is out of line with the nature of the things that the apostle is treating. The underlying thought of this chapter is that whether we do these things or do not do them, we serve the Lord. This must remain the underlying principle. We cannot go to wicked places and then say, "I am the Lord's." The strong man is not a man who does everything. He is one who says, "My life is regulated by the Word of God. I eat and drink everything."

Why We Must Receive Him

If the weaker brother comes to us, we must receive him. It is noteworthy that the apostle addresses the stronger brother. He tells him that he must receive the weaker brother. One more thing must not escape our attention. The apostle speaks of the weaker brother in the singular, but the stronger brothers he addresses in the plural: "Him [singular] that is weak in the faith receive ye [plural]." The implication is that the congregation consists of stronger brothers, and the weak brother is an exception. When you have a church that is weak from this point of view, it is in danger. In a church that is weak in this respect, the conscience becomes narrower and narrower. One says, "We may not have picnics." Another says, "We may not have banquets." A third says, "We may not have programs." A fourth says, "We may not go swimming." A fifth says, "Girls may not bob their hair." A congregation that consists of weaker brothers presently does not know how to move about anymore. There is a worse danger: that the weaker brothers make these indifferent things their religion, so that these things become a matter of principle, and people indulge in their weakness. Therefore, the apostle addresses the stronger brothers.

The admonition is that the stronger brothers receive the weaker brother. We are to receive him as a member in our midst. We are to receive him into our Christian fellowship. We are to let him come into our societies and our social gatherings. Receive him! Receive him in love! By receiving him in love, we may make the weak brother strong. This is possible. Rather than say to him, "You are silly," receive him.

The reason why we must receive him is that *God hath received him*. You and I do not determine who is to be received into the Christian fellowship of the church. We must remember this. That God has received him means that Christ died for that man. God has given to that man His grace. God has drawn him out of darkness into the light. God has made him our brother. If God has received him, shall we turn to him the cold shoulder? Receive him!

How We Ought to Receive Him

There is a limitation, however. We are to receive him, *but not to doubtful disputations*. The phrase is rather difficult. The Revised Version reads, "not for decision of scruples." The general meaning is plain. We can render it this way: "Receive him, but do not dispute with him about the considerations and motives as to why one does eat and another does not eat." This is plain from what follows. The stronger brother must not despise the weaker brother, and the weak brother must not judge the strong brother. That is, we must not judge one another in indifferent things. Of course, the apostle does not mean that we may not judge a drunkard. He is speaking of indifferent things. Indifferent things do not reveal whether we serve the Lord or not. And we should not judge the motives of one another. This is dangerous. This is the meaning of the words "Let not him *which eateth not* judge him that eateth." The danger is that the weaker brother does not understand that he is weak. He imagines that he is the stronger brother. Imagining that he is the stronger, he does not only say, "I dare not eat or drink," but he also says, "You shall not eat or drink either, and if you do, you are not a Christian." The other danger is that the stronger brother looks down on the weaker brother and despises him. Then there is contention in the church. The apostle says, "Nothing of the kind. Receive him." Still, the weaker brother must understand that he is weak. But the stronger brother must not lift himself up against the weaker brother.

Let this be the dominating principle in our life: whether we eat or not, we are the Lord's. If you can eat with thanksgiving, eat. If you can drink with thanksgiving, drink. If you cannot eat and give thanks, do not eat. But do all things unto the Lord, knowing that whether we live or whether we die, we are the Lord's.

Chapter Ninety-one

Always the Lord's

Romans 14:4 – 8
Who art thou that judgest another man's servant? to his own master he standeth or falleth. Yea, he shall be holden up: for God is able to make him stand.

One man esteemeth one day above another: another esteemeth every day alike. Let every man be fully persuaded in his own mind.

He that regardeth the day, regardeth it unto the Lord; and he that regardeth not the day, to the Lord he doth not regard it. He that eateth, eateth to the Lord, for he giveth God thanks; and he that eateth not, to the Lord he eateth not, and giveth God thanks.

For none of us liveth to himself, and no man dieth to himself.

For whether we live, we live unto the Lord; and whether we die, we die unto the Lord: whether we live therefore, or die, we are the Lord's.

In the last verse of the text is the underlying principle that must always guide us in all our life and walk, particularly with regard to those things known as the "indifferent things." There are things in our life that we do, or do not do, that cannot be determined by the question "May we do them, or may we not do them?" They are things that are indifferent in this respect: in doing them one may either serve the Lord, or sin. Conversely, one may not do them, and in not doing them he may either serve the Lord, or sin. In doing these indifferent things, or in not doing them, one may either serve the Lord, or one may sin. It all depends upon the attitude one assumes when he does them or does not do them. The things themselves are indifferent.

The apostle introduced the subject of the indifferent things [vv. 1–3] by addressing the church concerning the weaker brother. It is evident that the apostle had been informed that there were disputes in the church concerning such things. There were some in the church who said that one may not eat meat, that one may not drink a glass of wine, and that one must regard certain days. They were in danger of creating a certain pharisaical system of "precept upon precept." The apostle teaches that this is wrong. In itself, it makes no difference whether one does these things or does not do them. They are indifferent things. But the guiding principle of all of the life of the saints must be that we are the Lord's.

The Meaning

The Lord in the passage is Christ. This is evident from the context. In the verse that follows [v. 9] we read that Christ both died, and rose, that He might be Lord both of the dead and the living. The apostle speaks of Christ as Lord, because he wants to call attention to the relation in which Christ stands to His church. He is its Lord. Lordship had a different connotation in the apostle's day than it has today. In the apostle's day, a lord had proprietorship over his servant. A servant was the property of his master; his master owned him. In this sense the apostle speaks of Christ as Lord of His church. We are His. We are His property. We belong to Him. Therefore, there is nothing we have that is not to be consecrated to Him. Our body, our soul, our gifts, and our talents all belong to Him. We are His property. Not only our body, soul, and talents, but also all that we have belongs to Him. Our property, our business, our job, our family, and all our relationships belong to Christ.

There is a difference between the relation of an earthly master and his slave and the relation of Christ and His church. The relation between Christ and His church is a love relation. That Christ is our Lord is due to love. In love He was appointed to be our Lord. In love we were given to Him. In love we become His property. He bought us. He did not buy us with material things, such as gold or silver, nor did He buy us for a material purpose. Instead, He bought us with His own blood because He loved us. For this reason He purchased us in order to bless us. It is a relation of love. Not only is He our Lord because of love, but it was by the power of His love that we became His servants. We are His servants in this relationship of love.

The text emphasizes that we are *always* His. We are His, whether we live or die. This is not the same as saying that we are His *in life or death*. This, too, is true, but it is not what the text says. It says that we are the Lord's, whether we live or die. This is an active expression. Whether we actively live, or actively die, we are the Lord's. The expression *whether we live* covers all our life. It refers not only to our personal life, but also to our life in every relation. It refers to our relation to our family, our relation to the church, our relation to the world, our relation to our business, our relation to our employer—all the relations in which we live.

The same viewpoint is maintained when the text says, "whether we die." The text does not say *in death,* but *whether we die*. We should remember that even while we are living, we are also dying. Dying is the loss of everything that pertains to this present life. The text looks at dying from the viewpoint of our activity, from the viewpoint of our willingness to die. Whether we live or die, always we are the Lord's.

The apostle does not only say that we are the Lord's. He adds something. He says that we live and die *unto Him.* "For none of us liveth to himself, and no man dieth to himself." The words *no man,* of course, mean "no Christian." It is plain that the apostle does not refer to everybody. He refers to the member of the church, to the Christian. Whether Christians live, we live unto the Lord, and whether Christians die, we die unto the Lord. Whatever we do, in living and in dying, we do with a view to *Him.* Whatever we do *not* do with a view to Christ is sin, in living and in dying. Whatever we do that does not center in Christ is sin. To live unto ourselves is to seek ourselves, to glorify ourselves, to please ourselves. When we live unto ourselves, we set ourselves in the center and try to please ourselves. We eat to please ourselves; we drink to please ourselves; we do everything to please ourselves. And when we die unto ourselves, we set ourselves in the center. When sickness comes, we murmur, complain, and rebel.

The apostle teaches that we may not live unto ourselves, and we may not die unto ourselves. According to his inner principle, the Christian does not want to live unto himself, and he does not want to die unto himself. He wants to live and die unto Christ. He will ask what he can do to please Christ.

With regard to the indifferent things, which is the main thought in the passage, the fact that we are the Lord's must be our guiding principle. Then we will not ask whether we may do this or whether we may do that. Then we will not need consistory meetings and synods to lay down the rule for us. We can be safely guided by this principle: we are the Lord's. We must agree to let this principle guide us. We are the Lord's. This must determine all our life. This principle must always determine our behavior regarding the things indifferent.

Indifferent things, remember, are things that have no moral value in themselves. There were people in the congregation at Rome who supposed that one may not eat meat or drink a glass of wine, and that the members must observe certain days. They were the weaker brothers in the congregation. They were not the stronger brothers. Nor was the congregation dominated by these weaker brothers. It would be a miserable congregation that is dominated by weaker brothers. But in Rome there were people in the congregation who were weak with respect to things indifferent.

The text brings up yet another such indifferent thing. There were people who regarded certain *days*. In verse 5 we read, "One man esteemeth one day above another: another esteemeth every day alike." It is evident that when the apostle speaks of observing days, he does not refer to the sabbath day. But there were other days—holy days, feast days, new moons—which some insisted should be observed. When these people insisted on observing these days, they did not intend to merit righteousness in this way. If this had been the case, the apostle would have written differently, as he did, for example, to the Galatians. At Rome they did not observe days to merit righteousness, but they were weak. They could not stand in Christian liberty. They had need of certain precepts and ordinances. They wanted to please the Lord all right, but they thought that those days still had to be observed.

Its Application to the Indifferent Things

The principle that we are the Lord's is applied to the indifferent things. There are other indifferent things besides those mentioned in the passage. When these indifferent things become a matter of principle to the weaker brother, they become troublesome in the congregation. If we listen to the weaker brother, the condition of the church will be that we will not be able to move. Then one will say that a woman may not cut her hair. A second will say that a woman may not wear short skirts. A third will say that we may not go swimming. A fourth will say that we may not play ball. A fifth will say that we may not have banquets. A sixth will say that we may not have life insurance. A seventh will say that we may not have lightning rods on our barns. As a result, life will become so restricted that we will not be able to move. This must not happen.

The apostle addresses the stronger brothers. He lays down three important truths. In the first place, we must be persuaded in our own consciousness that we do these indifferent things, or do not do them, unto the Lord. This decides immediately whether we are dealing with indifferent things. If we are dealing with the theater or the movie or the dance, we do not do them unto the Lord. In such matters we are not dealing with indifferent things. The same principle determines whether in doing the things indifferent, or in not doing them, we serve the Lord. It may be an indifferent thing to wear short skirts, but if a woman wears short skirts from the principle of the corruption of the world, it is better for her to let her skirts drag on the ground. A lightning rod may be an indifferent thing, but if we seek our safety in it, we are sinning. If we eat meat to show our pride over against the weaker brother, we are sinning. This is why the apostle says that if one observes certain days or does not observe them, he does it unto the Lord. And if he does not observe days or refuses to observe days *unto the Lord,* he sins. If one eats or does not eat, he does it unto the Lord. And if he does not eat or refuses to eat *unto the Lord,* he sins. We are the Lord's, whether we live or whether we die. This is Christian liberty.

In the second place, from this the apostle deduces another truth, namely, that we do it with thanksgiving. Whatever we do or do not do, we must be able to give thanks. Our attitude has been such that we did it as unto the Lord. Therefore, we give thanks. A good test of right use of indifferent things is whether we can, and do, give thanks.

In the third place, from the fact that we are the Lord's, and from the fact that we do all things unto the Lord, the apostle draws this final truth: we may not judge one another. That is, we may not judge one another with regard to indifferent things. We may judge when someone walks in sin, but we may not judge with regard to things indifferent. We may not judge another man's servant. To his own master he stands or falls. That is, to Jesus only, as Lord, he remains faithful and stands, or he becomes unfaithful and falls. Does someone say, "That man will fall, and I want to save him"? The apostle says that he will not fall. The man who walks in Christian liberty will stand, for God will hold him up. Therefore, let this principle be our guide: whether we live or die, we are the Lord's.

Chapter Ninety-two

Always Living by Faith

Romans 14:23b
For whatsoever is not of faith is sin.

These words are the announcement of a general truth, but with a specific application. In this chapter the apostle has been writing about those things in the active life of the Christian that are known as the things "indifferent." They are activities that are in themselves neither good nor bad. They are such activities as eating meat, drinking a glass of wine, and observing certain days.

In the immediate context the apostle enunciated various principles with regard to these indifferent things. First, the apostle made plain that he takes sides with the stronger brothers. He takes sides with those who say that we may eat meat and drink a glass of wine. Second, with regard to the weaker brother, the apostle says that he may not judge the stronger brother. That is, he may not say to the stronger brother, "You may not eat meat, and you may not drink wine." He must say, "I may not eat meat, and I may not drink wine." Third, the apostle teaches that one who thinks a thing is wrong, and nevertheless does it, sins. If a man thinks that it is sinful to eat meat and nevertheless eats it, he sins. Things that are not sinful in themselves may in this way become sinful to the weaker brother. Fourth, the apostle warns that the stronger brother may not use these indifferent things in such a way that he becomes the cause of the weaker brother's falling into sin. Fifth, the apostle contends that if the use of these indifferent things by the stronger brother becomes the occasion for the weaker brother to stumble, the stronger brother must abstain from them.

Verse 23 applies to the matter of the indifferent things the general principle that *whatsoever is not of faith is sin.* There is a connection between the thought of verse 23 and that of verse 8, where we read that we do all things *unto the Lord.* For it is by faith that we belong to the Lord. That which we do unto the Lord, we do from the principle of faith. That which is not from the principle of faith is not unto the Lord and is, therefore, sin.

The Meaning

In the context of Romans 14, the truth that *whatsoever is not of faith is sin* has a specific application. As it occurs here, this truth is not a general doctrine. It specifically addresses the indifferent things. The meaning is that if one does not do these things out of faith, he is sinning. This is plain from the first part of this twenty-third verse: "He that doubteth is damned if he eat, because he eateth not of faith." Then follow the words *Whatsoever is not of faith is sin.* The thought of the text is this: we may not do these indifferent things unless we do them from a conscious faith. If we do not do them from a conscious faith, we sin.

Because the text has this specific application, many say that this Word of God cannot be understood as a general doctrine. On the basis of Romans 14:23b, Reformed interpreters have always maintained that whatever the unbeliever does is sin. All interpreters who have maintained the total depravity of man have always pointed to this text as proof: all that the unbeliever does is sin, because *whatsoever is not of faith is sin.* But interpreters who do not accept the total depravity of man, and who do not agree that the natural man always sins, insist that the text has a specific application only to the matter of indifferent things. According to them, the text is not a general doctrine that all the deeds of the unbeliever are sin. It is exclusively the teaching that if one doubts whether something is right, he must not do it, for if he does it anyway, he does not live from the conviction of his conscience.

This restriction of the text to its specific application is wrong for several reasons. First of all, it is not the same to say that "all that is not of faith is sin" and to say that "all that one is not sure of, all that is not from the conviction of one's conscience, is sin." A man may be perfectly sure that a thing is right and still sin when he does it. Second, it is evident that the apostle intends to teach that all is sin that does not have its source in the saving faith of Christ. Although it is true that he applies this general truth to the specific subject of indifferent things, the general truth nevertheless remains. Third, if the apostle can say of the Christian that all that he does not do out of faith is sin, how much more can this be said of the unbeliever! Therefore, this stands as a general doctrine: *whatsoever is not of faith is sin*. Every deed of the unbeliever is sin.

Why?

Sin is all that misses the mark. The word *sin* literally means "missing the mark." And the *mark*—the only right aim of our actions—is the glory of God. What is not to the glory of God and what is not from the motive of the glory of God, that is, all that misses this mark, God calls sin. This mark is never our aim by nature. "The carnal mind is enmity against God" [Rom. 8:7]. It does not aim at the glory of the Most High. The natural man, the sinful flesh, aims at self, at its own honor and glory. But it never aims at the glory of God. And if it doesn't, it sins. The only way in which this flesh is changed is through Christ. Christ in us, through His Spirit and grace, changes this flesh so that we again delight in God's precepts. This is from Christ. Therefore, only insofar as we are living out of Him do we live to the glory of God. All in us that is not out of Him is sin. Because all in us that is not out of Christ is sin, and because we are united with Christ by faith, all that is not of faith is sin. This stands as a general doctrine.

The Application to the Weaker Brother

This general principle is applied to life in the church. First, the apostle applies it to the weaker brother. Whatsoever is not of faith is sin for the weaker brother. If the weaker brother eats, even though he thinks it wrong, *whatsoever is not of faith is sin.* Verse 14 declares that "there is nothing unclean of itself: but to him that esteemeth any thing to be unclean, to him it is unclean." When Scripture says that nothing is unclean, the reference is to everything in creation. Of all that God gave in creation for us to use, nothing is unclean. Someone may respond, "If nothing is unclean, I do not sin if I use it." But verse 14 states that to him who thinks a thing is wrong, and who does it nevertheless, it is wrong. This strikes us as strange. Here is a man who thinks that there is something unclean in a piece of meat. If in this state of mind he eats it anyway, he sins. This is repeated in verse 20: "All things indeed are pure; but it is evil for that man who eateth with offence." Again, the reference is to all things that are in creation. All things in creation are pure, but it is evil to use them with offense. If, therefore, a man is confronted by a thing that is in itself pure, but his state of heart and mind is such that he cannot use it without offense in his heart, he sins if he uses it. The same is taught in verse 23: "He that doubteth is damned if he eat."

How can this be? How can anything that is in itself not sinful become sinful because of a certain subjective condition on the part of him who uses it? In other words, how can two men both do the same thing, and the one sin in doing it, while the other, doing the same thing, does not sin? We must remember that God does not look at the outward deed. We do. If we see two men doing the same thing, we conclude that both do good.

When two men both keep within the limits of the law, both are justified before the law of men. However, this is not true before God. The reason is that the issue before God is not whether an act conforms to the outward form of the law, but God looks at the heart. God does not ask only, "What did you do?" But He also asks, "Why did you do it?" And God never calls anything good unless it is good to the very heart. Accordingly, if two men jump into the water after a drowning child, and the one does it to the glory of God, but the other does it to receive praise of men, the one sins, and the other does not. God wants truth in the inward heart. He is never satisfied with an outward show.

Let us apply this to the weaker brother. He sits at the table with the strong man. The weak man says in his heart, "It is sinful to eat meat and to drink wine." In his heart he really is saying, "The Lord does not want me to eat and to drink." But he looks at the stronger brother. Because he does not want to be small in the eyes of that strong brother, he eats. What does he do? Outwardly, he does the same thing as the stronger brother, but inwardly he chooses his own honor, rather than the honor of Christ.

This specific application of the truth *whatsoever is not of faith is sin* can be expressed as a general rule for all of life. What cannot, in our own estimation, be done to the glory of God, we may not do. And if we do it anyway, we sin.

The Application to the Stronger Brother

The same principle applies just as well to the strong brother. It applies to him in his relation to the weak brother. In I Corinthians 10:23 we read, "All things are lawful for me, but all things are not expedient: all things are lawful for me, but all things edify not." Similarly, the apostle writes here that if the strong brother use his Christian liberty, and the weaker brother is hurt by the strong brother's use of his liberty, the strong brother must abstain from these things. In verse 13 the apostle forbids us to put a stumblingblock, or an occasion to fall, in our brother's way. He continues in verse 15: "But if thy brother be grieved with thy meat, now walkest thou not charitably. Destroy not him with thy meat, for whom Christ died." In verse 20 he admonishes, "For meat destroy not the work of God." And in verse 21 the apostle instructs us that "It is good neither to eat flesh, nor to drink wine, nor any thing whereby thy brother stumbleth, or is offended, or is made weak." What does all of this admonition to the stronger brother mean? What does it mean that by the use of our Christian liberty we may not offend the weaker brother? What does it mean that for the sake of the weaker brother we refrain from using our Christian liberty? Does it mean that we must refrain the moment the weaker brother says, "You may not do this or that"? Does it mean that the weaker brother is now the man who imposes his conscience upon the entire church? God forbid. Then life in the church would become such that presently we would not know how to move. The man who imposes his conscience upon us, saying, "You may not do this" or "You may not do that," is not a weak brother. He is a nuisance. The man who takes the yardstick of his own conscience and applies it to us is not a weak brother, but a nuisance. We must not listen to him.

The weak brother is not one who says, "*You* may not do this or that" but he is one who says, "*I* may not do this or that." To offend the weaker brother, then, is that you, by your activity, make him to sin. You can do this in many ways. You can do this in that by your eating you make him eat. Against this stands the text: *whatsoever is not of faith is sin*. By faith you do not do that which makes the brother sin.

There are many things we have a right to do that are limited by the love of the brother. This is the teaching of the apostle when he says, "For meat destroy not the work of God" [v. 20]. He adds, "Destroy not him with thy meat, for whom Christ died" [v. 15]. Often, because we do not want to refrain from doing certain things, we destroy the brother. That brother is God's work. God regenerated him, called him, delivered him. And we, on our part, do all we can to destroy the brother for things that we could just as well *not* do. For meat (and this means all things that amount to nothing), destroy not the brother. Christ died for him. Christ died for us. He gave all that He had, also for that brother. If Christ gave all that He had, shall not we give up meat to save that brother?

Therefore, the deep principle is this: let us love one another. Let all things be done to the edification of the brother. If we love one another, we will not destroy the brother, but we will do all things to the edification of each other. We will seek each other's salvation.

Chapter Ninety-three

Instruction unto the Hope

Romans 15:4
For whatsoever things were written aforetime were written for our learning, that we through patience and comfort of the scriptures might have hope.

A connection exists between Romans 15:4 with what precedes in chapters 14 and 15. The apostle is still speaking of the proper relation of the members of the church toward one another with a view to the indifferent things. He had admonished them not to please themselves, but to please one another. They ought to please one another not in the sickly and sentimental sense of catering to one another's whims, but in the sense of seeking one another's edification. The desire to serve the well-being of the church by seeking the well-being of one another ought to be the motive for using or not using things that in themselves are "indifferent." This motive required them to deny themselves for the sake of God's church and kingdom.

To urge them to bring this into practice, the apostle refers to the example of Christ, not as He walked among us while on earth, but as He was in the Old Testament. The apostle refers to Psalm 69:9: "For the zeal of thine house hath eaten me up; and the reproaches of them that reproached thee are fallen upon me" [Rom 15:3]. Thus, he comes to the general instruction that we receive from the Old Testament Scriptures when he says in Romans 15:4 that all things "written aforetime were written for our learning."

There are different elements in the text. The text speaks of the Old Testament, of instruction, of the patience and comfort of the Scriptures, and of our hope. These different elements are so related that the end and purpose of our instruction are expressed in the last part, namely, that we might have hope. The way in which we must attain this hope is indicated in the words *through patience and comfort,* and the source of this instruction is the Scriptures.

The End of This Instruction

The purpose of this part of Romans, and of the text in particular, is intensely practical. Chapters 12–16 constitute the practical section of the epistle. The practical purpose of verse 4 is evident from the preceding context. There the practicality is that we should be ready to serve the kingdom of God at all times. The text itself indicates the purpose: *that we . . . might have hope.* To have the hope is practical. The purpose of the text is to place us before the question "Do we have the hope?" And with this, the aim is to instruct us as to the way in which we will be able to say that we have the hope.

Romans 15:4 speaks of *the* hope.[1] The implication is that this hope is the only hope there is. There is no other hope. The world may speak of hope. It may hope for prosperity. It may hope for hope. But the hope of the world is always limited by death. Therefore, it is vain. If we are really to have hope, we must have something that can overcome death. Therefore, this hope of which the text speaks is the only hope. Hope in the text has the sense of "the act of hoping." When we read of hope in Scripture, the reference is sometimes to the object of our hope, to that for which we hope, but this is not the meaning in the text. Here the reference is to the grace the Christian has in his heart through the resurrection of Christ, which reveals itself in the act of hoping. The act of hoping really con-

---

1. The original Greek has the definite article. This is not reflected in the King James translation.

sists in the stretching forth of the new life that the Christian has in his heart to its own level—to the level of its source. Water always seeks its own level; it seeks the level of its source. In like manner the spiritual life of the Christian seeks the level of its own source, and its source is in heaven. The Christian has the beginning of the life that is from heaven, where Christ is, but he carries the beginning of this new life here in the world. He has this new life in the midst of sin, corruption, and death. This is why the tendency, the urge, of the Christian's life is to seek the level of the heavenly. This is why, if you explain the Christian's hope, if you ask why he is hoping, if you ask why he is not satisfied as he is, if you ask why he looks forward, the answer is that the urge of this life is to seek the level of its own source.

Analyzing the Christian's hope, we find that it is, first, an attitude of *waiting*. The Christian is expecting something. He waits for it. He waits for it in such a way that nothing can turn him from the object for which he waits. Second, there is in the Christian's hope the element of a *positive assurance*. Hope is not a doubt, so that you say, "I hope so, but I am not sure." Hope is certainty. It is the certainty of faith. In the deepest sense it is the certainty of love. It is the certainty of the knowledge that God loves us. Give me the assurance that God loves me, and I have all other certainty. Hope is certainty. It is certainty that the object of my hope is there, and it is certainty that it is for me. Third, there is in the Christian's hope the element of *longing*. The Christian hope is not just a cold waiting and a mere assurance. It is a longing for the final realization of that hope, so that the Christian sings that he is a stranger in the world and longs for the realization of that for which he hopes.

The text speaks of having this hope. Having this hope is not the same as having the mere principle of hope in the heart. The Christian always has the principle. He cannot lose this. However, this is not the same as having the hope itself. For this reason Scripture does not exhort us as to whether we *have* faith, but it exhorts us as to whether we are *in* the faith. So it is with hope. It is possible to have the hope in our heart and yet not be hoping. In fact, this is often the case, especially in our day. The apostle does not have this in mind. The church to which he is speaking had that hope. But the apostle is speaking of instruction in hope, so that we actively and consciously hope and so that that hope motivates all that we do. In this sense, do we have hope?

The Way in Which This End Is Attained

According to the text, this state of Christian hope is to be attained only *through patience and comfort:* ". . . that we *through patience and comfort* of the scriptures might have hope." This is the way to attain to the state in which we can say, "I live in the hope." What is this way? And why is it the way to the hope?

Patience is one of the most dynamic and powerful Christian virtues. Patience does not merely mean "to wait." If we want to know what patience is, we must understand that God's purpose with His people in this world is that they should represent His cause in the world. This is their calling. If there were no antithesis, there would be no place for patience. But it is the calling of God's people to represent His cause in the world. This includes every sphere of life. If it were not for this, God would take them out of the world. In connection with this calling, Scripture knows and proceeds on the assumption that when God's people are faithful in this calling, they have to suffer. This is plain from the context. Christ is also the example and motive of Christian patience: "The reproaches of them that reproached thee fell on me" [v. 3]. If we do not want this, we are not patient. We must expect reproach and suffering. We look up against reproach. We try to avoid it. But Scripture does not think anything of it. Scripture says that we must be willing to lose our life for Christ's sake. When we have to suffer, we are not to be pitied. Scripture says that we ought rather to rejoice. Patience, then, is the power whereby we say, "I will suffer," when we stand before the alternative of becoming unfaithful or suffering. The power to suffer for Christ's sake is patience.

Comfort, which is the second element on the way to the Christian hope, is closely related to patience. If we are to be patient, we must have comfort. Comfort is that the Christian holds on to the hope of the promise of God. If we hold on to the promise, we have comfort. God has promised His people eternal life and the possession of heaven and earth. Holding on to this promise of God is comfort.

If we walk in this way of patience and comfort, we arrive at *the hope.* We cannot attain to a joyful, conscious hope if we cannot be patient and if we have no comfort. If we stand before the choice of suffering or being unfaithful, and then choose to be unfaithful, we do not have hope. Then we do not give hope a chance. We become unfaithful before we give hope a chance to exercise itself. Give hope a chance! If you do, you will hold on to the promise, and you will increase more and more in the assurance of this hope. You will say, "I count all things but loss and dung for the excellency of the knowledge of Christ Jesus, my Lord" [Phil. 3:8]. That is hope. In other words, as long as you continue to halt between two opinions, you can never come to the state expressed in the text: having hope through the patience and comfort of the Scriptures.

The Source of This Instruction

Finally, the apostle says that we must learn this from Scripture. We may learn to have patience and comfort, and to possess hope, from Scripture. When the apostle speaks of the Scriptures, it is evident that he is speaking of the Old Testament. Some people think nothing of the Old Testament, but here the apostle is speaking of these Scriptures. It is true that at that time there was as yet no New Testament, but this is not the only reason. The words *whatsoever things were written aforetime were written for our learning* point out that the Old Testament Scriptures have a definite character. They are especially adapted to teach the New Testament people patience and comfort. The reason is plain. In the Old Testament the saints had nothing but the promise. We have much more. We have, in principle, the realization of the promise. Christ has come. However, everything the Old Testament saints had was a promise, and they took hold of it. For this promise they suffered shame, reproach, and death. They suffered willingly because they deemed the reproach of Christ greater riches than the world [Heb. 11:26]. They lived in patience as they suffered for the sake of the promise.

Because of this, the Old Testament Scriptures speak of patience and comfort unto hope in a threefold way. In the first place, they speak of this directly. To His saints in suffering, God spoke of patience, comfort, and hope. In the second place, patience and comfort are portrayed before our eyes by the Old Testament saints, as we read in Hebrews 11. Patience and comfort are portrayed before us by those who embraced the promise, those who confessed that they were strangers in the earth. They are examples not of what man can do, but of what the grace of God can do in His saints. In the third place, in the Old Testament Scriptures the saints sing of this patience, comfort, and hope. This is the Psalms. Why is it that in times of trouble the people of God, also in the New Testament, always sing Psalms? Because in the Psalms, the saints of the Old Testament sing of patience and comfort. Why is it that there is no collection of hymns that can compare with the Psalms? Because the saints of the Old Testament, in the Psalms, sing of patience and comfort.

So it is that the things written aforetime were written for our instruction. They were not written in order that we might know what patience, comfort, and hope are, but they were written in order that patience and hope might be given to us. The Old Testament saints had nothing but the promise. They suffered for the promise. Let us not be unfaithful. They looked for the promise. In a sense we also look for the promise, for in a sense it is still a promise. We look for the coming of the Lord. But we know that the promise will be realized. Let us therefore be faithful, that no one take our crown.

Chapter Ninety-four

The High Calling to Glorify God

Romans 15:5–9

Now the God of patience and consolation grant you to be likeminded one toward another according to Christ Jesus:

That ye may with one mind and one mouth glorify God, even the Father of our Lord Jesus Christ.

Wherefore receive ye one another, as Christ also received us to the glory of God.

Now I say that Jesus Christ was a minister of the circumcision for the truth of God, to confirm the promises made unto the fathers:

And that the Gentiles might glorify God for his mercy; as it is written, For this cause I will confess to thee among the Gentiles, and sing unto thy name.

Romans 15:5–9 is immediately connected with the preceding verse. There the apostle had written that the Old Testament Scriptures were written in order that we might learn the lesson of patience and comfort unto hope. It is impossible to attain to patience and comfort simply by reading the Scriptures. Therefore, the apostle continues in verse 5, "Now the God of patience and consolation grant you to be likeminded one toward another according to Christ Jesus."

The section covered by the text constitutes one whole. It is true that the discussion of the indifferent things really comes to an end in verse 7 of chapter 14, but the idea of the peace and unity of the church is so closely connected with the calling of the church to glorify God that the section cannot be broken up. It centers in the one thought that it is the calling of the church to glorify God.

Then the apostle goes on to show that it was the purpose of Christ in redeeming and receiving us to have us glorify God. Christ redeemed us in order that we should glorify God. Indeed, it was Christ's purpose in redeeming us that He should glorify God through us. To realize this calling to glorify God, it is necessary that we be likeminded one toward another.

The Purpose of Our Redemption

The purpose of our redemption is to glorify God. We read in verse 6, "That ye may with one mind and one mouth glorify the God and Father of our Lord Jesus Christ." Some interpreters would read it this way: "That ye may with one mind and one mouth glorify God, even the Father of our Lord Jesus Christ." They say that God is the Father of Christ, but He is not the God of Christ. But this is a mistake.[1] God is not only the Father, but also the God of Christ. God is the Father of the Second Person of the Trinity, but not His God. But it can be said that God is the Father and the God of Christ according to His human nature. The triune God ordained Christ. In this sense already, God is the God and Father of Christ. Not only did God ordain Christ, but He also formed Him. Christ calls God "My God" on the cross [Matt. 27:46]. When the text speaks of the God and Father of our Lord Jesus Christ, it refers not to the Second Person of the Trinity but to Christ in His human nature. God is the God and the Father of Christ according to His human nature. And we must glorify Him in this way. That is, we must glorify Him as the God and Father of our Lord Jesus Christ. In other words, the church must glorify God as the God of salvation.

---

1. The Greek text can be read either way. The King James Version translates it, "God, even the Father." Hoeksema prefers the other translation for the reason given.

"To glorify" means the same as similar phrases: "to purify" is to make pure, "to beautify" is to make beautiful. Likewise, "to glorify" is to make glorious. To glorify God, however, is not to add to the glory of God. We cannot make God more glorious than He is. God is glorious, and we cannot make Him more glorious. That God is glorious means that He is excellent and that His excellency shines forth. That is true among men. When we glorify one another, we do so with a view to some excellent accomplishment. When a man does something outstanding, so that his accomplishment stands out, we say that he is glorious. For his accomplishment he is glorified by the world. In a far more excellent sense, God is glorious.

We must add that God is the only glorious one. God is not common. God stands out. He stands alone in all His virtues. God stands alone not only in the sense that there is no one like Him, but also in the sense that all glory is His. There is no glory that is not His. All the glory among men is but a reflection of His glory. God is the only glorious one. This is why it is so corrupt to glorify men. We must not applaud men. God is the only one to be applauded.

God has revealed His glory. He has revealed it everywhere. He has revealed it in the works of His hands. If we only stop to think and to look at the things about us, we see that all declare His excellency. Take the flower with its beauty: its fragrance, its beauty, its life, is a reflection of the glory of God. Man cannot make a flower. He can imitate it. He can make a paper flower, but he cannot make a flower. Why? Because God is glorious.

There is a greater glory of God that the *church* knows. This is the glory of God in Christ. This is a greater glory, for in Christ, God has revealed that righteousness, mercy, and holiness whereby He calls light out of darkness, righteousness out of unrighteousness, life out of death. In creation God became manifest as the one who calls the things that are not as though they were. But in Christ God calls life out of death.

"That ye may with one mind and one mouth glorify the God

and Father of our Lord Jesus Christ" [v. 6] means that we who see, who experience, this glory of God in the redemption shall make this glory known. Mark you, we shall speak of the glory of *God*. In some evangelical circles they like to speak of the glory of Christ. This is all very well; we should speak of the glory of Christ. But this is not the main thing. This does not express the purpose that Christ seeks through the church, for even Christ did not seek His own glory. The purpose of Christ is to glorify God through the church.

We must not suppose that we glorify God only in our good works. Scripture emphasizes that the highest way of glorifying God is with our mouth: "That ye may with . . . one mouth glorify God." The highest way of glorifying God is to speak of God and to speak to God. To glorify God is to tell Him of His goodness, His mercy, His righteousness, His holiness, His power. It is also to confess Him, that is, to speak of His glory to one another and to the world. We fail here, don't we? We miserably fail here.

Nor may we think that this exhortation addresses only some of us. It does not come only to some developed Christians. This exhortation does not come only to grown-ups, so that our young people have nothing to do with it. The text says, "Glorify God *with one mind and one mouth*," that is, with one accord. This means all, young and old. This is our calling. This is the calling of the church. There is only one purpose for the church in the world: to glorify the God and Father of Christ with one mind and one mouth. This is a tremendous calling, especially because we must do this not only when we are together here for worship, but also when we are not together. We must do it in the world. We must do it in our schools. We ought to take this a little more seriously than we do.

The apostle enforces this exhortation by bringing to the church the thought that Christ redeemed and received them for the very purpose that they should glorify God. Or rather, His purpose was that He might have a medium to glorify God in the world. Notice what verses 8 and 9 say: "Jesus Christ was a minister of the circumcision for the truth of God, to confirm the promises made unto the fathers," and He was a minister of the mercy of God "that the Gentiles might glorify God for his mercy."

Some take the words *Christ was a minister of the circumcision* in the figurative sense. They understand the text to teach that Christ became a minister *of the Jews* for the truth of God, to confirm the promises made unto the fathers. But it is a mistake to explain *circumcision* as meaning the Jews. By circumcision, the apostle refers to the entire Old Testament dispensation. The circumcision is representative of the entire old dispensation. That Christ became a minister of the circumcision means that He came under the law of the old dispensation. He bore the curse of the law. He redeemed them of the old dispensation who were under the curse of that law and received them. At the same time He made an end of the law. And He threw the door open to the Gentiles.

In all of this, Christ revealed the excellency of God. He revealed especially two things. First, He revealed the mercy of God. Second, He revealed the truth of God. Christ became a minister of the circumcision with a view to the truth of God. He became a minister of the mercy of God that the Gentiles might be the objects of that mercy. He became a minister on behalf of the truth of God in order that the promises might be fulfilled. And He became a minister on behalf of the mercy of God in order that the Gentiles might be the objects of mercy. This is fitting. The circumcision always glorified God on behalf of His truth and faithfulness, and the Gentiles always glorify God on behalf of His mercy.

Our glorifying of God is Christ's purpose in redeeming us. It is also His purpose in receiving us. Christ did both. He redeemed us when He came under the law and entered into the suffering of death. Christ also received us. He received us when God gave us to Christ in His counsel. When Christ received us, we were nothing to be proud of, but Christ received us, and receives us in time, when the Father draws us to Christ.

We never come to Christ of ourselves. God draws us to Him. And Christ receives us: "Him that cometh to me I will in no wise cast out" [John 6:37]. Christ receives sinful men. It makes no difference how sinful you are; Christ will receive you. When He does receive us, He makes a glorious church of us by His grace. He sanctifies us, makes us righteous, and makes us holy.

Why does He do this? In man-made hymns, the basic note is that Christ loved us so. I have no objection to this. We may speak of the love of Christ. But this is not the final answer. If we want the answer to the question why Christ died in order to become *a minister of the circumcision* on behalf of the truth of God, and *a minister of mercy* on behalf of the mercy of God, the answer is because He wants to glorify *God*. We must not be *Christo*-centric in our conception. We must be *theo*-centric.

Passages from the Old Testament are introduced because Christ is represented as speaking there, especially in Psalm 18. The apostle quotes Psalm 18:49 as saying, "For this cause I will confess to thee among the Gentiles, and sing unto thy name." In Psalm 18 it was David speaking, but in Romans 15:9 it is Christ speaking. In Psalm 18 David spoke as representative of Christ. In the new dispensation Christ says, "It is My purpose to glorify Thee, O God."

How will He do it? Christ is in heaven. How will He do it? Through His church! The mouth of the church is Christ. The one who glorifies God is Christ, but He does it through the church. He does not do it through the church as dead instruments; no, He makes the church to be partakers of His grace and purpose. He wants the church consciously and willingly to participate in this glory of God.

An Incentive to Likemindedness

The calling of the church to glorify God is an incentive to likemindedness. Verse 5 declares, "Now the God of patience and consolation grant you to be likeminded one toward another according to Christ Jesus." Likemindedness is not that we all think the same, but it is that we all have the same aim and strive for the same thing. This one aim for which all must strive is the glory of God. When the apostle adds *according to Christ,* the meaning is that we must be likeminded according to the standard of Christ. It also implies that this likemindedness is limited by Christ. There is also likemindedness in the world, but we must not be likeminded according to the world. We must be likeminded according to the standard of Christ, and this means that we must be likeminded according to the truth.

Likemindedness is related to our calling to glorify God in such a way that if we are *not* likeminded, we *cannot* glorify the God and Father of Christ. The opposite of likemindedness is enmity and strife. If we argue about whether we may eat meat or drink wine or have life insurance or have lightning rods on our barns, what suffers is the glory of God. Therefore, let us make this prayer of the apostle our daily prayer: "The God of patience and consolation grant you to be likeminded one toward another according to Christ Jesus: That ye may with one mind and one mouth glorify the God and Father of our Lord Jesus Christ" [vv. 5, 6].

Chapter Ninety-five

The Church Filled with All Goodness

Romans 15:14

And I myself also am persuaded of you, my brethren, that ye also are full of goodness, filled with all knowledge, able also to admonish one another.

From the fourteenth verse to the end of this fifteenth chapter, we have a kind of conclusion or appendix, a kind of epilogue to the epistle. The doctrinal part of the epistle is found in chapters 1–11. The practical part of the epistle is contained in Romans 12:1–15:13. Then the apostle closes his epistle, in chapter 16, with a series of greetings.

The epilogue is what we would almost call an apology for what the apostle had written to the Romans. The apostle had never visited Rome. The church had not been founded by him. He had never labored there. Besides, the church was well established. Their faith was spoken of throughout the whole world. After having written this epistle, in which he admonishes them rather boldly in several places, the apostle feels that his message might be misinterpreted. At least they might draw the conclusion that the apostle did not think them able to admonish each other. Therefore, he writes in the text, "I . . . am persuaded of you, my brethren, that ye also are full of goodness, filled with all knowledge." He assures them, "You must not interpret my admonitions to you as if I thought that you are not able to admonish yourselves . . . But I am the apostle to the Gentiles, and as the apostle to the Gentiles I write to you" [vv. 14, 16]. He then expresses his desire to meet them [v. 23]. And he ends with blessing them [v. 33].

Verse 14 guards against misunderstanding. In it the apostle says that he is convinced that the church is full of goodness, filled with all knowledge, able to admonish one another. This Word is not only a Word for the church of Rome, but it is a Word for the church of all ages. Therefore, I can also address my congregation this way: "You are filled with all goodness and able to admonish one another."

Filled with What

Goodness in the text is not to be understood as it commonly is. It is not to be understood in the sense of doing good to one another. This idea is included in the word, but it is not the whole of its contents. Rather does the word *goodness* here have the same meaning that it has when the Lord says to the rich young ruler, "Why callest thou me *good?* none is good, save one, that is, God" [Luke 18:19]. In this sense, the word *goodness* means spiritual, moral, ethical perfection. Therefore, the apostle declares that the church is filled with all virtues, with all perfections.

The heart of this goodness is love, for love is the bond of perfectness [Col. 3:14]. It is the fulfillment of the law. Love is the essence of this goodness, love in the sense of the love of God and the love of the neighbor. From this principle spring all other goodnesses, such as the fear of God, righteousness, truth, holiness, and delight in the law of God. In relation to one another, out of love, arise such goodnesses as brotherly kindness, meekness, and patience. All of these virtues are included when Paul says, "I am persuaded of you, my brethren, that ye also are full of goodness." The apostle is saying, "Church of God, I am convinced that you are filled with righteousness, holiness, truth, love, kindness, and meekness."

In actual life, goodness is bound to reveal itself. A church cannot be filled with goodness without that goodness revealing itself. It reveals itself in relation to God in seeking of God, in walking in His ways, in having delight in His law, and in desiring to be pleasing in His sight. It reveals itself in relation to one another in seeking the well-being of the church and one another. It reveals itself in forbearing one another, forgiving one another, loving one another.

Goodness also reveals itself antithetically, for goodness never reveals itself alone. We never see goodness without also "badness." Antithetically, goodness reveals itself as fighting against sin, such sin as slander, backbiting, envy, maliciousness, covetousness, and hatred. When the church is filled with goodness, antithetically she fights all these sins as long as she is in the world.

This is a beautiful testimony to the church, yet it is not sufficient. The apostle adds that the church is filled with *all knowledge*. By *knowledge* the text refers to that which is worthy of the name knowledge. It does not refer to carnal knowledge. It does not refer to worldly knowledge. When Scripture speaks of knowledge, it refers principally to the knowledge of God. It refers to the knowledge of all things in the light of the knowledge of God. In that the text speaks of *all* knowledge, it is referring to the knowledge of the will of God concerning our whole life.

In the broad sense of the word, this knowledge is included in goodness. Although knowledge is included in goodness, the text specifically mentions knowledge. The reason is that goodness really belongs to man's will, while knowledge belongs to his mind. The two cannot be separated. We can distinguish between goodness and knowledge, but the two belong together. It is sometimes said that knowledge is virtue. This is not true. Knowledge is not virtue, but knowledge and goodness together are virtue. It is possible to have knowledge of the precepts of God and yet not have the will to do them, but where there is knowledge of the precepts of God and the will to do them, there is virtue. When the church is filled with goodness and knowledge, her condition is ideal.

The Way in Which She Is Filled

We might think that the apostle expresses himself too strongly. The church filled with goodness? The church filled with all knowledge? Can this be said of any church? We must understand that this testimony concerning the church of Rome is really a testimony concerning the marvelous power of God. It would indeed be dangerous to tell people, or even a church, that they are filled with goodness and all knowledge. This would make the church so conceited that the opposite would become manifest if it were not for the fact that the church has nothing of herself of which to boast. The church has nothing to boast of, because she has nothing of herself. To say that the church is filled with goodness and all knowledge is not praise of the church, but of Christ.

If we want to know what the church is of herself, we must turn to the first chapters of this epistle. There the apostle also speaks of a being filled: being filled with all unrighteousness, fornication, wickedness, covetousness, maliciousness; and full of envy, murder, debate, deceit, malignity [1:29]. This is what the Romans used to be. Therefore, they have nothing of which to boast. But the grace of Christ took hold of them. This grace of Christ cleaned house. If we want to know what the wonder of the grace of Christ is, we must read the first part of this epistle and the word of the text together. Then it is safe to speak of the church's being full of goodness and knowledge.

Even so, it may seem that the apostle is overstating the matter. Some people think so. They say that the apostle does not mean this in the literal sense; the text is an exaggeration. Others explain that this beautiful testimony is limited to the church of Rome.

However, the testimony is no exaggeration, and it applies to the church today, for either the grace of God fills us, or it never touches us at all. Principally, this testimony is certainly true of every saint and of every true church. The reason is that grace does not take hold of us at the circumference of our life in order to reform or improve us. This is impossible. Reformation never fills a man with goodness. And this is also true: a man is either filled with all "badness," or he is filled with all goodness. There is nothing in between. The reason is that a man is really as his heart is. The heart of man is the center of all his spiritual, moral life. From the heart are the issues of life. All of life finds its spiritual motive-power in the heart. One can throw sweet water on top of a fountain, but from that fountain springs forth bitter water. In the same way, one can try to reform a man from without; nevertheless, from the heart continue to come evil imaginations.

Grace takes hold of the heart, of the center of the fountain itself. It changes the heart radically. It turns the heart around. It changes the heart from darkness to light, from unrighteousness to righteousness. When grace gets through with changing the heart of a man, that man is filled with goodness. Nor does grace stop with changing the center of a man's life. Grace continues its work by causing the issues of the heart to take hold of the whole man. From the heart it influences the willing, the thinking, and the desiring. Therefore, the believer can say, "Old things are passed away; behold, all things are become new" [II Cor. 5:17].

This does not imply that the Christian no longer sins. As long as he is in this world, he is a sinful vessel, filled with goodness. The Christian is not a man with a new heart and an old heart. He has a new heart. But he has the new heart in a sinful vessel. Often the power of sin that is still in him fights his new heart so that the goodness cannot come to manifestation. When, therefore, the church is filled with goodness, goodness becomes at the same time a calling. When God fills us with goodness, our part is that we walk in all goodness. This is our calling in order that goodness may become manifest to the praise of Him who so filled us. This the church of Rome did.

The Practical Result of Being Filled

The purpose of the testimony is practical. The apostle wrote the text as a kind of apology. He had admonished the church of Rome rather boldly. Now he says, "You do not really need to be admonished. I did not admonish you because you are not able to admonish yourselves; you *are* able to admonish yourselves. I say that God has filled you with all goodness, and your calling is to walk in this goodness. The result is that you are able to admonish one another."

The word *admonish* in the text is not the same as our English word *admonish*. In the English language, to admonish is "to warn against something," but in the Greek, the word has a positive meaning: "to put someone in mind." What we must put in mind is the truth. To admonish is to put someone in mind and instruct each other regarding the truth. Because the church is imperfect, this putting in mind, this instruction, must also become a warning, but the essence of admonition is always instruction. A man admonishes when he says, "This is the truth." He admonishes when he puts someone in mind of the truth. This is the heart of admonition.

When the apostle writes that they are able to do this to one another, he has in mind the established church. Whenever the church puts people in mind of the truth, she is admonishing. The church must be busy with this. Nothing must ever take the place of it. It is not only through her offices that the church admonishes; we must admonish one another personally. When we are in conversation with one another, we must put each other in mind of the truth. We must do the same in our Bible study societies. This is the work of the church. Then we will become sound.

Now we can understand the relation in the text. Because we are filled with goodness and are full of knowledge, we can admonish each other. To be able to admonish, one must have knowledge. The man who is to be admonished also must have knowledge. You cannot admonish a fool. I do not like to preach to a dumb church. I would rather preach to spiritual college students.

Knowledge is not enough, however. To give and receive admonition, we must also be filled with goodness. If we are not filled with goodness, we have no moral right to admonish. I do not mean that a sinner cannot admonish. In fact, he must be a sinner in order to be able to admonish. But he must be so filled with goodness that he hates sin and fights it. Thus he will be able to give and receive admonition.

Thus, I deliver this Word to you, my congregation. In the first place, you are filled with all goodness, not your own goodness but the goodness of Christ. In the second place, it is your calling to walk in this goodness. In the third place, being filled with goodness, you are able to admonish one another.

Chapter Ninety-six

Christian Greetings

Romans 16:3-16
Greet Priscilla and Aquila my helpers in Christ Jesus:
Who have for my life laid down their own necks: unto whom not only I give thanks, but also all the churches of the Gentiles.
Likewise greet the church that is in their house. Salute my well-beloved Epaenetus, who is the firstfruits of Achaia unto Christ.
Greet Mary, who bestowed much labour on us.
Salute Andronicus and Junia, my kinsmen, and my fellowprisoners, who are of note among the apostles, who also were in Christ before me.
Greet Amplias my beloved in the Lord.
Salute Urbane, our helper in Christ, and Stachys my beloved.
Salute Apelles approved in Christ. Salute them which are of Aristobulus' household.
Salute Herodion my kinsman. Greet them that be of the household of Narcissus, which are in the Lord.
Salute Tryphena and Tryphosa, who labour in the Lord. Salute the beloved Persis, which laboured much in the Lord.
Salute Rufus chosen in the Lord, and his mother and mine.
Salute Asyncritus, Phlegon, Hermas, Patrobas, Hermes, and the brethren which are with them.
Salute Philologus, and Julia, Nereus, and his sister, and Olympas, and all the saints which are with them.
Salute one another with an holy kiss. The churches of Christ salute you.

The first two verses of chapter 16 mention Phebe, whom the apostle singles out as *our sister.* Of her, he writes that she is *a servant of the church which is at Cenchrea.* She had been a succourer of many saints, particularly of the apostle Paul himself. The meaning is that this woman had been, in a general way, laboring in the Lord. She did not labor in an official way, but she labored in such a way that she looked after the needs of the saints, took them into her home, and ministered unto the needy. The apostle commends her to the church at Rome. This implies that she was about to visit Rome. Therefore, it is very probable that she was the bearer of this epistle to the Romans. The apostle commends her to the church, and he exhorts the church to receive her in the Lord. They must receive her as saints, as it becomes saints to receive each other. And they must receive her with a reception of which a saint is worthy.

From verse 3 through verse 16 we have a long list of salutations. This is possibly due to the fact that the apostle had never been to Rome. There is also the fact that the apostle must have known an exceptionally large number of saints who were members of that church. The church of Rome was what we would call a "floating church." Due to persecution, people were driven about and finally settled in Rome. The apostle had come into contact with many of them.

It is not my intention to call attention to all the details of these saints. In fact, outside of Priscilla and Aquila we do not know any of them. But we must remember, especially since we have now gone through almost the entire epistle, that this part also is a part of the Word of God. We must not look at these greetings as mere greetings by the man Paul. They are inspired greetings. Not only are they greetings of the Spirit through Paul to the church, but they also contain practical lessons which, although not mentioned, are clearly implied.

Their Specific Character and Principle

The greetings and salutations in Scripture must not be put on a par with the common greetings with which we greet one another. When the apostle sends these greetings to the saints in Rome, he does not merely mean to say "Hello." Greeting in Scripture has a deeper meaning. This is plain from the word used in the original for *greeting,* which means "to bless." For example, when Jacob met Pharaoh, he blessed him, that is, he greeted him [Gen. 47:7]. That this is the meaning is evident from the formulas used by the saints when they greet one another. When the saints in Scripture greet one another, they use specific forms. They use forms such as "Peace be with thee" or "Peace be with thee, and thy house, and all that thou hast." When Boaz meets his laborers, he says, "The Lord be with you" [Ruth 2:4]. That this is the meaning of the biblical greeting is also strikingly plain from what the Lord says when He sends out His disciples. The Lord tells His disciples that when they shall enter into a house, they are to say, "Peace be to this house." That this is not merely an empty form is evident from what follows, for the Lord says, "If the son of peace be there, your peace shall rest upon it: if not, it shall turn to you again" [Luke 10:5, 6]. This is plain also from what the apostle John writes [II John 10]: "If there come any unto you, and bring not this doctrine, receive him not into your house." He adds, "Neither bid him God speed." In our day, we would say, "Do not say good-bye to him."

In this sense we must understand these greetings of the apostle. In this sense the Christian greeting means that by the word of the mouth we bestow on one another the blessing of the Lord. This implies, first, that we know one another in the capacity of saints. It implies that we know one another in Christ. We do not know one another according to social position. This makes no difference in the church. We do not know one another from the point of view of financial standing. We cannot salute one another as saints as long as we are in the carnal sphere. Second, it means that we live in the consciousness that saints are blessed. Third, the more the church suffers in the world, the more saints ought to salute one another. The more the world persecutes us, the more we ought to say to one another, "Peace be unto you." Is it not plain what this greeting meant to the church of Rome? When Nero took the saints and burned them alive, is it not plain what "Peace be unto thee" meant to them? It is a serious thing to greet one another as saints. When we meet as saints, we must not just say, "Hello." That, anybody can do. But when we greet as saints, we bless one another.

This is why the Christian greeting has a special principle. The principle from which the Christian greeting arises is the fact that the saints are in the Lord. Notice how often the expression *in the Lord* occurs here. When the apostle speaks of Phebe, he says, "Receive her *in the Lord*." Of Priscilla and Aquila he says that they are his helpers *in Christ Jesus*. Amplias he calls his beloved *in the Lord*. In the Lord—this is the basis for the Christian greeting.

To be in the Lord is to be in Christ. To be in Christ is to be in Him from both a legal and a spiritual, organic point of view. Legally, to be in Christ is to be members of the corporation of which He is the head. He died for us, redeemed us, and delivered us from the power of sin and guilt. The benefit is that we have peace with God. In the Lord there is peace. There is no peace outside the Lord. Peace with God is the only peace there is. In order to say to one another, "Peace be with you," we must be in the Lord.

To be in the Lord is also to have living contact with Him. The blessings of the kingdom of God flow to us from Him.

This is the distinctive character of the Christian greeting: *in the Lord*. Shall we greet one another this way? The time will come when we surely will.

Their Special Distinction

There is something else noteworthy about these greetings. This is the special distinction that is made between some of these saints and the church at large. Many of these saints we do not know. With the exception of Priscilla and Aquila, we do not know any of them. In the original, Priscilla is called Prisca. Priscilla means "little Prisca." This is why she is sometimes called Priscilla and sometimes Prisca. Priscilla is often mentioned before her husband. The apostle does not do so accidentally. Priscilla undoubtedly was the stronger character of the two. Priscilla and Aquila had left Rome and had gone to Corinth. There they had met the apostle Paul. They took Paul into their house. They and Paul were of the same trade, being tentmakers. This naturally drew them together. From Corinth, Priscilla and Aquila went to Ephesus. There they stayed a long time. They were strong Christians. This is evident from what we read of their meeting with Apollos. Apollos was a great speaker, but Priscilla and Aquila took him in and instructed him more fully in the way of the Lord. In verse 4 we read that they risked their necks for Paul. The apostle says that he owes them thanks for this.

The apostle refers to the church that is in their house. We read of this elsewhere as well. This gives us a picture of church-life in Rome. There was only one church in Rome, but they had no church property. Besides, it was not safe to have a central meeting place. Sometimes they met out in the open air. Later, when persecution increased, they met in the catacombs. We can imagine that the church as a whole did not meet very often. Members often met in someone's house. They came together in certain houses to worship, to pray, and to encourage one another. I often wonder what would become of us if it should become unsafe for us to meet in this building and we would have to meet in the house of Priscilla and Aquila. The apostle says, "Greet one another."

It is noteworthy that the apostle mentions so many women: nine in all. These women are said to labor in the Lord. This does not mean that they worked in an official capacity, but they performed all kinds of work, as our societies do, for example.[1]

---

1. At the time that Hoeksema was preaching these sermons, the women of First Church met regularly as a society, not only to study Scripture but also for the help of the needy in various ways. They baked and sewed for the poor. They visited the sick. They assisted mothers with special needs. Such a society was aptly named "Ladies Aid."

They sewed; they visited the sick; they ministered to the needs of the saints. The apostle characterizes this as *labour in the Lord*. One does not have to be an elder or a Sunday school teacher or a president of a Bible study society in order to labor in the Lord. Christ says that if we give a drink of water to a disciple, we labor in the Lord. These women receive special mention in Scripture. The Holy Spirit mentions them.

Finally, the apostle mentions some men. Some of these were especially known to him. He speaks of Amplias and Stachys as his *beloved* [vv. 8, 9]. This does not imply that the rest were not beloved, but there were some who were especially beloved of the apostle. Then he mentions those who helped him. He says, "Salute Urbane, our helper in Christ" [v. 9]. He also mentions those who had suffered in the Lord. Greet those who were my fellow prisoners, the apostle says [v. 7]. We don't know when this was; Paul had been in prison often. Of Apelles he says that he is *approved in Christ,* that is, he was tried of the Lord [v. 10].

It is striking that the apostle mentions some slaves: "Salute them which are of Aristobulus' household" [v. 10]. Implied is that Aristobulus was not a Christian; otherwise, the apostle would have said, "Greet Aristobulus." Instead, he greets those who are of the household of Aristobulus. They were slaves in the house of Aristobulus, and the apostle greeted them.

By these special greetings of certain members of the church, the apostle is glorifying Christ in His saints. It is not wrong to single out certain members in this way. If we do not glorify Christ in His saints, we do not glorify Him at all. Some people think that we may not give special attention to certain Christians, but this is contrary to Scripture. The Holy Spirit does it here. The apostle says, "Greet them." He makes special distinction between these saints and the church at large.

The church in Rome could take it, or else the apostle would not have risked it. If I should name a list of people and give them special mention, others would say, "I deserve special mention, too." The apostle makes special distinction here. It meant something to receive special mention from Paul. These people received praise in the Lord. When one receives praise in the Lord, the congregation rejoices. There is no jealousy in Christ. There is no jealousy in the church. The church in Rome could take it. And we ought to be able to take it also.

Their General Exercise

The apostle wants all the church to apply this admonition. He speaks of a general application of the Christian blessing. There is a beautiful manifestation of the unity of the church here. All the churches greet you, the apostle says. He was going to Rome. He had a commission from all the churches: all the churches greeted the church in Rome. There was as yet no schism in the church. Therefore, he could say, "All the saints greet you."

The church today is admonished to exercise Christian greeting: "Greet one another with an holy kiss." The kiss is an oriental custom. It is the way in which they greeted one another in Paul's time. We shake hands. It makes no difference. But it must be possible that every member greet everyone else with a holy kiss or with a handshake. If we meet someone whom we are not able to greet, there is something wrong. We must be able to greet one another with a holy kiss—not with a profane kiss, but with a kiss in the Lord.

Blessed is the church that has members who receive special mention, and the church that can take it. And blessed is the church in which the saints greet one another with a holy kiss.

Chapter Ninety-seven

The Glory of the Only Wise God

Romans 16:25-27
Now to him that is of power to stablish you according to my gospel, and the preaching of Jesus Christ, according to the revelation of the mystery, which was kept secret since the world began,

But now is made manifest, and by the scriptures of the prophets, according to the commandment of the everlasting God, made known to all nations for the obedience of faith:

To God only wise, be glory through Jesus Christ for ever. Amen.

This is a most fitting close to one of the richest and most beautiful parts of the Word of God. In distinction from some of the other epistles, the apostle closes this epistle with a doxology, or song of praise. He does not close this epistle with the customary benediction or blessing, but by a word of praise. It is not our purpose to enter into every one of the phrases that are literally piled up in this final word of praise. Our purpose is to catch the basic note and join in with this song of praise.

We have here one of those instances in which the apostle starts out by expressing a certain thought along a certain line, but is then so carried away by the wisdom and power of God manifested in all he has been considering that he concludes with something else. The apostle evidently had something in mind when he began, the main thought of which is expressed in that first clause of verse 25, namely, that God is of power to establish them. But as he meditates upon the riches and the depth of the wisdom of the work of God, he winds up with a song of praise that becomes the theme of the text.

The text is rather involved. These three verses constitute one long sentence. Many phrases are piled up, each of which contains enough material to make a separate sermon. The apostle starts out in verse 25 by saying, "To him that is of power to stablish you according to my gospel." *According to my gospel* is the same as saying *according to the preaching of Jesus Christ*. Again, this is the same as saying *according to the revelation of the mystery*.

This mystery had been hid since the world began, but is now made manifest, and by the Scriptures of the prophets has been made known. The making known of the mystery has for its purpose, first, the obedience of the faith of all nations; second, the establishment of the church; and finally, the glory of the only wise God.

The Wisdom of God That Is to Be Glorified

Glory to the only wise God is the main thought of the passage. We read, "To God only wise, through Jesus Christ, be glory forever." We must read the text this way. The idea is not that glory be given through Christ Jesus to the only wise God. Instead, the meaning is that to God only wise, through Christ Jesus, be glory forever. In other words, glory be to God only wise, as this wisdom became manifest in Christ Jesus.

Attention is called especially to the virtue of God's *wisdom*. Verse 27 calls attention to the wisdom of God as this wisdom was revealed to us in Christ. Wisdom is not separated from God's other virtues, but this virtue of God is emphasized. Although closely related to knowledge and understanding, wisdom is not the same as knowledge. Wisdom denotes that virtue whereby everything made by wisdom has purpose, design, and aim. It is the virtue by which that purpose, that aim, is attained. This is wisdom also among men. If a man goes about without aim and purpose, he is a fool. A wise man is a man who has aim and purpose and who knows how to make things subservient to his aim.

That God is *only wise* means that with regard to all things, God has set before His mind a purpose, an aim. God has set His mind upon a certain purpose. This purpose is the glory of His name. This purpose is the manifestation, the revelation, of His own divine being and life. This purpose, which is the highest purpose conceivable, must be attained by all things that are. Everything is made subservient to this purpose. This is God's wisdom.

When the text speaks of the *only wise* God and wants the church to join in singing this song of praise, the idea is not that Scripture merely means to tell us that God is all-wise. We know that God is all-wise, but that can never be an incentive actually to glorify and praise Him. At the close of his epistle, the apostle passes in review all the wisdom about which he had written. Beholding this wisdom, he sings a song of praise and says, "Glory be to the only wise God." God wants His people to *behold* His wisdom. God does not merely tell us in the abstract that He is wise, but He wants us to see the glory of His work from the viewpoint of His wisdom. We must glorify Him as we behold His wisdom as the only wise God.

However, we must behold Him as the only wise God through Jesus Christ: "To God only wise through Jesus Christ, be glory forever." Scripture also speaks of the wisdom of God in the works of His hands in this world. But that wisdom of God, as we now see it in the works of His hands in this world, is marred. The reason is that this wisdom becomes manifest in the individual creature in the midst of a world marred by sin. We can see this wisdom of God in the construction of the body. We can see it in the construction of the eye. We can see it in the construction of the ear. We can see it in all the works of God's hands. But the wisdom of God as it is in this world is so marred that men have blasphemously said that if they had made this world, they would have surpassed the Creator. They point to the foolishness of creation as it now is. They say, "God makes a tree, and then He makes a lightning bolt to strike it down." They say, "There is destruction and failure everywhere." They say that creation gets nowhere. Even the Bible tells us this. The Preacher tells us that outside of Christ, all is vanity. There is no purpose, no progress, in things. Everywhere there is vanity.

Where, then, is the wisdom of God? Everything is vain, without purpose. This is true as long as you do not put Christ in the very center of things. Take Christ out of God's work, and everything is vain and foolish. But put Christ there—put Him where He belongs, put Him where God put Him in the center of all things and around whom all is designed—and you see the wisdom of God.

The Revelation of This Wisdom

This is why verse 27 says, "Glory to God only wise through Jesus Christ"; that is, "Glory to God only wise as this wisdom became manifest through Christ." To this God give glory! This is not only because Christ spoke of God's wisdom. No, but Christ *Himself* is the manifestation of God's wisdom. He is the wisdom of God. Christ in His incarnation, in His work, in His suffering and death, in His resurrection, in His ascension, in His exaltation—this Christ, the historical Jesus Christ who came into the center of things in the years one to thirty-three, is the reason why things are not vain and why they have purpose. Jesus does not only remove sin, for then the question remains, "Why was sin ever there?" But sin must serve God's purpose. Death, corruption, war, and destruction must serve God's purpose. Things have a purpose, but then you must have Christ in the center. With Christ in the center, all things have a purpose. In Christ we behold the wisdom of God in all things.

In the new dispensation we can see that everything serves God's purpose. The apostle calls this the *mystery* [v. 25]. A mystery is not something absurd; it is not something contrary to the laws of our thinking, nor is it something that cannot be understood by us. A *mystery* is something that we can never find out along the common way of coming to the knowledge of things. In our common life we see things and hear things, but they are all limited by the scope of the earthly. We can never get beyond the scope of the earthly. A mystery is something that comes to us through special revelation concerning the other world. The Bible speaks of the things that eye hath not seen and ear hath not heard and that have not entered into the heart of man [I Cor. 2:9]. This does not mean that these things are so wonderful and so great that we cannot express them; rather, it means that they belong to the other world.

Verse 25 speaks of this mystery as having been hid from the time the world began. It was hid during the entire old dispensation. It was not hid in the sense that the saints in the old dispensation knew nothing about the mystery. There was some knowledge of it. There were the shadows, types, and symbols. But the mystery itself was not seen. The old dispensation was like a dark, cloudy day when the light of the sun is seen through the clouds, but one does not see the sun itself. Or it was like a moonlit night. The light of the moon is the reflection of the sun. You see the sunlight in the moon, that is, a reflection of it. Thus the people of the old dispensation looked at the reflection of the sun in the prophets, and they longed for the manifestation of the mystery.

But the mystery has now become manifest. Manifestation and revelation are not the same, but they are closely related. When a statue is unveiled, when the cover is taken off so that the statue becomes revealed, that is *revelation*. But when the sun is hid behind the clouds and then breaks through the clouds, that is *manifestation*. So the mystery manifested itself. It broke through the corruption and sin of this world when Christ came. For that, the saints of the old dispensation had longed. Isaiah cried out, "Oh that the heavens would rend" [Isa. 64:1], and they did. When they did, Christ came. He died, was resurrected, ascended into heaven, and was gone again. This is the manifestation of the mystery. This Christ solves every problem from the point of view of God's wisdom.

The Glory Due This Wisdom

If nothing else had happened, we would not glorify God for His wisdom, for while the mystery was made manifest, it disappeared again, and everything moves as it did before. It is not true that Christ changed the world. When we look about us in the world, we would say that no change was brought about in the foolishness of the world by Christ. If God had done nothing more, we would not say, "Glory be to God only wise," for Christ is gone, and we see Him no more.

But the apostle says that God made this mystery *known*. The mystery was not only made manifest, but it was also *preached*. This is why Christ, who is the revelation of the mystery, must be preached. He must be preached so that we may know the mystery. The church must know this. Above all, the church has the calling to glorify God, telling the world that things are not foolish, but that they are the manifestation of the all-wise God. The mystery was made known, verse 26 says, through the prophetic writings. Through the means of the prophetic writings, God made known the mystery. The apostles used the prophetic writings as a means in the proclamation of the gospel concerning the mystery. They combined their preaching with the prophetic writings, and thus the mystery was made known.

The making known of the mystery by the preaching of Christ has three grand purposes. The first purpose is that all nations might become obedient to the faith. All nations become obedient to the faith by repentance. The second purpose is the establishment of the church. The church must be established according to the gospel. In the knowledge of the mystery, the church is established. This is not only in order that we may have hope, but also in order that we should say, "Glory to God only wise." Even a human artist is insulted when he displays his painting and the crowd passes by and does not even notice it. God does not display the manifestation of His wisdom that we should pass it by. He displays it in order that the end of it may be that we say in word and deed, "Glory be to God."

If we, by our study of the book of Romans, may have attained a little more knowledge of God's wisdom by contemplating the mystery of God in Jesus Christ, God will be pleased, and we will rejoice.

Books in English by Herman Hoeksema
(published by the RFPA unless otherwise stated)

Behold, He Cometh! An Exposition of the Book of Revelation, Second Edition, edited and partially revised by by Homer C. Hoeksema. 2000.

Believers and Their Seed: Children in the Covenant. Revised edition, translated by Homer C. Hoeksema from the original work in Dutch, *De Geloovigen en Hun Zaad*. 1997.

The Clark-Van Til Controversy. Hobbs, New Mexico: The Trinity Foundation, 1995.

In the Sanctuary: Expository Sermons on the Lord's Prayer. 1981.

God's Eternal Good Pleasure. Edited by Homer C. Hoeksema. 1979.

God's Goodness Always Particular. Translated by the author from his original work in Dutch, *Dat Gods Goedheid Particulier Is.* [1939].

The Mystery of Bethlehem: Devotional Reading for the Christmas Season. Edited by Homer C. Hoeksema. 1986.

The Protestant Reformed Churches in America: Their Origin, Early History and Doctrine. Grand Rapids, Mich.: First Protestant Reformed Church of Grand Rapids, Mich., 1936.

Ready to Give an Answer: A Catechism of Reformed Distinctives, by Herman Hoeksema and Herman Hanko. 1997.

Righteous by Faith Alone: A Devotional Commentary on Romans, edited by David J. Engelsma. 2002.

Reformed Dogmatics. Edited by Homer C. Hoeksema. 1966.

The Triple Knowledge: An Exposition of the Heidelberg Catechism. Third Edition. 3 vols. 1970-1972.

When I Survey . . . : A Lenten Anthology. 1977.

"Whosoever Will." Second Edition, 2002.

The Wonder of Grace. 1982.

NOTE ON THE SCOPE OF HOEKSEMA'S WRITINGS: Herman Hoeksema (1886-1965), who was born in the Netherlands, also wrote a number of theological books in the Dutch language. One of them, *Van Zonde en Genade* (Concerning Sin and Grace), written with Henry Danhof, has been translated by Cornelius Hanko and edited by Herman Hanko. It will be published by the Reformed Free Publishing Association under the title *Sin and Grace*. Hoeksema also authored short pamphlets, monographs, and seminary materials on theological subjects. These may be read in the library of the Theological School of the Protestant Reformed Churches, Grandville, Michigan. Some of Hoeksema's pamphlets on theological subjects are still available today through the First Protestant Reformed Church, Grand Rapids, Michigan. As long-time editor of the *Standard Bearer* magazine from its inception in 1924, Hoeksema contributed a great number of religious articles. The *Standard Bearer* is still being published today, along with theological books, by the Reformed Free Publishing Association. To obtain a catalog of RFPA books or to subscribe to the *Standard Bearer,* see the contact information provided on the copyright page of this book.

Scripture Index

NOTE TO READER: Scripture from Romans that appears in italics as the text at the start a chapter is indexed as "chap.," followed by the chapter number. Such text is not indexed *within that chapter*. All other right-column entries represent page locations. If a Scripture is not referred to in the book by number, it is not usually indexed. Scripture verses from Romans that are not part of any italic opening text are usually expostited by the author in the chapter with a text nearest to that verse (or in the chapter just preceding or following).

Genesis
2:17	227
3:5	413
3:15	165, 485
9:8–17	165
15:5	143, 165, 166
15:6	142
17:17	564
22:2	365
25:22, 23	392
42:36	187, 362
47:7	682

Exodus
4:21	408
9	408
9:16	407, 408
32 thru. 34	401
32:32	400
32:32, 33	402
32:34	402
33:3	402
33:14	402
33:15	402
33:19	399, 400, 406

Leviticus
18:5	453

Numbers
15:17–21	540

Deuteronomy
27:26	267, 456
30:10–14	453
32:21	496
32:35	618

Ruth
2:4	682

I Kings
19:1–18	507

Psalms
18:49	671
19:1–4	489
32:1, 2	148–51, 154
44:22	377, 379
50:10	444
69:9	659
69:21	522
69:22, 23	522, 523
92:7	425
118:22	440

Isaiah
1:9	436
8:14	439

697

Isaiah (cont.)

10:22	436
10:22,23	435
11:10	542
28:16	439, 440, 469
52:7	484
53:1	483, 491
59:20	562
64:1	691
64:8	416
65:1	497
65:1, 2	498
65:2	497

Jeremiah

18:1–4	416
18:5, 6	416

Hosea

1	433
1:10	431, 433
2:23	431, 433

Joel

2:32	470, 480

Malachi

1:2, 3	393
1:4	396

Matthew

6:31	375
7:7	301, 518
16:25	581
21:33ff.	528
22:9	527
25:34	618
27:46	667
28:18–20	479

Mark

14:36	330
16:14–18	479

Luke

10:5, 6	682
14:26	394
15:17	531
18:1 thru. 8	618
18:8	558
18:19	674
22:32	371
23:34	523

John

1:17	85
3:16	177
5:22	369
6:37	473, 671
7:17	244
10:16	531
11:25	7, 212
12:31	205
12:32	476
14:6	7
14:15	614
15:18	337
16:13–15	333
16:33	341, 381
17:9	536
17:24	373

Acts

2	487
2:39	386
5:29	624
16:31	241, 274, 373

Romans

1	53–55
1 thru. 8	598
1:1–4	chap. 1
1:12	10
1:16	16
1:16, 17	chap. 2, 16, 51
1:18	chap. 3, 27, 29
1:19	21

Scripture Index

Romans (cont.)
1:19–23	chap. 4
1:24, 25	chap. 5, 39
1:24–27	40
1:28	chap. 6
1:29	42, 676
1:29, 30	40
1:29–31	43
1:30	42
1:32	chap. 7, 54, 273
2	55, 220
2:1	chap. 8, 61, 68, 82
2:3	61
2:4, 5	chap. 9
2:6–8	chap. 10
2:13	77
2:14, 15	chap. 11
2:17	55
2:17–21a	chap. 12
2:21–23	89
2:25	91
2:28, 29	chap. 13
3:2	98, 99
3:3, 4a	chap. 14
3:5	107
3:7, 8	chap. 15
3:9–18	chap. 16
3:10	115 note 1
3:20	119
3:21, 22	chap. 17
3:23	126
3:24	127
3:25, 26	chap. 18
3:27	chap. 19
3:31	141, 148
4:1	142
4:2	142
4:3	154
4:3–5	chap. 20
4:6–8	chap. 21
4:9	155, 169
4:10	155
4:11	chap. 22

Romans (cont.)
4:13	165
4:16	161, 169
4:17b	chap. 23
4:17–22	168
4:20	169
4:22	170
4:23, 24	chap. 24, 175
4:25	chap. 25
5:1	chap. 26, 67, 189, 191, 192
5:1, 2	193
5:2	chap. 27
5:2–4	196
5:3, 4	chap. 28
5:5	202, 207, 209, 631
5:6–8	chap. 29
5:8, 10	631
5:9	209, 210
5:10	chap. 30
5:11	217
5:12–14	chap. 31
5:12–21	217
5:14	224
5:15	chap. 32
5:18	chap. 33
5:20	237
5:21	chap. 34
6	248, 250
6:1	263, 264, 276, 281, 282, 284
6:1, 2	chap. 35, 250
6:3	251
6:4	chap. 36
6:5	254
6:10	257, 258
6:11	chap. 37, 255, 268
6:12	264, 268
6:13	175, 264
6:14	chap. 38, 276
6:15	276
6:17	175, 269
6:19	269

699

Romans (cont.)

6:22	175, 270
6:23	chap. 39
6, 7	244, 250
7	276, 277
7:1–3	277
7:4	chap. 40, 283
7:5, 6	chap. 41
7:7	277
7:9	289, 290
7:12, 14	277
7:15–17	chap. 42
7:18	290
7:19	290
7:20	290
7:23	311
7:24, 25a	chap. 43
7:25	302
8	244, 343
8:1	chap. 44, 309, 310, 312, 373
8:2	chap. 45
8:3	252, 265, 285
8:7	654
8:9	315
8:10	316, 318, 320
8:11	chap. 46
8:12, 13	328
8:12–15	322
8:13	322
8:14	chap. 47, 329
8:15, 16	chap. 48
8:16	335
8:17a	335
8:17, 18	342
8:17b, 18	chap. 49
8:18	346
8:19–22	chap. 50
8:21	349
8:23	324, 343, 344
8:25	349, 353
8:26	343
8:26, 27	chap. 51

Romans (cont.)

8:28	chap. 52
8:29	361, 425
8:30	235, 432
8:31	367
8:31, 32	chap. 53
8:32	177
8:33	367, 368
8:33, 34	381
8:34	chap. 54
8:35	367
8:35–39	chap. 55
8:38, 39	367
8:39	360
9	398
9 thru. 11	569
9:1–5	383
9:2, 3	391
9:3	101
9:6	390, 398, 534, 556
9:6, 8	436
9:6–8	chap. 56
9:10–13	chap. 57
9:14	406, 422
9:14–16	chap. 58
9:15	414
9:16	397
9:17	414
9:17, 18	chap. 59
9:18	415
9:19	422, 430
9:19–21	chap. 60
9:21	424
9:22, 23	chap. 61
9:24–29	chap. 62
9:30–33	chap. 63
10:3	445, 449
10:4	chap. 64, 453
10:4–9	454
10:5–8	chap. 65
10:6–8	459
10:8	477
10:9	chap. 66

~ *Scripture Index*

Romans (cont.)	
10:9, 10	468
10:11–13	chap. 67
10:14, 15	chap. 68
10:15	484
10:16–18	chap. 69
10:18	496
10:19	496
10:20, 21	chap. 70, 503
11	431, 569
11:1	503, 524
11:1–5	chap. 71, 510, 517
11:2–6	517
11:4	515
11:5	510, 511, 514, 563
11:6	chap. 72, 517
11:7	525
11:7–10	chap. 73
11:11	chap. 74, 540
11:11–15	532
11:12	534, 535, 561
11:13, 14	534
11:15	chap. 75, 540
11:16–21	chap. 76
11:17–24	554
11:18	547
11:20	546, 547
11:22–24	chap. 77
11:23, 24	554
11:25	534
11:25, 26a	chap. 78
11:26	561, 562
11:28	557, 560
11:28–31	chap. 79
11:32	569
11:33, 36	429
11:33–36	chap. 80
12, 13	640
12 thru. 16	576, 660
12	250, 612
12:1	576, 577, 591
12:1 thru. 15:13	673

Romans (cont.)	
12:2	chap. 81, 584, 590, 610
12:3–8	chap. 82
12:9	chap. 83
12:12	chap. 84, 605
12:16	chap. 85
12:17–21	620
12:19	chap. 86
13:1–5	chap. 87
13:8	chap. 88
13:10	629, 630
13:11, 12	chap. 89
14	640
14:1–3	chap. 90, 647
14:4–8	chap. 91
14:7	666
14:8	653
14:9	647
14:13	657
14:14	655
14:15	657
14:20	655, 657
14:21	642, 657
14:23b	chap. 92
14, 15	659
15:1–11	673
15:3	659, 662
15:4	chap. 93, 666
15:5–9	chap. 94
15:12	543
15:14	chap. 95
15:14, 16	674
15:14–33	673
15:23	674
15:33	674
16:1, 2	680
16:3–16	chap. 96
16:25–27	chap. 97

I Corinthians
1:31	135, 397, 444
2:9	691

701

I Corinthians (cont.)

3:21–23	366
10:23	656
13	593
15:20, 23	543
15:25	559
15:45	319
15:47	232
15:50	285
15:55	320
15:58	321

II Corinthians

5:10	369
5:17	249, 293, 677
5:18, 19	476
5:19	204
5:20	476
5:21	252
12:7–9	353

Galatians

3:10	456
4:4	534
4:6	330

Ephesians

4:13	534
4:27	616

Philippians

1:20–25	635
3:8	663
4:7	360

Colossians

1:24	338
3:1	609
3:14	674

II Thessalonians

2:2	635

II Timothy

4:7, 8	172

Hebrews

6:4–6	526
11	664
11:6	144
11:24–26	339
11:26	664
11:37, 38	338
12:2	339

James

1:2	195

I Peter

1:11	492
1:22	594
2:3, 4	440
2:4, 6–8	440
2:8	443
2:9	611
2:21–23	625

I John

2:15	536
2:18	636 & 636 note 1
3:2	194
3:9	293
14:17	371

II John

10	682

Revelation

5:5	543
6:9–11	618
9:6	270
13:8	129
22:16	543